A HISTORY OF
AMERICAN MAGAZINES
VOLUME II: 1850–1865

LONDON : HUMPHREY MILFORD
OXFORD UNIVERSITY PRESS

MAGAZINE EDITORS OF THE CIVIL WAR PERIOD

An Array of Editorial Talent, with Diverse Beards. Upper left: Robert Bon-
ner, *New York Ledger*. Upper right: James Russell Lowell, *Atlantic Monthly*.
Lower left: J. D. B. De Bow, *De Bow's Review*. Lower right: Fletcher Harper,
Harper's Monthly and *Weekly*. Center: Frank Leslie, *Frank Leslie's Gazette of
Fashions*, *Frank Leslie's Illustrated Newspaper*, etc.

A HISTORY OF
AMERICAN MAGAZINES

1850–1865

BY

FRANK LUTHER MOTT

DIRECTOR OF THE SCHOOL OF JOURNALISM
STATE UNIVERSITY OF IOWA

HARVARD UNIVERSITY PRESS
Cambridge, Massachusetts
1938

PN
4877
M7
v.2

PUBLISHED IN COÖPERATION WITH THE MODERN LANGUAGE
ASSOCIATION OF AMERICA, WITH THE ASSISTANCE OF A
GRANT AWARDED BY THE AMERICAN COUNCIL OF LEARNED
SOCIETIES FROM A FUND PROVIDED BY THE CARNEGIE
CORPORATION OF NEW YORK

English

47476

JUN 2 2 1944

PRINTED BY THE HARVARD UNIVERSITY PRESS
CAMBRIDGE, MASSACHUSETTS, U. S. A.

PREFACE

THERE is a certain fascination about old magazines. It springs, I think, from their personal quality. The distinctively human element is never long absent from their pages. Even the dull old *Bibliotheca Sacra* (to take a chance example) sometimes erupted into the fire and smoke of personal passion over a heresy trial. The magazines have always echoed popular ideologies, presented personal but representative emotional responses, interpreted the men and women of their own days.

This quality which the old magazines possess of holding the mirror up to human nature and popular movements is precious. Not even the newspapers present so effectively the veritable life of the times in which they were published. Historical investigation must increasingly look to the old weekly, monthly, and quarterly journals to discover what men and women were doing and thinking and feeling. For this reason a history of magazines must give a considerable share of its space to an analysis of magazine content. Editors and publishers, dates, titles, circulations, and so on, are important; but the real heart of the matter is reached in the answer to the question, "What did they print?"

In the following pages it has been my purpose to tell the story of the founding and the passing of all the magazines of importance in the period, calling attention to the phenomena of shifting popular favor; to detail the tendencies and movements in circulation, advertising, payment of authors and editors, and costs of publication; to describe the development of class journals, including those for the professions and trades; and finally — most important object of all — to analyze the contents of the magazines of the period considered according to ideas, literary types, and typographical and pictorial presentation.

The complexity of the pattern of American magazine history makes the mere ordering of its materials a difficult task. To trace the developments in magazine production, the permutations in form and techniques, and the course of editorial policies with respect to content in a given decade or period is clearly a chief obligation of the historian of magazines. Such treatment presents no very difficult problem in chronological handling. But in taking the story up by periods, one is almost sure to neglect or to obscure the individualities of the different magazines. This characteristic personality, which is the very soul of a periodical, can be shown only if the continuity of its history is preserved in a separate narrative or sketch. It is necessary, then, to provide for each period not only a "running history" but also a supplementary section of separate sketches covering the entire lives of the more important magazines which were founded in the period.

This was the method used in my previous volume, *A History of American Magazines, 1741–1850*, and it is here retained as the only device which allows a reasonably even pace to the "running history" and at the same time works no injustice to the individual magazines. Only two other methods are possible: (1) chopping the separate histories to fit the ends of the chronological divisions, in order that each period shall be neatly self-contained; (2) interpolating the whole of a magazine's story at the time its founding is noticed — tracing, for example, the *Atlantic Monthly* from Lowell to Weeks and then jumping agilely back to the fifties to record the founding of *Harper's Weekly*. These alternatives are obviously unsatisfactory, while the system used experimentally in the earlier volume seems to have enabled the general reader as well as the scholar to walk freely among the magazines without confusion as to paths or chronological fences.

But the reader is warned against two or three misconceptions regarding the work as a whole which may conceivably result from the method adopted. The "running history" in this volume covers the years 1850 to 1865, and therefore the book is called *A History of American Magazines, 1850–1865*, to mark its place in the series; but *many of the separate histories of magazines extend far beyond 1865*. To name but a few at random, the histories of *Harper's*, the *North American*, the *Atlantic*, the *Country Gentleman*, and the *Police Gazette* appear *in extenso* in this volume and serve to bring it down, so far as they are concerned, to the year 1938.

A further detail of arrangement rises from the principle that when a magazine, though founded in one period, reaches its chief importance much later, it should be treated in the Supplement attached to the history of the later period. Thus the sketch of the *North American Review*, begun in 1815, appears in the present volume, while that of the *Round Table*, which began in 1863, is postponed to Volume III; and the story of the *Saturday Evening Post*, founded in 1821, is held over to the final volume of the series. These variations from regular order are not very frequent, and the fact that all these magazines are properly fitted into their places in the "running history" prevents chronological confusion.

Perhaps the correction of another possible misapprehension may be permitted here. This volume represents, not merely a study of the magazines which have been given separate sketches here, but examination of the files and inquiry into the histories of hundreds of periodicals. A file running to many volumes has sometimes yielded no more than a line or two to the record.

I have incurred so many debts in connection with this study and have scattered these obligations over so long a period, that I despair of even listing all who have shown me special favors and made the work easier. To a few I wish to extend thanks for specific help, and the others I must include in a blanket expression of gratitude for all who are kind to toilers in libraries.

Professor Harrison John Thornton, of the University of Iowa, has been good enough to read the manuscript of the running history of this volume, and I am indebted to him for many helpful suggestions.

I am indebted also to the officials of many libraries, but chiefly, so far as this volume and its successor are concerned, to those of seven: the Library of Congress, the New York Public Library, the John Crerar Library, the Newberry Library, the Library of the State Historical Society of Wisconsin, the Iowa State Library, and the Library of the State University of Iowa. I remember gratefully the help and informed enthusiasm of Mr. V. Valta Parma, curator of the Rare Book Collection of the Library of Congress, and the hearty coöperation of Mr. Keyes D. Metcalf, then of the New York Public Library, and his staff. It is a pleasure to renew here an earlier acknowledgment of indebtedness to the late Mr. Johnson Brigham, of the Iowa State

Library. To Mr. Harold W. Hayden and Miss Irene L. Steidl, of the University of Iowa Library, I wish to make special acknowledgment for many favors. Librarians are a most patient and long-suffering race; I never cease to admire their devotion. I can only hope that these words may fall under the eyes of some of that small army of workers in many libraries whose names are unknown to me but who have unwittingly collaborated in this study, and that they will accept my thanks.

I have also a deep obligation to a group of scholars in the field of American literature who, in the course of arrangement for publication of this volume, examined the manuscript. This was no small task, and my debt is proportionately great to Professors Howard Mumford Jones, of Harvard University; Norman Foerster, of the State University of Iowa; Harry Hayden Clark, of the University of Wisconsin; and Gregory Paine, of the University of North Carolina. To this group was added Professor Arthur Meier Schlesinger, of Harvard University, whose encouragement in connection with the earlier volume as well as the present ones has meant much to me. Nor could I omit acknowledgment of my debt to Professor Percy Long, of New York University, secretary of the Modern Language Association of America, and to Dr. Donald Goodchild, secretary of the American Council of Learned Societies. The assistance of the two organizations just mentioned in the publication of these volumes is gratefully acknowledged.

Finally, a word about errors. John S. C. Abbott contributed much to the sensational success scored by the early *Harper's* through his long serial life of Napoleon. But he idolized and idealized the Corsican so egregiously that historians generally protested, and some of them came to Fletcher Harper and complained. Harper then undertook to induce Abbott to correct some rather obvious falsities, but in the course of the interview the historian (who was also a Congregational clergyman) drew himself up to his full height and said impressively: "Mr. Harper, I never write a line of my life of Napoleon without first getting down on my knees and asking Almighty God to keep me from errors." That ended the conversation. Nothing more could be said. For myself, though I cannot lay claim to the Reverend Mr. Abbott's piety, I have thought that I might forestall at least the more theological of the critics by suggesting a historians' addition to the Litany: "From mistakes of omission and commission, from slips in dates, from transposition of citations, from blunders obvious and recondite, Good Lord, deliver us!"

FRANK LUTHER MOTT

State University of Iowa
Iowa City, Iowa

CONTENTS

CHAPTER IV

THE GEOGRAPHY OF THE MAGAZINES

CHAPTER V

POLITICS AND WAR

CHAPTER VI
LITERARY TYPES AND JUDGMENTS

CHAPTER VII
ARTS, SPORTS, AND "ISMS"

SUPPLEMENT
SKETCHES OF CERTAIN IMPORTANT MAGAZINES
WHICH FLOURISHED 1850–1865

ILLUSTRATIONS

A HISTORY OF
AMERICAN MAGAZINES
1850–1865

CHAPTER I

THE BUSINESS OF MAGAZINE PUBLISHING

I T IS not the mere fact that 1850 marks the mid-century turn which causes that year to stand out as the beginning of a new era in the history of American magazines. That year and the two or three which followed it abounded in situations and events which spelled change. For example, the Compromise of 1850 seemed to dissipate the impending war cloud for a few months, but the threat soon darkened again and overshadowed much of the popular writing of the times; thus the year 1850 may be said to introduce the last and bitterest phase of the slavery debate. More special in its effect upon periodicals was an event of 1852 — the passage of a new Post Office Act reducing rates and effectively transferring postage charges from subscriber to publisher.[1] But doubtless the most definitely epochal happening of these years was the founding in 1850 of *Harper's New Monthly Magazine*, which was to affect, immediately and profoundly, the whole course of development of the American general magazine.

Other publishing ventures emphasized the fact that magazines were entering a new phase. *Putnam's Monthly* (to be followed by the *Atlantic*) introduced a finer and sounder literary quality than had been known before. The success of *Frank Leslie's Illustrated Newspaper*, and a little later of *Harper's Weekly*, gave the country a new kind of weekly miscellany, while the *New York Ledger* showed what could be done with the cheap story-paper.

Perhaps nothing illustrates better the fact that 1850 turns the page to a new chapter than the way in which a whole galaxy of earlier editors and magazine writers seem to be eclipsed at about this time by a group of newcomers. The great ones of the forties, such as Nathaniel Parker Willis, George Pope Morris, Lewis Gaylord Clark, George Rex Graham, were growing old, and were connected, for the most part, with failing magazines. Louis A. Godey and his editor Sarah Josepha Hale were almost

---

[1] See p. 18.

4 A HISTORY OF AMERICAN MAGAZINES

the only successful magazinists of the preceding decade to play important parts in the fifties, and *Godey's* was soon to be left behind by the younger *Peterson's*.

New and dominant figures were the scholarly, versatile, enthusiastic James Russell Lowell, of the *Atlantic Monthly*; the shrewd though unliterary Robert Bonner, of the *Ledger*; the vital and expansive Frank Leslie, founder of dozens of periodicals; the industrious J. D. B. De Bow, whose *Review* was the paramount spokesman of the South; and Henry Ward Beecher, a personality of great importance in the period, whose influence was exerted in no small degree through the *Independent*.

But a magazine is not always — perhaps not often — the lengthened shadow of an individual; its success is usually the result of many factors in combination. Among these factors, economic conditions bulk large, and our consideration of the magazines of the period from 1850 to 1865 may well begin with a brief account of the publishing situation in these years.

STATISTICAL ANALYSIS

Analysis of publication statistics in the seventh, eighth, and ninth census reports shows a downward swing in the number of periodicals (excluding newspapers) from approximately 685 in 1850 to about 575 in 1860. The curve did not resume the upward course of the forties and early fifties until about 1863.[2] Calculating the average life of these publications generously at four years, we may arrive at the guess that in the neighborhood of 2,500 periodicals other than newspapers were issued, however briefly or permanently, during the period of 1850–65.

The slight decrease in the number of magazines was owing to no decline of interest. There can be no doubt about that "passion for periodical literature which characterizes the age,"

[2] The eighth census (1860) shows a total of 3,383 weeklies, monthlies, and quarterlies, of which 2,694 were "political" weeklies and 171 "religious" weeklies. See *The Population of the United States* (Washington, 1866), pp. 321–322. It seems fair to suppose that practically all the "political" weeklies and some two-thirds of the "religious" weeklies were newspapers. Such a subtraction leaves 575 periodicals for 1860, while a similar method applied to the figures of the 1850 census yields a remainder of 685. See F. L. Mott, *A History of American Magazines, 1741–1850* (New York, 1930), p. 342. See *American Annual Cyclopaedia* (New York, 1863), p. 573, for a statement concerning the increase of magazines in 1863.

referred to by the *New York Quarterly* in 1854.[3] An obstacle to magazine development was offered, however, by the panic of 1857; and the Civil War, with its severe tests, prevented any very considerable growth before 1865.

TRIAL BY PANIC

The panic year of 1857 comes precisely midway of our period. Bank failures, unemployment, slow or impossible collections, and the other phenomena attending the close of an easy-credit era combined to embarrass publishers. The *National Era* frankly expressed the basic difficulty when it said:

> Many of our subscribers are among the intelligent mechanics and industrial classes of the North, and we hear by every mail that some of them, thrown out of employment, cannot find money to renew their subscriptions.[4]

Plans for expansion by established periodicals had to be curtailed, and projects for new ventures found a discouraging reception. The little local weeklies of literary miscellany, of which such a crop had sprouted in the early fifties, withered, and many of them died.

One of the chief casualties of the panic was *Graham's Magazine*, which had a history of thirty-two proud years. The *Knickerbocker*, too, was hard hit by the financial stringency and changed publishers twice in the period of depression, though it lived gaspingly through most of the war. The first *Putnam's* ended in the panic year; and *Emerson's*, which took over *Putnam's*, soon perished. The *Democratic Review*, whose pages had carried the work of the most famous writers of the country, and the *New York Mirror*, which had brightened the periodical history of a third of a century, gave up the ghost when the panic came. Many lesser losses could be named, and the list grew as the stringency continued to make itself felt through the years preceding the war. The South was largely exempt from the panic; its magazines were reserved for a severer trial.

Yet even in the depression some new barks ventured upon the troubled sea. Indeed, two of the most important periodicals of

---

[3] *New York Quarterly*, II, 689 (January 1854).
[4] *National Era*, XI, 194 (December 3, 1857).

the century — the *Atlantic Monthly* and *Harper's Weekly* — were begun in the very year of the panic, though they were launched before the hurricane struck. The *Atlantic* found itself involved in the bankruptcy of its publishers by the end of its second year; but it gained by its transfer to a more resourceful house.

NORTHERN MAGAZINES AND THE WAR

The war, when it came, brought with it far greater trials for the magazines than any presented by a temporary eclipse of the sunshine of prosperity. Here was a four-year darkness. "This is a bad time for newspaper and magazine owners," wrote the editor of the failing *Knickerbocker* in 1862. It was much worse for the magazines than for the newspapers; the latter were saved because the increased demand for their product — news — more than offset the increases in their expenses. But the *Knickerbocker* man was talking about the price of paper, which he said had risen 40 per cent in the latter months of 1862, "and there is every probability of the advance reaching fifty or one hundred per cent within a very short time." He was a true prophet, as is evidenced by a remark in the very next number of his magazine: the storm of war, he says then, is "blowing paper higher than a kite — to-wit, more than a hundred per cent above its usual price." [5]

Charles Hodge, editor of the *Princeton Review*, one of the greatest religious quarterlies of the times, looked back after the war was over and wrote, "We lost three hundred subscribers at one blow when hostilities commenced"; and when it is considered that reviews numbered subscribers by hundreds rather than by thousands, it will be realized how serious this blow was.

The war [continued Hodge] caused the price of paper to rise three-fold, while all the expenses were proportionally increased. Other journals suffered in the same way. Some were suspended, others decreased their size, while all called loudly for help. [6]

Virtually all, it may be added, were forced to use a poorer grade of paper.

[5] *Knickerbocker*, LX, 571 (December 1862), and LXI, 87 (January 1863).
[6] *Biblical Repertory and Princeton Review*, XXXVII, 657 (October 1865).

The *Princeton Review* was not affected by the 3 per cent tax on advertising imposed in 1862. Newspapers were, of course, the chief contributors under this tax; but it will be seen later that advertising had even before the war assumed some importance for magazines also. Postage rates were not raised during the Civil War as they had been in previous war periods. Moreover, the ability of the average reader to purchase magazines was probably not seriously impaired in the North during the war. Though prices of commodities rose out of all proportion to wage increases, the money in circulation was augmented by such items as soldiers' pay and bounties, as well as the issue of greenbacks; and "war-time prosperity" made for free spending.[7] There was a general tendency toward higher subscription prices, though many magazines went through the war without such increases.

The severest blow dealt the northern magazines by the war was the first of those noted by Hodge — the abrupt reduction of circulation area caused by the break in communication between the North and South. *Harper's* and *Godey's* had been especially popular south of the Mason-Dixon line, much to the oft expressed disgust of the promoters of a definitely southern periodical literature;[8] and the New York illustrated weeklies and some of the religious quarterlies had also found a considerable proportion of their readers in the states that seceded after Lincoln's election.

Many northern periodicals had, however, a circulation in the Federal army itself. Notes from readers in service may be found *passim* in the *Knickerbocker* (in the early years of the war), *Vanity Fair*, *Frank Leslie's Illustrated Weekly*, *Harper's Weekly*, and others. Even *Godey's Lady's Book* compliments the soldiers on their elegant taste as it notes its own popularity among them.[9] Such weeklies as *Leslie's*, the *Independent*, and *Harper's Weekly* profited by their handling of actual news and pictures from the theater of war. At least one miscellany, C. W. Alexander's *Soldier's Casket* (Philadelphia, 1865), was published solely for the men at the front.

[7] See Emerson David Fite's *Social and Industrial Conditions in the North During the Civil War* (New York, 1910), pp. 184–185.
[8] See pp. 108–109.   [9] Mott, *op. cit.*, p. 590.

SOUTHERN PERIODICALS DURING THE WAR

But if the war tried the stamina of northern periodicals, it made existence itself well-nigh impossible for those of the South. Accustomed to buy their paper, ink, and machinery from northern manufacturers, southern publishers were hard put to it to develop their own paper mills and ink factories on short notice. Coarse-fibered paper and inferior inks became the rule; it is said that even shoeblacking was used for ink, and there are well-known instances of wallpaper's having been employed as printing stock. Toward the end of the war, conscription interfered with the publishing business and made it almost impossible to secure labor. Postage rates were also very high.[10]

The leading general magazine in the Confederate States, the *Southern Literary Messenger*, managed to exist throughout most of the war, perishing in 1864, as Grant was approaching Richmond.[11] *De Bow's Review* was suspended in 1862.[12] The two oldest southern journals of medicine, the *New Orleans Medical and Surgical Journal* and the *Southern Medical and Surgical Journal*, of Augusta, were both suspended throughout the war. The *Danville Quarterly Review*, a religious periodical which was active in support of the union, survived until 1864, when wartime labor conditions caused its demise.[13] The *Review of the Methodist Church South* was suspended from 1862 to 1878.[14] And so the story ran in the Confederate States of America.

A few heroic southern periodicals, however, struggled through the war with practically unbroken files. The *Southern Presbyterian Review*, a quarterly published at Columbia, survived the crucial years without missing more than a few numbers, though it was much reduced in size because of the lack of paper.[15] William N. White, editor and publisher of the *Southern Cultivator*, was wont to boast after the war that his was "the

[10] Rabun Lee Brantley, *Georgia Journalism of the Civil War Period* (Nashville, 1929), pp. 87–95.

[11] Mott, *op. cit.*, p. 656.

[12] *De Bow's* published one issue, now rare, in July 1863 and resumed in 1866.

[13] See p. 539.

[14] See p. 14, footnote.

[15] The January and July numbers for 1864 were omitted (Vol. XVI). James Woodrow, president of the Theological Seminary at Columbia, was apparently the war editor. See p. 62 for a further note on this review.

only periodical in the South that never missed an issue throughout the four years of the war." [16] However that may have been,
there were others which managed to get through by reducing
size, doubling up issues, and suspending through brief periods.

Moreover, there were some publishers so optimistic or so fool-
hardy, or both, as to project new periodicals in the South amidst
the alarums of war. "Perhaps nothing has been more remarkable," observed one of them, the *Magnolia Weekly*,

than the great success that has attended literary enterprises in the
South during the war. At present it is very difficult to secure paper
and other materials for printing, and numerous causes combine to
make publishing an extremely hazardous undertaking. Notwith-
standing this, a number of new papers, daily and weekly, some literary and others political, have sprung up in various portions of the
South, and certain publishing houses have issued a perfect stream of
books from their presses.[17]

But these periodical "war babies" did not prosper; and the
Magnolia, six months later, was issuing a plaintive plea for
southern support of southern magazines, whose combined circulation, it was alleged, did not equal, at the beginning of 1864, the
number of copies the *New York Ledger* had sent into the South
weekly before the opening of the conflict.[18]

The devastation wrought by the war among southern periodicals cannot be said, however, to have affected the total magazine situation in America very greatly, for the seceding states
had no important publishing centers. But the interest in the
tragic struggles of these southern editors and publishers is dis-
proportionate to the financial investments and circulations involved.

CIRCULATIONS

The average circulation of American magazines appears to
have increased during the period under consideration, though it
must be remembered that circulation figures of the times are
highly unreliable, and practically the only sources are the occa-

[16] Brantley, *op. cit.*, p. 24.
[17] *Magnolia Weekly*, I, 224 (July 4, 1863).
[18] *Ibid.*, II, 132 (January 23, 1864).

sional boasts of successful publishers.[19] But according to the eighth census, the average circulation of the quarterlies in 1860 was about 3,370; that of the monthlies was about 12,000; while the weeklies, including newspapers, circulated an average of about 2,400 copies.

Doubtless the outstanding circulation success was that of Robert Bonner's *New York Ledger*, a popular literary miscellany which afforded weekly spice and variety for the lives of most of the nursemaids, cooks, and stableboys of the country, and offered vicarious escape besides to many a housewife and tired business man. But more of the *Ledger* later;[20] for the present it is necessary only to record the rumor that the paper sold 400,000 copies weekly. Rumor is all we have to go by in the matter, for Bonner, a man of extraordinary acumen in such things, was content to let rumor do the work, especially since the *Ledger* carried no advertising and had no necessity for circulation statements. Tucker's *Country Gentleman* boasted a quarter of a million in 1858. *Frank Leslie's Illustrated* had a circulation of 164,000 in 1860; and its special for May 12 of that year describing the Heenan-Sayers fight sold 347,000 copies. This, Leslie claimed, was the largest edition ever printed of an American periodical.[21] By 1850 the American Tract Society's *American Messenger* had 190,000, and another mass-circulation paper, the *Youth's Penny Gazette* of New York, had 100,000. *Harper's Weekly* reached a circulation of 120,000 by the end of 1861.[22] *Gleason's Pictorial* claimed 103,000 in 1856,[23] and the same publisher's *Flag of Our Union* had 100,000 somewhat earlier;[24] while the *New York Weekly* prob-

[19] The total circulation of newspapers and periodicals, grouped together, increased 117.61 per cent between 1850 and 1860, according to census figures; but this increase was owing chiefly to the increase in number and distribution of newspapers. The following directories of the period should be listed, though only the first quotes circulations: J. G. C. Kennedy, *Catalogue of the Newspapers and Periodicals Published in the United States. Compiled from the Census of 1850* (New York, 1852); Lay and Brother, *The Newspaper Record* (Philadelphia, 1856); Daniel J. Kenny, *The American Newspaper Directory and Record of the Press* (New York, 1861).

[20] See separate sketch 12.

[21] See pp. 458–459.

[22] See p. 475.   [23] See p. 411.

[24] See quotation of a statement by Gleason in the *Granite State Magazine*, III, 51 (February 1907).

ably had over 100,000 by the end of our period, and the New York *Sunday Mercury*, another story-paper, had 145,000 before the war.[25] Godey boasted 150,000 subscribers for his *Lady's Book* by 1860 and claimed the same through the war [26] — a figure doubtless equaled by *Peterson's Ladies' Magazine* a few years later.[27] *Harper's New Monthly* laid claim to an average of 110,000 for our period of 1850–65.[28] These thirteen are probably the only periodicals which achieved over 100,000 circulation during the years under consideration. For purposes of comparison, it may be noted that only two English periodicals were in this circulation class in 1850, and they were both penny papers.[29]

The *American Agriculturist* led the field of farm periodicals with 45,000 just before the war,[30] and the *Independent* headed the religious journals with something like the same figure at the end of the war.[31]

The home club system, by means of which a local solicitor might receive his own copy free by obtaining five to fifteen other subscriptions, was in general use. The club price was lower than the regular subscription and was often graduated according to the size of the club. *Godey's*, whose regular price was $3.00, was sold for $1.66 in clubs until 1863, when the increased cost of paper necessitated a rise to $2.00. The $2.00 magazines usually charged only $1.00 when sold in clubs of twenty. Premiums were sometimes offered to "the getter-up of a club"; Deacon & Peterson, for example, gave a sewing machine to any solicitor who sent them $60 of subscription money for either the *Saturday Evening Post* or the *Lady's Friend*. Premiums with individual subscriptions or small clubs were not common, however, until after the war.

Two circulation abuses may be noted: large exchange lists and delinquent subscriptions. Exchanges were post-free, and they were relied upon for favorable notices in newspapers; but

[25] *Journalist*, January 7, 1888, p. 1.
[26] See Mott, *op. cit.*, p. 581.
[27] See p. 309.   [28] See p. 391.
[29] They were the *Family Herald*, 175,000, and the *London Journal*, 170,000; while *Lloyd's Miscellany* had 95,000. See *Holden's Dollar Magazine*, VII, 233 (May 1851).
[30] See Mott, *op. cit.*, p. 730.   [31] See p. 372.

the free list grew out of all bounds in the cases of the more popular magazines, until it became a ruinous burden. *Graham's* had
2,100 country newspapers on its exchange list in 1853.[32] But
more exhausting yet was the drain from delinquents. Godey
tells with glee of receiving $30 in one subscription payment, to
settle an account apparently unpaid for ten years;[33] but most
subscribers who got so far behind were unlikely ever to pay anything. *Graham's* had $10,000 due in back subscriptions in Feb-
ruary 1852.

The delinquent subscriber continued for a long time the worst
enemy of the magazines, and dunning notices were frequent in
the departments of "Publisher's Notes." A religious weekly, in
the year after the publication of *Hiawatha*, printed an original
plea of this kind. It was widely copied by impecunious editors,
and may be printed once more:

TO OUR SUBSCRIBERS

Should you ask us why this dunning,
Why these sad complaints and murmurs,
Murmurs loud about delinquents
Who have read the paper weekly,
Read what they have never paid for,
Read with pleasure and with profit,
Read of church affairs and prospects . . .
We should answer, we should tell you:
From the printer, from the mailer,
From the kind old paper-maker,
From the landlord, from the carrier,
From the man who taxes letters
With a stamp from Uncle Samuel —
"Uncle Sam," the rowdies call him —
From them all there comes a message,
"Please to pay us what you owe us" . . .
Sad it is to turn the ledger,
Turn the leaves of this old ledger,
Turn and see what sums are due us . . .
Send us money — send us money —
SEND THE MONEY THAT YOU OWE US! [34]

---

[32] *Graham's Magazine*, XLIII, 554 (November 1853).
[33] *Godey's Lady's Book*, XXXIV, 270 (May 1847).
[34] Quoted in the *Saturday Evening Gazette*, December 27, 1856, p. 7, from
the *Methodist Protestant*.

The standard magazine price was $3.00 in 1850, though the *North American Review, De Bow's*, the *Southern Quarterly Review*, Silliman's *Journal of Science*, and others charged $5.00. The usual price for the weekly literary and religious journals was $2.00, and $2.00 monthlies were far from uncommon. There were some $1.00 and $1.50 monthlies. Increased subscription prices during the war have already been noted.

In the early fifties, organizations developed to take over the news-stand circulation of periodicals. These came under control of A. S. Tuttle in 1856, six years later to become the American News Company. The agency's charges were high, however, especially in the case of a struggling new periodical. The *American Freemason's Magazine* complained in 1860 of being required to pay half of its retail price for distribution.[35] But the agency served the publisher by relieving him of an expensive part of his distribution task.

ADVERTISING

Although magazine advertising made some progress during this period, it did not reach large proportions. George F. Rowell, founder of one of the first great advertising agencies, writing his recollections of the sixties, says that magazines were "not then thought to be at all worth the consideration of advertisers." [36] This is putting the matter too strongly or too sweepingly; both monthly and weekly magazines were used more or less by advertisers.

The *Atlantic Monthly* had fourteen pages of advertising in its number for December 1865, by no means all of it publishers' announcements. To advertise soap and print Bryant in the same number, as the *Atlantic* did, doubtless seemed sacrilege to some readers; but they became used to it. The *American Whig Review* did not find advertising beneath its dignity in its last year, 1851–52. Scott's reprints of the *Edinburgh Review* and other English magazines carried patent medicine advertising as early as 1865. *Emerson's* carried five or six pages of "ads" in each

---

[35] *American Freemason's Magazine*, V, 614 (June 1860).

[36] *Printer's Ink*, June 7, 1905, p. 11. This statement of Rowell's has misled many writers on magazine history who have examined only the bound files of magazines, from which the advertising pages have been omitted.

issue, and the *Knickerbocker* slightly less. The business reviews — *Hunt's* and *De Bow's* — had some advertising; the latter was carrying ten or a dozen pages of it just before the war. The women's periodicals nearly all carried advertising of house furnishings, musical instruments, silverware, sewing machines, schools, books, and so on. *Godey's* and *Peterson's* each had five or ten pages of it, and their example was followed by the *Ladies' Wreath*, the *Christian Parlor Magazine*, and others of the tribe.

With the weeklies, advertising was even more at home. *Harper's Weekly* and the *New York Illustrated News* each had three large quarto pages of advertising regularly by the end of the war. *Leslie's Illustrated* also had a good advertising business; on October 20, 1860, it ran a full folio page "ad" of Mason & Hamlin melodeons and organ harmoniums, with nine illustrations. The *Saturday Evening Post* and other story-papers each carried five or six columns of advertising; nor did the religious weeklies, including the *Independent*, disdain this addition to income. Of course the agricultural journals had their share.

But some periodicals eschewed advertising. *Harper's Monthly* reserved its advertising pages for announcements of the firm's own books.[37] Some of the literary miscellanies seemed to feel that they would lose caste by admitting advertisers. Bonner never took advertising for the *Ledger*. Gleason tried printing a page of advertising in his large quarto *Pictorial*, but soon abandoned the attempt. Doubtless some of the religious quarterlies would have been glad to accept such business, but their circulations were too small to make them profitable media.

Advertising rates were often low; $20 an octavo page, or fifteen cents a line for smaller advertisements was a not uncommon charge. The small literary and religious weeklies usually asked ten cents a line, and considerable reductions were generally made for yearly contracts. The *De Bow* rate before the war was $20 a page; *Emerson's* got $50. *The Saturday Evening Post* in war time was charging thirty cents a line. But *Harper's Weekly* could ask and receive $1.50 to $2.00 a line, according to position — a rate which brought it a weekly income from advertising of $3,500 to $4,000.

A staple of the advertising of these times, and indeed for

[37] See pp. 383–384.

many years thereafter, was the proprietary, or "patent" medicine.[38] The dignified *Whig Review* printed such advertising in quantities, and pills are to be found neighboring with sweetness and light in the chaste pages of the *Atlantic*. The proprietors of these medicines were among the cleverest advertisers of the day. From the inside cover of *Vanity Fair* comes this war-time gem:

<blockquote>
To Soldiers, Sailors, and the Public

THE PREVAILING DIFFICULTY

A general lassitude seizes the frame, which often resembles the torpor preceding death. . . . Now whether this be in

THE NORTH OR THE SOUTH

the remedy is the same. Take at once six or eight of Brandreth's Pills. . . .[39]
</blockquote>

The religious weeklies filled many columns with advertisements of bitters, pills, and "regulators"; while some of the lower class of story-papers gave publicity to contraceptives and drugs to produce abortion. Rarely is a voice raised against objectionable advertising. The *Family Visitor*, an informational weekly which had a certain connection with Western Reserve University, did, however, declare that its proprietors would not "be parties to a swindle": if the half which the patent-medicine people said was true, it was nothing less than "a crime ever to be sick." [40]

The publishers of the magazines were themselves sometimes extensive advertisers, and their prospectuses in the newspapers were often high-flown and exaggerated. Magazines' promises, observed *Norton's Literary Gazette* in 1852, were "a sort of paper currency without a specie basis." [41] Robert Bonner, publisher of the *Ledger*, and P. T. Barnum, proprietor of the famous museum and manager for Jenny Lind, were generally considered the two most effective advertisers in America. Frank Leslie called the former "the mammoth advertiser of the age" and said that "his unprecedented success clearly demonstrates the universality of the advertising medium." [42] Bonner would buy a

---

[38] See Frank Presbrey, *The History and Development of Advertising* (Garden City, 1929), pp. 289–301.

[39] *Vanity Fair*, VI, 50 (August 2, 1862).

[40] *Family Visitor*, III, 164 (September 28, 1852).

[41] *Norton's Literary Gazette*, III, 2 (January 15, 1852).

[42] *Frank Leslie's Illustrated Newspaper*, VII, 216 (March 5, 1859).

whole large folio page of the *New York Tribune* and repeat upon
it one sentence, after this fashion:

THE NEW YORK LEDGER
THE NEW YORK LEDGER
THE NEW YORK LEDGER
WILL BE FOR SALE
WILL BE FOR SALE
WILL BE FOR SALE
TOMORROW MORNING
TOMORROW MORNING
TOMORROW MORNING
THROUGHOUT THE
THROUGHOUT THE
THROUGHOUT THE
UNITED STATES
UNITED STATES
UNITED STATES
AND NEW JERSEY
AND NEW JERSEY
AND NEW JERSEY

Many repetitions of this would fill the whole of a closely printed
page. Bonner published what was probably the largest advertisement that had ever appeared in a newspaper when he took
seven pages of the *New York Herald* on May 6, 1858, for such
an "ad." He is said to have spent $1,000,000 with the advertis-
ing agency of S. M. Pettengill & Company to spread the gospel
of the *Ledger*.[43] He would sometimes print the first three or
four chapters of one of his enthralling serials in *Harper's
Weekly* or in a great daily, running perhaps two installments,
and then breaking the story off at the point at which the heroine
cries, "Unhand me, villain!" or something like that, and then
following it with the notice: "No more of this interesting story
will be printed in this paper. For the succeeding chapters, see
the *New York Ledger*, now on sale at all news depots." This
"teaser copy" was at first considered excellent "humbuggery,"
but it later provoked some resentment.[44]

---

[43] J. C. Derby, *Fifty Years Among Authors, Books and Publishers* (New
York, 1884), p. 201.

[44] See *National Era*, XIII, 42 (March 17, 1859). The *Era* published two
installments of Mrs. Southworth's *The Hidden Hand* in this manner and afterward apologized for the dereliction.

The art of advertising began to attract attention to itself in this period. Probably the first periodical devoted to the subject was *Pettengill's Reporter*, issued as a house organ by the New York agency of that name in 1851–59. *Vanity Fair* waxed satirical over the new art, as was its wont:

A model Advertisement-Writer in the *Herald* calls the Sewing Machine "a swift-fingered sister of love and charity." Let us hereafter speak of the Cooking-Range as the warm-hearted minister to appetite and contentment; of the Daguerreotype Apparatus as the bright-faced reflector of beauty and worth; and, among other ingenious contrivances, of the Model Advertisement-Writer as the soft-headed distributor of mellifluous soap.[45]

In somewhat the same vein Frank Leslie wrote in 1857:

The art of advertising is one of the arts most studied by our literary vendors of fancy soaps, philanthropic corn doctors, humanitarian pill-makers, and all the industrious professions which have an intense feeling for one's pockets. Every trick that can be resorted to for the purpose of inducing one to read an advertisement is practised, and, it must be confessed, very often with complete success. How often have we been seduced into the reading of some witty or sentimental verse, that finally led us, by slow degrees, to a knowledge that somebody sold cure-all pills or incomparable trousers.[46]

Such dodges to lure readers were the more necessary because papers refused to use display types, from a desire to protect the rights of the small advertiser. For example, *Porter's Spirit of the Times* announced at the head of its editorial column that "a uniform method of 'setting' will be adopted, in order that the ingenuity of one advertiser may not, by superior tact at display, get the better of another." This was Bennett's theory and rule for the *New York Herald*.[47] It was the necessity of working with agate type which caused Bonner to invent the kind of "iteration copy" which has already been noted. Not until the very end of our period did display lines make a general appearance in the papers; the change may be studied to advantage in *Harper's Weekly*.

The monthly magazines, however, had no such ban on dis-

[45] *Vanity Fair*, I, 37 (January 14, 1860).
[46] *Frank Leslie's Illustrated Newspaper*, IV, 284 (October 3, 1857).
[47] Presbrey, *op. cit.*, p. 232.

play. They had nothing to gain from the small advertisements of the many, as the newspapers fancied they had; they needed space copy — full pages and halves and quarters. Consequently, sizes corresponding to modern 18- and 24-point display are common, along with pictures sometimes a full page in size. Even the weeklies, which were closer to newspapers, were sometimes but little affected by the *Herald's* taboo upon all that was not agate.

THE OTHER SIDE OF THE ACCOUNT: OUTGO

Mechanical publication expense of the mid-century magazines is difficult to ascertain with any definiteness at this distance. Such statements as we have show great differences in aggregate costs — inevitable in view of the great diversity in the periodicals themselves. For example, among the monthlies we have a range from *De Bow's* $500 a month [48] to *Godey's* $8,000.[49] But De Bow used no illustrations and did not pay his contributors, while each number of the *Lady's Book* at this time contained two hand-colored steel plates, a mezzotint, and many woodcuts; and Godey paid some of his contributors very liberally. Likewise, in the field of the weekly, we may note a range from the *New York Evangelist*, a typical large folio of four pages, which cost $400 a week exclusive of editorial salary,[50] to *Ballou's Pictorial*, its sixteen large quarto pages copiously illustrated, on which its publisher lavished $1,700 a week until forced to suspend.[51] Average figures were probably lower than the lowest of those here set forth, for a publisher with modest expenses was not likely to boast of his economies to his subscribers; large expenses, on the other hand, might well be given publicity as an aid to collections or an excuse for failure.[52]

NEW POSTAL REGULATIONS

Postage became an expense of magazine publishing in the fifties. Before the Post Office Act of 1852 went into effect, on

---

[48] *De Bow's Review*, IX, 576 (November 1850).
[49] Mott, *op. cit.*, p. 581.   [50] *Zion's Herald*, XXII, 2 (January 1, 1851).
[51] *Ballou's Pictorial Drawing-Room Companion*, December 24, 1859.
[52] The *Southern Quarterly Review* is said to have cost $6,000 for its last four numbers, including payment to contributors. See *National Era*, XI, 90 (June 4, 1857).

September 30 of that year, the subscriber paid the postage on his magazine at the office of delivery. The new law not only reduced the postage rates materially, but allowed the payment of the fee at the office of mailing; thus the magazine publisher found it good policy to absorb the postage cost himself and relieve subscribers of the annoyance of their quarterly prepayments of these small sums at their own post offices. The average 96-page magazine, weighing five ounces, had cost six and a half cents to receive under the Post Office Act of 1845; now it cost one and a half cents to send.[53]

A new post office act in 1863 changed the rates somewhat, making a four-ounce magazine mailable for one cent and one weighing over four ounces and less than eight for two cents.[54]

RATES OF PAYMENT TO CONTRIBUTORS AND EDITORS

Payment to contributors remained on much the same level as during the preceding period.[55] Prices and wages were on an upward curve in the early fifties;[56] but, with the exception of Bonner's spectacular payments, there is no indication of any marked increase in what was paid for literary wares.

Some periodicals still paid nothing to contributors. These were the smaller literary miscellanies, the religious quarterlies, and the professional journals; and outside of these classes there were many free contributions, arising either from inability to pay or unwillingness to accept compensation for merely literary work. There was still something, here and there, of the old tradition that writing was not a trade but an avocation for gentlemen and ladies; but the rise of a fairly definite group of magazine writers[57] was rapidly erasing that pleasant old idea. These young writers wanted money. Gentle Alice Cary, writing

[53] There was a marked reduction of postage rates in the Post Office Act of 1851, but it carried a zoning provision which was bothersome, and it provided for payment of postage at the office of delivery. It was in force only fifteen months. For the rates of the Act of 1850 see *United States Statutes at Large*, 31st Congress, Session II, Chapter 20, Section 2; for those of the Act of 1852, *ibid.*, 32d Congress, Session I, Chapter 98, Section 1.

[54] *Ibid.*, 37th Congress, Session III, Chapter 71, Section 36.

[55] Mott, *op. cit.*, pp. 504–512.

[56] J. B. McMaster, *History of the People of the United States* (New York, 1913), VIII, 110.

[57] See p. 26.

to the *Western Literary Messenger*, which had no money for authors, promised naïvely, "If the *Messenger* will afford the most trifling remuneration, poems will be forwarded as often as desired." [58] Fitz-James O'Brien, the brilliant young Irish-American author, always out of funds, failed one day to move Fletcher Harper's heart in the matter of an advance, so he had a sign-painter make a large placard bearing the words:

ONE OF HARPER'S AUTHORS

I AM STARVING

And then he paraded up and down the street near the Harper building at Franklin Square bearing the sign sandwich-fashion until the public notice of it caused Mr. Harper to relent and pay the young writer what he asked.[59] Publishers were not allowed to forget that these newer writers wanted cash for their labor.

Putnam's Monthly paid its contributors, but on a low scale. Major Putnam writes:

> What was called the normal price for the earlier contributions to *Putnam's* was three dollars a page. The more important men received five dollars, and contributions of a special character were paid at as high a rate as ten dollars. . . . The rate for verse was from ten to twenty-five dollars a poem.[60]

The *Atlantic Monthly's* standard was a little higher. Its "mean rate" from its foundation in 1857 was $6.00 a page, though "in the case of a tyro" the figure would drop to $5.00; $50 a poem was a common price.[61] Emerson was paid $50 an essay, and his four poems in the first number seem to have been considered as one by the business office and bought for $50 — a bargain price for quantity.[62] The *Atlantic* paid Louisa M. Alcott $50 of "very happy money" for her first story in 1859

---

[58] Undated letter from E. W. Clement's collection of *Messenger* material.

[59] *Home Journal*, February 26, 1896.

[60] G. H. Putnam, *George Palmer Putnam* (New York, 1912), p. 174. Lowell, however, got as much as $50 a poem from *Putnam's*. See H. E. Scudder, *James Russell Lowell* (Boston, 1901), I, 350.

[61] Scudder, *op. cit.*, I, 421. See also Bliss Perry, *And Gladly Teach* (Boston, 1935), p. 180, in which he says the *Atlantic's* rate of $5.00 a page was founded upon *Blackwood's*.

[62] Scudder, *op. cit.*, I, 414, 416.

and steadily increased her rate thereafter, though it paid her only $10 for her poem "Thoreau's Flute" in 1863.[63] Lowell, who retired from the editorship in 1861, wrote four years later: "For some years I have had twice fifty dollars for whatever I write, and three or four times fifty for a long poem." [64] This was well enough for Lowell, who had written, when he was himself paymaster, to one of his "tyros": "You must be content. Six dollars a page is more than can be got elsewhere, and we only pay ten to the folks whose *names* are worth the other four dollars." [65]

Harper's relied on English writers for its serials, purchasing their work in "advance sheets," and in its earlier numbers it borrowed articles and short stories from the English magazines; but it soon began purchasing its brief fiction and its articles from American writers, paying the standard prices.[66]

Graham's and *Godey's*, leaders in the advancement of prices for magazine writing in the forties, were now out of the running. *Graham's* finished its career in 1858 after a decade or more of unsuccessful struggle. *Godey's* had largely abandoned famous names as an advertising device and had become much more a class periodical than a literary magazine. The *Knickerbocker* announced in 1859 that it was paying its contributors "from two to ten dollars a page." [67] It may be surmised that, for the high-class general monthly magazine, this range was representative, and that *Putnam's* "normal price" of $3.00 was probably not below an average.

Some of the weeklies paid fairly well. "The *Independent* has offered Mrs. Browning $100 for any scrap of her original poetry," wrote Mrs. Stedman from Europe to her son in 1860, "and she has already sent one new piece for them." [68] The *Independent* was to grow into an excellent poetry market. The *Round Table* offered Stedman himself $100 for a Christmas

[63] Belle Moses, *Louisa M. Alcott* (New York, 1909), pp. 115, 126, 151.

[64] C. E. Norton, ed., *Letters of James Russell Lowell* (Boston, 1894), I, 353. Letter dated December 21, 1865.

[65] Scudder, *op. cit.*, I, 421.

[66] See pp. 386–388.

[67] *Knickerbocker*, LIII, 222 (February 1859).

[68] Laura Stedman and G. M. Gould, *Life and Letters of Edmund Clarence Stedman* (New York, 1910), I, 212. Letter dated May 19, 1860.

poem in 1863;[69] it was another periodical whose literary success belongs to a later period. Dr. Gamaliel Bailey, editor and proprietor of the *National Era*, did the best he could with a slender capital to encourage such beginning writers as Lucy Larcom, Alice Cary, and "Gail Hamilton." He paid Mrs. Stowe $400 for the greatest fiction success of the period, which ran through more than forty numbers.[70]

Bailey told "Gail Hamilton" in 1856 that he was in financial straits, but promised her that if she would wait nine months for her money he would then pay her $50 for what she chose to write in the meantime. Thereupon "Gail," in a delighted letter to her sister, declared her intention of writing at the rate of $5.00 a column.[71] Yet after her nine months with the *National Era*, she was willing to take $3.00 a column from the *Independent*, to whose somewhat flirtatious office-editor the lively "Gail" writes that she thinks the compensation offered "quite enough for such quality of writing." [72] The next year she tells her sister about getting $2.00 for a story in the *Congregationalist* — "little enough, to be sure, but it didn't take long to write it, and twenty-five cents an hour isn't bad, particularly when you would not be doing anything else." [73] The willingness of the plucky and brilliant little schoolmistress to make the best of what was certainly not a good bargain is almost pathetic, and one is glad that her story of authorship had a happy ending. It may be followed in her sprightly letters; but it is impossible to resist the temptation to record here the ultimatum she was able to deliver to a questing publisher many years later: "Two hundred dollars an article without limit as to length. Free range as to themes over this world and the next." [74] "One ought not to write for money," observed "Gail," to clear her conscience, "but I consider it a first duty after one has written, to exact the highest price." [75]

In the South during the war, payments to magazine contrib-

---

[69] Stedman and Gould, *op. cit.*, p. 325.

[70] *Atlantic Monthly*, XVII, 748–749 (June 1866).

[71] H. Augusta Dodge, *Gail Hamilton's Life in Letters* (Boston, 1901), I, 117–118. Letter dated February 15, 1856.

[72] *Ibid.*, I, 130. Letter dated January 2, 1857.

[73] *Ibid.*, I, 153. Letter dated February 15, 1858.

[74] *Ibid.*, II, 885. Letter dated January 14, 1887.

[75] *Ibid.*, II, 1065.

utors were sometimes high, but they were made in depreciated currency when they were made at all.[76]

But Robert Bonner was the sensational paymaster of the period. It was in 1855 that the *Ledger's* lurid sun rose in the literary East, astonishing writers, shocking sober thinkers, and delighting hoi polloi. "Fanny Fern" had just published her *Fern Leaves*, and in her pert style and acute ideas Bonner saw just the drawing card he needed. He offered her the astounding price of $25 a column — and his columns were much shorter than those of the *National Era* and the larger folios. But "Fanny" was afraid of lowering her dignity by appearing in a cheap weekly and refused. That meant nothing to Bonner, who immediately doubled his offer. Again the lady said no; one wonders how such coyness could have been humanly possible. Bonner, warming to the chase, bid $75 a column; and "Fanny" still remained obdurate, though she was plainly weakening. When the editor suggested $100 a column, the force of cash overcame the resistance of pride; and "Fanny Fern" became a regular *Ledger* contributor to the day of her death. Her annual salary was $5,000.[77]

A similar achievement was the capture of Edward Everett for the *Ledger's* columns. To a large extent, Everett had inherited from the dead Webster the mantle of greatness which popular imagination had conferred upon that "God-like" orator. Able pulpiteer and lecturer, Greek scholar, early editor of the *North American Review*, Governor of Massachusetts, President of Harvard, Ambassador to the Court of St. James, United States Senator, Secretary of State, orator at the Gettysburg dedication, he had run the gamut. He was handsome, cultivated, polished, perfect. Bonner knew better than to approach the great man with offers of direct remuneration; but as an editor of many devices, he looked about for some effective indirect attack. Finally he found Everett's vulnerable heel in his presidency of the Mount Vernon Association. The saving of Washington's home as a national shrine was very close to Everett's

[76] See Joseph L. King, Jr., *George William Bagby* (New York, 1927), pp. 102–103.

[77] Derby, *op. cit.*, pp. 202–203. See James Parton, ed., *Fanny Fern: a Memorial Volume* (New York, 1873), and Robert P. Eckert, Jr., "Friendly, Fragrant Fanny Ferns," *Colophon*, Part 18 (September 1934).

heart, and when Bonner offered to donate $10,000 to the cause if Everett would contribute a short article to the *Ledger* every week for a year, the celebrity was captured. Everett took a month to think it over — and yielded. But many good people were shocked by the idea of their paragon's appearing in a story-paper alongside Mrs. Southworth and Sylvanus Cobb. *Vanity Fair* observed, with its wonted sarcasm, that Everett could now be called "Orator, Patriot, Sage, Cicero of America, Laudator of Washington, Apostle of Charity, High Priest of the Union, Friend of Mankind, and Writer for the *Ledger*!" [78]

Henry Ward Beecher, another of the most conspicuous Americans of the day, was added to Bonner's list of contributors by certain timely financial aid in a personal emergency, and the *Ledger* later paid him $30,000 for his serial novel *Norwood*.[79] To Longfellow, Bonner paid $3,000 for "The Hanging of the Crane"; and for Dickens' three-part *Hunted Down*, "written especially for the *New York Ledger*," he paid $5,000.[80] Bonner was an exploiter and something of a sensation-monger, but he did in the fifties and sixties somewhat the same service Graham and Godey had performed in the forties; he showed that good prices could be paid to writers with advantage to the periodical.

Editorial salaries were frequently undivided from owner's profits. Owners were editors of most of the literary and religious weeklies, and of many others of the periodicals. The outstanding editorial salary was the $2,500 paid annually to Lowell by the *Atlantic Monthly*.[81] Doubtless a chief object in supplanting Lowell with Fields in 1861 was the saving of this salary to Ticknor & Fields, publishers. Charles Godfrey Leland received $50 a month for editing *Graham's* in 1857,[82] and Dr. Bagby got half that sum for the same service on the *Southern Literary*

[78] *Vanity Fair*, I, 28 (January 7, 1860). *Yankee Notions* was even more unkind; see its VIII, 4 (January 1857). For the incident see Paul R. Frothingham, *Edward Everett* (Boston, 1925), p. 387; J. C. Derby, *op. cit.*, p. 471. Bonner is said to have paid, in the end, a total of $24,000 to the Mount Vernon Association for the Everett articles, which were later published in book form as *Mount Vernon Papers*. The Association's organ was the *Mount Vernon Record*, Philadelphia, 1858–60.

[79] Derby, *op. cit.*, pp. 207, 471.

[80] *Ibid.*, p. 203.

[81] Scudder, *op. cit.*, p. 421.

[82] C. G. Leland, *Memoirs* (London, 1893), II, 15.

Messenger.[83] Editing was indeed ill paid, and especially so when the magazine edited was in the doldrums.

The temptation to think of the sums mentioned above in terms of later living expenses must be resisted, however. Let it be remembered that Lowell was elected Smith Professor of Modern Languages at Harvard in 1855 at a salary of $1,200 a year.[84] "Gail Hamilton" was anxious in 1864 to accumulate $10,000 in order that, on the interest on that sum, she could live the rest of her life in the country "in a state of comparative ease and elegance." [85] Greeley allowed himself the munificent salary of $50 weekly in America's premier editorial position, while George William Curtis, his city editor, got $20; and Charles A. Dana, assistant editor, began at $14 in 1848.[86]

ANONYMITY

Closely connected with the matter of payment to writers is that of anonymity.

The number of more or less professional magazinists was growing; payment was more general; anonymity was gradually giving way to the signing of articles. Charles Astor Bristed exaggerated grossly when he stated in an English magazine in 1848 that "the names of *all* the contributors are generally paraded conspicuously on the covers" of American periodicals.[87] True, such representative magazines as *Graham's, Godey's,* and the *Christian Examiner* printed names, as did many others of the more obscure sort; but some of the most important American monthlies and quarterlies preserved the custom of anonymity, such as the *North American,* the *National Quarterly, Putnam's,* the *Atlantic,* and *Harper's Monthly* and *Weekly.* The *Atlantic,* however, sent to the press the names of the writers of all the articles in its first number, and printed on its back cover the names of promised contributors; and it was a common practice of the *New Englander,* the *New York Review,* and other "anonymous" journals to insert a slip containing the names of

[83] King, *op. cit.,* p. 78.
[84] Scudder, *op. cit.,* I, 377.
[85] Dodge, *op. cit.,* I, 410.
[86] Whitelaw Reid, *American and English Studies* (New York, 1913).
[87] *Blackwood's Magazine,* LXIII, 106 (January 1848).

contributors in the copies mailed to newspapers. The *New Englander* began to print the names of its authors in its annual index in 1858; *Harper's* and the *Atlantic* followed in 1860 and 1862, respectively.[88]

Under the system of anonymity, editors had plenary powers. It was a logical result of such a system that blue-penciling should be unrestrained. Many American editors doubtless followed the lead of Jeffrey, of the *Edinburgh Review*, who is said to have regarded a young contributor "as supplying raw material which might be rather arbitrarily altered by the editor." [89] Lowell, for example, created antagonisms on more than one occasion by censorious editing.

But in spite of the obstacle of anonymity, a new group of magazinists was winning recognition in the years 1850–65. The preceding decade had seen the rise of a discernible class of literary producers for the periodicals — the genus "magazinist" — but in the fifties these older writers were, to a large extent, being elbowed out by young men and women, most of whom were to win their larger reputations in the period of expansion following the Civil War. Such men as Richard Grant White, Thomas Bailey Aldrich, Edwin P. Whipple, Thomas Wentworth Higginson, Richard Henry Stoddard, Edmund Clarence Stedman — all destined to be voluminous contributors to the magazines for many years — now won their literary spurs. Such women writers of short stories as Mrs. Rebecca Harding Davis, Harriett Prescott, Caroline Chesebrough, and Rose Terry came forward.

[88] It is interesting to note in this connection that, as a result of anonymous publication, both Poole's earliest *Index* and Hill's *Rhetoric* credited John Burroughs' essay "Expression," published in the *Atlantic* for February 1860, to Emerson.

[89] Leslie Stephen, *Life of Sir James Fitzjames Stephen* (New York, 1895), p. 162.

CHAPTER II

PARADE OF LEADING GENERAL MAGAZINES

TO OBTAIN an adequate view of the general magazines of the years 1850–65 in their relations to one another, it will be necessary to survey them in their three classes — quarterlies, monthlies, and weeklies. As they march past, we shall observe that they are a mob rather than an army: some are bent and lean veterans, many are meanly clothed with but little semblance of uniforms, others are confident youthful recruits; but all march with that springing step which is the habit of optimism.

QUARTERLY REVIEWS

"We do not hear of any original American review of the first class which is doing much more than pay its publisher's expenses," wrote an observer in the *Literary World* in 1852, and added the suggestion that "in many instances" they are not doing that much.[1] A week later the same periodical remarked: "It has been the fashion to write of 'the poor old Quarterlies,' and attribute to them the same degree of influence which grandmothers possess in modern society."[2] Alas, it was but too true: the quarterlies seemed too slow for an age which was half-mad about railroads and Atlantic cables.

At the opening of our period in 1850, there was only one general quarterly in existence which could point to a history of more than eight years: that was the *North American Review*,[3] which for more than a third of a century had occupied a notable position in American periodical literature. Its editorial management had not been distinguished of late years, however, respectable as its clerical and professorial editors had been; and *De Bow's* eyes were not wholly blinded by southern prejudice when it declared of the *North American* in 1850: "That it is not the quarterly of other days . . . no one takes the trouble to

[1] *Literary World*, X, 103 (February 7, 1852).
[2] *Ibid.*, X, 121 (February 14, 1852).
[3] Treated more fully in sketch 1.

dispute."[4] The *Round Table*, a brash young New Yorker, recorded in 1863 a change in the editorship of the old review, which, it said, "for a long time has been living a life of dignified retirement."[5] This editorial change was to mark an improvement in the *North American's* fortunes, however; for the new editors, James Russell Lowell and Charles Eliot Norton, brought new prestige to the old journal.

Three other general quarterly reviews of importance were being issued in 1850: William Gilmore Simms was editing the *Southern Quarterly Review* with one eye on the slavery question and the other on southern literature;[6] Theodore Parker was publishing the last three numbers of the *Massachusetts Quarterly Review*;[7] and James Stryker was on the penultimate year of his statistical *American Quarterly Register*.[8]

In 1852 a new candidate entered the review field — the conservative *New-York Quarterly*, edited quite without distinction by A. G. Remington. Such men as Samuel Osgood, Charles L. Brace, and Adolph L. Koeppen wrote for it, but it lacked incisiveness and originality, and its articles were occasionally superficial. It perished in its third year.[9]

Then comes a gap until 1860: in this year three quarterlies of some interest were begun. Of the trio, far the most important was the *National Quarterly Review*, Edward I. Sears founder and editor. This journal was a real rival of the *North American* during much of its life of two decades. The cultivated but pugnacious personality of Sears pervades his occasionally brilliant review.[10] The *National Democratic Quarterly Review* published five numbers through the presidential campaign of 1860, leavening its politics with occasional literary articles.[11]

[4] *De Bow's Review*, IX, 125 (July 1850).

[5] *Round Table*, I, 6 (December 19, 1863).

[6] See Mott, *A History of American Magazines, 1741–1850*, pp. 721–727.

[7] *Ibid.*, pp. 775–779.

[8] *Ibid.*, p. 368.

[9] March 1852–July 1855. C. B. Norton and James G. Reed were successive publishers. It was a 156-page octavo and sold for $3.00 a year. Beginning April 1853, it published in each number a general literary review treating the books of the preceding quarter.

[10] Treated more fully in sketch 34.

[11] November 1859–November 1860. Thomas B. Florence and Isaac Lawrence were editors. The former had been a member of Congress and was allied with various reform movements.

Even briefer was the *Plantation*,[12] whose four numbers are extremely interesting to the student of slavery and prewar politics. Edited from a down-South plantation but published in New York, it was dedicated to "a defence of slavery, total, unqualified, unreserved." It printed many pages of politics, but also frequent sketches of southern life and southern characters, amusements, and industries. Its outlook upon the future was tragic: some of its pages remind one of those "ancestral voices prophesying war" which Kubla Khan heard; indeed, it definitely predicted war between the North and South in its initial article. Its editor was Joseph Addison Turner, a strong and many-sided character.[13]

Besides the general periodicals which have been mentioned, there were a score or more of sectarian journals published four times a year, and some professional and some learned publications, which will be treated in their proper categories. But before we leave the quarterlies, mention should be made of George Lippard's propagandic *White Banner*, of 1851, all four numbers of which were written by that erratic, vigorous sensationalist.[14]

GENERAL MONTHLIES: THE ADVENT OF *Harper's*

The monthly magazines were far more numerous and generally more prosperous than the "grandmotherly" quarterlies. The monthlies designed for the wider and more general audience may be here passed in review, omitting for the present the women's periodicals and the distinctively class and local magazines.

Of the general monthlies there were five in New York at the opening of our period in 1850: two politico-literary magazines, the *American Whig Review* [15] and the *United States Democratic Review*,[16] both declining toward the end of their careers in 1852

[12] March–December 1860. It was subtitled "A Southern Quarterly Journal of Literature, Politics, and General Miscellany." In form it was an octavo of 222 pages, and Pudney & Russell were the New York publishers.

[13] For Turner's *Countryman*, published on his plantation, see pp. 111–112.

[14] This periodical contains Lippard's mystical tale, "Adonai, the Pilgrim of Eternity," together with the constitution of Lippard's Brotherhood of the Union. "Adonai" has the elevation of labor as its theme.

[15] Mott, *op. cit.*, pp. 750–774.

[16] *Ibid.*, pp. 677–684.

and 1859, respectively; two cheap miscellanies, *Dwight's American Magazine* [17] and *Holden's Dollar Monthly*,[18] both to die in 1851; and the *Knickerbocker*, "Old *Knick*" to its faithful, which, after its editor of a quarter-century left it in 1860, had an inglorious five-year postscript to a distinguished career.[19] In Philadelphia there were two, *Sartain's* and *Graham's*. The former finished the race in 1852;[20] but *Graham's*, first under a return of George R. Graham's editorship and then under Charles Godfrey Leland's, lasted to the end of the war period.[21] In the South the old *Southern Literary Messenger*, under the excellent care of John R. Thompson, and the young *De Bow's Review*, in New Orleans, were the only important monthlies at the opening of our period. Dr. George W. Bagby took the *Messenger* over at the beginning of the war and conducted it, amidst the greatest difficulties, until 1864.[22] The West, though dotted with magazines of literary miscellany, offered none to a national audience. There were, then, only eight general monthlies of importance surviving from the preceding period, not one of which had enough vitality in it to give color or character to the magazine history of the new decade.

It was the founding of *Harper's New Monthly Magazine* that marked the end of the old era. The *Harper* formula was pictures from woodcuts, plus fiction from the great English novelists of the day, plus travel and biography, plus more pictures. Within a year or two after its first appearance in the field, the new magazine had achieved a phenomenal circulation for itself; had banished Godey's to the boudoir, where it had probably always belonged; had made *Graham's* and "Old *Knick*" back numbers; and had provoked a considerable amount of imitation, all of which fell short of the model. "The owners of *Harper's* have no right to win the stakes; they are rich enough already," wrote Graham plaintively in an advertisement in the *New York Tribune*,[23] thus admitting the victory of the newcomer. Though exceeded in literary distinction by the *Atlantic* and *Putnam's*,

---

[17] Mott, *op. cit.*, pp. 364–365.
[18] *Ibid.*, pp. 347–348.
[19] *Ibid.*, pp. 606–614.
[20] *Ibid.*, pp. 769–772.
[21] *Ibid.*, pp. 544–555.
[22] *Ibid.*, pp. 629–657.
[23] The advertisement in the *New York Weekly Tribune* is found on p. 7 of the issue for February 12, 1852. *Harper's Monthly* is treated more fully in sketch 16.

which came a little later, *Harper's* was the outstanding publishing success of the period in the monthly field.

Another newcomer in 1850 was the *International Monthly*,[24] edited by Rufus Wilmot Griswold in New York. Criticism was its specialty. Begun as a weekly eclectic, it broadened out within the year; but in 1852 it was merged with *Harper's*. In that year the Methodist church began in New York the publication of the *National Magazine* [25] with the aim of presenting the attractions of *Harper's* without those "morbid appeals to the passions" to be found in fiction. The Harper brothers were Methodists, too; but they did not share this official fear of the fiction bogey, and they prospered, while the *National* was discontinued in 1858 "for want of support."

The *National* undersold *Harper's*, as did a number of other monthlies started about this time. *Frank Leslie's New York Journal of Romance, General Literature, Science, and Art* [26] was a sixty-two page quarto on cheap paper which sold for $2.00 a year. It used English reprints chiefly and was illustrated by woodcuts during its five years of life. *Ballou's Dollar Monthly Magazine* was a Boston newcomer of 1855; it was octavo in form and throve on the work of Sylvanus Cobb and his kind for more than a third of a century.[27] Most of the cheaper periodicals, however, were weeklies.

In 1853 *Putnam's Monthly Magazine* [28] was founded by G. P. Putnam & Company, leading New York book publishers. Some of the best of established American writers were immediately

---

[24] Treated more fully in sketch 17.

[25] Monthly, July 1852–December 1858. Abel Stevens was editor 1852–56 and James Floy 1856–58; J. M. Reid was associate editor. It was chiefly eclectic, with departments of religious and literary news, illustrated by woodcuts.

[26] Begun in August 1853 by a Mr. Orvis as the *New York Journal* (caption and running title: *Illustrated New York Journal*); sold in December 1854 to Frank Leslie, who began a new series in January 1855, under the title *Frank Leslie's New York Journal of Romance, General Literature, Science, and Art;* bought by Samuel French in March 1857, who altered the title only by removing Leslie's name from it; merged with *Mrs. Stephens' Illustrated New Monthly* in January 1858.

[27] Founded by Maturin M. Ballou, who had just bought out Frederick Gleason's periodical publishing business; sold to Thomes & Talbot, publishers of the *American Union*, in 1872, and to George W. Studley in 1886. The word "Dollar" was dropped from the title when the price was raised to $1.50 in 1866. The file ends in 1893.   [28] Treated more fully in sketch 21.

enlisted as contributors, and several newer men won reputations in *Putnam's*. It was often brilliant and lively and always intelligent; it had variety and a real literary flavor. The enthusiasm of a dusty and often disappointed delver among old magazines leads the present writer to say, though with some diffidence, that *Putnam's* was the first genuinely civilized magazine in America; at any rate, it was the first American periodical that could be favorably compared with such English magazines as *Fraser's* or *Blackwood's*. But after less than five years of existence, and after experimenting, in a final bid for popularity, with woodcuts and other devices which had made its chief rival successful, it gave up the struggle.

It was *Emerson's Magazine*,[29] founded in 1854 as the *United States Magazine*, which took over *Putnam's* in 1857. J. M. Emerson had clearly intended it as a rival to *Harper's* at a lower price; it was well illustrated, but it publicly renounced English serials, which critics of *Harper's* were wont to find unpatriotic. Seba Smith was editor; and after the combination with *Putnam's*, he and his wife and sons were editors and proprietors. But it deteriorated, what with poor paper and poorer contents, until it ended in 1859 with a series under the title of the *Great Republic*.

Mrs. Stephens' Illustrated New Monthly[30] was the next attempt; it lasted two years, 1856–58. Mrs. Ann S. Stephens, the novelist, was editor; and her husband, Edward Stephens, a New York newspaper man, was publisher. The *Monthly* was a small quarto of sixty-four pages, illustrated by a few woodcuts, and filled with Mrs. Stephens' stories and essays, together with selected material.

This brings us to the founding of the *Atlantic Monthly*[31] in November 1857, with James Russell Lowell as editor. The *Atlantic's* Boston was a long way from *Harper's* New York — further than mere miles traced on a map would indicate. Boston had been the literary center of the United States for more than a decade, and most of the possessors of the period's great literary reputations lived within a half-day's journey (by one-horse

---

[29] Treated more fully in sketch 25.
[30] July 1856–June 1858, in four volumes.
[31] Treated more fully in sketch 30.

shay) of the Boston State House. Moreover, these literary great had all agreed to write for the *Atlantic*; and they made it immediately, so far as belles-lettres were concerned, the most important magazine in America. James T. Fields, who became Lowell's successor in 1861, wrote complacently two years later in his diary: "The *Atlantic Monthly* is a striking feature just now in American life. Purely literary as it is, it has a subscription list, daily increasing, of 32,000." [32]

The only southern magazine founded in these years to win wide recognition was begun in the same year with the *Atlantic*. This was *Russell's Magazine*,[33] edited in Charleston by Paul Hamilton Hayne. It was an excellent periodical, superior in the departments of poetry and criticism; but it perished on the eve of the war, after only three years of life. Likewise, the only new western magazine of distinction was Moncure D. Conway's *Dial*,[34] of Cincinnati, which, though it published only the twelve numbers of 1860, was so infused with the vigorous and original character of young Conway that it set a high standard. Politics, theology, belles-lettres, and criticism were the *Dial's* menu; Emerson was its most notable contributor.

Only one general monthly of any considerable significance was begun during the war. This was the *Continental Monthly*,[35] founded by James R. Gilmore with objects both political and literary, and edited during much of its three years by Charles Godfrey Leland. It owed a double allegiance to Boston and New York and had a distinguished list of contributors.

A WILDERNESS OF WEEKLIES

To find one's way surely among the weeklies of the mid-century is impossible. The story-papers and literary miscellanies were commonly in folio or large quarto form and thus difficult to preserve; moreover, a paper costing only a few cents seemed scarcely worth preserving.

The weeklies, however, were very important in these years.

---

[32] James T. Fields, *Biographical Notes and Personal Sketches* (Boston, 1881), p. 84.

[33] Treated more fully in sketch 29.

[34] Treated more fully in sketch 35.

[35] Treated more fully in sketch 37.

"The many weekly periodicals which peculiarly distinguish this nation and this age," to use the formal expression of one of them,[36] fall into a large number of classes. They will be found figuring in our subsequent study of religious, reform, agricultural, medical, legal, comic, juvenile, educational, and trade periodicals. They were of large importance in the field of women's magazines and the periodical literature especially designed for "the home." Though this latter class is difficult to separate from the more "general" miscellanies, an attempt will be made here to discuss some of the longer-lived and more widely circulated of those weeklies which made an appeal to the general reader.

SUNDAY PAPERS

Most of these were Sunday papers. They were not Sunday editions of dailies; they were miscellanies issued Saturday afternoon for Sunday reading. Much objection was offered by Sabbatarians against the "hawking" of these papers on Sunday, especially in New York and Philadelphia. Certain papers paid fines for this offense against the "blue laws" regularly every week,[37] flourishing in spite of courts and reformers. "At least one-half of the entire population of the city," writes a New York observer of the sixties, "occupies the early hours of the first day of the week in the eager perusal of literature prepared especially for Sunday." [38] This was not distinctively religious matter, though some of the papers had religious departments; on the other hand, some Sunday papers were sensational and vulgar. There were, of course, Sunday editions of some of the regular dailies, though this was comparatively uncommon until later; and these Sunday editions, nearly all begun during the war in order that there should be no interruption in the publication of the vitally interesting reports from the front, were distinctively *news*papers.[39] But the miscellanies for Sunday reading, many of which carried either the word *Sunday* or the word *Saturday*

[36] *Life Illustrated*, I, 2 (November 4, 1854).

[37] See New York Sabbath Committee, *The First Five Years of Sabbath Reform* [New York, 1862], pp. 7–8.

[38] Augustus Maverick, *Henry J. Raymond and the New York Press* (Hartford, 1870), p. 345.

[39] James Melvin Lee, *History of American Journalism* (Boston, 1917), p. 309; Alfred M. Lee, *The Daily Newspaper in America* (New York, 1937), Chapter XI.

COMING OUT OF A FASHIONABLE CHURCH

Drawn by E. I. Whitney to accompany a satirical sketch in *Harper's Weekly*, January 16, 1858.

in their titles, flourished everywhere. A Philadelphia guide-book of 1852 lists no less than sixteen weeklies of this type as being currently published in that city.[40] Every city of much size had one or more, and the veterans of the class were among the oldest of existing American periodicals. They printed either four blanket-size pages or eight in smaller folio, and commonly sold for $2.00 a year, though prices were increased — sometimes doubled — during the war.

Let us turn for example to the Boston *Saturday Evening Gazette*, an excellent paper of its kind, with its theatrical and other reviews, its amusing tales, its humor, and its "lighter gossip of Boston life." It was begun in 1814, and the William Warland Clapps, father and son, edited and published it for half a century. The younger Clapp, an authority on the American theater, published a serial "Records of the Boston Stage" in his paper. Adam Wallace Thaxter and Benjamin Penhallow Shillaber, the latter famous for his "Mrs. Partington" papers, were associate editors throughout the fifties. William Winter was New York correspondent for several years.[41]

There were many such papers in Boston. The *Flag of Our Union* (1846–70) had a rather notable history. Among its contributors were Poe, Mrs. Osgood, Mrs. Sigourney, Park Benjamin, Sylvanus Cobb, and Horatio Alger. In 1851 it was claiming to lead American weeklies in circulation, but it probably never distributed much over 100,000 copies. Gleason, its founder, claimed it made him $25,000 a year in profits.[42] The *American Union* [43] (1828–77) was less distinguished. Then there were

[40] R. A. Smith, *Philadelphia As It Is in 1852* (Philadelphia, 1852), pp. 239–241.

[41] It was founded by William Burdick and bought by Clapp, the founder of the *Daily Advertiser*, in 1817. It was called the *Boston Intelligencer*, 1816–18. The younger Clapp, succeeding to the property in 1847, had his brother, Charles J., associated with him for a time. He was succeeded in 1865 by B. G. Goodsell, who was followed by Col. Henry G. Parker. Parker conducted the paper 1871–93, adding society news and caustic dramatic and musical criticism. After his death the paper had various editors for short terms and was finally merged with the *Boston Budget* in 1906. See *Budget*, October 13, 1906, p. 6.

[42] See *Granite State Magazine*, III, 51 (February 1907). The *Flag* was founded by Frederick Gleason and sold to Maturin M. Ballou, the editor Gleason had employed, in 1854.

[43] William E. Graves and S. E. Weston were editors and publishers in the sixties, and Thomes and Talbot in the seventies.

the *Boston Museum* [44] (1848–60?), which was edited for some years by Ossian E. Dodge, the singer; the *Weekly Novelette* (1857–62), another Ballou periodical specializing in four-part stories, which is said to have suggested the dime-novel idea to Erastus Beadle; [45] the *True Flag* (1851–1908), edited for many years by John W. Nichols; and the *Yankee Blade* (1841–94), founded by William Mathews.[46]

A popular New England weekly of this class was the *Portland Transcript* (1837–1910), founded by Charles P. Ilsley, but conducted for nearly half a century by E. H. Elwell and associates. The *Portland Pleasure Boat* ran from 1845 to 1861. Down at Hartford, the fortnightly *Connecticut Courant Supplement* printed fiction and articles on small pages suitable for binding, from 1825 through 1878.

In Philadelphia the *Saturday Evening Post*,[47] thirty years old at the beginning of our period, was the veteran. It led the Philadelphia weeklies in 1850 with 42,000 circulation. Conducted by Edmund Deacon and Henry Peterson, it published Mrs. Southworth, T. S. Arthur, "Grace Greenwood," the Cary sisters, "Fanny Fern," and other popular writers, along with English serials. Another well-known Philadelphia miscellany for Sunday reading was (Joseph C.) *Neal's Saturday Gazette and Ladies'*

[44] Putnam & Mellen were early publishers, and William O. Eaton was an early editor. It was a sixteen-page quarto weekly at $2.00 a year. Dodge is said to have taken the paper with him to Cleveland when he moved there about 1858. It changed its title in 1852 to the *Literary Museum*, and the following year to *Dodge's Literary Museum*. It published serials by Sylvanus Cobb and others, much miscellany, and music by Dodge.

[45] See New York Public Library, *The Beadle Collection of Dime Novels* (New York, 1922), p. 17. This periodical was later revived by Thomes & Talbot, another firm of Boston dime-novel publishers, as the *Monthly Novelette* (1871–72).

[46] Mathews founded this paper in Waterville, Maine, in 1841 as the *Watervillonian*, but changed the awkward title to *Yankee Blade* in the second year. He published it in Gardiner, Maine, 1843–47, and then moved it to Boston, where he issued it as a semimonthly miscellany of excellent character until 1856. It was then merged with the *Port Folio*. The name was revived in 1862 in *Harry Hazel's Yankee Blade*, a Saturday story-paper. In the early eighties this paper dropped "Harry Hazel's" name and assumed the founding-date of Mathews' periodical. Cora Stuart Wheeler was editor for several years. It was published until 1894. Another "Harry Hazel" paper was the Boston *Yankee Privateer*, begun in 1852 and published as a story-miscellany for several years by J. Jones & Company.

[47] To be treated more fully in the final volume of this work.

Literary Museum (1836–53), which was carried on after Neal's death in 1847 by his widow, who was not yet twenty at that time. Mrs. Neal had become acquainted with her husband when she had brought her first contributions to the *Gazette* office. The *Gazette* published two famous humorous series — Neal's *Charcoal Sketches* and Mrs. Whitcher's *Widow Bedott Papers*. It was succeeded in December 1853 by the *Saturday Evening Mail*, with George R. Graham, who had just sold out *Graham's Magazine*, as editor, and Richard H. See as publisher. The *Mail* was strongly in favor of temperance and was largely eclectic. Other Philadelphia periodicals of this class in the fifties were the *Sunday Dispatch*, the *Sunday Mercury*, the *Sunday Transcript*, the *Sunday Morning Times*, and the *City Item*.

In New York the *Dispatch* (1845–1900) and the *Sunday Mercury* (1838–96) were the leading Sunday papers. Both of them are said to have "created ample fortunes for their proprietors." [48] The former was founded by A. J. Williamson and edited by him for many years. It was a large paper, full of crime stories and sensation fiction, with a few woodcuts; it was badly printed and published the advertising of contraceptives and abortion drugs. The *Mercury* [49] was on a higher plane. It printed stories and sketches by William Gilmore Simms, Bayard Taylor, Harriet Prescott Spofford, and such respectable writers, as well as the thrillers of J. H. Ingraham, "Ned Buntline," and J. H. Robinson — the last a favorite who was kept on salary. Humorists such as Artemus Ward, Josh Billings, Orpheus C. Kerr, and Miles O'Reilly are found in the *Mercury's* long columns; and F. O. C. Darley drew pictures for them. This paper gave much attention to sports. William Cauldwell bought it at the beginning of our period and published it for more than forty years, gaining for it a circulation of 145,000 before the war. Before coming to the *Mercury*, Cauldwell had been with the *Atlas* (1828–81), one of the oldest of the New York Sunday papers, long a labor advocate, and a much more serious period-

[48] Maverick, *op. cit.*, p. 345.
[49] Founded by Eldbridge G. Paige, clever versifier and sportsman, and Samuel Nichols, native Englishman and theatrical critic of ability. August Krauth was later taken into partnership. For full historical sketch of the *Mercury*, see *Journalist*, January 7, 1888, pp. 1–4.

ical than most of its kind.[50] Other prominent week-end papers in that city were the *Sunday Times*, the *Leader*, and the *Courier*.

The *New York Ledger* [51] was not originally designed for Sunday reading, but after the war it changed its publication day from Monday to Saturday in order to meet that demand. The *Ledger* was then feeling the competition of the *New York Weekly*. The younger paper had been founded in 1856 by A. J. Williamson, proprietor of the *Dispatch*, but it had reached only 28,000 circulation when it was bought just before the war by a firm composed of Francis S. Street and Francis S. Smith, the latter a writer of serials for it. The *Weekly* reached 100,000 circulation by 1865 and doubled that in five years more; it was the foundation upon which Street & Smith built their great business in dime novels.

After all, scoffers might poke fun at the *Ledger* and the *Weekly* and the *Sunday Mercury*, with their Mrs. Southworths and Sylvanus Cobbs and J. H. Robinsons; but the great American public had a positively insatiable appetite for such pabulum. The descending curve of illiteracy seems to have been matched by the ascending curve of popularity for the Sunday papers and dime novels.

THE SATURDAY PRESS

Among the weekly miscellanies published on Saturday, but scarcely of them, was that witty and sophisticated periodical, the *Saturday Press*. It was founded by Henry Clapp and Edward Howland on October 29, 1858. Clapp was a man of volatile temperament, caustic wit, and a freedom and courage in criticism of the American scene which were rare in those days. William Winter, his best apologist, has said of him that "he was wayward and erratic; but he possessed both the faculty of taste and the instinctive love of beauty, and, essentially, he was the apostle of freedom of thought." [52] He had been a militant aboli-

---

[50] Founded by T. D. Porter and Eustis Prescott; but the chief name connected with it for many years was that of Anson Herrick, at one time a member of Congress. Subtitle: "Literary, Historical and Commercial Reporter."

[51] Treated more fully in sketch 12.

[52] William Winter, *Old Friends* (New York, 1914), pp. 58–59. Also, Charles T. Congdon, *Reminiscences of a Journalist* (Boston, 1880), pp. 338–340; Albert Parry, *Garrets and Pretenders* (New York, 1933), Chapter IV.

tionist, prohibitionist, and Fourierist in New England in his earlier life and had later lived in France. At the time he began the *Saturday Press* he was in his prime; and in "Pfaff's Cellar," a chophouse conducted by Charles Ignatius Pfaff at 653 Broadway, where the young bloods in criticism and belles-lettres were wont to congregate, Clapp reigned as "Prince of the Bohemians." Two of these "Bohemians," Thomas Bailey Aldrich and Fitz-James O'Brien, were staff members of the *Press* organization from the beginning, the one writing about books and the other about the theater; but Aldrich remained with the paper only about three months and O'Brien an even shorter time. Perhaps their defection was responsible for a certain dryness in the remark which Clapp is said to have made after O'Brien was wounded during the early days of the war. The two younger men had both applied for the position of aide to General Lander; and though Aldrich got the appointment, through a piece of typical war-time hocus-pocus O'Brien actually took the place. "I see," said Clapp, when he heard the news of the casualty, "that Aldrich has been shot in O'Brien's shoulder." It was Clapp who described Horace Greeley as "a self-made man who worships his creator."

At Pfaff's, Clapp found and enlisted in the service of the *Press* such men as George Arnold, Charles Dawson Shanly, Walt Whitman, "Ada Clare," and William Winter. Whitman wrote "Out of the Cradle Endlessly Rocking" for the *Press*, where it was printed under the title, "A Child's Reminiscence." "Ada Clare," born Jane McElheney, whose poetic gift, such as it was, had been discovered by the *Atlas*, contributed both prose and verse to Clapp's paper: though she was sometimes called in the press of the period the "Queen of Bohemia," that sobriquet carries with it no implication of relationship between her and Clapp.[53] Winter was "sub-editor" of the *Press* during its last year.

The paper was always in hot water financially. Winter tells a story about locking the doors and hiding when Richard Henry Stoddard came to collect for a poem.[54] Aldrich tells one about

[53] For "Ada Clare," see *American Mercury*, XXI, 97–105 (September 1930). This article is elaborated in Parry, *op. cit.*, Chapters II–III.

[54] Winter, *op. cit.*, p. 294.

Clapp's getting all the advertising receipts for himself because he suffered from insomnia; such accounts were always settled in the mornings, and, while other members of the staff, like good Bohemians, lay abed till noon, Clapp was always abroad very early.[55] At length, in December 1860, the *Press* suspended publication. Five years later Clapp raised it from the dead with the following succinct announcement: "This paper was stopped in 1860 for want of means. It is now started again for the same reason." On November 18, 1865, it published Mark Twain's "The Celebrated Jumping Frog of Calaveras County," which presented a new humorist to New York and to America. In the same number it introduced "Josh Billings." "The young writers throughout the country were anxious to be seen in it," wrote Howells, himself a contributor, about the *Press*. "It was very nearly as well to be accepted by the *Press* as by the *Atlantic*." [56] But in 1866 it winked out again. Clapp died in poverty in 1875.

MISCELLANEOUS WEEKLIES

Among the weeklies which did not belong to the week-end group, two may be noted as holding over from the preceding period.[57] The *American Literary Gazette and Weekly Mirror*, the final incarnation of the old brilliant *New York Mirror*, lasted, with impaired influence, until about 1857. The aged Mrs. Anne Royall was still pursuing her Washington game in that remarkable last paper of hers — the *Huntress*.

Mrs. Royall was past eighty at the beginning of our period; and she and her paper died in 1854, shortly after she had bought a new printing outfit. The new material was sorely needed, for a worse set and worse printed sheet than the *Huntress* of the fifties would be hard to find. Yet, in spite of an appearance that would make a respectable printer tear his hair, there was something in the *Huntress* to excite genuine admiration. The character sketches in which the indomitable old lady-journalist

[55] J. C. Derby, *Fifty Years Among Authors, Books and Publishers* (New York, 1884), p. 232.

[56] W. D. Howells, *Literary Friends and Acquaintance* (New York, 1900), p. 70. Howells did not like Clapp or his group. See pp. 68–76, *op. cit.*

[57] A third was the *Literary American*, a pleasant miscellany edited by G. P. Quackenbos, professional literary agent, and published by A. J. Townsend. It was issued from July 8, 1848, to May 25, 1850.

specialized are really vivid, and she had bits of physical description of society personages and statesmen that are still most effective. There is personality in every ill-written and badly set line in the paper; through it all one cannot but see the bent old lady, wrinkled and tawdry, yet with sharp eyes and a flashing smile for everyone's quip, going about getting her material:

Many of our friends have been hurt that we did not — and have not called on them sooner. had a good rea*s*on to be. [She explains she has been ill.] *T*hen we are growing old though we would risk our life for our friends, which they well know, but would not suffer, Again — the *Congress Register* was not printed for six weeks after congress met, How could we find anyone, God *k*nows we were dying to see them.[58]

Who cares if old John Quincy Adams had called her a "virago errant, in enchanted armor"?[59] If the testimony introduced at the trial at which she was convicted of being a common scold is to be believed, and the judge thought it was, Mrs. Royall was an accomplished bestower of epithets herself. But now she was very old, and she hobbled about to see her friends, and wrote in her *Huntress* — rather more literary and much less scurrilous than her earlier *Paul Pry* — those character sketches that were still acute, though more and more slovenly in style.[60]

Several weeklies founded within the years 1850–65 must now be chronicled. The first is Donald G. Mitchell's *Lorgnette, or, Studies of the Town, by an Opera Goer.* This was not an operatic review, but a series of satires upon fashionable foibles in New York, illustrated capitally by F. O. C. Darley. It was reminiscent of *Salmagundi* and appeared throughout most of 1850.[61]

Second is the *Waverley Magazine* (1850–1908), for half a

[58] *Huntress*, March 4, 1848, p. 3.

[59] *American Historical Magazine and Tennessee Historical Society Quarterly*, IX, 343 (October 1904). Article by W. E. Beard.

[60] For *Paul Pry* and the *Huntress*, see Mott, *op. cit.*, p. 356. For Mrs. Royall's life and journalistic adventures, see Sarah H. Porter, *The Life and Times of Anne Royall* (Cedar Rapids, 1908); Richardson Wright, *Forgotten Ladies* (Philadelphia, 1928), pp. 156–186; and *American Mercury*, XII, 87 (September 1927), article by Heber Blankenhorn.

[61] First series is in twelve numbers, January 20–April 24; and the second of the same length, May 10–October 9. Stringer & Townsend and Henry Kernot were publishers. Its editor was given as "John Timon," and its real authorship was a fashionable mystery for some weeks.

century the favorite of amateur writers. Moses A. Dow, a Boston printer, purchased four hundred dollars' worth of type and machinery on credit in the early months of 1850, and created a magazine which he threw open to the unpaid contributions of schoolgirls and their swains. The *Waverley* was a success almost from the start, its contributors and their friends and admirers willingly paying their $3.00 a year to see these efforts in print. Circulation jumped to 50,000, later falling to about 20,000, which proved to be normal for many years. Dow is said to have enjoyed at one time an income of $50,000 to $60,000 a year from his magazine, which had a low ratio of expenditures. This is the style of its verse:

> I know a maid, a dark-eyed maid,
> Who's blithe and debonair,
> And on her face, her beaming face,
> Is pictured beauty rare.[62]

Perhaps we should forbear. It probably pleased the girl.[63]

The *American Miscellany* was founded in New York on February 1, 1851, by Albert Palmer, and in July of that year absorbed *Holden's Dollar Magazine*; it perished, however, a year later. Fowlers & Wells, publishers of literature on phrenology and other "isms," founded in 1854 a two-dollar weekly in four-page folio called *Life Illustrated*. It was not illustrated by pictures; but it was a highly departmentalized miscellany of "entertainment, improvement and progress," devoted to literature, mechanics, agriculture, photography, phonetic reform, and so on. The most important of its contributors was Walt Whitman, who wrote a few articles for it (as yet uncollected) in 1856. In the same year Whitman had contributed to Fowlers & Wells's *Phrenological Journal*, with which the less successful *Life Illustrated* was finally merged in 1861. The *American Register and International Journal*, John Hancock editor, was be-

---

[62] *Waverley Magazine*, III, 7 (July 12, 1851).
[63] John Ross Dix became assistant editor in 1853, but when they attempted to edit the magazine more severely, its circulation dropped; whereupon the early policy was resumed. The subscription price was raised to $5.00 in the sixties, but was later fixed at $4.00. Dow died in 1886, and the magazine used some material of the dime-novel type in the nineties, though it still clung more or less to its traditions. For some facts about Dow, see John W. Moore, *Historical, Biographical and Miscellaneous Gatherings* (Concord, 1886), p. 547.

gun in Boston on July 1, 1860, as a kind of continuation of the old *Niles' Register*, but it lasted only a little over a year. The *Irving Magazine* was a cheap weekly miscellany published in New York by Smith & Haney through 1860.

THE ILLUSTRATED WEEKLIES

Half a dozen copiously illustrated weeklies of general appeal must be grouped separately. It would not be inappropriate to classify these periodicals as newspapers, since they all relied much upon the reporting of current events: indeed, one of them called itself a newspaper in its title. But they were all very much more than newspapers, and they placed the emphasis on features of appeal which belonged more characteristically to the magazine than to the newspaper — namely, pictures and belles-lettres.

The first two of the group began in 1851. *Gleason's Pictorial Drawing-Room Companion* [64] issued its first number in Boston on May 3, and the *Illustrated American News* was born in New York June 7. Both printed many woodcuts, some of them dealing with news events, as well as much cheap fiction and some poetry by popular writers. The experiment with news pictures was scarcely successful, because of the time required for engraving the large blocks; the picture usually came three or four weeks after the event. Maturin M. Ballou, the editor of *Gleason's Pictorial*, bought the paper in 1855 and substituted his own name for Gleason's in the title. He continued the *Pictorial* until 1859,[65] but in the meantime his original New York rival had perished. T. W. Strong, the engraver, was the founder of the *Illustrated American News*, and he was assisted by such other workers on wood as Nathaniel and J. W. Orr, John Andrew, and A. V. S. Anthony. Their pictures were designed more often to illustrate the news than those of *Gleason's Pictorial*, and this may be the reason that the paper lasted only six months. It was revived, however, in the *Illustrated News*, published during 1853 by P. T. Barnum, the showman, and H. D.

---

[64] Treated more fully in sketch 18.

[65] It was followed by a story-paper, *Gleason's Literary Companion* (1860–70), a large folio of sixteen pages, in which the original publisher returned to the helm.

and A. E. Beach, of the *New York Sun*. Each of these men put $20,000 into the short-lived paper, and it gained 70,000 circulation before it was merged, without loss, in *Gleason's Pictorial*.[66] Their leading engraver wrote later that they had great difficulties in getting suitable wood and presses and in finding properly trained artists.[67] The editor of the paper was the famous anthologist Rufus W. Griswold, and Charles Godfrey Leland was his assistant.

At this point one of the period's most interesting figures enters the magazine publishing "game." Robert Carter, alias Frank Leslie, was an English engraver who had worked successively for Gleason, Strong, and Barnum; now, on December 15, 1855, he founded his own journal, which he called *Frank Leslie's Illustrated Newspaper*.[68] A fuller exposition of this large and exuberant personality must await later pages,[69] but it may be said here that J. C. Derby's ascription to him of the title "pioneer and founder of illustrated journalism in America" [70] is little or no exaggeration. The *Illustrated Newspaper* had a life of some sixty years, latterly as *Leslie's Weekly*.

Harper's Weekly,[71] begun in 1857, very nearly paralleled the life span of *Leslie's Weekly*. If we take into consideration the entire files of both journals, we must rank *Harper's* as of distinctly higher quality than *Leslie's*. The freshness and freedom from cant of *Leslie's* may be found very attractive, but *Harper's*

---

[66] Frederic Hudson, *History of Journalism in the United States from 1690 to 1872* (New York, 1873), p. 706; P. T. Barnum, *Struggles and Triumphs; or, Fifty Years' Recollections* (Buffalo, 1884), p. 140. The *Illustrated News* lasted from January 1 to November 28, 1853, and its predecessor from June 7, 1851, to March 12, 1852. Its engraving and printing were both good, but its pictures had little actual news value.

[67] *Frank Leslie's Illustrated Newspaper*, I, 6 (December 15, 1855). See also the not-too-dependable *Memoirs of Charles Godfrey Leland* (London, 1893), I, 278–292.

[68] Treated more fully in sketch 23.

[69] See pp. 452–462.

[70] Derby, *op. cit.*, p. 692. Leslie himself once pointed out that Chevalier Wikoff "made the first attempt to establish a pictorial journal in the United States" in a kind of supplement to his *Republic* newspaper called *The Picture Gallery*, an eight-page weekly which lasted but a short time in 1843. (*Illustrated Newspaper*, I, 6, December 15, 1855.) Of course there had been some illustrations in magazines for nearly a hundred years. See Mott, *op. cit.*, pp. 36–38, 208–210, 519–524.

[71] Treated more fully in sketch 28.

was better edited and better printed. The "Journal of Civilization," as *Harper's Weekly* called itself, was essentially "sound
and conservative." George William Curtis as editorial writer
and Thomas Nast as cartoonist added much to its power during
the war.

An imitator of *Harper's Weekly* appeared on November 12,
1859, again using the title, the *New York Illustrated News*.
John King was the first proprietor, but he sold to T. B. Leggett
after a year and a half. George S. Phillips, T. Smith Reed,
Mortimer Thompson, and Thomas Bailey Aldrich were successive editors. The woodcuts were good, and the paper looked much
like its model. Thomas Nast, Arthur Lumley, and A. R. Waud
were its chief artists in the early sixties. It carried many folding plates, one of which was as much as forty inches wide.[72] Its
war pictures were of the highest interest, but its fiction and its
printing were, on the whole, inferior to that of *Harper's Weekly*.
W. Jennings Demorest bought the paper at the beginning of
1864, called it *Demorest's New York Illustrated News,* and
added music, fashions and patterns, and a woman's department
by "Jennie June." It was merged with Mme. Demorest's *Mirror
of Fashion* after August 1864.

A brief but lavishly illustrated miscellany was *Gleason's Line-
of-Battle Ship*, published in Boston fourteen months from
November 1858.

There were also certain special holiday sheets such as the
Constellation, issued by George Roberts, former publisher of
the *Boston Notion*. The number of this series issued in New
York for the Fourth of July 1859 contained eight pages, each
of which measured four feet, two inches, by eight feet, four
inches. It was filled with large woodcuts and had a circulation
of over 50,000 copies.

[72] A battle scene in the issue for October 4, 1862.

CHAPTER III

CLASS PERIODICALS AND THEIR FIELDS

MAGAZINES AND THE "WOMAN QUESTION"

THE position of woman in the American society of 1850–65 was discussed not alone by the magazines designed mainly for the women themselves, but by quarterlies, monthlies, and weeklies of all descriptions. It may be interesting to preface a survey of the women's periodicals with a glance at this general comment on the ubiquitous "woman question." It appears to have had three chief phases: (1) the question of "female education"; (2) the matter of women's activities outside the home circle; and (3) the scandalous movement for dress reform.

To speak of "female education" would have offended Mrs. Sarah Josepha Hale, editor of *Godey's*, who maintained that the use of the word "female" was indelicate. But Mrs. Hale was not successful in this bit of speech reform until somewhat later; and in the war period we have the obnoxious word used widely, especially in connection with educational matters. There was the *Female Student*, published monthly 1859–60 by the students of Louisville Female College, to cite but one convenient example.

Matthew Vassar's gift for the foundation of a woman's college of high grade excited much attention. *Vanity Fair*, more or less serious for the nonce, thanks Vassar for "what bids fair to be the best educational institution for the Muslin Sex in America . . . giving the growing minds good solid pabulum." [1] But Mrs. E. S. Seager, late principal of the Female Department of Genesee Wesleyan Seminary, writes boldly in the *Monthly Literary Miscellany* demanding full coeducational privileges for girls — though she knows the proposal will "awaken ridicule and excite prejudice." [2] Fashionable girls' boarding schools, long an object of satire, received plenty of criticism in the fifties: a series of

[1] *Vanity Fair*, III, 82 (February 16, 1861).
[2] *Monthly Literary Miscellany*, VII, 398 (September 1852).

comic drawings depicting the life of such schools appeared in *Frank Leslie's Lady's Magazine* in 1863. Thomas Wentworth Higginson wrote learnedly in the *Atlantic Monthly* under the sarcastic heading, "Shall Women Learn the Alphabet?" [3] Indications of a new attitude, perhaps, were the riding schools and "gymnastic institutes" which advertised classes for ladies as well as gentlemen in *Frank Leslie's Ladies' Gazette of Fashions* in 1854. New also was the advice of a writer in a leading agricultural journal that women should read "good, moral, and sensible newspapers" in order to "govern, guide, and instruct" their children.[4]

But in the main, the same old arguments were rehashed. Henry James, writing on "Woman and the Woman's Movement" in *Putnam's*, had much to say of "woman's incapacity" and the "natural inequality" of the sexes.[5] Mrs. Kirkland, doing an article on "The American Ideal Woman" for the same magazine, said: "We are not for learned ladies, as such," though she believed in the cultivation of "every faculty." [6]

It may have been Mrs. Kirkland who also wrote, in connection with a review of Mrs. Browning's *Aurora Leigh*: "A woman may now enjoy the reputation of being clever without ceasing to be regarded as a woman. This is a glory of our age which should never be forgotten." [7] But there were others who regarded women's writing with disfavor. An anonymous contributor to the *United States Magazine* remarked that

France, England, Germany, Sweden, but most of all our own country, has furnished forth an army of women in the walks of literature. . . . Her literature has been more sensuous than intellectual. More than this, we are confident that the magnetism produced by her out-given heart-throbs has warmed into vitality a vast number of womanly men who, without manly force, or manly vigor of intellect, have given way to unmanly mawkishness and morbid complainings, Laura Matilda prettinesses and sentimentalisms, quite to the shame of manhood. . . . Our literature is growing rather fine than forceful, more elegant than original. . . . We are tired of the whole school of mosaic workers like

[3] *Atlantic Monthly*, III, 137 (February 1859).
[4] *Emery's Journal of Agriculture*, II, 29 (July 8, 1858).
[5] *Putnam's Monthly*, I, 279 (March 1853).
[6] *Ibid.*, II, 527 (November 1853).
[7] *Ibid.*, IX, 30 (January 1857).

Longfellow, and imitators like Bayard Taylor, and Curtis, and Stod-dard.[8]

The literature of the times did indeed need more virility in it; but women readers were doubtless more to blame for Long-fellow and the others than women writers, and back of the women readers in the chain of causes was the orthodox system of a sentimental education for girls.

If women are not to write, certainly they must keep clear of those even more dangerous fields — politics and the professions. A Dr. G. M. Wharton, writing in the *South-Western Monthly*, expresses the view that women do not have the self-possession and balance to deal with affairs.

Is there a thrill in the grasp of metaphysics [he asks rhetorically] or honey in the lips of transcendentalism? Your men-women run into the foolishest extremes! They want to live heaped in a phalanx, being Fourierites; they diet you on bread and water, being Grahamites; if they dose you, it is with next to no physic, being homœopathists; or they splash you like a hosepipe, being hydropathists; they are wonder-ful quacks invariably! In religion, they deny Christ, but avouch Davis, and substitute mesmerism and phrenology for the Old and New Testaments. They are Abolitionists; they would free the slaves of the South, only to enslave the Southerners themselves. . . .[9]

And so on; the doctor has a good time making women respon-sible for all the quackeries which his orthodox soul hates. But a few months later an anonymous lady who opposes women in politics defends women doctors;[10] she attacks Dr. Wharton's logic and rather "uses him up" — to employ the slang of that day.

For the South, this anonymous lady was an arrant extremist. Another lady is much more conventional when she indites the following verses in the *Southern Literary Messenger*:

> These reverend Misses, doctors in mob caps,
> And petticoated lecturers, are things
> Which make us loathe, like strange unnatural births,
> Nature's disordered works. Yon chirping thing
> That with cracked voice and mincing manners prates

---

[8] *United States Magazine*, III, 242 (September 1856).
[9] *South-Western Monthly*, I, 149 (March 1852).
[10] *Ibid.*, I, 273–277 (May 1852).

Of rights and duties, lecturing to the crowd,
And in strange nondescript of dress arrays
Unfettered limbs that modesty should hide . . .
Sweet sisters, call not that unsexed thing
By the pure name of woman.[11]

The same writer reviews Elizabeth Oakes Smith's *Woman and Her Needs* for *De Bow's,* insisting that "woman was made for duty, not for fame." She quotes a speech made at the first Worcester Convention by Mrs. Mehitable Haskell, who

> frankly acknowledges that "she does not know what are woman's rights, but for forty, nay, fifty years, she has known what woman's wrongs are, for she has felt them." . . . Alas! good Mrs. Mehitable, take home that earnest soul of thine. There is work for it elsewhere, but none here. Here is Babel-confusion, brawling presumption, restless vanity; no room for truth. Thy woman's wrongs, borne for fifty long years, canst thou not bear yet a little longer? Let suffering teach thee patience.[12]

Cold comfort, it may be feared, to Mrs. Mehitable, couched though it be in skillful Carlylese.

It was in the South, it will be perceived, that the new woman movement met its strongest opposition. "The madness, the frenzy, the absurdity of this spirit has not touched us here at the South," exclaimed Professor Joseph LeConte in his commencement address at the Laurensville Female College. "Woman has not unsexed herself here." [13] But in the North, opinion was changing, very slowly, to be sure, but perceptibly. "A little knowledge of *general* politics is necessary" to women, admitted the *Republic.*[14] The *Knickerbocker,* radical in its old age, published a startling article in 1863 demanding for women "entire equality on every point — politically, legally and socially." [15] There were several periodicals devoted more or less to political "rights" for women; they are an interesting lot and will bear rather close inspection.

[11] *Southern Literary Messenger,* XIX, 700–701 (November 1853).
[12] *De Bow's Review,* XIII, 270 (September 1852). The author was Mrs. Louisa S. McCord, wife of Colonel D. J. McCord, also a magazine writer.
[13] *Southern Presbyterian Review,* XIV, 63 (April 1861).
[14] *Republic,* I, 86 (February 1851).
[15] *Knickerbocker Magazine,* LXI, 381–388 (May 1863).

PERIODICALS OF THE WOMAN'S MOVEMENT

One of the earliest of American papers to be edited and published by a woman was the *Pittsburgh Saturday Visiter*,[16] by Jane Grey Swisshelm. It was primarily an antislavery journal, but the very boldness of its editress made it an argument in itself for woman's rights. Mrs. Swisshelm later wrote: "It was quite an insignificant looking sheet, but no sooner did the American eagle catch sight of it than he swooned and fell off his perch." And then she described amusingly the consternation of the average male editor when he first saw this new paper published by a woman:

> Instantly he sprang to his feet and clutched his pantaloons, shouted to the assistant editor, when he, too, read and grasped frantically at his cassimeres, called to the reporters, pressmen, typos and devils, who all rushed in, heard the news, seized their nether garments, and joined the general chorus, "My breeches! oh, my breeches!" Here was a woman resolved to steal their pantaloons! With one accord they shouted, "On to the breach, in defence of our breeches!" [17]

But the *Visiter* weathered the paragraphic wit directed at it, giving as good as it received, and set an example for many other ambitious women to aim at. "Small papers, owned and edited by women, sprang up all over the land, and like Jonah's gourd, perished in a night," says Mrs. Swisshelm.[18]

One of these, however, made a great stir in its day. The *Lily, A Ladies' Journal, Devoted to Temperance and Literature*, was founded January 1849, under the auspices of a women's temperance society of Seneca Falls, New York, by Mrs. Amelia Bloomer. It soon espoused the causes of female franchise and dress reform. The reformed costume which came to bear the name of Mrs. Bloomer was not designed by her,[19] but her advocacy of it in the *Lily* connected her with it in the public mind. It was certainly modest enough by later standards, though it was

---

[16] See p. 141.

[17] Jane Grey Swisshelm, *Half a Century* (Chicago, 1880), p. 113.

[18] *Ibid.*, p. 141.

[19] See *Sibyl*, I, 229 (September 1, 1857). Mrs. Chaplain, of Glen Haven, New York, is said to have been the first to adapt the costume from gymnasium wear for common use. Mrs. Miller, daughter of Gerrit Smith, adopted it soon afterward.

thought "suggestive" by some contemporaries. "A sort of hermaphrodite costume," said one commentator, "very pretty, very lascivious, very undignified." [20] But the descriptions and travesties of it were far more objectionable than the actual costume, which consisted of heavy, extremely wide trousers (sometimes bound at the bottom by an ankle cuff and sometimes open and practically covering the foot) and a heavy coat with its skirt coming well below the knees. Such was the Bloomer dress, which aroused storms of jeers and laughter — all of which, whatever it may have done for womankind, seems at least to have made the Bloomer name immortal in connection with a garment.

The *Lily*, having stirred up all this excitement, and having attained a circulation of 4,000, moved westward in 1854 to Mount Vernon, Ohio, where Mr. Bloomer had bought a half interest in E. S. S. Rouse's *Western Home Visitor* (1853–55). Once when the printers declared a strike because of the employment of a girl typesetter, Mrs. Bloomer discharged them all and hired a force of women. In 1855 the *Lily* was removed to Richmond, Indiana, and placed under the care of Mrs. Mary B. Birdsall. Elizabeth Cady Stanton "first came before the public as a writer for the *Lily*," [21] and Frances D. Gage, the Ohio poetess, was another contributor. The best *bon mot* in the whole file is one credited to "a San Francisco lady" and is about the Pilgrim Fathers:

The Pilgrim Fathers, forsooth! What had they to endure in comparison with the Pilgrim Mothers? It is true that they had hunger and cold and sickness and danger — foes without and foes within — but the unfortunate Pilgrim Mothers! They had not only these to endure, but they had the Pilgrim Fathers! [22]

The file of the *Lily* ends with 1856, after Mr. and Mrs. Bloomer had gone on west to Iowa.[23]

[20] *Republic*, II, 37 (July 1851).
[21] Mrs. Bloomer's manuscript note in the file of Lillian G. Browne, Seneca Falls, New York.
[22] *Lily*, V, 112 (July 15, 1853).
[23] The *Lily* was an eight-page quarto monthly, 1849–52; four-page folio semimonthly, 1853; eight-page quarto semimonthly, 1854–56. Volumes were yearly; subscription price, fifty cents. Anna C. Mattison's name was carried as joint editor for the first few months. Many years later Mrs. Bloomer wrote to

Another woman's rights paper was edited and published monthly 1852–54 by Mrs. E. A. Aldrich, of Cincinnati. It was called the *Genius of Liberty*, and after its suspension it became a department in Moore's *Western Lady's Book*. Anna W. Spencer's *Pioneer and Woman's Advocate* was published at Providence for a few years beginning in 1852. Paulina Wright Davis founded her *Una* in 1853 in Providence; it was later moved to Boston but survived only three or four years. Anna McDowell published the *Woman's Advocate*, owned, edited, and printed by women, in Philadelphia in 1855–60.

The *Sibyl: A Review of the Tastes, Errors and Fashions of Society* is quite as interesting as the *Lily*. It was founded at Middletown, New York, in July 1856, by Drs. Lydia Sayer, with John W. Hasbrouck as publisher. Note the *Drs.* before Miss Sayer's name; it stands for "Doctoress." Eventually the *s* was dropped in token of the claim that women had as much right as men to the title *Dr.* The *Sibyl* was the official journal of the National Dress Reform Association and reported its conventions in detail. The name plate contained a small picture of the editor wearing the new costume, which looks neat and sensible, though decidedly copious in comparison with modern styles. That there was great need of some kind of dress reform Drs. Sayer demonstrates from time to time. In her first number she writes:

We do decidedly object to such a pyramidal redundance as the present fashion suspends over hoops, destroying all idea of the beautiful form of woman; and since the bottom of the waist has been located just beneath the armpits, while the hoops reach above the hips, the once huge cone of dry goods looks more like a *hogshead* shuffled along by some propelling power save feet, (for such articles are not supposed to be on ladies nowadays,) while a pair of arms and a head stick out over this redundance of dry goods and cooperage.[24]

Miss Browne of the early days of the *Lily*: "I was a simple, young thing with no experience, no education for business, in no way fitted for such work; but some unseen power nerved me for the task and sustained me until such time as others were brought forward to take my place. I had a great struggle, but did the best I could." (MS. letter, March 21, 1893.) See article by E. Douglas Branch in *Colophon*, Part XII (December 1932); also D. C. Bloomer, *Life and Writings of Amelia Bloomer* (Boston, 1895).

[24] *Sibyl*, I, 3 (July 1, 1856).

The *Sibyl* advocated other reforms also: it was antitobacco and temperance, but it was not much interested in freeing Negroes so long as women were enslaved.[25] In the early numbers appeared a serial story detailing the trials of a femal reformer; it was doubtless largely an autobiography of the editor. The varied activities of Drs. Sayer are detailed from issue to issue: she was in demand as a "lecturess," and she took some part in politics. In the second month of the *Sibyl's* life she married her publisher, who was also the publisher of a local newspaper; and the newfangled vows the contracting parties took and the costume the bride wore make interesting reading for the *Sibyl's* pages. In 1859, when Mrs. Hasbrouck refused to pay taxes on her property to a government which withheld her "rights," a tax collector with a rude sense of humor levied on "one pair of Bloomer pants," which he took from her wardrobe during her absence. Of course the *Sibyl*, very properly, lambasted him in the next issue.[26] The paper continued almost through the war.[27] When it suspended, it recommended to its subscribers another dress-reform advocate, *Laws of Life*, edited by Drs. Austin and Jackson, the organ of the Jackson Sanatorium at Dansville, New York.[28]

ANOTHER INSTALLMENT OF AN ANCIENT SATIRE

Comment upon women's dress in this period, aside from the routine fashion notes in the women's magazines, was divided more or less equally between satires on current modes and satires on Mrs. Bloomer's proposal to reform those modes. What a writer in *Holden's* called "female pantaloonery" [29] was an almost universal object of remarks which ranged from ribaldry to invective. An article with woodcuts in *Sartain's Magazine* has the temerity to commend, as an independent American fashion,

[25] *Ibid.*, V, 956 (June 15, 1861).
[26] *Ibid.*, III, 516 (March 1, 1859).
[27] The *Sibyl's* dates are July 1, 1856–June 1864 (8 vols.). It was a semi-monthly until July 1861 (Vol. V), when it became a monthly. It was a handsome eight-page quarto and sold for a dollar a year as a semimonthly and fifty cents as a monthly.
[28] Published 1858–93 in thirty-six volumes.
[29] Miss F. L. Townsend on "Women in Male Attire," *Holden's Dollar Magazine*, V, 179 (March 1850). See also George William Curtis, "A 'Bloomer'," *Harper's Weekly*, IV, 483 (August 4, 1860).

"the Bloomer costume, as many call it — the Camilla costume, as some of its friends denominate it." [30] But most commentators were more severe: a writer in the *International Monthly*, for example, thinks that this "ridiculous and indecent dress" is never seen except "on the persons of an abandoned class, or on those of vulgar women whose inordinate love of notoriety is apt to display itself in ways that induce their exclusion from respectable society." [31] One episode in the Devil's visit to "Gotham" as narrated by a versifier in *Yankee Notions* runs:

> For dear Mrs. Bloomer he left his love,
> A well-meaning woman he thought her —
>   "But petticoats coming quite down to the knee
>   Is all mock modesty; tell her for me
> To cut them six inches shorter!" [32]

The Bloomer costume "of course does not thrive at the South. Our ladies blush that their sisters *anywhere* descend to such things." [33]

But which were worse — hoops or Bloomers? "The Horrors of Wearing Hoops" were frequently illustrated in Frank Leslie's paper [34] and in many other periodicals. A writer on "Female Cooperage" in *Putnam's* does not object to hoops for more formal dress, but does hate them at breakfast. He suspects that the ladies even sleep in them.[35] *Harper's Weekly* rejoiced in 1859 that "hoops are going out," [36] but it had been advertising Woodward's Patent (Premium) Columbian Skirt and Extenders, said to have banished "the great difficulty and many inconveniences experienced by Ladies wearing the Steel Hoop Skirts when entering and sitting in church, carriage, &c, and the too frequent inelegant displacement of their attire." [37] Perhaps it was this difficulty about getting through the church door which suggested to "Eudora," of the *Southern Literary Messenger*, her apt quotation from Beaumont and Fletcher:

[30] *Sartain's*, VI, 243 (September 1851).
[31] *International Monthly*, IV, 563 (November 1851).
[32] *Yankee Notions*, II, 127 (April 1853).
[33] *Southern Literary Messenger*, XX, 300 (May 1854).
[34] *Frank Leslie's Illustrated Newspaper*, IV, 64 (June 27, 1857).
[35] *Putnam's Monthly*, X, 123 (July 1857).
[36] *Harper's Weekly*, III, 818 (December 24, 1859).
[37] *Ibid.*, II, 287 (May 1, 1858).

FASHIONS IN BLOOMER DRESS

From *Peterson's Magazine*, January 1851. Following are the descriptions:

"BLOOMER EVENING DRESS. — Pantelettes of white satin; short, full skirt of pink silk, embroidered at the bottom. Corsage tight, open half way to the waist in front, over a worked chemisette. Loose sleeves, with white under-sleeves. White or pink satin boots.

"BLOOMER WALKING DRESS. — Full Turkish pantelettes of Mazarine blue silk, ruffled. Short, full skirt of blue silk, the same color as the pantelettes. Marseilles vest, open half way to the waist over a plaited linen bosom; small collar turned over. An over-dress of embroidered silk, high at the back, but open all the way in front, so as to show the vest. Loose sleeves, with full white under-sleeves. Hat of grey beaver with a rich plume."

I'm so honest,
I wish 'em all in heaven, and you know how hard, sir,
'Twill be to get in there with their great farthingals.[38]

Sibyl had complained of an undue prolongation of the communion service, because of the difficulty experienced when more
than a few behooped women knelt at the chancel rail at the same
time.[39]

"Trains" also found critics. "We venture a remonstrance
against the still prevalent practice of wearing trains in the
street," wrote the editor of *Godey's* in 1852, and he spoke of
"the skirts dragging their slow length along, cleaning the crossing at the expense of neatness, comfort, and good taste." [40]
Then the *Comic Bouquet* adds this fashion note:

But of all the achievements of which we can boast,
The most charming contrivance of all,
That projects out so neat
And makes all complete,
Is the patent adjustable bustle.[41]

MAGAZINES FOR WOMEN AND THE HOME

The number of periodicals of 1850–65 designed especially
for women is impossible to fix. It is, indeed, difficult to draw
the line between women's magazines and the large group of
periodicals calling themselves Home Journals, Family Visitors,
Household Monthlies, and the like. Moreover, not a few of the
Sunday papers already considered as a group [42] offered themselves as periodicals for the family and fireside. Many magazines were departmentalized for the various elements of home
life and appealed definitely to women, to children, and to young
people. For systematic consideration, all the distinctively home
magazines and women's and mothers' periodicals will be placed
in one classification here: at least thirty such had some importance in our period, and two or three times that number existed
obscurely for periods varying from three months to two years.

[38] *Southern Literary Messenger*, XXII, 214 (March, 1856).
[39] *Sibyl*, II, 332 (March 15, 1858).
[40] *Godey's Lady's Book*, XLIV, 412 (May 1852).
[41] *Comic Bouquet*, I, 68 (April 1859).
[42] See pp. 34–38.

Godey's [43] declined in literary quality in the fifties, though it kept up its charming illustration; *Peterson's*,[44] selling for a dollar less per year, was steadily overhauling it in the race for circulation. The *Ladies' Repository*,[45] of Cincinnati, was a Methodist magazine but had a circulation outside of church membership; and somewhat the same may be said of the Universalist *Ladies' Repository*,[46] of Boston. The *Home Journal*,[47] under the editorship of George P. Morris and Nathaniel P. Willis, won a large following in our period. It was more sophisticated and clever than other weeklies which carried the word "Home" in their titles, and the writing for it was better. Morris died in 1864, and Willis in 1867. All of these periodicals were under full sail in 1850 and were likewise on the top of the wave at the close of our period. Half a dozen others were not far behind them in 1850.[48]

And in that year Timothy Shay Arthur began *Arthur's Home Gazette* in Philadelphia. It was a two-dollar weekly and bore the subtitle, *A Journal of Pure Literature for Home Reading*. (The word *Pure* as used here did not mean unalloyed, but clean.) Three years later Arthur merged his weekly into a

---

[43] See Mott, *History of American Magazines, 1741–1850*, pp. 500–594.
[44] Treated more fully in sketch 6.   [45] Treated more fully in sketch 5.
[46] Titles: *Universalist*, 1832–38; *Universalist and Ladies' Repository*, 1839–42; *Ladies' Repository: A Universalist Monthly Magazine for the Home Circle*, 1843–73. Fifty volumes. George H. Emerson was editor in our period.
[47] Treated more fully in sketch 11.
[48] The *Ladies' Wreath*, 1846–55 (see Mott, *op. cit.*, p. 353); the *Rose of Sharon*, Boston, 1840–57, 18 volumes; the *Southern Lady's Companion*, Nashville, 1847–54, 8 volumes, published at the office of the *Nashville and Louisville Christian Advocate* and edited throughout most of its life by the Reverend M. M. Henkle; the *Home Weekly and Household Newspaper*, 1842–72, 31 volumes, formerly called the *Dollar Magazine* (see Mott, *op. cit.*, p. 365); the *Mothers' Magazine*, New York, 1833–88, 56 volumes, published by S. Whittelsey and edited by Mrs. A. G. Whittelsey until the Reverend D. Mead came in as publisher and joint editor in 1844, and edited and published by Mead with several variations in title after Mrs. Whittelsey left to start her own magazine in 1850; and *Mother's Journal and Family Visitant*, 1836–72, 37 volumes, edited successively by Mrs. Eliza C. Allen and Mrs. Elizabeth Sewell in New York, then moved to Philadelphia under the control of Mary G. Clarke 1851–56, and then back to New York, where Sheldon & Company became publishers and Mrs. Caroline O. Hiscox editor. Above were all monthlies except the *Home Weekly*. See Bertha-Monica Stearns, "Early Western Magazines for Ladies," *Mississippi Valley Historical Review*, XVIII, 319 (December 1931); and "Southern Magazines for Ladies," *South Atlantic Quarterly*, XXXI, 70 (January 1932).

monthly publication he had recently started under the name *Home Magazine*.[49] This prospered and continued for nearly half a century. The span of *Arthur's Home Gazette* was paralleled by that of *Mrs. Whittelsey's Magazine for Mothers*,[50] a dollar monthly to which J. S. C. Abbott, C. A. Goodrich, and other rather preachy writers contributed. The Covington *Kentucky Garland's* chief distinction was that it was edited, during its brief life in 1853, by "a widow with eight children" (Mrs. H. C. Lindsay). A neighbor was the *Ladies' Pearl* (1852–70), which published its latter volumes in St. Louis. Mrs. Electra Sheldon opposed woman suffrage in her *Western Literary Cabinet* (1853–54), of Detroit, though she stood for a broadening of women's vocations. *Frank Leslie's Gazette of Fashion*, forerunner of the popular *Frank Leslie's Lady's Magazine*,[51] began in New York in 1854. In the same year there were three newcomers from the provinces: the *Literary Journal*, edited by "Ella Wentworth" and others in Cincinnati; the *Western Lady's Book*,[52] of the same city, by A. and Mrs. H. G. Moore; and the Nashville *Home Circle*, by L. D. Huston. Of these, the first perished within the year, while the other two, using steel plates freely, continued until silenced by the first guns of the war.

The *Family Newspaper* is interesting for its claim that it was "the first and only successful paper ever published by a lady" — but it was not the first, and it was not successful. The lady in question was Marie Louise Hankins. Her paper was an eight-page illustrated folio — "a mammoth pictorial" — issued monthly in New York at seventy-five cents a year; it claimed a big circulation in 1855, but soon thereafter was lost to view. The Beadle Company, dime-novel publishers, made its first magazine venture with a well-edited periodical called *Home* [53]

[49] Treated more fully in sketch 20.

[50] January 1850–December 1852. The editor, Mrs. A. G. Whittelsey, was the founder of the *Mothers' Magazine* (see footnote 48 above). This magazine was not for mothers any more than for women generally; in its last year it added *and Daughters* to its title.

[51] Treated more fully in sketch 23.

[52] See W. H. Venable, *Beginnings of Literary Culture in the Ohio Valley* (Cincinnati, 1891), pp. 82–86.

[53] Treated more fully in sketch 27.

in 1856. It was abandoned after five years. In the same year appeared the *Kaleidoscope,* of Petersburg, Virginia, and the *North-Western Home Journal,* of Chicago. The former, edited by Mrs. R. B. Hicks, died the next year; while the latter, begun under James B. Merwin's editorship, became the *North-Western Home and School Journal* and lasted until 1862.

In 1858 the *Hesperian,* of San Francisco, first appeared, with editorial board and contributing staff composed chiefly of women. Mrs. F. H. Day was editor. Contents varied, as one later commentator remarks, "from sublime thoughts upon Milton to the best method of making muffins and embroidering flannel skirts." [54] The *Hesperian* carried on until 1862. Born in the same year with it were the very brief *Texian Monthly Magazine,* of Galveston, by Mrs. Eleanor Spann; and the *Household Monthly,* of Lynn, Massachusetts. Moving to Boston did not save the *Household Monthly,* and it died in 1860. The year 1859 saw the founding of a number of periodicals for women and the home, of which three may be mentioned here: the *Fireside Monthly,* of New York (1859–61), called in the first place *Hall's Fireside Monthly*; the *Kentucky Family Journal,* of Louisville (February–October 1859), which soon became the *Educational Monthly* (November 1859–July 1860); and the *Home Monthly,* of Buffalo, which was merged in a much longer-lived magazine of the same name at Boston.[55]

On the eve of the war a *Household Journal* and a *Household Magazine* were begun in New York,[56] after which there were few such periodicals founded until toward the end of the conflict. In 1864 a *Lady's Friend* was begun in Philadelphia, to be merged in 1873 in *Arthur's Home Magazine*; and the *Family Treasure* was founded in Pittsburgh, later to move to Cincinnati and publish in all six annual volumes.

---

[54] See Ella S. Cummins [Mighels], *The Story of the Files* (San Francisco, 1893).

[55] The Buffalo magazine published four volumes January 1859–September 1860. The Boston *Home Monthly* published thirty-nine volumes 1860–1908; it had a checkered career, what with suspensions and moving to New York.

[56] The *Household Journal of Popular Information, Amusement and Domestic Economy,* New York, October 6, 1860–September 1862; and the *Household Magazine,* January–June 1860, which became the *American Monthly,* July–December 1860.

THE RELIGIOUS PRESS

Even larger in totals than the group of women's periodicals was that sponsored by the religious sects. Every denomination had its publications, and usually a full complement of theological quarterly, home monthly, and regional weekly periodicals.

"Among the most marked signs of the times is the deep interest awakened among Protestants upon the great subject of Christian Union," [57] observed the *Protestant Episcopal Quarterly*, and it is true that all the religious journals discussed union; but they did not unite, and sometimes they engaged in highly acrimonious controversies among themselves. Thus they did not always set a good Christian example to other periodicals. *Putnam's*, *Russell's*, and *Frank Leslie's Illustrated*, as well as other secular periodicals, were wont to complain of the conduct and attitudes of the religious press.

The religious newspapers [said *Putnam's*] "exploit" the religious sentiment of the community; and, not infrequently, when manly and fair argument is wanting, they have recourse to the most dangerous and odious of all weapons in discussion — appeals to sectarianism and superstition.[58]

Russell's criticized them for their scurrilous language:

In many parts of the United States conductors of sectarian journals permit themselves and their correspondents a license of language and personal allusion which they would both hesitate to employ were they amenable to the rules of men of the world. . . . Such editors may be Christians, but they certainly are not gentlemen.[59]

As a matter of fact, the religious press was, in general, not of the highest character as either journalism or religion, though there were many excellent individual religious periodicals.

Far from marking a period of "Christian unity," the year 1850 saw divisions on the slavery question in effect in all the chief Protestant denominations except the Episcopal church, in which antislavery sentiment was restrained.[60] But on the other

[57] *Protestant Episcopal Quarterly*, VII, 385 (July 1860).
[58] *Putnam's Monthly*, IX, 524 (May 1857).
[59] *Russell's Magazine*, III, 376 (July 1858).
[60] *Liberator*, XX, 41 (March 1850). Calhoun's last speech in the Senate also pointed this out. See pp. 132–133.

hand, the work of the churches was stimulated by the religious revivals which followed upon the hard times of the late fifties.[61] It was in vain for *Leslie's* to complain that "Rational beings do not take religion as children take measles";[62] they put Leslie down as an atheist and went on getting converted.

Religious journals were very widely distributed. They sprang up in every state and territory. The war put an end to many such publications in the South, of course; but others managed in one fashion or another to survive. The *Methodist* gave a northern view of southern religious periodicals in 1861:

> Religious journals . . . were among the first to plunge madly into the current which was rapidly bearing the South on to anarchy, and they are now among the first to disappear.
>
> Without commenting on the Southern Baptist publications, of which seven have suspended, or those of Presbyterian and other denominations, which have suffered in a corresponding manner, let us note the condition of the Southern Methodist papers. [Eleven of them are then named.] Without a single exception these papers warmly espoused the rebel cause. The first three named [the *Southern Methodist Itinerant*, Parkersburg, Virginia; the *Intelligencer*, Holston, Tennessee; the *North Carolina Christian Advocate*, Greensboro] have ceased to exist — a sure and speedy retribution.[63]

The others, we are told, are filled with desperate appeals to avert their imminent end.

These comments were directed against the religious weeklies, which, it may be noted in passing, belong rather to the magazine than to the newspaper category by virtue of the general nature of their contents.[64] The course of the monthlies and quarterlies in the South was similar to that of the weeklies; but so far as the criticism of license is concerned, it is to be understood as applying mainly to the weeklies.

PRESBYTERIANS, BAPTISTS, METHODISTS

The Presbyterian, Baptist, Methodist, and Congregational denominations led the field in publishing activity during our

---

[61] *Democratic Review*, XLI, 364–372 (May 1858).

[62] *Frank Leslie's Illustrated Newspaper*, V, 282 (April 3, 1858).

[63] Quoted from the *Methodist* in the *Friends' Review*, XIV, 727 (July 20, 1861).

[64] See Mott, *op. cit.*, p. 137.

period. Each of them had from twenty-five to fifty periodicals. The religious journals, having a public ready made, as it were, enjoyed longer lives, in the average, than most other class publications.

There was not a time within our period when the Presbyterian bodies, for example, did not have at least a score of periodicals; and fourteen of them lasted throughout the whole period and longer. Their leading quarterly was the *Biblical Repertory*, later the *Princeton Review*.[65] The *Cumberland Presbyterian* [66] and the *Southern Presbyterian Review* [67] were both begun in the forties and lived long after the war period. These three Presbyterian quarterlies, representing regional and schismatic differences, were in full career in 1850. Two more came into the field in the next decade to favor reunion with the exscinded branch of the church and thus oppose the position of the old *Princeton Review*: they were the *American Theological Review* [68] and the *Presbyterian Quarterly Review*.[69] Then there was the *Danville Quarterly Review*,[70] especially interesting for its vigorous advocacy of the cause of the union in Kentucky during the war. In the monthly field there were the *Presbyterian Magazine* [71] (1851–60) and the more statistical *Presbyterian Monthly Record* (1850–86), both of Philadelphia; and the *Foreign Mission-*

[65] *Ibid.*, p. 529.

[66] This review began as the *Theological Medium* in 1845, at Uniontown, Pennsylvania, Milton Bird editor and publisher. He took it to Louisville in 1848. It was suspended during the war, but revived in 1871 at Nashville, with T. C. Blake as editor. In 1880 J. D. Kirkpatrick took it to Lebanon, Tennessee, where it was edited by the faculty of Cumberland University under the title *Cumberland Presbyterian Quarterly*. W. C. Logan took it to St. Louis in 1884, calling it the *Cumberland Presbyterian Review*, and it expired that year.

[67] Founded in Columbia, South Carolina, in 1847, it was published by "an association of ministers." It was merged in 1908 with other journals of the same faith to form the *Presbyterian of the South*, still current at Richmond.

[68] Later the *American Presbyterian Review*. Treated more fully in sketch 31.

[69] Published in Philadelphia, June 1852–October 1862, Benjamin J. Wallace editor. Associate editors were Albert Barnes, Thomas Brainerd, E. W. Gilbert, Joel Parker, and John Jenkins, "with the assistance of Professors in the New York Union, Auburn, and Lane Theological Seminaries." There was much of controversy with the Princeton theologians, against "excision." A few literary, philological, and historical articles appeared. This review was merged at the end of 1862 with the *American Theological Review*, New York, to form the *American Theological and Presbyterian Review*, later the *American Presbyterian Review*, q.v.

[70] Treated more fully in sketch 36.   [71] See Mott, *op. cit.*, p. 315.

ary (1842–86), of New York. The most prominent weeklies were the *Observer* and *Evangelist*, of New York, and the *Christian Observer* and the *Presbyterian*, of Philadelphia — all of them old and well established by 1850.[72] Philadelphia was a Presbyterian publishing center; it was the home of a dozen periodicals of that faith in our period, some of them belonging to the United Presbyterian branch.[73] Others were scattered all over the West and South.[74]

Though not so strong in their quarterlies, the Baptists were quite as active as the Presbyterians in the publication of periodicals. The *Christian Review*,[75] best of their quarterlies, survived until 1863. The *Western Baptist Review*, begun at Louisville in 1845, was merged six years later in *Ford's Christian Repository* (1852–1905), published monthly by S. H. Ford first at Louisville and then at St. Louis. The *Southern Baptist Review and Eclectic* (1855–61) was edited by J. R. Graves and J. M. Pendleton at Nashville. J. Q. Adams' *Christian* (1863–69) was a New York monthly devoted to the doctrine of sanctification. The *Baptist Missionary Magazine* [76] was the chief repre-

---

[72] For the first two, see Mott, *op. cit.*, p. 373; for the *Christian Observer*, *ibid.*, p. 137; and for the *Presbyterian*, a paper adhering to "the fundamental doctrines of evangelical Christianity," see its own centennial number for February 12, 1931, CI, 1–32. S. Irenaeus Prime was the great editor of the New York *Observer* in these years, and Henry M. Field of the *Evangelist.*

[73] The monthly *Evangelical Repository* (1842–91) and *Christian Instructor* (1844–1912) were in Philadelphia; but the church's chief weekly, the *United Presbyterian* (1842–current), and its brief *United Presbyterian Quarterly Review* (1860–61) came from Pittsburgh.

[74] To list some of the longest-lived of such weeklies, there were in the South: *Central Presbyterian* (1837–1908), Richmond, which furnished in 1908 the center for the general merger called the *Presbyterian of the South; Southern Presbyterian* (1847–93), founded at Milledgeville, Georgia, moved to Charleston and then to Columbia, where it was long edited by James Woodrow (see W. S. Hoole, *Check-List of Charleston Periodicals*, Durham, 1936, pp. 51–54); *North Carolina Presbyterian* (1858–1931), founded at Fayetteville, moved to Wilmington, and finally to Charlotte in 1898, where it became the *Presbyterian Standard; Presbyterian Herald* (1832–64), Bardstown, Kentucky, which made several moves, with changes of title, ending as the *True Presbyterian* at Louisville. At the West there were the *Presbyterian Banner* (current) founded in 1852 at Philadelphia, but merged three years later at Pittsburgh with the *Presbyterian Advocate* and through it tracing ancestry to the *Weekly Recorder*, Chillicothe, Ohio, founded in 1814 by John Andrews; the *Christian Herald* (1839–1920), Cincinnati, which in 1869 absorbed the *Presbyter* (1841–68, begun *Presbyterian of the West*) and became the *Herald and Presbyter*; and the *Oberlin Evangelist* (1836–62).   [75] See Mott, *op. cit.*, p. 666.   [76] *Ibid.*, p. 251.

sentative in the field of missions,[77] as it was the oldest of Baptist periodicals. Then there was the *Freewill Baptist Quarterly* (1853–69), of Providence, a well-printed review by William H. Bowen, George T. Day, and others.

But it was among the weeklies that the Baptists were most active. The *Watchman and Reflector*,[78] of Boston, was a great paper for New England. The *New York Examiner* [79] was edited through the war by Edward Bright, who is said to have made it "the foremost force in American Baptist journalism." [80] It absorbed, at the very end of our period, the *New York Chronicle*,[81] itself a distinguished periodical. Indeed the history of Baptist weeklies is a great sequence of consolidations.[82] The Southern Convention had many papers, all of which were either interrupted or ended by the war; two of the most famous were the *Religious Herald*,[83] of Richmond, and the peripatetic *Christian Index*.[84] The *Tennessee Baptist*,[85] long edited at Nashville

[77] The Southern Convention also had a missionary magazine — the *Foreign Missionary Journal* (1851–1916), of Richmond — and there was another Boston periodical in that field, the *Macedonian* (1842–1914), called *Helping Hand* after 1877; as well as the *Home Mission Herald* (1849–74) in New York.

[78] Mott, *op. cit.*, p. 138.

[79] Founded in Utica, New York, in 1823, under the name of the *New York Baptist Advocate*, it experienced several consolidations and variations in title before it was purchased by Edward Bright and S. S. Cutting in 1855 and the name changed to *Examiner*. Bright edited it forty years, 1855–94. See A. H. Newman, *A History of the Baptist Churches in the United States* (New York, 1894), for this and other periodicals. The *Examiner* was merged with the *Watchman* in 1913.

[80] *Watchman-Examiner*, VII, 600 (May 8, 1919).

[81] Founded in 1840 as a monthly by the American Bible Union; O. B. Judd made it a weekly in 1849. It came under the control in 1854 of J. S. Backus and Pharcellus Church. When Backus withdrew in 1863, Church united with it the *Christian Chronicle* (1846–63), of Philadelphia, only to sell the combination to the *Examiner* in 1865.

[82] See Volume III, Chapter III.

[83] Founded January 11, 1828, by William Sands, who remained as editor to the end of the Civil War. He was followed by A. E. Dickinson, 1865–1906. The present editor, R. H. Pitt, has been on the editorial staff since 1888. The *Herald* has been said to have made "the greatest contribution to life and progress of any southern Baptist journal." (Gaines Stanley Dobbins, "Southern Baptist Journalism," Thesis, 1914, Southern Baptist Seminary, p. 131.)

[84] See Mott, *op. cit.*, p. 138. For the most part, the *Index* has been connected with Mercer University. Perhaps its greatest editor was H. H. Tucker, 1878–89. See Dobbins, *op. cit.*

[85] Founded as the *Baptist* by R. C. B. Howell in 1835. In 1839 it was merged with other papers to form the *Baptist Banner and Western Pioneer* (see *Western*

by J. R. Graves, was the leading organ of what was called "Old Landmarkism"; the Boston *Morning Star* (1826–1911) was the chief paper of the Freewill Baptists; and *Zion's Advocate* (1853–1923), published monthly in various Southern towns but ending in Washington, spoke for the Primitive Baptists. Others there were in bewildering abundance.[86]

The Methodists of the fifties were quite as intent on publication as the Presbyterians and Baptists. They had two quarterlies — one for the parent church in the free states, and, two years after the division of 1844, one for the Methodist Church South.[87] The monthly *Ladies' Repository* [88] flourished, and the

---

Recorder in footnote 86, below) but his opposition to the Pedobaptists led Howell to resume publication, with J. R. Graves, a vigorous controversialist, as associate editor. In 1848 Graves became sole editor and changed the name to *Tennessee Baptist.* The circulation increased until the war came, giving this paper for a time the largest subscription list of all Baptist periodicals in the world. It was moved to Memphis in 1874 and merged with the *Baptist Reflector* in 1888. See Dobbins, *op. cit.*, p. 75.

[86] A few of the most important, grouped geographically, may be mentioned here: *American Baptist* (1846–88), founded in Boston as the *Christian Contributor and Free Missionary* by Cyrus P. Grosvenor and removed by him to Utica, New York, where it was merged in 1849 with the *Western Christian* (1846–49) and the name changed to *American Baptist;* edited under this title by Wareham Walker (moving to New York in 1857) until 1872, when it was bought by A. S. Patton and the name changed to the *Baptist Weekly; Zion's Advocate* (1828–1920), Portland, Maine; *Christian Secretary* (1824–96), Hartford, Connecticut, edited by Elisha Cushman throughout the war and later; *Journal and Messenger* (1831–1920), Cincinnati, founded as the *Baptist Weekly Journal of the Mississippi Valley*, and figuring in several consolidations and changes of title, being published in Columbus 1838–49; *Watchman of the Prairies* (1847–53), which gave place to the *Christian Times* (1853–67), Chicago; *Western Recorder* (1839–current), Louisville, begun as a consolidation of the Frankfort *Baptist Banner* (1825–38), the Nashville *Baptist* (1835–60), and the Alton (Illinois) *Western Pioneer* (1829–38) under the name *Baptist Banner and Western Pioneer*, becoming *Western Recorder* in 1851, bitterly opposing Old Landmarkism but growing into a family paper; *Biblical Recorder* (1833–current), Raleigh, North Carolina, begun as the monthly *Baptist Interpreter* at Edenton, moved to Raleigh, and made the weekly *Biblical Recorder* in 1835, edited (1833–51) by the able and influential Thomas Meredith and (1876–95) by C. P. Bailey; *Alabama Baptist* (1843–65), founded at Marion, later moved to Montgomery and Tuskegee, called *Southwestern Baptist* (1851–65), edited through the war by Samuel Henderson, an ardent secessionist, who was forced to discontinue it by federal authorities; *Southwestern Baptist Chronicle* (1847–66), New Orleans. See Dobbins, *op. cit.*; Newman, *op. cit.*; and the Centennial Number of the *Watchman-Examiner*, CI, 599–604 (May 8, 1919).

[87] For the northern quarterly, the *Methodist Review*, see Mott, *op. cit.*, p. 299. It was suspended with the May–June 1931 number, to be followed in 1932 by

National Magazine competed with the popular general periodicals. The Methodist weeklies, of which there were some thirty
in this period, usually employed the name *Christian Advocate*,
with a praenomen indicating the place of publication or the region in which it was circulated. The original *Christian Advocate* [89] had no such place-name attached, though it was often
referred to as the New York *Christian Advocate*: it was *the*
weekly of the church and accepted no regional limitation. The
Western Christian Advocate had been established by the General Conference, however, at Cincinnati in 1834; and in 1852 a
third official paper was set up in Chicago — the *Northwestern*

---

the quarterly *Religion in Life*. The *Quarterly Review of the Methodist Church
South* was founded January 1847 at Louisville, with H. B. Bascom, president of
Transylvania University, as editor. It was, like many reviews, rather heavy;
and its editor complained of a paucity of contributions. D. S. Doggett, of
Richmond, was placed in charge of it in 1851, and T. O. Summers, of Nashville,
in 1859; and the review followed its editors to those cities. After a war-time
suspension, 1862–70, A. T. Bledsoe's *Southern Review* (see Volume III, sketch 7)
was adopted by the church as its own quarterly, of which Bledsoe's vigorous
journal stands as a second series. After Bledsoe's death and the suspension of
his *Review* a few years later, a third series of the *Quarterly Review* began in
Nashville with J. W. Hinton as editor. Summers returned to the editorship in
1880–83, and then Hinton took it again for 1884–85, moving it to Macon,
Georgia. In 1886 the publishing house of the church assumed charge of it. A
fourth series was begun in 1886 with W. P. Harrison as editor, and the name
was changed to *Southern Methodist Review* for two years, after which the old
title was resumed. Harrison was succeeded in 1894 by John J. Tigert, later a
bishop of the church, who changed the name to the *Methodist Review* — a name
borne to the end except when the word *Quarterly* was inserted 1903–06. Tigert
also made it a bimonthly and brought it to a position of greater influence than
it had ever before enjoyed. It resumed quarterly publication in 1903, and four
years later Gross Alexander began an able editorship. He was followed by
Horace M. DuBose, 1916–18; Frank M. Thomas, 1919–21; Gilbert T. Rowe,
1922–28; and William P. King, 1929–30. The *Review* was suspended October
1930. For historical sketches, see LXXVII, 641 (October 1928), and LXXIX,
632 (October 1930).

[88] Treated more fully in sketch 5.

[89] Founded in 1826 by Nathan Bangs, publishing agent of the Methodist
Book Concern, and still issued. It has had a succession of notable editors,
elected by the General Conference of the Church — among them Bangs, 1828–
32 and 1834–36; the controversial Dr. Thomas E. Bond, 1840–48 and 1852–56;
Abel Stevens, 1856–60; C. H. Fowler, 1876–80, later bishop, who had the temerity to publish an E. P. Roe novel and Joseph Cook's Monday Lectures in the
Advocate; and, probably most important of all, the able James M. Buckley,
1880–1912. See Centennial Number, CI, 1091–1256 (September 9, 1926). Also
see, for all official Methodist periodicals, Chapter IX, "Periodicals of the Book
Concern," in H. C. Jennings, *The Methodist Book Concern* (New York, 1924).

Christian Advocate. In 1856 two more *Christian Advocates* were authorized by the General Conference — the *Central*[90] at St. Louis and the *Pacific*[91] at Portland. The *Northern Independent*,[92] an unofficial paper, had been founded to forward the abolition cause within the Methodist church,[93] and under the editorship of William Hosmer it advocated expelling all slave-holders from the communion. Not far behind it in antislavery opinion, but less violent, were the Boston *Zion's Herald*[94] under Daniel Wise's direction, and the *Northwestern* under J. V. Watson. But the standard Methodist paper, the New York *Christian Advocate*, was more conservative; indeed it was too mildly antislavery for the temper of the General Conference of 1860, which refused for that reason to reëlect Abel Stevens editor. Stevens and George R. Crooks thereupon started the New York *Methodist* (1860–82) — an influential paper of which Crooks was the chief editor until 1875. Throughout the war all the northern Methodist papers[95] were more militant.[96] In the mean-

[90] Charles Elliott, long editor of the *Pittsburgh Christian Advocate*, was editor during this period and sustained the antislavery cause in a border state with vigor. See William Warren Sweet, *The Methodist Episcopal Church and the Civil War* (Cincinnati, 1912), pp. 212 ff. The *Central* was moved to Kansas City in 1900. In 1932 the *Western, Central, Northwestern,* and *Pacific* were made regional editions of the church's *Christian Advocate*.

[91] The *Pacific Christian Advocate* had been begun privately the year before, at Salem, Oregon, but was moved to Portland in 1856. Thomas H. Pearne was editor 1855–64. It was unofficial 1880–92. In 1932 it was merged into the *Christian Advocate*.

[92] At Auburn, New York, 1856–61.

[93] *Northern Independent*, IV, 50 (November 1, 1860).

[94] See Mott, *op. cit.*, p. 138.

[95] Besides the papers mentioned in the North in this period, the Methodist parent church (as distinguished from the M. E. Church South) had the following unofficial representatives: *Northern Christian Advocate*, Syracuse, New York (1841–1917); *Buffalo Christian Advocate* (1850–1894); *Pittsburgh Christian Advocate*, founded in 1833, which was long "semiofficial," being published by local conferences while its editors were elected by the General Conference, but which came under the general management in 1932 and was merged in the New York *Christian Advocate* shortly thereafter; *California Christian Advocate*, founded in San Francisco in 1851 and continued since 1931 as the California edition of the *Christian Advocate; Baltimore Methodist*, founded in 1859, which became *Washington Christian Advocate* in 1922 and was merged with New York *Christian Advocate* in 1928; *Atlanta Christian Advocate*, founded in 1836, adopted by the General Conference in 1868, suspended 1885–92, revived as *Methodist Advocate Journal* at Chattanooga and later at Athens, Tennessee, 1893–1924, then changed in title to *Southeastern Christian Advocate* and later continued as southeastern edition of *Christian Advocate* until 1932. The United

time, the leading *Christian Advocates* of the Methodist Church South were those at Nashville, Richmond, and Charleston.[97] The Methodist Protestant church had its *Methodist Recorder* (1839–1929) at Pittsburgh, which was merged with the *Methodist Protestant* (1831–current) of Baltimore under the title *Methodist Protestant-Recorder*; and the Evangelical Association's organ was the *Evangelical Messenger* (1847–1936), of Cleveland.

PROTESTANT EPISCOPAL PERIODICALS

The Protestant Episcopal church had in the *Church Review*,[98] founded by N. S. Richardson at New Haven in 1848, a dignified and respected quarterly for the more conservative wing of the church. Richardson moved it to New York in 1861. The *Protestant Episcopal Quarterly and Church Register*,[99] published in New York 1854–61, was also "low church." It held a brief against Catholicism and also had much to say of the conflict between science and religion. The *Churchman's Monthly Magazine*, of New York, published six volumes 1854–59, with some

---

Brethren had the *Religious Telescope* (1834–current) at Dayton, Ohio; and the African M. E. Church had its *Christian Recorder* (1852–1931) in Philadelphia.

[96] See Chapter VI, "Methodist Periodicals During the War," in Sweet, *op. cit.*

[97] The Nashville *Christian Advocate* has been the leading general weekly of the Methodist Church South ever since the division, Nashville being the home of the church's publishing house. It was founded in 1836 as the *Southwestern Christian Advocate*. It bore the name of its city 1846–50, and the names of both Nashville and Louisville 1850–54; but since then it has been plain *Christian Advocate*. See historical sketch, LXXXVI, 498 (April 17, 1925). The *Richmond Christian Advocate* was born in 1832, in Baltimore, bearing the name of the latter city for a time, and then the names of both cities until 1900. The *Southern Christian Advocate* was founded in Charleston in 1837, under authorization of the General Conference, but it was moved about after the war, in 1886 to Columbia, and finally in 1919 to Columbia for a third time. (See Hoole, *op. cit.*, pp. 38–41.) The *Texas* and *North Carolina Christian Advocates* were begun respectively at Galveston in 1846 and at Greensboro in 1855, the former moving to Dallas in 1887. The *Pacific Methodist*, which later added *Advocate* to its name, was a lively paper founded by O. P. Fitzgerald in 1860 in San Francisco. All the above papers are still in existence except the *Texas Christian Advocate*, which was discontinued in 1931. The *St. Louis Christian Advocate* (1851–1928) was a storm center in war times. The *New Orleans Christian Advocate* was published in 1850–1926.

[98] Treated more fully in sketch 12.

[99] H. Dyer was publisher of all eight volumes, January 1854–October 1861. Bishop Meade's recollections of Virginia church history in Volumes II–IV, and Dr. Martin Paine's serial "Review of Theoretical Geology" in Volume III are notable contributions.

fiction mixed with its biography, essays, and expositions of Episcopal doctrine. It carried plates by J. N. Gimbrede, A. L. Dick, and others. It was the successor of *Evergreen* (1844–53), a New Haven monthly later moved to New York; William H. Onderdonk was proprietor. A more controversial monthly was the *True Catholic*, of Baltimore, edited and, in the main, written by Hugh Davey Evans, a lay theologian of high-church tendencies. It was begun in May 1843 and ended with the year 1856; it was immediately followed by the *American Church Monthly* (New York, 1857–58), to which Evans was a liberal contributor, though the editor was Henry Norman Hudson, Shakespearean scholar and former editor of the *Churchman*. The Boston *Church Monthly* (1861–70) was begun by George M. Randall and Frederick Dan Huntington, the latter a fresh proselyte from the Unitarians and both of them later bishops in the Episcopal church. This magazine contained some belles-lettres and much theology and denominational news; in later years, under less distinguished editorship, it lost prestige. In Chicago, James Grant Wilson began in 1857 the *Chicago Record*, a monthly of literary tone which printed criticism of books and art, Wilson's accounts of his European travels, and some church news. In 1859 it became a semimonthly and more definitely a church organ; it was called the *Church Record* 1858–60. When Wilson left for the war in 1862, he sold it to Thomas Smith, who used it as the foundation for his *Northwestern Church* (1862–65).

Strong as it was in its quarterlies and monthlies, the Protestant Episcopal church also had several weeklies of importance in our period. Chief among them were the New York *Churchman* (1831–61), advocate of the Oxford Movement, which had just passed from the distinguished editorship of Samuel Seabury at the beginning of our period; the New York *Church Journal* (1853–78), called by one authority "the best journal the Church has known," edited for fifteen years by John Henry Hopkins, son of the bishop of the same name; and the violently controversial Hartford *Calendar*, founded in 1845, which became *Connecticut Churchman* in 1866, and the next year plain *Churchman*, moving in 1878 to New York, where it is still published.[100] The veteran *Southern Churchman* was published in

[100] See "History of the *Churchman*" by Clifton H. Brewer, published serially

Alexandria, Virginia, during this period.[101] The Philadelphia *Episcopal Recorder* (1822–current) was chief organ of the Reformed Episcopal church. Other important weeklies were published in the South and West.[102]

Just before the war Wilson pointed out in his *Chicago Record* how vain had been the effort of the northern Episcopalians to keep peace and refrain from comment on slavery when "hearts ached to testify at the altar of God against its enormities" — all in the hope of avoiding division of the church. Alone of the major denominations, the Protestant Episcopal organization came up to the war years united, only to find its southern clergy leading in secession activities and thus forcing political division.[103]

CONGREGATIONALISTS AND UNITARIANS

The Congregational church was strong in its periodicals in the war period, though not so numerously represented as some other sects. It had four good quarterlies. Both the *New Englander*,[104] organ of the Yale theology, and *Bibliotheca Sacra*,[105] exponent of that of Andover, had been founded in 1843 and were now in the full tide of influence. The historical and statis-

---

beginning November 14, 1925, and also its "125th Anniversary" number of March 2, 1929. In spite of the fact that when the title *Churchman* was adopted in 1867, the numbering of the *Connecticut Churchman* was continued and it was acknowledged at the time as a continuation of that paper, the modern *Churchman* prefers to think of itself as the successor (after a suspension 1861–67) of the New York *Churchman* founded in 1831, and therefore the successor, through the *Episcopal Watchman* (which the New York *Churchman* had absorbed in 1833), of the old *Churchman's Monthly Magazine* (1804–27). The *Churchman* has absorbed half a dozen or more other Episcopal weeklies and has always been an important force in the church.

[101] It was founded at Richmond in 1835 and was returned there in 1879 by D. A. Sprigg, who remained its editor until 1899. William F. Lee was it founder.

[102] Some of the other more important Protestant Episcopal weeklies of the period 1850–65 are: *Protestant Churchman* (1843–75), New York, called the *Christian Times* in 1862 and moved to Philadelphia to become the *Episcopalian* in 1866; *Western Episcopalian* (1830–1908), which began as the *Gambier* (Ohio) *Observer* and after several changes became the Philadelphia *Church Standard;* *Christian Witness* (1835–72?), Boston; *Gospel Messenger* (1835–71?), Utica; *Church Advocate* (1835–current), Harrisburg; *Southern Episcopalian* (1854–63), Charleston; *American Churchman* (1861–71), Chicago. The monthly *Spirit of Missions* has been published in New York since 1836.

[103] *Church Record*, IV, 140 (December 15, 1860).

[104] Treated more fully in sketch 7.

[105] See Mott, *op. cit.*, p. 739.

tical *Congregational Quarterly*,[106] a semiofficial publication, was begun at Boston in 1859; and the *Boston Review*,[107] a bimonthly organ of the right wing of the church, in 1861. The Congregationalists also had three important missionary monthlies: the veteran *Missionary Herald*,[108] the *Home Missionary* (1829–1909), and the *American Missionary* (1846–1933). The greatest of the church's weeklies were three: the New York *Independent*,[109] of which Beecher was editor 1861–63; the old *Boston Recorder* (1816–67),[110] called during much of our period the *Puritan Recorder*; and the *Boston Congregationalist* (1849–current), which Henry M. Dexter, for forty years its editor, was in the process of making the great denominational paper of Congregationalism. Others there were in New England and the West.[111]

The great organ of Unitarianism was the *Christian Examiner*,[112] the Boston bimonthly, whose most important editors during the period under consideration were Frederick H. Hedge and

[106] This work was organized by Henry M. Dexter, historian of Congregationalism, and its files are a valuable repository of Puritan history and biography and of Congregational statistics. One of its chief functions was the publication of the official records of the church in each January number, and when this was taken away from it by the decision of the church to publish its own yearbook, the *Quarterly* suspended. The secretary of the American Congregational Union was an editor and part-owner in the successive persons of J. S. Clark, I. P. Langworthy, and Christopher Cushing. Dexter was chief editor 1859–65, being succeeded by A. H. Quint. The *Quarterly* featured a competent book review department. Its theological attitude was indulgent, except in the last three years, when, under the sole editorship of Cushing, it developed some taste for polemics in favor of orthodoxy. Twenty volumes, January 1859–October 1878.

[107] Treated more fully in sketch 32.

[108] See Mott, *op. cit.*, p. 134.

[109] Treated more fully in sketch 14.

[110] See Mott, *op. cit.*, p. 138.

[111] Notably *Christian Mirror* (1822–99), Portland, Maine; *Congregational Journal* (1819–62), Concord, New Hampshire, begun as *Concord Observer* and undergoing various alterations in title and in place of publication (see John W. Moore, *Moore's Historical, Biographical and Miscellaneous Gatherings*, Concord, 1886, p. 517); *Vermont Chronicle* (1826–94), Windsor, Montpelier; *Religious Herald* (1843–1900), Hartford, Connecticut; *Congregational Herald* (1859–63), Lawrence, Kansas; and *Prairie Herald* (1846–61), Chicago, which began as *Western Herald*, a Quaker paper, but became a Congregational organ in 1849 and finally changed title to *Congregational Herald* in 1853 (for this and for all Illinois periodicals of these years, see F. W. Scott, *Newspapers and Periodicals of Illinois*, Springfield, 1910); *Pacific* (1851–1928), San Francisco.

[112] See Mott, *op. cit.*, p. 284.

Joseph Henry Allen. The *Monthly Religious Magazine* [113] supplied family reading, and the *Monthly Journal of the American Unitarian Association* [114] supplied church news. The leading weeklies were the *Christian Register* [115] at Boston and the *Christian Inquirer* and the *Liberal Christian* [116] at New York.

OTHER PROTESTANT DENOMINATIONS

During most of the fifties the *Universalist Quarterly and General Review* [117] was under the editorship of its founder, the younger Hosea Ballou. The leading weekly of the denomination was the Boston *Trumpet and Universalist Magazine*, known 1862–78 as the *Universalist.*[118]

[113] This monthly began as an unpretentious but well-printed little pamphlet of religious miscellany published by Leonard C. Bowles in Boston — a sermon, a few book reviews, some short religious pieces. It started out as "strictly Unitarian in doctrine," but F. D. Huntington gradually developed a belief in trinitarianism and added *An Independent Journal* to the title in 1856. Huntington resigned his editorship at the end of 1858 and went into the Episcopal church, and his successors, E. H. Sears and Rufus Ellis, quietly removed the subtitle. Thereupon the magazine became more denominational and theological, answering to the name *Religious Magazine and Monthly Review* in 1870, and in 1874 to *Monthly Religious Magazine and Theological Review*. J. H. Morison was editor 1871–74. Fifty-one volumes were published, annually 1844–53, then semiannually; it began with January 1844 and ended February 1874, giving place to the *Unitarian Review*.

[114] It began as the *Quarterly Journal*, etc., in 1853, but changed to monthly in 1860, ending in 1869.

[115] See Mott, *op. cit.*, p. 138.

[116] *Ibid.*, p. 373.

[117] Hosea Ballou 2d, backed by Abel Tompkins as publisher, started this review in January 1844, "to represent the scholarship and literary culture of the Universalist Church, as well as its theology." Thus it was somewhat more literary than many of its class. Ballou's own blasts against slavery were a feature and an index of the *Review's* continuing interest in politics. Successive editors after Ballou were: George H. Emerson, 1857–63; Thomas B. Thayer, 1864–86; Richard Eddy, 1886–91. The *Review* was taken over by the Universalist Publishing House in 1865, but it continually lost money, in spite of the effort to boost circulation by the reduction of the subscription price to $2.00 in 1883, and it was discontinued after October 1891 for financial reasons.

[118] This denomination also had the *Christian Freeman* (1839–62), begun at Waltham but moved to Boston, the elder Sylvanus Cobb's famous abolition-prohibition-Universalist paper; the *Christian Repository* (1820–70), later the *Universalist Watchman*, at various Vermont cities; the *Utica* (New York) *Magazine* (1827–78), later the *Christian Leader; Gospel Advocate and Magazine* (1823–78), later the *Christian Gospel Banner* (1823–97), Augusta, Maine; *Star in the West* (1827–80), Cincinnati, merged in the following paper; and

The *Evangelical Review* [119] was established at Gettysburg, Pennsylvania, in 1849, the organ of the Evangelical Lutheran church. C. P. Krauth's was the leading name connected with it through most of the war period. At Philadelphia were published the *Lutheran Observer* (1831–1915) and the *Lutheran and Missionary* (1861–current), latterly the *Lutheran*.[120] The *Lutheran Standard* was issued from 1842 on from Columbus, Ohio, and the *Workman* from Pittsburgh 1839–93. The *Mercersburg Review* [121] was the great journal of the Reformed church (German). For the Reformed church (Dutch), the Philadelphia *Messenger* (1828–88), the New York *Christian*

New Covenant (1848–83), Chicago, edited by D. P. Livermore and his wife Mary A. Livermore 1857–69, and later by J. W. Hanson. These papers were all eventually merged into the *Universalist*, which was issued from 1882 on by the church's publication society. (See Vol. III for this paper in the next period; see also *Universalist Leader*, N.S., XXII, 16, January 4, 1919.) The one weekly never drawn into the *Universalist* net was the *Universalist Herald* (1848–current), long published at Notsulga, Alabama, by John C. Burruss, and later moved to Canon and Atlanta, Georgia. There was also the monthly *Manford's Magazine* (1856–96), published by Erasmus Manford and his wife, Mrs. H. B. Manford, first in Chicago and later in St. Louis.

[119] When it was begun in July 1849, six months after the *Mercersburg Review*, its founder, William M. Reynolds, hoped that it might be a bond of union in a greatly divided denomination and therefore made it "open to all." The special adherence of the editors, who were members of the faculty of Pennsylvania College at Gettysburg, to the General Synod, however, made it impossible to conciliate the General Council body of the church. Its bêtes noires were "Romanism and rationalism." President C. P. Krauth wrote much of German theology, and Martin L. Stoever of Lutheran history and biography. These men were the editors of the first series. The New Series, begun in 1871, under James A. Brown, for many years leader of the General Synod, and President Milton Valentine, marked a great advance and brought the *Quarterly Review of the Evangelical Lutheran Church*, as it was now called, to its position of greatest influence and circulation. (See N.S., XXVIII, 161, April 1898; and LVI, 129, April 1926.) It was not, however, very literary, though its later volumes inclined to economics, sociology, and science, while continuing its theological interest. The name was changed to *Lutheran Quarterly* in 1878. Later members of the editorial board were P. M. Bikle, Joseph W. Richard, Thomas C. Billheimer, F. G. Gotwald, J. A. Singmaster, Jacob A. Clutz. In 1926 the *Quarterly* passed from private control to that of the Lutheran Theological Seminary at Gettysburg, and two years later it was merged with the *Lutheran Church Review* (1882–1927), of the Lutheran Theological Seminary at Philadelphia, to form a new journal, the *Lutheran Church Quarterly*, organ of the United Lutheran church.

[120] It adopted the shorter name in 1882. In 1919, after a general merger, it began new numbering, but kept its former editor, title, and place of publication.

[121] Treated more fully in sketch 15.

Intelligencer (1830–1933), and the *Christian World* (1848–1935), Cleveland, were spokesmen.

The veteran and itinerant *Herald of Gospel Liberty*,[122] now sojourning in Newburyport, Massachusetts, and the *Christian Sun* (1844–current), of various North Carolina cities, spoke for the Christian church;[123] and Alexander Campbell's *Millennial Harbinger* (1830–70), of Bethany, Virginia, and the *American Christian Review* (1858–86), Cincinnati, represented the Disciples of Christ — though the difference between the two branches was chiefly in name. The Adventists had the *Advent Review* (1850–current), Washington; the *Advent Harbinger* (1844–54), Rochester; and the *Herald of Life* (1863–1931), founded in New York, but later moved to Springfield, Massachusetts, and later to Hartford. The *Friend*, the *Friends' Review*,[124] and the *Friend's Intelligencer* (1838–current), all published in Philadelphia, were the organs of the Society of Friends.

For the Swedenborgians, the *New Jerusalem Magazine* was published at Boston,[125] the weekly *New-Church Messenger* (1855–current) first at Chicago and then at New York, and the *New-Church Independent and Monthly Review* (1853–1904) at Chicago. The Harrisburg *Church Advocate* has represented the Church of God since 1835, and the *Moravian* has been published at Bethlehem, Pennsylvania, since 1856. The United Brethren have published the *Religious Telescope* at Dayton, Ohio, since 1834.

There were several Mormon periodicals.[126] The *Olive Branch* was issued by the Latter-Day Saints at Kirtland, Ohio, 1848–50, and the *Saints' Herald* in Iowa and Missouri towns since 1860. The *Western Standard* was edited by Elder George Q. Cannon in San Francisco 1855–57. The *Seer*, edited in

---

[122] See Mott, *op. cit.*, p. 137.

[123] For these periodicals, see J. Pressley Barrett, *A Century of Religious Journalism* (Dayton, Ohio, 1908).

[124] For the *Friend*, Mott, *op. cit.*, p. 562; for *Friends' Review*, *ibid.*, p. 773.

[125] Monthly, 1827–93. For historical sketch, see *New Jerusalem Magazine*, N.S., VI, 109 (February 1882). It was followed in 1894 by the quarterly *New-Church Review*.

[126] See Walter W. Smith, "Periodical Literature of the Latter-Day Saints," *Journal of History*, XIV, 257 (July 1921).

Washington by Orson Pratt 1853–54, referred in its title to
Joseph Smith, "the great Seer of the last days," and contained
the prophet's revelation on "Celestial Marriage" and his foretell-
ing of secession, confederacy, and war. For a long time the
weekly *Deseret News* (1850–current) was the only periodical
in Utah. Willard Richards was its first editor, and Cannon had
charge of it later. It was not primarily a newspaper, in spite of
its name, and the arts and sciences engaged much of its attention. In 1867 it became the first successful religious daily in the
English language. Mormonism furnished the topic for many
articles in the secular press, its sex feature having a peculiar
fascination.

Some interdenominational journals were published, such as
the *Theological and Literary Journal* [127] in New York and the
Theological Eclectic (1863–71) in Boston. The American Sunday School Union, Philadelphia, published the *Sunday School
Journal* (1831–58), which was succeeded by the *Sunday School
Times*.[128] The Union sold the *Times* to J. C. Garrigues in 1861
and in the same year began the *Sunday School World*, which it
still publishes. The *American Tract Society* issued its widely
circulated monthly *American Messenger* (1843–1923) and its
weekly *Christian Banner and Tract Journal* (1859–72) from
New York. The first Y.M.C.A. journal was the *Quarterly Reporter of Y.M.C.A.'s in North America*, begun at Buffalo in
1856 by N. A. Halbert, and changed in 1859 to the monthly
Young Men's Christian Journal.

[127] Edited by David N. Lord and published by Franklin Knight in thirteen
yearly volumes July 1848–April 1861, New York. There is but little to justify
the use of the word *Literary* in the title. The chief theme is the prophetic Scriptures. There are some articles of travel and politics, and much against contemporary geology. The editor wrote most of the review, but George Duffield,
R. W. Dickinson, and others afforded some assistance.
[128] An outgrowth of the revivalistic movements of the period, it was founded
in 1859. John S. Hart, famous educator and former editor of *Sartain's*, was its
editor until 1871, when John Wanamaker bought the property from Garrigues
and secured H. Clay Trumbull as editor and John D. Wattles as publisher.
Trumbull purchased the paper in 1877 and remained chief owner and editor until
1903, acquiring at one time 150,000 circulation. In 1903 the work was taken over
by Trumbull's son and son-in-law, Charles G. Trumbull, editor, and Philip E.
Howard, publisher, who are still in control. See "Golden Jubilee Number,"
January 2, 1909.

CATHOLIC PERIODICALS

In spite of much popular opposition, the Catholic church in America appeared to flourish. Bishop John Hughes, writing in the *Metropolitan* in 1856, pointed out that "the Catholics of the United States have been sorely tried within the last few years by the assaults made upon them on account of their religion," and he called attention to the common identification of Catholicism with what he called "Irishism." [129] This "Irishism," as will be seen later, touched various political, social, and economic questions, usually creating friction. The war forced another trial upon the church, since Catholics were largely allied with the Democratic party. But Catholic periodicals grew in number. A census taken in 1854 showed sixteen Catholic weeklies, two monthlies, and one quarterly.[130]

The quarterly was *Brownson's*,[131] a powerful, if sometimes quarrelsome, journal. The leading monthly was the *Metropolitan*,[132] a miscellaneous magazine of religion, literature, and information. The oldest of the Catholic weeklies of the war period was the *United States Catholic Miscellany* (1822–61), with which are identified the names of Bishops England, Reynolds, and Lynch;[133] and next to that was its New York rival, the *Truth-Teller* (1825–55). This latter was an offshoot of the London *Truth-Teller*, William E. Andrews being at first the conductor of both; and its purpose was to defend the Irish political cause and the Catholic faith together. But politics tended to crowd out religion, especially toward the end of its career.[134] The Boston *Pilot*, Patrick Donahoe proprietor, was also both Irish and Catholic; but his paper was conducted with more dignity and became the most influential periodical of the

[129] *Metropolitan*, IV, 652 (December 1856).
[130] *Ibid.*, II, 398, 453 (August–September 1854).
[131] See Mott, *op. cit.*, p. 685.
[132] Edited by M. J. Kearney and "A Committee of Literary Gentlemen." John Murphy & Company, publishers, February 1853–January 1859, Baltimore.
[133] See William L. King, *The Newspaper Press of Charleston, S. C.* (Charleston, 1872), pp. 166 ff.
[134] See Paul J. Foik, *Pioneer Catholic Journalism* (New York, 1930), p. 24. It was absorbed by the New York *Irish-American* (1849–1916), a religious and political weekly founded by Patrick Lynch and edited for half a century by his son-in-law, Patrick J. Meehan.

church.[135] It was strongly union during the war, as was the *Pittsburgh Catholic* (1844–current); but the same can scarcely be said of the *Catholic Mirror* (1850–1908), of Baltimore, or of the *Catholic Telegraph* (1831–current), of Cincinnati.[136] The *Freeman's Journal* (1840–1918), of New York, James A. Mc-Master editor, went so far in its opposition to the Federal government's conduct during the war that it was excluded from the mails for eight months and its editor thrown into prison.[137] Thomas D'Arcy McGee's *American Celt* (1852–57), of Boston, Buffalo, and New York successively, became at length the *Tablet*, a famous Catholic paper.[138]

There were other Catholic weeklies,[139] and for a short term (1857–61) a Baltimore literary periodical called the *Catholic Youth's Magazine*, edited by Martin J. Kearney and ended by his death.

The organ of the American and Foreign Christian Union, organized to "evangelize" Catholics, was the *Christian World* (1850–84), of New York.

NON-CHRISTIAN PERIODICALS

Several Jewish weeklies of the Civil War period should be mentioned. In New York two were prominent — Samuel H. Lewis' *Hebrew Leader* (1848–1906) and Samuel M. Isaacs' *Jewish Messenger* (1857–1903). Philadelphia had Isaac Leeser's *Occident and American Jewish Advocate* (1843–69). Leeser and Isaacs were doubtless the best-known orthodox rabbis in America. Further west there were the *American Israelite* (1854–current), founded by Isaac Mayer Wise and con-

---

[135] *Ibid.*, p. 169.
[136] *Ibid.*, p. 173.
[137] *Ibid.*, p. 204.
[138] It ran 1857–90. It was biweekly in later years and had many well-known contributors.
[139] Among them were the *Catholic Herald* (1833–63), Philadelphia; *Shepherd of the Valley* (1833–54), St. Louis, suspended 1839–50, a deserter to the Know-Nothings at the end; *Catholic Guardian* (1858–62), Louisville, revived as *Catholic Central Advocate* (1869–1900), L. H. Bell editor and publisher; *Metropolitan Record* (1859–73), founded by Archbishop Hughes, New York, and edited by John Mullaly, but repudiated by Hughes for its Civil War policy. For further list, see Apollinaris W. Baumgartner, *Catholic Journalism* (New York, 1931), pp. 19–20.

ducted by him for nearly half a century in Cincinnati;[140] and the San Francisco *Hebrew Observer* (1856–90).

The leading "freethinker's" periodical was the Boston *Investigator* (1835–1904), which gloried in the name "Infidel Paper." Horace Seaver was editor and Josiah P. Mendum publisher (1845–89). It will not be unsuitable to pair with the *Investigator* the Oneida *Circular*, published 1851–76 chiefly by J. H. Noyes for the Oneida Community and for communism and liberalism generally.[141]

SCIENTIFIC PERIODICALS

It may be true, as the religious magazines reiterated so frequently, that there was no real conflict between science and religion, or at least that there was no quarrel between true religion and sound science; but the clergyman can scarcely be said to have played Damon to the scientist's Pythias at the mid-century. The editor of the *Theological and Literary Journal*, for example, wrote and published a series of articles combatting contemporary geology through the years 1852–54. Editor Lord maintained that "the theory generally entertained by geologists respecting the great age of the earth would, if founded on just grounds, disprove the inspiration of the Bible." [142] But a writer in the *Biblical Repertory* took exception to this statement, and there was a controversy. Even the Agassiz series on glaciers in the *Atlantic Monthly* provoked criticism.

More important than the geological phase of the religio-scientific differences, however, was the discussion of Darwin's newly enunciated hypothesis of the origin of species. The *American Journal of Science* was perhaps the best exponent of that theory among the magazines. There Asa Gray, Theophilus Parsons, and Joseph D. Hooker set it forth throughout 1860, despite the opposition of Professor Agassiz. The *North American's* reviewer of Darwin's book rejected "the cosmogony" implied [143]

---

[140] Called *Israelite*, 1854–75. Wise was the founder of Reform Judaism in America. The *Israelite* has stood for Jewish religion and American nationalism. After the founder's death in 1900, it was edited by his sons until its sale in 1930 to A. L. and H. C. Segal.

[141] See p. 207.

[142] *Theological and Literary Journal*, IX, 251 (October 1856).

[143] *North American Review*, XC, 474 (April 1860).

and later replied to the *Journal of Science* articles. "The scientific world . . . has been thoroughly aroused by the publications of Mr. Darwin's speculations," he tells us.[144] Gray, writing in the *Atlantic*, maintained that the Darwinian theory was "very useful to science, and not harmful to religion." [145]

The voice of the clergy was heard much more variously than that of the scientist in this period. If, however, we include the periodicals devoted to the various fields of applied science — medicine, dentistry, pharmacy, engineering, mechanics, transportation, mining, agriculture, etc. — the scientific showing is considerable. There was an increasing tendency toward specialization in class periodicals, and the *American Journal of Science* [146] was virtually the only widely circulated review of general science in America. More specialized in content was the New York *Bulletin of the American Geographical and Statistical Society*,[147] an important magazine which printed much of the arctic explorations of Dr. E. K. Kane, sometime secretary of the Society. Kane's work was noticed in many periodicals and caused no little popular excitement. The *Mathematical Monthly* [148] and the *Astronomical Journal* [149] were both published at Cambridge. Of the latter periodical a *Putnam* reviewer said: "It sends its light to every quarter of the globe. . . . But wherever it goes, it sends back honor upon the United States." [150]

[144] *Ibid.*, XCI, 528 (October 1860).

[145] *Atlantic Monthly*, VI, 424 (October 1860). See B. J. Loewenberg, "The Controversy over Evolution in New England, 1859–73," *New England Quarterly*, VIII, 232 (June 1935), and "Reaction of American Scientists to Darwinianism," *American Historical Review*, XXXVIII, 686 (July 1933).

[146] See Mott, *op. cit.*, p. 302.

[147] Treated more fully in sketch 19.

[148] Edited by John D. Runkle. Three annual volumes quarto, October 1858–September 1861. The second volume was published in New York, though still printed in Cambridge. Simon Newcomb, O. T. Root, and Benjamin Peirce were frequent contributors.

[149] Founded November 1849 by Benjamin Apthorpe Gould, Jr., who edited it until 1861; it was then suspended until 1886, when Gould resumed it and edited it until his death in 1896. Seth C. Chandler edited it 1897–1908, after which Lewis Boss bought it and took it to Albany to publish in connection with the Dudley Observatory. Benjamin Boss has been editor since 1912. It had an annual deficit of $600 in its earlier years.

[150] *Putnam's Monthly*, II, 446 (October 1853).

MECHANICAL AND MINING ENGINEERING

In this period of amazing fecundity in invention, a number of periodicals were devoted to mechanics and patents.[151] The *Journal of the Franklin Institute* [152] was the veteran of this class; and the *Scientific American*,[153] which had been founded in 1845, was prominent. The *American Artisan and Patent Record*, published in New York 1864–75, was the only one of a group of similar periodicals to last more than two or three years. One of the ephemerals of this class, the *Inventor* (1855–57), of New York, printed in its first number an interesting account of a "steam carriage to be used on common roads" built by J. K. Fisher of that city. Experiments with it had been successful, and its inventor was "sanguine that it will supersede horse power," but the *Inventor* is "not prepared to say that this method of transportation will ever become general." [154] Some of the more general periodicals, especially the pictorials, published much comment on mechanical devices. The exhibition at the Crystal Palace in New York in 1853 was especially stimulating in this regard.

Related to these mechanical journals were half a dozen mining magazines and a number of periodicals devoted to railroad matters. Some of the mining journals were on the Pacific Coast and reflected the industry which had brought that region so melodramatically to the national consciousness. The *Mining and Scientific Press* began in 1860 and published 124 semi-annual volumes in San Francisco before it was merged with a New York journal in 1922; but the *Pacific Index*, of 1864, became the *American Mining Index*, of New York, after its first volume and lived only through 1867. New York also had the

---

[151] The *Scientific American* listed in 1854 fifteen mechanical periodicals which its editor remembered to have "come and gone." It added: "At present the *Scientific American* is the only weekly publication in this country devoted to mechanical and scientific subjects; and of the monthlies the old *Franklin Journal* and the young *Polytechnic* [*American Polytechnic Journal*, 1853–54, Washington] are the only representatives left. The *People's Journal* [New York, 1853–54, merged with *Scientific American*] was issued at one dollar per annum and undoubtedly attained the largest circulation of any of the monthlies." IX, 411 (September 9, 1854).

[152] See Mott, *op. cit.*, p. 556.

[153] Treated more fully in sketch 8.

[154] *Inventor*, I, 1 (September 1855).

Mining Magazine (1853–61) and the *American Mining Gazette and Geological Magazine* (1864–68). The *Mining Journal* (1845–78), of Marquette, Michigan, reflected the new iron, copper, and salt industries of its region. The general magazines continued to manifest their interest in the California gold fields,[155] and in the sixties some of them caught the Colorado gold craze.

The first successful oil well was drilled near Titusville, Pennsylvania, in 1859; and by the end of the year there were thousands of wells in that region, refineries had been placed in operation, and speculation in oil was rampant.[156] The *Petroleum Gazette and Scientific Journal* was issued in Cincinnati throughout most of 1865.

THE RAILROAD FEVER

The railroad journals begun in the fifties are a testimony to the great public interest in the building of new lines. The established periodical in this class was the *American Railroad Journal*,[157] of New York. In the same city were the *Railroad Advocate* (1854–57) and the *American Railway Review* (1859–62). The *American Railway Times* was published in Boston (1849–72), and the *United States Railway and Mining Register*[158] in Philadelphia (1856–1915). Cincinnati had its *Railroad Record* (1853–73), and Chicago its *Western Railroad Gazette*[159] (1857–1908). And so on.

These journals all argued eloquently for a railway to the Pacific Coast, as did many of the magazines not specifically dedicated to railroad extension. "We are impatient at being cut off from California," wrote Henry V. Poor, editor of the *American Railroad Journal*, in the *Bulletin of the American Geographical Society*. This society was much concerned with the projects for a transcontinental railroad; and Poor's article discussed the

[155] See p. 119.
[156] *Independent*, January 19, 1865.
[157] Treated more fully in sketch 4.
[158] Called the *Railway World*, 1875–1915. It began as the *Pennsylvania Railroad and Mining Register*, but dropped *Pennsylvania* for *United States* in November 1856. Fifty-nine annual volumes.
[159] *Western* dropped from title in 1870; moved to New York in 1882; merged with the *Railway Age* in 1908 as *Railroad Age Gazette*; called *Railway Age* in 1917.

geography of five proposed routes, based on a detailed map prepared by the society. But Poor foresaw great difficulties.

The proposition before us [he wrote] involves the construction of
a railroad for a distance of nearly 2,000 miles through an uninhabited,
and for the greater part, uninhabitable country, nearly destitute of
wood, extensive districts of it destitute of water; over mountain
ranges whose summits are white with eternal snows; over deserts
parched beneath an unclouded sky, and over yawning chasms which
the process of disintegration since the volcanic fires were put out, has
not yet filled up. How is a sufficient force to be maintained upon such
a work for its construction? And how is the road to be kept in repairs
and operated after it is built? How is the locomotive to be supplied
with its food, wood or water? These are some of the questions which
need to be discussed and solved, not the necessity which exists for the
work.[160]

De Bow's Review published hundreds of pages about railroad
building. De Bow himself was president of the Tennessee
Pacific Railway. His journal gave attention especially to southern projects and to the southwestern route to the Pacific. "The
rail-road fever appears to be at its height in the South-west," [161]
it observed in 1852, as the Southwestern Railroad convention
assembled at New Orleans; and a little later:

In every part of the South and South-west we have been emulating
the example of our thrifty neighbors in the North, and are beginning
to show a degree of enterprise and spirit, at least in the matter of railroads, not to be shamed in the comparison with their own.[162]

The *Review* had published a table of mileage in 1846 which
showed the Georgia Central to have more miles of road [163] than
any other company in the country — 190¼. These statements
illustrate the intense railroad rivalry which existed between
regions and the competing ambitions of certain cities which
aspired to be railroad centers.

[160] *Bulletin of the American Geographical Society*, I, 91 (Part 3, "for the year
1854"). Also see *Frank Leslie's Illustrated Newspaper*, December 15, 1855, *et seq.*
(first several numbers of the paper) for maps and sketches of Rocky Mountain
routes.
    [161] *De Bow's Review*, XII, 224 (January 1852).
    [162] *Ibid.*, XIII, 571 (December 1852).
    [163] *Ibid.*, I, 460–462 (May 1846). Tables reprinted from the *Railroad Journal.*

The growing number of railroad accidents caused some alarm. *Harper's Weekly* lamented the "wholesale slaughter upon railroads." [164] "Our railway trains are run too fast," complained the *New Era*. "Look at the recent disasters. . . . But the traveling public love to ride in one of those 'Lightning Runs,' which whizzes them over the track at a rate as dangerous as it is delightful." [165] The rate was twenty-five or thirty miles an hour.[166] An engineer writing in *De Bow's* gave one reason for the frequency of accidents when he complained that "roads have been found dropping to pieces three years after construction." [167]

Sleeping cars had been introduced by which seats for four passengers "are instantly, and while the cars are in full motion, converted into four perfect beds." [168] There were no dining cars, and coaches were badly lighted and heated. Dreamers were visioning all sorts of new developments, most of them relating to extensions and speed. "Jack Lantern," in *Putnam's*, will not listen to predictions of men flying, but he looks forward to great swiftness on the earth. "Let's leave the air to the prince of it," he urges. "If we fly, let it be as ostriches do, with our feet on the ground. . . . Hurrah for the *iron ostrich!* outstripping horses, antelopes, and the wild ass, and running neck and neck with the tornado!" [169] Boston's "Grand Rail-Road Celebration" of 1851 gave opportunity for no little indulgence in such rhapsodies.[170]

Railroads were generally prosperous during the war: the *Railroad Record* declared that "the year 1862 will ever be remembered in railroading as one of the most prosperous that has ever been known." [171] The *Stockholder*, a weekly devoted to railway investment, was founded in that year in New York, to last almost a half-century.

[164] *Harper's Weekly*, IX, 162 (March 18, 1865).

[165] *New Era*, XII, 124 (August 5, 1858).

[166] Emerson David Fite, *Social and Industrial Conditions in the North During the Civil War* (New York, 1910), p. 76.

[167] *De Bow's Review*, XIV, 146 (January 1853).

[168] *New Era*, XII, 71 (October 28, 1858).

[169] *Putnam's Monthly*, II, 34 (July 1853). See also II, 270–277 (September 1853), and II, 500–508 (November 1853), for articles on the Pacific Railway project. "Jack Lantern" was G. H. McMaster.

[170] See *Carpet-Bag*, September 20, 1851 — a Celebration number.

[171] *Railroad Record*, January 8, 1863.

MEDICAL JOURNALS

Another group of journals of applied science is composed of those designed for physicians. Of these the two oldest were the *American Journal of the Medical Sciences*,[172] of outstanding excellence, and throughout this period under the editorship of its founder in Philadelphia, Dr. Isaac Hays; and the *Boston Medical and Surgical Journal*,[173] a weekly which had distinguished itself just before our period begins by its contributions to the subject of the use of ether in surgery. Besides these, about a score of medical journals founded in the forties and located in important cities of various sections were in course of publication in 1850, but only five of them survived the war.[174] A dozen more were founded in the years 1850–60, scattered from Concord, New Hampshire, to Keokuk, Iowa; but most of these likewise succumbed to the stresses of the war.[175] The *Pacific Medical Journal* (1858–1917), of San Francisco, the *Iowa Medical Journal* (1853–69), of Keokuk, and the Philadelphia *Medical and Surgical Reporter* (1858–98) were longer-lived.

Such were the "regular" medical journals. There were at least seventeen of the homoeopathic persuasion, most of them

---

[172] See Mott, *op. cit.*, p. 566.

[173] *Ibid.*, p. 151, footnote. See also centennial number of the *Journal*, CXCVIII, 1–32 (February 23, 1928). Dr. J. V. C. Smith was editor 1835–57. It became *New England Journal of Medicine* in 1928.

[174] Survivors were *St. Louis Medical and Surgical Journal* (1843–1907); Lea and Blanchard's famous *Medical News* (1843–1905), Philadelphia, founded by Isaac Hays; *Northwestern Medical and Surgical Journal* (1844–89), which had published its first few volumes as the *Illinois Medical and Surgical Journal*, and by another change became *Chicago Medical Journal* in 1859; *Buffalo Medical Journal* (1845–1918); and *Ohio Medical and Surgical Journal* (1848–78), Columbus. The *New York Journal of Medicine* (1843–60), with its weekly continuation, *American Medical Times* (1860–64), did not quite outlast the war; but it was an important periodical. Four important southern medical journals were suspended during the war but were revived later: *Charleston Medical Journal and Review* (1846–77), *Nashville Journal of Medicine and Surgery* (1851–1920), *Atlanta Medical and Surgical Journal* (1855–99), and *New Orleans Medical and Surgical Journal* (1844–current). The last named was famous for its contributions to tropical medicine.

[175] The three of longest life were: *New Hampshire Journal of Medicine* (1850–59), Concord; *New York* (later *American*) *Medical Gazette* (1850–61); *American Medical Monthly* (1854–62), New York.

short-lived.[176] Outstanding were the *North American Journal of Homoeopathy*,[177] a quarterly founded by Dr. Constantine Hering and others in New York in 1851; and the Chicago *Medical Investigator*.[178] The eclectics were represented by the *Eclectic Medical Journal* (1836–current), of Cincinnati, and the *Eclectic Medical Journal of Pennsylvania* (1862–80), issued by the Eclectic College at Philadelphia. Dr. Joseph R. Buchanan, dean of a similar college at Cincinnati, whilom quack and reformer, published *Buchanan's Journal of Man* in that city 1849–56; it was a quasi-anthropological journal devoted largely to its editor's theories of "sarcognomy" and "psychometry." This was followed by the less erratic *College Journal of Medical Science* (1856–69), but Buchanan revived his *Journal* in Boston (1887–90). There were also such heretics as the *Journal of Medical Reform* (1854–57) in New York, and the *Southern Botanico-Medical Reformer* (1837–60), published with variations in title at Forsyth, Georgia, and other cities.

A few specialists appeared, like the *American Journal of Insanity* (1844–91), conducted by the staff of the New York State Lunatic Asylum in Utica; and the *American Journal of Ophthalmology* (1862–64), in New York.

The typical medical journal was described just before the beginning of the war period by Dr. Oliver Wendell Holmes, serv-

[176] From the group may be mentioned Dr. George E. Shipman's western pioneer, *Northwestern Journal of Homoeopathia* (1848–51), Chicago; Drs. S. R. Kirby's and R. A. Snow's *New York* (later *American*) *Journal of Homoeopathy* (1846–54); Dr. Henry M. Smith's *American Homoeopathic Review* (1858–66), a New York quarterly; Dr. William Tod Helmuth's *Western Homoeopathic Observer* (1863–71), St. Louis; and Dr. Edwin A. Lodge's *American Homoeopathic Observer* (1864–84), Detroit. See W. A. Dewey's "History of the Periodical Literature of the Homoeopathic School" in William Harvey King's *History of Homoeopathy and Its Institutions in America* (New York, 1905), II, 13–34.

[177] In its first year it was called *North American Homoeopathic Journal*. Dr. Samuel Lilienthal was editor 1871–85. It was a monthly after 1885. In 1919 it moved to Chicago, four years later changed title to *Pan-Therapist*, and ended in 1933.

[178] Begun in 1860, it started a new series in 1863. It was merged at the end of 1874 with the *United States Medical and Surgical Journal* (1865–74), a Chicago competitor, and changed from monthly to weekly publication under the name *United States Medical Investigator*. It became a monthly again in 1885. Dr. T. C. Duncan was its editor 1867–91. It tried quarterly publication in 1891, but ended in the next year.

ing as chairman of a committee on "medical literature" for the American Medical Society. It consisted, he said, of histories of epidemics and endemics, records of cases, accounts of operations, and book notices — with much eclectic material, so that "the ring of editors sit in each other's laps." [179] It is undeniable that there was little originality in these journals; but if they continued to ring the changes on the old subjects, it was because those subjects were still of great importance. For example, the *American Medical Times* observed in 1861 that "the subject of medical education is a trite and hackneyed theme . . . it would seem that no new aspect of the subject could be presented." [180] And yet such a matter could not be neglected. So also with regard to epidemics: in New Orleans in 1853–54, 254 victims died each day at the height of a yellow fever scourge which lasted for months.[181] There was no proper quarantine regulation in the cities, especially against smallpox, which was very prevalent. The *American Journal of the Medical Sciences* tells how patients suffering from this disease were allowed to spread it in public conveyances, factories, and streets.[182] The milk supply of New York City was not supervised, and the most spectacular campaign conducted by any journal in our period was that of *Leslie's* against the dairies which distributed milk from diseased cows to New York children.[183]

The medical service of the army (especially military surgery) occupied much space in the professional journals of the war years; and both this phase and the work of army sanitation attracted the attention of some of the general magazines. The *Sanitary Commission Bulletin* [184] was a special organ of importance; and the papers published briefly at the "sanitary fairs"

[179] *Transactions of American Medical Society* (Philadelphia, 1848), I, 256. This valuable report contains a history and a survey of medical periodicals, pp. 250–270.

[180] *American Medical Times*, III, 244 (October 12, 1861).

[181] *De Bow's Review*, XV, 595 (December 1853); XVI, 463 (May 1854); XVII, 39 (July 1854).

[182] *American Journal of the Medical Sciences*, N.S., XLVIII, 423 (January 1864).

[183] See pp. 456–458.

[184] Published November 1863 to August 1865, first in New York, then in Philadelphia, and lastly in Washington. E. L. Godkin was its editor for a time in 1864, but regarded his services as hack work. See Rollo Ogden, *Life and Letters of Edwin Lawrence Godkin* (New York, 1907), I, 228.

given all over the country in 1863–65 to raise money for the Commission were sometimes interesting for their contributions by famous writers.[185] An example was *Our Daily Fair*, edited for the Philadelphia Fair in June 1864 by Charles Godfrey Leland. It gives a history of the Sanitary Fair movement. In the South most of the medical journals suspended during all or a part of the war; but the *Confederate States Medical and Surgical Journal* was published for fourteen months from January 1864 at Richmond. "Amid the din of war's wild alarms," said the *Journal*, "the calm, peaceful voice of Science is heard." [186]

It was an age of "reforms," and the vegetarians, hydropathists, Grahamites, and phrenologists were active. *Hall's Journal of Health*, published in New York by Dr. William W. Hall (1854–94), was a standard popular magazine; it specialized in preventive medicine and in articles on consumption — Hall's specialty. The *American Vegetarian and Health Journal* (1850–54), a Philadelphia magazine, was of less importance. The *Herald of Health* was the new incarnation of the old *Water-Cure Journal*.[187] The hydropathists had also the *Water-Cure Monthly* (1859–60) at Yellow Springs, Ohio, and the *Water-Cure World: A Journal of Health and Herald of Reform* (1860–61) at Brattleboro, Vermont. A writer in *Putnam's* thought hydropathy a return to nature, correlated with enthusiasm for Wordsworth in poetry.[188] Not precisely Wordsworthian is the verse in which the *Knickerbocker* complains of the fad, however:

> It's water, water everywhere,
> And quarts to drink, if you can bear:
> 'Tis well that we are made of clay,
> For common dust would wash away![189]

The *American Phrenological Journal* [190] continued on its devoted way, though its cause showed signs of waning. One of the

---

[185] Besides *Our Daily Fair*, prominent papers were the *Drumbeat* (Brooklyn), the *Spirit of the Fair* (New York), and the *Haversack* (Philadelphia). See *American Annual Cyclopaedia*, 1864, p. 461.

[186] *Confederate States Medical and Surgical Journal*, I, 13 (January 1864).

[187] See Mott, *op. cit.*, p. 441.

[188] *Putnam's Monthly*, II, 66 (July 1853).

[189] *Knickerbocker Magazine*, XLI, 254 (March 1853).

[190] See Mott, *op. cit.*, p. 447.

best quips of those who saw only comedy in the elaborate charts of the phrenologists was that of "John Phoenix" in the San Francisco *Pioneer*. It consisted of a chart of John's own head made by "Flatbroke B. Dodge, professor of Phrenology and inventor proprietor of Dodge's Celebrated Hair Invigorator and Stimulator of Conscience and Arouser of the Mental Faculties." The chart showed the size of John's head to be 11, amativeness 11½, language 12, mirth 1, philoprogenetiveness 0, and so on — while his temperament was "lymphatic, nervous, bilious." [191]

AGRICULTURAL PERIODICALS

De Bow's Review, itself in some degree a planter's journal, was able to list in 1847 twenty-six agricultural periodicals then in course of publication; [192] and the report of the 1860 census stated that "forty papers and magazines, devoted almost exclusively to topics pertinent to farming and gardening, are published in the country." [193] Certainly more than a hundred periodicals of this class were published — some of them for only a year or two — in the years 1850–65.

Many agricultural periodicals founded in the thirties and forties continued throughout all or part of the war period.[194] The old *American Farmer*,[195] the widely circulated *American Agriculturist*,[196] and the Albany and Boston *Cultivators*, as well as several important southern and western papers,[197] held high rank in these years. Just before our period, in 1849, three suc-

[191] *Pioneer*, II, 127 (September 1854).

[192] *De Bow's Review*, IV, 444 (December 1847).

[193] Joseph C. Kennedy, *Preliminary Report of the Eighteenth Census, 1860* (Washington, 1862), p. 100.

[194] The most important of these will be found in Mott, *op. cit.*, pp. 441–444, where they are briefly described.

[195] *Ibid.*, p. 153.

[196] *Ibid.*, p. 728.

[197] For example, the *Genesee Farmer* (1831–65), Rochester; *Valley Farmer* (1848–1916), St. Louis; *Southern Planter* (1841–current), Richmond (now claiming to be "the oldest agricultural journal in America"); and *Southern Cultivator* (1843–1935), Athens, Georgia. For these, see Mott, *loc. cit.*; and for several of the early journals mentioned, see William Edward Ogilvie, *Pioneer Agricultural Journalists* (Chicago, 1927). For *Southern Planter*, see its Ninetieth Anniversary Number, January 1, 1930; for *Southern Cultivator*, see *A. L. A. Bulletin*, XXVII, 626 (December 15, 1933), article by James A. McMillen.

cessful farm journals were founded: the *Rural New Yorker*, edited at Rochester by D. D. T. Moore, which keeps to this day something of the luster of a well-loved name; the *Wisconsin Farmer* (1849–74), founded by Mark Miller at Racine and later moved to Janesville and Madison; and the *Working Farmer* (1849–75), of New York.

It was in 1853 that Luther Tucker (*nomen venerabile* in agricultural journalism) founded in Albany the *Country Gentleman*,[198] which was to acquire, many years later and in other hands, a wider fame. Meantime, from the South had come five shorter-lived but distinctive journals: the *Farmer and Planter Monthly* (1850–61), of Pendleton and Columbia, South Carolina; Joseph M. Chambers' *Soil of the South* (1851–57), at Columbus, Georgia; John F. Tompkins' *Farmer's Journal* (1852–54), at Bath, North Carolina; the *American Cotton Planter* (1853–61), of Montgomery, Alabama; and *Southern Field and Fireside* (1859–64), of Augusta, Georgia. The last was literary as well as agricultural. Its editor was William W. Mann, who had attracted attention by his letters from Paris in the *Southern Literary Messenger*; and John R. Thompson joined its staff after he sold the *Messenger* in 1860.

But it was from what was later called the Middle West that the flood of new farm journals came in the fifties and sixties. The *Ohio Farmer* (1851–current) was founded at Cleveland by Thomas Brown.[199] In 1856 four midwestern ventures were begun: the *Journal of Agriculture* (1856–1921), St. Louis; *Cincinnatus* (1856–61), a monthly octavo edited by the faculty of Farmer's College, near Cincinnati, but especially by F. G. Cary; the *Northwestern Farmer* (1856–71), at Indianapolis; and the *Northwestern Farmer and Horticultural Journal*, at Dubuque, Iowa. The last named was started by Mark Miller, founder of the *Wisconsin Farmer*, who five years later moved it across the prairie by wagon, and, combining it with the *Pioneer Farmer* (1853–61), of Des Moines, issued it as the *Iowa Homestead and Northwestern Farmer*.[200] The financial depression then

---

[198] Treated more fully in sketch 22.
[199] See *Ohio Farmer*, CLI, 1 (January 6, 1923). It claims 1848 as a beginning date through a consolidation, but Vol. I, No. 1, is dated January 1, 1851.
[200] See *Iowa Homestead*, LXIII, 283 (February 16, 1928); Ogilvie, *op. cit.*,

caused a break in the steady stream of new periodicals, and for a few years such farm papers as were founded were of short duration and small influence. But in 1862 two important Illinois papers were begun: H. N. F. Lewis' *Western Rural* (1862–1901), Chicago; and the *Western Farmer* (1862–82), Dixon. in 1863 the *Kansas Farmer* was founded at Topeka, where it is still published.

The roll may be ended, though not completed,[201] by naming two far-westerners of the period: the *California Farmer* (1854–84), by J. L. L. F. Warren, of San Francisco; and the *Oregon Farmer* (1858–61), by W. B. Taylor, of Portland.

Horticulture was represented by Thomas Meehan's delightful *Gardener's Monthly and Horticultural Advertiser* (1859–88), of Philadelphia; and by the *Horticulturist and Journal of Rural Art and Rural Taste* [202] (1846–75), founded by Luther Tucker at Albany, but subjected to various changes in homes and ownership before it was finally merged with its rival, the *Gardener's Monthly*.

---

pp. 112–120; *Palimpsest*, XI, 229–241 (June 1930); Gerald Seaman, "Some Early Iowa Farm Journals" (Iowa State College thesis, 1936). The date of the founding of the *Iowa Homestead* is usually given as 1855; but if the *Pioneer Farmer* is considered the progenitor, it should be 1853, since that paper was begun in Burlington, Iowa, as the *Iowa Farmer and Horticulturist* in 1853. (See D. C. Mott, "William Duane Wilson," in *Annals of Iowa*, 3d series, XX, 363, July 1936.) However, the *Homestead* continued the numbering of the *Northwestern*, which, according to Miller's statement, was founded in 1856. (See *Iowa Homestead*, VII, 1, January 29, 1862, and *Western Pomologist*, I, 1, January 1870.) The *Homestead* was consolidated with *Wallace's Farmer* in 1929 at a valuation of $2,000,000, which later forced the purchaser into a receivership.

[201] Four weeklies of long life should also be mentioned: *Practical Farmer* (1855–1922), Philadelphia, which became the *Heart of the Home* in 1923; *Rural American* (1856–69), of Utica, and later of New York; *Maryland Farmer* (1864–1902), Baltimore, called the *Farmer's and Planter's Guide* after 1877; *Mirror and Farmer* (1863–1918), Manchester, New Hampshire, which had been compounded of the *Dollar Weekly Mirror* (1851–63) and the *New Hampshire Journal of Agriculture* (1857–63).

[202] James Vick, the Rochester seedsman, bought it in 1853. In 1855 it went to Robert Pearsall Smith in Philadelphia, and in 1858 to C. M. Saxton in New York. It remained in New York, with George E. and F. W. Woodward editors and publishers, 1862–68, and Henry T. Williams, 1869–75. A. J. Downing, the famous landscape gardener, was editor during Tucker's ownership, and Patrick Barry, who had been horticultural editor of the *Genesee Farmer*, during Vick's. The magazine was notable under Downing for its articles on architecture (with engravings) and for imaginative writing, and under Barry for its hand-colored plates of fruits and flowers and handsome appearance. ·

For stock raisers there was D. S. Linsley's *American Stock Journal* (1859–64), New York, though all farm papers gave attention to stock. Apiarists had the *American Bee Journal* [203] (1861–current), founded in Philadelphia by Samuel Wagner.

This catalogue reflects the westward shift of the agricultural center of the country. The papers themselves reflect many other changes — one of the chief of them being the increasing use of machinery. This coming of the machine to the farm was hastened by the war, with its drain on man power. The McCormick reaper, for example, came into general use during the war. In 1863 the *Scientific American* declared that "the severe manual toil of mowing, raking, pitching, and cradling is now performed by machinery operated by horse-power." [204] During war years, women and children could operate these machines. "Yesterday I saw the wife of one of my parishioners driving the team in a reaper," wrote an Iowa clergyman to the *Home Missionary*.

Her husband is at Vicksburg. With what help she can secure and that of her little children, she is carrying on the farm. In another field was a little boy of ten years, similarly employed, and in another a little girl of about twelve, doing the same.[205]

The *Country Gentleman's* correspondents in the Midwest told a similar story.

TECHNICAL AND INDUSTRIAL

The most important of the dental journals of the period was the *Dental Cosmos*,[206] founded at Philadelphia in 1859 by J. D. White to succeed the quarterly *Dental News-Letter* (1847–59). There were more than half a dozen others.[207]

[203] See *American Bee Journal*, LXI, 15 (January 1921), Sixtieth Anniversary Number; and LXXV, 7 (January 1935) Seventy-fifth Anniversary Number. It was suspended 1862–65, published in Washington 1866–72, and then moved to Chicago and later to Hamilton, Illinois.

[204] *Scientific American*, IX, 9 (July 4, 1863).

[205] *Home Missionary*, XXXV, 209 (January 1863). See also the *Country Gentleman* for September 12, 1861, and February 4, 1864.

[206] The S. S. White Dental Supply Company (originally Jones & White) was publisher from the beginning to the end in 1936. Edward C. Kirk (1891–1930) had the longest editorial service. See *Dentistry Then and Now*, a booklet issued by *Dental Cosmos*.

[207] *American Journal of Dental Science* (1839–1909), New York, edited by

The *American Journal of Pharmacy* [208] continued on its way, a leader in its field. The *American Druggists' Circular and Chemical Gazette* [209] began in New York January 1857, to continue to the present. The *Journal of Materia Medica* (1858–96) was published in New Lebanon, New York, by George H. Tilden; falling into other hands, it was moved to Terre Haute, Indiana, for its last few years.

Various industries had their journals, all of them reflecting the great manufacturing progress of the period. The present *Blast Furnace*, of Pittsburgh, began in 1862 as *Trade of the West*.[210] *Age of Steel*, of St. Louis, began in 1857; and *Chicago Journal of Commerce*, later *Iron and Steel*, in 1863. These two periodicals were merged in 1902 under the name *Iron and Machinery World* (1902–06). The *Hardware Man's Newspaper and American Manufacturer's Circular*, New York, was founded in 1855 and adopted its present title, the *Iron Age*, in 1860. The *Coach-Makers' Magazine* (1858–71), notable for its lithographic plates; the *Hub*, founded in 1859, to become many years later, in the course of invention, the *Automotive Manufacturer* (ended 1929); and the *Harness and Carriage Journal* (1857–83) — all of New York — were the leading carriage manufacturers' journals.

The *American Telegraph Magazine* (1852–53) was published in New York, and the *Telegrapher* (1864–77) was a union weekly in the same city. The weekly *American Gas-Light Journal and Mining Reporter* was founded in 1859 and survives as the monthly *American Gas Journal*. The present *Dry Goods*

Chapin A. Harris in its first twenty years; *Dental Register* (1847–1923), Cincinnati, called during our period *Dental Register of the West; Dental Quarterly* (1862–67), Philadelphia; and the *Quarterly's* successor, *Dental Office and Laboratory* (1868–1908), may be mentioned.

[208] See Mott, *op. cit.*, p. 539.

[209] Founded by Henry Bridgman, "apothecary and druggist," but continued after eighteen months by L. V. Newton, and, after his death in 1880, by John Newton. In 1883 it was purchased by William O. Allison, founder of four other periodicals in the drug and paint trades. When he died in 1924 he was succeeded as president of the company by Harry J. Schnell. The *Circular* has fought nostrums and adulteration and for forty years has published annual directories of drug products. John H. Snively had the longest term as editor (1886–1904). See historical article, LI, 1–15 (January 1907).

[210] It was called *American Manufacturer and Iron World*, 1874–1905, and it has had several other variations of title.

Economist, of New York, was called the *United States Economist and Dry Goods Reporter* during our period.[211] Another veteran is the *Shoe and Leather Reporter,* founded in New York in 1857 and later moved to Boston.

Four printers' journals were begun in the fifties: Lay & Brother's quarterly *Ink Fountain* (1852–56) and the *Typographic Advertiser* (1855–92), of Philadelphia; the monthly *Printer* (1858–75), of New York; and the monthly *Round's Printer's Cabinet* (1856–88), of Chicago, later a quarterly advertising sheet.

LEGAL AND FINANCIAL PERIODICALS

Legal magazines were not particularly important or numerous during this period.[212] For the most part they were mere reporters of cases. The Boston *Monthly Law Reporter* (1836–66) was the oldest. The *Pennsylvania Law Journal* (1842–52), called the *American Law Journal* in its last five years, gave place in 1852 to the *American Law Register and Review;* in 1897 the state's university took it over, and it became the *University of Pennsylvania Law Review and American Law Register* and is now the oldest periodical of its class in the country. The *Pittsburgh Legal Journal* (1853–current) was the first of a long line of daily court papers,[213] and E. M. Haines's Chicago *Legal Adviser* (1861–1920) will serve to represent here the monthly advertising papers.

The phenomenal growth of life insurance attracted the attention of several periodical observers (notably that of the *National Quarterly Review*), and a score of insurance journals sprang up

---

[211] It was founded under the name *Dry Goods Reporter and Commercial Glance* by W. B. Burroughs, Jr., in 1846. For historical material, see Seventy-fifth Anniversary Number, November 19, 1921.

[212] For certain legal journals which held over from the forties, like the *Pennsylvania Law Journal, New York Legal Observer,* and *Western Law Journal,* see Mott, *op. cit.,* pp. 451–452. The Philadelphia *Legal Intelligencer* (1842–current) was established by William Wallace and conducted by him and his son, J. M. Power Wallace, until 1891, when it was purchased by Edward P. Allinson and others. Since Allinson's death in 1901 it has been conducted by Howard W. Page, Albert Branson Maris, and Harold C. Roberts in succession.

[213] See Lucius B. Morse, *The Daily Court Newspapers of the United States* (Philadelphia, 1929).

in this period.[214] The first general periodical in this field was *Tuckett's Insurance Journal* (1852–61), of Philadelphia.[215]

In the field of banking the leading periodical was the *Bankers' Magazine*,[216] which had been founded by I. Smith Homans in

[214] For a list of insurance periodicals 1852–68, see *Ninth Annual Report of the Superintendent of the Insurance Department, State of New York: Life Insurance* (Albany, 1868), p. clxi. The best list, however, is that of Marion V. Patch, "American Insurance Journals before 1900" (Thesis, Columbia University, 1930). The oldest of existing insurance journals is the *American Insurance Digest and Insurance Monitor*, born *Monitor* in New York in 1853, but after a few months called *Insurance Monitor and Commercial Register*, and then *Insurance Monitor and Wall Street Review* (1855–69). After that it was called merely *Insurance Monitor* for fifty years, adopting the present title when it was moved to Chicago in 1920. Editors: Thomas Jones, Jr., 1853–68; C. C. Hine, 1868–97; Walter S. Nichols, 1897–1920; John W. Petrie, 1920–current. Also founded in this period and still published is the *Weekly Underwriter and the Insurance Press*, founded 1859 as *Wall Street Underwriter and Joint Stock Register*, called *New York Underwriter* (1868–79). The Philadelphia monthly *American Exchange and Review* (1862–1931) was edited from its beginning to 1908 by J. A. Fowler. Other important insurance journals: *United States Insurance Gazette and Magazine* (1855–82), monthly, and *American Life Assurance Magazine and Journal of Actuaries* (1859–78), quarterly, both of New York and both edited by Gilbert E. Currie; *Philadelphia Intelligencer* (1857–1920), published variably as quarterly, monthly, weekly; *Legal and Insurance Reporter* (1859–99), Philadelphia, called during its first twenty years *Insurance Reporter*, edited for many years by C. A. Palmer; *New York Insurance Journal* (1862–1910), weekly and semimonthly, edited 1862–93 by T. and J. Slator; William Haddon's *New England Insurance Gazette and Monthly Financial Record* (1862–76); (Samuel) *Grierson's Underwriter's Weekly Circular* (1863–73), New York.

[215] However, "probably the first exclusively insurance journal published in America" was Alfred S. Gillett's *Insurance Advocate and Journal* (1850), of Chicopee, Massachusetts, an agency organ. See Daniel M. Handy, "Some Insurance Literature That Dates Back at Least Seventy Years," *Weekly Underwriter and Insurance Press*, CXX, 160 (May 25, 1929). Harvey G. Tuckett was a romantic figure; he achieved notoriety by his duel with the Earl of Cardigan in 1840. See Patch, *op. cit.*, pp. xi–xv. He was editor of *Tuckett's Insurance Journal* only during 1852–53.

[216] Conducted by Homans at Baltimore 1846–49; then moved to Boston, where it was published by Crosby, Nichols & Company under Homans' editorship until 1853, when Homans moved it to New York. There its editor became secretary of the Chamber of Commerce of the State of New York and financial editor of the *Courier and Enquirer*. I. Smith Homans, Jr., became editor and publisher in 1861, to be succeeded by Benjamin Homans in 1874. The Homans Publishing Company was owner and A. S. Bolles editor 1882–94. J. G. Floyd bought it in November 1894, but the next year it was acquired by Bradford Rhodes, who merged *Rhodes' Journal of Banking* (1873–95) with it under the name *Rhodes' Journal of Banking and the Bankers' Magazine*, doubling the size. It kept the serial numbering of the *Bankers' Magazine*, however (in addition to that of the *Journal*), and returned to its old name in 1896, dropping the *Journal's* numbering. In 1903 it passed to the Bankers Publishing Company, with

1846. The confusion in the currency caused by the issue of state bank notes of widely varying credit, the use of government notes of small denominations (called shinplasters in the slang of the day), the prosperity of counterfeiting, and the use of tokens issued by private business houses, altogether made an exasperating situation. The *Bankers' Magazine* set out the following table of currency in 1862:

> 10 omnibus tickets make a half dollar.
> 5 Schelke's beer tickets make a man drunk.
> 10 Krost's beer tickets made one city shinplaster.
> 1 handful of shinplasters (with the pictures
>   worn off) make a man cuss.
> 10 half dollars make a fool of a poor man.
> 25 beer tickets make half a cinq.
> 40 beer tickets, 10 omnibus tickets, 1 handful
>   of shinplasters, and nary half dollars make a
>   man steal.[217]

Thompson's Bank Note and Commercial Reporter was begun in 1836 as a daily bulletin to provide information on the rates of exchange of this currency. It later became a weekly and by the end of our period was issuing weekly, semimonthly, and monthly editions. Thus John Thompson laid the foundation of the later *American Banker*.[218] In 1853 he issued an "Auto-

---

George W. Englehardt as owner and E. H. Youngman, who had been with the magazine for ten years before, as editor. It has had a high standing from the first. Statistics have been a main feature, with legal decisions affecting banking, and articles by prominent financiers and economists. William B. Greene was a leading contributor through the nineties. For reviews of features of American financial history with which the magazine was associated, see CIII, 406 (September 1921), and CXXIII, 181 (August 1931).

[217] *Bankers' Magazine*, XVII, 604 (February 1862).

[218] Thompson retired from the editorship at the end of our period. He had been the first to organize a national bank in New York — the First National Bank, 1863. In 1877 he founded the Chase National Bank, named after Salmon P. Chase, Thompson's close friend and co-worker. In 1885 the monthly became *Thompson's Solvent Bank Report*, eventually a mere directory; while *Thompson's Weekly Reporter* became *Thompson's American Bank Report*, changing its name in 1887 to the *American Banker*. The weekly became very influential, working with the American Bankers' Association from the beginning of its organization and with the various state associations. A new management took control in 1918, with Charles Otis as president and C. B. Axford editor, and daily publication was begun in 1925.

graphical Counterfeit Detector" as a supplement to the *Reporter*, furnishing therein facsimiles of the signatures of bank presidents and cashiers of all the principal banks in the country. *Dye's Government Counterfeit Detector* (1850–1910) had already set the example in Philadelphia, to be followed in the same city by *Peterson's Counterfeit Detector* (1858–89). The passage of the act establishing the national banking system in 1863 simplified the situation, but Thompson's *Reporter* found a new sphere of usefulness in its records of the new banks in the West and of bank conditions generally, while the *Detectors* found enough to do as monthlies. Late in the period came the New York *Financier* (1863–current), many years later the *Banker and Financier*.

The two great general magazines of commerce were *Hunt's Merchants' Magazine*[219] and *De Bow's Review*.[220] Hodge's *National Journal of Finance* was published in New York 1856–66.

Educational problems were frequently discussed in the general magazines. The progress of free public schools, especially in New York and the Middle West, the amazing increase in the demand for textbooks,[221] and the popularity of W. H. McGuffey's "Eclectic Readers" and P. R. Spencer's "Spencerian System" copybooks were among the educational phenomena noted. Nineteen-twentieths of the New York children of school age were said to be in the public schools, and school age was four to ten or twelve years — after which "perhaps, a large majority of them are transferred to some mechanical pursuit or occupation which is to constitute their future livelihood, and the residue drafted to some higher literary institution, as a preparation for a professional career."[222] *De Bow's Review*,

---

[219] See Mott, *op. cit.*, p. 696.
[220] Treated more fully in sketch 10.
[221] *American Literary Gazette*, September 15, 1864. An interesting phase of the textbook development was the preparation of special school books for the South at the outbreak of the war. Note the review of the Reverend Allen M. Scott's revision of *Smith's English Grammar*, hailed as a "New Southern English Grammar," in the Richmond *Age*, I, 49 (January 1864).
[222] *Bulletin of the American Agricultural Society*, II, 214 (1856).

which had an educational department and reported the teachers' conventions, was continually advocating the public school system for the South. In 1851 *De Bow's* listed sixty southern colleges, only two of which — the University of Virginia and the College of South Carolina — had enrollments of over two hundred. Most of them had less than a hundred students.[223] Of course college attendance, North and South, was greatly reduced by the war.

Religious periodicals commonly gave no little space to educational problems, both within and without their churches. The *Northwestern Christian Advocate* pleaded for a better-educated clergy in its own denomination and declared boldly against an ignorant ministry. "What our young men want is education," it said. "Never was the demand for a properly qualified ministry so urgent." [224]

In the same city the Episcopal *Chicago Record* scored the clergy for objecting to lecture courses because of the prevalence of freethinking in them. The lecture lyceums had become a nationally important means of adult education. "Since the lecture-room has become so important an instrument for the dissemination of man's views," said Editor Wilson, the clergy should utilize it to their advantage.[225] "During the present and coming month," announced the *Record*, in January 1859, "E. P. Whipple, George Sumner, Herman Melville, George D. Prentice, E. H. Chapin, and Bayard Taylor will lecture before the Young Men's Association of this city." [226] "The lecture is the American theater," declared a writer in *Putnam's*.

It is the one institution in which we take our noses out of the hands of our English prototypes — the English whom we are always ridiculing and always following — and go alone. It has founded a new profession. It provides a weekly amusement in the smallest and remotest towns, and it secures to the insatiable Yankee the chance, an hour long, of seeing any notability about whom he was curious.[227]

---

[223] *De Bow's Review*, X, 477 (April 1851). See Edgar W. Knight, *Public Education in the South* (Boston, 1922), for growth of Southern public schools.
[224] *Northwestern Christian Advocate*, VI, 130 (August 18, 1858).
[225] *Chicago Record*, I, 68 (December 1, 1857).
[226] *Ibid.*, II, 152 (January 1859).
[227] *Putnam's Monthly*, IX, 317–321 (March 1857).

Even in the South the lyceum spread.[228] *Russell's Magazine* commented on its growth in South Carolina:

One of the signs of a slowly-awakening consciousness on the part of the people of South Carolina, that in all literary respects, they are lamentably behind the age, is to be found in the general establishment of Lyceums, and organized bodies for the discussion of literary and scientific subjects, in many of the towns and villages of the Interior.[229]

The multiplication of educational journals in the period was phenomenal. Seventy-six have been listed for the years 1850–65,[230] sixty-six appearing in the decade of the fifties. Twenty-five of the thirty-six states of the Union had one or more of these journals, many of which were prosperous. Thie chief reasons for this fecundity are found in the growth of the state teachers' organizations, of which many of these journals were organs, and in direct financial encouragement to the periodicals for teachers by certain of the states. Fifteen educational magazines were founded by state associations during our period, and others were adopted. State support had begun in Ohio and Michigan as early as 1838, probably in emulation of Prussian educational practice; the state legislature paid for copies of the chosen journal to be sent to teachers in its schools. In the forties Connecticut, Massachusetts, and New York adopted the system of state aid, and in the fifties Pennsylvania, Iowa, Wisconsin, North Carolina, Maine, and Rhode Island joined the procession. Some of these states made the necessary appropriations for short periods only, but others were more generous, Pennsylvania, for example, making considerable contributions up to recent times.[231]

The most important periodical of its class was Barnard's *American Journal of Education*,[232] and second to it only were the *Connecticut Common School Journal*,[233] also edited by Henry Barnard, and Horace Mann's Boston *Common School*

[228] See Mott, *op. cit.*, p. 489.
[229] *Russell's Magazine*, II, 565 (March 1858).
[230] Sheldon Emmor Davis, *Educational Periodicals During the Nineteenth Century* (Washington: Bureau of Education Bulletin, 1919, No. 28), pp. 96–99.
[231] *Ibid.*, pp. 25–30.
[232] Treated more fully in sketch 24.
[233] See Mott, *op. cit.*, p. 694.

Journal,[234] both begun in 1838. Other important educational journals were scattered from Massachusetts to California.[235]

COLLEGE AND AMATEUR PERIODICALS

There were many college literary magazines in our period, mostly short-lived, as is the habit of such periodicals. "The history of college periodical literature has been varied and dispiriting — a record of disaster," observed the *Round Table* in 1866; and it went on to point out that the *Yale Literary Magazine*,[236] "generally called the 'Yale Lit,' " was "the most successful of all college magazines." [237] The *Nassau Monthly* continued at Princeton. The *Harvard Magazine* began in December 1854, with an introduction signed by names not yet distinguished, such as Frank B. Sanborn, Phillips Brooks, and J. B. Greenough, and lasted for ten years. The long-lived *University of Virginia Magazine* (1856–1929) was founded as the *University Literary Magazine*. And there were the *Rutgers College Quarterly* (1858–61), the *Beloit College Monthly* (1853–75), and many others.[238] Several were from girls' schools, such as one called the *Cherokee Rosebud* (1848?–58?), by "The Scholars of the Park Hill Female Seminary" for Indians at Tahlequah, Indian Territory.[239] The *University Quarterly* was a journal conducted

[234] *Ibid.*, p. 491.
[235] Some of the most robust were: *Massachusetts Teacher* (1848–74), Boston; *American Educational Monthly* (1864–76), New York, by Schermerhorn, Bancroft & Company and to some extent a trade organ for its school supply business, but a widely circulated, practical journal, and at times the official journal of various state associations; *Ohio Journal of Education* (1852–1933), Columbus, called *Ohio Educational Monthly* after 1859; *Pennsylvania School Journal* (1852–current), begun at Lancaster, but later transferred to Harrisburg and edited by state superintendents; *National Educator* (1860–1905), published in various Pennsylvania towns; *Indiana School Journal* (1856–1900), Indianapolis; *Illinois Teacher* (1855–73), Peoria; *Wisconsin Journal of Education* (1856–current), founded at Racine and conducted there for two years before it was moved to Madison, suspended 1867–80; *Iowa Instructor* (1859–77), Davenport, variously titled and owned; *Kansas Educational Review* (1864–74), peripatetic; *California Teacher* (1863–76), San Francisco.
[236] See Mott, *op. cit.*, p. 488; also historical articles in the *Yale Literary Magazine*, Vol. CI (October and November 1935, January and February 1936).
[237] *Round Table*, III, 194 (March 31, 1866).
[238] See list in Irving Garwood, *American Periodicals from 1850 to 1860* (Macomb, Illinois, 1931), p. 46.
[239] See Grace Ernestine Ray, *Early Oklahoma Newspapers* (Norman, Oklahoma: University of Oklahoma Bulletin, 1928), p. 27. A selection of items

in 1860–61 at New Haven by "An Association of Collegiate and Professional Students in the United States and Europe." The *Round Table* called it a "ponderous platitude" which "went down in a cloud of debt and disappointed hopes." [240]

The swarm of amateur magazines had not yet descended. The *Waverley* [241] was such a periodical in these years, as were the *Pittsburgh Weekly Chronicle* (1841–1902), printed "for private circulation" in this period, and the *Opal*, published 1851–60 by the patients of the insane asylum at Utica. With this last it would seem that one should end the catalogue.

JUVENILES

There were a number of magazines for children. Several of the more important held over from the preceding period [242] — *Youth's Companion, Merry's Museum, Forrester's Boys and Girls*. The American Tract Society's *Child's Paper* (1852–97) was a monthly famous for its excellent wood engraving; the Society also published the *Child at Home* (1863–73). The *Youth's Casket* (1852–57) was Erastus Beadle's first publication; issued in Buffalo before its publisher originated the dime novel, it had Harley Thorne, J. O. Brayman, and H. E. G. Arey as successive editors. *Frank Leslie's Boys of America* was issued 1863–78. *Forrester's Playmate* was edited by "Mark Forrester" in New York 1854–64. The editors and publishers of the *Little Pilgrim* (1854–75) were Sarah J. Lippincott, best known as "Grace Greenwood," and her new husband Leander K. Lippincott: most of its contributions were by amateurs, including the children, and it sold its eight to sixteen pages monthly at fifty cents a year. Another famous juvenile was the *Student and Schoolmate*, of Boston, formed in 1855 by a union of the *Student*, founded in 1846,[243] and the *Schoolmate*, founded

---

from this paper was published in *Godey's Lady's Book*, June 1858, under the title "A Wreath of Cherokee Rosebuds."

[240] *Round Table*, III, 194 (March 31, 1866).

[241] See pp. 41–42.

[242] See Mott, *op. cit.*, pp. 492–493. The *Child's Friend* is there given the dates 1843–49, whereas it continued to be published until 1858; the second series ended, and Miss Follen resigned the editorship in 1849. For *Merry's Museum*, see Mott, p. 713; and for the *Youth's Companion*, sketch 2 of this volume.

[243] This became *Student and Family Miscellany* in 1850. N. A. Calkins was editor.

in 1852 — two New York papers. This periodical was edited by N. A. Calkins at first, and then by William T. Adams, known to the children as "Oliver Optic." In 1865 it introduced the Reverend Horatio Alger, Jr., to the world of juvenile readers. *Our Schoolday Visitor* (1857–75), Philadelphia, began as *Clark's School Visitor* and ended as the *Schoolday Magazine*.

Most religious denominations had their Sunday school papers, two of the oldest being the Episcopal *Children's Magazine* (1829–74), Washington, and the Congregational *Well-Spring* (1844–1931), Boston. The American Sunday-School Union still published its *Youth's Friend and Scholar's Magazine* (1823–64) in Philadelphia.

CHAPTER IV

THE GEOGRAPHY OF THE MAGAZINES

GEOGRAPHY, always important in the history of magazines, possesses an added value in the fifties and sixties because of the settlement of the Middle West and the Far West, and because of the sectional war for the Union. It is not merely the geographical allocation of the periodicals which is significant, but the regional attitudes and reactions found reflected in them, as well. Foreign relations, moreover, have a special interest in this period.

NATIONAL AND LOCAL MAGAZINES

Most of the American periodicals of 1850–65 were local or sectional in appeal and circulation. A few magazines had genuinely national circulation, like *Harper's Monthly, Godey's,* the *New York Ledger,* and *Frank Leslie's Illustrated.* Others carried such words as "National," "United States," and "North American" in their titles to show an intention of geographical breadth, but were unable to achieve widespread circulation. Perhaps *Peterson's Ladies' National Magazine* reached this goal by the outbreak of the war; if so, it was by means of a consciously national policy. "We have arranged," its publisher wrote in 1850, "for a tale of New England, a novel of the Middle States, a story of the South, a fiction of the West, a legend of the Border, and a romance of the South-West." [1] Here was a magazine awake to the fictional variety inherent in the national geography. *Putnam's Monthly* paid much attention to the West, though it alienated southern readers. The *North American Review* was largely by and for New England. The *Atlantic Monthly,* too, spoke with the voice of New England. [2] Especially was the *Atlantic* unpopular in the South, where Edmund Quincy's article "Where Will It End?" in the second number and Parke Godwin's successive political pronouncements were highly offensive. Phillips Brooks was attending a theological

---

[1] *Peterson's,* XVIII, 260 (December 1850).
[2] See pp. 495–498.

seminary in Virginia when the *Atlantic's* first number was issued, and the very next month we find his father writing him a warning letter advising him not to become involved in a difficulty that seems to have grown out of the action of some fellow students who had removed the *Atlantic* from the tables of the seminary library.[3] One conjectures that a burnt sacrifice had been offered up — not in Edmund Quincy's honor. The *Southern Literary Messenger*, after three numbers of the new magazine had appeared, spoke of "the violent abuse of the Southern people" which it contained.[4] Obviously, when the North and South were split asunder in 1861, a national magazine became impossible for some years.

Of course there were religious quarterlies and even weeklies, and medical, legal, and other technical periodicals, which aimed at a national audience; but few of them attained very large circulations. And after all, the great bulk of class publications were sectional or local in intention, and doubtless more than four-fifths of the periodicals of the time were designedly limited in geographical distribution. All the cities and many of the smaller towns in all the states and territories boasted literary or class periodicals, or both. The prevalence of the local story-paper, often designed for Sunday reading, has been mentioned.[5] Nowhere indeed is that variety in unity which is so typical of American literature and of the American scene in general better illustrated than in the magazine reaction to geographical variants. It will, therefore, be profitable to observe the relations of the magazines to certain cities and sections, noting by the way some of the more distinctively local and regional periodicals, especially in the South and West.

NEW YORK CITY AND THE MAGAZINES

The census of 1860 shows one-third of the aggregate periodical circulation of the country issuing from the state of New York — almost three times that of her nearest rival, Pennsylvania. New York City was firmly intrenched as the great publishing center of the nation. In population it had, by 1850,

[3] A. V. G. Allen, *Phillips Brooks* (New York, 1901), p. 60.
[4] *Southern Literary Messenger*, XXVI, 155 (February 1858).
[5] See p. 34.

passed the million mark; and in spite of a recent extension of Philadelphia's city limits, it had almost exactly double the population of its nearest rival.

New York's magazines were proud of their city. They satirized its foibles and attacked its abuses; but they sang paeans to its amazing exuberance and vitality. *Harper's Weekly* saw a concentration of "the intellect and energy of this country in this city."[6] *Putnam's* was dazzled by the effulgence of a planet larger and "more brilliant than the others" in the American constellation of cities.[7] The *Knickerbocker* became grandiloquent:

> The people of New York compose an illustrious sub-species of the great American family, instinct with energy and gifted with an almost unlimited spirit of enterprise, and endowed with the most exalted attributes of humanity. . . . They must attain a more glorious destiny than has yet been achieved among mankind.[8]

Putnam's, *Leslie's Illustrated*, and *Vanity Fair* are especially interesting in their attention to details of New York life and institutions. Theaters and music, dancing, observance of New Year's and Lent, extravagant living, election phenomena, abuses of transportation, fast driving, care of the streets, and tearing up the pavements to lay them again were topics that suggested articles, paragraphs, quips in abundance. *Putnam's* had an excellent department called "The World of New York," in which urban matters were retailed entertainingly for the country at large.

Leslie's gives us a remarkable social history of the city in its serial numbers. Suffering from growing pains, terribly misgoverned, dirty, violent, prosperous, ambitious for culture — it is all in *Leslie's* pages. Picturesque Mayor Fernando Wood "would make a good mountebank,"[9] we are told; he and "his army of idlers" do nothing to prevent gangs of outlaws terrorizing the city streets by night.[10] The destruction of the "pig-

[6] *Harper's Weekly*, I, 306 (May 16, 1857).

[7] *Putnam's Monthly*, VIII, 108 (July 1856).

[8] *Knickerbocker Magazine*, XL, 9 (July 1852). See also XLIII, 85 (January 1854).

[9] *Frank Leslie's Illustrated Newspaper*, I, 86 (January 19, 1856).

[10] *Ibid.*, I, 150 (February 16, 1856).

RACING ON A NEW YORK STREET

Characteristic *Yankee Notions* illustration (June 1852), drawn by John L. Magee. See p. 105.

geries," in which three thousand pigs were driven out of the city whose streets they had infested, is described in pictures and words; the Central Park project is encouraged; a snowstorm in the city is commemorated:

> Broadway, while the snow reigned supreme, was one continual exhibition of unchecked gaiety. The hotels vied with each other in fitting up splendid *cortèges*, magnificently appointed for the use of their guests. The omnibus lines, discarding wheels, put their long ships on runners. . . . Private sleighs of all sorts and sizes, belonging to everybody and nobody . . . filled up the interstices. . . . The sidewalks, meanwhile, were lined with an admiring crowd. . . . As night approached, the revel reigned supreme, and then were added to the glare of snow, the blaze of gaslight, the jostling multitude, the innumerable turnouts, a constant singing of song, of wit, and repartee — the population of the great American metropolis forgetting care, stocks, hard times, and "Jordan," agreed to be happy in Broadway.[11]

Nearly all commentators were pointing out the dangers of racing and fast driving in general on Broadway. Note the authentic accents of "Jonathan" in *Yankee Notions*: "Jewhilikins! they talk about relievin' Broadway! Why, darn my everlastin' buttons ef they ever kin. . . . It looks more like a grand run-away of everything than anything else." [12]

Crossing over from Broadway to Fifth Avenue, we find trade already rearing its unabashed head there. *Vanity Fair* laments:

> Eheu! Eheu! Eheu!
> There's a tailor in Fifth Avenue! [13]

Another writer in the same journal rebuked the horsecar conductors for keeping the doors open in cold weather while they joked with the drivers, for losing passengers' fares in the straw on the floor of the car, and for going into neighboring saloons when the car was stopped by some obstacle to traffic, to remain there until it was removed.[14] More seriously, perhaps, the *New-York Review* pointed out that more money had been spent to clean the streets in 1853 than ever before — and the streets had never been more neglected.[15]

[11] *Ibid.*, I, 118 (February 2, 1856).
[12] *Yankee Notions*, II, 332 (November 1853).
[13] *Vanity Fair*, I, 100 (February 11, 1860).
[14] *Ibid.*, I, 60 (January 21, 1860).
[15] *New-York Review*, III, 80 (April 1854).

JEALOUSY OF BOSTON

Philadelphia and Baltimore ranked next to New York in population, but the magazines of those cities gave no such attention to the life of their immediate environment as did those of New York.

Bostonians, however, gave some proof of pride in their city; and the *Atlantic Monthly*, the *North American Review*, and the *Christian Examiner* were closely connected with Boston's dearest institution — Harvard College. Oliver Wendell Holmes, mainstay of the *Atlantic*, said, "I would not take all the glory of all the greatest cities in the world for my birthright in the soil of little Boston." [16] But the closely knit literary hegemony of Boston writers excited much jealousy in New York and in the South.

> For years past [wrote a contributor to the *Southern Literary Messenger*], a coterie of very amiable and highly cultivated gentlemen living within cry of Harvard University have been engaged in the innocent occupation of puffing each other every three months in the *North American Review* . . . and at stated intervals meeting together to eat good dinners and "with one voice about the space of two hours" to cry out "Great is Diana of the Ephesians" — mighty and learned is this Boston of our building — what other city shall attain unto the glory thereof? [17]

The New York *Round Table* explained Boston snobbery thus: "There fine minds and noble characters have been warped by mutual flattery and cohesion. As they grow older their crochets are more crochetty, their poetry is less original, their philosophy more awry." [18] The unwillingness of Lowell and Fields to admit the gentiles into the sacred pages of the *Atlantic* [19] accounts for some of the feeling against the New England group. Edmund Clarence Stedman, for instance, writing to Bayard Taylor about his inability to get even his best work into the *Atlantic*, mourned that "a New York poet sings against the wind." [20]

---

[16] Caroline Ticknor, *Hawthorne and His Publisher* (Boston, 1913), p. 291.
[17] *Southern Literary Messenger*, XVIII, 756 (December 1852).
[18] *Round Table*, I, 73 (January 16, 1864).
[19] See pp. 497–498.
[20] Laura Stedman and G. M. Gould, *Life and Letters of Edmund Clarence Stedman* (New York, 1910), I, 343.

It was an admission that New York had nothing to compare in excellence with the *Atlantic*. Boston had its culture and New York its commerce; it is interesting to note that the best magazine presentation of New York's achievement of undisputed commercial leadership is found in Boston's *Atlantic Monthly* for January 1865.

MAGAZINES AT THE SOUTH

There were no southern cities to rival those of the Middle States and New England as publishing centers, though Richmond, Charleston, New Orleans, and Nashville had some distinction in that regard. Practically all southern periodicals were distinctly regional. More than thirty of them carried the word "Southern" in their titles during the period under consideration; and even *De Bow's Review* and the *Southern Literary Messenger*, which had some northern circulation, were southern in policy and contents. Undoubtedly the ardent southernism required of periodicals at the South prevented the attainment of national circulation and influence; yet it should be pointed out that there was a more nearly fundamental reason for the backwardness of southern magazines in the educational system of the South, which was notable both for its limitation in extent and for its emphasis on the classics. Obviously, the magazine genius is not of the classical kind, and most southern magazines seem stiff and pedantic.

The decade before the Civil War saw an unusual activity in the founding of southern magazines,[21] but with it all there were continual complaints of inadequate support. *De Bow's Review* asserted that not a single southern literary periodical repaid its proprietors "in any degree proportionate with their labors." [22] This lack of support of their own magazines frequently caused southern editors to turn savagely upon the northern periodicals which had large circulations in the South — an illogical but natural reaction. The *Southern Quarterly's* article "Northern Periodicals Against the South" is typical. It is an onslaught

[21] "In every State, new magazines show the growing activity of Southern intellect in the cultivation of letters. Journals and periodicals are multiplying all over the South." *Russell's Magazine*, III, 78 (April 1858).

[22] *De Bow's Review*, I, 2 (January 1846).

against *Harper's*, which, it calculates (in 1854) is receiving $150,000 from subscriptions. "Now we say fearlessly," declares Simms, "that one-third of that sum, centered annually upon almost any southern monthly or quarterly, would insure a better work than *Harper's* and *Putnam's* together." [23] And *De Bow* reviews the arguments in favor of northern periodicals:

Cheaper! Aye, if the price of our reputation, our property and our independence, bartered for the trash they give us, can be called a cheaper bargain than we can make at our own doors, we yield the point. But we get *more* for the value of our subscription money! More what? More trash, more abuse, more reports of anti-slavery conventions, of anti-Sabbath, anti-matrimony, and anti-everything-in-general mass meetings.[24]

Northern illustrated papers came in for special condemnation. A southern newspaper, in an attack on the *Illustrated News*, declared:

These Northern illustrated papers are all unworthy of respect. Frank Leslie's paper is as bad as the one before us and *Harper's Weekly* is not one whit better. Their sale at the South — and the *New York Ledger*, the *New York Mercury*, et id omne genus — should be interdicted. They are incendiary and pernicious, to say nothing of their demoralizing effect.[25]

None of these papers was abolitionist in principle before the war; against the abolition papers the feeling was even more bitter, and on at least one occasion antislavery publications were taken from the United States mails and publicly burned.[26]

At the various southern commercial conventions held from 1845 until 1862,[27] it was common to pass resolutions urging the claims of southern periodicals and books and deprecating the northern press, literature, and colleges. Such pronouncements by the Savannah convention of 1856 specifically attacked maga-

---

[23] *Southern Quarterly Review*, XXVI, 510–511 (October 1854).

[24] *De Bow's Review*, XX, 68 (January 1856).

[25] *Savannah News*, January 10, 1861.

[26] John Bach McMaster, *History of the People of the United States* (New York, 1913), VIII, 9.

[27] These conventions may be studied to advantage in *De Bow's*, where they were all faithfully reported. De Bow himself was president of the Memphis convention of 1857 and secretary of others.

zines holding antislavery sentiments, and this provoked one of them — *Putnam's Monthly* — to the retort satiric:

Of all the good jokes perpetrated by the Savannah Pickwickians none seems to us more purely humorous than the debate upon a "southern literature." Resolved, say these lovely wags, that there is no southern literature. Resolved, that there ought to be a southern literature. Resolved — this time the delighted reader is sure they are going to authorize W. Gilmore Simms, LL.D., to construct a southern literature.[28]

And they actually do appoint a committee to do so, says *Putnam's*. It seems rather a pity to take the point off so good a joke by explaining that the convention delegates were really not quite such fools: what they were asking their men of letters to do was to write textbooks untainted with northern principles for southern schools — a plan actually carried out.[29] *Putnam's* quotes from the debate over the resolutions the remark of one speaker who believed that the convention wasted its time "re-solving" over the magazine question: the ladies, for example, "would continue to read *Godey's Lady's Book* and *Arthur's Home Magazine*, no matter what sentiments they might advance; the ladies wanted their fashions and their hoops, and they would have them!" And the antislavery *National Era* observed matter-of-factly: "When the South will make good books and magazines, and pay for them, she will not be so troubled with the swarming literature of the Anti-Slavery States." [30]

But the neatest repartee was that which the *International Monthly* was able to make when the *Southern Literary Messenger*, in praising the work of H. S. Ellenwood, voiced its familiar complaint about unappreciated southern genius: "Had the gifted author been a native of Massachusetts, his name would be as familiar as household words; as it is, we doubt whether one in ten of readers has ever heard it." Griswold, expert where the lives and works of American authors were in question, re-plied in the *International*: "He *was* a native of Massachusetts.

[28] *Putnam's Monthly*, IX, 207–214 (February 1857).
[29] For a report of the proceedings of this convention see *De Bow's Review*, XXII, 100 (January 1857).
[30] *National Era*, XI, 90 (June 4, 1857).

. . . He was born in Salem, in the year of grace 1790. . . . We suspect that, in literature at least, all charges of injustice to the South are as ill founded as this." [31]

Northern periodicals printed many articles about the South, its cities, natural beauties, and society. Notable among these were "Porte Crayon's" series in *Harper's Monthly* in the early fifties, Dr. Augustus Rawlings' southern pictures in *Frank Leslie's Illustrated* in 1859, and the economic articles in *Hunt's Merchants' Magazine*.

The greater southern magazines — the *Messenger, Russell's,* the *Southern Quarterly,* and *De Bow's* — were ardently sectional beyond anything known to the periodicals of other regions. *De Bow's* became in the latter fifties a semiofficial spokesman for the southern cause. The large number of class periodicals in the South — religious, agricultural, professional — often exhibited sectional sympathies. The South also had its share of local literary periodicals (some of them aspiring to interest the larger southern audience), but the great majority of these lasted for only a year or two.[32] Two of somewhat longer endurance may be mentioned as typical of the group: the

[31] *International Monthly,* IV, 702 (December 1851). But Ellenwood is omitted even from the inclusive Alderman-Harris *Library of Southern Literature.*

[32] Some of these are worth naming. *Whitaker's Magazine: The Rights of the South* (1850), Charleston, was conducted by D. K. Whitaker, who had experimented disastrously with the *Southern Quarterly Review* and the *Southern Literary Journal* (see Mott, *A History of American Magazines, 1741–1850,* pp. 664, 721), and who now abandoned his new magazine after seven numbers, but, after a short interval, began a new series under the title *Whitaker's Southern Magazine,* at Columbia (1851–53). Whitaker then merged his magazine in the *Southern Eclectic* (1853–54), Augusta, Georgia, of which he became co-editor with J. H. Fitten. Oliver R. Baldwin's weekly *Magnolia* was published briefly in Richmond in 1851. The *Southern Literary Gazette* (1849–52) was founded in Athens, Georgia, by Walker C. Richards, assisted for a time by Paul Hamilton Hayne; it was moved to Charleston in 1850, taken over by Hayne in 1853, and issued under the title *Weekly News and Southern Literary Gazette* (1853–56). (See W. S. Hoole, *A Check-List and Finding List of Charleston Periodicals, 1732–1864,* Durham, North Carolina, 1936, pp. 55–56; Guy Cardwell, *Charleston Periodicals 1795–1860,* University of North Carolina dissertation, 1937.) *South-Western Monthly* (1852), Nashville, edited and published by Wales & Roberts, twelve numbers, largely eclectic, and notable for narratives of Indian wars and captivities; *Arkansas Magazine* (1854), Little Rock, by Newbern & Ringo; *Southern Times* (1855), Montgomery, Alabama. See also literary and "home" magazines for women, pp. 56–59; Frank McLean, "Periodicals Published in the South Before the Civil War" (University of Virginia dissertation, 1928); Gertrude C. Gilmer, *Checklist of Southern Periodicals to 1861* (Boston, 1934).

Southern Parlour Magazine, published, with slight variations of title, from 1852 to 1856 at Mobile and Memphis under the editorship of W. G. C. Clark; and the *Southern Literary Companion* (1859–64), of Newnan, Georgia.

The war-time magazines of the Confederacy seem to deserve detailed mention. The courageous effort in those years to maintain the existing magazines and to promote new ones is nowhere so well explained as in a sentence from the *Southern Monthly* of 1861:

"Sans le Nord, le Sud ne saurait lire" — said a shrewd French observer twenty-five years ago; and should this war last three years, nothing but Herculean energy will enable us to falsify this humiliating prophecy.[33]

Helping give the lie to that accusation was Hutton and Freligh's *Southern Monthly,* begun in Memphis in September 1861, but frightened out of that city by the fall of Fort Donelson in March 1862. It lasted but nine months, the last two numbers being published at Grenada, Mississippi; and this in spite of the declaration in its penultimate number that "it will cease but with the Confederacy which gave it birth." It had been intended to be the literary organ of the new nation, to supplant *Harper's* in the South; but it had its difficulties finding engravers, as well as the proper paper stock to print their work on.

J. A. Turner, a "miscellaneous genius," founded in 1861 his weekly literary miscellany, the *Countryman,* printed and published in his plantation, Turnwold, near Eatonton, Georgia. It was in this shop, with its old Washington handpress, and on this periodical, with its 2,000 southern subscribers, that Joel Chandler Harris, a lad of less than fourteen when the *Countryman* was begun, served his apprenticeship as printer and writer. Turnwold was a remarkable institution; it had a hat factory, a tannery, a distillery, a printing plant, a fine library, and 120 slaves. Here young Harris gathered the culture and materials which he was later to use in the *Uncle Remus* tales. It was in the path of Sherman's march from Atlanta; but the redheaded boy stuck to his presses, and when Sherman had gone on to the

[33] *Southern Monthly,* I, 1 (September 1861).

sea, though provisions were scarce, the printing plant was un-
harmed. The *Countryman* continued until 1865.[34]

Two new periodicals were begun in Richmond in September
1862 — the *Southern Illustrated News*,[35] second of its name,[36]
edited for a time by John R. Thompson; and the *Magnolia*,[37]
at least fourth of its name,[38] of which James D. McCabe, Jr.,
became editor. Both were weeklies and were intended to take
the place of popular northern periodicals now effectively removed from competition. To both of them the leading writers
of the South contributed — Simms, Hayne, Timrod, Bagby,
Thompson, Cooke. Both of the new weeklies were flourishing
at the end of 1862; both lasted through 1863, raising subscription prices to $20 at the end of that year; and both perished in
the latter months of the war. The *Bohemian* was a Richmond
attempt in the field of the literary miscellany; its first and last
issue was that for "Christmas, 1863."

But probably the height of publishing optimism was reached
when John W. Overall, a New Orleans newspaper man, appeared
at Richmond and founded a comic weekly called the *Southern
Punch* August 15, 1863.[39] It was not very funny or clever, and

[34] Julia Collier Harris, *The Life and Letters of Joel Chandler Harris* (Boston,
1918), pp. 23–52.

[35] Begun September 13, 1862, by Ayres & Wade, editors and proprietors. The
illustrations, through much of the file, consist of the portrait of a Confederate
general on the first page and a comic on the last page. In size the paper was an
eight-page quarto. There were serials by local writers, Miss Braddon, and others.
The last number recorded in the *Union List of Serials* is that for March 25, 1865.

[36] A *Southern Illustrated News* was appearing in Atlanta in 1860.

[37] Begun September 27, 1862, by Charles Bailie, as the *Magnolia: A Southern
Home Journal*. In March of the following year the paper was sold to Oakley P.
Haines and William A. J. Smith, and the name was changed to the *Magnolia
Weekly: A Home Journal of Literature and General News*. June 20 Haines retired, and Smith became proprietor and James D. McCabe, Jr., editor, with
H. C. Barrow associate editor. Haines had apparently been editor up to this
time. Smith and Barrow became joint owners January 9, 1864, and the young
novelist Charles P. J. Dimitry took the editorial chair the following March. The
Magnolia published a war serial by McCabe, Simms's play *Benedict Arnold*, some
of Hayne's war poems, serials by English writers, etc., as well as war news. It
was probably supplanted by *Smith and Barrow's Monthly*.

[38] The best-known periodical of this name was the one at Charleston in 1840–
43. (See Mott, *op. cit.*, p. 699.) Others were a semimonthly at Hudson, New
York (1833–34), and a weekly edited by Oliver R. Baldwin at Richmond in
1851. There were also later *Magnolias*.

[39] Overall, Campbell, Hughes & Company, publishers. The price was originally
$10, raised to $20 in April 1864; the format was that of an eight-page quarto

its satires upon the Richmond profiteers and extortioners were bitter. There were many army jokes: in one a Negro is brought before a white man:

Cuffy: I golly, massa! wot you tink? Dis nigga say he am de sofern corspondince fur ole Greeley's paper!

Master: Does he? I'll send him to Butler, who will put him in the front ranks of the Yankee army, to be shot on sight![40]

There was verse by the southern poets of the past, as well as by such contemporaries as A. B. Meek and Thomas Davis; and there were reviews of the Shakespearean and Greek productions at the New Richmond Theatre. The pictures, which were not numerous, were chiefly by John A. Elder.

Another brief Richmond venture was the monthly *Age: A Southern Eclectic Magazine*,[41] which was sold for $2.00 (Confederate currency) per number. In its number for April 1864 the editor wrote:

Richmond has been surrounded by a cloud of enemies, and editors and managers have dropped pen and ledger, and with musket on shoulder, lend their small but earnest aid at the front toward the discomfiture of this gigantic combination against our liberties. The grand issue of the conflict still lies among the unpublished edicts of Heaven.[42]

Thereafter there was a long silence until the final number, January 1865. Similar to the *Age* was *Smith and Barrow's Monthly*, which issued a number in July 1864. It was not hopeful enough to name a year's subscription price, but asked $10 for six months; if any subscriber paid for that long, he was disappointed. The Raleigh *Illustrated Mercury* was issued for several months in 1863–64.

WESTWARD THE COURSE OF MAGAZINES

The western magazines of literary inclinations and general appeal were practically all local: their mission was to bring the

---

paper. The last number in the Library of Congress file is the one for August 29, 1864.

[40] *Southern Punch*, April 30, 1864, p. 8.

[41] Ernest Lagarde & Company, publishers; William M. Burwell, editor, and Lagarde, associate. There were five numbers: January–April 1864, and January 1865. It was an octavo of eighty pages. It was the successor of the Richmond weekly *Record* of 1863, an eclectic by West and Johnson.

[42] *Age*, I, 317 (April 1864).

gentle charm of the arts into their brash and exuberant communities and so leaven the loaf of commercialism. But their forty-eight-page idealism usually starved to death in a dozen or two numbers. A wail from a dying magazine in Cincinnati may be quoted:

Magazines professing to be exponents of Western literature have been started, and have run their course, and in spite of most pitiful appeals to Western people, have died, in this city, at the rate of about one per year for the past twenty years.[43]

Yet Cincinnati was ranked fourth among American publishing centers by the census of 1850. There considerably more than a score of weekly and monthly journals, as well as a host of class periodicals, were issued during the period under consideration. Next to Conway's *Dial*[44] and the *Ladies' Repository*[45] (ill-assorted pair!) should be ranked among the Cincinnati magazines the *Genius of the West*,[46] from which the paragraph just quoted is taken. This interesting monthly was distinctively Ohioan, and its creditable contents demonstrate the fact that at least one western state could boast littérateurs of ability — the Cary sisters, Frances D. Gage, William T. Coggeshall, W. D. Gallagher, Coates Kinney, and the Orville J. Victors. But it lived only three years, and most of the other Cincinnati attempts did not wait even that long on the reaper's sickle.[47]

[43] Quoted from the *Cincinnati Commercial* in the *Genius of the West*, IV, 29 (January 1856).

[44] Treated more fully in sketch 35.

[45] Treated more fully in sketch 5.

[46] Founded October 1853 by Howard Durham, who later took the poet Coates Kinney into partnership. Coggeshall, later famous as anthologist and librarian, made a third in 1854, but was left alone when Durham retired a few months later and Kinney in 1855. Upon his appointment as state librarian early in 1856, Coggeshall sold to George True, who published the last number in August of that year. The magazine printed a good variety of material, its historical sketches and poetry meeting with special favor. See W. H. Venable, *Beginnings of Literary Culture in the Ohio Valley* (Cincinnati, 1891), p. 107, for a full account of the *Genius*, and for other Ohio magazines of the time. After Durham was crowded out of the editorship, he began a rival *New Western Magazine* January 1855. It lasted about six months.

[47] *Cist's Advertiser* was published by Charles Cist in two series, 1843–53, with several changes of name. It began as the *Western General Advertiser*. It was a historical, statistical, and literary paper. The *Columbian* (1849–50), by W. B. Shattuc and W. D. Tidball, was a literary miscellany which, by merger with E. Penrose Jones's *Great West* (1848–50), became the *Columbian and Great*

A second Ohio city was the home of several periodicals of some importance: Cleveland had its class and professional journals, as well as a *Western Literary Magazine* (a reprint, 1854–56, of a Columbus periodical of identical title) and the distinctive *Family Visitor*.[48] The latter was founded and edited through 1850–53 by members of the faculty of Western Reserve University, giving special attention to the natural history of the West and to educational and economic topics.

By 1860 Chicago, already claiming to be the foremost grain and lumber market of the world,[49] was running Cincinnati a close race as the western publishing center. There the *Gem of the Prairie* [50] was flourishing at the opening of our period. There *Sloan's Garden City*, which had been started as a kind of house organ for Sloan's liniments, was metamorphosed during 1853–54 into something less odorous by Oscar B. Sloan, son of the liniment proprietor and publisher. Well printed and very miscellaneous in character, its schoolgirlish poetry and milk-and-water fiction reflected little real credit upon Sloan's Horse Ointment. The commercial affiliations of the *Literary Budget* were more appropriate; its editor, W. W. Dannenhower, was a bookseller who began it as an aid to his business in January 1852. It was made a weekly in 1854, with the poet Benjamin F. Taylor as editor. It was definitely western in its contents and lasted nearly four years. Chicago also had some very creditable religious journals, as well as other class publications.[51]

West (1850–54). Methro Jackson's *Parlor Magazine*, which published two volumes 1853–54, had Alice Cary for an assistant editor. G. W. L. Bickley's *West American Review* published eight monthly numbers beginning April 1854, and then, absorbing the *Parlor Magazine*, issued a brief new series called the *West American Monthly* in 1855.

[48] Edited and published at Cleveland by Dr. Jared P. Kirtland, the naturalist, Samuel St. John, and O. H. Knapp. After April 4, 1850, it was printed at Hudson, Ohio, and edited by Kirtland and St. John. Samuel C. Bartlett, later of Dartmouth, was one of the founders. In September 1852 M. C. Read was placed in editorial charge, the others remaining contributors, along with Forrest Shepherd; the new publishers were Sawyer, Ingersoll & Company. The changes in editorship were caused by the departure of professors from Western Reserve. The dates are January 3, 1850, to May 10, 1853, after which a political newspaper continuator is said to have existed for some five years.

[49] *Putnam's Monthly*, VII, 606 (June 1856).

[50] See Mott, *op. cit.*, p. 389.

[51] See F. W. Scott, *Newspapers and Periodicals of Illinois, 1814–79* (Springfield, 1910), pp. 63–86.

Other "westerns" of some importance were the *Western Journal and Civilian*,[52] an informative though amateurish miscellany of some eight years' duration in St. Louis; George P. Buell's *Western Democratic Review* (1854–55), an Indianapolis monthly;[53] *Wellman's Literary Miscellany*,[54] of Detroit; and Jesse Clement's *Western Literary Messenger*, of Buffalo. This last was of the "family magazine" type and was largely eclectic; but it printed original work by such famous writers as R. H. Stoddard, Mrs. Sigourney, John G. Saxe, and T. H. Chivers.[55]

THE FAR WEST

A few magazines of special interest came from the California region, whither the gold rush had drawn a picturesque population. They were all published at San Francisco — a city which,

[52] January 1848–March 1856. The titles were as follows: *The Western Journal, of Agriculture, Manufactures, Mechanic Arts, Internal Improvement, Commerce, and General Literature* (January 1848–September 1851, Volumes I–VI); *The Western Journal and Civilian, Devoted to Agriculture, Manufactures, Mechanic Arts, Internal Improvement, Commerce, Public Policy, and Polite Literature* (October 1851–March 1856). T. F. Risk originated the project, but retired in August 1851 to found the monthly *Western Review* at St. Louis in the following year — one of several short-lived periodicals of that name. Risk's partner, Micajah Tarver, continued the magazine with the help of H. Cobb, who became joint editor and publisher. Cobb introduced some literary features to vary the monotony of informative material, using translations especially. Chateaubriand's *Atala* was printed serially in Volume VII. The file is valuable for articles on early railroad projects and material bearing on the development of the upper Mississippi valley. A few steel plates and woodcuts and several lithographs made by Schaerf & Brother in St. Louis serve for illustration.

[53] A continuation of the *Western Democratic Review* was published in Washington, D. C., in 1856, consisting of seven numbers edited by Buell under the title *National Democratic Review*. This is not to be confused with Florence's later *National Democratic Quarterly*.

[54] It was published from July 1849 to August 1854. The title was changed in March 1851 to the *Monthly Literary Miscellany: A Compendium of Literary, Philosophical, and Religious Knowledge*, and D. F. Quinby became editor, with Luther Beecher publisher. It was poorly printed on paper manufactured at Ann Arbor, and it sold for a dollar a year. See *Michigan History Magazine*, XIX, 399 (Autumn 1935).

[55] Published August 1841 through April 1857. It was weekly to August 1848; then monthly. E. W. Clement, of Floral Park, New York, is preparing a study of this magazine. It was founded by John S. Chadbourne, who sold a half-interest to Charles D. Ferris in 1842 and his other half to Charles Faxon, Jr., in 1846. Clement bought the Ferris interest in 1843. See F. H. Severance, "Periodical Press of Buffalo, 1811–1915," *Buffalo Historical Society Publications*, 1915, XIX, 277.

though "only five years old," observed a *Putnam* reviewer of the *Pioneer* in 1854, "supports two or three theatres, an opera, a monthly magazine, an Academy of Science, thirteen daily papers, and we don't know how many weeklies." [56] The *Golden Era* was more a literary weekly than a newspaper. Bret Harte, Mark Twain, Joaquin Miller, Charles Warren Stoddard, Fitz Hugh Ludlow, Orpheus C. Kerr, "Ada Clare," and many lesser lights were contributors to it. It was strong on racy sketches of mining life and a kind of gay and reckless dramatic criticism. The founders were J. MacDonough Foard, who had come to 'Frisco around the Horn, and Rollin M. Daggett, who had come across the Plains; they were twenty-one·and nineteen, respectively, when they pooled their liking for racy journalism and founded the *Golden Era* in 1852. It soon gained a circulation of 9,000 at $5.00 a year. The founders sold it in 1860; and it lived until 1893, when, having been transplanted to San Diego and shorn of its old free and easy ways, it was supplanted by the *Western Journal of Education*.[57]

The *Pioneer: or, California Monthly Magazine* claimed to be the first "periodical of a purely literary type" [58] in the Far West. It was founded by Ferdinand C. Ewer, a talented journalist who later became an Episcopal clergyman, in January 1854, and published four semiannual volumes. It was modeled on the *Knickerbocker*, even to the "Editor's Table." "John Phoenix" was one of the best contributors; others were the editor, Edward A. Pollock, Mrs. S. A. Donner, and so on. Dana Shirley wrote some good indigenous sketches, and John Swett, Mrs. Sigourney, and others contributed poems.[59]

Shortly before the *Pioneer* expired, James M. Hutchings began his San Francisco venture — *Hutchings' Illustrated California Magazine*. That was in July 1856; five annual volumes were published. *Hutchings'* sold for $3.00 a year — $2.00 less than the *Pioneer* — and it had some rather lively woodcuts, so

[56] *Putnam's Monthly*, III, 448 (April 1854).
[57] For the *Golden Era*, as well as the other California periodicals of the times, see (guarding against errors) Ella Sterling Cummins [Mighels], *The Story of the Files* (San Francisco, 1893).
[58] *Pioneer*, I, 1 (January 1854).
[59] Publishers: Vol. I, W. H. Brooks & Company; II–IV, LeCount & Strong. Title page of Vol. IV says VI by error. About sixty pages per issue, $5.00 a year.

it must have been strong competition for Ewer's magazine. "We wish to picture California and California life," said *Hutchings'* introductory article, and it did so with good autochthonous fiction and articles. Stories of the first discovery of gold and the earliest prospecting, by John A. Sutter, James W. Marshall, and J. D. Bothwick, are notable. Hutchings had himself been a miner, and his magazine was more indigenous than the *Pioneer*.

The roster of early San Francisco periodicals for this period [60] closes with the *Californian*,[61] one of several to bear this name at various times. It was founded and edited throughout most of its existence by Charles Henry Webb — the "John Paul" of many travesties and humorous sketches. Mark Twain, Bret Harte, Ina Coolbrith, and Charles Warren Stoddard were among the *Californian's* contributors; and Harte was for a time its editor.

THE EAST AND THE WEST

These western periodicals did not find their way eastward to any considerable extent. A writer in the English *Fraser's* in 1863 remarked "a curious law" governing the circulation of American periodicals.

All papers [he wrote] go from east to west, with the sun, and never in the opposite direction. The best possible magazine or weekly paper, if published in Cincinnati or the Ohio valley, would never cross the Alleghanies; while the West is covered with publications from the Atlantic seaboard.[62]

The explanation was, of course, that the western papers had neither great publishing houses nor settled reading publics be-

[60] The *Hesperian*, with its sketches of the early settlers of California and its "ornithology of the Pacific" by A. J. Grayson, has already been noted among women's periodicals (see p. 59). The *San Francisco News-Letter* (1856–1928), of which Frederick Marriott was founder and for many years the editor, was in some degree a newspaper. It became one of that class of urban weeklies of which there were examples in all the larger cities in later years, devoted to sports, society, the theater, and literature. Frederick Marriott, Jr., succeeded his father as editor in 1884, and Frederick Alfred Marriott in 1925. It was merged with the *Wasp* in 1928. The *Wide West* was a Sunday paper, issued from March 1854 to July 1858. For other Sunday papers, comics, and religious weeklies begun in San Francisco before 1859, see Douglas C. McMurtrie, ed., *A History of California Newspapers* (New York, 1927, reprinted from the *Sacramento Union* of December 25, 1858).   [61] Its file consists of seven volumes, 1864–68.

[62] *Fraser's Magazine*, LXVIII, 326 (September 1863).

hind them and were therefore inevitably local, or at most sectional, in their distribution.

Yet the zestful, full-flavored West and all its lively performances were of the highest interest to the East. The gold rush continued throughout the fifties to furnish good "copy" for the magazines, and later the movement of population toward the West, through Omaha to Colorado and Idaho caught their attention. It is true that the El Dorado enchantment lost some of its power as news came of repeated disappointments. "Mister," asks Nehemiah Slim of a returned miner in one of the *Yankee Notions* burlesques,

"hoo is this Elderader tha tauk so much about?"

"Wy," ses he, "haint you heerd? that's the gold country. Californy's all gold out and out; awl you hev to dew is jist go there and pick up as much as you want, and you kin lode the Ingins with it and fetch it hum, and live at eeze all your daze."

"Kin you?" ses I.[63]

And so Nehemiah goes west and returns sadder and wiser but no richer. *De Bow's,* which viewed the gold rush coolly in view of the exclusion of slavery from the new territories, was alarmed at "the extraordinary flow of gold from California," but concluded that the change in the proportions of gold and silver would be negligible.[64]

In this same article there is an interesting commentary upon the current reports of the impossible climate of the Far West. In view of the later pride of Californians in all that they have meteorologically, it is hard to believe that readers of 1850 "have been accustomed to the most unfavorable reports, in regard to the climate of California." But after all, Thomas Butler King thinks, "upon the whole, it will compare favorably with our Northern States, whatever may be the first impressions of settlers." [65] It was generally believed that the lands west of the Missouri were of no value for agriculture, or even for stock raising. Horace Greeley, writing in the *Continental Monthly,* after his western trip, said:

I cannot comprehend those who talk of the Plains and the more intensely arid wilds which mainly compose Utah and Nevada becom-

[63] *Yankee Notions,* IV, 174 (June 1855).
[64] *De Bow's Review,* VIII, 548 (June 1850). [65] *Ibid.,* VIII, 541 (June 1850).

ing a great stock-growing region. Even California . . . can never sustain so many animals to the square mile as the colder and more rugged hills of New York and New England, because of the intense protracted drouth of its summers.[66]

In a paper read before the American Geological Society and condensed in the *Journal* of that organization, John Jay the younger said that between the ninety-eighth meridian (which cuts through eastern Nebraska) and the Pacific slope, "generally the land is unfit for the support of an ordinary civilized community." [67] An article on the projected railroad to the Pacific in the *North American Review* at about the same time insisted that

Whatever route is selected for a railroad to the Pacific, it must wind the greater part of its length through a country destined to remain forever an uninhabited and dreary waste. . . . We may as well admit that Kansas and Nebraska are perfect deserts, except for the small strip of land on their eastern borders.[68]

And in these deserts dwelt pioneers whose morals gave much concern to certain writers. The Reverend T. Dwight Hunt, in a well-informed article in the *Journal of the American Geological Society* on "California, Oregon and Washington," says that the settlers in those territories

are *Americans let loose.* How better could I describe a fast people? . . . The haste to be rich has been desperate, the wreck of character has been fearful, but the amount of work accomplished within the time has been altogether without precedent. . . . Some of the world's best people have mingled with many of the world's worst.[69]

A writer in the *Boston Review* tells graphically of vigilance committees in Montana in 1865.[70] The Reverend Francis Wharton wrote of the settlers in the Trans-Mississippi region in the *Protestant Episcopal Quarterly Review.* His article shows a fine observation of western types, but he complains that steam-

---

[66] *Continental Monthly,* I, 83 (January 1862).
[67] *Journal of the American Geological Society,* I, 76 (March 1859).
[68] *North American Review,* LXXXII, 235, 236 (January 1856). Article by J. Wynne.
[69] *Journal of the American Geological Society,* I, 146 (May 1859).
[70] *Boston Review,* V, 128, 277 (March, May 1865).

boating on the Missouri stimulates "habits of reckless extravagance and excitability." A boat may produce in one season a greater net profit than its cost. It is "not unusual for pilots to receive eight hundred dollars a month." And he comments upon the fever for paper towns in Kansas and Nebraska and the phenomenal growth of the Mississippi river towns in Iowa.[71]

The Homestead Bill, a football of politics, excited some attention as "a blessed thing for the poor and landless." [72] *Frank Leslie's Illustrated* pictured the opening of the Overland Trail — "one of the greatest and most important achievements of the age. . . . The Pacific wagon road will build the railroad." [73]

Many eastern magazines besides those quoted exploited the attractiveness of western materials. *Putnam's* published a series of tales of the mining camps by J. W. Palmer, the journalist and poet, which were quite in the earlier manner of Bret Harte, with his elements of literary allusion, local color, and sentimentalism. Thus, said the editor of a later series of *Putnam's*, did Palmer "break the virgin soil of California as a literary field." [74] Both *Harper's Monthly* and *Harper's Weekly* showed by picture and text their interest in the romantic West. The Harper authors wrote not only *of* the West; to a certain extent they wrote also *to* the West. The *Monthly* especially had a good circulation in the pioneer regions. Anthony Trollope, traveling through America keen-eyed to see what he could see, found "Harper's everlasting magazine" in the humblest of cabins in a rude western country;[75] and Tilton once remarked in the *Independent*: "*Harper's* is, as someone has said, the pioneer of civilization at the West." [76] Fitz Hugh Ludlow's far-western articles in the *Atlantic* were notable. The *Spirit of the Times* was justly famous for its sketches of the West and Southwest; and some of the story-papers, like the Boston *Saturday Evening Gazette*, featured racy western material.

[71] *Protestant Episcopal Quarterly Review*, VI, 263–265 (April 1859).
[72] *Continental Review*, II, 635 (November 1862).
[73] *Frank Leslie's Illustrated Newspaper*, VI, 328 (October 23, 1858).
[74] *Putnam's Monthly*, V, 722 (June 1870).
[75] Anthony Trollope, *North America* (New York, 1862), p. 144.
[76] *Independent*, April 26, 1866.

THE WORLD VIEW

Interesting developments of European politics occupied many pages in American reviews and magazines in the fifties and sixties. The Crimean War, with the great American excitement at the fall of Sebastopol; the rise of Prussia and the emergence of Bismarck; Italian affairs and the personality of Cavour — these men and events all furnished absorbing topics for the magazines of our period. America was by no means isolated from the world at large.

"Questions of foreign policy have of late largely occupied public attention in the United States," wrote William H. Trescott in the *Southern Literary Messenger* in 1850, and he concludes his article by declaring that "we must become a great naval power." [77] In the ensuing fifteen years many international issues were to arise and subside, one of them carrying serious threat of war. Perry in Japan, Walker in Mexico, Lopez and other filibusters in Cuba, and finally the difficulties with England during the Civil War: these offered the chief problems to commentators in American magazines.

IMMIGRATION

But one great question which intimately involved foreign relationships rose to importance at the middle of the century and, showing no sign of abatement in our period, has remained to this day a troublesome problem. This is the question of immigration.

The hard times in Germany and perhaps the potato famine in Ireland, coupled with the unsuccessful revolutionary movements of 1848 and the years immediately following, resulted in the coming of thousands of refugees to American shores. The peak was reached in 1854, when 428,000 immigrants entered the United States, largely from Germany and Ireland. Not much over a million immigrants had come to America between 1775 and 1845, but in the decade 1845–55 about three million of them came. "Since the Gothic invasion of southern Europe," said the *Democratic Review* in 1852, "no migration of men has

[77] *Southern Literary Messenger*, XVI, 1 (January 1850).

occurred in the world at all similar to that which is pouring itself upon the shores of the United States." [78]

One of the early alarms was sounded in *De Bow's Review*, which advocated a period of probation for immigrants before enfranchisement.[79] *Putnam's*, however, pointed out that this great influx brought with it much old-world art, "whose elemental specialty we most need." [80] Most of the immigration went to the North, giving it an advantage in "the brute force of numbers" in the Civil War. This made the *Southern Literary Messenger* bitter against immigration in general;[81] and by the same token it made the *National Quarterly* think that the aid given the Federal side by the immigrants had justified the national policy in regard to them and overthrown the nativist theory.[82] The southern writer already quoted had much to say of the influence of the "low infidel classes of Germany," and there is no doubt that much of the theological controversy of this period and of later years is traceable to the importation of heterogeneous religious elements from Europe. The direct political effect of wholesale immigration in the formation of nativist groups was a feature of the times. The activities of one such group — the Order of United Americans — may be studied in the *Republic*, subtitled "a monthly magazine of American literature, politics and art," which was edited 1851–52 in New York by Thomas R. Whitney, at one time a representative of the American party in Congress. The Irish invasion of New England was an inescapable influence on Catholic periodicals,[83] and its social effects may be noted in many magazines, including the comics.[84]

VISITORS FROM HUNGARY AND JAPAN

President Louis Kossuth, then a refugee from the wrath of Emperor Francis Joseph, was the official guest of the United States in 1851–52. His coming was marked by tremendous

[78] *United States Magazine and Democratic Review*, XXX, 97 (February 1852).
[79] *De Bow's Review*, XIII, 455 (November 1852).
[80] *Putnam's Monthly*, III, 683 (June 1854).
[81] *Southern Literary Messenger*, XXXV, 463 (August 1863).
[82] *National Quarterly Review*, IX, 369 (September 1864).
[83] See p. 76.
[84] See pp. 178–179.

popular fervor; it was an event "destined to mark one of the brightest pages in the history of Liberty," [85] declared the *International Monthly*. Intervention in Hungarian affairs was seriously advocated; Secretary of State Webster's grandiloquent and insulting note to Austria in 1850 is a matter of history; and the *Republic* expressed a national feeling of exultation over the European upsets of 1848 when it said: "There is scarcely a crowned head in all Europe that has not trembled under the moral influence of our institutions." [86] The *Southern Literary Gazette* observed at the beginning of 1852 that there were practically none of its exchanges "in which we have not found, of late, something about *Intervention*." [87] All this emotion centered on Kossuth when he appeared in the eastern cities and was officially received by Congress; the patriot's personality and oratorical ability strengthened his cause and called forth ovation after ovation. "Of all orators who have yet strutted and fretted their hour before the public of Boston within the memory of the present generation," said the *Saturday Evening Gazette* a few years later, "Louis Kossuth was by all odds the greatest and best." [88] Lowell published in the *Anti-Slavery Standard* his poem in which the hero speaks these spirited words:

> "I Kossuth am: O Future, thou
>   That clear'st the just and blott'st the vile,
> O'er this small dust in reverence bow,
>   Remembering what I was erewhile.
>
> "I was the chosen trump wherethrough
>   Our God sent forth awakening breath;
> Came chains? Came death? The strain He blew
>   Sounds on, outliving chains and death." [89]

And Mrs. Mary Lowell Putnam, the poet's sister, printed a glowing appeal for Kossuth in the *Christian Examiner*,[90] while

[85] *International Monthly*, V, 2 (January 1852).
[86] *Republic*, I, 38 (January 1851).
[87] *Southern Literary Gazette*, January 24, 1852.
[88] *Saturday Evening Gazette*, May 30, 1857, p. 2.
[89] *National Anti-Slavery Standard*, X, 58 (September 6, 1849).
[90] *Christian Examiner*, XLVIII, 444 (May 1850).

a highly documented defense of him appeared in the *Democratic Review*.[91]

Kossuth had his enemies in America as at home, however. Catholic periodicals opposed him because of his enmity to their church; they generally took the broad position that he was only an adventurer using the banner of freedom as a cloak for personal and racial ambitions.[92] Such was indeed the opinion of some other observers, including Francis Bowen, editor of the *North American Review*. Bowen insisted that the American people had been "deceived by the prose dithyrambics of Kossuth, and by the romantic history, chivalrous daring, and theatrical garb of the Magyars." [93] The *Republic*, though strongly anti-Catholic, was also anti-Kossuth because it was preëminently nativist and must oppose everything from abroad. The *Liberator* berated the visitor because he would not take a stand against slavery.[94]

Another picturesque and official visit from abroad in our period was that of the Japanese embassy sent to deliver the first American-Japanese treaty. The doings of the "accomplished Japanners," as *Vanity Fair* called them, afforded a great fund of amusement for the American public, as may be seen by the perusal of such pictorials as *Harper's Weekly* and *Leslie's* in 1860. Behavior, costume, and language, oriental and ancient as they were, became comedy for America; and while the occidentals laughed at the simplicity of the visitors and regarded them as savages, the orientals may have reciprocated in kind behind their impassive faces. One of the ambassadors, nicknamed "Tommy" by the press, was indiscreet in certain of his amours and made some scandal. But an interest in things Japanese was aroused which did not subside for many years, if it ever has; and "sketches of the manners and customs of the Japanese" were numerous.[95]

[91] *Democratic Review*, XXXI, 505 (November–December 1852).

[92] *Brownson's Quarterly Review*, N.S., VI, 195 (April 1852); *Freeman's Journal*, XII, *passim* (1851).

[93] *North American Review*, LXX, 121 (January 1850).

[94] *Liberator*, XXI, 203 (December 19, 1851).

[95] *Vanity Fair*, I, 388 (June 16, 1860). These sketches are burlesqued.

RELATIONS WITH ENGLAND

Another official visitor was the Prince of Wales. The *Home Journal*, unequaled society monitor of these years, declared that "no ovation was ever tendered in this country, to any celebrity before, equal in brilliancy and effect" to the New York fête in honor of the English prince.[96] The periodicals were full of the royal progress through the eastern states and through Canada.

The Prince's marriage three years later attracted special attention because of the memories of this visit. The *Saturday Evening Post* published Artemus Ward's letter to Wales on the event of his marriage.

You remember me [he said], I saw you in Canady a few years ago. I remember you, too. I seldim forgit a person.

I hearn of your marriage to the Printcis Alexandry, and ment to writ you a congratoolatory letter at the time, but I've bin bildin a barn this summer and hain't had no time to write letters. . . .

My objec in now addressing you is to give you sum advice, friend Wales, about managin your wife, a bizness I've had over 30 years experience in.

As I sed, I manige my wife without any particular trouble. When I fust commenced trainin her I institooted a series of experiments, and them as didn't work I abandingd. You'd better do similar. Your wife may objeck to gittin up and buildin the fire in the morning, but if you commence with her at once you may be able to overkum this prejoodis. I regret to obsarve that I didn't commence arly enough. . . .

Remember me kindly to Mrs. Wales, and good luck to you both! . . .

A. Ward. [97]

Another event which tended to cement the affections of the two great English-speaking nations was the laying of the first Atlantic cable. Few incidents of that resounding decade of the fifties excited more attention than this. *Leslie's*, whose English-born editor was always rather concerned with Anglo-American relations, issued a special "Atlantic Telegraph Pictorial," with the motto: "Henceforth the world belongs to civilization and freedom — no longer to tyranny and war." [98]

[96] *Home Journal*, October 20, 1860, p. 2.
[97] *Saturday Evening Post*, September 12, 1863, p. 8.
[98] *Frank Leslie's Illustrated Newspaper*, VI, 216 (September 4, 1858).

If that motto was well chosen, perhaps there was something symbolical in the parting of the cable so soon after it was laid. Certainly troubles with England came on apace. Even in the fifties the imperialists tried to incite enmity toward that country. The *Democratic Review* tried to show in its serial argument "Who Owns British America?" in 1852 that the title to Canada was still vested in the descendants of the Earl of Stirling. It was much alarmed over the activities of England in Nicaragua and Honduras,[99] and it went so far as to state that "Cuba, Mexico, Central America, and all the islands of Central America must be ours." [100] In still another imperialistic article inspired by the Young America movement, it stated its "hope of a future Republican Empire, that travels with the sun, from a Northern to a Southern ocean, bearing upon its waters the commerce of a world." [101]

But it was early in the war that the ill feeling between England and America reached its height in the controversy over Mason and Slidell, not to subside for some years after Lee's surrender. "The thought of war with England has become a familiar one among us of late," observed a writer in the *North American Review* for 1865. "We are conscious of having been treated with contumely, even with insult," he continued, and then added the prediction that the attitude which England had maintained during the war• "will endanger for a long time the maintenance of friendly relations between the two countries." [102]

The Mason and Slidell matter was fully treated in the reviews [103] and the more serious monthlies, but the injustice of "the Cottonocracy of England" [104] was what rankled most. Lowell's famous "Biglow Paper" on Mason and Slidell, which appeared in the *Atlantic* early in 1862, closed with a remon-

[99] *Democratic Review*, XXXI, 337–352 (October 1852).

[100] *Ibid.*, XXXI, 624 (November–December 1852).

[101] *Ibid.*, XLII, 365 (November 1858).

[102] *North American Review*, C, 335 (April 1865). This was a commentary on Goldwin Smith's article in the *Atlantic Monthly*, "England and America," XIV, 749–769 (December 1864).

[103] See a legal examination of it, *North American Review*, XCIV, 196–258 (January 1862).

[104] *Atlantic Monthly*, VIII, 95–105 (July 1861).

strance addressed to John Bull by Brother Jonathan in which
the true issues of the war were stressed:

> We know we've got a cause, John,
>   Thet's honest, just, an' true;
> We thought 'twould win applause, John,
>   Ef nowheres else, from you.[105]

George Edward Ellis' *Atlantic* paper, "Why Has the North Felt
Aggrieved with England?" emphasized the animosity of the
English press and what was believed to be the failure of Eng-
lish opinion to rally to the support of a just cause.[106]

The *Albion*,[107] a New York weekly devoted chiefly to the reprinting of articles from the English journals, was not very loyal
to the North during the war. "The Federals have been systematically outgeneraled," [108] it asserted in the fall of 1862; but
when McClellan was removed, it placed "the crown of martyrdom" on his brow.[109] The *Scottish-American Journal* (1857–
65), a weekly published in New York by J. W. Finlay, kept out
of politics, though similar to the *Albion* in its appeal to citizens
not quite assimilated.

PROBLEMS OF INTERNATIONAL COPYRIGHT

A cause of frequent irritation between England and America,
especially among writers and publishers, was the pirating of
books and magazines. America depended less on books of English authorship in the fifties than it had in previous decades, because American literature was expanding; but the outstanding
magazine success of the times was made largely by the use of
English serials.[110] "The house of book-taker and book-seller,
Harper, of New York," said London *Punch*, "is a house built of
the skulls of English authors. . . . Harper makes his daily four
meals of the bones of English penmen." [111] Harper Brothers
soon began to pay well for advance sheets of the English novels

---

[105] *Atlantic Monthly*, IX, 270 (February 1862).
[106] *Ibid.*, VIII, 612–625 (November 1861).
[107] See Mott, *op. cit.*, p. 131.
[108] *Albion*, XL, 426 (September 6, 1862).
[109] *Ibid.*, p. 546 (November 15, 1862).
[110] See *Literary World*, IX, 506 (December 27, 1851).
[111] Quoted in *North American Miscellany*, I, 576 (April 19, 1851).

they used,[112] but that did not save them from abuse — especially from suffering competitors. "We are sure our patrons are all *patriots*," said Godey plaintively, "and will patronize American work." [113]

But the use of British serials, with or without payments to their authors, was by no means limited to the Harpers. It was very common. Besides the general monthlies and weeklies that helped themselves to such fare, there were the avowed eclectics. The *Living Age* [114] and the *Eclectic Magazine* [115] were each six years old in 1850; the omnivorous *Albion* was nearly forty. The *North American Miscellany* [116] (1851–52), of New York, and the *Panorama of Life and Literature* (1855–57), of Boston, were briefer experiments in eclecticism. Many of the more or less local weeklies placed large dependence on "selected" material.

Meantime the leading London and Edinburgh reviews continued to be reprinted in New York for American readers. It is not easy to realize now how large an American public the great English periodicals had before the Civil War. The *Edinburgh Review* was much more widely read in the United States than the *North American*. "In those days people of literary aspirations, especially young people, read the English magazines almost religiously," wrote Edward Everett Hale many years later.[117] The end of the war, marked as it was by strong feeling against England, found eight British magazines being regularly reprinted in America.[118] Leonard Scott & Company, of New York, early began such republication, pirating the reviews at first, and selling each at the low price of $2.00 a year. But in 1852 the publishers of the *Westminster Review* reprinted two articles from their magazine in the United States themselves and then copyrighted them, thus catching Scott in a suit for infringement by means of which they forced him to buy

[112] See pp. 385.
[113] *Godey's Lady's Book*, XLII, 203 (March 1851).
[114] See Mott, *op. cit.*, pp. 747–749.
[115] *Ibid.*, pp. 306–309.
[116] Combined with the *Dollar Magazine*, January 1852, and the name changed to *North American Miscellany and Dollar Magazine*.
[117] E. E. Hale, *James Russell Lowell and His Friends* (Boston, 1898), p. 160.
[118] *Round Table*, VI, 337 (November 23, 1867).

advance sheets from them. By 1860 Scott was advertising the *London Quarterly*, the *Edinburgh Review*, the *North British Review*, the *Westminster Review*, and *Blackwood's Edinburgh Magazine*, all printed in New York from advance sheets, at $3.00 a year each — the common rate for American magazines. Harpers, Lippincott, and other publishers reprinted some other more popular English periodicals.

Moreover, many American magazines were more or less close imitators of English periodicals. *Putnam's* and the *Atlantic* were modeled on *Blackwood's*; *Harper's Weekly* was formed on the *Illustrated London News*; Leslie, who had worked on the illustrated British papers, copied their characteristics for his American ventures; and Bonner's *Ledger* was much like the *London Journal*, which accumulated a half-million circulation on the popularity of J. F. Smith's serials.

On the other side, some American periodicals achieved London editions. Among these were *Brownson's Quarterly*, the *Bibliotheca Sacra*, and the *Free-Will Baptist Quarterly*. There were also some pirating miscellanies in London, such as the *American Magazine* (1851–52) and the *American Scrap-Book and Magazine of United States Literature* (1861–63), which drew their material largely from the *New York Ledger* and similar periodicals. But the outstanding example of English pirating was not based on magazines, but was afforded by the many publishers of *Uncle Tom's Cabin*, English editions of which were multiplied almost beyond belief.[119]

The leading advocate of international copyright laws among the American magazines was *Putnam's Monthly*, which urged them upon both governments repeatedly.[120]

[119] See pp. 142–143.
[120] *Putnam's Monthly*, I, 335 (March 1853); III, 96 (January 1854); VIII, 85 (January 1857).

CHAPTER V

POLITICS AND WAR

SLAVERY

THAT the dispute over slavery was dominant in the American mind during the years 1850–65 is amply shown by the magazines of the period. Here was a topic possessing unusual picturesqueness, an appeal to the sentiments, and possibilities for a variety of imaginative treatment. Thus it lent itself by its very nature to magazine handling, and the question of slavery was discussed with more fervor and with more white paper and printer's ink than any other topic before the people in these days.

And in spite of the fact that union *versus* secession was the paramount issue after the formation of the Confederate States of America in 1861, and that topics surrounding the actual progress of the war occupied much space in the public prints, slavery remained an important theme even through the war years. The desirability of freeing the slaves by public proclamation was an important subject of debate during the first two years of conflict; after the Emancipation Proclamation there was a necessary shift in point of view, and the question became, "What shall we do with the freedman?"

Add to the slavery brew such other ingredients as states rights, squatter sovereignty, nativism, and the tariff, and we have a political pot seething more furiously than any in earlier years of American history. That the chief interest of the period was political is evidenced by the statistics of magazines and newspapers. "The last decade in our civil history has been one of extraordinary political agitation," wrote Joseph C. G. Kennedy, superintendent of the eighth census, in 1862.

Accordingly, we find there has been a very large increase in the number of political papers and periodicals, as compared with the number of corresponding publications at the date of the preceding census. In 1850 their number was 1,630. In 1860 it was 3,242, being an increase of nearly 100 per cent.[1]

[1] Joseph C. G. Kennedy, *Preliminary Report of the Eighth Census, 1860*

These were "political papers and periodicals." What of
politics in the more general magazines? Though political discussions were taboo in *Harper's, Emerson's, Graham's,* the
women's magazines generally, and more or less in the religious
quarterlies, other periodicals more than made up for such
neglect. How could it be otherwise? Political questions per-
meated everything in the election year of 1856, complained an
editor of *Putnam's*:

Everything tastes of them, everything smells of them, everything
sounds of them; you can see nothing clearly till you have wiped them,
as it were, from its surface. They are in your viands at dinner, and
they are stronger than the aroma of your walnuts and your wine; at
the theatre they settle upon the scene; at church they blur the spectacles of the preacher; they are in the very tunes the street organs
grind.[2]

In the theater they actually interrupt the performance: *Yankee
Notions* tells of a gallery god who broke into Hamlet's "Alas,
poor Yorick! I knew him well," to inquire in a loud voice,
"Wot was his politics? Secesh?" [3]

It seemed impossible for the individual or the periodical to
keep away from politics altogether or for long. What the *Chicago Record* called "the demon of disputation" was abroad in
the land. Even the "quiet schoolhouses are turned into arenas
for the verbal tiltings of intellectual champions." [4] This made
a difficult situation for those general or class periodicals that
preferred not to take sides. There was the *United States Magazine of Science, Art, Manufactures, Agriculture, Commerce
and Trade*, into whose manifold fields politics were not intended
to enter. It tells the story of two Irishmen who fired off a cannon
"for a lark." At first they were afraid to do it, but Mike said
finally, "Never mind, Pat, I'll touch him off aisy so he won't
wake a cat!" And the *United States Magazine of Science, Art,
Manufactures, Agriculture, Commerce and Trade* continued:

(Washington, 1862), p. 103. The statement without change is later included in
the census publication, *Statistics of the United States in 1860* (Washington,
1866), p. 320.
    [2] *Putnam's Monthly*, VIII, 557 (November 1856).
    [3] *Yankee Notions*, X, 363 (December 1861).
    [4] *Chicago Record*, III, 140 (December 15, 1859).

We have our mortar all loaded, and charged with a huge shell. . . .
But our patrons, for whom the magazine is made, and by whose
patronage it exists, are in all sections, and of all parties; and how can
we fire off the piece without disturbing their equanimity or damaging
their interests? Surely, if we are resolved to talk politics in this journal we must "touch him off aisy" indeed, or we shall blow ourselves
up, if nothing worse.[5]

But the nonpolitical journals eventually found themselves
sucked into the whirlwind. The *Northwestern Christian Advocate* in 1859 declared:

We interfere with no man's politics or party relations, but the present alarming signs of the times demand that the Christian should come
forth from his closet to the duties of citizenship, asking "Lord, what
wilt thou have me to do?" As Methodists and as Methodist preachers,
our duty is plain.[6]

And that duty was to fight slavery.

In the meantime the campaign papers, the regular newspapers, the antislavery journals, and certain other periodicals
devoted wholly to politics were stirring the devil's brew with
all their collective might. One practice which had the effect of
emphasizing the sectional discord was the reprinting of the most
vitriolic articles of the other side in order to rouse the fighting
blood of readers. The *Liberator*, for example, had a regular department on its large front page headed "Refuge of Oppression," in which the worst of fire-eating southern editorials were
quoted. *Frederick Douglass' Paper* had a similar department
entitled "The Den of Villainy." In the South, *De Bow's Review*
sometimes collected inflammatory northern pronouncements
and gave them the title "The War Against the South."

ANTEBELLUM ISSUES

The political pages of magazines were filled not only with
discussions of slavery, but also with comment on such specific
issues as those presented by the Compromise of 1850 and later
by the Kansas-Nebraska Bill, on the Supreme Court's decision
in the Dred Scott case, on John Brown's raid, and on the

[5] *United States Magazine*, I, 84 (July 1854).
[6] *Northwestern Christian Advocate*, VII, 90 (June 8, 1859).

national presidential campaigns. The fundamental economic questions involved in the slavery dispute received less attention. True, such a journal as *De Bow's* was largely devoted to these matters; and Francis Lieber's article in that review on free trade, which he called "one of the great subjects of national theology," was a notable piece of work.[7] An essay in the *National Democratic Review* on "The Production of Cotton and Its Influence on Modern Civilization" is in the same class. No stronger tie than that of cotton, declared this writer, "need exist to preserve the permanency of the Union." [8] But events were to belie his claim. Both the *North American Review* and the *Atlantic Monthly* had articles on "King Cotton" in 1861;[9] and the *Merchants' Magazine* followed the international importance of cotton, and later of wheat, with some care.

The Compromise of 1850 was, of course, a main subject for comment at the beginning of our period. Outstanding among these comments, at least in the field of belles-lettres, is Whittier's poem "Ichabod" in the *National Era* [10] — a scathing denunciation of Webster's part in the Compromise. But Webster had very respectable support in Boston; and two years later Francis Bowen, editor of the *North American*, published in his review an elaborate defense based on a general review of Webster's speeches. "His fame will be a part of the inheritance of our children," concluded Bowen.[11]

But it was not long until the Kansas-Nebraska Bill struck at the foundations of the Compromise. "The infamous plot of the traitor Douglas" was what the violent sheet edited by the Douglass with two *s*'s to his name called the new proposal.[12] *De Bow's* followed this legislation carefully, later detailing the warfare in the territories involved and urging Southerners to go to the aid of their cause. The *Liberator*, on the other side, told the story of the organization of emigrants' aid societies in New England, with the raising of funds for the purchase of Sharp's

[7] *De Bow's Review*, XV, 53 (July 1853).
[8] *National Democratic Review*, I, 104 (November 1859).
[9] *North American Review*, XCII, 1 (January 1861); *Atlantic Monthly*, VII, 451 (April 1861).
[10] *National Era*, IV, 70 (May 2, 1850).
[11] *North American Review*, LXXV, 123 (July 1852).
[12] *Frederick Douglass' Paper*, March 10, 1854, p. 3.

rifles for free-soilers by Henry Ward Beecher, Theodore Parker, Gerrit Smith, and others.

Out on the plains west of the Missouri, where the immediate issues were being decided by guns and bayonets, several political periodicals (in which news was a very minor factor) were established — for example, the *Squatter Sovereign*,[13] on one side, begun in 1855 at Atchison by Dr. J. H. Stringfellow and Robert Skelly; and the *Herald of Freedom*, on the other, founded at Wakarusa by Dr. George W. Brown in 1854, but issued at Lawrence after its first number. The *Herald*'s office was destroyed by "Border Ruffians" in 1856, but that did not check it for long. It gave its type that same year to be used for molding the balls with which to charge a six-pound cannon for the attack on Fort Titus August 16, and the discharges of this cannon were accordingly called "new editions" of the *Herald of Freedom*.[14]

The decisions of the Supreme Court in the Dred Scott case did not go unnoticed in the magazines. *Putnam's*, for example, was in 1857 filled with criticism of the Court. The *Independent* denounced it weekly. In *Frederick Douglass' Paper* there appeared on at least one occasion an actual signed advertisement of a station of the "Underground Railway" at Syracuse.[15]

THE CAMPAIGNS OF 1856 AND 1860

The one-sided campaign of 1852 had far less attention in the general periodicals than that of 1856. During the latter contest *Putnam's* had a vivid sketch of a torchlight procession in New York.[16] *Sibyl* supported Gerrit Smith's candidacy enthusiastically because he favored dress reform;[17] and the feminine element also came into the campaign through an interest in "our Jessie" — Mrs. John C. Frémont. Here and there, repeatedly, is found an opposition to caucuses, conventions, and the secret

[13] Later owners made the *Squatter Sovereign* a free-state organ under the name *Freedom's Champion* in 1857. See William E. Connelly, *History of Kansas Newspapers* (Topeka, 1916), p. 141.

[14] *Ibid.*, p. 180; also see Douglas C. McMurtrie, "Pioneer Printing in Kansas," *National Printer Journalist*, LI, 27 (March 1933).

[15] *Frederick Douglass' Paper*, July 8, 1859.

[16] *Putnam's Monthly*, VIII, 665 (December 1856).

[17] *Sibyl*, I, 12 (July 15, 1856).

societies which the nativist movement had brought into the preceding campaign: "Each citizen should vote for the man whom he, individually and independently, thinks the best for the office." [18] *Putnam's* gives us the result of the election competently:

The great triangular contest is at an end, and the result, for the parties which were engaged in it, may be summed up in the following terms: that the Democratic, now the pro-slavery party, has gained its candidates, but damaged its cause; that the Republicans have lost their candidates, but furthered their cause; that the Americans, composed of the fragments of two old and decayed factions, have lost both candidates and cause, and that, seemingly, forever.[19]

But the new *Harper's Weekly* was delighted with the victory of Buchanan and consistently supported that statesman. Not so *Vanity Fair*, which, taking its text from Ecclesiastes, "Woe to that land whose ruler is a child," printed a sonnet which contained the following lines:

. . . Far more, where Age, with wisdom's empty show,
When storming blasts of bold-voiced treason blow,
And loud rebellious waves are dashing wild,
Clings to the swaying helm with nerveless hand,
Hugging a wretched mockery of command,
Worthless, though Peace through sky and ocean smiled. . . .[20]

The campaign of 1860, engaging as it did the thought, prejudice, and passion of all citizens, occupied many pages in the general magazines. The new *Atlantic Monthly*, speaking with the voice of its editor, James Russell Lowell, declared that this election was "a turning point in our history." [21] *Harper's Weekly*, disapproving the nomination of Lincoln in place of Seward, remained, for the most part, silent on the issues of the campaign. *Leslie's* and the comics *Momus* and *Vanity Fair* followed the conventions in detail. "Nihil's" account of the Charleston convention, for example, emphasized the drinking and disorderliness of the delegates. "A report was circulated toward evening"

[18] *Chicago Record*, III, 252 (September 6, 1855). The editor, however, does not agree with this statement.
[19] *Putnam's Monthly*, VIII, 647 (December 1856).
[20] *Vanity Fair*, III, 6 (February 9, 1861).
[21] *Atlantic Monthly*, VI, 494 (October 1860).

of Friday, it said, "that the hotels had run out of whisky, which caused general consternation" until contradicted from the floor [22] — a piece of reporting which probably should be taken with a grain of salt, or a little seltzer. The *North American Review* had no comment on the campaign of 1860, nor on that of 1856, though it had excellent articles on "Homer and His Heroines" and "The New Edition of the Septuagint" in these years.

The expectation of Republican victory, arising from Democratic divisions, intensified eastern disappointment in the nomination of Lincoln. It is clear that the Illinois rail splitter's personality was repugnant to the more refined and intellectual classes in the East. *Vanity Fair* described the Republican candidate as "a longitudinal person with a shambling gait . . . slab-sided. . . . He has a thin, almost nasal voice, and his grammar is not so far above suspicion as Caesar's wife is reported to have been." [23] The *Vanity Fair* burlesques of his speeches and "gags" make Lincoln out a clown and an ignoramus, though Artemus Ward's "Visit to Abe Lincoln" in that journal is kindlier than most of the comments with which it neighbors. General criticism did not cease with Lincoln's election; but thereafter, even in partisan organs, it flamed forth occasionally as if from the banked fires of disaffection.[24]

The 1860 campaign, enlivened by the "Wide Awakes," lent itself well to portrayal in the illustrated weeklies. There were, as usual, some campaign papers, like *Father Abraham*, of Lancaster, Pennsylvania, and the *Lincoln Clarion*, of Springfield, Illinois.

THE SLAVERY DEBATE

And all through the period the changes were rung on the slavery question. "What is coarsely but expressively described in the political slang of this country as '*The Everlasting Nigger-*

[22] *Momus*, May 1, 1860, p. 1.

[23] *Vanity Fair*, I, 349 (May 26, 1860). The Artemus Ward article appeared in II, 279 (December 8, 1860).

[24] Anti-Lincoln comment is exemplified in the following: *Momus*, May 22, 1860, p. 1; *National Quarterly Review*, X, 158 (December 1864); *Illustrated News*, IX, 354 (April 2, 1864), and IX, 418 (April 30, 1864). *Harper's Weekly* supported Lincoln in the 1864 campaign; see VIII, 402 (June 25, 1864).

Question' might perhaps be considered as exhausted as a topic of discussion if ever a topic was," wrote Charles Francis Adams in the *Atlantic*.[25] The controversy over the theory of the unity of mankind, upon the decision of which depended the Negro's right to cousinship with the Caucasian, was threshed threadbare. Denial of the descent of man from one parent stock by Professors J. C. Nott and Louis Agassiz, replies on the basis of Scripture, and rejoinders galore are to be found in *De Bow's*, the *North American Review*, *Putnam's*, and other periodicals.[26] In the years 1849–51, *De Bow's* ran four serial defenses of slavery, besides an important article by the editor in which he asserted that slavery was a personal relation, the idea of property being subordinate.[27] Apologizing for still another article a few months later, De Bow admitted that the discussions of the biblical basis of slavery were "growing hacknied." [28] J. A. Turner's *Plantation*, born and bred of the slavery controversy, knew not nor cared whether its readers thought its chief materials hackneyed or fresh: slavery was its conjuring word. It held the Negro to belong to a lower order of creation than the white, incapable of education, incapable of marriage, incapable of freedom.[29]

Another familiar argument was based on the contention of the superiority of the slave-labor system to that of hireling-labor. A writer in the *Southern Literary Messenger* prophesied that within a hundred years the North would be admittedly more despotic, with the enslavement of labor by capital, than the liberty-loving South, with her slaves.[30] In the same magazine a writer on "The Duty of Southern Authors" tells them that they must show to the world that slavery is "a great social, moral, and political blessing." [31] *Russell's Magazine*, on the other hand, was not inclined so much to defend slavery as to

[25] *Atlantic Monthly*, VII, 451 (April 1861).
[26] *De Bow's Review*, IX, 243 (August 1850); *North American Review*, LXXIII, 163 (July 1851); *Putnam's Monthly*, IV, 1 (July 1854).
[27] *De Bow's Review*, IX, 9 (July 1850).
[28] *Ibid.*, IX, 281 (September 1850).
[29] *Plantation*, II, 383 (December 1860).
[30] *Southern Literary Messenger*, XXII, 426–439 (June 1856).
[31] *Ibid.*, XXIII, 241–247 (October 1856).

accept it. "The fact of slavery is here," wrote the editor, "and a fact it must remain to the end of time." [32]

Nor was the "peculiar institution" of the South without defenders in other sections. From the Far West the *Pioneer* spoke in oratorical periods:

Slavery, authorized by God, permitted by Jesus Christ, sanctioned by the apostles, maintained by good men of all ages. . . . Abolition, born in fanaticism, nurtured in violence and disorder . . . dead to every feeling of patriotism and brotherly kindness, accomplishing nothing good. . . .[33]

From New England the Reverend Ephraim Peabody added his voice against abolitionism, in the *North American Review*. Such talk at the North he thought very harmful. "If slavery is ever done away with by human means," he added, "unless it be through revolution, insurrection, or civil war, it must be by southern men." [34] The idea was later reiterated in a *North American* commentary on *Uncle Tom's Cabin* by S. G. Fisher.[35]

Various solutions of the difficulty were suggested. The Reverend Abel Stevens, editor of the Methodists' *National Magazine*, thought that Divine Providence might be intending to end the slavery question in the United States by the importation of Chinese coolies — a practice which he understood was being followed in Cuba.[36] The *National Intelligencer* was advocating such measures, and they were discussed in *De Bow's* along with the advisability of resuming the slave trade. The *National Era* seemed really alarmed lest there should be a revival of the banned traffic.[37] Colonization was, of course, a widely discussed solution.

Plans for the annexation of Cuba, then struggling against the Spanish yoke, were included in various schemes for dealing with slavery — but chiefly for the object of southern expansion to offset the addition of free states to the North. Southern com-

---

[32] *Russell's Magazine*, I, 106 (May 1857). See also William Sumner Jenkins, *Pro-Slavery Thought in the Old South* (Chapel Hill, 1935), for the many angles and phases of this debate.   [33] *Pioneer*, II, 230 (October 1854).

[34] *North American Review*, LXXIII, 354 (October 1851).

[35] *Ibid.*, LXXVII, 466–493 (October 1853).

[36] *National Magazine*, VII, 87 (July 1855).

[37] *National Era*, XIII, 22 (February 10, 1859).

mentators did not always favor the project,[38] though the Charleston commercial convention endorsed it.[39] *De Bow's* printed many discussions of the matter, which it said in 1853 was "uppermost in everyone's thoughts." [40] It was the subject of the first article of the first number of *Putnam's*.

Most outspoken against slavery, among the general magazines, were *Putnam's* and the *Atlantic*, the latter founded in the year the former perished. Parke Godwin wrote political articles for both. In 1855 *Putnam's* claimed that abolitionism was no longer extremist, but that the cautious and the enthusiastic were joined in common cause.[41] It declared "there seems to be no probable issue but in civil war," five years before the firing on Fort Sumter.[42]

ANTISLAVERY PERIODICALS

Many of the northern church journals had a marked antislavery bias. Two New York Congregational papers, the *Independent* and the *Evangelist*, and two Methodist papers, the *Northern Independent* and *Zion's Herald*, may be named from the increasing crowd of abolitionists. The *Friends' Review* and the *Friend* record the course of the Quaker activity in opposition to slavery.

Of the considerable number of journals wholly devoted to the antislavery cause, the more important had been founded in earlier periods.[43] Outstanding were William Lloyd Garrison's *Liberator*,[44] Gamaliel Bailey's *National Era*,[45] Frederick Douglass' Paper,[46] and the American Anti-Slavery Society's *National*

[38] See *De Bow's Review*, VII, 539 (December 1849).

[39] See comment on this action in *Vanity Fair*, I, 312 (May 12, 1860).

[40] *De Bow's Review*, XIV, 63 (January 1853); see also XVII, 281 (October 1854), and XXX, 30 (January 1861); as well as *Danville Quarterly Review*, I, 260 (June 1861).

[41] *Putnam's Monthly*, VI, 425 (October 1855).

[42] *Ibid.*, VIII, 85 (July 1856).

[43] See Mott, *A History of American Magazines, 1741–1850*, pp. 162–456. See also Asa Earl Martin's "Pioneer Antislavery Press," *Mississippi Valley Historical Review*, II, 509 (March 1916).

[44] Treated more fully in sketch 3.

[45] See Mott, *op. cit.*, p. 457. The *National Era* was published 1847–59, being discontinued in the year of Bailey's death. A *New National Era* came ten years later.

[46] Founded in Rochester as the *North Star* in December 1847, with £500 given

Anti-Slavery Standard.[47] Mrs. Jane Grey Swisshelm's *Pittsburgh Saturday Visiter* (1848–52) was an ardent abolition sheet whose editor and publisher had learned to hate slavery during a two-year residence in Kentucky.[48] *Principia* (1859–66) was a New York weekly devoted largely to abolition; it was third in a series of such papers by the inveterate reformer-editor William Goodell,[49] its predecessors being *American Jubilee* (1854–55) and *Radical Abolitionist* (1855–58). Goodell was joined in 1862 by George B. Cheever. Among the colonization periodicals, the *African Repository* (1825–92) was the oldest; it was issued in Washington by the American Colonization Society. The *Colonization Herald* (1835–63) and the *New York Colonization Journal* (1850–63) were published by the Pennsylvania and New York societies, respectively. The *Boston Commonwealth* (1862–96) was founded by Moncure D. Conway and Frank B. Sanborn primarily as an antislavery journal, but it had many literary and religious affiliations and a long life after the passage of the Thirteenth Amendment to the Constitution. Among Negro periodicals, two were pre-eminent — *Frederick Douglass' Paper* and the *Anglo-African Magazine.*[50] The latter was edited by Thomas Hamilton in New York (1859–60), and was literary rather than political in purpose.

---

him by English friends. The name was changed in 1850. The paper was varied, bright, and attractive. It was merged in August 1860 with *Douglass' Monthly* (1858–60), which had been begun as a small magazine for English circulation. See Douglass, *Life and Times* (Hartford, 1882), pp. 264–270; F. M. Holland, *Frederick Douglass* (New York, 1891), Chapter VI; Vernon Loggins, *The Negro Author* (New York, 1931), pp. 151–154.

[47] Published in New York 1840–72; name changed to *National Standard* 1870. Lydia Maria Child, Oliver Johnson, Parker Pillsbury, and Aaron Powell were successive editors. It received $2,000 a year under an endowment in the will of Charles F. Hovey, which had stipulated that it should turn to the advocacy of woman suffrage once the slaves were freed; but it did not do so. See Ida Husted Harper, *Life and Work of Susan B. Anthony* (Indianapolis, 1898), Vol. I, *passim*.

[48] See Mrs. Swisshelm's *Half a Century* (Chicago, 1880), Chapters XI–XXXIV. See also p. 50.

[49] See *Dictionary of American Biography* (New York, 1931), VII, 385.

[50] See Loggins, *op. cit.*, p. 209; *Journal of Negro History*, XIII, 12 (January 1928); Irving G. Penn, *The Afro-American Press and Its Editors* (Springfield, Massachusetts, 1891); and Frederick G. Detwiler, *The Negro Press in the United States* (Chicago, 1922).

"The Negro, the Negro, the everlasting Negro!" exclaimed *Vanity Fair* in exasperation at the political exploitation of the race.[51] And it was a novel with a Negro as its hero that stirred the national feeling to its highest pitch.

SIMON LEGREE CRACKS HIS WHIP

Uncle Tom's Cabin was published serially in the *National Era* from June 5, 1851, to April 1, 1852. It excited a furore among readers of the *Era*,[52] but this interest was as nothing to that which it roused upon book publication. On March 20, 1852, it was issued in two volumes by Jewett & Company, of Boston. A few days later the *Liberator* predicted that "the effect of such a work upon all intelligent and humane minds . . . must be prodigious." [53] It was.

Within eight weeks the book had sold 50,000 copies, or 100,-000 volumes. "This is without precedent in the history of book publishing in this country," announced *Norton's Literary Gazette*.[54] But that was only a beginning. Three months later the *Gazette* told of 75,000 copies sold in America and three editions on the market in England.[55] By November there had been 120,000 copies sold on this side the water, and nineteen editions had been published in England (one of which had been distributed to the number of 180,000 copies); and the publishers, advertising a new cheap edition at 37½ cents, estimated a total distribution in America and Europe of a million copies within less than nine months.[56] By January 1853 the figure was at 200,000 copies for the United States, according to *Putnam's Monthly*, with thirty editions in England and Scotland, two translations in French, and one in German.[57]

In the meantime a flood of secondary Uncle Tom material was being published. "Uncle Tom literature is almost overwhelming the bookstores," noted *Norton's Gazette* in September.

[51] *Vanity Fair*, III, 70 (February 9, 1860).
[52] *Atlantic Monthly*, XVII, 748 (June 1866).
[53] *Liberator*, XXII, 50 (March 26, 1852).
[54] *Norton's Literary Gazette*, II, 108 (June 15, 1852).
[55] *Ibid.*, II, 168 (September 15, 1852).
[56] *Ibid.*, II, 212 (November 15, 1852).
[57] *Putnam's Monthly*, I, 98 (January 1853).

Within a few weeks, from North, South, East, and West, a host of pamphlets and volumes, old and new, good and bad, cheap and costly, pro and con, including facts, fictions, arguments, dramas, poetry, songs, all relating more or less to "Life Among the Lowly" of the southern portion of our land, have been issued from the Press.[58]

Twenty Uncle Tom songs, most of them in dialect, and seven other Uncle Tom novels had been published before the end of 1852; and before the theatrical season was over, a considerable proportion of the playhouses in England and America were producing Uncle Tom dramas. Legree was cracking his whip in six different London theaters at once, according to *Putnam's* for January 1853. "Never," exclaimed the editor of that magazine, "since books were first printed, has the success of *Uncle Tom* been equalled; the history of literature contains nothing parallel to it, or approaching it." [59]

The *Literary World* regretted this great success. "The Uncle Tom epidemic still rages with unabated virulence," it reported in December 1852.

No country is safe from its attack. . . . No age or sex is spared; no condition is exempt. The prevailing affection is universal, and all have the Uncle Toms. . . . Its influence is bad. The social evils of slavery have been exaggerated and presented in a form calculated to excite an inconsiderate popular feeling.[60]

Likewise, the *Democratic Review* in April of the next year declared that

the unparallelled popularity of *Uncle Tom's Cabin* in the United States and Europe . . . can only be accounted for by the simple fact that it was susceptible of being made a tool of abolition in one quarter and in the other a political instrument for undermining the influence of republican institutions. It is impossible for anyone who reads that book to account for its extraordinary sale . . . on the basis of mere literary merit.[61]

In the South there was a reaction yet more violent. It was reported in the antislavery papers that southern courts were

[58] *Norton's Literary Gazette*, II, 168 (September 15, 1852).
[59] *Putnam's Monthly*, I, 98 (January 1853).
[60] *Literary World*, XI, 355–358 (December 4, 1852).
[61] *Democratic Review*, XXXII, 200 (April 1853).

sentencing men to prison for long terms when they were found with the hated book in their possession.[62] Comment in southern magazines varied from abuse and threats to parody and banter.[63] Some thirty "anti-Uncle Toms" appeared,[64] but none of them attained much prominence.

Another book to attract wide attention in the fifties was H. R. Helper's *The Impending Crisis*, of 1857. This economic study of slavery by a Southerner was used as a campaign tract by the Republicans in 1860. *The Great Auction Sale of Slaves*, originally printed in the *New York Tribune* and later used as a tract by the antislavery societies, was also influential.[65]

THE FINANCIAL STRINGENCY OF 1857–60

Here we must interrupt the headlong rush of events toward armed conflict to hear the voice of the magazines upon the panic of 1857. That year "will be memorable in all future time for commercial disasters, the derangement of trade, the failure of banking institutions, and the suspensions of merchants and traders of all classes," declared the *National Magazine*.[66] The *Democratic Review* believed that this panic had "never had a counterpart." It had "devastated like a fearful scourge." [67] Nor did the clouds lift the next year; fourteen months later a religious journal observed that "the present winter has been the gloomiest and darkest ever experienced." [68]

Popular ideas about the hard times may be followed in that mirror of life in America in general and New York in particular — *Frank Leslie's Illustrated Newspaper*, known much later as *Leslie's Weekly*. The panic, said *Leslie's*, was "the natural end of the whole system of building railroads on loans and the contraction of floating debt." [69] And a series of cartoons in a later number depicted the history of a railroad company from

[62] *National Era*, XII, 170 (October 28, 1858).
[63] See Mott, *op. cit.*, p. 649. See also pp. 553–554.
[64] See article by Jeanette Tandy in *South Atlantic Quarterly*, XXI, 41 ff. (January, April 1922).
[65] *Atlantic Monthly*, IV, 386 (September 1859).
[66] *National Magazine*, XI, 561 (December 1857).
[67] *Democratic Review*, XLI, 367 (May 1858).
[68] *Northwestern Christian Advocate*, VII, 18 (February 2, 1859).
[69] *Frank Leslie's Illustrated Newspaper*, IV, 246 (September 19, 1857).

its inception in a beer saloon to its conclusion in a bankruptcy court.[70] "The money panic absorbs every other topic in every circle," we read in October 1857. "Everyone should immediately begin to retrench expenses. . . . The fearful and reckless extravagance in dress, exhibited by the women of America, is calling forth on all sides the condemnation of the right thinking of our people." [71] The New York theaters, however, seem unaffected, though Italian opera has been discontinued. "Large bands of men who have no work are daily gathered together in the Park and other public places, where addresses are made to them, and in some cases these are not couched in very soothing language." [72]

Others were somewhat less serious about the matter. Edmund Quincy wrote in his Boston correspondence to the *Anti-Slavery Standard*: "We have concluded, on the whole, to discontinue a habit which would be attended by the unpleasant incident of parting with our money. So we all stopped payment last week. The Giant Panic has devoured us." [73] Boucicault hurriedly revamped "Les Pauvres de Paris" to make a topical play called "The Money Panic of 1857," which was produced with fair success on the Boston stage at the holiday season.[74] The shoemakers' strike at Lynn, Massachusetts, in the winter of 1859–60 was treated rather lightly by *Leslie's*,[75] and other strikes of the time received little attention in the magazines.

In the South, where the panic was little felt, there was a tendency to make political capital out of it. *Russell's Magazine*, pointing out that "the present mob of New York demand bread or work," says that such are the dangers of "hireling states" when labor combines against capital. But, we are reminded, "no slave is thrown out of employment or compelled to hunt or beg for work or bread." [76]

[70] *Ibid.*, IV, 384 (November 14, 1857).
[71] *Ibid.*, IV, 294 (October 10, 1857).
[72] *Ibid.*, IV, 374 (November 14, 1857).
[73] *National Era*, XI, 178 (November 5, 1857). Quoted from the *Anti-Slavery Standard*. See also the *Saturday Evening Gazette*, November 7, 1857, p. 4.
[74] *Saturday Evening Gazette*, January 2, 1858, p. 2. The same play was called "The Poor of New York" when produced at Wallack's in that city the same month.
[75] *Frank Leslie's Illustrated Newspaper*, IX, 240 (March 17, 1860).
[76] *Russell's Magazine*, II, 260 (December 1857).

JOHN BROWN'S BODY

Meantime the raid at Harper's Ferry turned public attention to the "impending crisis." "Since the days of Aaron Burr," said *Leslie's*, "no public event has caused so widespread an excitement" as Brown's mad gesture.[77] *Leslie's* had no sympathy for Brown. "We blush for humanity," it exclaimed, "for our good name as a people, and for our profession as journalists, that any press through the land should be base enough to print one word in extenuation of the crime of these maniacs."[78] Of course many Republican newspapers did that very thing, and some of them printed many words to that end; but defense of Brown was rare in the nonpartisan periodicals. Even an abolition paper like the *National Era* declared that "No humane or reasonable man will for a moment sympathize with this effort to incite servile insurrection."[79] *Harper's Weekly* insisted that "the bulk of the Northern people have no sympathy with John Brown."[80] That journal, along with most of those of Democratic faith made political capital out of the event, though others claimed Brown was not himself a Republican. "It is but folly to believe," said the *National Democratic Quarterly*, that Republican leaders "are not the real authors of the mischief."[81]

But there were those among the church papers and antislavery journals that took up the cudgels for Brown, as the *Liberator* and the *Northern Independent*. True, the *Liberator* had at first called the raid "misguided, wild, and apparently insane," while allowing for Brown's good intentions.[82] Garrison was soon magnifying Brown as a hero, however: "if he shall be put to death, he will not die ignobly, but as a martyr . . . held in grateful and honorable remembrance by the latest posterity."[83] The *Atlantic Monthly* a few months later, in a review of James Redpath's *Public Life of John Brown* by Charles Eliot Norton, published the more temperate view of the man and his

[77] *Frank Leslie's Illustrated Newspaper*, VIII, 351 (November 5, 1859).
[78] *Ibid.*, VIII, 344 (October 29, 1859).
[79] *National Era*, XIII, 170 (October 27, 1859).
[80] *Harper's Weekly*, III, 802 (December 17, 1859).
[81] *National Democratic Quarterly Review*, I, 43 (November 1859).
[82] *Liberator*, XXIX, 166 (October 21, 1859).
[83] *Ibid.*, XXIX, 170 (October 28, 1859).

EXECUTION OF JOHN BROWN

This was a double-page spread in *Frank Leslie's Illustrated* for December 10, 1858. The volume binding makes it impossible to reproduce the picture without interference of the page-fold. "From an accurate sketch made on the spot by our own artist."

deed which eventually came to be rather generally accepted. "That John Brown was wrong in his attempt to break up slavery by violence," wrote Norton, "few will deny. But it was a wrong committed by a good man." [84]

These apologiae for Brown maddened the extremists on the other side. The *Old Guard*, referring somewhat later to the abolition excitement induced by the Harper's Ferry episode, charged the friends of the Negro in exaggerated terms with deifying Brown: "Do you not still minister at the bloody altars of your newly canonized saint, Ossawatomie? He was a burglar and a murderer. . . . One of you once said — 'John Brown has made the gallows more glorious than Jesus Christ has the cross.' " [85]

SECESSION

It will illustrate the complex nature of the causes of the Civil War if we turn from the moral and almost fanatical fervor attending the execution of Brown to a shrewd article on one of the financial phases of secession. It was written after the beginning of the war:

The North feels also that commercial dishonesty was potent among the influences which fomented this rebellion. Bankruptcy almost universal — planters immersed in debts for lands, for negroes, for food, for fabric — merchants overhead in debt to the importers and jobbers of the Northern sea-ports — everyone owing more or less, and few able to pay: such was the general pecuniary situation of the South at the outset of this subversion. It is no libel on the South to say that relief from the pressure of over-due obligations was primarily sought by an immense number, in plunging into the abyss of revolution. And a great proportion of the Southern merchants, with full intent to defraud their creditors, by lighting the flames of civil war, in 1860 swelled their indebtedness to their Northern friends to the utmost.[86]

Meanwhile, with the "Old Public Functionary" in the White House rather worse than helpless and hated and berated by both sides, with Seward's phrase "the irrepressible conflict"

[84] *Atlantic Monthly*, V, 380 (March 1860).

[85] *Old Guard*, I, 12 (January 1863). The "cross" misquotation was founded on a sentence from Emerson's lecture on "Courage," later deleted. Many southern periodicals quoted it. See *Plantation*, I, 13 (March 1860).

[86] *Continental Monthly*, II, 449 (October 1862).

daily justifying itself more fully, and with passion turning to hysteria in parts of the antislavery and southern press, Congress presented a spectacle of extraordinary license, corruption, and boordom. Conditions there did not miss the sharp eyes of *Vanity Fair*, which returned to the attack upon them again and again. F. B. Tucker wrote about them in *Putnam's*:

The capital is a nest of wickedness. . . . Bribery is rampant. Many men in Congress are for sale. We have ourselves heard legislators state the amount of gold which they have seen in the hands of members, and which such members have avowed to be their wages for such and such a vote. . . . Legislative discussion is maintained at the point of the knife and the muzzle of the pistol. Drunken orators uphold their cause with oaths, indecency, maundering, or inebriate laughter.[87]

After the first secessions in the winter of 1860–61, the paramount question north and south was the "right" to dissolve the ties of union. J. D. B. De Bow, who had advocated such dissolution before the alumni of the College of Charleston as early as 1858, was present at the secession conventions of South Carolina, Mississippi, and Louisiana;[88] and his *Review* was much occupied with "the right of secession." The *North American* printed a long article on that subject by General Joel Parker, later governor of New Jersey; he concluded that the alleged right did not exist.[89] Lowell wrote in the *Atlantic*: "It is time the North should learn that it has nothing left to compromise but the rest of its self-respect,"[90] and later he called for "a timely show of power."[91] But the more pacific *Vanity Fair* was opposed to that course, and one of its poets represented Uncle Sam speaking to the "Coercionist":

In the first place, then, good nephew, you can't keep it if you would; And the game ain't worth the powder to attempt it if you could.

And in the second place, said this writer, the Southerners are "your brothers."[92]

[87] *Putnam's Monthly*, V, 201 (February 1855).
[88] *De Bow's Review*, XXX, 251, 429 (April 1861).
[89] *North American Review*, XCIII, 212–244 (July 1861).
[90] *Atlantic Monthly*, VII, 121 (January 1861).
[91] *Ibid.*, VII, 246 (February 1861).
[92] *Vanity Fair*, III, 135 (March 23, 1861).

Then came the firing on Sumter. "The glorious action at Fort Sumter excited to enthusiasm the entire South," wrote De Bow.[93] In the North, the President's call for troops brought out not a little impassioned writing. "Three hundred thousand men are wanted, and that right away," said the new *Continental Monthly*. "We have it in our power to crush the rebellion, if our people will but arise in their might." [94] Theodore Tilton's "The Great Bell Roland" in the *Independent* [95] was only one of many poems echoing the call to arms.

MAGAZINES IN WAR TIMES

The leading quarterly reviews — Sears's *National Quarterly* and the *North American* on one side, and *De Bow's* on the other — gave more or less attention to the war. *De Bow's* gave a great deal, between suspensions; the *North American* used three to five of its long articles for war matters every year; the *National* gave about the same. The general monthlies practically all used war material in every issue. The *Atlantic* did so in political article, fiction, poetry, and reminiscence from the field. The *Knickerbocker's* pages had much of the war; but it became, before death mercifully put an end to its vagaries, violently "Copperhead." The *Continental Monthly* was also very warlike, with war serials, hortatory political articles, and so on. *Leslie's Monthly* printed many columns of war matter until a change of policy in 1863. The *Southern Literary Messenger*, the only important Confederate monthly during these dark years, was much concerned with the progress of the conflict. Even *Harper's Monthly* varied its serene sequence of biography, travel, and English serials with martial narratives in the latter years of the war. In the main, however, it may be said that the amount of war material used in the general magazines decreased as the conflict progressed.

The weeklies were rather closer to military affairs than the monthlies. The *New York Ledger*, for example, used some narratives from the field, a war serial, and Everett's editorials in 1862: this indicates the *Ledger* policy and that of the other

[93] *De Bow's Review*, XXX, 683 (June 1861).
[94] *Continental Monthly*, II, 243 (August 1862).
[95] *Independent*, XIII, 4 (April 18, 1861).

story-papers in general. In the *Home Journal* Willis wrote "Lookings-On at the War," and his partner Morris wrote battle songs. *Harper's Weekly* made up for its monthly sister's temerity by outdoing everybody else in pictures and articles about the war, though *Frank Leslie's Illustrated* was not far behind. *Vanity Fair*, so long as its plume waved, was in the thick of the battle.

Of the class periodicals, those of a religious nature generally gave some attention to war topics: the quarterlies made studied or fiery pronouncements according to temperament, and the weeklies were usually newspaperish enough to give regular reports of political and military developments. The women's periodicals, as a class, kept clear of war matters, though we may be sure their readers did not. The special trade and technical journals usually meddled with little outside their limited fields. Certain periodicals devoted to "isms" — as the Oneida *Circular* and *Sibyl* — though not precisely disloyal, were quite unsympathetic with either party to the conflict and made few comments on war matters. "We had almost forgotten about the War," confessed the *Circular* in 1864. "We have had so far, and are likely to have hereafter, but little to do with the War. . . . Curing slavery by war is like curing fever by calomel: the remedy, though effectual, remains in the system as a cause of disease." [96]

But one class of periodicals was by its nature wholly devoted to war matters — the group of military journals. The New York *Military Gazette* (1858–61) was a successor to the *Eclaireur* (1853–57) as an organ of the New York militia. Another state military journal was the *Connecticut War Record* (1863–65). The *Army and Navy Gazette* (1862–63) was succeeded by the *United States Army and Navy Journal*,[97] most important of its class, founded by the brothers Church. The *Army and Navy Official Gazette* (1863–65) was a Washington reporter of department orders and dispatches.

Very interesting are the brief files of certain papers issued irregularly by various units of the Federal army when some printer was able to secure a press during a period of leisure and

[96] *Circular*, N.S., I, 7 (March 21, 1864).
[97] Treated more fully in sketch 39.

opportunity for publication. The *Swamp Angel* was issued for the Federal garrison on Morris Island in Charleston Harbor in 1864. "The *American Union* will be issued daily when the movements of the army render this possible." The *Red River Rover* was "printed on board the steamer Des Moines, Uncle Samuel publisher," on ruled foolscap, by a printer of the Eighth Wisconsin. The *Camp Kettle* (1861–62) had an unusually long file, though erratic; it was "published at every opportunity by the Field and Staff Officers of the Roundhead Regiment" — the 100th Pennsylvania. The *Yazoo Daily Yankee* was "published semi-occasionally by Mr. Mudsill, Mr. Small-Fisted Farmer, Mr. Greasy Mechanic & Co." during the Vicksburg siege. The best-known southern paper of this war-born type comes from the same siege — the *Vicksburg Daily Citizen*, using wallpaper for the news stock which was unobtainable. Its issue of July 2, 1863, has several times been reproduced in facsimile. The *Old Flag* was printed by Union prisoners at Camp Ford, Tyler, Texas.

WAR TOPICS

The blessings of war were sometimes extolled in the army journals and in the *Continental Monthly*. Inventiveness and industry were found to have been stimulated, and devotion to "American Destiny" (a term which appears repeatedly in the *Continental*) had been enkindled.[98] Hatred of enemies was also fostered. One of the "outrages" of which much capital was made was the supposed use of the bones of Yankees killed in battle for mementos to adorn southern homes and southern toilettes. An unknown versifier perpetrated the following for the *Continental*:

> Silent the lady sat alone:
> In her ears were rings of dead men's bone;
> The brooch on her breast shone white and fine,
> 'Twas the polished joint of a Yankee's spine;
> The well-carved handle of her fan
> Was the finger-bone of a Lincoln man.
> She turned aside, a flower to cull
> From a vase which was made of a human skull;

[98] *Continental Monthly*, III, 411–420 (April 1863), article by the Hon. F. P. Stanton; also VI, 361–371 (October 1864), article by Hugh Miller.

For to make her forget the loss of her slaves
Her lovers had rifled dead men's graves.
Do you think I'm describing a witch or a ghoul?
There are no such things — and I'm not a fool,
Nor did she reside in Ashantee —
No, the lady fair was an F. F. V.[99]

But the *Continental's* chief thesis was immediate emancipation of the slaves. "The issue of our present struggle must be disunion or emancipation," it insisted;[100] and it kept that cry up until the Proclamation of September 22, 1862, was issued. The *Liberator* followed a similar course, though somewhat more violently. It quoted from a Roxbury, Massachusetts, sermon, "God has become an abolitionist!" and commented: "But Mr. Lincoln does not yet even see that God is an abolitionist."[101] And again: "President Lincoln, delay not at your peril!"[102] Nor is the *Liberator* quite satisfied either with the Emancipation Proclamation or with Lincoln's "conservatism" thereafter.

Indeed, there were many who were not satisfied with the President. Criticism of Lincoln and his generals by literary experts in tactics was so common that one of the comics of the times put forth the suggestion that the conduct of the war "be confided to a Board of Military Editors."[103]

"COPPERHEADS"

Argument over various proposed compromises grew very bitter, but there was always that conclusive answer so well stated by D. A. Wasson in the *Atlantic*: "We can propose no compromise, such as would end the war, without confessing that there was no occasion for beginning it."[104] More bitterly spoke *Vanity Fair*:

The veriest spawn of the Father of Lies
Is that creeping creature called Compromise.[105]

[99] *Continental Monthly*, II, 5 (July 1862).
[100] *Ibid.*, II, 450 (October 1862).
[101] *Liberator*, XXXII, 198 (December 12, 1862).
[102] *Ibid.*, XXXII, 43 (March 14, 1862).
[103] *Vanity Fair*, IV, 35 (July 20, 1861). But the critic sinned in this regard also.
[104] *Atlantic Monthly*, XI, 654 (May 1863).
[105] *Vanity Fair*, IV, 6 (July 6, 1861). See also *Yankee Notions*, X, 356 (December, 1861).

A LINCOLN CARTOON FROM *VANITY FAIR*

Henry L. Stephens represents Lincoln as Blondin crossing the Niagara over the Falls on a rotten plank (it should have been a tight rope). Blondin carried a man on his back; Lincoln here carries a Negro in a carpetbag, while Greeley from the shore calls out, "Don't drop the carpetbag!" *Vanity Fair*, June 9, 1860. See note on this cartoon, p. 523 and footnote.

The "peace democrats," who sat for a composite portrait by Francis Wayland in the *Atlantic*, labeled "a political monster," [106] were severely handled in many periodicals. Fernando Wood may be studied at length under the most unfavorable aspects in *Leslie's*. The political versifiers, who were very busy, described the peace party in the *Continental*:

> The piece of a party, called the party of peace,
> Like everything else which deceases,
> Has gone where the wicked from trouble shall cease,
> For the party of peace is in pieces.[107]

The two chief "Copperhead" journals were the daily and weekly *Day Book* and the monthly *Old Guard*. The *Day Book* was begun in New York in 1849 by N. R. Stimson to carry the war into the enemy's territory. The weekly edition made good its claim to be "saucy, racy, and spicy." It gave place in August 1861 to the weekly *Caucasian*, which was excluded from the mails for fifteen months from October 1861; it resumed in 1863, going back to its first name later in the year, but soon perished. As to the *Old Guard*,[108] it is a curiosity. In its first number it shouts:

> Let us begin to prepare epitaphs of eternal shame for the tombs of the traitors who dare lift up their hands, with Abraham Lincoln and his fellow-conspirators, against the Union and the Constitution! The terrible Danton once thundered in the French Assembly: *"Room, there! Room in Hell for Maximillian [sic] Robespierre!"* Read, O conspirators, your epitaph.[109]

What Editor Burr would have done without exclamation points and italics is difficult to surmise.

THE VOICE OF THE CONFEDERACY

In the South the reactions to the war were not dissimilar. After "the glorious action at Fort Sumter," the conflict was faced with a courage which was sometimes almost hysterical. "We have been coerced into a war," complained the *Southern Presbyterian Review*.

[106] *Atlantic Monthly*, XII, 784 (December 1863).
[107] *Continental Monthly*, I, 95 (January 1862).
[108] Treated more fully in sketch 38.
[109] *Old Guard*, I, 14 (January 1863).

We proceed . . . to show that in the events connected with the occupation, siege and fall of Fort Sumter, and the unconditional surrender of its garrison, we have a signal display of the powerful providence of God. . . . The usurpation of Lincoln, Scott & Company — the arbitrary, unconstitutional, tyrannous, unnatural, inhuman and diabolical course pursued by them — the barbarities perpetrated, the blood of patriot martyrs murdered, the curses of outraged women, the wailing of widows, the tears of orphans, cities subjugated, *all decency and civilization set at defiance by unlicensed lynx-eyed generals and soldiers.*[110]

This was written by the Reverend Thomas H. Smyth, Charleston minister, and long a leading contributor to church reviews. When Hodge published his famous article on the "State of the Country" in the *Princeton Review* in 1861, it was the Reverend John H. Rice, of Louisville, who replied to it in the *Southern Presbyterian*, contending that "the twin spirits of abolitionism and sectionalism" had forced the cotton states out of the union.[111] In the meantime Breckinridge in his *Danville Review* fought hard to keep Kentucky from secession.[112]

In *De Bow's* for January 1861 J. Quitman Moore wrote:

With all its attendant evils — with all its tragic horrors — with all its mighty retinue of sorrows, sufferings, and disasters — war — civil war — war of kindred races — is not the greatest calamity that can befall a people. . . . There is in war a sublime and awful beauty — a fearful and terrible loveliness. . . .[113]

And yet that saddest of comics, *Southern Punch*, paints a distressing picture of Richmond in September 1863. The city

is full of refugees. These unfortunate people have been driven from their homes by the Yankees, their property confiscated or given to the flames. . . . Cultivated gentlemen and accomplished ladies struggle daily for the means to keep themselves from absolute want. . . . Poor rooms, poorly furnished, are held at fabulous rates. Mammon, that accursed offspring of Satan, is everywhere rampant.[114]

---

[110] *Southern Presbyterian Review*, XIV, 365, 399 (October 1861).
[111] *Ibid.*, XIV, 1–44 (April 1861).
[112] See pp. 537–538.
[113] *De Bow's Review*, XXX, 52 (January 1861).
[114] *Southern Punch*, September 12, 1863, p. 5.

Hatred flamed high. "The more outrages they commit," remarked the *Southern Illustrated News* of the northern troops, "the worse we will hate them, and the more a people hate the Yankees, the wiser and better they will be." [115] And the *Southern Monthly* joined the ugly chorus of Yankeephobia: "They are a race too loathsome, too hateful, for us ever, under any circumstances, to be identified with them as one people." [116]

THE END OF THE WAR

The bonfires and processions by which the North celebrated Lee's surrender are pictured in *Harper's Weekly* and *Leslie's*, and echoes are found in the monthlies. But the rejoicing was soon stayed by the news of Lincoln's assassination. Then even the bitterest of the President's enemies held their peace for a time, and magazines and newspapers throughout the North were filled with laudation of the dead leader. Even the crude *Yankee Notions*, which had made him play the buffoon through its ill-printed pages for five years, said with simplicity in June 1865: "In every true American heart Abraham Lincoln has a monument." [117] Bancroft's article in the *Atlantic* for June 1865 on "The Place of Abraham Lincoln in History" contained somewhat the same ideas that were nobly expressed in Lowell's "Commemoration Ode," published in the same magazine in the following September: Lincoln was "the first American." And such has been the tenor of Lincolnian eulogy, with but few exceptions, in later American magazines.

[115] *Southern Illustrated News*, March 12, 1863, p. 2.
[116] *Hutton and Freligh's Southern Magazine*, II, 80 (May 1862).
[117] *Yankee Notions*, XIV, 178 (June 1865).

CHAPTER VI

LITERARY TYPES AND JUDGMENTS

"NEXT to that of Germany, the reading circle of the United States is the most extensive in the world," asserted the editor of *Putnam's Monthly* in 1856. "There are more writers in France, and better writing in England, no doubt, than among ourselves; but these nations cannot compare with us in the number of intelligent readers." [1] *Norton's Literary Gazette* gave statistics showing the publication of about a thousand books in the United States in 1852, one-third of them reprints — a figure doubled by 1855 and quadrupled by 1862. Lower prices for good books had much to do with this increase. "Twenty-five years ago, books sufficient to constitute a respectable library demanded a sum which few were able to spare," said *Church's Bizarre* in 1852. "Now a library adequate to the wants of even the professed littérateur may be had at a price within the means of all save the very poorest." [2]

LITERARY CRITICISM

This increasing flood of new books emphasized the need for good literary criticism. "That we have no 'organ' of criticism is painfully apparent," declared the *Cosmopolitan Art Journal*. "The monthlies painfully fail in their critical departments. . . . Their notices scarcely amount to anything else than good advertisements of their own or their friends' wares." [3] The *Criterion* joined the chorus: "An honest critical journal is viewed with apprehension by some few of the book trade. The facility with which puffs are procured, and the unblushing effrontery with which some of the newspaper press publish them are facts now well known." [4]

Three obstacles to honest criticism were commonly cited: the activity of the friends of authors and publishers, improper pres-

[1] *Putnam's Monthly*, VIII, 95 (July 1856).
[2] *Bizarre*, I, 18 (April 17, 1852).
[3] *Cosmopolitan Art Journal*, I, 77 (March 1857).
[4] *Criterion*, I, 41 (November 17, 1855).

sure by the advertisers of books, and the incompetence of reviewers. Of these the first was oftenest mentioned: so far did
puffery go that the editor of *Putnam's* was moved to quote one
complainant's forceful declaration: "I proclaim to all the inhabitants of the land that they cannot trust what the periodicals
say of new books!" [5] The practice of anonymity lent itself
naturally to puffery, for it was easy for a close friend of the
author, or even the author himself, to write and publish several
laudatory reviews without betraying his self-interest.[6] As to the
second obstacle to good criticism, the *Publishers' Circular*
claimed that the sinning was not all done by the publishers:
" 'Give us advertisements and we will give you good notices' is
a proposition every day made to publishers," it declared.[7] The
action of Ticknor & Fields in withdrawing their advertising
from the *Boston Traveler* following the publication of an unfavorable review of *Hiawatha* was widely commented upon.[8]

Yet there was some good reviewing. *Putnam's*, the *Atlantic
Monthly*, and the *Literary World* did some really excellent work
in that kind, as well as such short-lived periodicals as the *Criterion*, the *Crayon*, and *To-Day*. The more pretentious journals, such as the *North American* and the *National Quarterly*,
occasionally had good critical articles in special fields. Griswold's *International Monthly*, despite some conspicuous failures, printed much sound criticism.

The *Literary World*,[9] of New York, finished its career in
1853, under the editorship of Evert A. and George L. Duyckinck, having won golden opinions but little gold coin. Derby's
Literary Advertiser (1851–56), a Cincinnati semimonthly, was
devoted largely to biographical sketches. Norton's *Literary
Advertiser* was begun in New York by Charles B. Norton in
1851, changing its name the following year to *Norton's Literary
Gazette and Publishers' Circular*. George W. Childs, of Philadelphia, bought it in 1855 and continued it as the *American*

---

[5] *Putnam's Monthly*, V, 440 (April 1855).
[6] See Brander Matthews on this subject, *New York Times Book Review*,
August 14, 1921, p. 2.
[7] *Publishers' Circular*, December 1, 1855.
[8] *Criterion*, I, 73 (December 1, 1855).
[9] See Mott, *A History of American Magazines, 1741–1850*, pp. 766–768.

Publishers' Circular and Literary Gazette.[10]   Childs made R. Shelton Mackenzie editor. The *Circular* was mainly an advertising medium for the publishers, designed for circulation among booksellers. Similar in purpose was O. F. Parsons' *Monthly Trade Gazette* (1855–72), of New York.

To-Day: A Boston Literary Journal was edited weekly by Charles Hale, a brother of Edward Everett Hale, through the twelve months of 1852. It published excellent book reviews, notes on music, the drama, and fine arts, and essays on literary and artistic topics — no small part of the whole being from the pen of the talented editor. Its criticisms, as *Putnam's* observed, were admirable — "unsparing, yet kind and judicious." [11]   The *Criterion* (1855–56), by Charles R. Rode, was a New York critical weekly of high class, publishing really careful reviews, with notes on art, drama, and science. It was modeled on the *London Athenaeum*. Rode said he lost $4,000 on it during its nine months, before it was finally merged with the *Publishers' Circular*. A second venture by C. B. Norton was called *Norton's Literary Letter* (1857–60).[12]   It was chiefly bibliographical, and its subtitle describes its contents: "Comprising American papers of interest and a catalogue of rare and valuable books relative to America." Bibliographies of books pertaining to Maine, New Hampshire, and Vermont were notable features. Somewhat similar was the *Philobiblion* (1861–63), also of New York, which described itself as "A Monthly Bibliographical Journal, containing critical notices of, and extracts from, rare, curious, and valuable old books." Its editor was P. G. Philes, who had graduated from shoemaking into bookselling, and thence into criticism and editorship.

AMERICAN MAGAZINES ON ENGLISH LITERATURE

Much of the critical talent of American magazinists was expended on English works. Comment on Dickens, Thackeray, Carlyle, and Tennyson was especially prominent.

---

[10] See Volume III, sketch 23, for the *Publishers' Weekly*.

[11] *Putnam's Monthly*, I, 230 (February 1853).

[12] The voluming is irregular: I (October 1857); II (1858); III, IV (1859); N.S., I, II (1860). At the beginning of the new series it was intended to be a quarterly.

"No author was ever more popular in America than Dickens," declared a writer in *Putnam's*.[13] A decade of steady production of popular novels had dulled the memory of *American Notes*, with its injury to national pride. *Knickerbocker* thought the early fifties "the very hey-day of the renown of this great master." [14]

Thackeray visited the United States on lecture tours in 1852–53 and 1854–55. He spoke to large audiences everywhere and was reported to have made $12,000 from his second excursion; but the *Criterion* reported that his lectures "have not apparently fulfilled public expectation." [15] Critics generally were very generous in their treatment of him, however. "There are but three English novelists," declared J. F. Kirk dogmatically in the *North American Review* " — Fielding, Jane Austen, and Thackeray." [16] And even if audiences were sometimes disappointed in him, Thackeray seems to have made an excellent impression on those who met him personally. "A great, sweet, generous human heart," was George William Curtis' verdict in *Putnam's*.[17]

Another visitor was G. P. R. James, who came on an official mission. He landed in New York on July 4, 1850, "amid discharges of artillery, the huzzas of assembled thousands, and such an imposing military display as is rarely seen in this country except on occasions of great moment and universal interest." [18] The "assembled thousands" were, of course, celebrating Independence Day. Comment on James ranged from the eulogistic to the severe.

Bulwer was generally more highly esteemed. An enthusiastic commentator in the *National Democratic Quarterly* declared that he "is certainly one of the most extraordinary men, and one who has exerted the widest influence in his writings, that has arisen in any age." [19]

[13] *Putnam's Monthly*, VIII, 656 (December 1856). C. F. Briggs, editor of *Putnam's*, was not so enthusiastic. See II, 558 (November 1853). Compare article by G. F. Talbot, V, 263–272 (March 1855).

[14] *Knickerbocker*, XXXIX, 421 (May 1852).

[15] *Criterion*, I, 26 (November 10, 1855).

[16] *North American Review*, LXXVII, 200 (July 1853).

[17] *Putnam's Monthly*, I, 639 (June 1853).

[18] *International Weekly Miscellany*, I, 71 (July 15, 1850).

[19] *National Democratic Quarterly Review*, I, 159 (November 1859).

George Eliot, newest of the great English novelists, won encomiums. "The author of *Adam Bede*," said a writer in *Russell's Magazine* in 1859, "continues to baffle the efforts of the curious to discover his name. Whoever he is, he has achieved a success which is seldom gained, and still more rarely deserved." [20]

Among English writers of nonfiction prose, Carlyle received more attention than any of his fellows; but the great reputation which he had enjoyed in the forties shrank perceptibly in the next decades.[21] His *Friedrich* was less popular than the earlier works, and his tracts on slavery in America gave greatest offense in that part of the country where his "cult" had been most assiduously tended. "I accuse you," wrote D. A. Wasson to Carlyle in the *Atlantic*, "of narrowness and pettiness of understanding in regard to America. . . . You are beginning to suffer from yourself. You are threatening to perish of too much Thomas Carlyle." [22] Even in the South, where his sympathy with slavery might be expected to win him friends, the magazines were unkind to him. John Esten Cooke, writing in the *Southern Literary Messenger*, calls his *Latter-Day Pamphlets* "purely monstrous." [23]

The death of Wordsworth called forth much comment upon his work. Thomas Chase, the classical scholar, predicted in the *North American Review* that "Future ages will confirm the decision upon which this age has nearly agreed, that Wordsworth is the greatest poet since Milton, and in some sense the father of a nobler and loftier school of poetry than any which had before appeared." [24] The posthumous *Prelude* was "more generally read than any poem of equal length that has issued from the press in this age," [25] said another commentator.

After Wordsworth's death Tennyson was repeatedly hailed as the foremost of living English poets, "the acknowledged

[20] *Russell's Magazine*, V, 571 (September 1859).
[21] See F. L. Mott, "Carlyle's American Public," *Philological Quarterly*, IV, 245–264 (July 1925).
[22] *Atlantic Monthly*, XII, 497 (October 1863).
[23] *Southern Literary Messenger*, XVI, 330 (June 1850).
[24] *North American Review*, LXXIII, 474 (October 1851).
[25] *International Miscellany*, I, 196 (August 12, 1850). See also Annabelle Newton, *Wordsworth in Early American Criticism* (Chicago, 1928), and Norman Foerster's criticism of it in *Studies in Philology*, XXXVI, 85–95 (January 1929).

master of an original and popular school," "the leading poet of his generation," "preëminently *the* poet of our age." [26] Browning, on the other hand, is "little read, except by a circle of enthusiastic admirers; yet his fame and literary position are assured." [27] In 1861 the death of Mrs. Browning, who was always popular in America, called forth much praise of her work: *Putnam's* said her name was "a household word in the best and most cultivated homes of the Old World and the New." [28]

Bailey's *Festus* was the subject of controversy literary and religious. "Blasphemous rant and fustian," [29] declared Griswold's *International Magazine*; others were charmed by it. Writing after the smoke of battle had somewhat cleared, a *Putnam* critic said:

> Everybody read *Festus*: some it gladdened and some it saddened, and not a few it maddened. . . . the poem in England and America ran through editions as numerous as the loves of its hero. . . . [Bailey was] like a comet in the irregularity of his orbit, and somewhat like a shooting star in the sudden subsiding of his glory.[30]

FRENCH LITERATURE

Some progress was made during this period in American appreciation of current French literature: Dumas, Hugo, Balzac, and George Sand were the writers upon whom attention seemed mainly to be centered, though Sue, About, and de Kock received some comment.

The publication, in both the North and the South, of translations of *Les Misérables* distracted the American mind somewhat from civil war to sympathy with the poor in the person of Valjean. Contemporary estimates of the work ranged from the *Continental Monthly's* contemptuous "a mere sensation plot . . . a gross imitation of Eugene Sue," [31] to Charles

[26] *National Democratic Quarterly Review*, I, 133 (November 1859); *Presbyterian Quarterly Review*, VI, 656 (March 1858).

[27] *Putnam's Monthly*, VI, 655 (December 1855).

[28] *Ibid.*, VIII, 33 (January 1857). See also *Southern Monthly*, I, 75 (September 1861). The admiration of Alexander Smith in the latter is not representative.

[29] *International Magazine*, II, 453 (March 1851).

[30] *Putnam's Monthly*, VI, 660 (December 1855).

[31] *Continental Monthly*, II, 479 (October 1862). This referred to the third volume, "Marius."

Bohun's conclusion in *De Bow's* that "it is plainly stamped with the broad seal of genius." [32] The reception of the work in America was, on the whole, unfavorable; faults of bad reasoning, exaggeration, extravagance of style, confusion of materials, and lack of perspective were insisted upon. [33] The moral teaching was disapproved by E. P. Whipple in the *Atlantic*: "It will do infinitely more harm than good. The bigotries of virtue are better than the charities of vice." [34]

The death of Balzac in 1850 was the reason for the appearance of a few articles about the author of the *Comédie Humaine*. They were expository rather than critical. A writer in the *Democratic Review*, who called the subject of his sketch *Henri de Balzac*, said: "In England or America, he is far from being either generally read or appreciated. Few of his works have been translated." But this commentator thinks him "the greatest of novelists." [35] Motley had been far less cordial in the *North American* a few years before, refusing to recommend Balzac "for general circulation in this country." [36]

Dumas received some attention. His methods of composition furnished a subject for discussion; Winthrop Sargent called his works "literary impostures" in the *North American*.[37] John Esten Cooke named him "one of the most amusing writers of the present age" in the *Southern Literary Messenger*,[38] and Rufus Wilmot Griswold expressed the opinion in his *International Monthly* that "as a simple story writer," Dumas was "perhaps deserving of the highest place in the temple of letters." [39]

No French author, however, was more discussed than George Sand. Perhaps the best articles about her were a two-part essay in *Putnam's* by George Ripley [40] and a general review of

---

[32] *De Bow's Review*, After the War Series, II, 461 (November 1866).
[33] See Mrs. C. R. Corson's article on Hugo in the *New Englander*, XXIII, 477 (July 1864).
[34] *Atlantic Monthly*, X, 125 (July 1862).
[35] *Democratic Review*, XXXII, 325 (April 1853). See also *International Miscellany*, I, 316 (October 1, 1850).
[36] *North American Review*, LXV, 108 (July 1847).
[37] *Ibid.*, LXXVIII, 305–345 (April 1854).
[38] *Southern Literary Messenger*, XXVII, 303 (October 1858).
[39] *International Monthly*, IV, 125 (August 1851).
[40] *Putnam's Monthly*, IX, 175, 598 (February, June 1857).

her work and life in the *Atlantic Monthly* by Julia Ward Howe. "The hands might be sinful," admitted Mrs. Howe, "but the box they broke contained an exceeding precious ointment." [41]

This preoccupation with morals was characteristic of American comment on French literature. "Most of the French novels are liable to grave censures," thought the *National Democratic Quarterly*;[42] and the *Courant* declared: "French literature is immoral; literature is the 'expression of society,' hence, French society is immoral. Is not this the general idea that we have. in this country of French literature and French society? We think it is." [43] Henry Ward Beecher wrote in the *Independent*: "No man can read the reform literature of France, at least not such as Sue, and Sand, issue, and not regret to the day of his death that he ever touched it." [44]

GERMAN LITERATURE

Articles about German literature in American magazines mounted to a peak about 1850, but fell off soon thereafter; and during the latter two-thirds of our period German writers were given comparatively scant attention.[45] This decline of interest was probably partly in the nature of a reaction against the unbounded enthusiasm of the forties;[46] it was due also to a dearth of exciting German writers and to the disappearance of certain American magazines which had been especially interested in the Germans.

Goethe and Richter were the most prominent of the older German writers discussed in the American magazines of the fifties and sixties, and Heine of the "Young Germany." Lessing, Schiller, Rückert, Auerbach, and Ludwig got occasional attention. The *National Quarterly Review* published a series of careful and able articles on the German poets by its editor,

[41] *Atlantic Monthly*, VIII, 514 (November 1861). Howard Mumford Jones's "American Comment on George Sand, 1837–48," *American Literature*, III, 389 (January 1932), deals with the period immediately preceding the present study.
[42] *National Democratic Quarterly Review*, I, 153 (November 1859).
[43] *Courant*, I, 23 (May 19, 1859).
[44] *Independent*, February 16, 1854.
[45] Martin Henry Haertel, *German Literature in American Magazines* (Bulletin of the University of Wisconsin, No. 263; Philology and Literature Series, Vol. IV, No. 2, pp. 265–452. Madison, 1908).
[46] See Mott, *op. cit.*, pp. 401–403.

E. I. Sears, in the latter years of our period. During their short lives the *Dial*, *To-Day*, the *Criterion*, the *International Monthly*, and the *Continental Monthly* gave considerable space to the German writers; and the *Democratic Review* and the *Knickerbocker* continued their interest of past years in things Teutonic.

George Fitzhugh, writing in *De Bow's*, noted the sudden rise and the "equally sudden eclipse and decadence" of German literature and was well content with that waning because he thought that German writings were "made up, in great measure, of the horrible, the cruel, the impossible, the unnatural, and the supernatural." [47] Goethe continued to be the object of attacks on the ground of morality; one writer accused him of "undermining all that is honorable or holy among men." [48] Yet the *Southern Quarterly Review* praised *Wilhelm Meister's Apprenticeship and Travels*, the object of these strictures, very highly.[49]

The appearance of Leland's translation of Heine's *Pictures of Travel* in 1855 and the poet's death in the following year gave occasion for various articles about him. His skepticism and his errors of personal conduct were generally condemned,[50] but on the whole he fared well with the critics.

ESTIMATES OF AMERICAN WRITERS

There was rather more variation in the contemporary opinion of leading American writers as expressed in the magazines than in the accepted estimates of foreign authors, but in most cases a sentence or two may be culled from review or article to summarize more or less accurately the consensus of criticism.

Let us begin, then, with Irving, "the most favourite American author at home and abroad." [51] His life of Washington, published 1855–59, won almost universal praise.

---

[47] *De Bow's Review*, XXIX, 288 (September 1860).
[48] *Southern Literary Messenger*, XVII, 443 (July 1851).
[49] *Southern Quarterly Review*, XX, 248 (July 1851).
[50] See W. W. Hurlbut's article in the *North American Review*, LXIX, 216–249 (July 1849), and another in *Putnam's Monthly*, VIII, 517–526 (November 1856). The latter severely condemns Heine's character.
[51] *Southern Quarterly Review*, Third Series, I, 36 (April 1856).

Of Cooper, the *International Monthly* said in 1851:

> As a novelist, take him all in all, he is entitled to precedence of every other now living. . . . The great critics assign him a place among the foremost of the illustrious authors of the age.

Balzac's praise in the *Revue de Paris* is adduced and awkwardly translated: "Who is there writing English among our contemporaries, if not of him, of whom it can be said that he is a genius of the first order?" Cooper's death a few months after the appearance of this article brought out some appreciative criticism of his work: quarrels and litigation were then forgotten.[52]

Bryant was commonly considered the first of American poets. Griswold in his *International* called him "the greatest living poet who writes the English language"[53] in 1851; a writer in the *New York Quarterly* said "he rears his head preëminently over all competitors as the Bard of America";[54] and the *Southern Literary Messenger* nominated him for "president of the literary republic."[55]   Poe, his career ended, was still a subject for controversy. Griswold reprinted his venomous attack on the unfortunate poet's memory in the *International* for October 1850. Halleck's position was high and assured. One critic names Halleck, Bryant, and Poe as the supreme *artists* in American poetry.[56] Bayard Taylor was highly esteemed by some critics — "the finest of our poetical rhetoricians," wrote Griswold.[57] Nathaniel Parker Willis had clearly declined in popular esteem: perhaps what *Vanity Fair* called "his numerous and ingenious achievements in the elegant art of concealed puffery"[58] had something to do with the waning of his vogue.

Turning to New England, we find Emerson's reputation steadily growing.[59] "At last he has come out from the misty

---

[52] See *International Monthly*, III, 1 (April 1851) for quotation; also IV, 453 (November 1851); *North American Review* (Parkman), LXXIV, 147 (January 1852).

[53] *International Monthly*, IV, 388 (December 1851).

[54] *New York Quarterly*, III, 558 (January 1855).

[55] *Southern Literary Messenger*, XV, 44 (January 1849).

[56] *International Monthly*, III, 434 (July 1851).

[57] *Ibid.*, I, 485 (November 1850).

[58] *Vanity Fair*, I, 203 (March 4, 1860).

[59] See Nevius Ove Halvorson, "Growth of Emerson's Reputation up to the Time of His Death in 1882" (University of Iowa thesis, 1925), Chapters XII, XIII, and XIV.

twilight of Transcendentalism into the clear light of common sense," observed Delia M. Colton in the *Continental Monthly*.[60] Each of the three books Emerson published during this period was shown increasing favor by the critics; yet there was a constant undercurrent of objection from conservatives in theology and social theory.[61] Emerson's friend Thoreau seems to have been regarded as an interesting oddity by most reviewers. A *Knickerbocker* writer discussed *Walden* under the caption "Town and Rural Humbugs" and, though he praised the book, classed Thoreau with Barnum.[62] After the death of Thoreau, Emerson did justice to his memory in an admirable essay in the *Atlantic*; but Lowell, who had been kind to him in the *Massachusetts Quarterly* during his lifetime, was more severe in the *North American* after his death.[63]

Hawthorne was called "the greatest living American writer born in the present century" by the *International* in 1850.[64] That left Irving and Cooper out of the comparison. It was in 1850 that *The Scarlet Letter* was published; and the *International*, which is always quotable because of its assured, if dogmatic, generalizations, declared that "*The Scarlet Letter* will challenge consideration in the name of Art, in the best audience which in any age receives Cervantes, Le Sage, or Scott." [65]

Longfellow did not fare as well as might have been expected in the fifties and sixties. A reviewer in the *Southern Literary Messenger* wrote that "He has been over-praised by his co-workers and his disciples. He has been as much underrated by unfriendly critics," [66] and we are told that the poet was so much offended by this criticism that he asked to have the complimentary copy of the magazine which was being sent to him dis-

[60] *Continental Monthly*, I, 61 (January 1862).
[61] See Noah Porter's review of *Conduct of Life* in the *New Englander*, XIX, 496–508 (April 1861); also *Plantation*, I, 13 (March 1860).
[62] *Knickerbocker*, XLV, 236 (March 1855).
[63] Emerson's essay was in the *Atlantic Monthly*, X, 239 (August 1862). Lowell's articles are found in the *Massachusetts Quarterly Review*, III, 40 (December 1849); *North American Review*, CI, 597 (October 1865). Lowell was yet more severe in the essay in *My Study Windows* (1871).
[64] *International Miscellany*, II, 22 (December 1850).
[65] *Ibid.*, III, 158 (May 1851).
[66] *Southern Literary Messenger*, XV, 43 (January 1849).

continued.[67] Later another writer in the same magazine made amends, however, by asserting that "It cannot be denied that Henry W. Longfellow is the first of our living American poets." [68] *Hiawatha* appeared in 1855 and brought no little adverse criticism upon the devoted head of the author; the old charge of imitativeness was given a new lease of life in the *Criterion* and other periodicals.[69]

Lowell's activity just before 1850 had brought him strikingly before the public. After the *Biglow Papers* in 1848, "he leaped at once into the high tide of popularity," said one reviewer; but the novel elements in his work made most critics cautious.[70] Whittier, like Lowell, was condemned for lending his art to propaganda (term yet in the womb of *Muttersprache*); yet *Putnam's* asserted that his "place is as determined and distinctive as that of any of our acknowledged poets. . . . Many of his abolition poems are superb specimens of poetic indignation." [71]

Holmes was well liked. Francis Bowen in his *North American* called him "our old favorite . . . everybody's favorite," [72] and *Vanity Fair* declared, "If we were not *Vanity Fair* we would wish to be Dr. Holmes. From the earliest period of adolescence, his songs have been our delight." [73]

Whitman's *Leaves of Grass* was published in 1855. It was not widely reviewed in the magazines.[74] The practice of anonymity made it possible for the *Democratic Review* to print Whitman's own able apologia as a review of the volume,[75] and Edward Everett Hale wrote a singularly understanding notice of it for the *North American Review*.[76] The *Criterion*, on the

[67] B. B. Minor, *The Southern Literary Messenger* (New York, 1905), p. 166.
[68] *Southern Literary Messenger*, XXIII, 388 (November 1856).
[69] *Criterion*, I, 53 (November 24, 1855).
[70] *Continental Monthly*, I, 179 (February 1862).
[71] *Putnam's Monthly*, VIII, 26 (July 1856).
[72] *North American Review*, LXVIII, 201 (January 1849).
[73] *Vanity Fair*, IV, 256 (December 7, 1861).
[74] See Marion Reta Speaks, "Contemporary American Criticism of Walt Whitman, 1855–92" (University of Iowa thesis, 1926). It may be noted that Whitman himself had a journal, 1851–52, but it was primarily a newspaper. It was called the *Freeman* and was published in Brooklyn.
[75] *Democratic Review*, XXXVI, 205 (September 1855).
[76] *North American Review*, LXXXII, 275 (January 1856).

other hand, which would not have reviewed it at all had not
Emerson "unworthily recommended it," declared that "it is impossible to imagine how any man's fancy could have conceived
such a mass of stupid filth unless he were possessed of the soul
of a sentimental donkey that had died of disappointed love,"
and then decided to leave the matter to the officers of the law.[77]
A far better review appeared in *Putnam's*: faults are pointed
out sharply, and the poem is called "a mixture of Yankee
transcendentalism and New York rowdyism"; but the critic
acknowledges "an original conception of nature, a manly brawn,
and an epic directness" in the poem.[78] The *Southern Literary
Messenger* blames "the pantheism of Theodore Parker and
Ralph Waldo Emerson," which, it says, "pervades and pollutes
the entire literature of the North," for this "spasmodic idiocy
of Walt Whitman." [79]

Herman Melville, whose *Moby Dick* was published in 1851,
was treated kindly but firmly by the critics. He was told that
"*Typee* and *Omoo* were remarkable for freshness and a certain
artistic keeping," [80] though it was not right to abuse the mis-
sionaries as he had done in the latter; but *Moby Dick*
strained the patience of readers, and *Pierre* quite exhausted
it. "He totters on the edge of a precipice, over which all his
hard-earned fame may tumble," wrote Fitz-James O'Brien in
Putnam's.[81]

Laudatory articles about William Gilmore Simms were not
uncommon in the southern magazines. J. Q. Moore in *De
Bow's* attested the "reverence, esteem and admiration" for both
the character and the literary works of the dean of southern
literature. The republication of his Revolutionary romances,
which had "made his great reputation twenty years ago," was
the occasion for a survey of his work in the *Southern Literary
Messenger*; the author is called "one of our most worthy citi-

[77] *Criterion*, I, 24 (November 10, 1855).
[78] *Putnam's Monthly*, VI, 321 (September 1855).
[79] *Southern Literary Messenger*, XXI, 74 (July 1860).
[80] *International Miscellany*, I, 472 (November 1850).
[81] *Putnam's Monthly*, I, 164 (February 1853). See O. W. Riegel, "The Anatomy of Melville's Fame," *American Literature*, III, 195 (May 1931); and William Braswell, "A Note on 'The Anatomy of Melville's Fame,'" *ibid.*, V, 360
(January 1934).

zens and distinguished ornaments" of the South. The leading article in the *International Magazine*, of New York, for April 1, 1852, is a highly commendatory essay on Simms.[82]

H. H. Brownell, author of *Lyrics of a Day*, was hailed by the *North American Review* as the rival of the greatest war poets in literature: "His 'River-Fight' is the finest lyric of the kind since Drayton's 'Battle of Agincourt.' " [83] Holmes declared in the *Atlantic*: "*The Lyrics of a Day* are too modestly named. Our literature cannot forget the masterpieces in this little volume in a day, a year, or an age." [84] And yet it took only a decade to prove that Brownell had used a truer judgment in selecting his title than his critic had displayed in reviewing the volume.

Women were active in authorship in the fifties. "A most alarming avalanche of female authors has been pouring in upon us for the past three months," declared *Putnam's* in the summer of 1854. "The success of Uncle Tom and Fanny Fern has been the cause, doubtless." [85] Enough has been said in other places of the successes of Mrs. Stowe and Fanny Fern,[86] but some other "female authors" should be mentioned here. The *International Miscellany* declared that the poems of Alice Cary would "live among the contributions which this age offers to the permanent literary creation. Her younger sister, Phoebe Carey,[87] is also a woman of genius." [88] But *Putnam's*, which had praised the Cary sisters in its early numbers, later reproved them for "haste and carelessness" and found their verses "unreal, imitative . . . a sweet and cloying echo of an old song." [89] Mrs. Sigourney's reputation remained high with the average reader of verse. She died in 1865. Her poems, asserted the *Western Literary Messenger*,

---

[82] *De Bow's Review*, XXIX, 702 (December 1860); *Southern Literary Messenger*, XXVIII, 355 (May 1859); *International Magazine*, V, 432 (April 1, 1852), signed "P." — perhaps Philip C. Pendleton.

[83] *North American Review*, XCIX, 321 (July 1864).

[84] *Atlantic Monthly*, XV, 591 (May 1865).

[85] *Putnam's Monthly*, IV, 110 (July 1854).

[86] See pp. 142–144 and 23.

[87] The sisters spelled their name with an *e* in the early years of their authorship.

[88] *International Weekly Miscellany*, I, 14 (July 1, 1850).

[89] *Putnam's Monthly*, V, 328 (March 1855); VI, 48 (July 1855).

are laid on a million of memory's shelves. Children in our infant schools lisp her mellow canzonets; older youths recite her poems for riper minds in our grammar schools and academies; mothers pore over her pages of prose for counsel, and the aged of either sex draw consolation from the inspirations of her sanctified muse in their declining years.[90]

Maria G. Brooks, who had died shortly before the beginning of our period, was "admitted by masters of the literary art to have been the greatest poet of her sex who ever wrote in any language or in any age" — so we are told by a dealer in hyperboles in the *International Monthly*.[91]

MAGAZINE CRITICISM OF POPULAR NOVELS

Though *The Scarlet Letter* and *Moby Dick* belong to the fifties, the best sellers of that decade were chiefly by women: Susan Warner's *The Wide, Wide World* (1850), Mrs. Stowe's *Uncle Tom's Cabin* (1852), Mrs. E. D. E. N. Southworth's *The Curse of Clifton* (1853), Mary Jane Holmes's *Tempest and Sunshine* (1854), Maria S. Cummins' *The Lamplighter* (1856), Mrs. Maria J. McIntosh's *Violet* (1856), and Augusta Jane Evans' *Beulah* (1859). Forty thousand copies of *The Lamplighter* were sold in its first eight weeks.[92] Of Miss Warner's books, *Queechy* and *The Wide, Wide World*, Mrs. Kirkland wrote in the *North American*: "We know not where, in any language, we shall find their graphic truth excelled."[93] *Beulah* was "the welcome companion of every fireside."[94] It is not without reason that one of the historians of American literature speaks of "the feminine fifties."[95]

A few best sellers, however, were written by men — Donald G. Mitchell's *Reveries of a Bachelor*, T. S. Arthur's *Ten Nights in a Bar Room*, and Richard B. Kimball's *St. Leger*. In the early sixties came Edmund Kirke's *Among the Pines* and Edward S. Ellis' *Seth Jones*. The latter was perhaps the most

---

[90] *Western Literary Messenger*, XIV, 190 (June 1850).
[91] *International Monthly*, IV, 275 (September 1851).
[92] *Frederick Douglass' Paper*, May 26, 1854 (advertisement of John P. Jewett & Company, publishers).
[93] *North American Review*, LXXVI, 115 (January 1853).
[94] *Southern Literary Messenger*, XXXI, 241 (October 1860).
[95] F. L. Pattee, *The New American Literature* (New York, 1931), p. 381.

popular of the dime novels. But the women wrote dime novels, too; Mrs. Victor, Mrs. Stephens, and Mrs. Denison had best sellers in the Beadle lists.

Novels had become immensely popular. Most of the general magazines depended much upon serial fiction. The Harper periodicals, the eclectics, and the literary weeklies drew largely upon the British and French novelists. The *Atlantic*, the *Continental, Putnam's, Russell's*, and the *Southern Literary Messenger* relied upon the home product. Even the religious periodicals sometimes used serial stories; and a hot debate in all the panoply of theological polemics was waged in the *Protestant Episcopal Quarterly* over the question of the righteousness of the religious novel, one side arguing that "fiction is an agency that should not be given up exclusively to the use of the evil one;" and the other claiming that the religious novel is in itself "producing a very great evil." [96] *Putnam's*, in its later numbers, came to mistrust novel reading, which, "if systematically indulged in, and especially by girls," it thought might "result in the acquirement of those 'romantic notions' and 'false views of life' so much deprecated by the parents and guardians of youth." [97]

But the flood of novels swept on. "The time is now at hand," claimed a satirist in the *Southern Literary Messenger*, "when no gentleman or lady will be guilty of never having written a novel." [98] William Swinton, the journalist, wrote as follows in *Putnam's*:

Do you wish to instruct, to convince, to please? Write a novel! Have you a system of religion or politics or manners or social life to inculcate? Write a novel! Would you have the "world" split its sides with laughter, or set all the damsels in the land abreaking their hearts? Write a novel! Would you lay bare the secret workings of your heart, or have you a friend to whom you would render that office? Write a novel! . . . Do you wish to create a sensation? Why, write a novel! And lastly, not least, but loftiest, would you make money? Then, in Pluto's and Mammon's names! write a novel! [99]

[96] *Protestant Episcopal Quarterly Review*, III, 108 (January 1856); III, 538 (July 1856); V, 477 (October 1858).
[97] *Putnam's Monthly*, X, 90 (July 1857); X, 384 (September 1857).
[98] *Southern Literary Messenger*, XXVIII, 441 (June 1859).
[99] *Putnam's Monthly*, IV, 396 (October 1854).

SHORTER FICTION

Although the short story was as yet recognized by few as a distinctive literary type, it must be mentioned here because of the increasing dependence of magazines upon it.

The great stream of short fiction continued to be of the sentimental *Godey* type. Poe was dead, and Hawthorne had turned to the longer forms after 1851; neither seemed to have made much impress upon the American short story. There was a racy, genuine note in certain anecdote-stories that were coming out of the West and Southwest, as in those which the *Spirit of the Times* published from the pen of Thomas B. Thorpe, but most magazines would have recoiled in dismay from such rudeness.

The *Atlantic Monthly*, however, went counter to the general honeyed stickiness with its very first numbers. It published many of Rose Terry's forthright stories of New England life; it published Rebecca Harding Davis' grimly realistic "Life in the Iron Mills." It enlisted Fitz-James O'Brien, Caroline Chesebrough, Harriett Prescott, and Edward Everett Hale. In short, it printed better stories than any other magazine in the country, and it relied upon them rather than on English serials. Its editor had written to his friend Briggs in 1853, "I do abhor sentimentality from the depth of my soul";[100] and the stories he and his successor Fields selected for the magazine were, for the most part, of a realistic trend. To take one representative example, Miss E. P. Appleton's "A Half-Life and Half a Life," in the number for February 1864, is a convincing and memorable picture of pioneer life on the Kentucky border. The characters are relentlessly described, the scenes of the story are as effectively real as they are simple, and even the narrator herself confesses to her plainness.

Melville, Simms, Curtis, Mitchell, Ludlow, and Trowbridge were among the short story writers of the times, and O'Brien was much admired; but most of the best as well as the worst work was done by women. "America is now wholly given over to a damned mob of scribbling women," wrote Hawthorne to Ticknor [101] — and the mob all wrote short stories.

[100] C. E. Norton, ed., *Letters of James Russell Lowell* (New York, 1894), I, 205.

[101] Caroline Ticknor, *Hawthorne and His Publisher* (Boston, 1913), p. 141.

THE MAGAZINES AND POETRY

If the feminine note was conspicuous in fiction, it was even more so in poetry. There "the Lilies and the Lizzies — the sighing swains and rhyming milkmaids" [102] were busiest. "The poets all used to chime in with 'The Lay of the Last Minstrel,' " observed the *Democratic Review*; "then they caroled nothing but love ditties like Moore, then imitated Byron; and now they whimper like Tennyson." [103] The banality of contemporary poetry worried the critics continually. "Dear Aunts, do put a little more metal in your poetry!" begged the *Southern Literary Messenger* of those poetesses of uncertain age who were responsible for much of the magazine verse:

> When you write poetry, make an effort to *say* something. If you have nothing to say, do not *write* "Poetry." No: knit stockings — knit stockings in all such cases. You must not be satisfied with inditing mere words of liquid sounds, or fashionable gracefulness of sentences. You must talk of *things*.[104]

Aldrich's lachrymose masterpiece in infant-obituary verse, "Babie Bell," was a great popular success in 1856. It was reprinted in thousands of periodicals and newspapers.[105] "You have come in good time, Walt Whitman!" aptly exclaimed Whitman himself in a review of his own work.[106]

In the better magazines the war served to put some iron into current verse, though the popular war songs were oozy with sentiment. "Sing of the war and the times, O poets!" beseeched the editor of the *Knickerbocker* in 1861, "and spare us for a brief season those sweet Lines to —— and Stanzas to the Moon." [107] The best offering of war poetry is to be found in the pages of the *Atlantic*, where Mrs. Howe's "Battle Hymn of

[102] *Sartain's Monthly*, VI, 99 (January 1850).
[103] *Democratic Review*, XXXII, 528 (June 1853).
[104] *Southern Literary Messenger*, XIX, 660 (November 1853).
[105] See Ferris Greenslet, *The Life of Thomas Bailey Aldrich* (Boston, 1908), pp. 26–28. Evidence that the better magazines were conducted on a plane somewhat superior to the popular taste is afforded by Aldrich's statement that this poem was "declined by all the leading magazines in the country" before its publication in a newspaper (p. 28).
[106] *Democratic Review*, XXXVI, 212 (September 1855).
[107] *Knickerbocker*, LVIII, 470 (November 1861).

WHAT THE WELL DRESSED GENTLEMAN WORE IN 1855

From *Frank Leslie's Gazette of Fashions*, December 1855. Following are the descriptions, left to right:

Walking Suit. — Unbuttoned surtout, exhibiting underneath the front of a frock coat closely buttoned. Pants of plain cassimere.

Youth's Walking Costume. — The coat is straight sack with flowing sleeves; pants of small-check cassimere and boots of glazed leather.

Walking Suit. — Very popular among our fashionables. Frock coat fitting the figure neatly. Vest of fine-figured plush cut double-breasted. Pants of green cassimere in large plaids.

Walking Suit. — Sleeve talma, cut single-breasted, with fly in front. The material is usually brown Duffal beaver-cloth, which makes a graceful, stylish garment. The pants are of heavy check cassimere.

the Republic," Emerson's "Voluntaries," Whittier's "Barbara
Frietchie," Holmes's "Brother Jonathan to Sister Caroline,"
Longfellow's "Killed at the Ford," and Lowell's second series
of "Biglow Papers" and "Commemoration Ode" were all published. The *Independent* was already gaining a reputation for
good poetry, and such abolition papers as the *Anti-Slavery
Standard* and the *National Era* published some excellent verse.

HISTORY, BIOGRAPHY, AND TRAVEL

The fifties were a great decade in historical writing. Bancroft, Prescott, Motley, and Hildreth were in full tide of production. "The American seems to have a peculiar genius in one
department of art and one of literature," observed a *Putnam*
critic. "He is a good sculptor and a good historian." [108] Apparently there was a popular demand for history, and when
Macaulay's great work appeared, 200,000 volumes of it were
sold in the United States in a few months.[109] Reviews gave hundreds of pages to discussion of contemporary historical works.

The first successful historical journal of general scope was
the *Historical Magazine*,[110] founded in Boston in 1857 by C. B.
Richardson. It was moved to New York the next year, J. D. G.
Shea soon becoming its editor. It was a monthly offshoot of the
New England Historical and Genealogical Register,[111] the out-

[108] *Putnam's Monthly*, IX, 549 (May 1857).
[109] *Harper's Weekly*, III, 803 (December 17, 1859).
[110] *The Historical Magazine, and Notes and Queries Concerning the Antiqui-
ties, History and Biography of America*. Publication was suspended September–
December 1871; April 1872–March 1873; April 1874–March 1875. Extra numbers March and December 1874, and January, March, and May 1875. Shea
became publisher in 1864, and Henry B. Dawson (Morrisania, New York) in
1866. Editors: John W. Dean, 1857; George Folsom, 1858; J. D. G. Shea,
1859–65; Henry R. Stiles, 1866; Henry B. Dawson, 1866–75. The last number
was for June 1875 (3d series, Vol. III, Extra Number V). Among contributors
were Bancroft, Sparks, Force, Lossing, Schoolcraft, and Simms. The file contains a large amount of historical, biographical, and archaeological material not
elsewhere available.
[111] *The New-England Historical and Genealogical Register and Antiquarian
Journal*. The latter part of the title was used on the cover from the beginning
and on title pages 1869–73. Published quarterly in Boston from January 1847
"under the patronage of the New-England Historic-Genealogical Society."
There was a committee of guarantors until the fall of 1874, when financial
responsibility was assumed by the Society. Editors: William Cogswell, 1847;
Samuel G. Drake (with, for short periods, William T. Harris, N. B. Shurtleff,

standing periodical of its class, which flourished throughout
these years under the care of the antiquarian Samuel G. Drake.
There were eight or ten local and state historical journals in
addition to these of wider scope.[112]

Biography was also popular. The success of *Harper's
Monthly* was owing in some measure to the long serial life of
Napoleon by John S. C. Abbott, and biography was staple in
other periodicals. The *Portrait Monthly* (1863–64) relied
chiefly on woodcuts of Civil War generals accompanied by
biographical sketches. Irving, Simms, Parton were busy biographers; and many other writers dipped into this field from
time to time. In an article on "The Biographical Mania" in the
Saturday Evening Gazette in 1857, we are plausibly assured
that "the partiality of the reading community for biographies
has been greatly increasing." [113]

"Not many years ago a man could acquire quite a reputation
by crossing the Atlantic," observed a writer in *Gleason's Pictorial* in 1853; but "it does not set a man up very high to travel

Joseph B. Felt, T. Farrar, and W. B. Trask), 1848–61; John W. Dean (with
Trask, Elias Nason, and Charles Hudson for various numbers), 1862–64; William B. Trask, 1864–65; Elias Nason, 1866–67; Albert H. Hoyt, 1868–75; John
W. Dean, 1876–1901; Henry E. Woods, 1901–07; Francis A. Foster, 1908–12;
Henry E. Scott, 1913–current. Drake, the founder of the journal, was first
secretary and then president of the Society. He was a bookseller and "had no
superior in this country as an antiquary." The *Register* was designed to publish
(see Preface to Vol. I) biographies of persons who came to New England before
1700, genealogical tables, statistical and biographical accounts of officials, ancient
documents and lists of names, descriptions of costumes, dwellings and utensils
of the past, cemetery inscriptions, heraldic devices, and portraits. There are also
records from family Bibles, interleaved almanacs, and private journals; old ballads, book reviews, etc. The indexes are elaborate (see Library of Congress
cards). William Cullen Bryant wrote that the *Register*, "in a country like ours,
where all of us are peers of the realm, is, for the New-England states, the Book
of the Peerage." (Cover, July 1873.) For a brief history of this journal see
XXX, 184 (April 1876).

[112] For a list compiled by Augustus H. Shearer, see *Annual Report of the
American Historical Association for the Year 1916* (Washington, 1919), I, 477.
Of these, the journals of longest life were *Annals of Iowa*, begun in 1863 as
*Annals of the State Historical Society of Iowa; Essex Institute Historical Collec-
tions*, begun in 1859 at Salem; and *New Jersey Historical Society Proceedings*,
begun in 1845 at Newark. All three are quarterlies and still current. The *Firelands Pioneer* was published 1858–78 by the Firelands Historical Society at Norwalk, Ohio; it was revived in 1882 at Sandusky. *Cist's Advertiser* published
much historical matter; see p. 114, footnote.

[113] *Saturday Evening Gazette*, July 4, 1857, p. 4.

nowadays: everybody travels." [114] And nearly everybody wrote about what he had seen after he got home. There was scarcely a periodical which did not print travel sketches, review travel books, and describe foreign and domestic journeys. The pictorials had an advantage in this kind, for they could make their travel articles doubly attractive.

THE WAR OF THE DICTIONARIES

Another interesting phase of the bookishness of the sixties was the current discussion of the merits of two rival dictionaries. Some years before, the *Southern Literary Messenger* had adverted to the "increased attention" given to "the philosophy of language," which it ascribed to the recent work of Archbishop Trench and named as "one of the most marked of the literary aspects of the times." [115] This was chiefly a scholarly interest; but upon the appearance of the quarto edition of *Worcester's Dictionary* in 1860, there set in a rivalry between Webster and Worcester in which nearly every literate person took sides. "The schoolmen have been much exercised of late by the dictionary war," observed *Vanity Fair.* " 'A Webster! A Webster!' and 'Worcester to the rescue!' have been the battle cries heard above the cannon of Napoleon III." [116] The *Old Guard* took the side of Worcester, violently, as was its character, and referred to *Webster's Dictionary* as "that immense monument of ignorance, folly and fraud!" [117] But the *Knickerbocker* refused to become excited over the matter: "Worcester or Webster? Well, they are both stirring books; and if t'other dear charmer were away we could be perfectly happy with either." [118]

HUMOR

Many periodicals had their humorous departments — some modeled upon Clark's "Table Talk" in the *Knickerbocker*, some imitating the "Editor's Drawer" in *Harper's*, and some mere

[114] *Gleason's Pictorial Drawing-Room Companion*, IV, 333 (May 21, 1853). See also *New-York Quarterly*, II, 318 (July 1853) to the same effect.
[115] *Southern Literary Messenger*, XXI, 24 (April 1855).
[116] *Vanity Fair*, I, 210 (March 24, 1860).
[117] *Old Guard*, VII, 876 (November 1869).
[118] *Knickerbocker*, LX, 185 (August 1862).

"Joke Corners." Many of the weeklies helped themselves to comic stories which went the rounds of the newspaper press; such tales were in demand. The *Home Journal* advertised in 1859 "fresh, spicy, amusing, original comic stories, which smack and relish of the wit, humor, raciness, brilliancy, and sparkle of the times." The *Spirit of the Times* was famous for its humorous sketches.

A perusal of these departments and of the contemporary comic periodicals shows that the humor of the mid-century was of two chief kinds: (1) the frontier humor, and (2) the urban humor.

The first class frequently had a fresh raciness which gave it a value that the other more conventional kind did not possess. Frontier humor depended upon exaggeration, incongruity, and dialect for much of its effect. Mark Twain's very first efforts occur in our period; John Phoenix died in 1861; Artemus Ward, Petroleum V. Nasby, and Bill Arp were at their best in the sixties. These writers commonly used all three of the elements mentioned — sometimes all together. Their wit was often rough, and their incongruities were frequently the result of a crude treatment of sacred matters; but their buffoonery often had real point, and they were sworn enemies of sham.

The second class — that of urban comedy — habitually used more worn materials. It is not difficult to list the standard jokes:

The fish story joke	The boarding-house (or hash)
The bedbug joke	joke
The English fop (later dude) joke	The wedding night joke
The drunkard's return joke	The old maid joke
a. The lamp post joke	The bashful suitor joke
b. The keyhole joke	The boy-under-the-sofa joke
The unwelcome suitor (or kick-in-the-pants) joke	The beaten scholar joke
The sleeping policeman joke	The newly rich joke
The roof cat joke	The dog-and-tramp joke
The black eye joke	The love letter joke
The watered milk joke	The crinoline joke
	The peddler joke

The Biddy joke

A few of these last have vanished from the later comics, but most of them bloom perennially. Scholars are no longer beaten; crinoline has passed, giving place to fashions just as useful to paragraphers; peddlers are less frequent, perhaps. The Biddy joke, which was derived from the stupidity of Irish emigrant girls employed as house servants, now masquerades as the new-maid joke. *Momus* had a series of articles on comic types in 1860 — Bridget, the cockney, the boarding-house widow, and so on.

As a variant to any of the above forms, cacography might be used: it was frequent in our period. And parodies and bur-lesques were common. "The two poems that have been most parodied in this country," said the *International* in 1851, have been "Woodman, Spare That Tree" and "The Raven." [119]

Of the two-score comic periodicals begun during the period under consideration, only six outlived a second year. The best of the lot — *Diogenes hys Lanterne* and *Vanity Fair* — sur-vived for eighteen months and three and a half years, respec-tively.

Only one of the six had lived over from the preceding period — the *New York Picayune* (1847–60). It had been founded by Dr. Richard B. Hutchings and Joseph Woodward in order to advertise Hutchings' Dyspepsia Bitters, and the jokes which had been inserted to carry the advertising proved more success-ful in curing dyspepsia than the bitters. So medicine yielded to comedy, the paper was enlarged, and that brilliant and eccentric journalist, Joseph A. Scoville, was employed as editor. But Scoville quarreled with the proprietors in 1852; and W. H. Levison, John Harrington, and John D. Vose became joint editors for a few years. After that, Frank Bellew, the artist, and Mortimer Thomson, the humorist, did the editorial work. Hutchings was ousted from the management in 1853, and Woodward, Levison, and Robert Gun were successive propri-etors. There was much satire on local fads and types. Levi-son's burlesque Negro sermons by "Professor Julius Caesar Hannibal" became famous, and "The Diary of a Broadway Dandy" was a successful serial in the paper's first year. The

[119] *International Monthly*, IV, 24 (August 1851).

woodcuts were few, but prominently displayed; the price was fifty cents a year.[120]

Figaro! or Corbyn's Chronicle of Amusements (1850–51), though primarily a journal of the New York theater, must be placed among the comics because of the wit of its editor, Wardell Corbyn, and some of his contributors. Corbyn was soon joined in the editorship by J. W. S. Hows, dramatic critic of the *Albion* and a competent writer. A feature of *Figaro!* was its Lind-madness, for its five months of existence fell within the time of the visit of the Swedish Nightingale to America.

Of longer life was the New York *Reveille* (1851–54), a small folio with woodcuts, founded by two Englishmen, Charles and Barton, and later edited by Cornelius Matthews, of "Puffer Hopkins" fame. T. B. Gunn, formerly of the *Picayune*, did some of its later pictures.

The *Carpet-Bag* (1851–53), of Boston, described itself as "a literary journal published weekly for the amusement of its readers." Its editors were S. W. Wilder and Benjamin Penhallow Shillaber, the latter famous as the creator of Mrs. Partington and her interesting family; John T. Trowbridge was an assistant at one time, and Charles G. Halpine came to it from Barnum, whose secretary he had been for a few months. To the *Carpet-Bag* shop came also Charles F. Brown, who had not then acquired the final *e* on his name or thought of signing himself "Artemus Ward," and got a job as a typesetter. He was "a sandy-haired, thin-featured youth [of seventeen], with a long nose and a pale complexion." [121] Putting the work of Shillaber, Trowbridge, Halpine, "John Phoenix," "M. Quad," and John G. Saxe into type, the boy was inspired to do some things of his own, which, Franklin-like, he got into the hands of the editor without disclosing his authorship of them; and he

---

[120] Hutchings sold his business to Woodward & Company after a few years, and when Woodward had to leave town because of domestic troubles, Levison and Thaddeus Glover became owners. Upon the death of Levison, Jesse Haney, who had been an assistant editor, conducted the paper for the widow until it was sold to Thomson. It was a small folio at first, but Thomson made it a quarto, in conformity to the comic paper tradition. See T. B. Connery, "American Comic Journalism," *Once a Week*, XV, 10 (June 6, 1895).

[121] John T. Trowbridge, *My Own Story* (Boston, 1903), p. 181.

was delighted to see them appear in print over the pen name "Lieutenant Chubb." The first known contribution of the sixteen-year-old Sam Clemens appeared in the *Carpet-Bag* May 1, 1852. Well printed on eight small folio pages, and sparsely illustrated by woodcuts, the paper sold for $2.00 a year. At the outset the *Carpet-Bag* had not tried "to be exclusively funny," but, as its sub-title indicated, to be a light miscellany. The contributors it attracted, however, were funny men; their laughter was contagious, and they soon had the whole paper chuckling. "Our correspondents — jolly fellows — have had it their own way," said an editorial in the first number of the second volume.[122] Its satire, with a few exceptions, was mild, and its comedy was not so crude as that of many of its compeers.[123]

Diogenes hys Lanterne (1852–53) was a New York weekly edited by John Brougham, the comic actor. George G. Foster and Thomas Dunn English, who had been editors of the older *John Donkey*, were leading contributors. It was an offshoot of the New York *Picayune*, and Dr. Hutchings is said to have been the founder.[124] Frank Bellew, Thomas Butler Gunn, and George Woodward, all of the *Picayune* staff, became connected with the *Lantern*, as it was called on the cover, the first two as artists and the last as publisher. There was an unbacked cartoon, usually political and often clever, in each number. Thomas Powell, an Englishman who was said to have been the model, or one of the models, for Mr. Micawber, joined Brougham as editor in the fall of 1852. Fitz-James O'Brien and Charles Seymour were among the writers enlisted. With all this talent the paper should have succeeded; but Diogenes, as of old, was unpopular, and the paper perished after eighteen months. A story used to be told to the effect that soon after the

---

[122] *Carpet-Bag*, March 27, 1852.

[123] George K. Snow and Silas W. Wilder were the original publishers. They were also publishers of the *Boston Pathfinder* and the *Pathfinder Railway Guide*. When their partnership was dissolved in September 1851, Wilder, Shillaber, and S. T. Pickard became editors and proprietors of the *Carpet-Bag*. They were joined by Silas D. Hancock in April 1852, and two months later Halpine bought Pickard's quarter-interest. There were two annual volumes — March 29, 1851–March 26, 1853. See Franklin J. Meine's excellent sketch of this paper in the *Collector's Journal*, II, 411 (October–December 1933).

[124] See Scoville's comment in *Pick*, February 5, 1853, p. 4.

Lantern was started Brougham and a companion were dining at a café when William E. Burton, a fellow actor who had once had a magazine of his own, entered and seated himself at their table. The friend asked Burton if he ever read the new comic and received the emphatic reply: "Never, except when I am drunk!" Brougham then rose and bowed, and replied, "Then thank God, we are always sure of one faithful reader!" But whatever Burton's opinion, the *Lantern* was a high-grade comic as long as its oil held out. "It was the best comic paper ever published in America," declared one authority.[125]

Another humorous sheet begun in New York in 1852 was *Young Sam*, edited through twelve weekly numbers by Thomas Powell, who later went to the *Lantern*. Henry C. Watson, the music critic, and George Arnold, the poet, were contributors; and Charles Rosenberg was the chief illustrator.

T. W. Strong also entered the field in 1852, with *Yankee Notions*, a paper which lived past the end of our period.[126] It was cheaply printed, and its wit was usually cheap also. It was copiously illustrated with rather crude woodcuts. The picture of an Irish servant displaying to the young man of the house a big turtle which he had hidden in her bed, with the declaration that she had at last caught the bug which had been disturbing her slumbers, may have produced uproarious laughter in the good old days. In 1853 Strong began a comic of somewhat higher grade called *Young America*, under the editor-

[125] L. W. Kingman in the *American Bibliopolist*, VII, 264 (December 1875). See also T. B. Connery in *Once a Week*, XV, 11 (May 2, 1895); and William Murrell, *History of American Graphic Humor* (New York, 1933), pp. 181–182.

[126] Ended in 1875. Strong was an engraver, and many woodcuts were used — sometimes as many as a hundred a month. John McLenan, Frank Bellew, and J. H. Howard were three of the artists employed. Strong claimed to have paid $20,000 to artists and engravers in the first year (see I, 380, December 1852). But the pictures were chiefly of the old-fashioned repulsive comic-valentine sort; Strong was a manufacturer of these valentine horrors, too. The monthly had a circulation of 15,000 at $1.25 a year at the end of its first year and twice that at the end of its second. It claimed the incredible figure of 150,000 in 1858. R. M. DeWitt took it over in June 1866, after which it deteriorated in paper, printing, and "art." At its best it had "P. B. Doesticks" and "Petroleum V. Nasby" for contributors. It did much clipping from the newspapers, and it satirized public affairs often. Probably its frontier material was the best stuff it published. It had a music and theater department in the late fifties. It was originally founded on the satire of the Yankees, and its subtitle was "Whittlings from Jonathan's Jack-Knife."

ship of Charles Gayler, the playwright. Fitz-James O'Brien was among its contributors, and McLenan and Hoppin were the artists. In 1854 it was sued for libel by an offended druggist, and discontinued; but it was revived for several months in 1856 under the name *Yankee Doodle; or, Young America*.

Hint, edited and illustrated by William North in New York in 1854, was the first comic daily; it published six numbers at that frequency, then two as a weekly. It has been hinted that the paper died of overindulgence in puns.

Cozzens' Wine Press (1854-61), of New York, was a trade journal; but its editor, Frederick S. Cozzens, had such a gift of humor that his monthly should be listed with the comics. It had only eight octavo pages, and much of that space was given to lists of the wines, brandies, and "segars" offered for sale by Cozzens and by the Ohio Longworths; but the correspondence of "Lorenzo Pinchbeck," the editor's "vinous anecdotes," and the essays on related subjects enabled the little periodical to live up to its subtitle, "A Vinous, Vivacious Monthly." The *Wine Press* cellar at No. 74 Warren Street was often the meeting place of the literary lights: Irving and Halleck liked to go there, and Gulian Verplanck, Gaylord Clark, and T. B. Thorp. It was Thorp who wrote some years later in *Harper's*: "There were rare gatherings in his [Cozzens'] cellar, where wit was expended that was as rich and mellow as his own 'best brands.' " [127]

When Joseph A. Scoville left the *Picayune* early in 1852, he started a weekly of his own in folio called the *Pick*. It gained a good circulation at once, but lasted only about two years. John McLenan was its chief artist, but it used many old *New York Herald* cuts. Dr. Hutchings became business manager in March 1853; but a few months later he inaugurated a new venture of his own — the *New York Time-Piece*, a four-page miscellany in folio with a few comic woodcuts. It had only a very brief existence.

The *Comic World* (1855) was a sixteen-page quarto published monthly by Leland, Clay & Company, of New York, and sold at first for only twenty-five cents a year. *Nick Nax for All Creation* (1856-75) was also of New York. Its pub-

[127] *Harper's Monthly*, XLVIII, 590 (March 1874).

lishers were M. A. Levison and J. C. Haney, the former being editor. It published twice as many pages as the *Comic World* and sold for $1.25 a year.

Frank Leslie's Budget of Fun (1858–96) was the longest-lived of the group. It was a well-printed monthly quarto of sixteen pages, carrying many woodcuts of humorous intent and often crude drawing, at a dollar a year. It usually had a large political cartoon on the front page and printed criticism of the theater and of art.[128]

Vanity Fair[129] was probably the best of American comics before the Civil War. W. H. Stephens, C. D. Shanly, Artemus Ward, and Charles Godfrey Leland had editorial connections with it; and its good art and spicy comment on affairs made it always attractive.

The two years 1859 and 1860, with their lowering war clouds, saw no less than seven comic periodicals founded — of which *Vanity Fair* was the most important. Two other New Yorkers greatly exceeded it in longevity: the *Comic Monthly*, published 1859–81 by J. C. Haney at seventy-five cents a year, and later by Jesse Haney at somewhat higher prices; and the *Phunny Phellow*, issued 1859–76 by Okie, Dayton & Jones at sixty cents a year. Later, Ross & Tousey were distributors of *Phunny Phellow*, while Street & Smith appear to have owned it. To both these cheap papers Nast contributed drawings — to the former in 1860 and to the latter in 1866. Bellew and Beard were leading *Comic Monthly* artists. *Phunny Phellow* practically filled eight of its sixteen pages with woodcuts. It was a phree borrower of phoolery; consequently its jokes were not so bad as its cuts.

It was in 1860 that *Momus* had its brief career of one month as a daily and three months as a weekly. It was edited by an English-born bookseller named Addie and included comment upon politics and such events as the visit of the Japanese, the national conventions, the Heenan-Sayers fight, and the Prince of Wales's tour. It had a full-page political cartoon nearly

---

[128] In 1878 the name was shortened to *Frank Leslie's Budget*, and new numbering was adopted without greatly changing the character of the publication. It was later called *Frank Leslie's Budget of Wit*. Thomas Powell was editor in the years just after the close of the Civil War.

[129] Treated more fully in sketch 29.

every day, drawn chiefly by Frank Bellew and William North. The introductory poem, written but not signed by Charles T. Congdon, began:

I am Momus, god of Giggle — I am son of ancient Nox;
From Nox taking knocks, head-breaking still I give to modern blocks;
Over-grinning was my sinning — itching still the gods to hector;
Cachinnation my vocation — too much nonsense spoiled my nectar.[130]

The *Southern Punch* has been mentioned in another connection.[131] A second comic of the Confederacy was the *Bugle-Horn of Liberty*, which published three monthly numbers in Griffin, Georgia, in the fall of 1863. "Bill Arp" was a contributor, and "Elihu Squiggs" wrote "Letters from the Army." A cut of a half-naked Hindu was printed one month and labeled "Abraham Lincoln"; next month the same cut was used again with the name of Horace Greeley under it.

There were other brief and less significant experiments in comic journalism in our period, especially in the early fifties.[132]

CHEAP AND NASTY

Cheap, and even vulgar, though some of these papers were, they were scarcely vicious. There were, however, undoubtedly some *sub rosa* periodicals designed for sly circulation in resorts of questionable character, but it is now impossible to learn much of them. Lambert A. Wilmer, in his attack upon the journalism of the day entitled *Our Press Gang*, speaks of those

---

[130] *Momus*, April 28, 1860, p. 2. See Charles T. Congdon, *Reminiscences of a Journalist* (Boston, 1880), p. 345.

[131] See pp. 112–113.

[132] *Hombre* (1851), a weekly quarto of San Francisco; *Humbug's American Museum* (1852), a New York satire on Barnum; *Budget* (1852–53), New York; *City Budget* (1853–54), possibly a continuation of the *Budget; Bubble* (1853), New York, pricked after two numbers; *Everybody's Own* (1853), Buffalo; *O. K.* (1853), New York; *Curiosity Shop* (1854), San Francisco; *Quampeag Coyote* (1855), Mokelumne Hill, Calaveras County, California; *Shanghai* (1855–56), Ellicott's Mills, Maryland; *Wang Doodle* (1858–59), Chicago, four monthly numbers; *Comic Bouquet* (1859), Philadelphia, a monthly with lithographed cover and mediocre contents by J. L. Magee; *Innocent Weekly Owl* (1860), New York; *Jolly Joker* (1862–77), a New York monthly, later semi-monthly; *Merryman's Monthly* (1863–77), a quarto by Jesse Haney and Company, illustrated by Frank Beard and others. See the informed but very inaccurate article on the American comics in *Bookman*, XXII, 81 (September 1905).

"typographical reptiles" and names the *Cytherean Miscellany,*
the *Alligator,* and *Paul Pry.*[133] One also finds references to
Thomas L. Nichols' *Arena* and George L. Woodridge's *Libertine,* which were suppressed and their editors punished. *Flash*
also had a stormy career.

There was much railing against vicious literature, but most
of it was directed against fiction dealing more or less realistically with phases of life of which the critics disapproved. The
frequent condemnation of Sue, Sand, Hugo, and Balzac, as
well as of deKock, has been noted; Ainsworth, Reade, and other
English writers came in for some criticism of this kind. This
was the period of Solon Richardson's *Hot Corn* and G. G. Foster's *New York by Gas-Light,* each of which made a *succès du
scandale* with its morally pointed portrayal of New York street
life. The clerical editor of the *National Magazine,* writing on
"Satanic Literature" in 1853, said:

> The extent of this nefarious literature . . . is seen wherever we
> travel, through the land. Agencies and depôts are organized for it
> everywhere. It is the most omnipresent product of the press except
> the newspapers.[134]

The indictment was clearly too inclusive. A writer in *Russell's
Magazine* inveighs against "cheap literature" in somewhat the
same vein:

> It lifts the floodgates of vice and pours its desolating waters upon
> the land . . . at all events, sentiments of the grossest materialism,
> pictures of the darkest scenes of life, are so dexterously inwrought
> into the body of some works as to . . . be like slow poison diffused
> through our daily bread, slowly but surely to work our death. And it
> is a great misfortune that works of this class are most eagerly sought
> by the unthinking masses. . . .[135]

A *National Quarterly* critic is somewhat more definite:

> "Sensation stories" are now all the rage. Nine out of every ten (nay,
> we may say ninety-nine out of every hundred) persons prefer the

---

[133] Lambert A. Wilmer, *Our Press Gang* (Philadelphia, 1859), p. 175. The
Paul Pry referred to was not, of course, that of Mrs. Royall, which had been
discontinued in 1836.
[134] *National Magazine,* II, 25 (January 1853).
[135] *Russell's Magazine,* I, 418 (August 1857).

stories of Sylvanus Cobb, Jr., to the noble productions of Miss Muloch and George Elliott [sic]. *The Hidden Hand* and *The Gunmaker of Moscow* are far more universally read than *John Halifax* and *The Mill on the Floss*. Even the great Bulwer is voted a bore, while Emmerson Bennet is considered charming.[136]

The police gazettes were not precisely in this category: they were crime reporters, but not until after the war were they especially devoted to sex crimes and to the exploitation of sex scandals. There were three of them — the *National Police Gazette*,[137] of New York; the *California Police Gazette* (1859–77), of San Francisco; and the *Illustrated Police News* (1860–1904), of Boston.

[136] *National Quarterly Review*, II, 33 (December 1860).
[137] Treated more fully in sketch 9.

CHAPTER VII

ARTS, SPORTS, AND "ISMS"

COMMENT ON ART

ART comment was fairly common in the magazines of the fifties and sixties, though most of it took the form of news notes rather than that of more formal criticism. Exhibitions were reviewed in the *International Monthly*, *Putnam's*, and *Sartain's*; they were occasionally noticed in the illustrated weeklies; and of course they had an important place in the journals specifically devoted to art. *Vanity Fair*, the *Lantern*, and *Momus* also reviewed them, with satire sometimes too severe. But with most journals, not severity but fulsome praise was the rule, and the *Bulletin of the American Art-Union* complained of "that tone of indiscriminate laudation which is even more common" than undue harshness.[1]

The exhibitions at the National Academy of Design, the American Art-Union, the Artists' Association, and the Düsseldorf Gallery in New York received special attention. *Russell's Magazine* noted the activities of the Carolina Art Association. The "Great Exhibition" at the New York Crystal Palace in 1853–54 was widely discussed,[2] and illustrators presented its best sculpture and painting to the readers of the pictorials.

The National Academy came in for much adverse criticism. "It has stood still while the rest of the world has been rushing forward," complained *Putnam's*. "It has given us no architects. . . . Among its members are some very clever painters of landscapes and portraits, but the works it has produced have been mere toys in private houses."[3]

The *International* agreed that American art excelled in landscape, naming such painters as Durand, Kensett, Cropsey, Church, Cranch, Boutelle and Gifford.[4] The new feeling for

---

[1] *Bulletin of the American Art-Union*, Series 1850, p. 2 (April 1850).

[2] *Cosmopolitan Art Journal*, V, 505 (May 1855); *North American Review*, LXXV, 357 (October 1852).

[3] *Putnam's Monthly*, I, 700 (June 1853).

[4] *International Monthly*, III, 327 (June 1851).

color was often discussed. "This is emphatically an age of color among painters," declared the *Saturday Evening Gazette*.

The pre-Raphaelites have sprung up in England and dazzled the eyes of men with an intensity of coloring: iconoclasm runs rampant in France . . . our cloud of witnesses are the works of Brown and Stillman, the Niagara and Heart of the Andes.[5]

The architecture of public buildings was frequently illustrated in the pictorials. But Augustus J. Hoppin declared with much truth in the *Bulletin of the American Art-Union* that "As to public buildings, we have few if any architectural pretensions." [6]

Pride in American sculpture was common, but W. J. Stillman declared in the *Cosmopolitan Art Journal* that most of it was idle and frivolous.

Richard Greenough's Franklin is one of the few genuine works to which we should be inclined to assign a permanent value. . . . Hiram Powers startled the art-world with a completeness of realization of his subjects hitherto even unattempted. . . . But he is a pure actualist; his work is all surface, and beyond that point he had not the ability to pass.[7]

There was no little discussion of the Jackson equestrian statue by Clark Mills. *Vanity Fair* disapproved it. "Mr. Mills has gained the reputation he deserved," said that lively periodical. "His hind legs are famous, and will remain famous." Then Mills executed an equestrian of Washington, with the horse on three legs, which *Vanity Fair* dubbed "the horse and Washington statue." [8]

"Our artists suffer a total eclipse three-fourths of the year, for the lack of a suitable place to exhibit their performances in," complained *Putnam's*.[9] And after the war had begun, the *Knickerbocker* noted that "Little or nothing is now being done in the studios. Many of our artists have shouldered muskets." [10] Apparently this depression did not last, however.[11]

[5] *Saturday Evening Gazette*, January 26, 1861, p. 1.
[6] *Bulletin of the American Art-Union*, Series 1850, p. 55 (July 1850).
[7] *Cosmopolitan Art Journal*, IV, 3, 4 (March 1860).
[8] *Vanity Fair*, I, 157 (March 3, 1860).
[9] *Putnam's Monthly*, I, 351 (March 1853).
[10] *Knickerbocker*, LVIII, 48 (July 1861).
[11] *Ibid.*, LXI, 175 (February 1863).

The problem of the popularization of art was given some attention. "In a republic like ours," declared *Gleason's Pictorial*, "it can never be expected or desired that many individuals will become rich enough to emulate the prodigious patronage bestowed in the palmiest days of art in Europe upon painters, sculptors, and architects." [12] But a commentator in the *United States Magazine* found that the America of the times

has a positive taste for the arts of the sculptor, the painter and the engraver, as almost every house, however humble, can testify, and this taste has been for the last fifteen or twenty years steadily advancing to a high state of cultivation. We must have works of art . . . and the time has gone by when poor ones will content us. The old "mourning pieces," "samplers," "shepherdesses," and "Charlottes at the tomb of Werther," which were wont to grace the boudoirs of our grandmothers, have long since been assigned to attics.[13]

Where today, a twentieth-century writer may add, they are eagerly sought by collectors of antiques.

One agency for the democratization of art came to its end, however, in this period — the art union.[14] "The utter extinction of the American Art-Union, by a decision of our courts, has had a temporarily depressing effect on the cause of art in this country," observed *Putnam's* in 1853.[15] This, the largest of the art unions, had found itself unable to present the prizes offered in 1852 because of an unexpected decline in membership.[16] The ill-feeling engendered by that situation finally resulted in a court action to enjoin the union's activities under the law forbidding lotteries. The *National Police Gazette* boasted of having been the first to "open the eyes of the people" to the swindle and humbug practiced by the union, and rejoiced in the action of the courts.[17] Certain cliques and jealousies among artists undoubtedly helped to destroy this agency for bringing art home to the people; and the *International*, justly enough,

[12] *Gleason's Pictorial Drawing-Room Companion*, I, 365 (October 4, 1851).

[13] *United States Magazine*, III, 413 (November 1856).

[14] See Mott, *A History of American Magazines, 1741–1850*, p. 437.

[15] *Putnam's Monthly*, I, 120 (January 1853).

[16] *International Monthly*, V, 277 (February 1852).

[17] *National Police Gazette*, June 26, 1852. The union's troubles may also be followed in *Figaro!*

attacked the union system as "hot-bed methods of cultivating an appreciation of art and rewarding its professors." [18] The failure of the oldest and largest of the art unions [19] hastened the disaster which eventually overtook them all. The New-England Art-Union, which was organized in 1851; the Western Art-Union, at Cincinnati; the Philadelphia Art-Union, most successful of all; [20] and other more local organizations, such as the Chicago Art Union, which made its first distribution in 1861, perished before the end of our period. The Cosmopolitan Art Association, organized in New York in 1854, was somewhat different in plan from the unions: it furnished one of the standard magazines as a return for the three-dollar membership fee, and then offered "an extensive list of premiums" consisting of paintings, marbles, and other art objects, to be drawn by lot in the fashion used by the unions. Thus evading the lottery law, this association became the successor of the American Art-Union and grew in membership until the war put an end to it. [21] For one of its distributions it bought Powers' "Greek Slave" and, after giving it away, repurchased it at $6,000 and gave it away again.

Photography excited a wide popular interest. "Daguerreotyping," said the *Cosmpolitan Art Journal*, "though not regarded as a *legitimate* child of Art, has done much to advance her cause with the people. There is scarcely the humblest cottage but has some beautiful and correct image of friend or relative." [22] Mathew B. Brady became famous for his photographs of war scenes and of national leaders during the Civil War. Willis praised his work in the *Home Journal*, and "Gail Hamilton" did likewise in the *National Era*. "This wonderful art of Photography, this true child of the sun, last-born and fairest," rhapsodized "Gail," "has caught expression and traced form and feature with a most delicate and accurate pencil." [23] Another phase of democratic art was the diorama, or pano-

---

[18] *International Monthly*, II, 194 (January 1851).

[19] See *Bulletin of the American Art-Union*, Series 1851, p. 17 (April 1851) for a history of this organization.

[20] *Graham's Magazine*, XL, 325–326 (March 1852).

[21] *Cosmopolitan Art Journal*, supplement to Vol. IV.

[22] *Ibid.*, I, 34 (November 1856).

[23] *National Era*, XIII, 46 (March 24, 1859).

rama. This type of exhibition became very popular, was abused, and was travestied successfully by Artemus Ward and others. The *Southern Literary Messenger* describes it:

> What is most improperly called a "Panorama," a long moving picture of striking scenery or imposing events, such as we shall very soon have of the war in Italy, is just now a popular entertainment in our cities. As the canvass rolls by, unfolding to our view Alps and oceans, cathedrals and battles, coronations, conflagrations, volcanic eruptions, etc., we hear, in the pauses of a cracked piano, the voice of the Showman, as of one crying in the Wilderness, who tells us all about the localities represented, with a good deal of pleasant information to be obtained in no other manner, because it is improvised for the occasion.[24]

ILLUSTRATION

"The 'illustration' mania is upon our people," observed the *Cosmopolitan Art Journal* in 1857.

> Nothing but "illustrated" works are profitable to publishers; while the illustrated magazines and newspapers are vastly popular. Harpers initiated the era, by their illustrated Bible. . . . Then the Magazines followed suit — *Harper's* keeping, as it still does, the lead, and the page that had the best picture was esteemed the best.[25]

In spite of the inroads of wood engraving, steel and copper kept their place as the proper mediums for the higher type of engraving throughout this period. The annuals, long a stronghold for line engraving, stipple, and mezzotint, had declined by the fifties,[26] but the magazines continued good patrons of the engravers of plates. Portraits in the *Eclectic Magazine*, in the *Democratic Review*, and in *De Bow's* of the early fifties; and sentimental pictures and landscapes in *Godey's*, *Peterson's*, the *Ladies' Repository*, and *Sartain's* (to name but a few among many) were usually on steel. *Godey's*, *Peterson's*, and *Frank Leslie's Ladies' Gazette* used hand-colored fashion plates, some of them so large as to necessitate folding in to fit the magazine. Folding plates began in 1861 in *Godey's*.

[24] *Southern Literary Messenger*, XXIX, 151 (August 1859).
[25] *Cosmopolitan Art Journal*, I, 111 (January 1857).
[26] See Ralph Thompson, *American Literary Annuals and Gift Books, 1825–1865* (New York, 1936), Chapter IV.

But engraving on wood blocks was surely making its way. By 1853 a *Knickerbocker* writer could say of wood engraving:

To such a degree and beauty has it been brought that in a great measure it supersedes the copper and steel engravings which used formerly to be employed. And though it is doubtful whether wood engraving can ever be brought to equal the delicacy of the plates, yet for figures, for views of places and things, for landscapes, and especially for vignettes of the most exquisite finish and beauty, wood engravings are now almost universally used.[27]

In 1865 *Harper's Monthly* claimed that it had printed "something more than ten thousand engravings [on wood], the cost of which will average about thirty dollars each." [28] Such pictorial weeklies as *Leslie's Illustrated*, *Harper's Weekly*, and *Gleason's Pictorial* did much to stimulate wood engraving; and the comics, juveniles, and mechanical journals used many woodcuts. The women's magazines commonly used both wood engraving and steel plates.

ART JOURNALS

Certain of the art unions had their publications, chief of which was the *Bulletin of the American Art-Union* (1847–53). The *Cosmopolitan Art Journal* was the quarterly organ of the Cosmopolitan Art Association, of New York. It began as a mere bulletin in July 1856, but was enlarged to a more pretentious format and more inclusive contents at the end of 1858. O. J. Victor was editor, and he enlisted an excellent group of contributors. A prominent feature of the magazine was a series of "life sketches" of artists and writers. A steel engraving adorned each number, and many woodcuts were used. It ended March 1861.

The *Crayon* [29] was the best art journal of the period. It was founded and edited by W. J. Stillman and John Durand; Durand was left alone in the work after the second year. Broad in its scope, handsomely printed, it was written with a certain authority. Bryant and Lowell were among its contributors.

[27] *Knickerbocker*, XLI, 51–57 (January 1853).
[28] *Harper's Monthly*, XXXII, 1 (December 1865).
[29] It published seven volumes and seven numbers of an eighth, from January 3, 1855, to July 1861. There were two volumes in 1855 and one each year thereafter. It was a weekly in 1855, and then a monthly.

Alexander Montgomery published an American edition of his
Illustrated Monthly Magazine of Art in New York (1853–54).
It was distinguished by copious and able wood engraving, some
of it by W. J. Linton. There were several short-lived western
art journals and a group of periodicals devoted to daguerreo-
typy and photography.[30]

MUSIC AND THE MAGAZINES

"Our country has been almost over-run with musical artists
recently," remarked a critic in *To-Day* in 1852. "Musical enthusiasm has rather drawn away attention from the drama." [31]
The chief of these "musical artists" was, of course, the "Swedish
Nightingale," Jenny Lind, who came to America under the
management of P. T. Barnum in the autumn of 1850 and remained for about a year. Her concerts constituted "a triumph
unprecedented in the history of artistic success," declared the
International.[32] Her arrival in New York, well prepared for by
the master showman, called forth tremendous enthusiasm. "She
has taken the town by storm," said the *Knickerbocker* editor.
"She has had a continued ovation." [33] In another magazine we
read: "The excitement is of the hottest temperature. It is universally conceded that Jenny Lind is the greatest woman, Barnum is the greatest man, Genin the greatest hatter, and New
York the greatest place in the world." [34] Genin, the hatter, it
must be explained, had paid $225 at auction for the first ticket
to Jenny Lind's first concert — an artistic-financial function
which brought $26,500 into the box office. With this beginning,
the Lind-Barnum tour could not but make a great success in

[30] *Western Art Journal* was edited by W. P. Strickland, in Cincinnati, in 1855.
In the same city the *Pen and Pencil* was published in 1853, and another periodical
of the same name was issued in Chicago three years later. Among the journals
devoted to photography were *Humphrey's Journal of Photography* (1850–70),
of New York, begun as the *Daguerreian Journal* by S. D. Humphrey; *Photographic Art Journal* (1851–60), called after its third year the *Photographic and
Fine Art Journal; American Journal of Photography and the Allied Arts and
Sciences* (1852–67), New York; *Philadelphia Photographer* (1864–1923), which
moved to New York in 1885, became (Edward L.) *Wilson's Photographic Magazine* in 1889, and *Photographic Journal of America* in 1915.
[31] *To-Day*, I, 16 (January 3, 1852).
[32] *International Monthly*, III, 471 (July 1851).
[33] *Knickerbocker*, XXXVI, 378 (October 1850).
[34] *Holden's Dollar Magazine*, VI, 638 (October 1850).

other cities. The populace was Lind-mad. "It was the most universal influenza ever known," said *Figaro!* [35] "We have had Jenny Lind hats, umbrellas, shoes, cabbages, apples, and chestnuts," the *Republic* records; "but the last article we have seen laying claim to this popular soubriquet was a *Jenny Lind Ashbox!*" [36] From this it will be seen that some commentators were inclined to wax satirical. Some complained outspokenly of the press-agentry attending the tours of the "Nightingale." The *Western Literary Messenger* editor refused to attend the Buffalo concert because the tickets were "double the price they should be." [37]

Madame Sontag's appearance in opera was a sequel to Jenny Lind's success.[38] Madame Alboni's in the same year was a comparative failure.[39] Ole Bull on a second American tour, Julien and his orchestra, and Salvi were all greeted with enthusiasm; but it was Adelina Patti, in 1860, who duplicated the successes of Jenny Lind and Ole Bull. *Momus* sums up the attitude of America toward Patti's art in a dialect poem, "Jonathan to Adelina," beginning:

> No use-t a talkin' — you're the gal for me!
> No wonder all the airth with praise is ringin'! [40]

Such Americans as Louis M. Gottschalk and Clara Louise Kellogg were also very popular, the former as a pianist with Patti, and the latter in various grand opera parts but chiefly as Marguerite in "Faust."

The progress of Italian opera in New York was followed more or less closely by many periodicals. Prices were raised in 1855 to $2.00 a seat, with $1.50 for standing room; and small houses resulted. These prices were reduced in the middle of the 1856 season, but the operatic fortunes did not mend.[41] *Porter's Spirit of the Times* printed Director Maretzek's letter of resignation,

[35] *Figaro!*, I, 40 (September 28, 1850). *Figaro!* is a good periodical in which to follow the craze.

[36] *Republic*, I, 89 (February 1851).

[37] *Western Literary Messenger*, XVII, 48 (September 1851).

[38] *Putnam's Monthly*, I, 117 (January 1853).

[39] *Ibid.*, I, 589 (May 1853).

[40] *Momus*, May 3, 1860, p. 3.

[41] *Frank Leslie's Gazette of Fashion*, V, 4 (January 1856).

in which it was alleged that the difficulties of the opera arose from the demand of stockholders for free admission.[42] Maurice Strakosch was the new director, but the panic of 1857 interrupted the season of that year and closed the Italian Opera House on Fourteenth Street.

Opera in Boston, with the visits of Patti, Brignoli, Alboni, and others, was chronicled by *Dwight's Musical Journal*, the *Saturday Evening Gazette, Gleason's Pictorial*, and *To-Day*. "Boston is more than sharing our musical enthusiasm," admitted the New York *Putnam's* in 1853. "It has fairly beaten us this winter."[43] Italian and German opera was also successful on tours which extended even to the Middle West.

So pervasive was Italian opera in these days that it affected even the colored minstrel show, according to *Leslie's*.[44] But the minstrels kept their peculiar character in the long run, and their popularity as well. Such favorite songs as "Jim Crow," "Zip Coon," "Long-Tailed Blue," "Ol' Virginny Neber Tire," "Settin' on a Rail," were known by nearly everyone and sung by thousands. The Christy and Woods minstrels in New York, with a theater seating twenty-five hundred "in spite of crinoline";[45] the Prendergast Minstrels, who came to town in the panic year; and three or four other shows of the same genre in New York comprised a kind of institution. Two "groups of sable performers warble nightly to appreciative audiences"[46] in Boston, and there were resident troupes in most of the larger cities.[47]

Chief among the popular songs of the fifties were those of Stephen C. Foster — "Oh! Susannah" and "Old Uncle Ned" (1848), "Nelly Was a Lady" (1849), "Old Folks at Home" (1851), "Massa's in the Cold, Cold, Ground" (1852), "My Old Kentucky Home" (1853), and "Old Black Joe" (1860). "His songs," said a writer in the *Atlantic* of the sixties, "had an unparalleled success."[48]

[42] *Porter's Spirit of the Times*, I, 104 (October 11, 1856).
[43] *Putnam's Monthly*, I, 351 (March 1853).
[44] *Frank Leslie's Illustrated Newspaper*, I, 54 (January 5, 1856).
[45] *Ibid.*, IV, 324 (October 24, 1857).
[46] *Saturday Evening Gazette*, February 20, 1858, p. 2.
[47] See "Negro Minstrelsy," *Putnam's Monthly*, V, 72 (January 1855).
[48] *Atlantic Monthly*, XX, 614 (November 1867). See also *Dwight's Journal of Music*, October 2, 1852; September 17, 1853; and November 19, 1853.

THE FASHIONABLE SINGING–CLASS

From *Frank Leslie's Gazette of Fashions* (accompanying *Frank Leslie's Monthly*) for July 1862.

Popular songs of the war were many and various. "When This Cruel War Is Over" is said by the *Musical Review* to have sold a half-million copies almost immediately upon publication. "Mother Waiting for the News" and "When Will My Darling Boy Return?" were other hits.[49]

Of the musical journals current in this period, two had begun in 1849 — *Saroni's Musical Times* (1849–52), founded by Herman S. Saroni in New York, and later owned by Eugene Lies, who dropped Saroni's name from the title; and the *Musical World* (1849–60), which, beginning life with the picturesque name *Message Bird*, used various titles during its decade of existence. Another which changed titles with disconcerting frequency was Mason Brothers' *New-York Musical Review and Gazette* (1850–73), which began as *Choral Advocate*, with Lowell Mason, George F. Root, and William B. Bradbury chief contributors, and ended as the *New York Weekly Review*.[50] I. B. Woodbury was its editor during its early years, when it was devoted especially to church music.

But the best musical magazine of the times was *Dwight's Journal of Music*[51] (1852–81), of Boston. John Sullivan Dwight was one of the country's foremost music critics and had been contributing a monthly musical article to *Sartain's*. His *Journal* was authoritative and dignified. *Watson's Weekly Art Journal* was begun in 1864, but its history belongs to later periods.[52] Several periodicals were devoted chiefly to singing schools and church choirs.[53]

[49] *Musical Review*, November 19, December 17, 1864.
[50] See Volume III, Chapter VIII.
[51] Subtitled "A Paper of Art and Literature," in 41 volumes, mostly semi-annual, April 10, 1852–September 3, 1881. Dwight was proprietor until 1858, when he sold it to Oliver Ditson, the music publisher. It was a weekly except during the war, when it was issued fortnightly. It gave special attention to Boston music, but carried New York correspondence, and had notes from abroad. It published some notable poetry by Holmes, Whittier, and Cranch; and C. C. Perkins, W. S. B. Matthews, William F. Apthorpe, Julia Ward Howe, and A. W. Thayer were other contributors. In 1878 Dwight accomplished the transfer of the magazine to Houghton, Osgood & Company in order to remove it from connection with the music publishing business; but in spite of a testimonial concert by Boston friends which brought in $6,000, it was forced to suspend. See George Willis Cooke, *John Sullivan Dwight* (Boston, 1898), Chapters VI and VIII.
[52] See Volume III, Chapter VIII.
[53] Four of those of longer life may be listed: I. B. Woodbury's *New York*

THEATERS AND MAGAZINES

Of periodicals devoted wholly to the drama, there were very few in our period. *Figaro!* was chiefly theatrical, but it ranges itself also with the comics;[54] and, by the same token, the humorous periodicals almost always took an interest in the theaters. The *Spirit of the Times* and the *New York Clipper*, both devoted in these years primarily to sports, gave much attention to the theater before 1865. So did such pictorials as *Leslie's* and *Gleason's*. The *Saturday Evening Gazette*, of Boston, advertised itself in 1857, not without some show of justice, as "the best theatrical journal in the country." Other weeklies, such as the *Home Journal* and *Albion*, reviewed plays; and some of the monthlies, notably *Putnam's* and *Emerson's*, were interested in the drama. Theaters flourished in the Far West, and the *San Francisco Chronicle* began in 1865 as a theatrical sheet.[55]

Dramatic critics generally agreed that American drama was in a parlous state — perhaps even nonexistent. The American theater was "bound hand and foot to the 'Old Country,' " according to the *Democratic Review*.[56] A later writer in the same magazine said that "It is generally conceded that the American drama, as a national institution, is as yet unborn. So far we have been almost entirely dependent upon foreign productions."[57] And to a surprising extent upon foreign actors, he might have added. "That the drama is in a state most deplorably low at the present time few will take upon themselves to deny," asserted a critic in *Emerson's* in 1858;[58] and Conway declared in his *Dial*: "Still does the Drama sit with the mob; still is Pegasus yoked with the ox."[59]

"Uncle Tom" and "Hot Corn" were creating furores in the

Musical Pioneer and Chorister's Budget (1855–71); *Boston Musical Times* (1860–71); *Southern Musical Advocate* (1859–69), suspended during the war 1861–66, and succeeded by *Musical Million* (1870–1913), Singer's Glen, Virginia; *Musical World* (1863–90), Cleveland.

[54] See p. 180.
[55] John P. Young, *Journalism in California* (San Francisco, 1915), p. 64.
[56] *Democratic Review*, XXXIV, 122 (August 1854).
[57] *Ibid.*, XL, 557 (December 1857).
[58] *Emerson's Magazine*, VI, 304 (March 1858). See also *Figaro!*, I, 5 (August 31, 1850).   [59] *Dial*, I, 376 (December 1860).

lower-class theaters in the middle fifties. In 1855 the *United States Magazine* described the theatrical situation in New York as follows:

Some fourteen or fifteen places of amusement have been crowded almost nightly. We have Rachel, in French classic drama, at the Metropolitan. Forrest, in the heavier parts of English drama, at the Broadway. Mme. LaGrange, in Italian opera, at the Academy of Music. Charming Louisa Pyne, in English opera, at Niblo's — Mr. Bristow's new opera of Rip Van Winkle having been presented there at least three times each week. At Wallack's, sterling comedy is presented in its greatest perfection; and at Burton's the ridiculous is drawing crowded houses. Mrs. Duffield is "starring" at the Bowery; black opera flourishes; and one or two of the new Broadway establishments are, we understand, fitted up in palacious [*sic*] splendor. Each of the minor establishments has its peculiar star and attractions. From an estimate in one of our dailies we perceive that over twelve thousand dollars per night is expended in this species of amusement alone in our city.[60]

This star system was frequently condemned. "It is now an indisputable fact, that, unless some prominent star is under engagement, not a theatre from one end of the country to the other pays its expenses," declared *Gleason's Pictorial*.[61] But such stars as Forrest, more popular than ever after his feud with Macready and his divorce scandal, and Rachel, who made her American début September 3, 1855, were objects of great popular enthusiasm and were given many pages of discussion in the periodicals.

There was no little adverse criticism of Dion Boucicault and his piratical habits; the comics were especially active in this warfare, though they occasionally acknowledged the enemy's effectiveness.[62] "Aut scissors aut nullus" was the motto suggested for Boucicault by *Momus*.[63]

The war interfered but little with the theaters in the North. "The God of War does not frown upon popular amusements at the present time," said the "Dramatic Gossip" department of

[60] *United States Magazine*, II, 206 (November 1855). See also *Frank Leslie's Illustrated Newspaper*, I, 11 (December 15, 1855).
[61] *Gleason's Pictorial Drawing-Room Companion*, II, 285 (May 1, 1852).
[62] *Yankee Notions*, VII, 100 (April 1858).
[63] *Momus*, May 1, 1860, p. 2.

the *Knickerbocker* in 1863. "The theatres have teemed with pleasure seekers, and managers are making money as fast as hotel keepers. No matter how poor the quality of the dramatic dish provided, there is no lack of dollars and cents to pay for it." [64] In the South during war time the *Southern Illustrated News* and the *Magnolia* reviewed dramatic productions in Richmond and other southern cities. "The Maiden's Vow," a war play by James D. McCabe, Jr., was produced at the Broad Street Theater in Richmond in April 1863. On the same page with an account of the defeat at Vicksburg, the *Magnolia* said:

> Art, music, and the drama are putting on gay attire. . . . The New Richmond Theater has been enjoying a fine business. , . . The management has turned its attention, we believe, to the light dramatic literature. . . . The Varieties has been doing a tolerable business . . . has lately been inclined predominantly to the amusing, and has gotten off some happy burlesques. *Vive la bagatelle!*[65]

The familiar clerical ban on theaters persisted. The *Chicago Record*, an Episcopal journal, declared in the course of a controversy that not one of the Chicago clergy "has ever attended a theatrical exhibition in Chicago." [66] In New York the Unitarian Henry W. Bellows had a good word to say for the theater, and he was thereupon taken to task by the Congregational Henry Ward Beecher. *Leslie's* said:

> The Rev. Dr. Beecher handled the Rev. Dr. Bellows without gloves. Dion Boucicault returned the compliment and mauled the Rev. Dr. Beecher, without even washing his hands. To this the Rev. Dr. Beecher utterly fails to reply, but makes one compromise and gives one invitation. He offers to see Mr. Boucicault as often as he (Mr. Boucicault) hears him (Dr. Beecher) preach. If this was affected, it would be a terrible infliction on both.[67]

The objection to theaters was widespread, however. The *Youth's Companion*, in its laudatory editorial on Lincoln immediately after his assassination, said, "We are sorry that he should have received his death-wound in a theatre." [68]

[64] *Knickerbocker*, LXI, 82, 83 (January 1863).
[65] *Magnolia Weekly*, I, 192 (June 6, 1863).
[66] *Chicago Record*, III, 180 (March 1, 1860).
[67] *Frank Leslie's Illustrated Newspaper*, III, 403 (May 30, 1857).
[68] *Youth's Companion*, XXXVIII, 58 (April 27, 1865).

POPULAR SPORTS

Horse racing and prize fighting were the spectacular sports of the day. Physical culture exercises made gains in some educational institutions, but the total effect was not impressive. "Physical culture is on the top of the wave," wrote one of the leaders of the movement, Dr. Dio Lewis, in the *Atlantic* in 1862, "but it is as yet in the talk stage. Millions praise the gymnasium; hundreds seek its blessings." [69] Harvard, Yale, and Amherst built gymnasiums in 1859 — the first of any adequacy in the country. [70]

About sports in which people in general could participate one reads comparatively little in the magazines of the times. There were some beginnings, but the wave of popular sport interest did not break over America until after the war. The Autocrat wrote in the *Atlantic Monthly* just before that conflict:

I am satisfied that such a set of black-coated, stiff-jointed, soft-muscled, paste-complexioned youth as we can boast in our Atlantic cities never before sprang from the loins of Anglo-Saxon lineage. . . . We have a few good boatmen, no good horsemen that I hear of, nothing remarkable I believe in cricketing; and as for any great athletic feat performed by a gentleman in these latitudes, society would drop a man who would run around the Common in five minutes. [71]

Interest in horse racing grew almost to a frenzy at some of the meets during the war, when money was plentiful. The sport may be followed best in the *Spirit of the Times*. Flora Temple trotted a mile in 2.19¾ in 1859; and Dexter, for which Robert Bonner of the *New York Ledger* later paid $33,000, beat that mark in 1865 with 2.18¼. Bonner and Commodore Vanderbilt were rivals among nonprofessional drivers of fast trotters: at an exhibition contest between them (no money being wagered, as Bonner never bet on a horse race) Bonner drove a team two miles [72] in 5.01¼.

But the greatest popular excitement in sports was aroused by

[69] *Atlantic Monthly*, X, 129 (August 1862).
[70] *Science*, VIII, 1 (July 2, 1886).
[71] *Atlantic Monthly*, I, 881 (May 1858).
[72] *Science*, XXI, 523 (May 1868).

certain prize fights of the period. The outstanding hero of fisti-
cuffs in these years was the "Benecia Boy" — John C. Heenan.
The Morrissey-Heenan bout in 1858, the drawn battle between
Heenan and Sayers in England in 1860, and the Heenan-King
fight in 1863 were the high points of the period. When Heenan
lost to the Englishman King after twenty-five rounds, there was
as much mourning in some quarters as over a lost battle in the
Civil War. When Heenan left for England in 1860 to encounter
Tom Sayers, *Vanity Fair* published "The Benecia Boy's Farewell," ending:

> I'll wind our colors 'round my loins —
> The blue and crimson bars —
> And if Tom does not feel the stripes,
> I'll make him see the stars! [73]

Leslie's Lady's Magazine printed a picture of two boys caught
fighting and explaining their black eyes to their mammas:
"We've only been playing at being Tom Sayers and the Benecia
Boy!" [74] There was, of course, much moral indignation vented
against the brutality of these fights. *Leslie's Illustrated* began
by condemning prize fighting as "identified with all the coarsest,
lowest vice of our cities" and declaring it "the very last subject
that should be mentioned in a paper which finds its way into
decent families"; [75] but it ended by sending a special correspondent and a trained artist to London to report the Heenan-
Sayers battle and by giving many pages to affairs of the ring.
Religious and other journals generally attacked prize fighting,
however: the Heenan-King bout was "disgraceful to England
and not much less so to America," concluded the *Northwestern
Christian Advocate*. [76]

Baseball was showing its first indications of popularity. We
read of games of twenty or thirty innings, with scores of seventy
to fifty and thereabout. Pitchers are warned against pitching
too wildly; umpires are commended for firmness. "Carriages
surrounded the grounds, and the smiles of the fair encouraged
the players." A Chicago correspondent of *Porter's Spirit of*

[73] *Vanity Fair*, I, 45 (January 14, 1860).
[74] *Frank Leslie's Lady's Magazine*, XV, 288 (October 1864).
[75] *Frank Leslie's Illustrated Newspaper*, IX, 66 (December 31, 1859).
[76] *Northwestern Christian Advocate*, XII, 6 (January 6, 1864).

CROQUET IN THE COSTUMES OF THE SIXTIES

Charles G. Bush's picture of a croquet game published in *Harper's Weekly*, November 3, 1866. A full-page woodcut.

the Times says: "The Excelsior is the pioneer ball club of the city; it was organized a year ago this Spring [i.e., 1858]. We have now four clubs that play under the New York rules, and one or two in process of organization." [77] The same journal, which ordinarily reported baseball games alongside cricket matches, recorded the founding of the first important league — the National Association:

> The first convention was, it will be remembered, held last year [1857] to devise a new set of Rules and Laws for Baseball. The call originated with the old Knickerbocker Club. . . . A strong effort will be made [this year] to have eleven fielders on a side.[78]

The *Sunday Mercury*, of New York, claimed the title "the Father of Baseball," as it had been the first to encourage the sport by reporting matches.[79]

Boat races, especially in intercollegiate sport, and chess and billiards were followed in the *Spirit of the Times* and, after 1853, in Frank Queen's *New York Clipper*. Croquet was a new fad, just imported from England. The "stirring, healthful conflict" of this game, as played by women in hoopskirts and men in top-hats, was decidedly picturesque.[80] As to billiards, the *Round Table* remarked in 1865: "There is no more exquisite foolery of our day than the mania for playing billiards which has developed itself in this country in the last five or six years." [81] The *Billiard Cue* (1856–74) was a modest monthly of four folio pages edited by the famous billiardist, Michael Phelan, as a house organ for his manufacturing business. The *Chess Monthly* (1857–61) was also a New Yorker.

The greatest general sports periodical of these years was *Wilkes' Spirit of the Times*, which was begun in 1859 by George Wilkes, founder of the *National Police Gazette* and a former editor of *Porter's Spirit of the Times*. Within two years Wilkes's paper, aided by the beginning of the war, had put the old *Spirit* out of business.[82] Racing, field sports, and the stage came

---

[77] *Porter's Spirit of the Times*, VI, 216 (June 25, 1859).

[78] *Ibid.*, IV, 21 (March 13, 1858).

[79] See *Journalist*, January 7, 1888, p. 3.

[80] *Saturday Evening Post*, December 26, 1863, pp. 1, 4.

[81] *Round Table*, II, 88 (October 14, 1865).

[82] See Mott, *op. cit.*, p. 480. But note the following data: Porter withdrew from the original *Spirit of the Times* in 1856 and, with George Wilkes as associate

within the purview of *Wilkes' Spirit of the Times*. The *California Spirit of the Times* was a sports weekly in San Francisco.[83] The *New York Clipper* was founded in 1853 by Frank Queen as a sporting and amusement journal; but it was very miscellaneous and printed some fiction, verse, and music. Eventually it became the great news journal of professional performers on the stage, in circus rings, and on athletic fields. Its news of all sports and of the details of the stage in many cities makes it an invaluable record up to the middle eighties.[84] Ed James's *Sportsman* was a New York periodical of 1863.

NEWSPAPERS OF THE PERIOD

The fifties and sixties represent a period of newspaper growth, improvement in news-gathering facilities, political controversy, and the dominance of great editorial personalities. American reporters, declares an anonymous journalist in *Harper's Monthly*, beat the world in speed, if not in good writing;

---

editor, founded *Porter's Spirit of the Times* (1856–59). Porter died in 1858, and Theodore E. Tomlinson and other friends continued to conduct the paper. With these men Wilkes soon disagreed, and he withdrew angrily from association with them and began on September 10, 1859, *Wilkes' Spirit of the Times*. *Porter's Spirit of the Times* suspended some weeks later, and the original *Spirit of the Times* ended June 22, 1861, leaving Wilkes in command of the field. He dropped his own name from the title in 1868, and in 1873 adopted numbering to conform to his claim that his was the original *Spirit of the Times*. (As to numbering, see Mott, *op. cit.*, p. 480 n. The assumption of that footnote that the *Spirits* were all in one line was owing to Wilkes's own purposely misleading statements.) See *New York Clipper*, XXX, 521 (October 28, 1882), which, though incorrect in details of the origin of the first *Spirit*, is helpful. Wilkes's paper, from which Wilkes himself retired in 1875, leaving E. A. Buck as half owner and editor, was merged in the *Horseman* in 1902. See George P. Rowell & Company, *Centennial Newspaper Exhibition* (New York, 1876), p. 186.

[83] It began as the *Fireman's Journal*, giving special attention to sports. In 1878 it became an insurance journal, under the name *California Spirit of the Times and Underwriter's Journal*. The inclusive dates are 1854–94.

[84] Harrison Trent was owner for the first two years, and James Jones was part owner 1856–57; otherwise Queen was editor and publisher until his death in 1882. T. Allston Brown was on the editorial staff and furnished a series of sketches of actors for early volumes. After Queen's death the estate conducted the *Clipper* for a time, with Benjamin Garno as managing editor, after which A. J. Borie became editor and publisher. The paper deteriorated and was purchased by *Variety* in 1923. See *Variety*, CI, 10, 51 (December 31, 1930); but for its history before the death of Queen, see *Clipper*, XXX, 521 (October 28, 1882).

and he gives accounts of how the visits of the Japanese embassy and the Prince of Wales had been covered.[85]

Horace Greeley's *Tribune* had acquired great influence; its weekly edition enjoyed the phenomenal circulation of some two hundred thousand subscribers. "The public know that Mr. Greeley edits the most widely circulated and influential paper in the world," asserted a writer in the *Southern Literary Messenger*,[86] which could not be accused of favoring that editor. Indeed, Greeley had many bitter enemies. He was an easy butt for ridicule. From an extended travesty in the *Day Book* we may quote a sample paragraph:

No one that we have ever heard of has as yet attempted to give any information relative to Horace Greeley's birth or parentage, and for the reason, probably, that he never had any. The first that was seen of him, he was coming out of a field of tall rye, his white head bobbing up and down like a tall mullen waving in the wind. No one had ever seen or heard of such a thing before, and for a long time naturalists were in doubt whether he belonged to the animal or the vegetable kingdom. . . . From his appearance it was believed that he had just begun to walk upright. Further than this, nothing is or ever was known of the origin of Horace Greeley.[87]

The other editors of the greater papers were also public figures and frequent subjects for discussion and comment. *Vanity Fair*, which, as a kind of *arbiter morum*, found it necessary to correct the papers rather often, condemned the activities of Bennett severely and repeatedly. "As a scurrilist perhaps James Gordon Bennett was unequalled," ran an epitaph for him as suggested by *Vanity Fair*. "His career enriched his pocket at the expense of his character and that of the profession he followed only to degrade." [88] This comic journal printed a picture of a pair of scissors to express its opinion of the *Courier and Enquirer*, and said of the *Post* that it "is conducted by a poet and two reporters. . . . The general impression is that the managers send out for three pages of matter and rely upon the telegraph news to make out a fourth." [89] The *Herald's* mat-

[85] *Harper's Monthly*, XXVI, 361–367 (February 1863).
[86] *Southern Literary Messenger*, XXXI, 212 (September 1860).
[87] *Day Book*, June 9, 1852, p. 2.
[88] *Vanity Fair*, IV, 155 (September 28, 1861).
[89] *Ibid.*, I, 246 (April 14, 1860).

rimonial advertisements came in for condemnation as mere facilities for assignations. *Porter's Spirit of the Times* was almost alone in taking a lenient view of them as a "slick and convenient mode of popping the question," quite suitable to "this progressive, dashing, gay, and frisky old nineteenth century." [90]

The increasing number of weekly papers in the West was one of the noticeable phenomena of the times. It is often difficult to distinguish between weekly newspapers and those weeklies which found in politics, literature, or some reform movement their *raison d'être*. The census of 1850 carried a classification of "political weeklies" separate from that for "newspapers." Certainly many of such local weeklies gave no more attention to news than did some of the story-papers, like the *New York Ledger*, and far less than most of the religious weeklies, such as the *Independent* and the *Christian Advocate*.

"ISMS" OF THE PERIOD

The interest in new social, ethical, and artistic theories was a feature of the war period which greatly alarmed conservative minds. The author of an article in the *Southern Literary Messenger* called "The Country in 1950" wrote fearfully:

> The increasing spread of lawless theories and the constant rise of dangerous vagaries of the mind and passions, denominated "isms," whose apt prototypes may be found in Milton's yelling hounds of hell, that kennel in the womb of Sin — are alarming evidence that the ground is thick strewn with the seeds of anarchy.[91]

The *Messenger* writer used the device of prophecy to get a general view of the country's tendencies; *Momus* gave its readers a series of articles on America by one "Sli-po-kum," a mythical member of the Japanese embassy, and was thus enabled to satirize "re-dress" for woman, spiritualism, "free-love and other Nastifications," and so on.[92] *De Bow's* was quite as conservative but less imaginative and satirical; it spoke directly: "The rank hot-bed of civilization seems to send forth poisonous plants even more profusely than useful ones. Millerism, Mes-

[90] *Porter's Spirit of the Times*, I, 1 (September 1856).
[91] *Southern Literary Messenger*, XXII, 430 (January 1856).
[92] *Momus*, May 12, 1860, p. 1.

merism, Mormonism, Bloomerism, and Spiritualism, all have
flourished amazingly among us." [93]
"The infamous doctrines of Fourier" [94] were attacked by
many and defended by a few. The *Spirit of the Age* (1849–50),
a successor of the *Harbinger*,[95] was a New York weekly devoted
to the advocacy of "confederated communities," prison reform,
antislavery, and other reforms.[96] William H. Channing was its
editor, and such men as Albert Brisbane, Charles A. Dana,
Thomas L. Harris, and the elder Henry James were contributors. The socialist Joseph Weydemeyer published two numbers of *Revolution* in New York in the spring of 1852; it gave
first printing to Karl Marx's famous essay, "The 18th Brumaire
of Louis Napoleon." The *Social Republic* (1858–60) was the
official organ of William Weitling's General Working-Men's
League. The Oneida *Circular* [97] was the organ of the perfectionist communities founded by J. H. Noyes. In it Noyes expounded his doctrines of spiritualism, communism, and free
love; though uneven in its editing, it was often well written
and interesting. The free love doctrines of certain communist
groups aroused wide popular antagonism, and the police raid
on Albert Brisbane's Progressive Union Club in New York,

[93] *De Bow's Review*, XVI, 369 (April 1854).
[94] *Ibid.*, XXII, 633–644 (June 1857).
[95] See Mott, *op. cit.*, p. 763.
[96] See Clarence L. F. Gohdes, *Periodicals of American Transcendentalism*
(Durham, North Carolina, 1931), Chapter VI.
[97] The *Circular* was preceded by three or four other periodicals edited by
J. H. Noyes and published by the communities with which he was associated.
The *Perfectionist* was published in New Haven in 1834 and was the first of the
series. There followed, at Putney, Vermont, the *Spiritual Magazine*, the *Perfectionist*, and the *Witness*. After the perfectionist community was driven out
of Putney, two other colonies were established — one at Oneida, New York, and
the other at Wallingford, Connecticut. The *Free Church Circular* was issued
from Oneida 1847–51. Its plant was destroyed by fire in 1851, and a new series
under the title *Circular*, with entirely new numbering, was begun at Brooklyn,
November 6, 1851, and published for a year as a weekly, changing then to
semiweekly publication; after two annual volumes, it was moved to Oneida,
where it was published for a decade (1854–64). It was then published for four
years at Wallingford (Mount Tom), after which it spent its last years at
Oneida. Theodore L. Pitt, George W. Noyes, and Alfred Barron were editors at
various times; but John Humphrey Noyes was its leading spirit. For the most
part it was weekly, small folio. Its peculiar brand of spiritualism, Noyes's free
love doctrines, and communism were its chief topics. It was followed by the
American Socialist (1876–79) at Oneida.

after columns of exposé in the newspapers of that city, produced an excitement which *Leslie's* said was "only equalled by the fall of Sevastopol and the arrival from Arctic regions of Dr. Kane." [98]

The spread of belief in spiritualism in the fifties was extraordinary. Spiritualistic societies "are being organized all over the Union under the title 'Harmonial Brotherhood,' " stated the *Democratic Review* in 1853.[99] "Everybody has read at least one of the two volumes on Spiritualism published in New York in 1853–55, by Judge J. W. Edmonds and Dr. George T. Dexter — both strenuous advocates of the new religion," observed the California *Pioneer*.[100] Horace Greeley wrote an article on the subject for *Putnam's* in which he adjured his readers: "Let us not fear to open our eyes lest we see something contrary to our preconceptions." [101] Even the Methodist clergyman-editor of the *National Magazine* was intrigued by "the Odic force" behind the spirit rappings.[102]

But most periodicals attacked the new movement, while recognizing the strength of its support. The *Southern Literary Messenger* pointed out that

It is no longer the impostures or buffoonery of the Foxes and Fishes [Kate and Margaret Fox and their sister Mrs. Anna Fish, of the "Rochester knockings"] which invite our ridicule or provoke our censure; but large numbers of both sexes, persons frequently of decent position and respectable education, have yielded to the seductions of superstition and rendered us apprehensive that the torrent of delusion will flow on with increasing volume.[103]

The *Police Gazette* followed this torrent with a serial account of "The Spiritual Humbug: Its Progress and Influence." The *Knickerbocker's* burlesque newspaper, "The Bunkum Flagstaff," became a "mejum" for purposes of satire.[104] The scientific hocus-pocus of the believers in the rappings was parodied

---

[98] *Frank Leslie's Illustrated Newspaper*, II, 204 (November 1855).

[99] *Democratic Review*, XXXII, 268–273 (March 1853).

[100] *Pioneer*, IV, 193 (October 1855). This was in connection with a famous spiritistic hoax by the editor.

[101] *Putnam's Monthly*, I, 63 (January 1853).

[102] *National Magazine*, passim in 1853, especially Vol. III.

[103] *Southern Literary Messenger*, XIX, 385 (July 1853).

[104] *Knickerbocker*, XLIV, 190–192 (August 1854).

by the *Carpet-Bag*: "The obtuseness of the abdominal abdicator causes the cartilaginous compressor to coagulate into the diaphragm and depresses the duodenum into the fandango," it explains learnedly.[105] This was all very well for the light-minded, but the religious papers naturally took the heresy more seriously:

If you wish to embrace the system it is only necessary for you to turn Jehovah out of the universe, and put matter and motion on His throne; deride the idea of moral accountability; deem yourself on a par with a vegetable; regard the marriage contract as a figment of "priestcraft" standing in the way of "free-love societies," and scoff at future retribution as a legend of antiquated ignorance.[106]

But the spiritualists themselves were not silent. "There have been issued, and still continue to be," observed the *New Englander*, "a score or more of periodicals devoted exclusively, or nearly so, to the defence and propagation of the new faith." [107] Thus the sponsors of the new doctrines were able to reply to their detractors and, according to the *Spiritual Telegraph*, render the "uncharitable and abusive" attacks of the orthodox clergy ineffectual. This paper was published in New York (1853–57) by Charles Partridge and S. B. Brittan "on behalf of the spirits who desire to speak to their mourning friends on earth";[108] the title was apt, for the telegraph had been a miracle of the preceding decade. Brittan had published before this a spiritualistic quarterly called the *Shekinah* at Bridgeport, Connecticut, in 1851–53; and he and Partridge published a monthly, the *Sacred Circle* (1854–56), of which Judge Edmonds, Dr. Dexter, and O. G. Warren were joint editors. Brittan was further interested in the *Banner of Light* (1857–1907), a Boston "Weekly Journal of Romance, Literature and General Intelligence," which lived to publish a hundred semiannual volumes of spiritualistic propaganda. Brittan was allied with Thomas Lake Harris and Carlos Stuart in the editorship of the

---

[105] *Carpet-Bag*, II, 7 (April 17, 1852).

[106] R. Gilbert, of Business Corner, Iowa, in a series of articles in the *Northwestern Christian Advocate*, Vol. IV. Quotation from issue of March 26, 1856.

[107] *New Englander*, XVI, 669 (August 1858).

[108] *Spiritual Telegraph's* prospectus, published in all early numbers. S. D. Brittan was editor. In its last volume it was called *Chas. Partridge's Spiritual Library*.

American People's Journal, a Swedenborgian paper of the early fifties. Harris, brilliant speaker and poet, edited one of the most remarkable periodicals of this group, the monthly *Herald of Light* (1857–61) in New York. It printed a good deal of verse, including, in the number for July 1857, the spirit poems of Edgar Poe. Harris was also associated with the *Mountain Cove Journal and Spiritual Harbinger*, published 1852–53 by the spiritualistic colony at Mountain Cove, Virginia, which was "dictated by Spirits out of the flesh, and by them edited, superintended, and controlled." This was the first of a number of spiritualistic papers in folio;[109] its most famous successor was the New York *Herald of Progress* (1860–64), by Andrew Jackson Davis, "the Poughkeepsie seer."

MISCELLANEOUS REFORMERS

Davis got in some blows for abolition, and many of the abolitionists, suffragists, dress reformers, and such sympathized with other reform movements of the time.

The temperance cause made great gains in converts, societies, and periodical organs. By the middle fifties, thirteen of the thirty-one states had passed laws of a prohibitory character, and Maine's liquor laws furnished a storm center for controversy. Well over a score of temperance periodicals may be counted in the period. Most of them, however, were of short life; apparently only two lived to count ten years — the *Journal of the American Temperance Union* (1837–65), New York; and the *Templar's Magazine* (1850–74), Cincinnati, which moved to Philadelphia after a war-time suspension. Two of the early-dying kind should be mentioned for the originality of their titles: the *Crystal Fountain* (1852), Allegheny, Penn-

---

[109] Such as the *Christian Spiritualist* (1854–55), New York, and the *New England Spiritualist* (1855–56), Boston. William H. Channing's *Spirit of the Age* (see p. 207, above) had spiritualistic leanings and published some of Thomas Lake Harris' work. The Oneida *Circular* (see footnote 97, above) was also a spiritualistic organ of a sort, its first name having been the *Spiritual Magazine*. *Bizarre, for Fireside and Wayside* (1852–55), conducted by Joseph M. Church in Philadelphia and at first called *Church's Bizarre*, was a dollar monthly in octavo. It satirized spiritualism while under Church's editorship, but later gave much space to "Spiritual Manifestations." It had some good contributors in its earlier and better years. Finally, R. P. Ambler's *Spirit Messenger and Harmonial Guide* (1850–51), a weekly quarto of Springfield, Massachusetts, must be listed.

sylvania, and the *Old Oaken Bucket* (1849–52), Racine, Wisconsin. "Temperance," wrote the editor of the *New-York Quarterly*, "has often been a fruitful theme for enthusiasts and demagogues, and as discussed by many has provoked contempt from liberal minds. It has had its orator in every New England village." [110] The following from *Cozzens' Wine Press* is reproduced here not as propaganda, but in order to placate the ghost of Frederick ("Sparrowgrass") Cozzens, who in life looked forward to this occasion:

When some future Livy [*Ecce!*] shall trace the events of this century, . . . he will turn with admiration and confidence to the perennial pages of the *Wine Press* and say: "Behold a proof of the high civilization of the period! Here we discover a bold, sagacious, enterprising people resolutely pursuing the path of empire, yet not unmindful of the gentler amenities of life. Here we perceive that even amid the rapid progress of Commerce, the arts were not neglected; that social virtues and the courtesies of a polished nation existed in happy proportion; for in those days *they drank good wine like gentlemen and Christians!*" [111]

And this in spite of the *Old Oaken Bucket*.

The American Peace Society continued to publish its *Advocate of Peace*,[112] concentrating its effort during the Civil War upon opposition to international conflict. The American Female Guardian Society continued its *Advocate of Moral Reform* (1832–current) in New York.[113] Prison reform had its *Pris-*

[110] *New York Quarterly*, I, 10 (June 1852). Several temperance papers edited by women are named by Bertha-Monica Stearns, "Reform Periodicals and Female Reformers," *American Historical Review*, XXXVII, 678 (July 1932).

[111] *Cozzens' Wine Press*, III, 1 (June 1856).

[112] Begun May 1828 by William Ladd, secretary of the Society, under the name *Harbinger of Peace*, it was changed three years later to *Calumet*. In 1835 it was merged with William Watson's *American Advocate of Peace* (1834–35) at Hartford, which the Society took over, adopting the *Advocate's* name. It was moved to Boston two years later and thereafter called *Advocate of Peace*, beginning a new series. Secretary George Beckwith was editor for many years, and Holmes, Whittier, and Bryant were contributors. It moved to Washington, where it is now published under the title *World Affairs*, in 1910. See historical sketch in the number for March 1928.

[113] Later (1887) called *Advocate and Family Guardian*. It was founded by John R. McDowall and edited, by Sarah Towne Smith, Helen E. Brown, Mrs. S. R. I. Bennett, and others in succession. A similar journal was the *Friend of Virtue*, later *Home Guardian* (1838–92), of Boston. Both of these were, in their beginnings, sensational anti-vice papers. See Bertha-Monica Stearns's article cited in note 110.

oner's Friend (1845–57), a Boston weekly which had borne the gruesome and propagandic title of the *Hangman*, and which numbered Charles Sumner, Dr. S. G. Howe, and Dr. Walter Channing among its contributors. The *Journal of Prison Discipline and Philanthropy* (1845–1919) was published by the Pennsylvania Prison Society in Philadelphia.

Labor unionism, which made great gains during the sixties, received some attention from the general periodicals, and publications like Lippard's *White Banner* [114] were especially interested in labor. J. C. Fincher, secretary of the machinists' and blacksmiths' union, published *Fincher's Trades Review* in Philadelphia 1863–66; and in 1864 Blake & Hayde founded their *Workingmen's Advocate* in Chicago, where it became an important journal.[115] The iron molders' and cigar makers' unions had their journals.[116]

Spelling and alphabet reform also attracted devotees. "A spirit is being cultured and cherished by the public which will within a few years demand the adoption of phonetic instead of the ordinary print," thought *Life Illustrated*, which gave a department to what it called "phonotypy." Phonography, later called shorthand, had several journals, chiefly in New York and Cincinnati; but none of them enjoyed a long life. More or less connected with them were three or four "phonetic" journals, including a curious Cincinnati monthly called *Type of the Times* (1848–59), with a running title *Tip of de timz*, which was "devoted to the spelling and writing reform." Lucius A. Hines, the socialist, was one of the editors. Stephen Pearl Andrews edited first the *Fonetic Propagandist* (1850–52) and later the *Anglo-Saxon* (1855–57), both in New York; the latter was printed in phonetic type. The *Literary Locomotive and Phonetic Paragon* (1858–59), of Newburgh, New York, undoubtedly had a name too difficult to live up to.

Reformers occasionally had time to get in a blow or two against the "tobacco evil," as witness the *Chicago Record's*

[114] See p. 29.
[115] See Volume III, Chapter X.
[116] *Iron Molders' Journal* (1863–current), Cincinnati, published as a small bulletin until its enlargement in 1895, called since 1907 the *International Molders' Journal;* and *Cigar Makers' Official Journal* (1864–current), Chicago. The *Daily Press*, of Baltimore, published in 1853, was first of the labor union dailies.

article against the smoking clergy,[117] and a long doggerel poem in *Sibyl* which ran like this:

Chewing in the parlor
Smoking in the street,
Choking with cigar-smoke
Everyone you meet,[118]

and so on and on. But C. Pfirshing set out his *Tobacco Leaf* in 1865 in New York, and it still sprouts weekly.

BARNUM, BEARDS, AND BATHS

These attempts at reform betray, as a rule, a sensitiveness to possible criticism — a kind of national introspection which has been characteristic of America. *Putnam's* article, "What Impression Do We, and Should We, Make Abroad?" is typical.[119] Most magazines printed more or less about the criticisms of America made by foreign visitors. Perhaps a general consciousness of imperfection was the chief reason why certain institutions, habits, and persons were pilloried — the perennial tendency to offer a vicarious sacrifice.

Phineas T. Barnum, whom everyone condemned as the personification of Humbug, but to whom nearly everyone paid cash tribute, is a case in point. *Vanity Fair*, which always displayed a gift for wedding clever phrase to just statement, had an apostrophe to Barnum which closed thus: "Barnum, you are the Self-Offered American Moral Sacrifice, and National Columbian Scape-Goat of the Century." [120] The great showman seldom failed in his projects. We have noted the Jenny Lind success; it followed that with "Tom Thumb," which made Barnum's American Museum a famous place of resort. "Even grave senators cannot pass through the city without calling on his Excellency General Tom Thumb," said the *Literary American*.[121] The wedding of "Tom Thumb" with Lavinia Warren, another dwarf long exhibited by Barnum, was a national event of 1863. Barnum's baby show shocked the sensibilities of some

---

[117] *Chicago Record*, I, 10 (May 1857).
[118] *Sibyl*, I, 32 (August 15, 1856).
[119] *Putnam's Monthly*, II, 345–354 (October 1853).
[120] *Vanity Fair*, II, 306 (December 22, 1860).
[121] *Literary American*, I, 124 (August 26, 1848).

moralists, but it was a great success nevertheless. *Frank Leslie's Ladies' Gazette* defended it, claiming that there was "nothing in it to shock the most delicate or fastidious minds," and that it was "the first step toward the development of a new but most important branch of physiological science." [122]

The "beard question" had to be discussed: "In this country, since the Mexican War and the California adventure, the beard is quite generally worn — at least in the cities and large towns," said a *Putnam* observer.[123] Winter baths, conjuring up "horrible ideas of chills and arctic shiverings," were generally avoided; but a physician writing in the *Mother's Journal* maintained that "The idea that bathing or washing in the winter may be omitted on account of the cold weather is a great mistake." [124] Parties were often "wildly extravagant, full of senseless display," according to George William Curtis.[125] And finally, it may be mentioned that duels were still defended by "many respectable opinions openly avowed" as "a very desirable substitute for rough fighting." [126]

SECRET SOCIETIES

The growth of secret societies in the fifties was notable, especially among the Masons and Odd Fellows. The *American Quarterly Review of Freemasonry* observed in 1857:

> The present state of the public mind in regard to secret societies is unprecedented, and their popularity unparalleled in the history of the country. . . . [They are] the universal panacea by which not only man, but woman-kind, is to be "redeemed, regenerated, and disenthralled." [127]

The leading Masonic bibliography lists forty-five periodicals which represented that order at one time or another from 1850 to 1865.[128] Most of these were briefly burning tapers, but there

---

[122] *Frank Leslie's Ladies' Gazette of Fashion*, IV, 3 (July 1855).
[123] *Putnam's Monthly*, III, 338 (March 1854).
[124] *Mother's Journal*, XXIX, 306 (December 1864).
[125] *Putnam's Monthly*, I, 178 (February 1853). "Potiphar Papers."
[126] *Russell's Magazine*, I, 133 (May 1857), and *Democratic Review*, XXIX, 548 (December 1851).
[127] *American Quarterly Review of Freemasonry*, I, 136 (July 1857).
[128] Josiah H. Drummond, *Masonic Historical and Bibliographical Memoranda* (Brooksville, Kentucky, 1822), pp. 74–106. Very helpful also are the chrono-

was scarcely a time within the period when half a dozen or more Masonic journals were not in course of publication. When the *American Freemason* began in 1853, it listed nine similar periodicals already in the field.[129] "Within the past few years," asserted one journal, "Freemasonry has taken an imposing place in the literature of the times." [130] The four most important Masonic journals before 1870 may be noticed briefly.

The *Freemasons' Monthly Magazine* (1841–73), edited in Boston by Charles W. Moore, secretary of the Massachusetts Grand Lodge, was the pioneer periodical to devote itself wholly to Masonry, to the exclusion of outside news and miscellany; its specialty was Masonic jurisprudence. It ended with the death of its editor. The *Masonic Review* (1845–99) was founded in Cincinnati by Cornelius Moore, who continued as editor until 1877. The *American Quarterly Review of Freemasonry* (1857–59), though it exists in a file of only two volumes, is one of the Masonic classics. Edited by Albert G. Mackey in New York, its list of contributors included the greatest Masonic scholars of the times. Albert Pike, Rob. Morris, Giles F. Yates, and Finlay M. King were constant writers for it. The *Voice of Masonry* (1862–99), of Chicago, was a continuation by Morris of his Louisville journal of the same name published through 1859–61. It used considerable miscellany and reflected the versatility of its editor.

For the I. O. O. F., one of the most important journals was the *Golden Rule and Odd Fellows' Family Companion* (1844–52), founded in New York by E. and J. Winchester. It was highly miscellaneous in character. In 1849 it prefaced its already long title with the name *Gazette of the Union*. The *American Odd Fellow* (1862–74) was edited and published in New York by John W. Orr, the engraver on wood.

---

logical, geographical, and alphabetical card indexes in the Masonic Library at Cedar Rapids, Iowa.

[129] *American Freemason*, III, 5 (September 15, 1854). This journal was at first called the *Kentucky Freemason:* Rob. Morris was its editor.

[130] *American Quarterly Review of Freemasonry*, I, 5 (July 1857).

SUPPLEMENT

SKETCHES OF CERTAIN IMPORTANT MAGAZINES
WHICH FLOURISHED 1850–1865

[For an explanation of the organization of the Supplement, see the Preface to the present volume; and for comment on the method of the bibliographical note which appears as footnote 1 of each sketch, the reader is referred to the first volume of the series, *A History of American Magazines, 1741–1850*, page 69.]

CHRONOLOGICAL CHART OF THE MORE IMPORTANT AMERICAN
MAGAZINES 1850-1865

The following magazines were published during the whole of the period:

American Agriculturist
American Journal of Medical Sciences
American Journal of Science
American Railroad Journal
Bibliotheca Sacra
Christian Examiner
Church Review
Connecticut Common School Journal
Eclectic Magazine
Friend
Friends' Review
Godey's Lady's Book
Home Journal
Hunt's Merchants' Magazine
Independent
Journal of Franklin Institute
Ladies' Repository
Liberator
Littell's Living Age
Mercersburg Review
Merry's Museum
Methodist Quarterly Review
National Police Gazette
New Englander
New York Ledger
North American Review
Peterson's Ladies' Magazine
Princeton Review
Saturday Evening Post
Scientific American
Youth's Companion

THE NORTH AMERICAN REVIEW [1]

WHEN that group of young professional men of Boston and Cambridge who supported the *Monthly Anthology* decided to give up their periodical, they must have done so with deep regret. True, it had never produced sufficient profits even to pay for the club's weekly suppers; and when slight profits became large deficits, the end was indicated. And whatever the pride in the *Anthology* may have been, those suppers of "widgeon and teal," "very good claret, without ice (*tant pis*)," "segars," and "much pleasant talk and good

[1] TITLES: *The North-American Review and Miscellaneous Journal*, 1815–21; *The North American Review*, 1821–current.
FIRST ISSUE: May 1815. Current.
PERIODICITY: Bimonthly, May 1815–September 1818; quarterly, December 1818–October 1876; bimonthly, January 1877–December 1878; monthly, January 1879–August 1906; fortnightly, September 7, 1906–August 16, 1907; monthly, September 1907–June 1924; quarterly, September 1924–June 1927; monthly, September 1927–March 1935; quarterly, June 1935–current. I–VII (May 1815–September 1818), semiannual volumes, three numbers each; VIII, December 1818, March 1819; IX, June, September 1819; X–CLXXXIII (1820–1906), regular semiannual volumes (X–XXX also called New Series, I–XXI); CLXXIV, January 4–April 19, 1907; CLXXXV, May 3–August 16, 1907; CLXXXVI, September–December 1907; CLXXXVII–CCXXI (January 1908–June 1925), regular semiannual volumes; CCXXII, September 1925–February 1926; CCXXIII, March 1926–February 1927; CCXXIV, March–December 1927; CCXXV–current (1928–current), regular semiannual volumes.
PUBLISHERS: Wells & Lilly, Boston (William Tudor, owner), 1815–16; Cummings & Hilliard, Boston (North American Review Club, owners), 1817–20, 1824; Oliver Everett, Boston (North American Review Club, 1821–23; Jared Sparks, 1823–24, owners), 1821–24; Frederick T. Gray, Boston (Jared Sparks and F. T. Gray, owners), 1825–28; Gray & Bowen, Boston (Jared Sparks, F. T. Gray, and Charles Bowen, owners), 1828–30; Gray & Bowen, Boston (A. H. Everett, F. T. Gray, and Charles Bowen, owners), 1830–31; Charles Bowen, Boston (A. H. Everett and Charles Bowen, owners), 1832–36; Otis, Broaders & Company, Boston (J. G. Palfrey, chief owner, 1836–42; Francis Bowen, chief owner, 1843–52), 1837–38, 1843–47; Ferdinand Andrews, Boston (J. G. Palfrey, chief owner), 1838–40; James Munroe & Company, Boston (J. G. Palfrey, chief owner), 1840–41; David H. Williams, Boston (J. G. Palfrey, chief owner), 1842; Charles C. Little & James Brown, Boston (Francis Bowen, chief owner), 1848–52; Crosby, Nichols & Company, Boston, 1853–63; Ticknor & Fields, Boston, 1864–67; Fields, Osgood & Company, Boston, 1868–69; James R. Osgood & Company, Boston (A. T. Rice, owner, 1877), 1870–77; D. Appleton & Company, New York (A. T. Rice, owner), 1878–80; A. T. Rice, New York, 1881–89;

humor" [2] were occasions which supplied a flow of wit and scholarship all too rare even in Boston.

Therefore the bonds of the fellowship which the *Anthology* had created were not entirely dissolved when the magazine was suspended. The group saw the founding of Andrews Norton's *General Repository* six months after the abandonment of the *Anthology*, and assisted the editor in filling its Unitarian pages; indeed some of the members of the old group edited the last two numbers of the *Repository*.[3] But it lasted only two years. After the *Repository* was given up in 1813, members of the old *Anthology* group planned a new magazine to be called the *New England Magazine and Review* and to be edited by Willard Phillips — then a young Harvard tutor but later a prominent lawyer. This project, apparently originated by President Kirkland and Professor Channing, of Harvard, met with opposition when William Tudor, another member of the old group, returned from abroad with his head full of plans for starting such

---

Lloyd Bryce, New York, 1889–94; North American Review Publishing Company, New York, 1895–1915; North American Review Corporation, New York, 1915–current. (George B. M. Harvey, chief owner during his editorship; W. B. Mahony, chief owner 1926–current.)

EDITORS: William Tudor, 1815–17; Jared Sparks, 1817–18; Edward Tyrrel Channing, 1818–19; Edward Everett, 1820–23; Jared Sparks, 1824–30; Alexander Hill Everett, 1830–35; John Gorham Palfrey, 1836–42; Francis Bowen, 1843–53; Andrew Preston Peabody, 1853–63; James Russell Lowell, 1863–72 (with Charles Eliot Norton, 1863–68; E. W. Gurney, 1868–70; Henry Adams, 1870–72); Henry Adams (with Thomas Sergeant Perry as assistant editor, 1872–73; Henry Cabot Lodge assistant editor, 1873–76), 1872–76; Allen Thorndike Rice, 1877–89; Lloyd Bryce, 1889–96; David A. Munro, 1896–99; George B. M. Harvey, 1899–1926; Walter Butler Mahony, 1926–35; John H. G. Pell, 1935–current.

INDEXES: *General Index*, 1815–26 (Boston, 1827); William Cushing, *Index*, 1815–77 (Cambridge, 1878); *Supplementary Index*, 1878–80; indexed in *Poole's, Poole's Abridged, Readers' Guide, Annual Library Index, Cumulative Index, Jones' Index, Review of Reviews Index, Engineering Index, Dramatic Index.*

REFERENCES: Herbert B. Adams, *Life and Writings of Jared Sparks* (Boston, 1893), Chapters V, VIII–XI; George E. DeMille, *Literary Criticism in America* (New York, 1931), Chapter I; Algernon Tassin, *The Magazine in America* (New York, 1916), Chapter II; *North American Review*, CCI, 123 ff. (January 1915), and C, 315–330 (January 1865); *Historical Magazine*, III, 343–345 (November 1859).

[2] See Mott, *A History of American Magazines, 1741–1850*, p. 256. Quoted phrases are taken from *Anthology Society: Journal of the Proceedings* (Boston, 1910), edited by M. A. DeWolfe Howe.

[3] Mott, *op. cit.*, p. 278.

a magazine himself.[4] It was agreed to leave the field to Tudor; and, accordingly, the *North-American Review and Miscellaneous Journal*, a bimonthly, appeared in May 1815, with Tudor as editor and Wells & Lilly as publishers.

The new journal was a neat duodecimo of 144 pages, issued at $4.00 a year. Its contents were far more varied than in later years. It swung between the English review type, as exemplified by the *Edinburgh*, and the more miscellaneous magazines such as the London *Gentleman's* and the Philadelphia *Port Folio*. On the whole, the magazine tendency had rather the better of it for the first two or three years.

The initial number began with a series of comments on old American books and pamphlets, written by Tudor. This "catalogue raisonnée" ran serially through the numbers of the first three years of the magazine; two seventeenth-century pamphlets on Virginia were considered in the first number, and later other colonial guidebooks and such histories as Hubbard's *Indian Wars*, Price's *New England*, and Mather's *Magnalia* were reviewed. This was under the title "Books Relating to America," and it was followed, in that initial number, by several brief letters to the editor signed by such names as "Scipio Africanus," and "A Friend to Improvement." One of these proposed to change the second Sunday service from afternoon to evening, averring that "the middle of the day, so oppressive in summer, should be left to meditation and repose."[5] This apparent surrender of sanctity to somnolence may have been one of the items that caused Robert Walsh to condemn the new journal in his *National Gazette* as "lax in its religious tone."[6] Or perhaps it was the letter of "C. G." objecting to the application of force by officers called "tythingmen" to compel attendance at church, or indeed the request of another unknown to be supplied with a list of all the plays thus far produced in America. Certainly none could object to the censorious words of "Charles Surface" anent "idle gossip and mischievous tattling," or to the remarks of "Aristippus" against sitting

[4] *North American Review*, C, 318 (January 1865). Anniversary article by Judge Willard Phillips.
[5] *North American Review*, I, 15 (May 1815).
[6] The *North American* is defended against this aspersion in the *Western Review*, IV, 94 (March 1821).

crosslegged in company or using a soiled silk handkerchief for a napkin.

No gentleman [dogmatizes "Aristippus"] is to lean back to support his chair on its hind legs, except in his own room: in a parlour with a small circle it borders on extreme familiarity, and in a drawing room filled with company, it betokens a complete want of respect for society. Besides, it weakens the chairs, and with perseverance, infallibly makes a hole in the carpet.[7]

Other communications in this first number are scientific and agricultural in character. The letters are followed by two mediocre poems — a satire and a descriptive piece. Then comes a thirty-two page notice of Baron de Grimm's *Memoirs*, much of it devoted to anecdotes extracted from that work. Similar space is given to the *Quarterly Review's* attack on American manners and morals in its famous review of *Inchiquin's Letters*, the article using James K. Paulding's contribution to the controversy, *The United States and England,* as its basis. Thus the *North American* began in its very first number its participation in the third war with England — the paper war. The other two reviews deal with the political situation in France and with Lydia Huntley's poems. Nine of Miss Huntley's poems are printed, which, "if not sublime," are at least allowed to be "exquisitely beautiful and pathetick." [8] Miss Huntley (later Mrs. Sigourney) came to be, in the next year, a contributor of original verse to the *North American.* The reviews are followed by four or five pages of meteorological tables, after which the number is closed by fourteen pages of "Miscellaneous and Literary Intelligence" and four of obituaries. The "Intelligence" department contains an account of the induction of the Reverend Edward Everett (then twenty-one years old) into a new Greek professorship at Harvard, as well as the announcements of Boston publishers. The obituaries are all from abroad and include that of Lady Hamilton, "famous for her beauty, her accomplishments, and her frailty." [9]

Virtually all of this first number and a good three-fourths

[7] *North American Review*, I, 21 (May 1815).
[8] *Ibid.*, I, 120 (May 1815).
[9] *Ibid.*, I, 143 (May 1815).

of the first four volumes were written by the editor himself. "I began it without arrangement for aid from others," he wrote later, "and was in consequence obliged to write more myself than was suitable for a work of this description." [10] The magazine was Bostonian, Harvardian, Unitarian. And yet Tudor wrote to Sparks: "My object was to abstract myself from the narrow prejudices of locality, however I might feel them. I considered the work written for the citizens of the United States, and not for the district of New England." [11]

As to how well he succeeded in giving a national scope to the review, opinions may differ. Too much attention was given to Harvard, to Boston publishers, to New England writers, and to the proceedings of learned societies in Boston and Cambridge. This indeed continued long after Tudor had relinquished all connection with the magazine: the March 1818 number carried the entire prospectus of Harvard, the Harvard Phi Beta Kappa addresses were frequently printed, and Harvard professors continued to edit the journal for more than half a century. This devotion to its college and city angered its critics, and for many years they called it "provincial and parochial." [12] Said the New York *Broadway Journal* in 1845: "That the *North American Review* has worked religiously for New England, her sons, her institutions, her claims of every sort, there is no question." [13] Simms's *Southern and Western Magazine* echoed the accusation: "None can deny the exclusive and jealous vigilance with which it insists on the pretensions of Massachusetts Bay." [14]

On the other hand, Tudor did give some attention to other parts of the country; and, as we shall see, Sparks later made an especial effort to broaden the geographical scope of the journal. From the beginning, foreign affairs were watched with interest. Tudor even went so far as to clip generously from foreign periodicals because of his lack of correspondents abroad; fortunately for the *Review*, however, scissoring did not become a

---

[10] William Tudor, *Miscellanies* (New York, 1821), p. 52.
[11] Adams, *op. cit.*, I, 229. Letter to Sparks dated March 12, 1817.
[12] *Literary World*, April 24, 1847.
[13] *Broadway Journal*, I, 337 (May 31, 1845).
[14] *Southern and Western Magazine*, I, 297 (May 1845).

permanent policy. And in one other respect the magazine did achieve a national scope: it was a spokesman for nationality, not only against the attacks of the English reviews upon American life and character, but also in its advocacy of a national literature and a national art.[15]

At the end of his first year's editorship, Tudor transferred the ownership of the *North American* to the old literary group which had descended from *Anthology* days. This now consisted of John Gallison, a lawyer and newspaper editor; Nathan Hale, editor of the *Boston Daily Advertiser*; Richard Henry Dana, a young lawyer of high literary promise; Edward T. Channing, another young lawyer of literary proclivities, Dana's cousin and a brother of William Ellery Channing; William P. Mason, a fourth lawyer; Jared Sparks, a Harvard tutor; and Willard Phillips, who had been a tutor at Harvard, but had just entered the practice of law. F. C. Gray was not a member, but often attended.

> We held weekly meetings [wrote Judge Phillips many years later] at Gallison's rooms, at which our own articles and those of friends and correspondents were read, criticized, and decided upon. . . . We also solicited articles upon particular subjects from literary friends at a distance.[16]

Tudor remained as managing editor without pay for another year, though the club took the responsibility of providing a large part of the reviews and of supporting the venture financially. In 1817, however, he severed his connection with the journal. It is frequently said that he was succeeded by Phillips; but it is certain that, though Phillips was the club's leader, the managing editorship devolved upon Sparks. Sparks wrote to his lifelong friend, Miss Storrow, on February 21, 1817:

> . . . I have engaged to take charge of the *North American Review* after the next number, when Mr. Tudor resigns. I was desired to do this by several gentlemen, and by the particular advice of the president. Mr. Phillips declines, as it interferes too much with his profession.[17]

---

[15] See Gregory Paine's "Cooper and the *North American Review*," *Studies in Philology*, XXVIII, 799 (October 1931).

[16] *North American Review*, C, 318 (January 1865).

[17] Adams, *op. cit.*, I, 99.

Sparks remained editor for only one year, although he was later to return for a more extended and distinguished editorship; at this time he was drawn away from editorial work by his desire to devote himself to theology. His impress upon the *North American* of 1817–18 is seen chiefly in the emphasis on American history and on travels in Africa, in both of which fields he had an enthusiastic personal interest.

As we now look back upon Sparks's six bimonthly numbers, it is easy for us to see that the most important single piece in them was Bryant's "Thanatopsis." This poem, which had been written some six years earlier, was left at Phillips' home in the summer of 1817 by the poet's father, without title or author's name, one of a group of five submitted for publication. Two of these, "Thanatopsis" and four stanzas on death, were in the father's handwriting; and Phillips, who knew both father and son, supposed the two were by Dr. Bryant and the other three by Cullen. At any rate, the club was delighted by all of them. When Dana heard "Thanatopsis" read, he interrupted with the exclamation, "That was never written on this side of the water!" They gave the poem its title "Thanatopsis," but they supposed the lines on death were intended as a prelude to the blank verse and so printed them; and in the same number — that for September 1817 — they published the other three poems. All were, of course, like everything else in the *North American*, anonymous; and not until after the poems were published did any member of the club know that all five poems were by William Cullen Bryant. "To a Waterfowl" was published in the *North American* in March 1818; and four reviews from Bryant's pen appeared within the next two years.[18]

Channing followed Sparks as editor. The *Review* had been growing less and less magazinish; and in December 1818 it discarded its news notes, general essays, and poetry, and adopted quarterly publication, though it retained its subtitle *and Miscellaneous Journal* for three years longer. The change

---

[18] See Tremaine McDowell's "Bryant and the *North American Review*," *American Literature*, I, 14 (March 1929); also McDowell's "Bryant's Practice in Composition and Revision," *P.M.L.A.*, LII, 474; and Carl Van Doren's "The Growth of Thanatopsis," *Nation*, CI, 432. "Thanatopsis" as published in the *North American* did not include the beginning and ending which Bryant wrote for it on the publication of his volume of poems in 1821.

was scarcely perceptible. Channing was elected Boylston professor of rhetoric and oratory at Harvard at the end of 1819.
Dana, who had been his chief assistant, expected to be appointed editor in his stead, but the club thought Dana too unpopular among probable contributors to make a successful
editor. He naturally resented this decision, and he and Channing left the club.[19] Some of his friends also resented it —
among them Bryant, who said that if the *North American* "had
remained in Dana's hands, he would have imparted a character
of originality and decision to its critical articles which no other
man of the country was at that time qualified to give it." [20]
And for many years the critics of the *North American* —
or at least those of them who knew about this episode — were
wont to exclaim, "What a wonderful journal it might have
been if only the poet Dana had been made editor back in
1820!" [21]

But it was upon a brilliant young Greek professor that the
choice fell — Edward Everett. The new editor had gained remarkable prestige as a scholar, orator, and writer. John Neal
wrote in *Blackwood's* that Everett was "among the first young
men of the age" [22] — a high-sounding but rather cloudy phrase.
Hall, of the *Port Folio*, was more definite: he said that Everett
possessed "a combination of talents surpassing anything that
has been exhibited in the brief annals of our literature in the
person of any individual." [23] Of course there were malcon-
tents, even aside from those displeased by the slap at Dana;
the critic W. A. Jones, of *Arcturus*, called Everett, some years
later, "an incarnation of the very spirit of elegance" — which
sounds well enough until one reads Jones's definition of "ele-

[19] Evert A. and George L. Duyckinck, *Cyclopaedia of American Literature*
(rev. ed.; Philadelphia, 1881), I, 785. That Channing's resignation was owing
to resentment is by no means certain. Duyckinck does not say so. See Adams,
op. cit., I, 234. Palfrey took Channing's place in the club. William P. Mason, a
Boston lawyer, took the place of either Gallison, who died in 1820, or Dana.
Van Wyck Brooks points out that one cause of Dana's unpopularity was his
championship of the new romantic poetry. See *The Flowering of New England*
(New York, 1936), p. 115.
[20] James Grant Wilson, *Bryant and His Friends* (New York, 1886), p. 189.
[21] See *Arcturus*, III, 405 (May 1842).
[22] *Blackwood's Edinburgh Magazine*, XVI, 570 (November 1824).
[23] *Port Folio*, No. 2 of 1820, p. 463.

gance" as "safe mediocrity, 'content to dwell in decencies forever.' " [24]

However, Everett was the most successful of the *Review's* editors up to that time. Griswold, in his *Prose Writers*, speaks of the "unprecedented popularity" of the journal under Everett. Certainly the number of readers increased. Everett himself later wrote that it had 500 or 600 circulation when he took it over;[25] it had some 2,500 two years later and continued to increase slightly.[26] The publishing responsibility, which the club had placed in the hands of Cummings & Hilliard shortly after Wells & Lilly gave it up in 1816, Everett transferred to his brother Oliver, who had a large family and was in indigent circumstances.[27]

Everett himself was a voluminous writer for the *Review*. He heads the *Boston Journal* list of contributors [28] to the first forty-five years of the *Review* with 116 articles. Moreover, he brought into his journal some important new contributors. Before his editorship, the following writers, in addition to the members of the club already listed and the editors, had done most of the writing: Everett himself, who was an important contributor before he was made editor; his brother Alexander H., a later owner and editor; John G. Palfrey, who was also a later editor; ex-President John Adams; Judge Joseph Story; Andrews Norton, the famous Unitarian; Dr. Walter Channing, a brother of Edward T.; Dr. Enoch Hale, a brother of Nathan, one of the club members; Francis C. Gray, a Boston lawyer who had been John Quincy Adams' secretary in his mission to Russia; George Ticknor, professor of modern languages at Harvard; Samuel Gilman, a Harvard tutor who became the Unitarian minister at Charleston, South Carolina; Sidney Willard, professor of Hebrew at Harvard; Theophilus Parsons and Franklin Dexter, literary Boston lawyers; John Farrar, professor of mathematics at Harvard; and John Pickering, Salem lawyer and philologist. Daniel Webster contributed a few

---

[24] *Arcturus*, II, 223 (September 1841).

[25] *North American Review*, C, 320 (January 1865).

[26] Paul Revere Frothingham, *Edward Everett* (Boston, 1925), p. 68. In 1826 it had nearly 3,000; see Adams, *op. cit.*, I, 360.

[27] Frothingham, *op. cit.*, p. 69.

[28] See *Historical Magazine*, III, 343–345 (November 1859).

articles, notably one on Bunker Hill in July 1818. Everett introduced into the pages of the *North American* such writers as Caleb Cushing, then a Newburyport lawyer, who wrote on topics in many fields; W. H. Prescott, who wrote a great deal of what he himself referred to rather too contemptuously as "thin porridge" [29] for the "Old *North*"; Nathaniel Bowditch, famous Salem mathematician; Professor John W. Webster, of the Harvard chair of chemistry and mineralogy; Joseph G. Cogswell, Harvard professor of geology and later master of the Round Hill School; and Charles W. Upham, a Salem clergyman.

The type of contents continued much the same as under Sparks and Channing. The club was still active; Everett was inclined to resent its overlordship [30] and gradually achieved an independence from it. "The sole editorship gradually passed into my hands," he wrote later.[31] Of politics the *Review* published comparatively little, except as certain social and economic discussions verged upon the political. Perhaps the most important ventures in that field were two discussions published in 1820: Chief Justice Lemuel Shaw's article on "Slavery and the Missouri Question" appeared in January of that year, and James T. Austin's "The American Tariff" in October. Of science there was more, especially in the field of geology. F. C. Gray had an elaborate review of "systems of Geology" in the number for March 1819, which closed with the expression of a hope that "our University will soon be roused from its long neglect of this study." [32] It was. Dr. John Ware wrote occasionally on medical and chemical subjects; and Cushing, who had taught natural history at Harvard, sometimes wrote on botany. Law was a well-tilled field in the *Review*; Joseph Story, Henry Wheaton, and Theron Metcalf composed, with the lawyer members of the club, a distinguished legal staff for the journal. Travel books received much attention.

European literature, society, and politics occupied hundreds and eventually thousands of pages of the *North American*.

---

[29] Rollo Ogden, *William Hickling Prescott* (Boston, 1905), p. 66.
[30] Adams, *op. cit.*, I, 341.
[31] *North American Review*, C, 320 (January 1865).
[32] *North American Review*, VIII, 414 (March 1819).

Everett came to his editorship fresh from European travel and
with his head full of European ideas. A typical number of the
review — that for July 1822 — contained articles on Rousseau's
life and Mirabeau's speeches by Alexander H. Everett, a review
of Sismondi's *Julia Sévéra* by Edward Everett, a disquisition on
Italian literature by James Marsh, a review of C. A. G. Goede's
England by Edward Brooks, and one of *Europe, by a Citizen
of the United States*, by F. C. Gray. To show the attempt to
balance the foreign cargo by American materials, the remainder
of the contents of the number should be listed: Edward Everett's review of *Bracebridge Hall*, William Howard Gardiner's
review of *The Spy*, J. G. Cogswell on *Schoolcraft's Journal*,
Caleb Cushing on Webster's Plymouth oration, and Theron
Metcalf's review of Greenleaf's *Cases Overruled*.

That Everett recognized his neglect of American themes
there can be no question; but he was Europe-minded in these
years, and so were his associates. When Sparks wrote him
from Baltimore criticizing the *Review* for want of Americanism, Everett arranged his defense under three points:

1st. You cannot pour anything out of a vessel but what is in it. I am
obliged to depend on myself more than on any other person, and I
must write that which will run fastest. 2d. There is really a dearth of
American topics; the American books are too poor to praise, and to
abuse them will not do. 3d. The people round here, our most numerous and oldest friends, have not the raging Americanism that reigns
in your quarter.[33]

This seems an expression of unbelievable narrowness. A dearth
of American topics! It was the period of vast westward movement, of the Monroe doctrine, of sectional rivalry, of the
Missouri Compromise, of the United States Bank question, and
of early antislavery agitation. American books were, of course,
few; though it was the day of Irving, Cooper, and Bryant.

But Everett did not, after all, completely forget the doctrine
of the exploitation of nationality upon which Tudor and Sparks
had founded the review he now edited. He never quite made it
deserve the derisive title, "the *North Unamerican*." He ran a series of articles on internal improvements in the southern states.

[33] Adams, *op. cit.*, I, 243.

He gave attention to the work being done in American history and biography. He published many articles on American science and American law. He became one of the leaders in the curiously undignified controversy between English and American journalists over the question of whether the *Quarterly Review's* declaration that Americans were "inherently inferior" to Englishmen was sound,[34] defending American ideals with vigor.

The *North American's* literary criticism, if not always acute, if sometimes warped by the prejudices of its special culture-group, was generally discriminating and honest. There was no outstanding literary critic among its contributors, but most of them wrote on belles-lettres occasionally. One modern reader of the old volumes of our review believes that "the work of these men is so homogeneous that one can almost treat them as a composite critic."[35] This is itself uncritical, though it is true that prejudices and predilections alike were often shared, and that the editing of the times often brought diverse views into line. Bryant's few reviews, notable for their plain speaking and clear apprehension of standards, and Dana's, not much more numerous, require special mention. Everett was more inclined to speak of faults lightly while he showed enthusiasm for features he could praise; like many another critic of the time, he felt that he was watering a growing plant. Franklin Dexter said of Pierpont's *Airs of Palestine*, "the applause it has received is given as much to animate as to reward."[36] Most of the *Review's* writers plead, sometimes rather naïvely, for more and better American literature.[37] Among English writers, Scott was upheld as the great figure, in a series of reviews by various pens. Toward Byron the attitude was not consistent: Tudor condemned his lack of morals,[38] Phillips rebuked his disorder and disproportion,[39] and A. H. Everett praised him[40] beyond the liking of many readers of the *Review*.[41] Moore's verse,

[34] See Mott, *op. cit.*, p. 189.
[35] De Mille, *op. cit.*, p. 21.
[36] *North American Review*, IV, 409 (March 1817).
[37] Paine, *op. cit.*, pp. 801–802.
[38] *North American Review*, IV, 369 (March 1817).
[39] *Ibid.*, V, 98–110 (May 1817).
[40] *Ibid.*, XX, 1 (January 1825). Everett condemned his immoralities, however.
[41] Adams, *op. cit.*, I, 349. Ticknor to Sparks: "The review of Lord Byron was universally disapproved."

though popular, was said by Channing to be "little more than a mixture of musick, conceit, and debauchery." [42] One article on German literature must be mentioned — Edward Everett's masterly review of Goethe's *Dichtung und Wahrheit* in the number for January 1817.

Everett worked hard at his editorial task. After he had relinquished it, he wrote to his successor: "You must do what your predecessor did — sit down with tired fingers, aching head, and sad heart, and write for your life." [43] And later: "On one occasion, being desirous of reviewing Dean Funes' *History of Paraguay* . . . and having no knowledge of Spanish, I took lessons for three weeks . . . and at the end of that time the article was written." [44] But he had his reward, not only in the growing power and prosperity of his journal, but in such praises as that of the *Edinburgh Review*, which declared that the *North American* was

by far the best and most promising production of the press of that country that has ever come to our hands. It is written with great spirit, learning, and ability, on a great variety of subjects.[45]

The praise of the master.

But the ambitious Everett could not be satisfied long in the confinement of editorial work, and at the end of 1823 he resigned to enter politics. Jared Sparks, who had been in charge of a Unitarian congregation at Baltimore, was thereupon invited to return to the post he had occupied in 1817–18. He accepted, on condition that he be allowed to purchase the property from the club; the purchase was made, at $10,900 [46] — approximately the annual receipts from subscriptions. Three years later Sparks sold a quarter-interest to F. T. Gray, his publisher, for $4,000.[47] The circulation increased slightly throughout Sparks's editorship: it was 2,932 in 1826, 3,063 in 1828, and about 3,200 in 1830.[48] The last figure was destined

[42] *North American Review*, VI, 1 (November 1817).
[43] Adams, *op. cit.*, I, 341.
[44] *North American Review*, C, 320 (January 1865).
[45] *Edinburgh Review*, XXXIV, 161, footnote (August 1820).
[46] Adams, *op. cit.*, I, 361.
[47] *Ibid.*, I, 360.
[48] *Ibid.*, I, 360, 362, 363.

232 A HISTORY OF AMERICAN MAGAZINES [Sketch

to remain the high point of the *Review's* subscription list until after the Civil War.

In spite of a circulation that now seems of negligible size, the *North American* had reached a position of acknowledged power and influence in the country. It was read by the leading men and was available in all the important reading rooms. Over a hundred copies went to England, but it was banned in France by the Bourbon monarchy.[49] A. H. Everett, now minister to Spain, wrote Sparks that its editorship was an office honorable enough to "satisfy the ambitions of any individual," and thought it better than the old *Edinburgh*.[50] Governor Cass wrote from Detroit: "The reputation of the *North American Review* is the property of the nation." [51] George Ticknor, visiting in Philadelphia, told of the high respect for it there.[52]

Sparks, emphasizing American topics more than Everett had, retaining most of the older spheres of interest and developing new ones, kept quite as high a standard as his predecessor.[53] The policy of paying a dollar a page to contributors, adopted in 1823 as a substitute for the gentlemanly custom of unrewarded literary labor, apparently had little effect on the contents of the journal. The older, prized contributors continued — the Everetts, Story (who refused his dollar a page),[54] the Hales, Ticknor, Prescott, Cushing, Cogswell. George Bancroft, who had made his first contribution just before Sparks took charge, became a valued writer of articles and book reviews in the next few years. Lewis Cass wrote some influential articles on the American Indian policy. F. W. P. Greenwood, Sparks's successor as Unitarian minister at Baltimore, wrote for the April 1824 number an article on Wordsworth which was at the same time appreciative and discriminating; this was the first of sev-

---

[49] Adams, *op. cit.*, I, 284–285.
[50] *Ibid.*, I, 287.
[51] *Ibid.*, I, 274.
[52] *Ibid.*, I, 350.
[53] It is impossible to accept the summary dictum of Julius H. Ward in the centennial number that the *Review* "distinctly fell off" during Sparks's administration from "the high reputation for strong and widely varied articles which it had during Mr. Everett's career as editor." See *North American Review*, CCI, 127 (January 1915). This statement is repeated in Tassin, *op. cit.*, p. 38.
[54] Adams, *op. cit.*, I, 358.

eral good essays in literary criticism by Greenwood, who was under contract for fifty pages a year.[55] Peter Hoffman Cruse, also of Baltimore, and editor of the *American* there, was another valuable and regular contributor. Other newcomers were Orville Dewey, Unitarian minister at New Bedford; Jeremiah Evarts, editor of the *Missionary Herald*; Samuel A. Eliot, a Boston merchant and politician; J. L. Kingsley, professor of ancient languages at Yale; Moses Stuart, professor of sacred literature at Andover; and Captain (later General) Henry Whiting. The Tuesday Evening Club, of which Prescott, his brother-in-law Franklin Dexter, and W. H. Gardiner were leading spirits, helped supply material.

Sparks himself wrote much on South American countries, and on Mexico and Panama. He learned Spanish and kept up a correspondence with several men in South America. R. C. Anderson, American minister to Colombia, had an article on the constitution of that country in the number for October 1826. Sparks also wrote a number of articles on colonization of the blacks. He gave no little attention to the South; his article on Baltimore in January 1825 won much favor. He advocated the hands-off policy with regard to slavery [56] — an attitude maintained by the *North American* for many years. Samuel Gilman, of Charleston, was a frequent contributor.

Travel, history and biography, political economy, science, philosophy, poetry, and fiction were prominent topics in Sparks's *North American*. European affairs had less space than formerly, though both Everetts wrote upon them. But Edward Everett wrote also on American questions; his argument against the protective tariff in the number for July 1824 became almost a classic.

Sparks was accustomed to taking great editorial liberties with the manuscripts of his contributors. When Bancroft complained of alterations, Sparks wrote:

I have made it a practice without a single exception to strike out of any article such parts, as I did not like; and I have hardly printed an article in which I did not omit something, nor do I remember writing an article for the N. A. R. while it was in other hands from which

[55] *Ibid.*, I, 357.
[56] *Ibid.*, I, 263.

some parts were not struck out. I *add* nothing without the consent of the author, but I omit in all cases where I think it ought to be done. You are the only person who has complained.

That he was too sweeping in his statement that he added nothing, is fully apparent from his correspondence.[57]

Sparks traveled much during his editorship, and his editorial work was done in his absence by Palfrey, Gray, or Folsom. During his sojourn in Europe in 1828, Edward Everett had charge. In 1830 Sparks sold his three-quarters interest in the *Review* to A. H. Everett for $15,000.[58] Sparks had become engrossed in historical projects; Everett had just returned from Spain, where he had been minister from the United States.

Alexander Hill Everett made the years 1830 to 1836 the high point of the *North American's* first half-century. He surpassed his brother's editorship by keeping the journal abreast of American political problems, and he excelled Sparks by his more adequate treatment of European topics.

> In every respect [said the *Knickerbocker Magazine* in 1835] the *North American Review* is an honor to the country. In politics it is liberal and impartial. We hail it as the sole exponent, in its peculiar sphere, of our national mind, character and progress; and are proud to see it sent abroad . . . as an evidence of indigenous talent, high moral worth, and republican feeling.[59]

In the second number under the new editor, Edward Everett, now a member of Congress, wrote a long article on the double subject of the Webster-Hayne debate and nullification; it filled eighty-four pages. In January 1831 the editor discussed "The American System," and Bancroft wrote on "The Bank of the United States." The latter article was followed in April by a discussion of the same subject from the pen of William B. Lawrence, of New York, who was just beginning a distinguished legal and political career. In January 1833 the editor printed his own seventy-page dissertation on nullification, and in July

[57] See John Spencer Bassett, ed., *Correspondence of George Bancroft and Jared Sparks, 1823–1832* (Smith College Studies in History, Vol. II, No. 2, January 1917). The quotation is found on p. 96, and other complaints and replies on pp. 87–89 and 120–125.

[58] Adams, *op. cit.*, I, 290, footnote, and I, 364.

[59] *Knickerbocker Magazine*, V, 465 (May 1835).

of that year a strong article on "The Union and the States." These had the same theme, which may be expressed in the Jacksonian phrase with which the former ended: "THE FEDERAL UNION: IT MUST BE PRESERVED." [60] Two years later the *Review* published a discussion of Mrs. Child's *Appeal* by Emory Washburn, a Worcester lawyer, which contained language that defines the position of the journal at this time:

That we must be rid of slavery some day seems to be the decided conviction of almost every honest mind. If in a struggle for this end the Union should be dissolved, it needs not the gift of prophecy to foresee that our country will be plunged into that gulf which, in the language of another, "is full of the fire and the blood of civil war, and of the thick darkness of general political disgrace, ignominy, and ruin." . . . We regret to see the abolitionists of the day seizing upon the cruelties and abuses of power by a few slave-owners in regard to their slaves in order to excite odium against slave-holders as a class.[61]

It was an attempt, not too successful, to wed antislavery idealism with antiabolition moderation, and its main purpose was to record the *North American's* opposition to immediate emancipation.

The editor, who had come home with well-filled notebooks, wrote much of European politics, personalities, and literature. In April 1830, after he had bought the review but before he had wholly taken over its editorship, he had a general article on "The Politics of Europe." In the next number he published his discussion of "The Tone of British Criticism," which ended the truce that Sparks had declared between the *North American* and the English reviews. Irving made his sole contribution to the *North American* in October 1832, when he wrote on the history of the Northmen. Longfellow made his début in the journal in April 1831, with an article on the history of the French language; this was followed by articles on the Italian, Spanish, and Anglo-Saxon languages, and a much more interesting "Defence of Poetry" in January 1832.

Two other literary critics who became constant contributors to the *Review* in the thirties were the twin brothers, W. B. O.

[60] *North American Review*, XLI, 193 (January 1833).
[61] *Ibid.*, LXXXVIII, 170–190 (July 1835).

and O. W. B. Peabody. They were identical, wrote Palfrey later,

in handwriting, face, form, mien, voice, manner. I never knew them apart. Both were copious writers in poetry and prose. Their style was very marked . . . but it seemed absolutely the same in both.[62]

W. B. O. contributed an article on "The Decline of Poetry" to the January 1829 number of the *Review*; but his brother did not appear until October 1830, when he contributed "Studies in Poetry." O. W. B. was a brother-in-law of the new editor and became his assistant. Though conservative and lacking in originality, the Peabodys were capable reviewers.

Other writers of importance who matriculated in the *North American* during A. H. Everett's editorship were Charles Francis Adams, who wrote on history and economics; Professor C. C. Felton, most of whose work was in the field of literary criticism; and George S. Hillard, whose forte was biography.

It was shortly before the end of Everett's editorship that his curious article on *Sartor Resartus* was published (October 1835).

It was not at all an unfriendly review [wrote Carlyle to Emerson] but had an opacity of matter-of-fact in it that filled me with amazement. Since the Irish bishop who said there were some things in Gulliver on which he for one would keep his belief *suspended*, nothing equal to it, on that side, has come athwart us. However, he has made out that Teufelsdröckh is, in all human probability, a fictitious character, which is always something, for an inquirer into Truth.[63]

It does seem, indeed, that the reviewer feels he has done a tremendously clever piece of literary detective work in discovering that the character of Teufelsdröckh is fictitious. Perhaps, however, he is only giving a rather heavily humorous account of the mystification element in *Sartor*. This review is the only favorable notice of Carlyle that appeared in the *North American*, which was not kind to transcendentalism.

Throughout his editorship Everett was a member of the Massachusetts Senate, and in 1836 he sold his holdings in the

---

[62] *North American Review*, C, 326 (January 1865).
[63] C. E. Norton, ed., *Correspondence Between Thomas Carlyle and Ralph Waldo Emerson* (Boston, 1883), I, 112.

Review and withdrew from editorial work on it, in order to become a candidate for Congress. The new editor and chief proprietor was John Gorham Palfrey, a Harvard graduate, the successor of Edward Everett as minister of the Brattle Street Unitarian Church, Boston, and now professor of sacred literature at Harvard.

Palfrey, like Sparks, was much interested in historical studies; and he sometimes allowed too much space to articles in this favorite field. In April 1838, for a typical example, there were papers on "Historical Romance in Italy," "Periodical Essays of the Age of Anne," "The Last Years of Maria Louisa," "The Early History of Canada," "Memoirs of Sir Walter Scott," and "The Documentary History of the Revolution." Only two other articles appeared in this number, in addition to the brief "Critical Notices" — one on a Hebrew lexicon, and the other on a geographical topic. Sparks, Prescott, C. F. Adams, and the editor himself were among the leading contributors of historical material.

Politics, which had occupied unusual space under his predecessor, Palfrey saw fit, in the main, to exclude. It was not that he was uninterested in such matters, for when he finally withdrew from his editorship it was to follow the example of the two Everetts and enter active politics; but he apparently thought to place the *Review* outside controversy and partisanship.

Next to history, literature occupied the most space in Palfrey's *North American*. Professor Felton, who seems to have been an assistant editor, wrote frequent reviews of novels, poetry, and essays. Felton was not well equipped for the criticism of belles-lettres; he judged too often according to standards not at all literary. He was in the habit of quoting at length, which often made his articles readable, but gave them the appearance of magazine hack work rather than the dignity of criticism. Palfrey often followed the same method. Longfellow's reviewing was sometimes incisive and forthright — note the introduction to his article on a book about London:

"Any amusement which is innocent," says Paley, "is better than none; as the writing of a book, the building of a house, the laying out of a garden, the digging of a fish-pond, even the raising of a cucumber." If these are the pastimes which the author of *The Great Metropolis* has within his reach, our opinion is, that, when he is next in want of an innocent amusement, he had better raise a cucumber.[64]

This is, at least, much cleverer than the great body of *North American* writing; most of the reviewers for that journal would have felt called upon to go back to the founding of London by the ancient Britons, and to trace its history laboriously down to the nineteenth century. Palfrey published one article ninety pages in length — Gardiner's review of Prescott's *Ferdinand and Isabella.*

Palfrey established the department of shorter "Critical Notices," which continued for many decades to fill the "back of the book." Some of the old club members continued to write for the *Review* — Tudor, Phillips, Channing, Hale, Edward Everett. But there were also some new recruits, of whom perhaps the most important, as events turned out, was Francis Bowen, Harvard teacher of "intellectual philosophy" and political economy, who wrote chiefly on philosophical subjects for these first contributions. Andrew P. Peabody, another later editor, also became a contributor in these years; as did Henry T. Tuckerman, who was later to achieve a high reputation as literary and art critic. Henry R. Cleveland, one of the "Five of Clubs" at Cambridge (the other four being Longfellow, Sumner, Felton, and Hillard) was another newcomer to the *Review*, with J. H. Perkins, of Cincinnati; William B. Reed, of Philadelphia; and George W. Greene, consul at Rome. The first woman to contribute extensively to the *Review* was Mrs. Therese A. L. von J. Robinson, wife of Edward Robinson, the biblical scholar; she was a talented writer and had an excellent knowledge of both German and Russian. Some of the lectures which Signor L. Mariotti delivered in Boston in 1840 were printed in the *Review*.

Emerson's lecture on Michael Angelo was published in the number for January 1837, and the one on Milton in that for July of the next year. Otherwise, there was little echo from the movement that was being called transcendentalism. There

[64] *North American Review*, XLIV, 46 (April 1837).

was a deep gulf fixed between the group that supported the *North American Review* and that which projected and wrote the *Dial* in 1840 to 1844. One looks in vain for the names of Margaret Fuller, Alcott, Ripley, Parker, Thoreau, and Cranch in *Review* indexes.

Clearly, the *North American* lost ground while Palfrey was editor. It reflected great contemporary movements less adequately; it probably declined somewhat in circulation.[65] There is some truth in Miss Martineau's arraignment of it, in her book on America:

> The *North American* had once some reputation in England; but it has sunk at home and abroad, less from want of talent than of principle. If it has any principle whatever at present, it is to praise every book it mentions, and to fall in as dexterously as possible with popular prejudices.[66]

Even Parkman, a leading contributor, found the number for the fall of 1837 "uncommonly weak and waterish." He thought this owing in part to the "paltry price the *North* pays (all it can bear, too, I believe)" — yet "for a' that, the Old *North* is the best periodical we have ever had." [67] The *London Monthly Review* presented some refutation of such criticisms by cribbing wholesale from its American contemporary — a proceeding which Palfrey exposed with glee in the number for October 1842.

Francis Bowen purchased the controlling interest in the *North American* at the end of 1842. He had returned to Cambridge in 1841 from a two-year European residence. He was a man of broad learning and varied interests; but he was prejudiced, belligerent, and far too unmindful of his audience. He was anti-low-tariff, anti-transcendental, anti-British. He retained the editorship, however, longer than any of his predecessors — a full decade, whereas the others had averaged less than four years.

[65] No figures are available, but this was the common gossip — spread, to be sure, by critics of the *Review*. Palfrey denies it, not very definitely (C, 325, January 1865). Note the statement in the *Southern Quarterly Review*, I, 38 (January 1842).

[66] Harriet Martineau, *Society in America* (London, 1837), II, 308.

[67] George Ticknor, *Life of William Hickling Prescott* (Boston, 1864), p. 255, footnote.

Bowen, supported by Felton, who continued active as a staff contributor, carried on against the English traducers of America, trying to beat them at their own game. An article by the two called "Morals, Manners and Poetry of England" in July 1844 begins: "The earliest notices we have of Britain represent it as fruitful in barbarians, tin, and lead. It has continued so ever since." [68] This was probably popular enough; but some of the magazine's other lines of conduct produced unfavorable repercussions. When in January 1850 Bowen published a long article attacking the Hungarian patriots at the very time that Kossuth was being hailed in America — and in Boston itself — as an apostle of human liberty, the *North American* suffered much criticism. Robert Carter, brilliant Boston journalist, published a series of articles in the Boston *Atlas* refuting Bowen's arguments. This came just at the moment of Bowen's election to the McLean chair of history at Harvard; and the overseers of the college, impressed by the attack on the candidate's learning, vetoed the election.

Bowen's literary criticism was also sometimes of the tomahawk variety. Cooper was his bête noire. His first article in the *North American*, in January 1838, had been a review of Cooper's *Gleanings from Europe*; this was a general criticism of Cooper's work, many of its points well taken, but willfully oblivious to the better qualities of the novelist. This was followed by other reviews of Cooper in a similar spirit and by a prejudiced article on the *Naval History* by A. S. Mackenzie. Felton also wielded the tomahawk, notably upon William Gilmore Simms, in October 1846.

Bowen had a taste for French fiction. He reviewed George Sand, Paul de Kock, and Dumas with a good deal of appreciation in the *North American*, and printed a really distinguished article on Balzac by Motley in his number for July 1847. Reviews of novels were comparatively prominent in these years. Lowell's first contribution was an article on Frederika Bremer's work. E. P. Whipple made his first appearance in the *Review* of 1843 and soon became its best reviewer of fiction and poetry; he took criticism itself seriously, he had a historical sense, and he wrote well.

[68] *North American Review*, LIX, 1 (July 1844).

There were a number of articles in these years on charities, including the provision for the blind and the insane. Papers on educational topics and on military affairs were not infrequent. Lorenzo Sabine wrote occasionally on various industries. Politics were sometimes touched upon, though not regularly: when the Oregon question came up with England, Bowen demonstrated at length that the Oregon country was "a contemptible possession" and not worth fighting over.[69] "Slavery in the United States" was reconsidered in October 1851, in an article by Ephraim Peabody, and the former position restated. Edward Everett Hale, who had first written for the *Review* in 1840, at eighteen years of age, continued in its pages. George E. Ellis, the Unitarian leader, first appeared there in 1846. Mrs. Mary Lowell Putnam began a series of articles on Hungarian and Polish literature in 1848.

But "the torpid and respectable *North American Review*," as the *Literary World* called it,[70] was getting a bad name for dullness. An occasional brandishing of the tomahawk was not enough to arouse any general interest in the current numbers. The men who had grown up with it still swore by it, but the bright young men were more likely to swear at it. Said a satirist in the Boston *Chronotype* in 1849:

> The N. A. is a slowcoach, yet it certainly goes ahead, as any man may satisfy himself by taking a series of observations for a few years. As we look in at the coach window at the present time, to be sure, the passengers seem to have been taking a social nap, and the driver probably held up, not to disturb their slumbers. Europe is on fire, and questions of moment are welding-hot in our own country, yet this *North American Review* is either admiring the tails of tenth-rate comets, or sprinkling a little Attic salt without any pepper on a dish of cucumbers.[71]

Other contemporaries joined the chorus of insult. "What venerable cobweb is that," asked Thoreau, who had boasted that he never wrote for the *Review*, "which has hitherto escaped the broom . . . but the *North American Review?*" [72]

---

[69] *Ibid.*, LXII, 252 (January 1846).
[70] *Literary World*, I, 197 (April 3, 1847).
[71] Quoted *ibid.*, V, 54 (July 21, 1849).
[72] H. D. Thoreau, *Writings* (Boston, 1906), XI, 38, and X, 427. See also

Bowen was appointed to a Harvard professorship in 1853, and this time unanimously confirmed by the overseers; he thereupon sold the *North American* to Crosby, Nichols & Company, Boston publishers, who named as the new editor Andrew P. Peabody, Unitarian minister in Portsmouth, New Hampshire. He, too, was appointed to a Harvard professorship in 1860; but he filled out his decade as editor. Peabody was an improvement on Bowen, but he could not lift the pall of general dullness that had settled upon it. Perhaps it was really no duller than it had been from the first, if it were possible to measure such things by an absolute standard; but it suffered from the brighter magazines that sprang up and won readers away from it, while it continued to rely upon the old ponderous review style and the old academic subjects.

Readers who had taxed their eyesight for forty years on the ophthalmologically vile pages of the *North American* were encouraged, however, by a change to large, easily read type; and *Norton's Literary Gazette* observed with pleasure in 1854 that the new editorship had been "marked by a wider range of material." [73] One of the most important of the early articles was Sidney G. Fisher's review of *Uncle Tom's Cabin* in October 1853, which accepted the doctrine that the Negro was "naturally the servant of the white man," [74] found emancipation therefore impossible, and proposed legal remedies for abuses of slaves. Edward Everett Hale's article on "Kanzas and Nebraska," however, in January 1855, encouraged the emigration of "freemen" to that battleground. Two years later Judge Timothy Farrar attacked the Taney decision in the Dred Scott case with vigor and dignity. As late as April 1861 another of the *Review's* labored articles on the institution of slavery restated the now traditional position of the journal against immediate emancipation; and a year later the exigencies of war had driven it only to a lukewarm assent to an emancipation limited to blacks fighting in the union army. [75]

International Monthly, IV, 128 (August 1851); *Democratic Review*, XV, 244 (September 1844); *De Bow's Review*, IX, 125 (July 1850).

[73] *Norton's Literary Gazette*, N.S., I, 79 (February 15, 1854).

[74] *North American Review*, LXXVII, 477 (October 1853).

[75] *Ibid.*, XCV, 533 (October 1862).

During the war there was a political or war article in nearly every number, occasionally critical of the conduct of military affairs.

In literary criticism Whipple continued to do the *North American's* best work. Professor C. C. Everett wrote on Ruskin, Mrs. Browning, and others. A Mrs. E. V. Smith wrote on Poe in 1856; it was a true Bostonian view of Poe, relying on Griswold for facts of personal life, shocked by some of the extreme Gothic elements in Poe's work, but admiring "The Raven" and "Annabelle Lee." It ended with the tender-minded declaration: "Rather than remember all, we would choose to forget all that he has ever written." [76] French literature was given very special attention for several years, with the Countess De Bury as the chief writer in this field.

There was some science. Dr. O. W. Holmes contributed a physiological article or two; Bowen argued against Darwin's new *Origin of Species* in April 1860; Wilson Flagg wrote some delightful essays on nature, landscape art, and such topics; Asa Gray wrote on botany.

More and more one finds unknown and fifth-rate writers in the pages of the "Old *North.*" The new *Atlantic Monthly* was attracting some of the articles that would normally have gone into the older periodical; yet contributors like Motley, Holmes, Whipple, Norton, and the newcomers Richard Henry Dana, Jr. and Thomas Wentworth Higginson, with Arthur Hugh Clough from England, did much to raise the average.

But the energy and genius commonly required to give flying starts to as many as three new magazines will usually fail to rejuvenate a single moribund journal. What to do with a periodical to which Carl Benson could casually refer as "that singular fossil, the *North American Review*"? [77] Argument, indignation only advertised the libel. What the publishers did do was to secure as editors two men of very high literary standing. James Russell Lowell was one of the three or four most important literary men in America; Charles Eliot Norton had won a reputation as a writer on social questions and on Italian litera-

[76] *Ibid.*, LXXXIII, 455 (October 1856).

[77] Charles Astor Bristed ("Carl Benson"), *Pieces of a Broken-Down Critic* (New York, 1874), p. 15. Letter dated February 11, 1864.

ture, and as an industrious editor. Their work on the *North
American* began with the issue for January 1864.

Lowell declared later that all he had promised Crosby and
Nichols "was my name on the cover." [78] What he actually delivered was a small amount of editorial work and two series of
notable articles, the first political in nature and the second literary.[79] His editorial work began with a few letters to prospective contributors of importance. To Motley he wrote some
months after a beginning had been made:

> You have heard that Norton and I have undertaken to edit the
> *North American,* — a rather Sisyphian job, you will say. It wanted
> three chief elements to be successful. It wasn't thoroughly, that is,
> thickly and thinly, loyal, it wasn't lively, and it had no particular
> opinions on any particular subject. It was an eminently safe period-
> ical, and accordingly was in great danger of running aground. It was
> an easy matter, of course, to make it loyal, — even to give it opinions
> (such as they were), but to make it alive is more difficult.[80]

Through the efforts of Norton and Lowell, a staff of contributors was built up which rivaled that of earlier years: Edwin L.
Godkin, of the *Nation*, which Norton had helped to found;
Emerson, who now followed his two earlier contributions with
a second essay on "Character" and one on "Quotation and
Originality"; Charles Francis Adams, Jr., whose articles on
railroads were genuinely important; James Parton, writing on
political and biographical topics; George William Curtis, editor
of *Harper's Weekly*; Goldwin Smith, English publicist, who
visited the United States in 1864 — and many others of equal
weight. Payment to contributors was increased from $2.50 to
$5.00 a page;[81] other high-grade magazines were paying ten.[82]
As the clever Theodore Tilton remarked of the *Review's* rate of

---

[78] Horace E. Scudder, *James Russell Lowell* (Boston, 1901), II, 124.
[79] In *ibid.*, Chapters X–XI, will be found an excellent review of these articles.
[80] G. W. Curtis, ed., *Correspondence of John Lothrop Motley* (Boston, 1889),
II, 167. Quoted in Scudder, *op. cit.*, II, 48; C. E. Norton, ed., *Letters of James
Russell Lowell* (Boston, 1894), I, 334; *North American Review*, CCI, 131 (January 1915).
[81] Sara Norton and M. A. DeWolfe Howe, eds., *Letters of Charles Eliot
Norton* (Boston, 1913), I, 266; *Education of Henry Adams* (Boston, 1918),
p. 296.
[82] See Volume III, Chapter I.

payment to contributors in 1866: "In this respect it labors, like Rabelais' Panurge, 'under an incurable disease, which at that time they called lack of money.' " [83]

Lowell's own articles were of prime importance. His first was an estimate of Lincoln, in the first number under the new editorship; in the second number he assessed General McClellan; and in the fourth number, which appeared on the eve of the presidential election, he answered his question "Lincoln or McClellan?" in favor of the former. A noble paper on "Reconstruction" came in April 1865; and in July a rather discursive essay entitled "Scotch the Snake, or Kill It?" centered upon the problem of the freedmen. Two papers on President Johnson's troubles were published in 1866. "After the pressure of war-time was lifted," says Lowell's biographer, "he made the *Review* the vehicle for more strictly literary articles; and it was plainly a relief to him to spring back to subjects more congenial to his nature." [84] First of these papers was his review, in January 1865, of the third volume of Palfrey's *History of New England*; it is a remarkable summation of the New England creed. Then followed a series of essays on Lessing, Rousseau, Dante, Shakespeare, Milton, Chaucer, Spenser, Dryden, Pope, Wordsworth, Carlyle, and Emerson — drawn largely from his lecture notes — which made the foundation for Lowell's reputation as a critic.

Norton, besides doing most of the editorial work, wrote a number of articles himself. In January 1864 there was a paper of his on "Immorality in Politics" which combatted the biblical defenses of slavery; in July 1864, an article about the heroism of soldiers in the field; in January 1865, a paper on Lincoln; and in the following October, one entitled "American Political Ideals."

In October 1864 Ticknor & Fields, leading Boston publishers and owners of the *Atlantic Monthly*, purchased the *Review*. They were doubtless encouraged to make the venture by what Norton called the efforts "to put some life into the old dry bones of the quarterly." [85] Norton had high editorial ideals; he

---

[83] *Independent*, April 26, 1866, editorial.
[84] Scudder, *op. cit.*, II, 78.
[85] Norton and Howe, *op. cit.*, I, 266.

saw before him "an opportunity now to make the *North American* one of the means of developing the nation, of stimulating its
better sense, of holding up to it its own ideal." [86] But he de-
spaired of lightening the sheer specific gravity of the *Review's*
pages. He wrote to Lowell in July, 1864:

> The July *North American* seems to me good, but too heavy. How
> can we make it lighter? People will write on the heavy subjects; and
> all our authors are destitute of humor. Nobody but you knows how to
> say witty things lightly.[87]

In the summer of 1868, Norton resigned to go abroad on a
literary mission, and Professor E. W. Gurney was put in his
place. At once troubles began to accumulate. But let us allow
Lowell's playful but vexed letter to his publisher tell the story:

> The express has just brought your note asking for the log of the
> *North American* on her present voyage. The *N. A.* is teak-built, her
> extreme length from stem to stern-post 299 feet 6 inches, and her
> beam (I mean her breadth of beam) 286 feet 7 inches and a quarter.
> She is an A–1 *risk* at the Antediluvian. These statements will enable
> you to reckon her possible rate of sailing. During the present trip
> I should say that all the knots she made were Gordian, and of the
> tightest sort. I extract from log as follows:
>
> 11 July. Lat. 42° 1′, the first officer, Mr. Norton, lost overboard in
> a fog, with the compass, caboose, and studden-sails in his pocket, also
> the key of the spirit-room.
>
> 25 July. Lat. 42° 10′, spoke the Ark, Captain Noah, and got the
> latest news. 26, 27, 28, dead calm. 29, 30, 31, and 1 August, head
> winds N.N.E. to N.E. by N.
>
> 15 August. Double reef in foretopsl, spoke the good ship Argo,
> Jason commander, from Colchos with wool.
>
> 17 August, dead calm, Schooner Pinta, Capt. Columbus, bound for
> the New World, and a market, bearing Sou Sou West half South on
> our weather bow. Got some stores from him.
>
> 20. Capt. Lowell cut his throat with the fluke of the sheet anchor.
> So far the log.
>
> Now for the comment. Toward the 1st September I received notice
> that the *Review* was at a standstill. Mr. Gurney was at Beverly, ill
> and engaged to be married. I had not a line of copy, nor knew where
> to get one. I communicated with G. and got what he had — viz: two

[86] Norton and Howe, *op. cit.*, I, 268.
[87] *Ibid.*, I, 272.

articles, one on Herbert Spencer, and t'other on Leibnitz. I put the former in type, but did not dare follow with the latter, for I thought it would be too much even for the readers of the N. A. By and by, I raked together one or two more, — not what I *would* have but what I *could*. . . . We want *something* interesting, and we must have some literary notices. . . .

A few days later he wrote to Fields again:

Correct estimates from log thus: 25 September. Lat. 42° 10'. Captain Lowell committed suicide by blowing out his brains with the gaff-topsl halyards. There can be no doubt of the fact, as the 2d officer recognized the brains for his (Cap. L.'s), he being familiar with them.

30 September. Captain L. reappeared on deck, having been below only to oversee the storage of ballast, whereof on this trip the lading mainly consists. What was thought to be his brains turns out to be pumpkin pie, though the second officer was unconvinced and the Captain himself could not make up his mind.

The fact is I was cross, and did not quite like being brought up with such a round turn at my time of life. . . . Gurney will take hold of the next number, and it will all go right.[88]

Gurney did "take hold" and kept hold for two years, after which he surrendered his grasp of the tiller to young Henry Adams.

The new editor was a grandson of President John Adams, who had been a contributor to the *North American Review* in 1817; a son of Charles Francis Adams the elder, who had written more than a dozen articles for the journal; and a brother of the second Charles Francis Adams, now doing papers on the railroads for it.[89] It is no wonder that he regarded the "Old *North*" as a kind of family heirloom; he wrote to a friend that it was "a species of medieval relic, handed down as a sacred trust from the times of our remotest ancestors."[90] Lowell and Norton had done much to restore the former public esteem for it; but it was still an unprofitable "relic," with a circulation of three or four hundred and an annual deficit.[91] Its articles were still long and heavy. Henry Adams wrote,

[88] Scudder, *op. cit.*, II, 122–125.
[89] Charles F. Thwing points this out in his review of the index volume of the *North American*, in *Literary Review*, VIII, 179 (March 1878).
[90] W. C. Ford, ed., *Letters of Henry Adams* (Boston, 1930), p. 219.
[91] *Education of Henry Adams*, p. 234.

years later, in his autobiography: "Not many men even in England or France could write a good thirty-page article, and practically no one in America read them." [92] His brother accomplished such a task, however, in July 1869, with "A Chapter of Erie," followed by "An Erie Raid" two years later — written "with infinite pains, sparing no labor," [93] and later published in book form for a larger audience.

In 1872 Lowell went abroad, resigning his connection with the *North American*. Adams was now left in full charge; but he, too, soon went off to Europe, leaving Thomas Sergeant Perry to get out three numbers in 1872–73.[94] Returning in the summer of 1873, Adams made his former pupil in history, Henry Cabot Lodge, assistant editor;[95] and the two edited the journal through 1876.

Again the *Review* emphasized history. The editors were specialists in that field, and they had help from Parkman, Fiske, Charles Kendall Adams, and others. The first number, in 1876, contained a remarkable series of articles on American historical topics to celebrate the centennial. But the *Review* was not devoted to history to the exclusion of other material. Indeed, Adams gave it more "bite" than it had had for a long time — perhaps more than it had ever had before. Lowell remarked that Adams was making the old tea kettle think it was a steam engine.[96] There were political articles in nearly every number by the editor, his brother, and others. Charles F. Wingate summed up the battle against the Tammany Ring in a series in 1874–76. Chauncy Wright wrote his brilliant contributions to the developing theory of evolution for the *North American* in the late sixties and early seventies. Simon Newcomb wrote on science and W. D. Whitney on philology. Among the leading writers of literary criticism were Francis A. Palgrave, William Dean Howells, Henry James, Karl Hillebrand, and H. H. Boyesen. The book notices at the end of each number were often distinguished: "not seldom," said the *Nation*,

[92] *Education of Henry Adams*, p. 234.
[93] C. F. Adams, *An Autobiography* (Boston, 1916), p. 172.
[94] *North American Review*, CCI, 137 (January 1915).
[95] See H. C. Lodge, *Early Memories* (Boston, 1914), and the quotation from it in *North American Review*, CCI, 753 (May 1915).
[96] *North American Review*, CCI, 136 (January 1915).

such a review was "a literary product capable of standing by itself." [97] No longer was the reader in doubt about authorship, for the cloak of anonymity was lifted in 1868.

But it was all hack work — "hopeless drudgery" [98] — to Adams. He saw no future in it: "My terror," he once wrote to his assistant, "is lest it should die on my hands." [99] The publishers, now James R. Osgood & Company, sometimes interfered with the editor, as when Adams was not kind enough to Bayard Taylor's *Faust*, which Osgood had published. [100]

In October 1876 Adams published a political article, "The Independents in the Political Canvass," which advocated support of Tilden by the new nonpartisan group. To this number — which was nearly all politics and history — the publishers attached a disclaimer and a notice that the editors had resigned. The young editors had involved the old "relic" in a runaway — though miraculously they had almost brought it to life.

It had been known in publishing circles for several years that the *North American* was for sale, though all it had to sell was a historic name and an annual deficit. There was also a persistent rumor that it was to be discontinued. [101] It was offered to Edward Everett Hale when he started *Old and New* in 1870. Henry Holt and E. L. Godkin were planning to buy it and bring it to New York, [102] when Osgood suddenly announced that it had been sold to Allen Thorndike Rice. Rice was a young man of twenty-three, Boston-born but a recent graduate of Oxford, wealthy, energetic, and lively-minded. Gladstone called him "the most fascinating" young man he had ever met. [103] He paid $3,000 for the old journal, [104] which now had a circulation of 1,200. [105] At once he made it a bimonthly. Julius H. Ward, an Episcopal clergyman who had been nominated by Osgood to succeed Adams, was Rice's first managing editor; after a few months he was followed by Laurence Oliphant, English author

[97] *Nation*, XVI, 99 (February 6, 1873).
[98] *Education of Henry Adams*, p. 308.
[99] Ford, *op. cit.*, p. 267.
[100] See *Atlantic Monthly*, CXXVII, 140 (January 1921).
[101] See *American Annual Cyclopaedia* for 1870, p. 448.
[102] See *Nation*, CI, 47 (July 8, 1915).
[103] *North American Review*, CXLIX, 117 (July 1889).
[104] See *Current Literature*, II, 448 (May 1889).
[105] *North American Review*, CXLIX, 113 (July 1889).

and communist then residing in America. Then in 1878 Rice moved the magazine to New York; and L. S. Metcalf, a trained journalist, took charge of the editorial work. D. Appleton & Company succeeded James R. Osgood & Company as "publishers." Finally, in 1879 the magazine was made a monthly.

Thus were the successive stages of the revolution accomplished. Boston was left sorrowing for her errant daughter, and for the first time in sixty years men who had never entered Harvard Square were in charge. But the significant feature of the change was not geographical or institutional: the really important alteration was in the contents of the magazine. Within a year or two the *North American* became a free forum, welcoming all important expressions of opinion. It was almost as close to current events as a newspaper. Rice's frequently expressed aim was "to make the *Review* an arena wherein any man having something valuable to say could be heard." [106] If the "Old *North*" had been for decades dignified and retiring, it was now plunged bodily into the very maelstrom of contemporaneity, sucked into controversy, bobbing on the surge of the latest doctrine. Metcalf, who was allowed the fullest liberty in the selection of material, said later:

> But I knew that there was a certain preference for articles which tended to the sensational, and I allowed myself to be considerably influenced by Mr. Rice's undoubted belief in the practical business advantage of such contributions.[107]

This sounds very commercial; but it should be noted that Rice had a free mind himself and desired to promote free discussion. Further, for the word "sensational" it would be better to substitute such terms as "unconventional" and "intellectually exciting." Of course Rice obviously thought that fresh writing on lively topics would be profitable: his whole venture was founded upon that belief.

So far as partisan politics were concerned, Rice kept the *Review* more or less neutral, presenting both sides of most questions. There is some Republican bias to be seen in the presidential campaign of 1880, and some opposition to Blaine in

[106] *North American Review*, CXLIX, 110.
[107] *Review of Reviews*, III, 288 (April 1891).

1884. The *Review* was stoutly against Cleveland's antiprotectionism, however; and in 1888 it printed several articles on the Republican side and only one with Democratic leanings. By this time Metcalf had left to found the *Forum*; and James Redpath, journalist and lyceum organizer, had become, in 1886, managing editor of the *Review*.

But political discussion was not limited to the presidential campaigns, and every number included politics and economics. Radical views were presented along with conservative opinions, and controversy became the settled policy of the magazine. For example, when Judge Jeremiah S. Black presented the Tilden side of the electoral question in July 1877, E. W. Stoughton, one of the Hayes counsel, set forth the other side in the next number. The symposium — a device for presenting variant attitudes and views concurrently — made its appearance as the vehicle of a discussion of the resumption of specie payments in November 1877.[108] The writers in the *North American's* symposia were authorities — or at least well known. In the one on resumption, for example, there were Secretary of the Treasury Sherman, former Secretary McCulloch, Congressmen William D. Kelley and Thomas Ewing, and the well-known economist David A. Wells. There was no waiting upon voluntary contributions now; the editors chose their men and offered adequate remuneration and thus were able to present a monthly array of names known to all their readers. Among political matters frequently discussed were the silver question, civil service reform, and the third presidential term. The "southern question" was reviewed by Southerners (by Charles Gayarré in November 1877, and Henry Watterson in January 1879) as well as by Northerners.

Related industrial and social problems crowded the pages of the new *North American*. "A Striker" and the president of the Pennsylvania Railroad appeared in the same number — September 1877. "Land and Taxation: a Conversation" was the joint production of two frequent contributors — Henry George and David Dudley Field. An attack on woman suffrage by

---

[108] The device was probably imitated from the *Nineteenth Century's* recent "Modern Symposium" on evolution, which had been reprinted in this country in *Popular Science Monthly Supplement*.

Parkman in October 1879 drew forth a symposium of replies in the next number by Julia Ward Howe, T. W. Higginson, Lucy Stone, Elizabeth Cady Stanton, and Wendell Phillips; a rejoinder by Parkman followed in January 1880. Many articles on women and their position appeared in the eighties; their dress, health, occupations, religion were discussed.

Religion ranked next to politics in Rice's magazine. Beginning with an article on "Reformed Judaism" by Felix Adler in July 1877, discussion ran the gamut of belief and unbelief. A symposium on "The Doctrine of Eternal Punishment," in March 1878, and another on "What Is Inspiration?" in September of the same year enlisted some of the leading clerical writers of America. The question of evolution was linked with theology in "An Advertisement for a New Religion by an Evolutionist" in July 1878, and in the symposium "Law and Design in Nature" in June 1879. J. A. Froude's two-part article on "Romanism and the Irish Race in the United States" was balanced by Cardinal Manning's "The Catholic Church and Modern Society." Sunday observance was discussed more than once.

Freethinkers and infidels were represented repeatedly in the late seventies, and in August 1881 Robert G. Ingersoll and Jeremiah S. Black, two famous lawyers, debated the Christian religion. Black, who had shown some temper in the debate, showed more when he was unable to get his rejoinder to the second part of Ingersoll's argument into the same number with it; he refused to go on, but wrote an angry letter to the *Philadelphia Press* calling the *North American* "a treacherous concern." [109] Loud were the protests, indeed, against the Ingersoll articles from all quarters. "The *North American Review* has sold out to Ingersoll," said the *Chautauquan*, and predicted a great loss of subscriptions.[110] The Reverend George P. Fisher contributed a reply to Ingersoll which he said was not a reply, in the number of February 1882. Hostilities were renewed five years later when Henry M. Field, editor of the *Evangelist*, addressed an open letter in the *North American* to the now famous agnostic. The debate which followed was climaxed by a review of the subject by William E. Gladstone. Gladstone was

[109] See *Critic*, I, 322 (November 19, 1881).
[110] *Chautauquan*, II, 185 (December 1881).

one of the greatest figures in the English-speaking world, and the publication of a paper on Christianity by him, as a part of this debate, was one of the greatest "hits" ever made by the *Review*. One other religious series excited some interest; in it various well-known persons gave reasons for the faith that was in them. It began in 1886 with Edward Everett Hale's "Why I Am a Unitarian" and ran for four years. It included even "Why I Am a Heathen," by Wong Chin Foo; and it ended with Ingersoll's "Why I Am an Agnostic" in 1890, with its aftermath of replies by Canon Farrar, Lyman Abbott, and others.

More literary phases were not entirely neglected. Three of Emerson's later lectures were published in 1877–78, Bryant's essay on Cowley in May 1877, and Taylor's on Halleck in the following number. Whitman contributed several essays in the eighties. The Shakespeare-Bacon controversy was exploited in the latter part of the same decade, Ignatius Donnelly being the chief exploiter. The traditional section of brief book notices was abandoned in 1881; a later review department was conducted through 1887–89.

The drama was given some attention, from Boucicault's articles, which began in 1878, onward. Richard Wagner contributed a two-part autobiographical article in 1879. There were articles on science (especially on the evolutionary hypothesis), on educational problems, on art, and on foreign affairs. The list of foreign contributors was led by Gladstone, whose first article, on "Kin Beyond the Sea," in September 1878 was followed by perhaps a dozen more in later years; Froude, Trollope, Bryce, and Goldwin Smith were other English writers prominent in the magazine in the eighties. The *North American* also caught the fever, then epidemic among the magazines, of publishing Civil War memoirs; it printed General Beauregard's reminiscences and a number of letters dealing with the struggle.

Thus it will be seen that Rice's magazine had incalculably more variety than the "Old *North*." It even went so far, in April 1888, as to publish a lively defense of prize fighting by Duffield Osborne. A typical number in the early eighties (February 1881) contained the following leading articles: "The Nicaragua Canal," by U. S. Grant; "The Pulpit and the Pew," by O. W. Holmes; "Aaron's Rod in Politics" (advocating public education in the South), by A. W. Tourgée; "Did Shakespeare Write Bacon's Works?" by J. F. Clarke; "Partisanship in the Supreme Court," by Senator John T. Morgan; an installment of her "Ruins of Central America" (result of an expedition partially financed by the *Review*), by Désiré Charnay; "The Poetry of the Future," by Walt Whitman.

The magazine's circulation advanced to 7,500 by 1880, and to 17,000 by the time of Rice's untimely death in 1889. It was then making its owner an annual profit of $50,000.[111] Rice left a controlling interest in the *Review* to Lloyd Bryce, who had been a friend of his at Oxford; and Bryce immediately purchased the remaining stock.[112] Bryce was a Democrat in politics, while his predecessor had been a Republican; but the *Review* was kept nonpartisan — or rather bipartisan, for it continued to present both sides of most controversial questions. The new editor was a man of wealth, a novelist, a liberal, and a member of Congress from New York. From Rice's régime he inherited the journalist William H. Rideing as managing editor; and David A. Munro, who had received his earlier training in *Harper's* publishing house, was later added to the staff.

There was little or no change of policy in the *Review* under Bryce. The same emphasis on controversy, the same use of the symposium and joint debate, the same exploitation of problems from forum and market place continued to characterize the magazine. There was, perhaps, more discussion of foreign affairs than formerly, especially by the middle nineties. In the number for January 1895, for example, exactly half the pages are devoted to foreign questions. One of the big features of Bryce's earlier editorship was the debate on free trade by Gladstone and Blaine, in the number for January 1890; it was followed by articles on the same subject by Roger Q. Mills and Joseph S. Morrill. Another was the debate between the Duke of Argyll and Gladstone on home rule for Ireland in August and October 1892. Gladstone's series on immortality in 1896 also attracted wide attention. Other leading English writers

[111] See pamphlet, "The Oldest Magazine in America and the Youngest," published by the North American Review Corporation, 1930.

[112] *Journalist*, XII, 1 (March 14, 1891).

were Balfour, McCarthy, Sir Charles Dilke, James Bryce, Labouchère, Lang, and Gosse.

Prominent American topics were the powers of the speaker of the House of Representatives, discussed by Speaker Reed, a favorite contributor, and others; labor questions, on which T. V. Powderly, also a frequent writer for the *Review*, was an authority; free silver, in the discussion of which the editor seems to have given the advantage to the gold men; immigration, Catholicism, military and naval armaments, life insurance, the Columbian Exposition, and Hawaiian annexation. When the Venezuelan question came up, James Bryce and Andrew Carnegie, both frequent writers on Anglo-American relations, discussed it with sanity and insight.

The *Review* came more and more to cultivate a clever and somewhat sophisticated type of essay on contemporary social life, manners, and fads. Gail Hamilton had become a regular contributor in 1886. Ouida came a few years later; and Max O'Rell, Jules Clarètie, Sarah Grand, and Grant Allen wrote such pieces. The servant girl problem, the man and the girl "of the period," courtship and marriage, and the amusements and sports of the day furnished unlimited opportunities for this kind of writing. More serious was the discussion of divorce, which was analyzed in more than one symposium. Mark Twain became one of the *Review's* most valued contributors; most of his writing done for its pages was basically serious, and even bitter — though commonly winged with barbs of wit. His "In Defense of Harriet Shelley" and his "Fenimore Cooper's Literary Offences" belong to the mid-nineties. The chief literary critics were Howells, Gosse, and Lang; but the magazine did not make a practice of reviewing new books.

By 1891 the *Review* had reached its high peak of circulation, at 76,000, with a subscription price of $5.00. In that year the *Review of Reviews* said:

It is unquestionably true that the *North American* is regarded by more people, in all parts of the country, as at once the highest and most impartial platform upon which current public issues can be discussed, than is any other magazine or review.[113]

---

[113] *Review of Reviews*, III, 394 (May 1891).

It lost circulation, however, in the hard times of the middle nineties.

In 1895 the publishing company was reorganized; and the next year Bryce turned the editorship over to Munro, who conducted the magazine for the next three years. Though still filled with valuable material, the *North American* under Munro declined in freshness and vitality. There were few exciting articles, and some tendency to get in a rut and stay there. Cuba was, of course, an absorbing topic; and the expansion question occupied many pages. General Miles's review of the Spanish War was one of the best features. Symposia were less frequent, and the *Review's* pages were no longer an arena for single combats and group melees.

Then in 1899 Colonel George Harvey bought a controlling interest in the *North American* and became its editor. Harvey had been managing editor of Pulitzer's *World* in the early nineties and had later made a fortune in electric railways. The next year after he purchased the *North American* he became president of the reorganized Harper & Brothers, but he did not publish his magazine under the aegis of that house. He did become editor of *Harper's Weekly* from 1901 to 1913, however, conducting the two periodicals simultaneously.

Harvey's first number — that for July 1899 — opened with a long poem by Swinburne. He continued to publish poems — usually rather long ones — throughout his editorship. He published Henley and Yeats in his first year; but probably the most famous poem he ever printed was Alan Seeger's "I Have a Rendezvous with Death" in October 1916.

For the first year or two of Harvey's editorship the leading topic of the *Review* was England's war with the Boers, which was treated from the various international points of view by European and American writers. The Philippine question was also prominent; Harvey made a special effort to put the Filipino attitude before the American people. In October 1900 there was an old-fashioned symposium on the presidential issues; but Bryan's articles before and after the election give the *Review* of this year a definitely Democratic bias.

In the meantime there had been much foreign material — not only foreign politics, but European letters and art. Tolstoi,

D'Annunzio, and Maeterlinck became contributors. H. G. Wells's "Anticipations: An Adventure in Prophecy," a serial of 1901, is even more interesting a third of a century after its writing than it could have been to its first readers in the *Review*. A "World Politics" department was begun in 1904, with correspondence from the leading European capitals.

Three of the chief American contributors in these years were Howells, James, and Mark Twain. Mark wrote his famous essay "To the Person Sitting in Darkness" for the February 1901 number. It was one of the bitterest excoriations of "civilization" ever printed; it made a great furore and called for a second address "To My Missionary Critics" in a later number. Mark's dissertation on Christian Science in 1902–03 also drew much criticism and an official answer by W. D. McCrackan. McCrackan had appeared in the *Review* as an apologist for Christian Science some two years earlier, in connection with a joint debate on the subject between himself and J. M. Buckley, editor of the Methodist *Christian Advocate*. Mark Twain's "Chapters from My Autobiography" appeared in 1906 and 1907. It was three years before this that the *North American* serialized Henry James's *The Ambassadors* — its first work of fiction in nearly a century of existence. James was far from popular, but he seemed to belong to the *North American*: "he has come to his own," said *Life*, "and his own has taken him in." [114] *The Ambassadors* was followed by Howells' *A Son of Royal Langbrith*, and Conrad's *Under Western Eyes* appeared in 1910–11. About this time Harvey became interested in the promotion of Esperanto as an international language, and for several years he published supplements to the *Review* designed to forward this cause.

The campaign of 1904 found the *North American* clearly sympathetic to the candidacy of Theodore Roosevelt, though trying, as usual, to present both sides of the contest to its readers. Trusts were the theme of many articles in these years. A notable symposium discussed the Supreme Court decision in the Standard Oil case in 1911. But in 1906 Harvey had turned against "T. R." and his high-handed ways. In that year the *Review* became a fortnightly and began a regular editorial de-

---

[114] *Life*, XLI, 26 (January 8, 1903).

partment called "The Editor's Diary." It was a very readable department; its editorial comments ranged from disquisitions on constitutional questions to essays on such topics as "The Theory and Practice of Osculation." Thus Harvey made the *North American,* as his biographer observes, a personal organ for the first time in its history.[115] A new department of book reviews was begun at the same time. But fortnightly publication lasted only a year, after which the *Review* once more became a monthly. The editorial department, however, was retained until 1909. The campaign of 1908 did not interest the *Review* very much; indeed, there was a distinct decline in the enterprise and liveliness of the magazine beginning at about this time. The circulation appears to have been stationary at about twenty-five thousand. A larger type was adopted at the end of 1910, but the printing was sometimes inferior.

In April 1906 Harvey published an article called "Whom Will the Democrats Next Nominate for President?" in which Mayo W. Hazeltine suggested the name of Woodrow Wilson, of Princeton University, for that office. This was more than six years before Wilson's actual nomination, but a month after Harvey had first conspicuously pointed out his availability.[116] The *North American,* with *Harper's Weekly,* continued to build up the Wilsonian candidacy. In the quadrennial presidential candidates' symposium in October 1912 there were articles for Taft, Roosevelt, and Wilson; but editorially the *Review* was Democratic.

A year later Harvey began the custom of making the first article in his magazine an editorial pronouncement, usually political. He was greatly disturbed by Wilson's handling of the Mexican situation and by the war against Villa; and the campaign of 1916 found him supporting Hughes and condemning Wilson for meddlesomeness in Mexico, for violations of the merit system, and for what he called in his summing-up article in October, "a fatuous timidity in dealing with belligerent [European] powers."

The *Review* was a fighting magazine during the war. "Our

[115] Willis Fletcher Johnson, *George Harvey* (Boston, 1929), p. 67.

[116] Harvey had made a similar suggestion the month before in his editorial page in *Harper's Weekly,* March 10, 1906.

chief duty before God and man is to KILL HUNS," Harvey shouted.[117] Impatient of monthly publication, he began the *North American Review's War Weekly*, later called *Harvey's Weekly* (1918–20). He disapproved of Wilson's "fourteen commandments," his work at Versailles, and the formation of the League. He supported Harding in 1920 and was the next year appointed ambassador to Great Britain. While he was abroad, Elizabeth B. Cutting, who had been an associate editor since 1910, edited the *Review*. Lawrence Gilman, who had been with the magazine since 1915, continued as literary and dramatic critic; and Willis Fletcher Johnson was an associate editor. David Jayne Hill, an authority on international questions, wrote many of the leading articles. Harvey returned to New York in time to take part in the presidential canvass of 1924; his leading *North American* campaign article was entitled "Coolidge or Chaos." The chief feature of the following year consisted of two symposia on "Five Years of Prohibition"; to the one in June the "drys" contributed, and the "wets" were heard in September.

When Harvey came home in 1924, he found the *Review's* circulation down to 13,000. In the fall of that year he changed to quarterly publication, at $4.00; this took the magazine off the newsstands, which have seldom been friendly to quarterlies.

In 1926 the *Review* was purchased by William Butler Mahony, lawyer and financier, who made it a monthly again in the following year, and much more attractive typographically. Associated with him in the editorship were Miss Cutting, who remained until 1927; W. F. Johnson, who continued as a contributing editor; Herschel Brickell, who became the magazine's chief reviewer in 1927; and Kenneth Wilcox Payne, who came to the *Review* in 1928 from *McClure's* and other magazines.

The magazine under Mahony was devoted to articles on social, economic, political, literary, and art problems, with a few short stories in each number, and departments of book reviews, light essays, and finance. It printed many well-known writers, but in general it followed the policy of seeking new and varied talent rather than repeating authors. In an era of social, financial, and political upset, the *Review* kept an extraor-

[117] *North American Review*, CCVIII, 15 (July 1918).

dinarily even keel, swinging far neither to the right nor to the
left, interpreting situations and tendencies quietly and interestingly month after month. Among its political commentators
were Vice-President Dawes, Theodore Roosevelt, Jr., and Senators Albert C. Ritchie, Atlee Pomerene, Arthur Capper, and
George H. Moses. Such English writers as Dean W. R. Inge,
V. Sackville-West, Gilbert K. Chesterton, and Siegfried Sas-
soon contributed to its pages; and Conrad Aiken, Amy Lowell,
Lincoln Steffens, Struthers Burt, and John Erskine lent distinction to its tables of contents from time to time.

The *Review* in June 1935 came under the editorial control of
John H. G. Pell, known for his writings on early American history, and a great-great-grandson of Edward T. Channing, third
editor of the magazine. Mahony retained a financial interest.
As associate editor came Richard Dana Skinner, formerly dramatic editor of the *Commonweal*, and a great grandson of that
Richard Henry Dana who, as so many thought, should have
been the *Review's* fourth editor. Quarterly publication, which
has been the rule for a little more than half the magazine's history, was resumed.

The 120 years of publication celebrated by the *North American Review* in 1935 were cut precisely in half by the revolution
effected in its policies by Allen Thorndike Rice in 1876. In its
first sixty years it was dignified, ponderous, respected; its list
of contributors contained the names of most New Englanders
who were prominent in literature, scholarship, and public affairs.
Though it occasionally tried to widen its horizons, it was definitely provincial, maintaining close relationships with Harvard
College and Boston. It was often really scholarly, though sometimes an encyclopedic dullness masqueraded as learning in its
pages. Under Sparks and the Everetts it achieved a fair circulation for the times, after which its business affairs declined, in
spite of the brilliance of Lowell, Norton, and Adams, past helping by anything short of radical change. After such a change in
1876, it became a scintillating and lively journal, featuring
many of the world's great names, and filled with clash of
opinion on politics, economics, science, religion, and social problems. It reached its peak of prosperity in the eighties, though it

was later distinguished through the long editorship of George Harvey for its political influence and its international outlook. Its total file, amounting now to approximately 120,000 pages, is a remarkable repository, unmatched by that of any other magazine of American thought through nearly a century and a quarter of our national life.

2

THE YOUTH'S COMPANION [1]

NATHANIEL WILLIS once wrote the following autobiographical note to his son, Nathaniel Parker Willis,
the poet. He referred to himself in the third person:

He was in the habit of teaching his children, statedly, the Assembly's Catechism; and to encourage them to commit to memory the
answers, he rewarded them by telling them stories from scriptural
history, without giving names. The result was that the Catechism
was all committed to memory by the children, and the idea occurred
of a children's department in the *Recorder*. This department being

[1] TITLES: *The Youth's Companion*, 1827–34, 1836–1929; *Youth's Companion
and Sabbath School Recorder*, 1834–36.

FIRST ISSUE: April 16, 1827. LAST ISSUE: September 1929 (but see footnote 18 below).

PERIODICITY: Weekly, 1827–1927; monthly, 1928–29. I–XXIX, annual volumes ending in May 1827–56; XXX, June–December 1856; XXXI–CII, regular
annual volumes, 1857–1928; CIII, January–September 1929 (but see footnote 18 below). No issue between April 16 and June 6, 1827. In numbering the
volumes, LXVII was omitted.

PUBLISHERS: Nathaniel Willis and Asa Rand, Boston, 1827–30; Nathaniel
Willis, Boston, 1830–56; Olmstead & Company (John W. Olmstead and Daniel S.
Ford), Boston, 1857–67; Perry Mason & Company (later Perry Mason Com-
pany), Boston, 1867–1929. (D. S. Ford was president of Perry Mason & Com-
pany, 1867–99; Seth Mendell, 1900–12; Charles E. Kelsey, 1912–25. The Atlantic
Monthly Company, Ellery Sedgwick president, was owner of Perry Mason
Company, 1925–29.)

EDITORS: Nathaniel Willis, 1827–56; Daniel Sharp Ford and Nathaniel Willis,
1857–62; D. S. Ford, 1863–70; D. S. Ford and Hezekiah Butterworth, 1870–86;
D. S. Ford, H. Butterworth, and Edward Stanwood, 1887–94; D. S. Ford and
E. Stanwood, 1894–99; E. Stanwood, 1900–11; Charles Miner Thompson, 1911–
25; Harford W. H. Powel, Jr., 1925–29. Associate, assistant, and contributing
editors: William E. Barton (1900–17, 1925–29), Theron Brown (1870–1914),
Joseph Edgar Chamberlin (1890–1901), Thomas Hart Clay, George William
Douglas (1902–14), Roswell Martin Field (1900–02), Charles Macomb Flandrau,
Isaac Nelson Ford, Paul P. Foster (1894–1925), Edward Williston Frentz,
Will N. Harben (1891–93), Jefferson L. Harbour (1884–1901), Heloise E. Hersey
(1901–12), M. A. DeWolfe Howe (1888–93, 1899–1913), Ira Rich Kent (1900–
25), John Macy (1901–09), John Clair Minot (1909–19), John L. Mathews,
James Parton (seventies), Arthur Stanwood Pier (1896–1925), William H. Ri-
deing (1881–1919), Walter Leon Sawyer (1892–1901), Ellery Sedgwick (1896–
1900), Dallas Lore Sharp (1900–03), Charles Asbury Stephens (1870–1929),
Charles Miner Thompson (1890–1901), Edward William Thomson (1891–1901),

much sought for by the children, it suggested the experiment of having a paper exclusively for children.[2]

The *Recorder* referred to was a Boston Congregational paper, one of the earliest of the religious weeklies,[3] which Willis had helped to found after a journalistic experience in Portland, Maine. The reasons thus given for beginning the *Companion* go far to explain its early character.

A specimen number was issued under the date of April 16, 1827, by Willis and Asa Rand, his partner in the publication of the *Recorder*. In their prospectus they explain that they are unable to find room in the older paper for all the good pieces of a juvenile character which they could clip "from the various publications which we receive and peruse." Moreover,

This is a day of peculiar care for Youth. . . . Our children are born to higher destinies than their fathers; they will be actors in a far advanced period of the church and the world. . . . The contents of the proposed work will be miscellaneous, though articles of a religious character will be most numerous. . . . This publication, so far as we know, is of a new kind.

There were however, as the publishers hastened to admit, tract and Sunday school periodicals and unreligious literary magazines for children then being published,[4] as well as "others for mere amusement, whose influence is unfavorable to religion and morals." But the *Youth's Companion*, though unconnected with the Sunday schools and tract societies, was to be instructive as well as entertaining, and was to "warn against the ways of transgression, error and ruin, and allure to those of virtue and piety." [5]

Bradford Torrey (1886–1901), George M. Towle (seventies), J. H. Woodbury (1874–90).

REFERENCES: "The *Companion's* Seventy-Fifth Birthday," *Youth's Companion*, LXXV, 205 (April 18, 1901); M. A. DeWolfe Howe, "The Hundredth Anniversary of the *Youth's Companion*," *Youth's Companion*, C, 822 (November 4, 1926); Sherwin Lawrence Cook, "One Hundred Years of the *Youth's Companion*," *Boston Evening Transcript*, August 10, 1929, Book Section, pp. 1–2; C. A. Stephens, "When the *Youth's Companion* Was Young," *Stories of My Home Folks* (Boston, 1926), pp. 1–15.
[2] Henry A. Beers, *Nathaniel Parker Willis* (Boston, 1885), p. 9; *Youth's Companion*, C, 822 (November 4, 1926).
[3] See Mott, *A History of American Magazines, 1741–1850*, p. 138.
[4] *Ibid.*, p. 144.   [5] *Youth's Companion*, I, 1 (April 16, 1827).

The specimen number was filled with precisely the kind of material which distinguished the *Companion* for the next thirty years; therefore it will be worth while to list its contents. The prospectus and terms were followed by a review on the first page of *Nina, An Icelandic Tale*, "by a Mother," in which some of the phenomena of Iceland are detailed. On later pages we have "A Death Bed Scene of a Child of Six Years Old," "A Child's Prayer for His Minister," three moral anecdotes, and "Hints on Education." There are several poems on the fourth and last page — one by "Roy," the pen name of the youthful Nathaniel Parker Willis; Mrs. Hemans' "To an Infant"; some verses "To a Child Who Forgot to Pray"; and some others entitled "One Warning More," ending with the minatory line, "This night may thy soul be required of thee!" There is a department of "Variety," which includes "a little Hymn" to be used as a prayer:

> Now I lay me down to sleep,
> I pray the Lord my soul to keep;
> If I should die before I wake,
> I pray the Lord my soul to take.

The paper was a four-page quarto, to be published weekly at $1.50 a year; but the price was reduced to $1.00 before the second number was issued. That second number was rather long in coming, for the publishers did not care to venture until they had built up a subscription list; it was issued at last on June 6. The circulation was doubtless local and Congregational.[6]

Willis took complete charge of the editorial work in the *Companion* from the first,[7] consisting chiefly as it did of the industrious use of shears and paste pot. His partner Rand withdrew entirely after three years. "Roy" finished college and quit contributing to the *Companion* after a year or two.

There was enough edifying matter about dead and dying infants in those early volumes to satisfy even the most morbid religionist. Narrative gradually displaced the essay-sermon in

---

[6] A New York *Youth's Companion* (1832–34) published two annual volumes. Its use of the same name indicates that its owners either did not know of the Boston paper, or thought the two fields would not overlap.

[7] Frederic Hudson, *Journalism in the United States from 1690 to 1872* (New York, 1873), p. 293. Willis' autobiographical sketch is quoted.

the place of honor in the paper, and the first serial was printed in three parts in July and August 1829. Some original pieces appeared among the "selections" by the end of 1831. Daniel Clement Colesworthy, a Portland printer and writer for the young, was the first "leading contributor" to the paper; and he wrote its first serial stories, such as "The Orphan," as well as the later series, "Advice to Apprentices." His contributions are marked by his initials, which must have become familiar to many New England children of the thirties. He later moved to Boston and conducted a bookstore there. Another improvement which occurred in 1831, after Rand's withdrawal from the partnership, was the occasional insertion of a small woodcut. These were borrowed from James Loring, the book publisher, and portrayed the races of men, natural history subjects, children praying or dying, and so on. They were crude cuts and poorly printed, and sometimes were placed on end to fit them into a column without breaking the make-up.

In the fall of 1834 the words *Sabbath School Recorder* were added to the title of the paper, evidently in an attempt to make it available for Sunday school use; but the subtitle was dropped in a little less than two years, though the paper continued to print much Sunday school matter. "Roy" was back in 1837, and Lydia H. Sigourney also became an occasional contributor.

A new "dress" improved the paper in the early forties, and the contents seem more interesting. The page was enlarged to small folio in 1843. Departments were headed Moral Tales, Religion, Obituary, Morality, Biography, Natural History, Nursery, Parental, Educational. During these years the motto carried under the name plate read: "Devoted to Piety, Morality, Brotherly Love. No sectarianism, no controversy." The contents were still largely eclectic; but Professor Joseph Alden, of Williams College, was a frequent contributor of original sketches. And by the middle fifties "Estelle" was contributing so much that it is easy to think she had a staff position. "Estelle" was the pen name of Elizabeth Bogart, who had gained some fame as a writer of both verse and fiction by her contributions to N. P. Willis' *New York Mirror*.

From 1834 to 1846 the paper was said to be "published" in Portland as well as in Boston, because Willis' agent there, William Hyde, delivered it to its considerable Portland subscription list post-free. The regular postage on the *Companion,* paid by subscribers, was twenty-six cents a year in Massachusetts and half as much again outside of the state.[8] Shortly before the Postal Act of 1852 went into effect, the *Companion* thought to save something by reducing the size of its sheet to quarto again; but in 1853 it was back to a small folio.

In 1857 Nathaniel Willis, then in his seventy-eighth year, sold his paper to John W. Olmstead and Daniel Sharp Ford, the proprietors of the *Watchman and Reflector,* a leading Baptist paper. Ten years later Olmstead and Ford dissolved partnership, the former taking over the *Watchman and Reflector* and the latter the *Youth's Companion.* Ford remained the *Companion's* chief owner and leading spirit until his death in 1899. Rather than place his own name at the masthead of the paper, Ford invented a name for the publishing company — Perry Mason & Company. There never was any Perry Mason; but the thousands of children who imagined Mr. Mason as a benevolent old gentleman with mutton-chop whiskers were not far wrong after all, for that was what Ford looked like in his later years.

Willis remained as "senior editor" until 1862; he survived for eight years longer, "familiarly called 'the tough old deacon,' "[9] and died at the age of ninety. But Ford was the real editor from the time that Olmstead & Company bought the paper. He made fiction more important and bought more original material; he made the *Companion* less a Sunday school paper, though the moral emphasis continued very strong. The size of the page was increased somewhat, and larger type was adopted, to the undoubted benefit of youthful eyes. Circulation — about 4,800 when Olmstead & Company purchased the paper — was ten times that a decade later. Advertising, which Willis had refused, now appeared, including that for sarsaparillas and pain killers.

On the whole, the sixties seem to have been a prosperous decade for the *Companion.* The war caused a slight decrease in size, but in 1869 the paper came out as an eight-page quarto at $1.50, nearly all original. Anonymity vanished with shears and

---

[8] *Youth's Companion,* I, 7 (June 6, 1827).
[9] *Maine Historical and Genealogical Recorder,* III, 222 (No. 4, 1886).

paste pot by the end of the decade, and famous names began to
be seen in the paper's columns. Harriet Beecher Stowe, Elizabeth Stuart Phelps, Louise Chandler Moulton, Virginia F.
Townsend, Mrs. P. P. Bonney, Hezekiah Butterworth, and
John Denison Champlin (signed by initials only) were contributors of the later sixties. Butterworth and Champlin wrote
much for the paper; and the former became an assistant editor
in 1870, continuing a popular writer of both fiction and nonfiction until his death in 1894. The "Children's Column" for
the little folks, which later became a page, began in the sixties,
followed later in the same decade by such long-continued features as the puzzle corner and the anecdote department.

The *Youth's Companion* anecdotes deserve a special mention.
From those "moral anecdotes" in the first specimen number all
through Willis' editorship, there had been brief bits of narrative
each furnished with an appropriate moral. Sometimes the story
was excellent but the moral not very obvious: when that occurred, the fault was corrected by a particularly emphatic
statement of the teaching, however banal. Ford now, in 1869,
devised a set form for these anecdotes, prefacing each with a
stated moral in leaded type, followed by the anecdote set solid.
The reason for the typography was, of course, that it was desired to invite the eye to the statement of the ethical principle
by the opener type, while it was taken for granted that the
longer solid-black paragraphs which followed would not deter
readers who had learned what choice morsels of humor would
reward them at the end. But youthful readers learned how to
circumvent the canny moralistic editor; generation after generation of them, as soon as they learned to read, learned also to
skip the beautifully leaded introductions and plunge into the
fine print of the real anecdote. Editors are said to have combed
thousands of printed pages for these anecdotes every week, but
the result was well worth the effort.

Another *Youth's Companion* institution which began in the
later sixties was the "Premium List." Immediately after the
Civil War, all the periodical publishers seem to have discovered,
at about the same time, the efficacy of premiums to be given
with annual subscriptions.[10] But of them all, the *Youth's Com-*

[10] See Volume III, Chapter I.

panion used premiums intensively for the longest time. Year
after year for half a century and more, it sent out its annual
"Premium List Number," late in October, to the delight of hundreds of thousands of boys and girls who saw in the pictured
treasures available "for three new subscriptions," or more or
less, the realization of their fondest dreams of possession. The
great list, which by the early eighties had reached thirty-six
pages of the regular *Companion* size, and by the nineties twice
that, was even more eagerly awaited than the next number of
a continued story by C. A. Stephens — and that sounds like
hyperbole. How these multitudes of children would pore over
the pictures and descriptions of the chests of tools, the scroll
saws, the magic lanterns, the chemical cabinets, the electric
equipment, the small printing presses, the dolls, the Elsie books
and Henty books and books of biography and adventure, the
Bibles, atlases, histories! And how subscriptions must have
rolled in upon Perry Mason following each premium list issue!
The "Magic Scroll Saw" alone is said to have added 40,000
subscribers.[11] The premium lists began in 1867; the circulation was quoted at 50,000 the next year, and it gained an average of about 10,000 annually for the next ten years. After that,
its annual gain was more like 25,000, until it reached about
400,000 in 1887. It hovered around the half-million mark in the
nineties, passing it in 1898. For almost half a century, beginning
in 1870, the subscription rate was fixed at the unusual figure
of $1.75.

Apparently three factors were chiefly responsible for the
Youth's Companion's popularity: premiums, continued stories
with real appeal to youth, and the cultivation of the interests of
the whole family.

The good Colesworthy and others had done some short serials
for the early *Companion*, but Virginia F. Townsend's stories in
the late sixties were the first of the type which were later to win
popularity for the paper. One should not, perhaps, speak of "a
type" of *Companion* serial, for there were at least two well-
defined types — the domestic story of a family of real boys and
girls, such as those written so successfully in the nineties by
Sophie Swett; and the outdoor adventure story, of which

[11] Stephens, *op. cit.*, p. 8.

Stephens was the master. The former doubtless appealed most to girls, but boys read it, too; the latter was probably intended for boys, but girls and all the family read it. Charles Asbury Stephens wrote convincing tales of hunting, fishing, exploring, and so on, in which boys figured as the heroes. In the seventies and eighties he traveled widely to gather materials for articles and stories, half his expenses being paid by the paper and the other half met by his receipts from the stories;[12] but later he developed a vein of delightful short tales in series, founded upon true incidents of his own youth and upon stories told him by New England acquaintances — an early and superior type of the "true story."[13] For half a century C. A. Stephens was a joy to *Companion* readers. In an autobiographical note written many years later, he tells of how, one January day in the later sixties, he brought his first stories to the editor of the *Companion*. He was then not yet twenty, but he had resolved to "live by the use of his pen"; and he was delighted by the honorarium of $7.00 apiece which Ford allowed him for his stories. The next week he brought in two more, for which he was paid $10 each. With these riches he made a trip to Washington to see what he could see in the nation's capital to interest young people. This was the beginning of the Stephens travels for the *Companion*.[14] Butterworth also did some traveling for the paper, of which his popular *Zig-Zag Journeys* were the result.

The third factor in the success of the paper was Ford's far-seeing policy of making it a journal for the whole family. A publisher of *St. Nicholas*, later to become a monthly competitor of the *Companion*, once stated that the life of a subscription to his magazine averaged three years, children having a way of growing up and putting aside childish things.[15] This was never true of the *Companion* after Ford took full charge in 1867. Father and Mother read it as well as the children, and it was always well worth their reading. Possibly articles by Gladstone, Blaine, Speaker Reed, Lord Bryce, Chief Justice Brewer, Hardy, Kipling, Presidents Dwight, Low, Gilman, and Hadley,

[12] *Ibid.*, p. 7.
[13] *Ibid.*, pp. 12–15.
[14] *Ibid.*, pp. 1–4.
[15] W. W. Ellsworth, *A Golden Age of Authors* (Boston, 1919), p. 93.

Professors Tyndall, Huxley, and Flammarion, and Henry Ward Beecher and Edwin Lawrence Godkin were sometimes a bit over the heads of the youngsters; but the names gave tone to the paper, ambitious boys and girls read the articles, and many an adult liked the simpler manner which these great adopted for the benefit of the *Companion* readers.

But for some years Ford was satisfied with less glamorous names. Champlin, Mrs. C. W. Flanders, Ruth Chesterfield, and Mrs. Mary A. Denison were favorites. Then in 1872 Louisa M. Alcott and Rebecca Harding Davis appeared in the paper, the latter to become an editorial contributor. The *Companion* absorbed *Merry's Museum* in December of that year. Gradually the famous names were acquired, and others added through the years — William Dean Howells, Jules Verne, Charles Reade, Justin McCarthy, to name but a few. John T. Trowbridge was a favorite writer in the seventies; and James Parton, son-in-law of the founder, was a staff contributor.

It was in 1870 that Ford began building up the extensive editorial staff that was to make the *Youth's Companion* an exceptionally well-edited paper. In that year Butterworth and Stephens both began their work as members of the staff, and the Reverend Theron Brown began his long connection with the paper, which ended only with his death in 1914. Parton and George M. Towle were staff members in the seventies. J. H. Woodbury came to the staff in 1874, remaining until his death in 1890; while William H. Rideing came in 1881, to be especially helpful for a third of a century and more in procuring famous contributors from his native England. Jefferson L. Harbour, well-known writer for boys, was an editor 1884–1901; Bradford Torrey, the ornithologist, was on the staff 1886–1901; and Edward Stanwood, who came to the paper in 1884, was managing editor for a quarter of a century beginning in 1887. Charles A. Dana is said to have declared the *Companion* the best-edited paper he knew — and he knew most of them.[16]

In the eighties the size was twelve pages, small folio. This was the decade in which the *Companion* began its policy of obtaining articles on their specialities by world-famous celebrities,

[16] *Youth's Companion*, LXXXI, 189 (April 18, 1907). Here is found an incomplete list of "Some Editors and Staff Contributors" without dates.

especially statesmen, scientists, and explorers. Besides the famous men already mentioned, the eighties and nineties saw the publication of really excellent little articles by Theodore Roosevelt, Grover Cleveland, Carl Schurz, George F. Hoar, Wu Ting Fang, Booker T. Washington, Ira F. Remsen, Andrew D. White, Henry M. Stanley, Robert E. Peary, Nelson A. Miles, Sir John Lubbock, Max Müller, Lillian Nordica, and Marcella Sembrich. What a list! And it could be made much longer without impairment of quality.

In fiction the paper was somewhat less distinguished, but quite as attractive. Stephens, Trowbridge, Butterworth, Horace E. Scudder, George Egbert Craddock, Frances Hodgson Burnett, and H. H. Boyesen were among the writers of serials. Ford knew what he wanted in *Companion* fiction and what he did not want. He wanted liveliness, action, humor, and convincing youthful characters; he rigidly maintained a taboo against love-making, crime (especially murders), the slightest emphasis on immoralities, and improper language. Melodrama was commoner in the early *Companion* than in the paper of the nineties. Adventures gradually became less exotic and more convincing, often relating to hunting, fishing, and games. In the middle eighties the editor had tried offering cash prizes for serials and short stories, but he soon found that it was hard to get exactly what he needed in that way. He was always friendly to beginning writers; and many a budding author sent his first attempt to the *Youth's Companion*, receiving, if he asked for it, a criticism of the manuscript along with the rejection slip when it was returned. For example, young Jack London found in the *Youth's Companion* one of his first and most hospitable markets in the years from 1899 to 1905. What is perhaps his best short story, "To Build a Fire," was published in the number for May 29, 1902; and his series of stories of the Fish Patrol appeared in the *Companion* in 1905.

There were poems in each issue — two or three on the anecdote page and two or three on the "Children's Page." Tennyson, Longfellow, Whittier, Whitman, Aldrich, and Stedman were among the more famous contributors of verse. The anecdote page usually began with a poem — *the* poem of the issue — and followed it with a little religious essay, frequently by

Theron Brown. There was also a column of current events. The last page always led off with a short medical article, of the kind that later came to be syndicated for the daily press. For a long time these were written by Stephens, who took a medical degree in the eighties chiefly in order that he might be qualified to write them. Dr. Thomas Lathrop Stedman was also a staff contributor.

History was always prominent in the *Companion*. Parkman, Fiske, Taine, Froude, Freeman, Hale, and Wilson were famous historians and biographers who wrote for it. William Garrot Brown, the southern historian, was for a time a contributing editor.

The paper was well illustrated from the sixties onward, first by woodcuts, and after the eighties by half tones after wash drawings. Russell & Richardson were early engravers for the *Companion*. Jacob Russell became art director for the paper and was followed by Frederick O. Sylvester.

In the nineties a procession of associate and assistant editors passed through the *Companion* office. M. A. DeWolfe Howe was there through 1888–93 and again in 1899–1913. Joseph Edgar Chamberlin, later well known as literary editor of the *Boston Transcript*, was on the *Companion* staff 1890–1901. Charles Miner Thompson came from the *Boston Advertiser*, also in 1890, to remain for more than a third of a century. Edward W. Thompson, Will N. Harben, and Walter Leon Sawyer were editors in the nineties. Paul P. Foster came to the paper in 1894 and after 1911 wrote the scientific notes which had become a feature. Ellery Sedgwick was an assistant editor in 1896–1900; and Arthur Stanwood Pier, who wrote many continued stories for the paper, occupied a similar position in 1896–1925.

On the day before Christmas, in 1899, Daniel S. Ford died. In spite of many benefactions, his estate was worth some two million dollars at the time of his death. Seth Mendell, Ford's chief partner for many years, succeeded him as president of the Perry Mason Company, serving in that position until 1912, and later as director. Stanwood, managing editor since 1887, continued to head the staff, with Rideing, Howe, and Thompson as associates for the next decade or more. During this time there

was no change in the policy of the paper. Famous writers, such
as Sir Gilbert Parker, Israel Zangwill, Margaret Deland, Hamlin Garland, Lyman Abbott, and Woodrow Wilson gave its
pages high-sounding names and valuable articles; while Stephens, Pier, Sophie Swett, and Stewart Edward White provided
the fascinating serials that did so much to maintain a *Companion* popularity now almost traditional. Circulation kept
well above the half-million mark until 1907, when the panic
of that year brought it down a little. Premiums were still
efficacious.

During the first decade of the new century the following men
joined the editorial staff, to remain for longer or shorter periods:
William E. Barton, Ira Rich Kent, Dallas Lore Sharp, Roswell
Martin Field, John Macy, Heloise E. Hersey, George William
Douglas, and John Clair Minot. When Stanwood reached the
age of seventy, in 1911, he retired as editor of the *Companion*,
to be followed by Charles Miner Thompson. Thompson had
then been on the staff of the paper for twenty-two years; he
now became part owner as well as editor-in-chief. Mendell retired from the presidency, giving place to Charles E. Kelsey,
who had been connected with the paper since 1889 and for a
number of years secretary of the publishing company.

A gradual decline of the *Companion's* circulation and advertising had already begun. It is never easy to explain the failing
prosperity of a periodical which has long been popular. The
experts themselves cannot do it, or they would know what to
prescribe. For a time the *Companion* tried issuing a special
New England edition for regional advertisers. There were some
experiments in changing the editorial policy; but the old subscribers demanded a continuance of the traditional combination of serial, short stories, articles by famous men and women,
anecdotes, science, and puzzles. The great women's magazines
offered strong competition in the "family journal" class, but the
Companion was unwilling to abandon its long-standing policy
of editing for the whole family circle. A commentator on the
subsequent demise of the paper observed:

Ford's youths of fiction were like the forgotten boys of Adams and
Alger and Castlemon. . . . Ford's strictness was never entirely

escaped. The modern *Youth's Companion*, whether or not the staff was aware of it, had inhibitions which held it back, quite imperceptibly perhaps.[17]

Most of the staff, business and editorial, had been with the paper for many years and were trained in its traditions.

The subscription price was advanced to $2.00 at the time of the reorganization in 1912, and another half-dollar was added because of increasing costs in 1919. Two years later the size was reduced to quarto. In 1925, with the circulation down to 300,000, the Perry Mason Company was purchased by the Atlantic Monthly Company, of which two former assistant editors of the *Companion*, Sedgwick and Howe, were respectively president and vice-president. Harford W. H. Powel, Jr., who had been editor of *Collier's*, was placed in editorial charge.

The general family appeal was now largely relinquished, and the *Companion* was edited for modern boys and girls. The old "inhibitions" were, for the most part, abandoned. This was not wholly successful, for old friends resented the new changes. In 1928 the paper was made a monthly; and such innovations as fashions for girls, young people's clubs, and love stories were adopted. The last number appeared in September 1929, after which the centenarian was merged with the *American Boy*, of Detroit.[18]

Many an older man and woman sorrowed at the passing of the *Youth's Companion*, recalling the happy hours spent with it each week throughout childhood and youth. That it was an excellent educational influence cannot be doubted. There has never been another periodical quite like it, and in the opinion of the oldsters there can never be another so good.

[17] Cook, *op. cit.*, p. 2.

[18] Technically, the *American Boy* after September 1929, continued the *Youth's Companion* as a part of the file of the latter, since it took over the serial numbering of the *Youth's Companion* and has continued it. The cover title was changed at the time of the merger to the *Youth's Companion Combined with American Boy*, with the words *American Boy* given much more prominent type display than the remainder of the title; the page caption reads *American Boy–Youth's Companion*, and the paper is referred to editorially and in advertising as the *American Boy*. No changes in editorial policy were made in 1929, and the paper is clearly the *American Boy* and not the *Youth's Companion*. It seems proper, therefore, in fairness to both papers, to treat the *Companion* as a historical unit ending September 1929.

3

THE LIBERATOR [1]

WHEN he founded the *Liberator* in January 1831, William Lloyd Garrison was not yet twenty-six years old; but he had already been connected with five papers, and he had gained a wide reputation as a fire-eating young abolitionist. He had served an apprenticeship with his home-town weekly in Newburyport, Massachusetts, and had then founded the *Free Press* in the same town before he had reached his majority. He had discovered John G. Whittier, another youngster, and made him a regular contributor to the paper; but that had not prevented its demise after three months. He had then edited for nine months a Boston temperance paper called the *National Philanthropist*;[2] in Bennington, Vermont, he had conducted a political paper, the *Journal of the Times*, for six months, continuing his advocacy of teetotalism and inveighing strongly against slavery and war. Finally, at the solicitation of Benjamin Lundy, proprietor of the first of the great anti-slavery periodicals, the *Genius of Universal Emancipation*,[3] he had joined in the editorship of that paper in Baltimore. In the *Genius* Garrison had gone further than Lundy, urging immediate instead of gradual emancipation, and black-listing those engaged in the domestic slave trade. As a result of one of these black-listings, Garrison had been prosecuted and cast into jail, where he had languished for seven weeks.

This record indicates the restless vigor and the boldness of

[1] TITLE: *The Liberator.*
FIRST ISSUE: January 1, 1831. LAST ISSUE: December 29, 1865.
PERIODICITY: Weekly. Regular annual volumes.
PUBLISHERS: William Lloyd Garrison and Isaac Knapp, 1831–34; Isaac Knapp, 1835–36; Massachusetts Anti-slavery Society, 1837; Isaac Knapp, 1838–39; William Lloyd Garrison, 1840–65 (with William Bassett, Francis Jackson, Ellis Gray Loring, Samuel Philbrick, and Edmund Quincy as a Finance Committee).
EDITOR: William Lloyd Garrison.
REFERENCE: Wendell P. and Francis J. Garrison, *William Lloyd Garrison, 1805–1879: The Story of His Life* (New York, 1885–94), 4 vols.
[2] See Mott, *A History of American Magazines, 1741–1850*, p. 165.
[3] *Ibid.*, p. 162.

the young reformer. He was ambitious, too: when John Neal attacked him in the *Yankee* and called him a nobody, he replied in the *National Philanthropist*:

> If my life shall be spared, my name shall one day be known so extensively as to render private enquiry unnecessary; and known, too, in a praiseworthy manner. I speak in the spirit of prophecy, not of vainglory — with a strong pulse, a flashing eye, and a glow of the heart.[4]

The story of Garrison's youth indicates but little, however, of that steadfastness, that persistence in sharp attack, that continued reiteration of violent invective directed chiefly at one object, which distinguish the great work of his life — the *Liberator*.

Released from the Baltimore jail, Garrison found his old position with the *Genius* no longer open to him. Lundy and he disagreed on some fundamental principles — colonization, for instance, and immediacy; and besides, the *Genius* was in financial straits and must needs be reduced to a monthly, and a monthly Lundy could edit alone. Garrison thereupon resolved upon an immediate-abolition paper of his own, to be issued from the national capital and called the *Public Liberator and Journal of the Times*, and he issued a prospectus to that effect in August 1830. "The primary object of this publication," said Garrison, "will be the abolition of slavery, and the moral and intellectual elevation of our colored population." He also pledged his "zealous support" to "the cause of Peace and the promotion of Temperance," and he promised a "fair proportion" of literary miscellany and news.[5] But before the end of the year Lundy moved the *Genius* to Washington, and Garrison decided to launch his paper in Boston. During a speech-making tour through New England, Garrison had found "prejudice more stubborn, apathy more frozen, than among slave owners themselves" — which made him think his paper was more needed "within sight of Bunker Hill and in the birthplace of

---

[4] Quoted from the *National Philanthropist* of August 22, 1828, by Garrison, *op. cit.*, I, 100.

[5] Garrison, *op. cit.*, I, 199–201. This prospectus was not reprinted in the *Liberator*, since it had been widely circulated, but its promises were specifically renewed in the "salutatory."

LIBERATOR NAME PLATE, WITH SLAVE AUCTION CUT

Top one-third of an early number of the *Liberator*. The auction block is labeled: "SLAVES, HORSES & OTHER CATTLE TO BE SOLD AT 12 O'C."

liberty" than at the capital of government.[6] Besides, he had made a decision very important in the technique of this reform movement: he had resolved to keep free of politics and make his appeal on high ethical grounds. Another reason for going to Boston was that Garrison and his partner Knapp were Massachusetts boys, and they found a young print-shop owner named Stephen Foster who was willing to issue their paper in return for the work of Garrison and Knapp regularly at the cases in his shop.

Garrison had become acquainted with Isaac Knapp, his future partner, when they were both printer's apprentices at Newburyport; Knapp had followed his friend to Baltimore to work on the *Genius*. He, too, was an enthusiastic abolitionist; but he had no talent for writing, and his habits were irregular. He was Garrison's associate in the printing and publishing part of the business, sharing financial responsibility; but his help on the editorial side was never important.

The first number of the *Liberator* (for the longer title originally proposed had been discarded in favor of the single significant word) was a quarto of four pages, with four columns to the page, priced at two dollars a year. It was dated with the first day of the new year, 1831. Made part of the name plate and extending above it was a cut depicting a slave auction. On the first page, following some salutatory verses, appeared Garrison's famous initial address "To the Public," which contained the following paragraph:

I am aware that many object to the severity of my language; but is there not cause for severity? I *will be* as harsh as truth, and as uncompromising as justice. On this subject, I do not wish to think or speak, or write, with moderation. No! no! Tell a man whose house is on fire to give a moderate alarm; tell him to moderately rescue his wife from the hands of the ravisher; tell the mother to gradually extricate her babe from the fire into which it has fallen; — but urge me not to use moderation in a cause like the present. I am in earnest — I will not equivocate — I will not excuse — I will not retreat a single inch — AND I WILL BE HEARD. . . .

[6] *Liberator*, I, 1 (January 1, 1831). This address "To the Public" is reprinted in Garrison, *op. cit.*, I, 224–226. The whole of the first number is reproduced in *Old South Leaflets*, No. 78.

The remainder of the first page was devoted to two articles about slavery in the District of Columbia, and the second page to an account of the editor's Baltimore trial, followed by a poem on "Universal Emancipation" by G——n. The third page was headed "Journal of the Times" in memory of Garrison's old Vermont paper; it began with an editorial rhapsody on the New Year, followed by "Correspondence" and some paragraphs of comment. The last page was headed "Literary, Miscellaneous and Moral." There was some adversion to the peace movement and to the cause of the Indian; but in the main the first number of the *Liberator* was a rattling volley against the institution of slavery.

The significance of this volley cannot be understood without a realization of the fact that the doctrine of immediate abolition had, in 1831, little or no standing even among antislavery advocates. There were several antislavery periodicals being published,[7] but none which took the advanced ground occupied so belligerently by the *Liberator*.

Bitter antagonism was at once aroused in many quarters, but particularly in the South. As the little paper continued, week after week, firing its carefully aimed charges of grapeshot upon the "peculiar institution" of the southern states, defenders of slavery were stung to action. In October the corporation of Georgetown, D. C., enacted legislation forbidding any Negro to take the *Liberator* from the post office, subject to fine and imprisonment; and if the fine or jail fees were not paid, directing that the offender be sold into slavery for four months.[8] A vigilance committee of Columbia, South Carolina, offered a reward of $1,500 for any white person found circulating the hated paper.[9] A Raleigh, North Carolina, grand jury indicted Garrison and Knapp for the circulation of their paper "in this county, in contravention to the act of the last General Assembly."[10] The legislature of Georgia passed a resolution offering a reward of $5,000 for the arrest and conviction of Garrison or Knapp or "any other person or persons who shall utter, publish, or circulate within the limits of this State said paper called the

[7] See Mott, *op. cit.*, p. 456.
[8] *Liberator*, I, 171 (October 22, 1831).
[9] *Ibid.*   [10] *Ibid.*

Liberator." [11] The governor of Massachusetts and the mayor of Boston were called upon by the governors of Virginia, South Carolina, and Georgia at various times to extinguish the firebrand. Mayor Harrison Gray Otis later explained:

It appeared on enquiry no member of the city government, nor any person of my acquaintance, had ever heard of the publication. Some time afterward [after the complaints of the governors] it was reported to me by the city officers that they had ferreted out the paper and its editor; that his office was an obscure hole, his only visible auxiliary a negro boy, and his supporters a very few insignificant persons of all colors. This information, with the consent of the aldermen, I communicated to the above-named governors, with an assurance of my belief that the new fanaticism had not made, nor was likely to make, proselytes among the respectable class of our people. In this, however, I was mistaken.[12]

But in respect to the humble conditions under which the *Liberator* was produced, Mayor Otis was quite correct. The arrangement with Foster for printing the paper lasted for only three weeks, after which the two partners took a room in the attic of the old "Merchants' Hall," where they installed a few cases of worn type, an imposing stone, an old press, a long table, and a bed. There they lived and edited and published their paper, with some assistance after the first year from a Negro boy. "The publishers of the *Liberator*," they announced in their first number, "have formed their copartnership with a determination to print the paper as long as they can subsist upon bread and water, or their hands find employment." Their fare actually was not much more than bread and water, and even then they had difficulty in paying their paper bills; without occasional gifts from Samuel E. Sewall and Ellis Gray Loring, Garrison could not have gone forward during the earlier years of the *Liberator*. Lowell wrote realistically in his poem "To W. L. Garrison":

> In a small chamber, friendless and unseen,
>   Toiled o'er his types one poor, unlearned young man;
> The place was dark, unfurnitured and mean; —
>   Yet there the freedom of a race began.

[11] *Liberator*, III, 123 (August 3, 1833); Garrison, *op. cit.*, I, 247.
[12] *Ibid.*, XVIII, 162 (October 13, 1848).

Help came but slowly; surely no man yet
Put lever to the heavy world with less:
What need of help? He knew how types were set;
He had a dauntless spirit and a press.[13]

No inconsiderable proportion of the *Liberator's* support came from the free Negroes of the North. They were in accord with Garrison's opposition to colonization, and they wrote acceptable contributions for the paper. In its fourth year the publishers stated that nearly three-fourths of the actual subscribers were Negroes.[14]

Opposition to colonization occupied many pages in the *Liberator*. The Colonization Society, Garrison wrote,

has inflicted great injury upon the free and slave population: first, by strengthening the prejudices of the people; secondly, by discouraging the education of those who are free; thirdly, by inducing the passage of severe legislative enactments; and, finally, by lulling the whole country into deep sleep.[15]

A project which Garrison did approve, however, was that of boycotting the products of slavery — a method in vogue among antislavery Quakers. "*Entire abstinence* from the products of slavery is the duty of every individual," he insisted.[16] Peace and temperance received some attention in these early years of the *Liberator*. The paper attacked the saloon keeper with burning indignation. "God is my witness," exclaimed its editor, "that great as is my detestation of slavery, I had rather be a slaveholder — yea, a kidnapper on the African coast — than sell this poison to my fellow creatures for common consumption." [17]

The New-England Anti-Slavery Society was organized at the beginning of 1832, with Garrison as corresponding secretary; and in August it sent him on a speaking tour in New England. The *Liberator*, which now had 500 subscribers,[18] was enlarged

---

[13] *Anti-Slavery Standard*, October 16, 1848. First called "The Day of Small Things."

[14] In a circular issued in April 1834. Quoted in Garrison, *op. cit.*, I, 432.

[15] *Liberator*, I, 126 (August 6, 1831).

[16] *Ibid.*, I, 121 (July 30, 1831).

[17] *Ibid.*, II, 101 (June 30, 1832).

[18] Garrison, *op. cit.*, I, 430.

to a small folio, five columns to the page; and small woodcuts illustrating distressing scenes incident to slavery appeared occasionally. John Rankin's "Letters on American Slavery" were printed serially in the second volume. In the third we have much of the Prudence Crandall matter — the persecution of a Connecticut school teacher who was conducting a school for colored children. In this connection Garrison was sued for libel by five men who had been responsible for jailing Miss Crandall and whom the *Liberator* attacked so viciously that the heroine of the whole episode, justifying her Christian name, reminded the vitriolic editor that "Soft words turn away wrath, but grievous words stir up anger." [19] But Garrison could not use "soft words." Only a few weeks later he took occasion to defend the *Liberator's* sharp speaking thus:

But the *Liberator* uses very hard language, and calls a great many bad names, and is very harsh and abusive. Precious cant, indeed! And what has been so efficacious as this hard language? Now, I am satisfied that its strength of denunciation bears no proportion to the enormous guilt of the slave system. The English language is lamentably weak and deficient in regard to this matter. I wish its epithets were heavier — I wish it would not break so easily — I wish I could denounce slavery, and all its abettors, in terms equal to their infamy.[20]

The summer of 1833 Garrison spent in England, enlisting aid there in the fight against American slavery. In charge of the *Liberator* during his absence was Oliver Johnson, a printer who had had some training in religious journalism, and a stout-hearted abolitionist. It was natural enough that slavery advocates should resent Garrison's carrying the American dispute to England; at any rate, this excursion gave James Watson Webb's *Courier and Enquirer* and William L. Stone's *Commercial Advertiser* ammunition with which to attack bitterly the abolitionists who, just as the ship bringing Garrison home docked at New York, were gathering to organize the New York Anti-Slavery Society. Those papers did much to incite the mob violence which broke up the organization meeting, and their chief text was that Garrison had been "traducing" his country abroad. The office of the *Liberator* in Boston was mobbed, too;

[19] Garrison, *op. cit.*, I, 322.
[20] *Address Before the Free People of Color* (New York, 1833), p. 11.

but altogether the various mobs did little harm, and Garrison
was quick to assert in his paper:

> To the charge made against me by the cowardly ruffian who con-
> ducts the New York *Courier and Enquirer*, and by the miserable liar
> and murderous hypocrite of the New York *Commercial Advertiser*, of
> having slandered my country abroad, I reply that it is false.[21]

He took care to give his readers, thereupon, a full account of his
"mission" to England, especially regarding his "slanderous"
utterances.

The antislavery movement was now gaining momentum as
never before; and the *Liberator* had been, to a large extent, the
cause of the increasing interest. The American Anti-Slavery
Society was organized in Philadelphia December 5, 1833, with
Garrison as foreign corresponding secretary. But the little
Liberator hoed a hard row financially, and in the spring of 1834
the publishers decided to make a special appeal for financial
help from its friends and the friends, in general, of abolition.
Help was the more necessary at this juncture because Garrison
was soon to marry and set up a home. The appeal took the form
of a circular headed "Shall the *Liberator* Die?" The circulation
was now over 2,000, but the publishers had suffered from the
delinquent-subscriber curse, from the necessity of paying
agents' commissions, and from the fact that the subscription
price of $2.00 was too low for so small a circulation. The annual
deficit was calculated at $1,700, allowing for an editorial salary
of $700.[22] The only result of the circular was to stimulate
efforts of friends to increase the subscription list; no more direct
aid was forthcoming. In 1835 and 1836 the responsibility for
the paper was divided, Knapp becoming publisher and assuming
the financial burden, while Garrison remained as editor, his
salary being provided by gifts.[23] Garrison was absent from the
Boston office much of the time because of illness; he spent
months together at his summer home in Brooklyn, Connecticut,
and he made many trips attending conventions and delivering
lectures. In his absence Charles Burleigh did most of the ed-

---

[21] *Liberator*, III, 163 (October 12, 1833).
[22] Garrison, *op. cit.*, I, 430–432.
[23] *Ibid.*, II, 84; *Liberator*, VI, 191 (November 26, 1836).

itorial work,[24] and Oliver Johnson was for several years a strong
support for the paper. But there was much irregularity in the
1835 issues, though no numbers were missed.[25] For some
months Knapp had no print shop of his own.[26]

The great feature of the 1834 volume of the *Liberator* was
the record of the visit to America of the English abolitionist,
George Thompson, with the mob violence and the speech-
making incident to it. In 1835 came the Faneuil Hall pro-
slavery meeting, followed somewhat later by the mobbing of
Garrison at the antislavery headquarters. The story of this mob
and of how Garrison was dragged through the streets of Boston
— "the Cradle of Liberty, the city of Hancock and Adams, the
headquarters of refinement, literature, intelligence and religion"
— is fully told by the editor himself in his paper;[27] and the
responsibility for the outrage is disputed through many issues.
In the next volume (1836) the big story is that of George
Thompson's antislavery journeys through England and Scotland. In the meantime, one of the paper's departments, "The
Refuge of Oppression," attracted no little attention. It had
been started in 1834, to succeed the earlier "Slavery Record."
Into it, said the editor sarcastically, "we propose to copy some
of the choicest specimens of anti-abolition morality, decency,
logic, and humanity." [28] As a matter of fact, it was filled with
the most extreme statements into which fury betrayed the more
reckless defenders of slavery, and thus it became an arsenal of
extraordinarily effective boomerangs.

In 1837 the Massachusetts Anti-Slavery Society took over
the financial responsibility for the *Liberator*, retaining Knapp
as its printer. The paper was enlarged, and the price raised to
$2.50 a year. It was not to be the organ of the Society, however,
but was to continue the mouthpiece of William Lloyd Garrison.[29]
Obviously, this arrangement could not continue, especially in
view of the fact that the editor was coming more and more to
place before his readers the cogitations of a liberal mind upon

[24] Garrison, *op. cit.*, II, 84.
[25] *Ibid.*, I, 468.
[26] *Ibid.*, II, 43.
[27] *Liberator*, V, 179 (November 7, 1835).
[28] *Ibid.*, IV, 3 (January 4, 1834).
[29] Garrison, *op. cit.*, II, 122.

subjects other than slavery. But the Society supported the paper through that year, bringing the circulation to 3,000 and enlarging the page again.[30] In 1838 Knapp resumed the responsibilities of publisher, which he retained for two years; but, as before, he had his hands full in paying paper and labor bills, and left the editor without salary. Moreover, his habits became more and more "irregular." In 1840 a committee bargained with him to give up for two years his claim upon the publication of the *Liberator* and on its subscription list, which he did for the sum [31] of $175. A finance committee of Garrison's friends was then set up to raise the money to pay deficits, and Garrison became both publisher and editor — an arrangement maintained until the end. The philanthropic committee consisted of William Bassett, Francis Jackson, Ellis Gray Loring, Samuel Philbrick, and Edmund Quincy; they all remained faithful through many years of money-raising, though only two of them — Bassett and Quincy — survived the paper. Oliver Johnson became "general agent," or circulation manager, in 1840, but he soon was called to the editorship of the *Anti-Slavery Standard* in New York. Knapp showed himself anxious to resume his former relation with the *Liberator* after the two-year agreement had expired, though he had never made more than wages out of it. Repulsed by the finance committee and by Garrison, he defiantly issued one number of *Knapp's Liberator* on January 8, 1842, and disappeared from the scene;[32] he died obscurely some two years later.

Those heresies and "vagaries" of the *Liberator* which had made it impracticable to look to the Massachusetts Society for Garrisonian support gradually increased in number. From the first, peace and temperance had shared with abolitionism the fire of Garrison's reformatory zeal. Both Elijah P. Lovejoy and John Brown, though esteemed martyrs, were condemned for carrying arms;[33] and Garrison was the leader in the formation in 1838 of a Non-Resistance Society,[34] whose propaganda came

[30] *Ibid.*, II, 123.
[31] *Ibid.*, II, 331–332.
[32] *Ibid.*, III, 37–42.
[33] *Liberator*, VII, 191 (November 24, 1837); XXIX, 166 (October 21, 1859).
[34] *Ibid.*, VIII, 154 (September 28, 1838).

to occupy a considerable part of the *Liberator's* columns. Most of the fourth page was devoted to nonresistance in 1838, with the results of protests and loss of subscriptions from more militant abolitionists. The pressure was removed in January 1839 by the weekly *Non-Resistant*, which became the organ of the Society; Garrison was a nominal editor of it throughout its three and a half years. So far as Garrison himself was concerned, the whole peace question was knit up with a set of beliefs known as "perfectionism," and derived, in some part at least, from John H. Noyes, the Oneida communist.[35]

Another upsetting doctrine which readers of the *Liberator* found creeping into their paper was the sabbatical heresy. This was a revolt against what Edmund Quincy once called the "Puritanico-Judaic Sabbath," and it was climaxed by an Anti-Sabbath Convention called early in 1848 by Garrison and some of his closest friends.[36] Following this came a worse heresy (if worse there could be) in mutterings against the doctrine of the inspiration of the Scriptures. This also culminated in a mass meeting — the famous Bible Convention held at Hartford in 1853. Garrison published the call for this meeting[37] and took part in its deliberations.

Antislavery and antiliquor suited *Liberator* readers very well indeed; antiwar raised some dissenters; but anti-Sabbath and anti-Bible brought a storm of disapproval on Garrison's devoted head. But here was a man who had been born a reformer, bred up to controversy, and educated in the clash of dissension. Infirm in body, he was a raging warrior in the battles of words, breathing challenges and imprecations. The growing enmity of New England clergy, fostered not only by Garrison's heresies but also by his attacks on the churches for their opposition to abolitionism, came to a head in the "Pastoral Letter" of 1837.[38] Garrison was absent when this attack appeared, and it was answered briefly by Oliver Johnson, editor in charge; but next week there were sixteen columns of reply, half of it by Gar-

[35] For Noyes and his paper, see p. 207 above; for influence of Noyes on Garrison, see Garrison, *op. cit.*, II, 148, and *Liberator*, VII, 203 (December 23, 1837).

[36] *Liberator*, XVIII, 11 (January 21, 1848).

[37] *Ibid.*, XXIII, 63 (April 22, 1853).

[38] *Ibid.*, VII, 129 (August 11, 1837).

rison himself.[39] This brought out other letters signed by groups
of clergymen, and other rejoinders. The acrimonious debate
served at length to solidify the Garrisonites, and to make the
editor of the *Liberator* more than ever the dictator of the increasing group of antislavery extremists; and it also brought
about eventually a schism among Garrison's enemies. One
clerical opponent asserted that the hero-worship bestowed upon
Garrison was nothing less than "IDOLATRY — the worship of
another being than Jehovah" and that the mad leader aimed to
"make himself the Universal Lord, and make all men slaves to
him." [40] Of course, there was a new organization and a new
paper — the *Massachusetts Abolitionist* (1839–41). Since this
competitor was priced at a dollar a year, Garrison thought it
necessary to begin the *Cradle of Liberty*, a monthly filled with
selections from the *Liberator* and selling at seventy-five cents a
year, or fifty cents in quantities.[41]

The great schism of 1840 followed, at the convention of the
American Society in New York. There the "New Organization"
faction had tried to capture the Society for political action —
a purpose abhorrent to Garrison. After this battle, the editor
sailed for England to attend the World Antislavery Convention,
from which he sent back accounts of its proceedings for his
paper.

Throughout all these contests over religious and social questions, throughout the contests for leadership and the rivalry of
societies and the quarrels over policy, the *Liberator* never
lost sight of its one arch-enemy, slavery; it continually reiterated its attack upon the slaveholders and charged atrocities
against them; it maintained its testimony for immediate emancipation. The chief reason for the paper's opposition to political
action by the abolitionists was its repudiation of the Constitution and the government erected upon that compact. Garrison
rejected an instrument which tolerated slavery, denied his loyalty to a government built upon such a foundation, and refused
to vote or to take part in political activities.

[39] *Ibid.*, VII, 133 (August 18, 1837).
[40] *Ibid.*, IX, 44 (March 15, 1839).
[41] It began March 23, 1839; the second issue came April 6, after which it
appeared weekly through July 18, 1840; then it gave way to the *Monthly
Offering*.

So far as the Union, now and forever, was concerned, Garrison had written, in the first volume of the *Liberator*: "If the bodies and souls of millions of rational beings must be sacrificed as the price of the Union, better, far better, that a separation should take place." [42] His advocacy of disunion gradually increased in definiteness and boldness, until in 1842 he impressed upon the coming antislavery meeting in New York "the duty of making REPEAL OF THE UNION between the North and the South the grand rallying-point until it be accomplished or slavery cease to pollute our soil." [43] Accordingly, the following "flag" was carried at the head of the *Liberator's* editorial column during the last eight months of 1842:

> A REPEAL OF THE UNION BETWEEN NORTHERN LIBERTY
> AND SOUTHERN SLAVERY IS ESSENTIAL TO THE ABOLITION
> OF THE ONE AND THE PRESERVATION OF THE OTHER.

It was in this year that Garrison quoted in the *Liberator* the passage from Isaiah which was later to furnish the phrase with which he led his attack on the Constitution:

> Hear the word of the Lord, ye scornful men that rule this people. Because ye have said, We have made a covenant with DEATH, and with HELL are we at agreement, when the overflowing scourge shall pass through it shall not come unto us. . . . And your covenant with DEATH *shall be annulled,* and your agreement with HELL *shall not stand*; when the overflowing scourge shall pass through, then shall ye be trodden down by it.[44]

At the 1843 meeting of the Massachusetts Anti-Slavery Society, Garrison presented the following resolution, which was then hoisted to the *Liberator's* masthead, taking the place of the former more matter-of-fact declaration:

> *Resolved,* That the compact which exists between the North and the South is "a covenant with DEATH and an agreement with HELL" — involving both parties in atrocious criminality — and should be immediately annulled.

Two years later, facing the crisis caused by the addition to the slave power afforded by the annexation of Texas, Garrison ut-

---

[42] *Liberator*, I, 165 (October 15, 1831).
[43] *Ibid.*, XII, 63 (April 22, 1842).
[44] *Ibid.*, XII, 71 (May 6, 1842); Isaiah xxviii: 14–18.

tered these words at a mass meeting, and later published them in his paper:

"But who are we," men will ask, "that talk of such things? Are we enough to make a revolution?" No, Sir; but we are enough to *begin* one, and, once begun, it never can be turned back. I am for revolution, were I utterly alone. I am there because I *must* be there. I *must* cleave to the right. I cannot choose but obey the voice of God. *Now,* there are but few who do not cling to their agreement with hell, and obey the voice of the devil; but soon their number will be multitudinous as the stars of heaven.[45]

Nothing could better illustrate the essential Hebraism of Garrison than this whole episode. Not only must he obey the "voice of God," but he expresses himself most naturally in a kind of prophetic fervor, and the idioms and rhythms of Scripture are his. Nor was there at any moment the slightest doubt in his devoted mind that he was right — so right that he could face martyrdom with equanimity.

But for the routine of editorship Garrison was not well fitted. His frequent invalidism and his occasional long speaking trips — a third English "mission" in 1847 and an extended western tour in 1848 — caused him to neglect his editorial duties. Edmund Quincy, resigning a temporary co-editorship entered into during one of Garrison's periods of illness in 1843, congratulated him upon his recovery and then proceeded to scold him gently for his slipshod editorial methods:

We think that the paper often bears the marks of haste and carelessness in its getting up; that the matter seems to be hastily selected and put in higgledy-piggledy, without any very apparent reason why it should be in at all, or what it should be in the place where it is.[46]

But there is no sign that this protest was much heeded. After all, Garrison was no mere editor, to be bound to a desk; and his uncertain health did prevent his doing all he wished to do. He was ill for long periods in 1847 and again in 1848, and Quincy helped out once more. The subscription price of the paper was brought down again to two dollars in 1847 — an unwise policy,

---

[45] *Ibid.*, XV, 158 (October 3, 1845).
[46] Garrison, *op. cit.*, III, 85. Letter dated November 6, 1843.

for it did not stimulate circulation. There was by this time severe competition among abolition papers.

The *Liberator's* antipolitical position did not seem to call for the same abuse of the Free-Soilers that had been heaped upon the Liberty party;[47] the difference was one of personalities, for the earlier party had been led by the enemies of the Garrisonians. Political developments shared in the *Liberator's* columns with such matters as the visit of Father Mathew, the Irish temperance advocate, in 1849. Father Mathew refused to commit himself to antislavery during his visit, and many pages of Garrison's paper were given to a discussion of this dereliction, and to the printing, for contrast, of utterances of Daniel O'Connell, advocate of both temperance and abolition. A similar matter came up with the visit of the Hungarian patriot Kossuth to America three years later. In an article headed "Kossuth Fallen!" Garrison wrote:

Like recreant Father Mathew, to subserve his own purposes, and to secure the favor of a slave-holding and slave-breeding people, Kossuth skulks, dodges, plays fast and loose; he refuses to see any stain on the American character, any inconsistency in pretending to adore liberty and at the same time multiplying human beings for the auction-block and the slave shambles![48]

In the meantime, the *Liberator* was calling for open violation of the fugitive slave law and condemning the Compromise of 1850. Webster's seventh-of-March speech was called "indescribably base and wicked."[49] Longfellow's "The Building of the Ship," with its invocation beginning

Thou too sail on, O Ship of State!

was condemned as "a eulogy dripping with the blood of imbruted humanity";[50] that ship was already, said Garrison

rotting through all her timbers, leaking from stem to stern, laboring heavily on a storm-tossed sea, surrounded by clouds of disastrous portent, navigated by those whose object is a piratical one (namely, the extension and perpetuity of slavery), and destined to go down

[47] *Liberator*, XVIII, 126 (August 11, 1848).
[48] *Ibid.*, XXI, 203 (December 19, 1851).
[49] *Ibid.*, XX, 43 (March 15, 1850).
[50] *Ibid.*, XX, 11 (January 18, 1850).

"full many a fathom deep," to the joy and exultation of all who are yearning for the deliverance of a groaning world.[51]

It was in this year, also, that the *Liberator* carried its interesting account of the mob incited by the New York *Herald* and led by Captain Rynders against the annual antislavery meeting in New York.[52]

The twentieth anniversary of the *Liberator* was celebrated by a "soiree" at Cochituate Hall in Boston on January 24, 1851; Garrison was eulogized by all the speakers,[53] and most gratifyingly by George Thompson, returned to these shores to make more abolition speeches. Thompson, hero of a hundred mobs, now a member of the British parliament, was the great feature of the *Liberator* in 1851. In the next volume there was not only the Kossuth incident to record, but also the comment upon the publication of *Uncle Tom's Cabin* and its prodigious success.[54]

The work of women for abolition had occupied a very important place in the reform for several years, and the result had been to link the women's rights reform with the antislavery movement. Garrison had promised his support to women's rights as early as 1837;[55] in 1849 he declared that "the denial of the elective franchise to women in this Commonwealth, on account of their sex, is an act of folly, injustice, usurpation, and tyranny";[56] and he participated in the National Women's Rights Convention in Cleveland in 1853.

The *Liberator* took no part in urging emigration to Kansas in 1855. It held to its nonresistance views, and it had no faith in Kansas "as a breakwater against the inundation of the dark waters of oppression."[57] When it came to the election of 1856, Garrison found himself somewhat embarrassed by his nonparticipation creed; he would have liked to support Frémont as against Buchanan,[58] but Frémont was a unionist, and the *Liberator* was carrying the motto: "NO UNION WITH SLAVE–

[51] *Ibid.*, XX, 19 (February 1, 1850).
[52] *Ibid.*, XX, 81 (May 24, 1850).
[53] *Ibid.*, XXI, 18 (January 31, 1851).
[54] Cf. pp. 142–144.
[55] *Liberator*, VII, 203 (December 15, 1837).
[56] *Ibid.*, XIX, 199 (December 14, 1849).
[57] *Ibid.*, XXV, 86 (June 1, 1855).
[58] *Ibid.*, XXVI, 174 (October 31, 1856).

HOLDERS!" So he refrained from active support of the Free-Soil candidate.

The storm which Garrison and his paper had done so much to raise now grew more threatening. John Brown's raid, which of course the *Liberator* could not countenance, added its threat to the growing excitement. "The 'battle waxes at the gate,'" quoted Garrison, to whom prophetical language was natural in times of stress, "and all the signs of the times are indicating that a great revolution is at hand." [59] But Garrison himself was often confined to his bed by bronchitis and fever, Charles K. Whipple being left at such times as editor in charge of the *Liberator*.[60] To Wendell Phillips fell the supposed duty of exposing Abraham Lincoln's antiabolition record, which he did in a savage article headed "Abraham Lincoln, the Slave-Hound of Illinois" and beginning: "We gibbet a northern hound today, side by side with the infamous Mason of Virginia." [61] There were defenses of Lincoln published in the *Liberator* during the campaign, but it must be admitted that the Republican nominee fared ill in its pages.

Garrison was one Northerner who hailed the secession of South Carolina with joy. In his New Year's editorial for the 1861 volume of the *Liberator* he wrote:

All Union-saving efforts are simply idiotic. At last "the covenant with death" is annulled, and "the agreement with hell" broken — at least by the action of South Carolina, and ere long by all the slave-holding states, for their doom is one.[62]

Six weeks later, he declared again for the acceptance of secession:

Now, then, let there be a CONVENTION OF THE FREE STATES called to organize an independent government on free and just principles; and let them say to the slave states — "Though you are without excuse for your treasonable conduct, depart in peace! . . . And if nothing but the possession of the Capital will appease you, take even that, without a struggle!" Let the line be drawn between where free institutions and slave institutions begin![63]

---

[59] *Liberator*, XXX, 2 (January 6, 1860).   [60] Garrison, *op. cit.*, III, 498.
[61] *Liberator*, XXX, 99 (June 22, 1860).
[62] *Ibid.*, XXXI, 2 (January 4, 1861).
[63] *Ibid.*, XXXI, 27 (February 15, 1861).

After the secession of South Carolina, Garrison was at his post as the editor of the *Liberator*. He had no more time for invalidism. Every number of the paper was imbued with his vigorous spirit; the editorial page was an ever flowing well of eloquence.

As he faced the fact of the beginning of the war for the preservation of the Union, Garrison found himself in an ethical dilemma. If he supported the war, he would have to give up two of the chief principles which the *Liberator* had held through many years — the belief in disunion, and the doctrine of peace at any cost. On the other hand, if he opposed the war, he would be ungratefully rejecting the one and only practical reformer, and he did not hesitate in his choice.

Let nothing be done [he wrote] at this solemn crisis, needlessly to check or divert the mighty current of popular feeling which is now sweeping southward with the strength and impetuosity of a thousand Niagaras, in direct conflict with that haughty and perfidious Slave Power which has so long ruled the republic with a rod of iron for its own base and satanic purposes.[64]

He justified his support of the government's armed interference with the secession of the southern states by pointing out that what he had been arguing for through many volumes was the duty of the free states to secede in order to defeat the designs of the slave power; but that the southern states, whose peculiar institution had not even been threatened by the party or candidate which had just won the election, had no moral right or legal claim to secede. Along this line Garrison continued to urge the North to separate, at the same time that he supported the effort to prevent southern secession.[65] But by the end of 1861 the *Liberator* had flung casuistry aside; and it had displaced its old motto, "The United States Constitution is a covenant with death and an agreement with hell," by the more loyal "Proclaim Liberty throughout all the land, to all the inhabitants thereof."

Garrison did not wholly discard his peace principles, however. "But this is obviously not the time," he wrote, "to expect

[64] *Ibid.*, XXXI, 66 (April 26, 1861).
[65] *Ibid.*, XXXI, 63 (April 19, 1861).

a dispassionate hearing on this subject. . . . The war must go on to its consummation." [66] The son whom Garrison had named after George Thompson enlisted in the war and won a lieutenancy in service.

From the beginning of the war, the *Liberator* urged, exhorted, prayed President Lincoln to free the slaves by presidential proclamation. In the fall of 1861 it tried to bring the matter home to the President after this fashion:

> *To refuse to deliver those captive millions who are now legally in your power, is tantamount to the crime of their original enslavement;* and their blood shall a righteous God require at your hands. Put the trump of jubilee to your lips! [67]

And a few months later: "President Lincoln, delay not at your peril! Execute judgment in the morning — break every yoke — let the oppressed go free." [68] When the President, in September 1862, announced emancipation for the first of the next January, Garrison did not ring the bells and blow the trumpets; he accepted the proclamation as "an act of immense historic consequence," [69] but he was disappointed at its reservations and proposed delays. In the first number of the *Liberator* for 1863, we have Garrison's "Glory Hallelujah!" editorial, in which he calls the Emancipation Proclamation "sublime in its magnitude, momentous and beneficent in its far-reaching consequences." [70]

During the campaign of 1864 the *Liberator* was free to take part in politics for the first time in its history; no longer was its editor deprived of his franchise by his resolution not to support a slavery government. The paper supported Lincoln for re-election. It had criticized many of his acts, but it was grateful to him for emancipation. [71] During the campaign Garrison was invited to call upon Lincoln at the White House and had a satisfactory interview with him.

The *Liberator* was much concerned now with abolition in the border states and with the Negro regiments in the Federal serv-

[66] *Liberator*, XXXI, 94 (June 14, 1861).
[67] *Ibid.*, XXXI, 162 (October 11, 1861).
[68] *Ibid.*, XXXII, 42 (March 14, 1862).
[69] *Ibid.*, XXXII, 154 (September 26, 1862).
[70] *Ibid.*, XXXIII, 3 (January 2, 1863).
[71] *Ibid.*, XXXIV, 46 (March 18, 1864).

ice. It printed occasional letters from colored officers and soldiers. A few communications from nonresistants got into the paper, but they were infrequent.

It was with the adoption of the thirteenth amendment to the Constitution, forever abolishing slavery in the United States, that the *Liberator*, in common with all the abolition societies and periodicals, enjoyed its great day of triumph. "With devout thanksgiving to God, and emotions of joy that no language can express," the paper announced the passage of the amendment by the House of Representatives.[72] Throughout that year of 1865 one state after another ratified the amendment, until on December 18 Secretary Seward was able to issue the proclamation officially acknowledging it as a part of the Constitution. William Lloyd Garrison then went to the office of the *Liberator*, and taking his composing stick in hand, himself set in type the words of the proclamation, for the issue about to go to press; and to the official edict he added these words of his own:

At last the old "covenant with death" is annulled, and the "agreement with hell" no longer stands. . . . It is, consequently, a complete triumph as well as the utter termination of the antislavery struggle, as such. Rejoice and give praise and glory to God, ye who have so long and untiringly participated in the trials and vicissitudes of that mighty conflict! Having sown in tears, now reap in joy! Hail, redeemed, regenerated America! . . . Hail, ye ransomed millions, no more to be chained, scourged, mutilated, bought and sold in the market! . . . Great and marvellous are thy works, Lord God Almighty![73]

This paean appeared in the penultimate number of the *Liberator*. For Garrison had decided in March 1865 not to "prolong the existence of the paper beyond this YEAR OF JUBILEE."[74] As it said in its very title, the *Liberator* was begun in order to free the slaves; that done, its work was over, and it had no further reasons for being. Besides, there were very practical reasons for discontinuance. It had never made money; but on the contrary, it had been kept going only by the activities of a finance committee which had managed to collect funds for it because it was invaluable to the abolition cause. Of that

[72] *Ibid.*, XXXV, 18 (February 3, 1865).
[73] *Ibid.*, XXXV, 202 (December 22, 1865).
[74] *Ibid.*, XXXV, 46 (March 24, 1865).

committee, three had died. The paper had suffered from the economic conditions of war time: it had been forced to raise its price to three dollars in 1862, and its circulation had declined.[75] It was more than once in financial straits, and as late as November 1865 Garrison had to undertake a lecture tour to raise funds which would enable him to carry on publication until the last volume was completed.[76] Throughout these trying years — and, indeed, since the late forties, when he had first been employed by the *Liberator* — J. B. Yerrinton, the paper's printer, had proved himself a reliable friend.

The last number of the *Liberator* was issued on December 29, 1865. It contained many letters of eulogy and farewell from long-time friends of the paper and its editor, and Garrison's eloquent valedictory, in which he stated with pride that he had begun the paper without money and without a subscriber, and now ended it without having realized a cent of profit from it. A few weeks after the paper was suspended, admirers of Garrison began the collection of a "National Testimonial" to him, which amounted, before it was turned over to him two years later, to over $31,000.[77]

From among the many comments on the career of the *Liberator* which appeared at the time of its demise, the following remarks by O. B. Frothingham, published in the *Nation*, may fittingly close this history:

It expired last Friday in the arms of victory. . . . The paper has finished its course because it has reached its goal. . . . It was supported by principle; it lived on its nerve. If want of money could have killed it, the paper would have been starved out long ago. If hate and loathing could have destroyed it, it could not have lived a twelvemonth. All the packs were in full cry after it the instant it was discovered, and it seemed a very small thing to kill. . . . The paper has not much more than doubled since then; but steadily, week by week, never failing in a single instance to come to time, it has dropped its water upon the nation's marble heart. Its tenacity has been as wonderful as its intensity. . . . There was a stern monotony in its issues that was like the pressure of fate. It was an unvarying soliloquy thirty-five years long. It is perhaps the most remarkable instance on record of a single-hearted devotion to a cause. . . .[78]

[75] Garrison, *op. cit.*, IV, 65 (footnote); IV, 125.
[76] *Ibid.*, IV, 166.   [77] *Ibid.*, IV, 183.   [78] *Nation*, II, 7 (January 4, 1866).

AMERICAN
RAILROAD JOURNAL.

RAILROAD JOURNAL,
AND ADVOCATE OF INTERNAL IMPROVEMENTS.

AMERICAN RAILROAD JOURNAL,
AND ADVOCATE OF INTERNAL IMPROVEMENTS.

AMERICAN RAILROAD JOURNAL,
AND ADVOCATE OF INTERNAL IMPROVEMENTS.

EARLY HEADINGS OF THE *RAILROAD JOURNAL*

Showing primitive locomotives and coaches.

THE AMERICAN RAILROAD JOURNAL [1]

IN JANUARY 1832 there were twelve railroads in the United States, but they were operating only two hundred miles of road. There were only three locomotives in use, nine of the roads relying upon horsepower. Yet in this month and year D. Kimball Minor, part proprietor of the *New-York American*, a daily paper, began the pioneer American railway periodical, the *American Railroad Journal*. It was a sixteen-page quarto, made up like a newspaper, and issued weekly at $3.00 a year. To the wits of the town the idea of a railroad paper was very funny. "You might as well have an *Aqueduct*

---

[1] TITLES: (1) *Rail-Road Journal*, January 2, 1832, only; (2) *American Railroad Journal*, January 7, August 25, 1832; (3) *American Railroad Journal and Advocate of Internal Improvements*, September 1, 1832–December 23, 1837; (4) *American Railroad Magazine and Mechanics' Magazine*, July 1, 1838–December 1844; (5) *American Railroad Journal and General Advertiser for Railroads, Canals, Machinery, Steam Boats and Mines*, January 16, 1845–January 1848; (6) *American Railroad Journal and Iron Manufacturer's and Mining Gazette*, January 8, 1848–1849, 1875–86; (7) *American Railroad Journal: Steam, Navigation, Commerce, Mining, Manufactures* (subtitle varies), 1849–74; (8) *The Railroad and Engineering Journal*, 1887–92; (9) *American Engineering and Railroad Journal*, 1893–95, 1899–1911; (10) *American Engineer, Car Builder and Railroad Journal*, 1896–98; (11) *American Engineer: The Railway Mechanical Monthly*, 1912; (12) *Railway Age Gazette: Mechanical Edition, Including the American Engineer*, 1913–15; (13) *Railway Mechanical Engineer*, 1916–current.

FIRST ISSUE: January 2, 1832. Current.

PERIODICITY: Weekly, 1832–37, 1845–83; semimonthly, 1838–42; monthly, 1843–44, 1883–current. [First Series], I–VI, January 2, 1832–December 23, 1837 (last number actually published March 1838); suspended January–June 1838; New [Second] Series, I–IX (VII–XV), July 1, 1838–December 24, 1842; Third Series, I–II (XVI–XVII), 1842–44; Second Quarto [Fourth] Series, I–XLIII (XVIII–LX), 1845–86; New [Fifth] Series, I–IX (LXI–LXIX), 1887–95; LXX–current, 1896–current. Annual volumes, except VII–XV, which were semiannual.

PUBLISHERS: Same as editors, 1832–48; J. H. Schultz & Company, 1849–82; George F. Swain, 1882–86; Mathias N. Forney, 1886–96; R. M. Van Arsdale, 1896–1911; Simmons-Boardman Publishing Company, 1911–current. All New York, except Philadelphia, 1846–48.

EDITORS: D. Kimball Minor, 1832–39, 1843–48 (with George C. Schaeffer, 1836–39, 1843–44); George C. Schaeffer, 1840–43 (with Egbert Hedge, 1840–42); Henry V. Poor, 1849–62; J. H. Schultz, 1862–79; Harlan A. Pierce, 1879–84; J. Bruen Miller, 1884–86; Mathias N. Forney, 1886–97 (with W. H. Marshall,

Chronicle, or a *Turnpike Commentator!*" they laughed.[2] But Minor believed in the future of the iron roads: "they must," he insisted, "in a few years entirely take the place of Canals, where new works are to be constructed."[3]

In its first number the *Journal* listed twenty new railways under construction, and within a few months the New York legislature granted a charter for a line from New York City to Lake Erie with a $10,000,000 capitalization. Minor saw his dream of railroad networks coming true, but his own small publishing project did not prosper. He obtained only a few hundred subscribers and lost $1,000 on the *Journal* during its first two years.[4] Then came the great fire of 1835 which almost put an end to the struggling paper and to the other periodicals that Minor was by this time publishing. But he hung on, taking George C. Schaeffer, a practical engineer, into partnership. Two years after the fire came the panic of 1837, and this time it did look as if the *Railroad Journal* were doomed; it suspended that autumn, but it managed to get out the issues to fill its 1837 volume early the next year, and in July 1838 it resumed as a semimonthly. Minor had to withdraw in 1839, however, and seek financial success in other fields, leaving Schaeffer in charge; but he was back in 1843, was sole proprietor the next year, and in 1845 restored the paper to its original weekly issue at $5.00 a year.

The pages of the *Journal* were not wholly devoted to railroad affairs. During its first four years its editor maintained his connection with the daily *American,* and much of the literary miscellany from that paper was "lifted" for use in the weekly *Journal.* Moreover, although Minor left no doubt about which side he had chosen in the contest between canals and railroads, he gave large space to the advocates of canals. His paper's subtitle read *Advocate of Internal Improvements,* and official re-

---

1896–97); W. H. Marshall, 1897–98; George M. Basford, 1899–1904; Roy V. Wright, 1905–10, 1912–current (with E. A. Averill, 1906–10); E. A. Averill, 1910–11.

INDEXES: LVIII–LXXXVII (1884–1930) in *Engineering Index;* LXXXVII–current in *Industrial Arts Index.*

REFERENCES: *Railway Mechanical Engineer,* CV, 385–435 (October 1932); Centennial Number, *Railroad and Engineering Journal,* LXI, 1–4 (January 1887).

[2] *American Railroad Journal,* January 14, 1832.

[3] *Ibid.,* January 2, 1832.

[4] *Railway Mechanical Engineer,* CV, 387 (October 1932).

ports on canals and highways, as well as on railroads, occupied much of his space.

In 1846 Minor took the *Journal* to Philadelphia, installing its office in a hotel which he was operating in that city; but he brought it back to New York late in 1848 in order to sell it the next year to John H. Schultz. Schultz gave the editorial charge over to Henry V. Poor, who thus entered the field of railway statistics with which his name is connected. Under his supervision the *Journal* came to be devoted chiefly to railway finance; and *Poor's Manual*, a yearly reference work, was an offshoot of this interest. When Poor left the *Journal* in 1862 to devote all his time to his manuals, Schultz took over the editorial work and carried the paper on without change in policy.

But in 1879 Schultz put Harlan A. Pierce in editorial charge, and the paper entered upon the discussion of the political questions which had become so important in the railway field. In 1882 Schultz retired and was succeeded by George F. Swain, who had been secretary of the publishing company; and in the next year the *Journal* became a monthly. There were another new editor and another new editorial policy in 1884: J. Bruen Miller turned the magazine to the discussion of railway construction and management problems, making it a review for railway managers and engineers. Thus it fell in line with the need for specialization within its field. Its transformation was complete with its purchase in 1886 by Mathias N. Forney and the change of title the next year to *Railroad and Engineering Journal*.

Forney was thoroughly trained both in mechanical engineering and in journalism; he was secretary of the Master Car Builders' Association. Car building was his specialty, and the *Journal* served that industry. In 1887 Forney purchased *Van Nostrand's Engineering Magazine*, consolidating it with the *Journal*.

There has been little change in the policy of the magazine since that time, though there have been several changes in titles and ownership as well as editorship. Two of its editors were later taken by the American Locomotive Company to be made presidents of that concern — W. H. Marshall and George M. Basford. R. M. Van Arsdale, publisher of the magazine's chief competitor, the *National Car Builder*, purchased the *Journal* from Forney in 1896, consolidating the two magazines but retaining the numbering of the *Journal* for the new periodical. After Van Arsdale's death, the Simmons-Boardman Company, publishers of the *Railway Age Gazette*, bought the *Journal* in 1911 and later gave it the name *Railway Age Gazette: Mechanical Edition.* Roy V. Wright, a former editor who had gone to the *Age Gazette*, was put in charge. The present title, *Railway Mechanical Engineer*, was adopted in 1916.

On the occasion of its centenary, the magazine summarized its history as follows:

> Organized as an advocate of the development of railways, it continued for seventeen years to foster and stimulate public interest in the growth of the great transportation system of the United States. Next began a thirty-year period in which railway financial management and the interests of the investors became its major preoccupation. With the gradual broadening of the scope of the daily press to deal more with financial affairs, the value of the *Journal* to the outside public declined, and it began to devote itself exclusively to the interests of those within the industry. Then came the need for specialization, and for the past forty-five years its columns have been devoted to the service of the equipment departments of the steam railroads.[5]

[5] *Railway Mechanical Engineer*, CV, 401 (October 1932).

THE LADIES' REPOSITORY [1]

THE idea of the *Ladies' Repository* originated with Samuel Williams,[2] a Cincinnati Methodist, who thought that Christian women needed some magazine less worldly than *Godey's Lady's Book* and Snowden's *Lady's Companion*, with their sentimental tales of silly love affairs and their fashions "direct from Paris." Williams urged the enterprise upon the western agents of the Methodist Book Concern, who were established at Cincinnati; he saw that the Ohio Conference recommended it to the General Conference of 1840; he was instrumental, through the book agents, in obtaining the approval of the General Conference. Accordingly, the *Ladies' Repository, and Gatherings of the West* appeared in January 1841, a thirty-two page magazine. The editor was the Reverend L. L. Hamline, a prominent minister who later became a bishop of the Methodist Church.

It was an exceptionally well-printed little magazine, with large octavo pages. It contained sober, earnest, and rather well-written essays of a moral character, plenty of poetry such as it was, some articles on historical and scientific matters, and book reviews. It was nearly all original, though the contributors were not well known. "The *Repository* will aim to entertain as well as to instruct," declared the editor in his opening number.

But although it will not always preserve the gravity of a sermon, yet it will never, as is hoped, become the vehicle of silly jests and sicken-

---

[1] TITLES: *The Ladies' Repository, and Gatherings of the West*, 1841–48; *The Ladies' Repository*, 1849–76. Subtitle: *A Monthly Periodical Devoted to Literature and Religion* (*Art* was inserted after *Literature* in 1876).
FIRST ISSUE: January 1841. LAST ISSUE: December 1876.
PERIODICITY: Monthly. I–XXVII, 1841–67, regular annual volumes; XXVIII–XXXIV, 1868–74, New Series, I–XIV, regular annual volumes for the whole numbers but semiannual volumes for the New Series numbering; XXV–XXXVI, 1875–76, Third Series, I–IV, voluming as in New Series.
PUBLISHERS: Agents of Methodist Book Concern, Cincinnati.
EDITORS: Leonidas Leut Hamline, 1841–44; Edward Thomson, 1844–46; Benjamin Franklin Tefft, 1846–52; William Clark Larrabee, 1852–53; Davis Wasgatt Clark, 1853–63; Isaac William Wiley, 1864–72; E. Wentworth, 1872–76; Daniel Curry, 1876.
[2] *Ladies' Repository*, XXXVI, 570 (December 1876).

ing tales, to offend the chaste sobriety of the wise, and feed the fro-
ward merriment of the simple.[3]

Its subtitle suggested a western note in the magazine's contents, and a number of western writers were enlisted — chiefly
Ohioans. Prominent among them was Alice Cary, who, all in
all, contributed over a hundred sketches and poems to the magazine. Her sister Phoebe was also a frequent contributor, as
were Otway Curry, Moncure D. Conway, Joshua R. Giddings,
Meta V. Fuller, Julia L. Dumont, and other Westerners of those
years. But the publishers decided to make their periodical more
national in its scope, and *Gatherings of the West* was dropped
from its title at the end of 1848. It was always, however, rather
distinctively a magazine of that midwestern region where Methodistic power had concentrated.

In its second year engravings were made a part of the magazine and (with some exceptions) appeared monthly to the end
of the file. The initial picture, in the January 1842 number,
showed a railway train and engineer; the accompanying description said the rails were of wood and predicted a speed of thirty
miles an hour for the new vehicle.

The editors from beginning to end were Methodist preachers
who added the editorial task to their regular pastoral duties.
The first editor kept to his job for three and a half years; he
was followed by Edward Thomson, who served for two years,
giving place to B. F. Tefft, who stuck to it for six years. Tefft
wrote in 1847:

Added to our official relations to the *Repository*, we are the responsible editor of the books of the general catalogue published at the
Western Book Concern. . . . We have had strength enough left to
preach the blessed Gospel every Sabbath.[4]

In spite of the ministerial editorship, however, the magazine
was, barring a constant testimony against fiction, reasonably
tolerant.

Among New Englanders who became contributors to the magazine were Mrs. Sigourney, the omnipresent; John S. C. Abbott,
busy writer of essays and of a romantic kind of history; Hannah

[3] *Ladies' Repository*, I, 7 (January 1841).
[4] *Ibid.*, VI, 375 (December 1847).

F. Gould, the poetess; and Julia C. R. Dorr, the Vermont magazinist. From Chicago wrote Emily C. Huntington, later editor of the famous *Little Corporal*; Professor William H. Wells, who sent travel articles; and Frances E. Willard, founder of the W.C.T.U. Frances D. Gage, the Ohio poetess, was a frequent contributor, as were Virginia I. Townsend, subsequently editor of *Arthur's Home Magazine*, and Charles Nordhoff, later associated with *Harper's New Monthly*.

In 1851 the magazine began to publish a piece of music with each number — a practice continued until 1855. At this time there were two steel plates with each issue, costing the publishers about $250 apiece.[5] Such engravers as William Wellstood and R. Hinshelwood did some excellent work for the *Repository*. The subjects were chiefly landscapes and portraits, though there were some more sentimental domestic and romantic pieces. A series of portraits of literary women appeared in 1855 and later: that of Mrs. Sigourney was severely criticized by some readers because the lady wore short sleeves. In spite of the early warning against "silly jests," a department of "Apothegm, Wit, Repartee, and Anecdote" made a welcome appearance in 1853.

It was in that year that Davis W. Clark, later a bishop of the church, began an editorship that lasted until the war was nearly over. Davis was probably the best editor the *Repository* had in its whole sequence of overworked ministers. Under his care the magazine became brighter and attained a paid-up circulation of 40,000. Clark made it a magazine for the whole family. He did not share the horror of his predecessors for fiction: in the first year of his incumbency there were moralized little sketches and tales by William T. Coggeshall and Alice Cary, and by 1860 short stories were printed unblushingly. Moreover, there was not quite so much preaching by men about the duties of women, though clergymen and college presidents still occupied many pages.

The *Repository* lost circulation at the beginning of the Civil War — it had enjoyed thirty to forty thousand — but regained most of it before 1865. The price was raised in the war years from $2.00 to $3.50. There were some war poems and stories of

[5] *Ibid.*, XIX, 761 (December 1859).

life in the field. The number for August 1863 was delayed because Cincinnati was under martial law as a result of one of Morgan's raids.

But after the war the magazine declined, and the profits which it had made in the fifties and sixties were turned into deficits. It still made a brave appearance, however. The New Series of 1868 had eighty large pages to each issue, illustrated by good woodcuts. It was now "a religious family magazine" of fairly general appeal. It began publishing serial fiction in 1873. "Art Notes" also took their place in the magazine in the early seventies. But the circulation steadily declined, and the illustration had to be curtailed.

The General Conference of 1876 decided that the *Repository's* "range" was too narrow and "directed that instead there should be issued a magazine of wider scope and higher character to take its place." From this statement and from the type of magazine which supplanted the old *Ladies' Repository*, it is evident that the diagnosis of the General Conference was to the effect that the "range" had been too narrow both in geographical extent and in scope of contents.

And so the old magazine died, and from its ashes rose the *National Repository*,[6] a handsome octavo of ninety-six pages "devoted to general and religious literature." Daniel Curry, who had been editor of the *Ladies' Repository* in its last year, was editor of the new phoenix. "It makes its advent into the world of letters," he wrote, "as a friendly competitor for a place among the great literary monthlies of the day." [7] But there was, apparently, a conflict of opinion between editor and publishers over the new magazine's policy. As a matter of fact, it was not greatly different from its predecessor, though it gave more attention to public affairs. Curry wrote in 1880 that "more money and a broader policy" were needed to make the *Repository* a success, "but for reasons satisfactory to themselves . . . the

---

[6] TITLE: The *National Repository, Devoted to General and Religious Literature, Criticism and Art*.
FIRST ISSUE: January 1877. LAST ISSUE: December 1880.
PERIODICITY: Monthly. Regular semiannual volumes.
PUBLISHERS: Agents of the Methodist Book Concern, Cincinnati.
EDITOR: Daniel Curry.
[7] *National Repository*, I, 93 (January 1877).

publishers chose to pursue the old and beaten track." [8] The publishers' final statement in December 1880 explained that changes "designed to make the *Repository* a competitor in the field of illustrated literary magazines" were followed by "a rapid decline in circulation," and that success depended "upon being wisely, if need be, solely, adapted to the field of Methodism." [9] Their logic was irrefutable, but it could not recall the *Repository* to life and prosperity.

In its best days the *Ladies' Repository* was an excellent representative of the Methodistic mind and heart. Its essays, sketches, and poems (which now seem quaint and stilted), its good steel engravings, and its careful moral tone give it a character of its own, and a pleasant, though slightly musty, fragrance.

[8] *Ibid.*, VII, 383 (April 1880).
[9] *Ibid.*, VIII, 576 (December 1880).

6

PETERSON'S MAGAZINE [1]

IN 1842 Charles J. Peterson was a partner of George R. Graham in the ownership and management of the *Saturday Evening Post* and in the editorship of *Graham's Magazine*. Louis A. Godey had recently made an outstanding success of his *Lady's Book*, with its hand-colored fashion plates, its sentimental engravings, and its miscellany of innocuous essays, poems, and tales. Peterson and Graham talked the matter over and agreed that a two-dollar competitor for Godey's three-dollar women's journal would be a likely venture.[2] *Graham's*, though not an avowed women's magazine, had been forced to publish colored fashions in order to compete on the three-dollar basis; Graham evidently anticipated that a cheaper fashion magazine would cut into his rival's rising circulation without hurting his own somewhat more general magazine. At any rate,

[1] TITLES: (1) *Ladies' National Magazine* (title pages), 1842–48; (2) *The Lady's World of Literature and Fashion* (type title page January–June; engraved title page has No. 1), 1843; (3) *The Lady's World* (half title January–May; page captions February–May), 1843; (4) *The Lady's World and Artists' Magazine* (page captions April), 1843; (5) *The Artist and Lady's World*, June 1843; (6) *Peterson's Magazine* (half titles), 1848; (7) *Peterson's Ladies' National Magazine* (all titles except as in Nos. 8 and 9 following), 1848–54; (8) *Peterson's Magazine of Art, Literature and Fashion* (type title pages), 1849–50; (9) *Peterson's Magazine* (engraved title pages), 1851–53; (10) *Peterson's Magazine* (all titles except as in No. 11), 1855–92; (11) *Peterson's Ladies' National Magazine* (cover title), 1855–77 (?); (12) *The New Peterson Magazine*, 1892–94; (13) *The Peterson Magazine of Illustrated Literature*, 1894–98.
FIRST ISSUE: January 1842. LAST ISSUE: April 1898.
PERIODICITY: Monthly. I–CII, semiannual volumes, 1842–92; CIII (New Series, I), January–June 1893; CIV (New Series, II), July–December 1893; CV (New Series, III–IV), 1894; CVI (New Series, V [January–June 1895]–VI [July 1895–December 1896]), 1895–96; [CVII] New Series, VII, 1897; [CVIII] New Series, VIII, January–April 1898.
PUBLISHERS: Charles J. Peterson, Philadelphia, 1842–87; Peterson Magazine Company, Philadelphia, 1888–93; Penfield Publishing Company, Philadelphia, 1894–95, New York, 1895; Peterson Company, New York, 1895–98.
EDITORS: Charles J. Peterson and Mrs. Ann S. Stephens, 1842–53; Charles J. Peterson, 1854–87; Mrs. Charles J. Peterson, 1887–92; Frank Lee Benedict, 1892–93; Roderic Campbell Penfield, 1894–98.
[2] Albert H. Smyth, *The Philadelphia Magazines and Their Contributors, 1741–1850* (Philadelphia, 1892), p. 225.

Peterson founded his new *Ladies' National Magazine* while still associated with Graham — that is, in January 1842. In the next year, however, the venture appearing to be a success, Peterson resigned from *Graham's* and sold his interest in the *Post*.

Peterson's new magazine had the same large octavo page size as *Godey's* and *Graham's*, and three engravings with each issue — some of them colored — but only thirty-six pages of letter-press. It made much, in its promotion, of its engravings and of its $2.00 price — or $1.25 in clubs of eight. "Our aim," it said, "is to combine cheapness with real merit." [3]

The chief contributor in the early numbers, and indeed in the whole of the magazine's first decade, was Mrs. Ann S. Stephens. She had been an associate editor on *Graham's* and was now advertised as editor of the *Ladies' National*. Peterson himself was really the editor of his magazine, and his name was some-times printed with Mrs. Stephens' on the title pages of the vol-umes, but there was an attempt for several years to produce the effect of a magazine edited and written both by and for women. "We shall rely chiefly, if not altogether, on female pens," wrote the editor in 1834.[4] But that Mrs. Stephens was never chief editor of the magazine is amply proved by a note which ap-peared in it a few months after her death and a few months be-fore the death of Peterson:

This is the place to correct an error into which many of our con-temporaries have fallen, in saying that Mrs. Stephens was the editor of this magazine. She never officiated in that capacity, all her time being occupied on her writings.[5]

But in view of the facts that her name appeared on the maga-zine's title pages up to and including that of 1847, that she is referred to in publishers' notices after that as "our co-editor," [6] and that she undoubtedly wrote an editorial department in the forties, it seems fair to call her an associate, or perhaps a con-tributing, editor. Contribute she certainly did, with amazing fecundity. Serial after serial streamed from her pen, dealing

[3] *Ladies' National Magazine*, III, 128 (April 1843).
[4] *Ibid.*, IV, 208 (December 1843).
[5] *Peterson's Magazine*, XC, 456 (November 1886).
[6] *Ibid.*, XIV, 215 (December 1848) ; etc.

much in characterization, in picturesque description, and in situations of a melodramatic sort. "Of the numerous female writers of our country, Mrs. Stephens is deservedly classed among the first," wrote a critic in the *American Literary Magazine*.[7] She spent some time abroad in 1850, and three or four years later she left *Peterson's*.

Emily H. May was Mrs. Stephens' nearest competitor in prolific contribution to the *Ladies' National Magazine*; but others of greater literary reputations wrote much for it. Frances S. Osgood, Elizabeth Oakes Smith, Mrs. E. F. Ellett, Mrs. Sigourney, Lydia June Pierson, Mrs. A. M. F. Annan, and Mrs. Mary V. Spencer were familiar names in the magazine's pages. In this company T. S. Arthur was not out of place, but there were other male writers, as Thomas Buchanan Read and John T. Trowbridge. A typical number consisted of installments of two or three serials — "novelets," they were called — four or five short stories, several poems, a pattern department, and some publisher's notes and book reviews. Music was sometimes published. The letterpress was not unattractive, though printed on cheap paper. In 1850 the number of pages was increased to forty-eight, five years later to eighty, and after the war to ninety-two. The increase of size brought no change in contents: it merely gave more of the same fare.

In the early years of the magazine Peterson seems to have had a difficult time making up his mind what to call it. *Ladies' National Magazine* generally appeared on the title pages, though *The Lady's World* furnished it competition in some half titles and page captions. An engraved title page was furnished annually, and it sometimes disagreed with the typographical title page in the name of the magazine. In the middle of 1843 Peterson bought the *Artist*; and an attempt to combine its title with that of the *Lady's World* further complicated matters. Five different titles were used in 1843. In 1848 the publisher began using his own name in the title, first as *Peterson's Ladies' National Magazine*, and later as *Peterson's Magazine*; the latter title became fixed from 1855 until the changes of the nineties.

Some excellent mezzotints were published in the middle forties; but in the fifties the number of engravings on steel and

---

[7] *American Literary Magazine*, II, 335 (June 1848).

copper decreased, and some poor woodcuts were introduced, with a general deterioration in the illustration. Apparently the circulation kept up, however: the magazine "never has declined in circulation, but always advanced," averred the publisher in 1852.[8] By the time of the Civil War it had undoubtedly overtaken *Godey's* in the circulation race, and its claim in 1866 that "*Peterson's* has now, and has had for years the largest circulation of any ladies' periodical in the United States, or even in the world"[9] was truthful. The figure quoted for *Peterson's* in the first Rowell directory (1869) was 140,000, and a few years later it went to 165,000.

The magazine was slimmer during the war, but it looked more prosperous after peace was declared. By 1870 it was advertising a thousand pages of letterpress a year, with fourteen steel plates, twelve double-page folding colored fashion plates, and a thousand wood engravings. There were five or six serials a year, monthly departments of fancywork, recipes, etc., and plenty of short stories and poems. "All the popular female writers of America" contributed, including, besides the old stand-bys, Mrs. Kirkland, Mrs. Southworth, Mrs. Rebecca Harding Davis, Louise Chandler Moulton, and Jane G. Austin. Fannie Hodgson, later to become so popular as Frances Hodgson Burnett, was a constant contributor; and Ella Wheeler made her début in *Peterson's*. Beginning in 1878 and continuing for fifteen years, there was issued with each number, as a "supplement," a large folded pattern "for polonaise, cloak, mantilla, jacket, waist, or some other article of a lady's costume, in the very latest fashion."

Peterson's was thus a combination of fashions and light literature. The stories were all very much alike: virtue in poverty, a broken heart, the dangers of frivolity, with occasionally a thrilling incident like a runaway or a rescue. In the number for January 1844 appeared a story by Mrs. M. A. Browne Gray, a sister of Mrs. Hemans — no less — entitled "Sarah Burnett." In it the poor heroine "died of a weary spirit and of a slowly broken heart." The editor says that "it cannot, we think, be read without tears," and he promises "a sweet poem from her

[8] *Peterson's Magazine*, XXII, 296 (December 1852).
[9] *Ibid.*, L, 436 (December 1866).

pen." The editor-publisher was himself a poet, and occasionally he favored his readers with dithyrambs like this:

> Oh! let us go a-maying. We will away from the dull, brick-town: we will away into the country, the fresh, green, breezy country. Through our open casement the cool air comes in gushes, fragrant with blowing violets and budding trees. We can hear the rustle of the lilacs in the garden, as they scatter their perfume around. Hark! the whistle of a bird — and with the sound we are away, climbing the hill-side and watching for the early nests as when we were a boy. We are in the country — in imagination at least — idling in sylvan glades, listening to gurgling streams, bathing our temples in the soft, south wind, and loitering among green meadows where the dewey footprints of April have left flowers at every step. . . . Oh! let us go a-maying.[10]

There was, however, some relief from treacle: Mrs. Davis and Mrs. Kirkland occasionally contributed a fresh breath of realism or humor; and there were a few Indian tales. Marietta Holley's stories of "Josiah Allen's Wife" were published in *Peterson's*. Frank Lee Benedict's society stories had some bite of satire in them.

Peterson died in 1887, and his widow took over both the business and editorial management of the magazine.[11] Lucy H. Hooper's Paris letter and her articles and serials were a feature of the eighties. Edgar Fawcett, Julian Hawthorne, and Howard Seely were prominent contributors. Steel engravings were continued throughout that decade, and patterns and fashion notes were still paramount; but the circulation had declined to 100,-000 by the time of Peterson's death.

In 1890 the steel engravings were discontinued, the typography was improved, and a better grade of paper was adopted. Two years later Mrs. Peterson disposed of the magazine to a stock company headed by Roderic Penfield, who abandoned fashions for literature, art, and the theater, and changed the name to the *New Peterson Magazine*. Frank Lee Benedict was editor for two years, after which Penfield was editor as well as publisher. Henry L. Stoddard was a contributing editor. The price was lowered to a dollar a year in 1894, to compete with

[10] *Peterson's Magazine*, III, 129 (May 1843).
[11] *Journalist*, October 15, 1887, p. 4.

other popular magazines of the early nineties; and the name was changed again to the *Peterson Magazine of Illustrated Literature*. In the next year Penfield moved it to New York, selling it within a few months to a stock company.

For a magazine that had been running on a fairly even keel for half a century, this was a storm of activity. And the worst of it was that the ship was in for bad weather, if the circulation barometer afforded any indication. There were no serials now, but a great deal of art and the stage, with pictures in half tone. Arthur Hornblow had a theatrical department in 1896, and Henry L. Stoddard wrote a department of editorial comment. Gertrude Atherton, Octave Thanet, and Opie Reed were contributors. The magazine was very strong in biography; it published serial lives of Washington and Lee, of American naval heroes, of the border warriors, and of early American authors. It was just beginning a life of John Brown in 1898, when Frank Munsey bought it and merged it into his *Argosy*.

Though not of any considerable literary importance, *Peterson's Magazine* was for some two decades the most popular women's magazine in America. Its hand-colored fashion plates were equal to those of *Godey's*. When the pages of its earlier volumes are opened today to its tender sentimentalism of picture, story, and poem, it brings us, in spite of dust and broken bindings, the authentic atmosphere of a phase of early Victorianism which is not without charm.

7

THE NEW ENGLANDER [1]

EDWARD ROYALL TYLER, founder of the *New Englander*, was a son of that Royall Tyler who was the author of the first American comedy, "The Contrast," and who was later a chief justice in Vermont. The son was a Yale graduate, a Congregational minister, an antislavery agitator, and a former editor of the *Connecticut Observer* at Hartford.

Planned and formed to "give utterance to the New England way of thinking," [2] the new quarterly was, through and through, exactly what its title designated. This meant Congregationalism in theology, a tendency to whiggery in politics, enthusiasm for antislavery, the promotion of education, and adherence to strictly orthodox morals — loyalty, in short, to what a later editor called "those political and religious principles which are dear to the children of New England." [3] The life of the *New Englander* covered the period of the great western exodus from the region which it served, and in its circulation campaigns it continually appealed to the "sons of New England" whithersoever they had wandered.

[1] TITLES: *The New Englander*, 1843–85; *The New Englander and Yale Review*, 1885–92.
FIRST ISSUE: January 1843. LAST ISSUE: March 1892.
PERIODICITY: Quarterly, 1843–77; bimonthly, 1878–85; monthly, 1886–92. I–IV [First Series], 1843–48; VII–XII (New Series, I–VI), 1849–54; XIII–XXXVI, 1855–77; XXXVII–LVI (New Series, I–XX), 1878–92. Annual volumes, 1843–86; semiannual volumes, 1887–92. Final volume (LVI) incomplete with three numbers, January–March 1892.
PUBLISHERS: A. H. Maltby, New Haven, 1843–48; John B. Carrington, New Haven, 1849–50; S. W. Benedict, New York, 1851; F. W. Northrup, New Haven, 1852–55; D. Mead, New Haven, 1856–57; W. L. Kingsley, New Haven, 1857–92.
EDITORS: Edward Royall Tyler, 1843–48; New Englander Association (including from time to time William T. Bacon, Leonard Bacon, Theodore D. Woolsey, Horace Bushnell, Noah Porter, William A. Larned, Joseph P. Thompson, and S. W. S. Dutton), 1849–50, 1852–57; S. W. Benedict, 1851; W. L. Kingsley, 1857–92 (with George P. Fisher and Timothy Dwight, 1866–75).
INDEXES: Vol. XX is an index to Vols. I–XIX; *Poole's; Jones' Index*.
[2] *New Englander*, I, 1 (January 1843).
[3] Prospectus, 1870.

More specifically, the *New Englander* was the child of Yale. Associated with Tyler in establishing the journal were Theodore D. Woolsey, three years later made president of Yale; Noah Porter, who was Woolsey's successor in the presidency; William T. Bacon, a Yale graduate engaged in religious journalism; Leonard Bacon, Joseph P. Thompson, and S. W. S. Dutton, the three leading New Haven ministers, all Yale men; William Larned, Yale professor of rhetoric; and Horace Bushnell, former Yale tutor, now a Hartford minister. These men formed an association to support the quarterly by their contributions. After the death of Tyler in 1848, the association conducted the journal jointly for two years, after which they allowed S. W. Benedict to buy it from John B. Carrington, the New Haven publisher, and move it to New York. But it remained in the metropolis for only a year; F. W. Northrup then purchased it and brought it back to New Haven, placing it once more under the guidance of the association. In these years President Woolsey was generally supposed to be the chief editor, though it was later revealed that Larned had been editor in 1854–55.[4] In 1857 the review was purchased by William L. Kingsley, who served as editorial chief from that time until the end in 1892. Kingsley was also a Yale man and a Congregational clergyman; but he was essentially an editor, and he was able to retain the original association members as contributors to the journal and to add other leading clergymen and professors as the years went on.

The *New Englander* was never primarily a theological review. But with such a staff, there was theology aplenty in its pages, of course; and in its early years, especially, it gave space to controversy. It championed the cause of Horace Bushnell, one of its editors, when he was attacked; it gave space to Leonard Bacon's war on certain of the church societies; it trained heavy guns on Catholicism; it criticized "the transcendentalism, the rationalism — or to call things by their right names, the downright German pantheism — of some men about Boston who pretend to be Christian preachers."[5] Moreover, practically every article had a clerical taste: historical articles, even when

---

[4] *New Englander*, XXI, 331 (April 1862).
[5] *Ibid.*, I, 6 (January 1843).

not dealing directly with church or Bible, made much of an overruling Providence; fiction and poetry were regarded largely from moral and religious angles; discussions of politics and economics stressed the ethical and ecclesiastical phases.

Politics were discussed rather frequently. In the early volumes Editor Tyler had a brief political article for each number. A strong position was taken against slavery. The Mexican War was believed to be "unchristian," though probably good politics.[6] The *New Englander* was never partisan, though the Whigs had the better of its discussions. During the Civil War it was intensely loyal, each number carrying some article relating to public affairs.

It had no good literary critics in its early years, and few even at the end. It reviewed belles-lettres, however; and there were occasional full-length articles on literary topics by Larned, Dutton, or the Reverend Increase N. Tarbox. In its first volume the review had some amusing strictures upon the *Dial* and its authors.[7] The classics were often the subject of learned articles from the pens of Woolsey and others.

There was some science in the *New Englander*. Professor Denison Olmsted wrote thoughtfully on astronomical and similar topics, and James Dwight Dana was a later contributor. The conflict between science and revealed religion was resolved frequently in favor of the latter. History, education, and temperance were other favorite fields. The variety of the review's pages is an enduring tribute to the broad interests of the leading contributors. Of these, Leonard Bacon was the most prolific, followed by Woolsey and Thompson; Tyler, Larned, and Porter come next, with Dutton, Olmsted, and President Samuel Harris of Bowdoin in a third group.[8]

A typical number — the one for January 1847 — contained the following articles: a review of Perdicaris' *Greece*, by Wool-

---

[6] *New Englander*, V, 141 (January 1847).
[7] *Ibid.*, I, 502 (October 1843).
[8] Statistics are in the index which appears in the file as Vol. XX, pp. 15–16. Articles were more or less anonymous. Initials were signed 1844–48; later, slips were inserted in editorial and other copies to give authors' names. Names were printed in the advertising section beginning in 1859, but they did not appear with the articles until 1886. The index volume indicates authorship in most instances.

sey; "Unitarianism in New York," by Thompson; "Responsibility in the Management of Church Societies," by Bacon; "The True Spirit of Devotion," by S. W. Andrews; an article on Hawthorne, by Dutton; "Life and Eloquence of Sylvester Larned," by Bushnell; "Le Verrier's Planet," by Olmsted; "The American Catholic Church," by Tyler; and "The Mexican War," also by Tyler.

After the war, Professor George P. Fisher and Timothy Dwight were co-editors with Kingsley for a decade. The old group continued to write for the review, and there were such newcomers as Borden P. Bowne, Henry N. Day, M. Stuart Phelps, Thomas R. Lounsbury, and Charles F. Thwing. A consistent attempt was made to westernize the journal in order to appeal to the New England *émigrés*; and in 1872–73 President A. L. Chapin, of Beloit College, and Professor S. C. Bartlett, of Chicago Theological Seminary, were associate editors, while William W. Patton, of Chicago, and H. M. Goodwin, of Olivet College, became frequent contributors.

The *New Englander* was made a bimonthly in 1878 and a monthly in 1885. The appeal to Yale alumni became more marked in the eighties; and when monthly publication was adopted, a subtitle *and Yale Review* was added, with a department of "University Topics." The magazine appears never to have been very prosperous and probably never exceeded a circulation of 1,000.[9] It was always well printed, however, and in its early volumes sometimes furnished a portrait on steel; the first one was, appropriately, that of Elihu Yale. The review was priced at $3.00 a year; and it furnished, as a quarterly, some two hundred pages a number. It did not pay for contributions.

The *New Englander* was discontinued in 1892, to give place to the *Yale Review*, a radically different periodical with new serial numbering, and under new management. For half a century the older journal had maintained a respectable and influential position. In spite of its faults of occasional heaviness and mediocrity, it had set a remarkably varied table and had kept its eyes open to the changes in the American scene. It was one of the best of the religious quarterlies.

[9] See the Ayer and Rowell directories.

SCIENTIFIC AMERICAN [1]

T HE founder of the *Scientific American* was one of those inventive Yankees whose versatility, "handiness," and restless "projecting" life have made his type a legend. Rufus Porter was apprenticed to a shoemaker at fifteen, but cobbling was too dull for him; he liked better to play the fife for military companies on their field days and the fiddle for dancing parties. So he ran away from his cobbling. Then he was apprenticed to a housepainter, and during the War of 1812 he painted gunboats and fifed for the Portland light infantry. Later he painted sleighs, beat the drum for the soldiers, taught drumming and wrote a manual on the subject, and then became a country schoolmaster until his wandering feet and impatient mind took him away from the schoolhouse. In 1820 he invented a camera obscura with mirrors so arranged that with its aid he could draw a satisfactory portrait in fifteen minutes. This gave him a motive for the wandering life which he craved. Soon he added a revolving almanac to peddle as a sideline. Experiments with a horsepower boat ate up his savings, and he

[1] TITLE: *Scientific American*
FIRST ISSUE: August 28, 1845. Current.
PERIODICITY: Weekly, 1845–October 15, 1921; monthly, November 1921–current. I, August 28, 1845–September 19, 1846; II–XIII, annual volumes, September 26, 1846–September 4, 1858; XIV, September 11, 1858–June 25, 1859. New Series, I–current, July 2, 1859–current, semiannual volumes. (The notation "New Series" was dropped after July 1888.)
PUBLISHERS: Rufus Porter, New York, 1845–46; Munn & Company, New York, 1846–current (under the name of Scientific American Publishing Company, 1919–32).
EDITORS: Rufus Porter, 1845–47; Orson Desaix Munn and Alfred Ely Beach, 1847–48; O. D. Munn, Salem Howe Wales, and A. E. Beach, 1848–71; O. D. Munn and A. E. Beach, 1871–96; O. D. Munn and Frederick Converse Beach, 1896–1907; Charles Allen Munn and F. C. Beach, 1907–18; C. A. Munn, 1919–24; Orson Desaix Munn [II], 1925–current. (Managing editors: Waldemar Bernhard Kaempffert, 1911–15; Austin C. Lescarboura, 1919–24.)
INDEXES: *Readers' Guide, Cumulative Index, Engineering Index, Annual Library Index.*
REFERENCE: "Seventy Years of the *Scientific American*," in the Seventieth Anniversary Number of the *Scientific American*, CXII, 540–546 (June 5, 1915).

returned to portrait painting and later to landscape painting. But his itch for invention would not let him rest; and he produced in succession a cord-making machine, a patent clock, a steam carriage, a portable horsepower, a corn sheller, a churn, a washing machine (of course), a signal telegraph, a fire alarm, a revolving rifle, a flying ship, a trip hammer, a fog whistle, an engine lathe, a rotary plow, a portable house, and many other devices. Some of these were successful and gave him the funds to sink in failures.

In the intervals of invention, Porter edited the *New York Mechanic* in 1840, moving it to Boston the following year and calling it the *American Mechanic*; but he left it in 1842 to do some more inventing. He returned to the editorial field, however, in 1845; and while experimenting with electrotyping processes in New York he founded a weekly paper which he called the *Scientific American*. The first number, a four-page small folio at $2.00 a year, was issued on August 28, 1845. It was illustrated by a few woodcuts and bore the subtitle: "The Advocate of Industry and Journal of Mechanical and Other Improvements." It was devoted primarily to new inventions, but it also contained some fragmentary essays on moral subjects "selected" from other periodicals, as well as some poetical "pieces," the choice of which reflect no credit on the editor's literary judgment. Circulation amounted to only a few hundred.[2] It would have been too much to expect of Porter that he should stick to his new paper for very long; and accordingly he sold it for a few hundred dollars in July 1846, though his name was carried as editor for ten months longer.

The purchasers were Orson Desaix Munn and Alfred Ely Beach. Beach was the son of Moses Y. Beach, famous editor and publisher of the *New York Sun*. The elder Beach was himself an inventor of importance, and the son inherited his mechanical interests and ability. When the younger Beach, not yet twenty-one, working with his father on the *Sun*, heard that the *Scientific American* was for sale, he suggested to his old schoolmate Munn, then conducting a mercantile business in a small Massachusetts town, that they should go into it together. Thus

[2] George P. Rowell & Company, *Centennial Newspaper Exhibit* (New York, 1876), p. 223.

was the firm of Munn & Company organized, issuing its first number July 23, 1846.

As the publisher of a paper devoted chiefly to patents, Munn & Company found themselves in close contact with inventors of all sorts and besieged by questions about the methods of patenting and about patent law. A patent agency was accordingly set up. Unlike many others of its class, it was conducted on high principles and gave honest advice, and in the course of a decade or two it became a very prosperous concern and the largest agency of the kind in the world. Its relation to the *Scientific American* was one of mutual helpfulness. When A. B. Wilson brought the model of his sewing machine (later the Wheeler and Wilson) to Munn & Company in 1849, it was written up for the *American*. In the same way, Thomas A. Edison got a good story on his new talking machine in 1877. The leading inventors of America were patrons of Munn & Company — Samuel F. B. Morse, Elias Howe, Captain James B. Eads, Captain John Ericsson, Dr. R. J. Gatling, Peter Cooper Hewitt, Thomas A. Edison.[3] And even the obscure and unsuccessful inventions, of which the *Scientific American* publicized thousands (for every patron of Munn & Company got at least a few lines in the paper) were often interesting and sometimes significant in illustrating trends of experimentation.

The *American* featured these articles, and one of its most important departments was the weekly publication of the official list of patents, "with the claims annexed," received directly from the United States Patent Office; but the contents of the paper were not limited to matters about inventions. The new publishers had enlarged the weekly issue to eight pages, and a variety of information of mechanical and scientific nature was presented.

And that we may furnish an acceptable family newspaper [said the editors at the beginning of the second volume] we shall continue to give in brief and condensed form the most useful and interesting intelligence of passing events — not omitting a small portion of serious matter, suitable for Sunday reading — but avoiding the disgusting and pernicious details of crime.[4]

[3] *Scientific American*, CXII, 540 (June 5, 1915).
[4] *Ibid.*, II, 5 (September 26, 1846).

Some advertising was printed from the first; but each advertisement was limited to sixteen lines, without display or illustration.

Circulation came but slowly at first; but it passed 10,000 in 1848 and 20,000 in 1852. The next year it reached 30,000 — approximately its circulation for the next decade. In 1848 Munn and Beach had been joined in their venture by Salem Howe Wales, another New Englander come to New York to make his fortune. Wales was active in the editorial work; his letters from the Paris Exposition in 1855 attracted wide attention.

In July 1859 the *Scientific American* began a new series, with semiannual volumes. It then changed from a small folio of eight pages to a large quarto of sixteen, keeping the price at $2.00. The editorial policy remained about the same. The general miscellany had faded out of the picture several years earlier. Now the illustrated articles on new inventions came first, as always, followed by news and commentary on patent law, the patent claim list, some general scientific notes, a query column, a few clippings of a scientific nature, and a page of advertising. There was but little interest shown in such fields as biology and geology; but there was some astronomy, and chemistry and medicine had occasional innings. Agriculture was given some attention; and fields in which applied physics played a large rôle, like transportation and manufacturing, occupied much space. Munn & Company had prospered and now had their Washington bureau, with Judge Charles Mason, former commissioner of patents, as their legal adviser.

The Civil War brought more matter about arms and naval devices — a field in which the paper had always maintained a considerable interest. The subscription rate was increased to $3.00 in 1863. Two years after the close of the war, the page size was increased to small folio once more in order to accommodate increased advertising; better paper, press work, and engraving made a decidedly handsomer periodical.

The *Scientific American* was a journal of opinions. It fought fakirs and quacks, including perpetual motion cranks and all their tribe. On the other hand, it was a firm believer from the beginning in aviation. Porter had indeed built a kind of forerunner of the modern dirigible during his editorship of the paper.

Ballooning was followed closely. As aeronautics developed, the *American* opposed the impractical flapping-wing boats and the screw fliers; but when Langley conducted his experiments in 1903, it was one of the few observers to lend him encouragement even in his failure. It was a strong partisan of the Wrights. It offered a $2,500 trophy for flights by heavier-than-air machines, which was finally won by Glenn H. Curtiss in 1910; and through the magazine Edwin Gould offered his $15,000 prize for a heavier-than-air machine with two power plants.

Another early enthusiasm of the paper was that for subway transportation. In 1849 it told of a project for "An Underground Railroad in Broadway" as follows:

The plan is to tunnel Broadway through the whole length, with openings in stairways at every corner. The subterranean passage is to be laid down with a double track, with a road for foot-passengers on either side — the whole to be brilliantly lighted with gas. The cars, which are to be drawn by horses, will stop ten seconds at every corner, thus performing the trip up and down, including stoppages, in about an hour.[5]

But no progress was made along these lines because of the unfriendliness of the city government and the ridicule of New York newspapers. At last Beach secured legislative authority to build a short underground pneumatic tube, somewhat after the London plan, and this he proceeded to do secretly and without Tammany's franchise. In six nights early in February 1870 a large gang of workmen dug an eight-foot tunnel under Broadway from Warren Street to Murray, the dirt being carried off through the cellar of a building whose owner sympathized with the project. But just as the work was being rushed to an end, the *Tribune* discovered what was going on, through a reporter who had disguised himself as a workman; and it exposed the whole scheme. Beach then utilized the publicity which had been given the *Scientific American* tunnel to charge the curious twenty-five cents a head for a view of the subway and the pneumatic machine. They saw the cylindrical tunnel, twenty-one feet below Broadway, with a car that fitted it like the carrier in a pneumatic tube (which it was) and held eighteen persons;

[5] *Scientific American*, V, 104 (November 3, 1849).

the car was blown from one end of the subway to the other and then sucked back when the compressed-air engine was reversed. For a full year this experimental tube was in use; many persons were convinced, and some of the newspapers, but Tammany was able ultimately to kill the bill authorizing a subway and obtain the enactment of one calling for a five-million-dollar elevated steam road.[6]

It was about this time that Wales left the *Scientific American* to hold various positions in the city administration. The sons of the remaining proprietors entered the organization in the late seventies and early eighties; especially to be noted because they were later to control the property are Charles A. Munn and Frederick C. Beach. In order to take care of a flood of material about the Centennial at Philadelphia, it was decided to launch another periodical at the beginning of 1876; this was the origin of the weekly *Scientific American Supplement.*[7] Besides the articles and illustrations bearing on the great exposition, the *Supplement* printed much of scientific thought abroad, and especially of scientific discussion which was "more technical and special in nature." There seemed to be a place for such a periodical after the exposition was over. Though it published some material very similar to that which appeared in the parent magazine, it was not devoted primarily to mechanics and was generally more interested in pure science. Then in 1885 Munn & Company founded a monthly *Scientific American: Architects' and Builders' Edition*, later called *Scientific American Building Monthly*,[8] in order to meet the growing demand for specialized periodicals and to take advantage of the large advertising business in the construction lines. The *Building Monthly* was a well-illustrated forty-page magazine which featured building plans; in connection with it Munn & Company maintained a staff of architects who furnished plans and

[6] *Ibid.*, CXII, 541 (June 5, 1915).
[7] Published January 1, 1876–December 27, 1919, in 88 volumes. Edited and published throughout by Munn & Company.
[8] The change in title occurred in 1902. This periodical was begun November 1885 and was supplanted January 1905 by *American Homes and Gardens*, subtitled "New Series of *Scientific American Building Monthly.*" The new periodical was also monthly, and was a profusely illustrated high-grade magazine. It was absorbed in September 1915 by *House and Garden*.

specifications to prospective builders by mail. Monthly export and Spanish editions completed the family of *Scientific American* periodicals.

The parent paper had a circulation of 40,000 by 1880, and it came very near to 50,000 before the hard times of the early nineties affected it. That retardation was only temporary, and in a few years it was again forging forward to new high levels. Advertising was copious and profitable.

The World's Fair at Chicago occupied many pages of the paper in the nineties. Electrical developments, the experiments in aeronautics, and the advent of the automobile furnished the feature serials of those years. The automobile vehicle had been a familiar idea to readers of the *Scientific American* for many years when it first startled pedestrians and frightened horses on our city streets just after the turn of the century. No year had passed for more than half a century that this journal had not exhibited plans and pictures for horseless carriages moved by all sorts of power. The experiments of such foreign inventors as Cugnot, Trevethick, Guerney, Church, and Lenoir had been duly chronicled. When the motor car really came to stay, the *Scientific American* was for some years a chief periodical of the industry.

A. E. Beach died in 1896 and was succeeded as secretary of the company by his son F. C. Beach. O. D. Munn lived until 1907, though his work devolved, in his last years, largely upon his son C. A. Munn, who followed him as president. Circulation ran up to 75,000, and in 1911 the paper was enlarged to twenty-four small-folio pages. A "midmonth number" was still larger; it was usually devoted to a specialty, such as an automobile review or an agricultural issue, and had a colored cover. A little later all numbers came to have the bright covers, and after a few years the midmonth special was abandoned. Articles were now signed, commonly by the names of government bureau heads or officers of industrial concerns, but occasionally by university professors. Waldemar B. Kaempffert was an assistant editor from 1897, and managing editor 1911–15. Illustration, now almost entirely by half tone, was copious. In 1915 a seventieth anniversary number was issued which detailed the progress of mechanical improvement along many lines.

The World War brought into the pages of the *Scientific American* many articles about arms, aircraft, submarines, and chemical warfare. The subscription price was raised in 1917 to $4.00, and two years later the page size was changed to quarto to conform with the more popular magazine format. The printers' strike of 1919 forced the *American*, in common with several other periodicals, to resort to the use of plates made from typewritten sheets. The same disturbance was the occasion for the suspension of the weekly *Supplement*, which was supplanted by the *Scientific American Monthly*.

It was perhaps owing to the increasing force of specialized competition that the circulation of the *American* declined somewhat during and following the war. Whatever the cause, the fact of the decline, added to the increasing costs of an inflationary period, determined Munn & Company (which now took the name of Scientific American Publishing Company for its periodical business) to make the *Scientific American* a monthly and to consolidate with it the magazine called the *Scientific American Monthly*. This was done November 1921. The editorial staff through these years was composed of J. Bernard Walker, Austin C. Lescarboura, J. Malcolm Bird, Albert A. Hopkins (who had come to the paper in 1890), and others; while C. A. Munn, O. D. Munn (II), and Allan C. Hoffman were officers of the company and the conductors of the journal. In 1924, following the death of C. A. Munn, the second Orson D. Munn, grandson of the founder of Munn & Company, succeeded his uncle as chief editor and publisher.

Patent lists, once a chief feature of the *Scientific American*, dwindled in these later years and finally disappeared, though a department of legal news remained. After the changes of 1921, the scope of the magazine broadened; its articles about new inventions had been decreasing for some years, and now its function as a purveyor of science to the people became paramount. It was no longer the inventor's paper, but a periodical of popular science. "It has been the constant aim of this journal," said the editor in 1910, "to impress the fact that science is not inherently dull, heavy or abstruse, but that it is essentially fascinating, understandable, and full of undeniable charm." [9] This

[9] *Scientific American*, CIII, 514 (December 31, 1910).

the *Scientific American* has succeeded in doing, not only in its early history but in its later years. It has met the two requirements of good scientific writing — reliability and readability.

One of the values of the *Scientific American* which endeared it to several generations of boys and young men was a kind of personal quality difficult to account for. Its columns of queries and answers, its willingness to answer correspondents by letter, its lucidity, and its appeal to the ambitious youth of a machine age — all may help to explain this feeling which many of the subscribers to the paper had for it. The boy Thomas Edison walked three miles to get his copy each week,[10] and doubtless many other inventors and industrialists were equally stimulated by it in a formative period. In this respect it is probable that the *Scientific American* had a significance — at least for its first sixty or seventy years — unapproached in kind and effect by any other periodical.

[10] *Scientific American*, CXII, 543 (June 5, 1915).

THE NATIONAL POLICE GAZETTE [1]

THAT stormy petrel, George Wilkes, started a little four-page paper called the *Subterranean* in 1844 to burrow beneath the nefarious politics of New York City and bring forth into the light of day the monstrosities of vice which it dug up. Wilkes was only twenty-four and very active, so that he managed to dodge assassins and escape the police for nearly a year; but after his sixth arrest, his paper died. To him, as he languished in the Tombs, came Enoch E. Camp, a lawyer, and proposed that the two of them start a police gazette modeled on the English papers of that character, such as the *Penny Sunday Times and People's Police Gazette, Bell's Penny Dispatch, Sporting and Police Gazette*, and *Clark's Weekly Dispatch*. This suited Wilkes perfectly, and with Camp furnishing the funds and Wilkes the editorial enterprise, the *National Police Gazette* made its appearance on September 13, 1845.[2]

Like its models, the new paper carried one woodcut across the tops of the three middle columns of its front page; but that was its only illustration. It had eight large quarto pages and

[1] TITLE: *The National Police Gazette.*
FIRST ISSUE: September 13, 1845. Current.
PERIODICITY: Weekly, 1845–1934; semimonthly, 1934–35; monthly, 1935–current. I–XXXII (1845–77), annual volumes; thereafter semiannual volumes. Suspended February 11, 1932–September 5, 1933.
PUBLISHERS: Enoch E. Camp and George Wilkes, 1845–48; George Wilkes, 1848–66; George W. Matsell & Company, 1866–74; Herbert R. Mooney and Charles A. Lederer, 1874–77; Richard K. Fox, 1877–1922; Charles J. Fox, 1922–32; Police Gazette Corporation, owned by editors (see below), 1933–current. All of New York.
EDITORS: Same as publishers, 1845–1922; Ralph D. Robinson, 1923–32; Mrs. Merle W. Hersey, 1933–35; Edward E. Eagle and Harold H. Roswell, 1935–37; H. H. Roswell, 1937–current.
REFERENCES: Walter Davenport, "The Nickel Shocker," *Collier's*, Vol. LXXXI, March 10, 17, 24; Edward Van Every, *Sins of New York as "Exposed" by the Police Gazette* (New York, 1930), and *Sins of America as "Exposed" by the Police Gazette* (New York, 1931).
[2] The earliest number in the Library of Congress file is that for October 11, but it is No. 5. The first four numbers were republished under date of October 16.

sold at first for ten cents — later reduced to five and then to four. It featured "The Lives of the Felons," a series of biographies of criminals drawn from police records. Number One was the story of Robert Sutton, known as "Bob the Wheeler," pugilist and swindler. But the "Life" which bulked largest, running through most of 1846 and 1847 was that of John A. Murrell, the "land pirate." [3] The ostensible purpose of the paper was to "spot" offenders and thus make it impossible for them to ply their trades of swindling and thievery.

It will be our object [said the prospectus] to strip them of the advantage of a professional incognito, by publishing a minute description of their names, aliases, and persons; a succinct history of their previous career, their place of residence at the time of writing, and a current account of their movements from time to time.[4]

This procedure was bold and was bound to expose the *Gazette* and its editors to assault and perhaps worse. Indeed, within a few months "Bob the Wheeler," now out of jail, gathered together certain choice spirits, including James Downer "the Resurrectionist" (grave robber), Dingdong Kelly, and John J. Betterton the Blockman; and they made a concerted attack on the office of the *Gazette*, then situated in the basement of a building at 27 Centre Street. In the fighting that ensued, Downer was duly prepared for "resurrection"; two other mobsters were killed with him, and, among the defenders of the *Gazette* shop, "Sergeant" Belcher suffered a broken arm. The sergeant and Tim "Keel-layer" Mooney were Wilkes's two bodyguards, and they saved him from a broken head many a time. The tradition was that Mooney had once killed two London "bobbies" with their own truncheons in a free-for-all; at least, the reputation stood him in good stead in his present occupation.

This was all good advertising for the new paper, and circulation boomed to 15,000 in a short time. The Mexican War came on, and the *Gazette* made a business of printing the names and descriptions of deserters from the army; the Secretary of War thereupon authorized a large subscription for distribution

---

[3] This was published in book form with paper covers in 1847 (Sabin 51553).
[4] *National Police Gazette*, September 13, 1845, p. 4.

among the soldiers. It is a mistake to think that the *Police Gazette* featured sex scandals in these early years; that was to come later.

In the fall of 1847 the size of the page was enlarged; and the next year the *Gazette* was made a four-page blanket sheet, each page having eight wide columns. By this time Camp had retired, and Wilkes was waging war with New York hoodlum gangs on one side and with the police department on the other. He did not hesitate to attack Chief of Police George W. Matsell himself. In 1850 came an assault on the *Gazette* office which resulted in six deaths, among them that of Andrew Frost, the paper's star reporter. Wilkes and the redoubtable "Sergeant" Belcher were both carried to a hospital, and the plant was demolished. Such was life in New York in the "good old days."

In a short time, however, the paper was going at full blast again. Among the leading stories carried by the *Gazette* in the forties and fifties were that of the Macready mob at the Astor Place Theatre; those of its own crusades against gambling dives and lotteries; the exposure of Madame Restall the abortionist; the Daniel E. Sickles story, and the attack on John B. Gough, who had been found drunk in a bawdy house. Correspondents in other cities sent crime news, but New York was preëminent. Frank descriptions of houses of criminal resort in that city were frequent. Here is an example:

One of the first and worst in the area [Five Points] is the tough concert saloon at 50 Houston Street and of which the proprietor, Charley Sturges, is well known to the entire crooked brigade of both sexes. At this place plots are hatched to break into banks, flood the country with "queer," spirit some pal out of prison, to put away some principal or witness, or to square it with the police. Here not a little counterfeit engraving is turned out by that first-class workman, "Cooley" Keyes.[5]

But it was too stiff a pace for any paper to keep up; and besides, Wilkes became an assistant editor of the *Spirit of the Times*, a high-class sporting paper, in 1850, later becoming joint proprietor and finally owner and editor of it.[6] The *Police*

[5] Quoted from the *Gazette* in Van Every, *op. cit.*, p. 14.
[6] See pp. 203–204.

Gazette declined throughout the Civil War, and in 1866 Wilkes sold it — to none other than Chief Matsell, his erstwhile enemy.

Matsell provided more pictures and proceeded to sensation-alize the paper to the tune of sex. Advertising followed this lead, and we have the advent of offers of "photographic cards for gentlemen," "manhood restored" nostrums, and transparent cards. Pictures came to cover practically all of the big first page; in October 1867 the page was reduced to a reasonable size and eight pages were provided, the first devoted to a single picture. A corps of correspondents was again set up to cover the crime and scandal of the whole country and thus justify the word *National* in the paper's title. For the first time the theater entered the pages of the *Police Gazette*, in a column headed "Choses Dramatique" [*sic*]. Lydia Thompson and her English beauties bulked large in the paper. And now the prize ring, which Wilkes had attacked as barbarous, made its appearance, accompanied by some other sporting items. A succession of big crime and scandal stories furnished pabulum for the paper in these years — Daniel McFarland's murder of A. D. Richard-son, a famous journalist, and his acquittal by a jury which justified the act on the "injured husband" grounds; the Nathan murder mystery, still unsolved; exposures of John H. Noyes and his "perfectionists"; and the great Beecher-Tilton scandal. This last was heaven-sent for the *Gazette's* purposes: it liked nothing so much as a good juicy sex triangle involving the clergy, and here was the most famous clergyman in America inextricably caught in the very most shocking of situations. Such fun! chortled the *Gazette*.

But after all, appetites for the morbid were being fairly satis-fied by the newspapers in the seventies, and the newspapers could give daily installments of the latest infamy. Why wait for the weekly feast and starve for details of vice between whiles? So the *Gazette* declined again, and in 1874 Matsell, having run up a tremendous bill for woodcuts, paid it by making over the whole paper to his engravers, Mooney & Lederer. Theaters and sports had been dropped by this time, but the Beecher-Tilton affair was going full gallop. Even this, however, did not rejuvenate the failing journal.

In 1874 Richard K. Fox, an Irish journalist, arrived in New

York with only a few shillings in his pocket but with some ideas in his head and unlimited energy in his sturdy frame. Within a year he was business manager of the *Police Gazette*, which he had found a paper of low reputation, small sales, and large debts. It was unable to pay him his salary or advertising commissions in full; but he got along somehow, and three years later he was proprietor of the paper — still debt-encumbered, but his own. He borrowed some more money and early in 1878 made the *Gazette* a sixteen-page quarto printed on pale pink stock — the format in which it was to become famous. He plunged deeper than ever into Sex with a capital S — sex scandals, sex crimes, sex pictures, sex advertising. He made reduced subscription rates for saloon keepers, barber shops, and hotel keepers. Circulation boomed as never before.

A typical number of our pink sensation-monger might spread over its front page a woodcut of a scene in one of New York's "sinks of iniquity" which made much of the shapely limbs and buxom bosoms of the feminine habitués. The *Gazette* artists had no eye for sylphid forms (when waists were slender they were obviously made so by tight lacing), but their tastes ran to the voluptuous and well fed. Turning over the leaf, we come upon an editorial page devoted to comment on crime — perhaps a defense of capital punishment, a sharp criticism of hypocrisy among the clergy, or an attack on the incompetence of the police of Chicago or Kankakee. There are answers to correspondents about criminal records — a department later devoted to sports. On the third page are crime stories with glaring headlines:

SNARED BY A SCOUNDREL.

An Innocent Country Beauty, on
Her Travels, Encounters
Her Fate in an Ad-
venture

OF THE WORST TYPE.

His Easy Conquest of the Unsophis-
ticated Girl Through a Grand
but Diaphanous Yarn,

AND HER SUBSEQUENT SAD FATE

and one like this:

EGGCITING EGGSPLOIT.

Miss Esther Scattergood, Employed
at Georgia House in Desh-
ler, Ohio,

EATS 50 RAW EGGS IN 50 MINUTES

For a wager of a Calico Dress
and the Price of the Eggs

Some of the stories come from English and German papers: wherever lurid or weird news flowered, there sucked the *Gazette* bee, and what a strange and sometimes sickening honey it made! On the fourth and fifth pages were more pictures. Some were mere unexciting portraits, but the eye was inevitably taken by some action scene — "A Purse-Heavy Citizen, Out for a Night's Frolic, Wheels a Dizzy Disciple of Terpsichore Through the Streets on a Wager" — and in a wheelbarrow. "Would-Be Voters: A Bevy of Strong-Minded Amazons Make a Sensation at a New York Polling Place." The sixth page might have a lurid account of a hanging, or another chapter in the mystery of poor kidnaped Charley Ross, the seventh an account of how two rustic beauties in Keokuk fought and gouged and pulled hair for the favor of a local swain, and one would expect on the next two pages the artist's vivid presentation of both the hanging and the amazonian conflict.

Perhaps this is far enough to go in our sample number, but it would be a mistake to stop short of "Glimpses of Gotham" by "Paul Prowler." Paul was Samuel A. Mackeever, the *Gazette's* star writer, who did some ten columns for the paper every week. He prowled about all of New York's most unsavory places and described them most effectively in his articles, and (what is more remarkable) named and identified them by street and number. Like his exemplar, the "London Spy," he was always strictly moral in these peregrinations; and he lectured his companion Charley most edifyingly upon the dangers of the primrose path. Mackeever also wrote under the names of "Colonel Lynx" and "The Old Rounder." Nor should we miss the installment of the serial by Bracebridge Hemyng, who was the author, in other periodicals, of the Jack Harkaway

THE NATIONAL
POLICE GAZETTE
THE OLDEST ILLUSTRATED WEEKLY. ESTABLISHED 1846

Entered according to Act of Congress, in the Year 1879, by the Publisher of The National Police Gazette, in the Office of the Librarian of Congress at Washington.

Vol. XXXIV.—No. 96.   NEW YORK, SATURDAY, JULY 26, 1879   Price Ten Cents.

A MASHER MASHED—HOW A CHICAGO YOUTH, OF THE "TOO-AWFULLY-SWEET-FOR-ANYTHING" VARIETY, WHILE ESSAYING THE ROLE OF A LADY-KILLER, WAS TAKEN IN AND DONE FOR, LIKE THE VERIEST COUNTRYMAN, BY A BRACE OF SHARP DAMSELS AND THEIR MALE ACCOMPLICE. See Page 7.

A TYPICAL *POLICE GAZETTE* COVER OF THE SEVENTIES

Three scenes depicting the story of a Chicago youth who, "while essaying the role of a lady-killer," was "taken in and done for" by "a brace of sharp damsels."

stories, but here the proud fabulist of "Steps to Ruin; or, Gaslight Temptations." Nor would it do to neglect those olios for the morbid which sported startling headlines and were made up of scores of choice bits selected from the more sensational news columns of two continents. The most familiar was:

VICE'S VARIETIES.
An Assorted Lot of Evil Deeds
of Evil Doers
Collected by Gazette Correspondents
in All Quarters.

Others were "Noose Notes," in which appeared brief accounts of hangings; and "Crimes of the Clergy," and "Homicidal Horrors." The *Gazette* reported a hanging with as much heavy gaiety as the old-fashioned home weekly used to give to the story of a family reunion, and a clergyman caught *in flagrante delicto* was sweet on its tongue.

There were a few theatrical notes in 1878, and in the next year there were more; but not until the "Stage Whispers" column of 1883 did the *Gazette* really go in for theatrical reporting. From then on it exploited popular actresses regularly, especially such as displayed their charms in tights. The busy Mackeever wrote of the theaters under the pen name of "The Marquis of Lorgnette." In the nineties, burlesque queens alternated with ring champions and race horses in the adornment of that show window of the *Police Gazette* — its flashy front page.

It was in 1879 that sports became a part of the paper's regular fare, and in the following year such a success was made of reporting the Ryan-Goss prize fight that the ring bade fair to eclipse crime in the *Gazette*. Not that there was much difference between the ring and crime; prize fighting was certainly illegal, and the bare-knuckle contests were savage enough. They were fought under London prize ring rules, which permitted wrestling, gouging, kicking, and scratching. The match with which the *Gazette* made such a hit in 1880 was that between Paddy Ryan, the Troy Terror, and Joe Goss, the English champion. The battle was to have been fought in Canada, but both bruisers lost to the British redcoats, who drove them back to American soil. The meeting eventually took place at Collier's Station,

West Virginia, where Ryan became champion after eighty-seven
bloody rounds. The newspapers did not give the battle much
prominence, but Fox detailed several of his writers and artists
to cover it, including Arthur Lumley, a star reporter, and William
H. Harding, sports editor. The demand for the issue containing
the story of the fight required an edition of 400,000
copies, and this popularity determined Fox to make his paper
the leading prize ring authority in America. As part of his plan,
he became the chief backer of the new champion.

William Muldoon, famous wrestler and friend of Fox, had
recently been on a barnstorming tour to Boston; and there he
had seen one John L. Sullivan, the "Strong Boy of Boston," in
action. He had thereupon brought Sullivan to New York, where
the "Strong Boy" had proceeded to knock out Steve Taylor with
éclat and a left-hand punch. Sullivan wanted a match with
Ryan at once, but the Trojan told him to get a reputation first.
One night Fox and his sports editor came into Harry Hill's
place on Houston Street, to find Sullivan the center of attraction
there, engaged in informing a large circle of admirers what a
great fighter he was. Fox sent a waiter over to invite Sullivan
to his table; Sullivan sent the waiter back with a message to the
effect that anybody who wanted to see him could (hic) travel
across the room to his table. Now Fox had become a man of
position and dignity, and this was an affront which he never forgave.
He resolved to humble the Bostonian pride, and he fixed
on the Trojan prowess to do it. He backed Paddy Ryan for a
$5,000 stake.

The great fight took place at Mississippi City, a hundred
miles from New Orleans, on February 7, 1882. A special train
was run from New York. The Police Gazette was filled for
weeks with news of the training of the fighters and other "advance
dope." The contest made Sullivan champion, and brought
him the Fox diamond-studded championship belt,[7] which the
unforgiving "Jawn L." contemptuously referred to as a "dog
collar." [8] The Gazette got out a special fight supplement on
February 14, capitalizing its disappointment.

Fox's next move was to bring Tug Wilson from England, but

[7] R. F. Dibble, *John L. Sullivan* (Boston, 1925), p. 38.
[8] Van Every, *op. cit.*, p. 265.

Tug was so small that the champion would not meet him in a regular fight. He did bet a thousand dollars, however, that he could knock the Englishman out in four rounds. This he failed to do because his opponent crawled around on the floor and would not stand up to be slugged. This match was fought in Madison Square Garden and attracted the first of the great fight crowds. The next year Fox brought over Charley Mitchell from England, who knocked Sullivan down in the first round but was in a dazed condition when police stopped the contest at the end of the third round. Another match was arranged between Sullivan and Mitchell a year later, but the "Strong Boy" was drunk as a lord when he appeared, in full dress clothes, at the ring; and the 13,500 disappointed customers were turned away without a refund. Other Fox importations designed to put Sullivan in his place were dealt with more summarily — Slade from Australia and Greenfield from Birmingham, England.

The *Police Gazette*, with a circulation of 150,000, was now a power in the sporting world; and Fox put all its influence behind an effort to force Sullivan to meet Jem Smith, who in 1887 was the British champion. But all its attempts were fruitless. Finally Fox picked up an American fighter, John Joseph Killion, who, under the name of Jake Kilrain, rapidly gained prestige and was eventually matched with the great Jem. The international fracas took place near London early in January 1888; the American won in 106 rounds, and the *Gazette* proclaimed him champion of the world. Thus ran the headlines:

EXTRA!/ THE BATTLE./ Jake Kilrain's Wonderful Mastery of the British Champion./ MORE DETAILS./ The Dauntless Representative of America Lays Out the Englishman./ FOUL PLAY./ Charley Mitchell Strikes a Strong Blow for Square Dealing./ A VIVID PICTURE./ Kilrain's Marvelous Performance Fully Described by a Graphic Spectator./ "NIGHT OF BLUCHER."/ The Briton Gasps a Hope for the Shades of Darkness./ Echoes from Abroad./ The Best Description of the Fight.[9]

Of course the next step was to match Kilrain with Sullivan, which was a matter of many months and much printer's ink. But Fox finally put up $10,000 as Kilrain's half of the purse,

[9] *National Police Gazette*, January 7, 1888.

and on July 8, 1889, as Vachel Lindsay wrote many years later —

> On an emerald plain,
> Nigh New Orleans,
> John L. Sullivan, the Strong Boy of Boston,
> Fought seventy-five red rounds with Jake Kilrain

— and effectively knocked him out.

Thus ended the feud of Mr. Fox and Mr. Sullivan; and what Mr. Fox's many champions could not do, John Barleycorn accomplished in short order. But though Fox had failed in his immediate objective, he had maneuvered his paper into a position which made it extremely profitable; and by the nineties he was rated a millionaire. He backed the court defenses of prize fighters which resulted in giving the ring a legal status in New York.[10] He donated diamond and gold medals and belts right and left, not only to prize fighters but to pedestrian racers, club swingers, female rifle shooters, rowers, wrestlers, weight lifters, swimmers, foot racers, fencers, and so on. It is estimated that he spent a million dollars on such awards.[11] Nor did he confine his generosity to athletes. He gave *Police Gazette* belts to champion singers, champion dancers, champion rat catchers, champion oyster openers, and champion steeple climbers. Of course he did not forget the *Gazette's* best friends, the bartenders and barbers: he gave medals to the champion drink mixer and the champion hair cutter, too. The latter is said to have cut a head of hair in less than thirty seconds, with the customer scared but satisfied.

By 1890 the paper was carrying two full pages of small ads, most of them of a disreputable kind. It still featured crime (the Mafia in New Orleans, Harry Hayward the Minneapolis hypnotist murderer, Durrant of San Francisco), as well as scandals, hangings, and weird "news," along with pictures of burlesque queens in tights, ring news and history, racing, cockfighting, and so on. It was not offered for sale at the more reputable newsstands, but it was to be found at practically every barroom and barber shop in America. It got into trouble with

[10] Van Every, *op. cit.*, pp. 270–274.
[11] G. H. Genzmer in the *Dictionary of American Biography*, VI, 572.

the Society for the Suppression of Vice, and Anthony Com-
stock once secured a conviction of its editor, with a fine of
$500.[12] There were plenty of private suits based on libel allega-
tions as well; within six months in 1885 suits totaling over
$3,000,000 were either threatened or filed, including one by the
beautiful Lillian Russell for $20,000.[13]

The *Gazette's* art work was doubtless more important than
its text. Among Fox's earlier artists were the English Matt
Morgan; Charles Kendrick, who had a fresh sense of humor;
Philip G. Cusacha, at one time art director of New York's
illustrated daily, the *Graphic*; George G. White, author of a
handbook on drawing; and George E. McEvoy, cartoonist.
Most of the pictures were far from distinguished artistically,
and as a rule they were not signed; but some — especially the
composite pages with inserts — were attractive. In the latter
nineties half-tone engravings were frequently used, though they
had not wholly displaced line cuts; in 1901, however, even the
big front-page pictures were in half tone.

The *Gazette* issued picture supplements in the eighties —
reproductions on heavy white paper of its actress and champion subjects. It also did a thriving business in "cabinet size,
exquisitely finished photographs" of actresses, pugilists, baseball heroes, wrestlers, jockeys, pedestrians, swimmers, race
horses, fighting dogs, and fighting cocks. It issued a sporting
annual, with records in all departments, and manuals of the
ring, baseball, jiu jitsu, et cetera; as well as "Fox's Sensational
Series," which consisted largely of such things as "Paul
Prowler's" disclosures.

Mostly malodorous, but it paid. In 1883 the *Gazette* moved
into a new quarter-million dollar building at Pearl and Dover
Streets. It kept its 150,000 circulation almost through the nineties; but about the time of the Spanish War it began to decline,
slightly at first, then more rapidly, until by the time of the
World War it was down to 60,000. It still boasted "the snap-
piest of all girl pictures" and "breezy paragraphs of doings in
the legitimate and variety houses." To this it now added movie
gossip. It continued its traditional news pictures of sporting

[12] Van Every, *op. cit.*, p. 153.
[13] *Ibid.*, p. 158.

events — in which it was now inevitably inferior to the news-papers. It featured "famous battles of prize-ring history reviewed" and its "always reliable and authentic sporting record." Of the crime features, once a mainstay, only a little was left; the Sunday newspaper magazine sections had supplanted the *Gazette* in that commodity, and the news of Dr. Cronin, Mrs. Lurtgert, and Harry Thaw seemed second hand.

The adoption of the eighteenth amendment was a solar plexus for the *Police Gazette*, for it cut off with one blow its entire barroom circulation. The new speakeasies which eventually sprang up knew not the *Gazette*. Richard K. Fox died in 1922, and in that very year came another shattering blow: women began to bob their hair. Now when this fashion became common, the barber shops — last refuge of the *Police Gazette* — were thrown open to women; and women must not find naughty pictures lying about while they waited their turns in the chair of the hairdresser. For years the *Police Gazette* had been the "barber shop Bible." It had helped make barber shops the centers of sports interest in all the small towns; it had been passed around in the free-and-easy crowds of men waiting for shaves on Saturday nights. "Have you seen the last *Police Gazette*?" ran the vaudeville gag. "No, I shave myself." But now, Dame Fashion, transformed into one of the female pugilists whom the *Gazette* used to feature, had delivered a right uppercut to the chin of the old pink paper which left it as groggy as Kilrain in his seventy-fifth round "nigh New Orleans."

Charles J. Fox, son of the old master, had been director of the *Gazette* for some years. He put Ralph D. Robinson in as editor. At last the paper got a "break" with the phenomenal increase of interest in prize fighting during and following the war. The Dempsey-Willard contest in 1919 and the two Dempsey-Tunney fights in 1926 and 1927 enlisted amazing popular interest. The *Police Gazette* soared to over 200,000 circulation in 1926, but this prosperity was only temporary. The freedom of discussion of sex matters which was also an aftermath of the war reacted adversely to the old paper. Whereas it had been virtually unique in its suggestion of ribaldry in the eighties and nineties, it now had competition aplenty from the "confession" and "spicy" magazines. Under the flood it went down irretrievably. In February 1932 it was sold out as a bankrupt for $545.

A year and a half later an attempt was made to revive it, with the archaic heading and the old pink paper, by Mrs. Merle Williams Hersey, daughter of a Methodist clergyman and publisher of several other "hot" magazines. It was filled with confession stories and pictures of almost-nudes; its leading feature was the autobiography of a burlesque "strip artist." There seemed little demand for this particular kind of inanity, and the *Gazette* was made a semimonthly in May 1934, and a monthly the next year, with further changes of ownership in 1935 and 1937. It lingers on.

DE BOW'S REVIEW [1]

YOUNG James D. B. De Bow, recently graduated from
Charleston College and still more recently admitted to
the bar, attended the Commercial Convention of the
Southern and Western States which was held at Memphis in
1845 and presided over by John C. Calhoun. He was made one
of the secretaries of the convention and was tremendously im-

[1] TITLES: (1) *The Commercial Review of the South and West*, 1846–50 (cover
title, *De Bow's Commercial Review of the South and West*, 1847–50); (2) *De
Bow's Review of the Southern and Western States*, 1850–52; (3) *De Bow's Review and Industrial Resources, Statistics, etc.*, 1853–64; (4) *De Bow's Review,
Devoted to the Restoration of the Southern States*, 1866–67; (5) *De Bow's Review. . . . Agricultural, Commercial, Industrial Progress & Resources*, 1868–80
(cover title, *De Bow's New Orleans Monthly Review*, 1869–70).
FIRST ISSUE: January 1846. LAST ISSUE: June 1880.
PERIODICITY: Monthly, I–VI, semiannual volumes, 1846–48 (omits August
1847; doubles August–September 1846, June–July 1847, May–June, October–
November 1848); suspended January–June 1849; VII–VIII (New Series, I–II),
July 1849–June 1850; IX–X (New Series, I, IV), July 1850–June 1851 (separate
monthly issues carry numbers of original series IX–X; Second Series, III–IV;
and Third Series, I–II); XI–XII (New Series, IV–V [V–VI]), July 1851–June
1852; XIII (New Series, I), July–December 1852; XIV (New Series, I), January–June 1853; XV–XVI (New Series, I–II), July 1853–June 1854 (separate
monthly issues carry New Series, II–III); XVII (New Series, IV), July–December 1858; XXVI–XXXI (Enlarged Series, I–VI), 1859–61 (double numbers: May–June, October–November 1861); XXXII (Enlarged Series, VII),
January–February, March–April 1862; XXXIII (Enlarged Series, VIII), May–
August 1862, in one number; suspended September 1862–June 1864; XXXIV
(Enlarged Series, I, New Series), July–August 1864, in one number; suspended
September 1864–December 1865; [XXXV–XLII] After the War Series, I–VIII
(whole numbers, XXXII–XXXIX), 1866–July 1870 (doubles April–May, July–
August 1867, May–June 1868); suspended August 1870–September 1879;
[XLIII] New Series, I, October, November, December 1879, June 1880 (omits
January–May 1880). See collation by Selma Nachman in *Bulletin of the Biblio-
graphical Society of America*, IV, 27 (January–April 1912).
PUBLISHERS: J. D. B. De Bow, 1846 (at New Orleans, 1846–52, 1859–61;
Washington, 1853–58; Charleston, 1861–62; Columbia, 1864; Nashville, 1866–
67); Heirs of J. D. B. De Bow, Nashville, 1867–68; William M. Burwell, New
Orleans, 1868–70; L. Graham & Company, New Orleans, 1879–80.
EDITORS: James Dunwoody Brownson De Bow, 1846–67; R. G. Barnwell and
Edwin Q. Bell, 1867–68; William MacCreary Burwell, 1868–80.
INDEXES: I–II in II, I–IV in IV, I–X in X, XI–XX in XX; also I–
XXXIII in *Poole's, Jones'*, and *A. L. A. Portrait*. After the War Series in
Poole's.
REFERENCES: Lillian Viola Doty, *De Bow's Review* (University of South

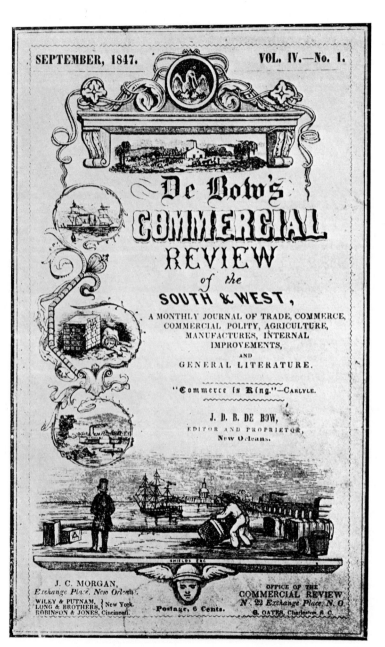

SEPTEMBER, 1847.

VOL. IV.—No. 1.

De Bow's
COMMERCIAL
REVIEW
of the
SOUTH & WEST,

A MONTHLY JOURNAL OF TRADE, COMMERCE,
COMMERCIAL POLITY, AGRICULTURE,
MANUFACTURES, INTERNAL
IMPROVEMENTS,
AND
GENERAL LITERATURE.

"Commerce is King."—CARLYLE.

J. D. B. DE BOW,
EDITOR AND PROPRIETOR,
New Orleans.

SHIELDS ENG

J. C. MORGAN,
Exchange Place, New Orleans.
WILEY & PUTNAM, } New York.
LONG & BROTHERS,
ROBINSON & JONES, Cincinnati.

Postage, 6 Cents.

OFFICE OF THE
COMMERCIAL REVIEW
N. 22 Exchange Place, N. O.
G. OATES, Charleston S. C.

AN EARLY COVER OF *DE BOW'S REVIEW*

pressed by its importance.[2] The central principle of this and later southern commercial conventions was that the South, lagging behind the North in the development of transportation, manufacturing, and agriculture, could best realize all its glorious potentialities not by political action so much as by united industrial effort. De Bow committed himself wholly to this principle and immediately began to lay plans for the establishment of a journal to exploit it.[3]

It was natural that De Bow's mind should turn at once to the project of a journal. He had been, for the past year or two, assistant to D. K. Whitaker, the owner of the *Southern Quarterly Review*,[4] of Charleston; he had written several articles for it, and at least one had attracted wide attention.[5] In spite of a rather sketchy preparation for the law, he felt that his career lay in magazine journalism.

It was equally natural that he should think of Charleston, his home, as the seat of the new periodical; and the prospectus for the *Commercial Review of the South and West* was issued there, late in 1845. But when the first number appeared in January 1846, it bore the name of New Orleans on its cover. De Bow said later that he was attracted to the Louisiana city by the success of the *Southern Medical Journal* there.[6] Certainly Charleston had been the graveyard of many magazines.

The first number was an octavo of ninety-six pages, not especially well printed (*De Bow's* was never notable typographically), but filled with useful information about southern and western commerce and resources. It was modeled upon *Hunt's Merchants' Magazine*,[7] but as yet it did not approach the copiousness of materials to be found in that journal. Most of it was

---

Carolina thesis, 1930); Charles Gayarré, "James Dunwoody Brownson De Bow," in After the War Series, III, 497–506 (June 1867); Edward Reinhold Rogers, *Four Southern Magazines* (University of Virginia, Studies in Southern Literature, Second Series, 1902); Herman Clarence Nixon, "De Bow's Review," in *Sewanee Review*, XXXIX, 54–61 (January–March 1931).

[2] See his article about the convention, *De Bow's Review*, I, 7–21 (January 1846).

[3] *Ibid.*, IV, 122 (September 1847).

[4] See Mott, *A History of American Magazines, 1741–1850*, p. 721.

[5] *De Bow's Review*, After the War Series, III, 499 (June 1867).

[6] *Ibid.*, XXXIII, 109 (July 1866).

[7] Mott, *op. cit.*, p. 696. De Bow speaks of *Hunt's* in his introductory article.

written by the editor. In his introduction, "Position of the *Commercial Review*," De Bow promised a journal of trade and commerce, of agriculture, manufactures, and internal improvements. "Literature," he wrote, "cannot be entirely neglected"; and he would offer biographical sketches occasionally, as well as news of the "book-trade." But "party movements and maneuvering and party tactics" he abjured, declaring for "an active neutrality." In closing, he asked for "an extended circulation." Other articles in this first number consisted of De Bow's account of the Memphis convention, a piece on railroads composed in part of Gadsden's report on the subject at Memphis and in part of an extract from *Hunt's Merchants' Magazine*, a description of Oregon and California which De Bow had written the year before for the *Southern Quarterly*, a brief article on "Louisiana Sugar" by E. J. Forstall, and other statistical pieces on the foreign grain trade, Charleston and New Orleans, and postal reforms. The last twenty pages of the magazine, in smaller type, gave "Southern and Western Statistics," figures on foreign trade, market news, and brief notes on publication.

It was not a bad beginning, and it received a warm greeting in the newspaper press; but the months went by, each bringing a new number filled with facts and statistics, with a certain amount of that high-flown rhetoric which the editor loved, and with passages on commerce among the ancients which gave an air of learning — and yet that "extended circulation" for which the young publisher had prayed did not come. A sign of financial distress was the omission of the August issue, which waited on the next month for a "double number." The same thing happened again in June of the next year, and the August 1847 issue was entirely omitted. The fact is that De Bow, who had begun his journal almost wholly upon credit, expecting to succeed because such a work was needed, had about exhausted the patience of his creditors. Doing much of the writing himself and all of a publisher's work, and living on next to nothing, he had found magazine making a hard trade — almost impossible, indeed. "Our funds are very low," he gasped in November 1848;[8] and with the next number the magazine was suspended.

It was at this desperate juncture that Maunsell White, a

---

[8] *De Bow's Review*, VI, 378 (October–November 1848).

wealthy sugar planter, came to De Bow's rescue. He believed in the young man and advanced funds sufficient to warrant another trial with the *Review*. De Bow now revived the journal after it had slumbered for six months, attacking the job with a zeal and industry that no hardship could daunt. At this time he was a tall, gaunt young man nearing thirty, with a great shock of black hair and a rather wild-looking black beard, out of the midst of which stared keen eyes (obscured by spectacles in later years, for he injured his eyes badly by the overwork of this period), while a large beaked nose thrust out belligerently. Judge Charles Gayarré later told of the young editor's way of living just after the *Review* was revived by White's generosity.

Many a night [he says] De Bow and a friend who assisted him [9] toiled until nearly dawn in a small office in Exchange Alley, No. 2. At that critical time they both slept in a room which had been given them by J. C. Morgan, the well known bookseller of the epoch. The bare walls of that room above the bookstore looked on no other furniture than a modest mattress lying on the floor, on which the two companions rested at night. They literally lived on bread alone, with a little butter, however, to soften its dryness. Never did two persons exist on so small an expenditure, their daily outlays rarely exceeding twenty cents — that is, ten cents for each.[10]

"A little butter" rather spoils the rhetoric, but we cannot begrudge it them.

A better publishing arrangement, with Weld & Company, was entered into; there were some encouraging subscription checks; and the outlook brightened. Best of all, they found two good subscription solicitors, whom Gayarré describes with a flow of language that demands quotation:

. . . one, a plausible Down-Easter, named Foster; the other a fine specimen of the Louisiana backwoodsman, called Price. Into them Mr. De Bow breathed his own indomitable spirit, and they both started for conquest like two war-steeds. Price scoured plantations on rivers and bayous and in the most retired parts of the country through swamps, morasses, and interminable piney woods. Foster swooped

[9] Rogers (*op. cit.*, p. 24) surmises that the friend was Gayarré himself; but this seems impossible, for Gayarré was at this time a man of established position. It was more likely R. G. Barnwell.
[10] Gayarré, *op. cit.*, p. 500.

over cities and villages, knocking at every door, and, with an address that admitted of no refusal, subdued reluctance, cajoled opposition, warmed up indifference into giving tokens of approbation, and goaded avarice itself into liberality.[11]

With such solicitors in the field, it is no wonder that business picked up. In 1851 Benjamin Franklin De Bow came on from Charleston to assist his brother in the publishing department; of his competence there is some question, for he had poor health and was very deaf. In August 1851 it is noted that the *Review* has set a goal of 5,000 circulation, but is "yet far from it." [12] A few months later the editor notes a large increase. As a matter of fact, the tide had definitely set in toward the *Review*; and though figures are never given, there can be no doubt that it achieved in the early sixties, at $5.00 a year, by far the largest circulation among southern magazines.

Its operating costs were about six thousand dollars a year in the early fifties,[13] and it was soon enabled not only to pay off the debts of those first years before the suspension, but to repay Benefactor White. Advertising was very light and rates low. Twenty dollars a page, with large reductions on contract, represented little income in the fifties; but it was considerably better in the sixties, with half- and full-page advertisements for sewing machines, pianos, machinery, liquors, patent medicines, insurance, and books to the extent of a dozen pages.

From the beginning there had been far more of the South in *De Bow's* than of the West, in spite of the early aims and title of the journal. Nor did circulation spread to the West, though there was a large subscription list of New York business men. In 1853 the West disappeared from the title, which became simply *De Bow's Review*.

Cotton was, of course, a prominent topic. Cotton mills for the South were advocated, but more important was the project to control the cotton market by coöperative selling. The "Florida plan" was a scheme for a holding company with state charters to handle the whole southern cotton crop.[14] There were

---

[11] Gayarré, *op. cit.*, p. 501.
[12] *De Bow's Review*, XI, 225 (August 1851).
[13] *Ibid.*, IX, 578 (November 1850).
[14] *Ibid.*, XI, 497 (November 1854); XII, 123 (February 1852).

other ideas to reduce planting.[15] *De Bow's* looked upon the low price of cotton as the great problem of the South.

Agricultural material is abundant in the file. Rice growing, soils, forestry, and plantation management were subjects discussed in addition to cotton culture. Education was a common topic from the first; and when a department was assigned to that subject in 1855, it chronicled the effort to install the public school system in Georgia and other southern states. Railways, canals, river control, and plank roads also received much attention from the beginning. The various southern commercial conventions were reported in detail in *De Bow's*; the series makes a valuable history of southern thinking on economic problems before the war.

Literature was originally relegated to a very humble place in the *Review*, as has been noted; but in 1850 a literary department was introduced by a poem from the pen of Paul Hamilton Hayne. Thereafter appeared some stories of the southwest border and other localities, poems by Hayne and A. B. Meek, occasional literary criticism, and some travel articles dealing especially with Mexico, Cuba, and South America. Book notices were brief. It must be said that *De Bow's* was never distinguished in literature and that the editor's own taste was far from trustworthy. He was always interested in history and was one of the founders of the Louisiana Historical Society; he published in the *Review* a number of articles on the past of his state and region.

Another department which was outside the original plan for the magazine came eventually to be of great importance; politics entered after the suspension of 1849. De Bow was not much interested in candidacies and elections, but it was not to be expected that he would keep cool in the great intersectional quarrel that was brewing. It was all tied in with his favorite commercial idea: he thought that only industrial activity would

prepare us for this crisis which it needs no seer's eye to see will, in the event, be precipitated upon us by the reckless fanaticism or ignorant zeal of the "cordon of free states" surrounding us on every hand. . . . Before heaven! we have work before us now. Who conducts our commerce, builds for us ships, and navigates them on the high seas? *The*

[15] *Ibid.*, XI, 73 (January 1852).

North! . . . Who supplies the material and the engineers for our railroads, where we have any, and gives to us books and periodicals, newspapers and authors, without any limit or end? *The North!*

After several such rhetorical questions, followed always by the answering blast — *"The North!"* — De Bow proclaims to the South: "Action! *Action!!* ACTION!!! — not in the rhetoric of Congress, but in the busy hum of mechanism, and in the thrifty operations of the hammer and anvil." [16]

Political action soon came to be included in De Bow's creed, however; and he became one of the earliest of the confirmed secessionists. *"The cup of endurance is full!"* he cried in January 1851 and called for a southern convention at once: it "could not endanger the Union unless its further preservation would be a crime." [17] From month to month the *Review* discussed secession and slavery with eloquence and often with passion. It becomes almost a textbook on the southern view of the slavery question; in the historical essay, the theological dissertation, the ethnological argument, the political editorial, in verse, satire, fiction, sermon, the changes are rung on the defense of human slavery.

In 1853 President Pierce appointed De Bow superintendent of the census, and he moved the *Review* with him to Washington and published it there during his four years in office. In those years it contained less of editorial comment and was more national. It printed more articles about nothern commerce than it had used formerly. In 1855 it attempted a division into five departments: literature and miscellany; agriculture; commerce and statistics; mining, manufactures, and internal improvements; and education. The topic of slavery appears to find no place in these categories, but as a matter of fact it found place in all of them. In January 1856 De Bow wrote: "It is our intention to make the *Review* a repository of all the valuable papers that have been prepared on the subject of southern slavery and in vindication of the rights of the South." [18] This he proceeded to do, devoting a large proportion of his pages to the great controversy. In 1860 he promised to keep the matter within limits,[19] but he did not hold to that resolution for long.

[16] *De Bow's Review*, IX, 120 (July 1850).
[17] *Ibid.*, X, 106 (January 1851).   [18] *Ibid.*, XX, 118 (January 1856).
[19] *Ibid.*, XXVIII, 123 (January 1860).

He was president in 1857 of the Knoxville convention, at which
he advocated the reopening of the African slave trade.[20] Two
years later at the Vicksburg convention, the African Labor
Supply Association was organized with De Bow as president.[21]
At this latter meeting De Bow argued that if the Union cramped
southern industry, another government might be better.[22]

Throughout these years, commercial and agricultural statistics, news, and information were not neglected. A series of volumes containing materials from the *Review's* file was published
in the fifties.[23] For a short time early in 1858 *De Bow's Weekly
Press*, "devoted to light literature, politics, and information,"
was issued in New Orleans; but it was a failure. Among the
chief writers for the *Review* were Joel R. Poinsett, J. W. Mon-
ette, Charles Gayarré, C. G. Forshey, Josiah C. Nott, George
Frederick Holmes, M. F. Maury, George Fitzhugh, Edmund
Ruffin, B. B. Minor, Brantz Mayer, James W. Legaré, and D. J.
McCord. There were some portraits on steel, appearing regularly in 1851–53, and occasional woodcuts.

After Harper's Ferry, *De Bow's* was full of talk of secession
and the approaching conflict. In January 1860 George Fitzhugh, well-known Virginia apologist for the slave-labor system,
proposed "disunion within the Union" by a boycott of the
North; but an editorial note expressed the opinion that *"disunion out of it* when the issue comes" would be the better
policy.[24] An article the next month on "The Manufacture of
Arms at the South" began: "In these darksome times it becomes
the South to keep her arms properly burnished and her powder
dry." [25] An essay in praise of war appeared in the next number. In April 1860 came an appeal calling on the South to
secede and form a great empire including Texas, Mexico, Central America, and Cuba.[26] Thus, often wildly and always enthusiastically, the *Review* looked forward to approaching civil
war, though it was more prosperous than ever before, its num-

[20] *Ibid.*, XXIII–XXV, *passim;* XXVII, 205 (August 1859).
[21] *Ibid.*, XXVII, 120 (July 1859).
[22] *Ibid.*, XXVII, 469 (September 1859).
[23] *The Industrial Resources of the Southern and Western States*, three volumes, 1853; *The Southern States Agricultural Miscellanies*, 1857.
[24] *De Bow's Review*, XXVIII, 1–7 (January 1860).
[25] *Ibid.*, XXVIII, 234 (February 1860).
[26] *Ibid.*, XXVIII, 367 (April 1860).

bers were larger, and its subscription lists longer — in fact, "at the very meridian of success." [27]

Secession became a reality, and with it war. De Bow was appointed cotton-purchasing agent for the Confederacy and moved his editorial headquarters to Richmond, while his brother moved the publication office to Charleston. De Bow, Fitzhugh, J. Quitman Moore, and J. H. Thornwell wrote most of the magazine. A department called "The Southern Confederacy" had been instituted in March to publish the documents of the new government. There was now but little emphasis on economics: the *Review* was nearly all politics and literary miscellany. Southern attacks upon the Confederacy for inefficient conduct of the war were stoutly deprecated; [28] southern commerce was shown to have been stimulated by war operations; [29] new Confederate textbooks were advertised. But that signal of distress, the double number, appeared and reappeared, the paper and printing grew steadily worse, and finally there was a quadruple number in August 1862, and then complete suspension. It was explained in this last issue that "more than half of our subscribers are in Texas, Louisiana, Arkansas, and in parts of the other states held by the enemy, and to them, for some time to come, it may be our fate to be voiceless." [30] Voiceless to all was the *Review* from then until after the end of the war, except for a single number in July 1864. This number was issued by Evans & Cogswell, of Columbia, South Carolina, and contained contributions by De Bow, Fitzhugh, John Tyler, Jr., and B. R. Welford, of Virginia; and a Dr. Coleman, of Mississippi.

In January 1866 De Bow revived his *Review* in an "After the War Series" (sometimes called "Revived Series"), at $6.00 a year. He had received his pardon from the President for his part in the Confederacy, had been made president of a projected railway to the west coast to be called the Tennessee & Pacific, and had gone to live in Nashville. It was there that he resumed publication of the *Review*, with offices in New York in care of his brother. Circulation was difficult, but advertising was good. There had been a time when De Bow had refused to take adver-

[27] *De Bow's Review*, XXIX, 400 (September 1860).
[28] *Ibid.*, XXXII, 139–146 (January–February 1862).
[29] *Ibid.*, XXXII, 158 (January–February 1862).
[30] *Ibid.*, XXXIII, 96 (May–August 1862).

tising from "abolitionists," [31] but now it was the advertising of northern firms anxious to enter the "reconstructed" South that filled *De Bow's* at the rate of twenty or thirty pages a month, and, on December 1866, to a total of sixty-seven pages in the one issue.

For *De Bow's*, too, was "reconstructed." It defended, even eulogized, President Johnson, and declared in the first number of the new series that his "policy of reconstruction has worked most admirably so far." [32] Defenses of slavery are over. "The people of the South, universally," we are told, "are willing to give a fair and honest trial to the experiment of negro emancipation." [33] Later there is less optimism about the situation, political action seems hopeless, and De Bow counsels his readers to "abandon all interest in politics" and devote themselves to "the development of the wealth and resources of the country" [34] — the doctrine with which the *Review* started out in 1846.

De Bow's accounts in the After the War Series of his travels through the South are often illuminating. The labor question is discussed *passim*; free Negro labor is found to be useless, and the question is raised whether coolies could be imported from India.[35] Readers made trouble when an article was published in July 1867 advocating acceptance of black equality before the law.[36] There were many articles and two or three series on the history of the war just past, with recollections of hardships both in the field and at home.

But to reëstablish a magazine, difficult enough at any time, is a thirteenth labor of Hercules in a devastated, poverty-stricken country. The last lines which De Bow wrote for his journal were the following:

The expenses of the *Review* are three times what they were in former days! Even the most trifling sums are gratefully received. We know, and make all allowances for, the necessities of the country; but there are numbers who, by a very small effort, or sacrifice, might aid us in this contingency.[37]

[31] *Ibid.*, XXI, 442 (October 1856).
[32] *Ibid.*, After the War Series, I, 25 (January 1866).   [33] *Ibid.*, p. 7.
[34] *Ibid.*, After the War Series, II, 559 (November 1866).
[35] *Ibid.*, After the War Series, I, 224 (February 1866); II, 215 (August 1866).
[36] *Ibid.*, After the War Series, IV, 13 (July 1867).
[37] *Ibid.*, After the War Series, III, 336 (March 1867).

In February 1867 De Bow was summoned to the bedside of his brother, mortally ill at Elizabeth, New Jersey. A cold taken on the journey developed into a pleurisy of which he died a week later; his brother, long business manager of the *Review*, died the next month.

The magazine was continued by Mrs. De Bow for several months, under the editorship of R. G. Barnwell, who had been connected with it almost since its beginning and who had recently been associate editor, and Edwin Q. Bell, a brother-in-law of De Bow and also a long-time member of the staff.[38] In March 1868 William MacCreary Burwell, a writer on economics, bought the journal and became its editor. He moved it to New Orleans again. Claiming for it a circulation of 3,000, he was able to obtain twenty or thirty pages of low-rate advertising a month. But *De Bow's New Orleans Monthly Review*, as it was now called, declined rapidly. There was much on economic topics, edited without much system, but far less commercial and industrial news, statistics, and information than formerly. Reconstruction news was given under the heading "Exodus." In July 1870 the journal was again suspended.

Nine years later it was once more revived, but for only four numbers. These were published in New Orleans by L. Graham & Company, October–December 1879, and June 1880. They were edited by Burwell and were of the same cast as his numbers a decade earlier. At the beginning of 1884 the property, chiefly goodwill, was transferred to the *Agricultural Review*, of New York, which itself perished before the year was out.

The importance of *De Bow's Review* lies in its value as an interpreter of the antebellum South, especially on the economic side. De Bow himself was more talented as a statistician than as a writer or as an economist. His was not an original mind, though it had a certain sweep of imagination. The influence of *De Bow's* on its times is problematical; probably it did something to accelerate the dominant movements. But the file as it now exists in libraries makes accessible masses of information of great value to investigators.

[38] *De Bow's Review*, After the War Series, III, 484 (April–May 1867).

11

THE HOME JOURNAL [1]

NATHANIEL PARKER WILLIS and George Pope Morris had been associated in the publication of the *New York Mirror* and the *New Mirror* [2] before they undertook the publication of the *Home Journal*. The *Mirror* passed to other control in 1845, and on St. Valentine's Day of 1846 the partners founded the *National Press: A Home Journal* in New York. Willis was in England at the moment, but arrived in New York a few weeks after the new paper had been launched. The name proved to be unsatisfactory, carrying no connotation of the special character of the periodical; so nine months later the subtitle alone was run up at the masthead.

Willis was a poet and essayist of established reputation. His light and musical style, his wit, and his habit of gossip made him an entertaining writer for any periodical. He was forty years of age when the *Home Journal* was begun, but he was already old; his health was unreliable, and his important literary work was done. He still wrote as cleverly, however, as in his precocious youth, and he was still the aesthete and the dandy. General Morris was the most popular song writer of his times, author of one oft-parodied poem which is still remembered —

---

[1] TITLES: (1) *The National Press: A Home Journal*, February 14–November 14, 1846; (2) *The Home Journal*, November 21, 1846–March 23, 1901; (3) *Town and Country*, March 30, 1901–current.

FIRST ISSUE: February 14, 1846. Current.

PERIODICITY: Weekly. Annual volumes designated only by year numerals until February 14, 1900, which began Vol. LV.

PUBLISHERS: Morris & Willis, New York, 1846–64; Willis & Phillips, New York, 1864–67; Morris Phillips & Company, New York, 1867–1901; Stuyvesant Company, New York, 1901–current.

EDITORS: George Pope Morris and Nathaniel Parker Willis, 1846–64; Nathaniel Parker Willis and Morris Phillips, 1864–67; Morris Phillips and George Perry, 1867–90; Morris Phillips, 1890–1900; William Frederick Dix, 1900–08; Henry J. Whigham, 1909–35; Henry A. Bull, 1935–current.

REFERENCES: Henry A. Beers, *Nathaniel Parker Willis* (Boston, 1885), Chapter VII; Semicentennial Jubilee Number of *Home Journal*, February 26, 1896; Ninetieth Anniversary Number of *Town and Country*, December 1936.

[2] See Mott, *A History of American Magazines, 1741–1850*, p. 320.

"Woodman, Spare That Tree." He was the business man of the partnership, for Willis never looked inside a ledger.

The new paper was a big folio of four pages, with seven wide columns to the page and no illustrations. In it

> Mr. Willis gives at the moment of prominence in public interest personal sketches of public characters . . . stirring scenes in New York. . . . There are a chronicle of the news for ladies . . . fashions and fashionable gossip . . . the sparkle of theatrical news. . . . It leaves the details of politics and heavier matters to the daily newspapers.[3]

Willis' biographer, in an excellent characterization of the editorial work on the *Home Journal*, says that there Willis set himself "to portray the town":

> He became a sort of Knickerbocker Spectator, and his *Ephemera*, published in book form in 1854, is a running record of the notabilities of New York for a dozen years. He chronicled the operas and theatres: Ole Bull, Jenny Lind, and Macready; the shops, the omnibuses, the endless procession of Broadway, the museum, the art galleries, the Tombs, the Alhambra, the Five Points, the Croton water, the cafés, the hotels, the balls and receptions, the changes in equipages, customs, dress. He grew to be a recognized *arbiter elegantiarum*, and his correspondence columns were crowded with appeals on knotty points of etiquette or costume. . . . He was a skillful paragrapher; he had unfailing tact and knew where to stop. Above all, he was eminently human; his gregariousness and his cheerful philosophy cast a gleam of their own on this looking-glass of urban life. He imported a rural air into the city, watched how April greened the grass in the public squares and June spread the leaves in Trinity churchyard, stopped to pick "a clovertop or an aggravating dandelion 'twixt post-office and city hall." [4]

Willis, as long as he lived, was the chief attraction of the *Home Journal*; though he might not visit the office for weeks· at a stretch, he wrote for the paper regularly and voluminously. When he was forced to make a journey for the sake of his health, he sent in his stint in the form of travel letters. In the late fifties Morris' health failed to such an extent that Willis was forced to give more attention to the details of the work than be-

[3] *Home Journal*, January 1, 1848, p. 1.
[4] Beers, *op. cit.*, p. 288.

fore. He translated French stories and skits for the *Journal*;
he did a series for it called "The Belles of Our Time"; he wrote
a serial story, *Paul Fane*, for it; he republished in it some of his

PORTRAIT CHARGÉ OF GEORGE POPE MORRIS

Vanity Fair (July 12, 1862) draws General Morris, editor of the *Home
Journal* singing his famous lyric, and makes a laborious pun in calling him "The
Bard who best gives Timbre to song."

work that had appeared in old numbers of *Graham's* and in some
of his books.

Besides Willis' work and the news of society and fashions,
there was much miscellany of an entertaining kind in the *Home
Journal*. For a long time there was a department called "Gossip
and News of Parisian Journals," and another of "Returned

Love Letters." In this latter the utterances of the sighing swains and smitten maidens seem so real that one almost has to accept them as genuine: surely nobody could have written them in cold blood. There were many selections borrowed from other journals, and occasionally a pirated English novel — as *Dombey and Son*, issued in monthly supplements in 1848. In the semicentennial number, it was claimed that Irving, Halleck, Paulding, and others were early contributors;[5] but such pieces by famous contributors as appeared in the *Home Journal* were commonly taken from other publications. The *Journal* paid nothing to contributors, except in a few instances. "Grace Greenwood," Mrs. Ellett, Marian M. Pullam, Anne Lynch, and "Barry Gray" probably received compensation. The series of "Popular Songs and Ballads" with music was by Morris. Julia Willis, sister of the editor and a woman of exceptional abilities, wrote many of the literary notices. Edgar Allan Poe "was employed by us, for several months, as critic and sub-editor," says the editor in an obituary sketch. "He was invariably punctual and industrious." [6]

The paper was successful. "The *Home Journal* has become universal," boasted the editors, with large gesture, in 1858. "It is read, we believe, wherever run the gold threads of domestic happiness and true moral refinement, which are woven so thickly into the strong and coarser web of our country's industry and energetic prosperity." [7] In 1852 the proprietors had hired an assistant editor in the person of James Parton, then a young schoolteacher with journalistic aspirations, whose first contribution to any journal had been accepted by Willis and printed with a complimentary foreword which served very well for payment in lieu of cash.[8] Parton served acceptably with pen and scissors for three years, but at the end of that time he quarreled with Willis over the nonacceptance of some work of Sara P. Willis, another sister of the editor. Sara, who had been left a widow by her first husband and a *divorcée* by her second, had turned to literature and was writing some spirited sketches un-

[5] *Home Journal*, February 26, 1896, p. 1.
[6] *Ibid.*, October 20, 1849.
[7] *Ibid.*, January 2, 1858, p. 1.
[8] J. C. Derby, *Fifty Years among Authors, Books and Publishers* (New York, 1884), pp. 221, 222.

der the pen name of "Fanny Fern." She was deeply indignant at her brother's refusal to print her work in the *Home Journal*; and Parton, who quickly yielded to the charm of the vivacious young authoress, took her part, left the *Journal* in a huff, married the offended lady, and later encouraged her to write a novel in which Willis was held up to public contempt.

Parton was succeeded by Thomas Bailey Aldrich, a stripling of nineteen who had already published one volume of poems, written literary notices for the *Evening Mirror*, and perpetrated a saccharine but immensely popular piece of obituary verse called "The Ballad of Babie Bell." Aldrich fitted in well at the *Journal* office, worked hard, and practically ran the paper himself during the invalidism of both proprietors. One day as he sat in the office with his feet on the desk, reading exchanges, he was startled by the unannounced entrance of a tall, handsome stranger, who inquired, "Is this Mr. Aldrich? My name is Willis." [9] Aldrich became interested in the *Saturday Press* [10] a few years later and resigned his position with the *Journal* in 1859. Another young poet, Richard Henry Stoddard, was a loyal disciple of Willis and a frequent contributor to his paper; but it is doubtful if, as has been asserted, he was at any time assistant editor. [11]

The most exciting episode in the early history of the *Home Journal* was its part in the Edwin Forrest divorce proceedings. Only the high lights of it can be recorded here. After Forrest's petition for divorce had been filed in Pennsylvania and its accusations against Mrs. Forrest's character made public, Willis published, April 6, 1850, a signed statement defending her, attacking Forrest's motives, and indignantly protesting against the attempt to "sully her fair name by cheap and easy falsehood, that he can throw her off like a mistress paid up to parting." Forrest retaliated by naming Willis as one of nine corespondents and then personally attacking him in Washington Square, knocking him down and beating him. Forrest was a man of imposing physique, and Willis was almost an invalid. Out of

[9] *Ibid.*, p. 231.
[10] See p. 39.
[11] It is so asserted in the Semicentennial Number, but Stoddard's autobiography, though rich in reminiscences of Willis and the *Home Journal*, mentions no such connection.

this grew an action at law against Forrest, charging assault and battery; a verdict for $2,500 and costs was awarded by the first jury, but the case was sent back for a new trial and the damages reduced to $1.00. Forrest in the meantime sued Willis for libel in the *Home Journal* article and recovered $500 damages. The divorce suits were decided in Mrs. Forrest's favor; and after five appeals, Forrest paid his wife $64,000 in alimony.[12]

It may be conjectured, anent the violence of Washington Square, that it would have been a better fight if Forrest had attacked the senior partner; for General Morris was a robust figure of a man, of whom R. H. Stoddard says: "He had a broad, padded chest and a bulky waist, whose amplitude of girth was encircled by a military belt, which supported the long and dangerous weapon that dangled from it." [13]

Morris died in 1864. Willis thereupon took into partnership the adopted son of his old friend, Morris Phillips, who remained the efficient director of the paper for a third of a century. When Willis died, three years after Morris, Phillips took as partner George Perry, who bought a quarter-interest and was joint editor until his death in 1890.

The *Journal's* circulation had suffered during the Civil War, when it was forced to raise its subscription rate from $2.00 to $3.00; but Phillips reduced it to $2.00 in the seventies, added illustrations, and advertised it as "devoted to art, literature, and society." Still the circulation declined, sticking at about 16,000 through most of the eighties, and dipping to 10,000 in the nineties. The *Home Journal* in these years became one of a considerable class of urban papers, flourishing upon a comparatively small number of rather wealthy subscribers, devoted to society news, art and letters, styles, gossip about amusements, and light essays and verse — all prepared for a more or less local audience. Though the *Journal* was a good paper of this kind, there was nothing distinctively literary about it after Willis' departure from the scene.

At the beginning of the nineties the paper reduced its page

[12] For full accounts of these matters, see Beers, *op. cit.*, and William R. Alger, *Life of Edwin Forrest* (New York, 1875).
[13] R. H. Stoddard, *Recollections* (New York, 1893), p. 87.

from the absurd blanket sheet to an ordinary folio, and added more pages; ten years later it became a quarto. In 1900 it was purchased by William B. Howland; and early the next year, when Howland turned his attention to the *Outlook*, the Stuyvesant Company was organized to take over the *Home Journal*, with J. A. McKay as president. The name was thereupon changed to *Town and Country*; the price was raised first to $3.00, then to $5.00, and finally to $7.50; the illustration and number of pages were increased; and the emphasis was placed strongly upon articles and pictures portraying fine homes in city and country. The circulation soon increased to 20,000 or more. Henry J. Whigham became editor in 1909, and two years later he and Franklin Coe bought the paper. In 1925 W. R. Hearst's International Magazine Company purchased the property, retaining the corporate name, Whigham as editor, and Coe as publisher. Ten years later Henry Adsit Bull became editor and Joseph Bryan III managing editor. The magazine has retained its devotion to fashionable life, the personalities of the Social Register, and fashionable sports and amusements. It is by no means limited to New York, but has correspondents in the leading social centers. Its art director since 1935, Louis-Marie Eude, has given distinction to its make-up and pictures.[14]

[14] See *Time* for December 7, 1936, p. 64.

THE NEW YORK LEDGER [1]

ROBERT BONNER was born in Ireland, near Londonderry, in 1824. He was a lad of fifteen when he came to America to live with an uncle at Hartford and learn the printer's trade in the office of the *Courant*. Five years later he went to New York to read proof and set advertisements in the office of Morris and Willis' *Evening Mirror*. Bonner was a pushing young fellow and soon had a modest print shop of his own. Among the jobs that he did there was the printing of a weekly mercantile paper called the *Merchant's Ledger and Statistical Record*, published by a retired merchant named D. Anson Pratt. It was not a success; and Pratt, after four years of effort, was about to discontinue it at the end of 1850, when Bonner, loath to lose the printing of it, offered to take it off his hands for $900 — the amount of his savings.

Thus the *Merchant's Ledger* changed hands, and gradually it changed character as well. Bonner began to put into it some pieces of fiction and verse and to make it more and more a general family journal. The popular if sentimental poems of Mrs. Sigourney began to appear in it in 1853, with some selected material of a general nature. In 1855 Bonner threw out the price quotations and market news, and even the advertising,

---

[1] TITLES: *The Merchant's Ledger* (subtitles vary), 1847–55; *The New York Ledger*, 1855–98; *The Ledger Monthly*, 1898–1903.

FIRST ISSUE: The earliest issue located is Vol. I, No. 29, dated August 1, 1847; with regular weekly publication, this would place the first issue on January 20, 1847. LAST ISSUE: December 1903.

PERIODICITY: Weekly, 1847–98; monthly, 1898–1903.

PUBLISHERS: D. Anson Pratt and Abram Requa, 1847–50; Robert Bonner, 1851–87; Robert Bonner's Sons, 1887–1901; Ledger Company, 1901–03. All of New York.

EDITORS: D. Anson Pratt, 1847–50; Robert Bonner, 1851–87; Mayo W. Haseltine, 1887–94 (?); Robert E. Bonner, 1894(?)–1901(?).

REFERENCES: Frederic Hudson, *Journalism in the United States from 1690 to 1872* (New York, 1873), Chapter XL; J. C. Derby, *Fifty Years among Authors, Books and Publishers* (New York, 1884), Chapters IX–X; James L. Ford, *The Literary Shop* (New York, 1895), Chapters I–III; George P. Rowell & Company, *Centennial Newspaper Exhibition* (New York, 1876), pp. 225–227.

shortened the name to the *New York Ledger,* and filled the
paper with fiction, moral essays, and verse. What he had in
mind undoubtedly was the achievement of a success like that of
the current *London Journal,* which had reached half a million
circulation by means of the amazing vogue, among clerks,
scullery-maids, and literate coachmen, of the serials of J. F.
Smith.

But Bonner was not content to wait for the slow accretion of
a subscription list; he must make a sensation. He saw his opportunity in the sudden popularity of the work of Sara Willis,
who had become known to all up-to-date readers of the current
prints as "Fanny Fern." Her *Fern Leaves* was a contemporary
best seller. These little essays, *Putnam's Monthly* said,

are acute, crisp, sprightly, knowing, and, though sometimes rude,
evince much genuine and original talent, a keen power of observation,
lively fancy, and humorous, as well as pathetic sensibilities. . . .
There are certain bold, masculine expressions that we should like to
see chastened.[2]

In other words, the fern leaves sometimes looked rather like sour
dock, but they always kept their greenness. The *Democratic
Review,* a severer critic, said in a tone of exasperation, "Fanny
is a charming little humbug. She ought to have married Barnum."[3] But a writer who could be paired with Barnum, even
in this off-hand way, was just the writer Bonner needed. He
brought her, much to her own surprise and the surprise of the
public, into the pages of the *Ledger* by the payment of the
astounding sum of $100 a column.[4]

And into these columns her work continued to flow for many
years. In 1872 she dedicated one of her frequent collections of
sketches (this one called *Folly As It Flies; Hit at*)

To my friend Robert Bonner, Editor of the *New York Ledger.*
For seventeen years, the team of Bonner and Fern, has trotted over
the road at 2.40 pace, without a snap of the harness, or a hitch of the
wheels — Plenty of oats, and a skilful rein, the secret.

[2] *Putnam's Monthly,* I, 103 (July 1853).
[3] *Democratic Review,* XXXIII, 187 (August 1853).
[4] See p. 23.

The extraordinary metaphor of this dedication is explained by Bonner's interest in horses, which, as will be pointed out, developed eventually in a spectacular way.

But this was only a beginning. Early in 1856 Bonner enlisted Sylvanus Cobb, Jr., who had been writing for *Gleason's Pictorial* in Boston. For the *Ledger* Cobb wrote *The Gunmaker of Moscow* and many other prime favorites of romance-hungry but not very discriminating readers. Cobb wrote steadily for the *Ledger* from 1856 until his death in 1887, contributing to it no less than 130 serials, 834 short stories and sketches of adventure, and 2,305 shorter items. Among these were many "forest sketches," and more than 50 "scraps of adventure from An Old Sailor's log-book."[5] "Mr. Bonner," said the *Aldine Press*, "should not treat his readers worse than he does his horses: give them a little more corn and a little less Cobb."[6] But *Ledger* readers apparently liked their Cobb. Bonner also engaged the services of Mrs. Emma D. E. N. Southworth, whose *The Curse of Clifton* had recently made a big hit; and she also continued to write for the *Ledger* for many years, at an honorarium of $10,000 a year.[7]

Having thus recruited a staff of popular writers, Bonner set out to advertise his paper. His advertising made the whole country gasp, and then chuckle, and then rush out to newsstands to buy copies of the *Ledger*. This advertising was of two kinds: iteration copy, in which a single sentence was repeated thousands of times to fill a whole page of small print in the *Herald* or *Tribune*; and the publication of samples of the *Ledger's* wares, such as a chapter from one of Cobb's thrillers.[8] A contemporary historian wrote:

The proprietor of the *Ledger* has paid as high as $27,000 for one week's advertising; he has paid $150,000 in one year; yet, strange to say, not an advertisement is inserted in the *Ledger*, and no money will obtain the insertion of one. He once paid the *Herald* $2000 for a single advertisement. . . .[9]

[5] G. H. Genzmer, in *Dictionary of American Biography*, IV, 246.
[6] *Aldine Press*, III, 26 (March 1870).
[7] *Critic*, XI, 31 (July 16, 1887).
[8] See pp. 15–16.
[9] Hudson, *op. cit.*, p. 649.

Bonner used a certain amount of wit and humor in his advertisements — some of it "dated" and now not so funny. It was the
fashion to laugh at New Jersey, where so many of the com-
muters lived: when the *Ledger* plant was burned out in 1860,
and Bonner farmed out his printing and got the paper out
promptly in spite of his misfortune, he advertised, "Unless we
are burned out more than once a week, the *New York Ledger*
will be ready Monday mornings on all news-stands of the United
States, Sandwich Islands, and New Jersey." This bon mot he
repeated some thousands of times in a big advertisement.

The *Ledger's* success was one of the wonders of the times. In
days when circulations of not ten periodicals in the country
reached 100,000, the *Ledger* leaped far beyond its closest competitor with 400,000.[10] It sold for $2.00 a year — a small folio
of eight five-column pages, well printed in small type.

In spite of the fact that the *Ledger* flourished on "thrillers,"
its stories were never salacious or even improper.

> When I first bought the *Ledger* [said Bonner upon his retirement]
> I pictured to myself an old lady in Westchester with three daughters,
> aged about twenty, sixteen and twelve, respectively. Of an evening
> they come home from a prayer meeting, and not being sleepy, the
> mother takes up the *Ledger* and reads aloud to the girls. From the
> first day I got the *Ledger* to the present time there has never appeared
> one line which the old lady in Westchester County would not like to
> read to her daughters.[11]

The humorist James L. Ford once wrote out the following anecdote to illustrate *Ledger* editorial methods:

> One day a maker of prose and verse received from the hands of the
> great editor a story which he had submitted the week before.
> "If you please," said the poet politely, "I should like to know why
> you cannot use my story, so that I may be guided in the future by
> your preferences."
> "Certainly," replied Mr. Bonner. "This story will not do for me
> because you have in it the marriage of a man with his cousin."
> "But," protested the young author, "cousins do marry in real life
> very often."

[10] See advertisement in *Harper's Weekly*, January 7, 1860.
[11] Quoted in *Current Literature*, I, 196 (September 1888).

"In real life, yes," cried the editor; "but not in the *New York Ledger*!" [12]

If this story is not true, it might well have been. "Real life" and the columns of the *Ledger* were not complete strangers, perhaps; but they were not familiarly acquainted. Innocuous romance, innocuous adventure, innocuous sentiment: such was the *Ledger's* program.

A sample number in the spring of 1859 carried a sentimental poem on the beauty of homeliness on the front page, with a chapter of Mrs. Southworth's *The Hidden Hand* illustrated by a woodcut three columns wide and some four inches deep. Later two or three more woodcuts were used in each number, but for a long time there was only one; the *Ledger* was never notable for its illustration. The serial was carried over to the second page, which also provided some miscellany for children. The third page was introduced by a piece of verse, followed by "leaves" from the moral Mrs. Seaton's journal, a bit of travesty by John G. Saxe, and a chapter from a serial history of Plymouth. Page four was the editorial page. In the number before us "Fortune Telling and Spiritualism" are both condemned rather pleasantly; the value of patience is extolled in a piece called "Watch and Wait," and "grand parties" are rejected in favor of simpler entertainments. Page five is dominated by one of Edward Everett's "Mount Vernon Papers," which is followed by verses by Alice Cary and a moral essay by Mrs. Ritchie. Then comes Chapter I of Cobb's famous "Gunmaker," which runs over to occupy all of the next page as well. Page seven is made up in the typical *Ledger* manner, with a poem in fine print in the upper left-hand corner; then the final installment of another Cobb romance, with its last column (the fourth on the page) filled out by one of the ballads of George P. Morris. This leaves a column for some mildly amusing "Wit and Wisdom." The last page has its poem, a short story of adventure, and two columns of "Notices to Correspondents."

In later years there were more short stories and less nonfiction. But the serials were always the great attraction of the paper. The columns on the last page containing the answers to

---

[12] Ford, *op. cit.*, p. 13.

correspondents were an interesting feature. In the main they were devoted to that old journalistic artifice — advice to the lovelorn. For example:

J. D. F. — If you have engaged yourself to a young lady unknown to your parents and they object, we can only say, had you referred the question to them before this took place, you might not have had to refer it to us.

LONG BEARD AND PHELIX. — We imagine our opinion on "the propriety of their kissing" would make but very little difference to a pair of lovers. If you choose to pick all the plums out of your cake before Christmas, don't expect to relish it on that anniversary.[13]

Bonner made capital out of capturing big names and then advertising them. "Fanny Fern" was the first; she was followed by Edward Everett, a figure of great dignity and prestige, who was obtained by an appeal to his devotion to the Mount Vernon project.[14] General Grant's father wrote a life of his son for the *Ledger*, and Horace Greeley wrote his autobiographical papers for it. Henry Ward Beecher wrote his novel *Norwood* for Bonner, who paid him well in the time of Beecher's need.[15] William Cullen Bryant, Henry W. Longfellow, George Bancroft, and Harriet Beecher Stowe succumbed to golden temptation, together with "the presidents of the twelve chief colleges of the United States," and the "twelve leading clergymen" of the country. "The influence which Mr. Robert Bonner possesses with eminent men is something miraculous," said *Vanity Fair*, in referring to the promise of articles from President Buchanan's pen as soon as he should leave the White House.[16] The secret of Bonner's influence was simple, however: it lay in a willingness to spend money for names. Having conceived the idea of getting articles from the three great newspaper editors of the period — Greeley, Bennett, and Raymond — Bonner obtained the articles and then astonished his public by printing all three in the same issue. Of course he advertised his coup lavishly.

Dickens and Tennyson were English authors represented.

[13] *Ledger*, March 12, 1859, p. 8.
[14] See p. 23.
[15] See p. 24.
[16] *Vanity Fair*, II, 207 (October 27, 1860).

John Bigelow said proudly and emphatically to his London friends in 1860 that the *Ledger*

paid literary men of the first class better than they were paid anywhere else; by its vast circulation it brought the brains of the highest and lowest intellectual strata into contact and sympathy, and, as an illustration of this, had published within a month a better poem than had appeared in the British press in the previous thirty years.[17]

But these headliners were only headliners; the *Ledger* continued to rely on Cobb and Southworth and their kind for its popularity. Bonner's authors were, in the main, third or fourth rate. They were men and women who, in the words of the forgotten J. R. Dennett, are now remembered as forgotten. John S. C. Abbott, Emerson Bennett, T. S. Arthur, and F. A. Durivage were prominent among them. George D. Prentice, famous editor-poet of the time, conducted the paper's column of wit and humor from 1867 until his death in 1870.

The *Ledger* office was burned in 1860. "Never," said *Vanity Fair* unkindly, "was the *Ledger* so brilliant and sparkling" as on that occasion.[18] Shortly afterward Bonner erected a marble building on the corner of Spruce and William streets to house his paper. His wealth increased. The *Ledger's* newsstand sales alone ran to 350,000.[19] Always fond of horseflesh, Bonner began buying fine race horses; but when he bought one he would always retire it from track competition, because he did not believe in racing for stakes. What he liked to do best was to drive a race in competition with Commodore Vanderbilt on a fine country road. He became the owner of such world-famous horses as Dexter, Maude S., Rarus, Pocahontas, and Peerless, and at one time had over a quarter of a million dollars invested in his stables.[20]

Bonner retired in 1887, the year of Sylvanus Cobb's death, turning the *Ledger* over to his three sons. By this time the paper had already begun to decline. Its writers in the nineties were, for the most part, unknowns. Eben E. Rexford was a regular

[17] John Bigelow, *Retrospections of an Active Life* (New York, 1909), I, 265. The poem referred to was Bryant's "The Cloud on the Way."

[18] *Vanity Fair*, I, 107 (February 11, 1860).

[19] Hudson, *op. cit.*, p. 654.

[20] Derby, *op. cit.*, p. 206.

contributor, and Margaret Deland had a serial in the paper in 1898; but the *Ledger* had become just another cheap paper. Its competitors, taking advantage of advertising offered by mail-order concerns, outdistanced it.

In 1898 it was made a fifty-cent monthly, under the title of the *Ledger Monthly*. Robert E. Bonner had been editor for several years. It was now a magazine much like the early *Ladies' Home Journal*, with various family departments. In 1902 it was sold to a stock company and reduced to a smaller quarto size, but it survived the change only one year.

THE CHURCH REVIEW [1]

OF THE several reviews that have owed allegiance to the Protestant Episcopal church in America, the *Church Review* appears to have had the greatest vitality and the most distinguished career. A checkered career it was, to be sure, for it was published under five variations of title; it was at various times quarterly, bimonthly, and monthly; and it was most erratic in its arrangement in volumes. But it had for its contributors all the great men of its church in America, as well as prominent laymen in the fields of letters, law, science, philosophy, and education.[2] Among leading contributors of literary criticism were the poets Arthur Cleveland Coxe (Bishop Coxe after 1865) and Clement C. Moore, of whose single-poem fame we are reminded annually. Francis L. Hawks, orator, antiquary, journalist of experience, and church historian, was

[1] TITLES: (1) *The Church Review and Ecclesiastical Register*, 1848–April 1858, April–October 1889; (2) *The American Quarterly Church Review and Ecclesiastical Register*, July 1858–January 1870; (3) *The American Quarterly Church Review*, April 1870–October 1871; (4) *The American Church Review*, 1872–April 1885; (5) *The Church Review*, July 1885–January 1889, 1890–91. FIRST ISSUE: April 1848. LAST ISSUE: October 1891.
PERIODICITY: Quarterly, 1848–78, 1881–82, October 1884–April 1886, 1889–91; bimonthly, 1879–80, July 1886–1888; monthly, 1883–March 1884. I–XIII, annual volumes, April 1848–January 1861; XIV, April, July 1861, January, July 1862 (omits October 1861; April, October 1862; January 1863); XV–XXII, annual volumes, April 1863–January 1871; XXIII, April, July, October 1871; XXIV–XXXII, annual volumes, 1872–80; XXXIII–XL, quarterly volumes, 1881–82; XLI–XLII, semiannual volumes, 1883; XLIII, January, February, March 1884; XLIV, October 1884 (omits April–September 1884); XLV–LII, semiannual volumes, 1885–88; LIII–LXIII, quarterly volumes, April 1889–91 (omits LXI–LXII, April, July 1891).
PUBLISHERS: George B. Bassett, New Haven, 1848–59; George Tuttle, New Haven, 1859–61; N. S. Richardson, New York, 1861–68; John M. Leavitt, New York, 1868–71; M. H. Mallory, New York, 1872–74; Edward B. Boggs, New York, 1875–80; James Pott, New York, 1881; American Church Review Press, New York, 1881–91; Macmillan Company, New York, 1891.
EDITORS: Nathaniel Smith Richardson, 1848–68; John McDowell Leavitt, 1868–71; M. H. Mallory, 1872–74; Edward B. Boggs, 1875–80; Henry Mason Baum, 1881–91.
INDEXED in *Poole's*.
[2] Lists of contributors may be found in VII, 642 (January 1855), and LIII, 3 (April 1889). Authors' names were not printed with their articles until 1874.

a leading contributor for several years. Bishops Hopkins, Doane, Whittingham, Henshaw, Potter, and Kip were prominent in the *Review's* pages; most of the leading bishops throughout almost a half-century were represented. Though religion and theology held the foremost place in the tables of contents, literature, education, and social questions gave variety and scope. A literary paper found place in nearly every number, and book reviews dealing with general literature were not neglected.

The founder and first editor, N. S. Richardson, had polemical tendencies. His statement of aims and principles in the first number (April 1848) had such a bellicose ring that he was constrained to add in the second that the *Review* had "no wish to wage religious controversy." The position of the journal was generally upon the right: in it "the conservative part of the church spoke." [3] Richardson was editor and owner for twenty years, moving the quarterly from New Haven, its first home, to New York in 1861.

John M. Leavitt bought the *Review* in 1868. He had been trained in law, but had taken church orders in the year the *Review* was founded; he was later to establish the *International Review*.[4] He kept the *Church Review* for only three years and a half, and then passed it on to M. H. Mallory, who was editor and owner for an even shorter period. Edward B. Boggs followed with an undistinguished editorship of six years, during which the journal was made a bimonthly; and then Henry Mason Baum gained control of it. Baum brought it again to a position commanding respect. In 1883 an episcopal circular commending it was signed by all the bishops of the church.

At the head of our current literature [runs the circular] stands the *Church Review*. During the last few years and under its current editorship, it has won a deservedly high place in the country. It is as comprehensive in its tone as the Church itself. All the schools of thought that may lawfully claim recognition are welcome in its pages. The most vital questions of the day have been discussed by it with dignity, learning, and commanding ability.[5]

[3] Julius H. Ward in William Stevens Perry, *History of the American Episcopal Church* (Boston, 1885), II, 62.
[4] See Volume III, Chapter II.   [5] *Church Review*, LIII, Preface, p. 2.

The *Review* was criticized, however, for presenting "all sides" of the questions it discussed instead of taking positive positions.[6]

In 1889 Baum engaged in an unusual experiment in magazine making. For two years he issued the quarterly numbers each as a separate volume bound in cloth or paper; the series of books was designed to form nuclei of parish libraries all over the country. An editorial committee was organized, composed of representatives of all the church's theological seminaries. The plan was not a financial success, however, excellent as the numbers were; and after a brief suspension in 1891, the Macmillan Company experimented with one number, then abandoned it.

During its first forty years the *Church Review* was said to have lost $100,000, much of which was made up to the owners by friends who believed the journal to be a valuable asset to the church.[7] But when the efforts of Baum failed to give it financial independence, thumbs were turned down.

[6] *Ibid.*, XLII, 307 (October 1883). N. S. Richardson, former editor and owner, was one of the critics.
[7] *Ibid.*, LIII, Preface, p. 3.

14

THE INDEPENDENT [1]

D URING the 1840's no little dissatisfaction developed among Congregationalists over the workings of the old "Plan of Union" between Presbyterian and Congregational churches in the West. Originally conceived merely as an economy in missionary activity, it had resulted in turning most of the western societies into the Presbyterian fold. When the seriousness of this situation was grasped by the Congregationalists, efforts followed to establish churches of their own outside of New England. For example, the Broadway Tabernacle was changed from Presbyterian to Congregational auspi-

[1] TITLE: *The Independent.* Subtitles: (1) *and the Weekly Review*, October 1921–April 1922; (2) *A Fortnightly Journal of Information and Discussion*, May 1922–August 16, 1924; (3) *A Fortnightly Journal of Free Opinion*, August 30–September 13, 1924; (4) *A Weekly Journal of Free Opinion*, September 27, 1924–October 13, 1928.

FIRST ISSUE: December 7, 1848. LAST ISSUE: October 13, 1928.

PERIODICITY: Weekly, except May 27, 1922–September 13, 1924, when it was fortnightly. I, December 1848–1849; II–LV, 1850–1903, annual volumes; LVI–LXXIV, 1904–June 1913, semiannual volumes; LXXV–CIV, July 1913–1920, quarterly volumes; CV, January–June 1921; CVI–CVII, July–December 1921, quarterly volumes; CVIII–CXXI, 1922–October 13, 1928, semiannual volumes. Omissions: October 11, 18, 25, November 22, 1919; July 2, 16, 30, August 13, 27, September 10, 1921. Last volume incomplete with 16 numbers.

PUBLISHERS: Henry Chandler Bowen, Theodore McNamee, Jonathan Hunt, Seth B. Hunt, and Simeon Chittenden, New York, 1848–96; Clarence W. Bowen, New York, 1896–1912; Independent Corporation, New York (Hamilton Holt, president, 1912–14; Karl V. S. Howland, president, 1914–20; Wesley W. Ferrin, president, 1920–21), 1913–21; Weekly Review Corporation, New York (Fabian Franklin, president), 1921–24; Independent Publications, Inc., Boston ("owned by its editors." — CXIV, 570), 1924–28.

EDITORS: Leonard Bacon, Joseph P. Thompson, Richard S. Storrs, 1848–61; Henry Ward Beecher, 1861–63; Theodore Tilton, 1863–70; Henry Chandler Bowen, 1870–96; William Hayes Ward, 1896–1914; Hamilton Holt, 1914–20; Harold DeWolf Fuller (with Fabian Franklin, October–December 1921), 1921–24; Richard Ely Danielson and Christian A. Herter, 1924–28.

INDEXES: *Poole's, Readers' Guide, Cumulative Index, Dramatic Index, Annual Library Index.*

REFERENCES: Sixtieth Anniversary Number of *Independent*, December 10, 1908; Lyman Abbott, *Henry Ward Beecher* (Boston, 1903), Chapter XIV; Benjamin W. Bacon, *Leonard Bacon* (New Haven, 1931), Chapters IX, XI–XIV, XVI.

ces, with Joseph P. Thompson as minister; the Church of the Pilgrims was set up in Brooklyn, with Richard S. Storrs in charge; and Plymouth Church was built and Henry Ward Beecher called to it from western Presbyterianism. But these out-of-New-England churches had no periodical organ, and Thompson and Storrs felt this lack keenly. Their feeling was shared by Henry C. Bowen, of the firm of Bowen & McNamee, wholesale dealers in silks, who had been the leader in founding Plymouth Church.

Out of these circumstances sprang the *Independent*. Bowen & McNamee, with three other merchants of similar church affiliations, advanced the capital; while Thompson and Storrs, joining with them Leonard ·Bacon, pastor of the First Church at New Haven and a foremost Congregationalist, became editors. Bacon once stated the purpose of the *Independent* as being "to establish the right of Congregationalists to remain so beyond the Byram River" [2] — which approximates the southernmost boundary between Connecticut and New York — and this remained a major purpose for more than a decade. But there was a second purpose. Thompson, when he was trying to persuade Bacon to join in the enterprise, wrote to him, "We are all free-soilers"; [3] and antislavery was a second principle on which the *Independent* was founded.

It was a weekly "religious newspaper" which Bowen and his associates founded. The "religious newspaper" was a type of publication which flourished in America from the second to the eighth decades, [4] and in some cases a little later; it printed denominational and other "religious intelligence," but its miscellany and editorial discussions were, on the whole, more important than its news. The *Independent* began as a big four-page folio, with eight wide columns on each page, selling at $2.00 a year. The first page was occupied chiefly by miscellany of a religious cast, the second page by editorials and news, the third by news and advertising, and the fourth by advertising.

Bowen, having chosen his editors and agreed to pay each of them $100 a quarter, kept his hands off the editorial policy.

---

[2] Bacon, *op. cit.*, p. 470.
[3] *Ibid.*, p. 306.
[4] See Mott, *A History of American Magazines, 1741–1850*, p. 136.

Bacon, greatest of the triumvirate in prestige, was called the "senior editor"; but Thompson was the most active and far the most consistent contributor.[5] Bacon seldom came to New York, though he kept in touch with the office and with Thompson by correspondence. Storrs, the orator and debater, was scarcely a journalist. Henry Ward Beecher, pastor of Bowen's church, was thoroughly a journalist; and he soon became a regular contributor. His work was all signed, not with his name or initials, but with an asterisk: that signature quickly became known, and Beecher came to be called the "star contributor." But the managing editor, whom Bowen paid $1,000 a year and who laid out the issues and selected the material, was Joshua Leavitt, former editor of the *Evangelist* and the *Emancipator* and one of the organizers of the Free Soil party.

"We wish to be, in the highest sense, an independent journal," said an editorial in the first issue. But independents who renounce the adventitious aids which organizations give to principles offend not only those who oppose the principles but the organizations that support them, and the *Independent* soon felt itself considerably kicked about. "The Democratic journals abhor us," said an editorial in 1851. The reason was, of course, the *Independent's* opposition to slavery. "The Whigs count us reprobates," continued the editorial: this was because of the paper's enmity against the fugitive slave law. And even "the Free Soil party regard us as entirely unreliable," on account of the editors' rejection of party ties. The tale of woe goes on:

Old School friends distrust our orthodoxy. . . . New School brothers . . . find us sometimes veering toward the Old School side. . . . Yet the circulation of the *Independent* has been from the first continually increasing.[6]

It did not increase very fast, however, for several years; the public had to catch up with it. Its extreme position with regard to the fugitive slave law almost wrecked it in its second year: it advised not only noncompliance with the law by antislavery men, but armed resistance to it by the fugitives themselves.

[5] *Independent*, LXV, 1359 (January 10, 1908).
[6] *Ibid.*, V, 42 (March 17, 1853).

When the great Castle Garden peace meeting in New York was called in 1850, Bowen & McNamee refused to list themselves among the five thousand merchants who signed the call. The motive of the signers was frankly commercial; New York was protecting its southern trade by aligning itself against abolition and with the law. Bowen & McNamee, wholesale silk, with a large southern business, were denounced in the New York *Journal of Commerce* for refusing to sign the call, and they thereupon inserted in the *Herald* of October 28 the following "Card":

> The public, including the New York *Journal of Commerce*, are informed that we are silk merchants, and keep an extensive and well-assorted stock of goods which we offer to responsible buyers on reasonable terms. As individuals we entertain our own views on the various religious, moral, and political questions of the day, which we are neither afraid nor ashamed to declare on all proper occasions. But we wish it distinctly understood that our goods and not our principles are in the market. The attempt to punish us as merchants for the exercise of our liberty as citizens we leave to the judgment of the community.
>
> BOWEN & MCNAMEE.

Standing by their guns lost the proprietors of the *Independent* about half their subscription list of 6,000, but it brought them some 5,000 new subscribers; so they gained by the transaction.[7] But Simeon Chittenden, one of the paper's backers, was frightened by the incident, withdrew, and at once published a statement denying sympathy with abolition; and Bowen & McNamee soon bought out the Hunt brothers, who had a half-interest. In this latter transaction the *Independent* was valued at $6,000, which was exactly three-fourths of the average yearly deficit.[8] Bowen & McNamee were now sole owners of a losing property, and their silk business was declining. But they kept stubbornly on.

The *Independent* welcomed *Uncle Tom's Cabin* with enthusiasm and immediately made Mrs. Stowe a leading contributor. When the Nebraska bill was passed, it urged antislavery men

---

[7] Bacon, *op. cit.*, p. 343.
[8] *Independent*, LXV, 1380 (January 10, 1908).

to emigrate to the contested territory and help make free states. Beecher's articles against slavery were powerful. In the meantime, the *Independent* accomplished one of its great objectives when the Albany conference of 1852 embarked Congregationalism upon a church-building program in the West. It supported Horace Bushnell during his trial for heresy; and it was active both in the attack upon the American Tract Society for its failure to take a stand against slavery, and in that upon the American Board for its toleration of slavery in connection with missions.

The paper claimed 10,000 circulation on January 1, 1852, 22,000 by the end of 1855, and 25,000 a year later. In 1854 it was enlarged to eight pages. By the beginning of the war it had at last reached a paying basis, with over 35,000 subscribers. But Bowen & McNamee had in the meantime failed in their silk business in the panic of 1857; and when the opening of the war shut off the possibility of collections in the South, they were forced into a second bankruptcy. To save the *Independent*, now a valuable property, they assigned it to Bowen's father-in-law, Lewis Tappan, before the crash. This disposal of the paper angered the editors, and they all resigned. Tappan had been critical of certain phases of the paper's editorial policy; and, moreover, though they had no financial standing in the management, the editors felt they had a moral interest in it and should have been consulted about the change in ownership. Leavitt remained, however.

Tappan's control was only nominal and temporary. Bowen soon found a temerarious and unknown investor who put him on his feet again, and the *Independent* was launched upon its second phase, and its great success.

Henry Ward Beecher was made editor. His star editorials had already made him popular with the paper's growing audience; he was a famous man and continually in the public eye; and his emotional nature, functioning always along the lines of popular sentiment, made him almost a national idol. He did comparatively little work on the paper, for he could not tie himself down to a desk; but that little was important. His assistant editor was Theodore Tilton, a young poet and lecturer and a brilliant writer, who paid his chief the homage of imitation.

Tilton had already been on the staff for several years, and he now wrote many of the editorials and came increasingly to direct the paper's policy. Leavitt was retired to the department of religious news; and Oliver Johnson, one of the founders of Garrison's antislavery society, and long an assistant editor of the *Liberator*, became "office editor."

The *Independent* gradually forgot its championship of Congregationalism under this new management; in his salutatory, Beecher said that it would stand for "vital godliness rather than sectarianism." [9] But the state of the country called for political and secular editorials, and Tilton had little interest in religious matters; thus the paper lost its strong religious fervor. The war was on, and the *Independent* was heart and soul in the midst of it. Beecher was very impatient with President Lincoln; for the man whom he was later to eulogize in an eloquent funeral sermon he had now but scant respect:

> Certainly neither Mr. Lincoln nor his cabinet have proved leaders. Fear was stronger than faith! And never was a time when men's prayers so fervently asked God for a Leader! He has refused our petition! . . . Not a spark of genius has he; not an element for leadership. Not one particle of heroic enthusiasm.[10]

And throughout his editorship Beecher kept pounding away at the President to emancipate the slaves, and emancipate them at once.

When Beecher was sent to England in 1863 to speak for the Union to English audiences, he willingly surrendered the editorial chair to his assistant. Tilton's name did not appear as editor until two years later, but he and Johnson ran the paper after September 1863. Circulation had fallen off for a year or two at the beginning of the war; but now, with the war tide running in favor of the Union, with Beecher's "Star Papers" still a feature, and with the strong staff of contributors that Tilton had built up, it rapidly ascended to around 75,000. Advertising was abundant; Bowen was sometimes criticized for allowing it to encroach on the reading matter, and also for accepting questionable patent medicine copy.

[9] *Independent*, December 19, 1861.
[10] *Ibid.*, August 7, 1862.

In some respects Tilton was an excellent editor. He wrote brilliantly, but floridly and with too much use of personalities.[11] He was clever rather than profound, and he liked controversy. "Tilton is his name and tilting his profession," said *Vanity Fair*.[12] With slavery a dead issue, he took up woman suffrage to make it the favorite reform of the paper: He gathered a fine group of contributors — Whittier, Lowell, Greeley, Taylor, Garrison, Phillips, Mrs. Browning, Kossuth. Mrs. Stowe's *Pearl of Orr's Island* appeared serially in 1861–62.

But "a religious article in its columns is an accident," complained the *Round Table* in 1865,[13] and the *Springfield Republican* said the paper was edited by "infidels and Unitarians." [14] But though Johnson was a Unitarian, Tilton was not quite an infidel: once when his faith was questioned, he printed the Sermon on the Mount as his religious creed.

Tilton was a vigorous opponent of Andrew Johnson's policies. When Beecher wrote his famous Cleveland convention letter, aligning himself with some of those policies as endorsed by the soldiers' and sailors' meeting in that city, Tilton wrote:

With profound surprise and grief we have read Mr. Beecher's letter. . . . No man's notives are purer . . . an unhappy blindness. . . . He has done more injury to the American republic than has been done by any other citizen except Andrew Johnson.[15]

Not only did the *Independent* thereupon set up a running editorial criticism of Beecher's position, but it stopped printing the Beecher sermons. In retaliation, Beecher stopped furnishing not only the sermons but also the "Star Papers," which had long been a leading *Independent* feature — a series of moral essays signed by Beecher's asterisk. When Tilton demanded that he continue the "Star Papers" according to contract, Beecher refused on the ground that the contract had been broken by the paper's action in regard to the sermons, and he

[11] See Eugene Benson's brilliant analysis of Tilton's journalistic qualities, *Galaxy*, VIII, 255 (September 1869).

[12] *Vanity Fair*, I, 215 (March 31, 1859).

[13] *Round Table*, December 23, 1865.

[14] Quoted by George Ripley, who was an anonymous contributor to the *Independent*, in a letter to his sister, February 12, 1867. O. B. Frothingham, *George Ripley* (Boston, 1883), p. 255.

[15] *Independent*, September 6, 1866.

had no wish to renew it. A few years later the *Christian Union* was started as Beecher's own organ.

Meanwhile Bowen, the publisher, grew less and less pleased with the erratic course of his editor. The *Watchman and Reflector* thus taunted him in 1868:

> The publisher of the *Independent* finds himself powerless to control his own paper. . . . It is painful to contemplate the fall of the *Independent*. A year ago some of the leading Congregational minds at the West had strong hopes of at least saving it to evangelical religion.[16]

The "leading Congregational minds" that participated in this interesting incident of religious journalism — "seven learned doctors," the *Evangelist* called them — were Edward Beecher, T. M. Post, A. L. Chapin, J. M. Sturtevant, John P. Gulliver, G. F. Magoun, and S. C. Bartlett. They were truly the western leaders of Congregationalism. They met in Chicago in December 1867, and after two days of what an amused and unregenerate critic referred to as "a solemn inquest on the soul of the *Independent*," [17] they received Bowen's pledge to make his paper a champion of evangelical religion. But he could not do it with Tilton as editor. At the end of 1870, Tilton therefore retired, saying frankly but in good spirit that he did so because of differences in opinion on political, social, and religious questions.[18] This forced retirement of Tilton was probably connected with charges of immorality against the young editor; at any rate it was quickly followed by countercharges which involved Beecher, and which eventually were aired in the most famous of scandalous American trials.[19]

After Tilton's resignation, Bowen himself became both editor and publisher and remained so until his death in 1896. Edward Eggleston was managing editor for a year or two and was then succeeded by William Hayes Ward, who retained the position until Bowen's death, after which he became editor-in-chief. Samuel T. Spear succeeded Johnson as associate editor, remaining with the paper until his death twenty years later.

[16] *Watchman and Reflector*, December 24, 1868.

[17] Frederic Hudson, *Journalism in the United States from 1690 to 1872* (New York, 1873), p. 299. The Chicago *Advance* was started a little later; see Volume III, Chapter III.

[18] *Independent*, December 22, 1870.

[19] See the various lives of Beecher, and Bacon, *op. cit.*, Chapter XVI.

In 1870 the paper was at its high point of circulation. It claimed an advertising patronage three times that of any other religious newspaper and more than that of any secular paper, number for number.[20] From November 1868 through 1871 it had printed the famous blanket sheet of nine columns, giving twelve pages and offering a monthly "illustrated edition" adorned with large sentimental woodcuts. These big sheets were furnished uncut, and many readers who thought them too sacred to mutilate by trimming found that in order to get at the inside pages it was necessary to lay the sheet down in the middle of the floor of a good-sized room to fold the pages back. Subscribers complained that Congregationalists were becoming differentiated from people of other faiths by their long arms, a peculiarity superinduced by holding out the *Independent* for reading. So, after reviewing these manifold tribulations caused by the blanket sheet, the *Independent* changed in 1872 to a thirty-two page, four-column illustrated quarto. The example had been set it by Beecher's *Christian Union*. With this change to a more magazinish form came a corresponding change in content. The paper had been growing somewhat more literary; Justin McCarthy had been "literary editor" in 1868–69. In the latter year Bowen had boasted:

The *Independent* is the only religious newspaper in the country that can employ the best talent on a large scale. Other papers now and then have a good writer, but our columns are filled weekly with the most popular names known, and at a cost which would sink any other journal.[21]

It sounds like ballyhoo, but it is substantially fact. Moreover, while the paper maintained its literary standing after 1870, it renewed its religious flavor. Washington Gladden joined the staff as "religious editor," to remain for five years.[22]

Then into this atmosphere of high hopes and fine prospects stalked the specter of unbelievable scandal and discord. In the Beecher-Tilton imbroglio, Bowen took sides against Beecher. He withdrew his membership in Plymouth Church, and he engaged the *Independent* in the ugly quarrel. It may be said that

[20] *Independent*, LXV, 1383 (January 10, 1908).
[21] *Ibid.*, LXV, 1382 (January 10, 1908).
[22] See Washington Gladden, *Recollections* (Boston, 1909), Chapters XII–XVI.

nearly everybody who participated in that most painful of defamatory orgies suffered, and the *Independent* was no exception: by 1877 its circulation was down to 15,000. Then, in the eighties, as it was beginning to regain some of its lost ground, came the Andover troubles in the Congregational church, with the accompanying heresy trials. Bowen, while still proposing the paper as undenominational, had given it about the same Congregational character it had held before the war; and, his feelings being strongly enlisted with the heresy-hunters, he aligned the *Independent* on the orthodox side. "For seven years this conflict lasted," writes William Hayes Ward, who was Bowen's assistant from 1868 on, "and Mr. Bowen cared more for his view of truth than for the interests of the *Independent*, and many who had been its progressive friends left it and went elsewhere." [23]

But in spite of these handicaps to circulation growth, which kept the paper down to less than a third of the subscription list it had enjoyed in the sixties, the *Independent* maintained an important position among American periodicals. It was one of a very small group of religious papers to hold a comparatively general audience in a period which saw most such periodicals degenerate into denominational news letters. Its departments of religious news were strong (and now interdenominational); but it also gave attention to general events and to questions of the day discussed by well-known writers, such as Theodore L. Cuyler, Helen Hunt Jackson, William Winter, Presidents Eliot and Gilman, George William Curtis, Cardinal Gibbons, W. E. Gladstone. It supported the Republican candidates for president at each election, except in that of 1884. Then Bowen was noncommittal, Twining was for Cleveland, and Spears favored Blaine; accordingly, Bowen did not allow the paper to favor either candidate, but gave his sub-editors leave each to lambast the opposition — and both did so vigorously. The paper was highly departmentalized: it had sections devoted to science, the fine arts, music, education, Sunday school, farm and garden, and literature. A department for the children occupied two or three pages. Literary editors in the seventies and eighties were Titus M. Coan, Professors C. F. Richardson and C. H. Toy, Kinsley

BEECHER AMONG SYMPATHIZING FRIENDS

The *Police Gazette* published this picture, and explained: "Reference to the scandal causes the gushing pastor, Beecher, to weep.—His lady-members come to the rescue and soothe the old dominie in his tearful trouble."

Twining, and Maurice Thompson. In poetry the journal became notable. Bryant, Longfellow, Holmes, Stoddard, Stedman, Taylor, Gilder, Aldrich, Harte, Hovey, Riley, Joaquin Miller, Emily Dickinson, Lucy Larcom, the Cary sisters, "H. H.," Celia Thaxter — the roll of *Independent* contributors reads like a list of the chief poets of the time, which it is. Sidney Lanier found here his most cordial market; "Sunrise," sometimes considered his masterpiece, was published in the *Independent* with sixteen other poems of his at various times. Hayne, too, appeared frequently. English poets represented, besides Mrs. Browning, were Tennyson, Kingsley, Jean Ingelow, Swinburne, Lang, Dobson, Gosse, Locker, and Stevenson. In 1885 the *Independent* printed 241 poems, and in 1886, 226.

Bowen died in 1896 at the age of eighty-two, vigorous to the last. Ward, his successor as editor, and Clarence W. Bowen, his son and his successor as publisher, carried on along the same lines for two years; then they made the journal an octavo of a more secular cast. It kept its annual review of progress in the various denominations, written by an authority from each; but once more the *Independent* had dropped its emphasis on religious matters. Each issue now began with a "Survey of the World"; and there were articles on current problems by competent men and women, some fiction, and a little illustration. This latter feature increased, especially after 1902. Politically the paper maintained its Republican affiliation through the nineties. It opposed Bryan strongly, and its editorial about the McKinley victory in 1896 began, "Praise the Lord!" [24] But partisanship in the editorial columns grew less marked, and from the campaign of 1900 on, the *Independent* made a practice of printing statements by all the candidates shortly before the election. The journal was, however, wholly committed to the policy of "expansion" and "taking up the white man's burden." Two new reforms were added to the list of the *Independent's* historic "causes" — one of minor and the other of major importance. The minor reform was that of simplified spelling, which was adopted both in theory and practice. The other was that of a league of nations, which the journal early

[24] *Ibid.*, November 5, 1896.

espoused: it sent an editorial correspondent to the Hague Conference of 1899.

But the journal did not thrive, and in 1913 it was sold to a new company of which Hamilton Holt, a grandson of H. C. Bowen, and managing editor since 1897, was president; in the following year Holt succeeded Ward as editor, and Karl V. S. Howland became president of the publishing company. The form was changed to a small quarto, and illustration became abundant. There were many articles by prominent statesmen and officials: Taft contributed a series on governmental questions shortly after his retirement from the presidency. Three prominent periodicals were absorbed in these years — the *Chautauquan* on June 1, 1914; *Harper's Weekly*, May 22, 1916; *Countryside* (founded as *Suburban Life*), January 1, 1917. Edwin E. Slosson was an associate editor from 1903 to 1921 and contributed many attractive scientific features. Howard J. Howland was an associate editor 1913–20. The circulation went to 60,000 in three years after the 1913 change in management. During the war the paper printed many pictures of the conflict, somewhat in the manner *Harper's Weekly* might have employed; and Holt was its European correspondent.

The *Independent* played an important part in the development of American sentiment in favor of the League of Nations. Holt himself was, as the contrary-minded *Nation* observed, "filled with a passion for the League of Nations surpassed by that of no one else." [25] He had printed in 1914 a disarmament plan which he described five years later as "the first attempt in the United States after the war broke out and as far as we know anywhere to formulate in concrete detail the basic principles of a League of Nations." [26] That editorial led to the formation of the League to Enforce Peace, which created an undoubtedly effective propaganda. It was about a year after Holt published his plan that President Wilson espoused its main features. The *Independent* supported the Wilson covenant ardently and opposed Harding in 1920 on that issue.

The printers' strike caused the *Independent* to miss several issues in 1919. The rising paper and labor costs were embar-

---

[25] *Nation*, CXIII, 366 (October 5, 1921).
[26] *Independent*, XCVIII, 235 (May 17, 1919).

rassing. For a time in 1920–21 Wesley W. Ferrin was president
of the publishing company, and an editorial board consisting
of Franklin H. Giddings, Norman Hapgood, Shailer Mathews,
E. E. Slosson, Talcott Williams, and John Spargo had charge.
But this was too unwieldy. In October 1921 the journal was
sold to Fabian Franklin and Harold DeWolf Fuller, editors
and publishers of the *Weekly Review,* which was thereupon
consolidated with the older paper. The *Review* was a conservative journal, founded largely to combat the *New Republic* and
Nation and such liberals. Now the paper which had opposed
Harding in 1920 because of his opposition to the League of
Nations supported his administration with vigor. It opposed
the Volstead laws; it fought "radicalism." But it was very
wobbly financially in 1921, missing some issues; and in May
1922 it became a fortnightly.

In February 1924 the *Independent* changed hands again,
passing to Richard Ely Danielson and Christian A. Herter,
who moved it in April to Boston. Herter had been in the diplomatic service and later had served as assistant to Herbert
Hoover, then Secretary of Commerce. The new editors signed
a statement declaring themselves "earnest seekers after truth,"
and saying that "contributions should meet the criteria of significance, intelligence, and sincerity." But their high ideals
were destined to failure; although they published a journal of
genuine importance, it was doomed. In October 1928 it was
merged in the *Outlook,* whose name was now changed to the
Outlook and Independent. This was the paper which Beecher
had started in 1870 as the *Christian Union.*[27] For many years
it had paralleled the *Independent* in various phases, and the
union of these two journals of high character and noble history
seemed fitting and proper.

[27] See Volume III, sketch 16.

15

THE MERCERSBURG REVIEW [1]

THE periodical latterly called the *Reformed Church Review*, but in the palmy days of theological controversy known as the *Mercersburg Review*, was begun in 1849 to champion the views dubbed, after the name of the theological seminary which gave them currency, "the Mercersburg theology." Philip Schaff, who afterward won a place as perhaps the foremost of American church historians, had a few years before been summoned from Germany to succeed F. A. Rauch, the founder and first president of Marshall College, at Mercersburg, as a teacher of theology. Here he joined forces with John W. Nevin and others in propounding views which strongly emphasized the historical basis of Christianity. The chief object of attack on the part of objectors was the Mercersburg belief that

[1] TITLES: (1) *The Mercersburg Review*, 1849–52, 1857–78; (2) *The Mercersburg Quarterly Review*, 1853–56; (3) *The Reformed Quarterly Review*, 1879–96; (4) *The Reformed Church Review*, 1897–1926. Subtitle, 1862–68: *An Organ for Christological, Historical and Positive Theology.*

FIRST ISSUE: January 1849. LAST ISSUE: October 1926.

PERIODICITY: Bimonthly, 1849–52; quarterly, 1853–1926. Suspended 1862–66. Annual volumes. New Series, 1867–78, I–XII (whole numbers, XIV–XXV; N. s. numbers on covers only); New Series, 1879–96, I–XVIII (whole numbers XXVI–XLIII; N. s. numbers on covers only); Fourth Series, 1897–1921, I–XXV [whole numbers, XLIV–LXVIII]; Fifth Series, 1922–26, I–V [whole numbers, LXIX–LXXIII].

PUBLISHERS: Alumni of Marshall College, Mercersburg, Pennsylvania, 1849–52; Alumni of Marshall College (after 1855, Franklin and Marshall College), Chambersburg, Pennsylvania, 1853–58; George B. Russell (for Alumni), Pittsburgh, 1859–61; S. R. Fisher & Company, Philadelphia, 1867–68; Reformed Church Publishing Board, Philadelphia and Lancaster, 1869–1926.

EDITORS: J. W. Nevin, 1849–52; Theodore Apple, 1853–56; E. V. Gerhart and Philip Schaff, 1857–61; H. Harbaugh, 1867; T. G. Apple, 1868–96 (with E. E. Higbee, 1875–78; John M. Titzell, 1883–96; William Rupp, 1893–96); William Rupp, 1897–1904; George W. Richards, 1904–12 (with John S. Stahr, 1905–12); Theodore F. Herman, 1912–26 (with John S. Stahr, 1912–16); George W. Richards, 1918–26.

REFERENCES: "The New Review," *Reformed Church Review*, Fifth Series, I, 1 (January 1922); David S. Schaff, *Life of Philip Schaff* (New York, 1897).

INDEXES: General index for 1849–70 in XVIII (1871); general index for 1849–1911 issued as number for October 1911 (Fourth Series, XIV); general index for 1912–20 in Fourth Series, XXIV (1920). Also in *Poole's.*

the history of the Christian church shows Protestantism to be a historical link rather than a final form.

The *Mercersburg Review* saw "theology as a living process in the life of the church." It had, in the period before its suspension during the war, "no strictly denominational character," [2] though the ministry of the Reformed Church was especially invited to contribute. The three adjectives *Christological, historical*, and *positive* (or *churchly*) are used repeatedly, and for a time in a subtitle, to state the *Review's* aims. It never had any quarrel with science or history; it accepted the doctrines of evolution; and it boasted that it was "never the organ of the cloister or the oracle of a cult." [3]

In its early days the *Review* was filled with the noise of the battle. It was conducted, to use the words of one of its chief opponents, Orestes A. Brownson, "with spirit, learning and ability," and Brownson goes on to pay it a high if egotistical compliment: he asserts that it is "almost the only direct opponent we have ever had that we did not feel it a sort of degradation to meet." [4] The editor who revived the *Review* after the war spoke rather quaintly of this conflict so earnestly engaged in as "those somewhat impatient, if not carnal, polemics, which, during the first theological panic, were waged against what was by its enemies, with unfriendly intent, baptized as Mercersburg theology." [5] Along with this warfare of defense was an attack on the rationalism that came in from Germany.

The *Review* was founded by the alumni of Marshall College and for some years edited by a committee of that organization. But the editors-in-chief were in the main the professors of systematic theology and the presidents of the seminary, first at Mercersburg, and then at Lancaster. The periodical began with 100 subscribers, "a Moses' rod stretched over a sea of doubt." With a circulation of 300 it was self-sustaining, and for nearly half a century it kept on with no more than 500 subscribers. During its early years the *Review* published some poetry, some familiar essays (chiefly by its first editor, J. W. Nevin), and

---

[2] *Mercersburg Review*, I, 8 (January 1849)
[3] *Reformed Church Review*, Fifth Series, I, 2 (January 1922).
[4] *Brownson's Quarterly Review*, New Series, IV, 191 (April 1850).
[5] *Mercersburg Review*, XIV, 6 (January 1867).

some comment on politics. It was against antislavery agitation, as its location would lead one to expect, saying as late as April 1861: "The less the people of the North meddle with the system in the way of political agitation and uncharitable abuse, the sooner this desirable end [the 'civilization' and conversion of Negroes] will be reached."[6] But in the next issue the editor had a strong war editorial establishing, upon a historical basis, the sovereignty of the Union.

Forced to suspend during the war, the *Review* was resumed in 1867 by T. G. Apple. It was less fresh and attractive than it had been before, Dr. Apple's ideas of the "scientific and classical form of a theological review" being a little severe; but its tendency was more conciliatory, and it was a strong influence toward the basis of agreement presented in 1881 to the Reformed Church by the Peace Commission, of which Dr. Apple was a member. The name "*Mercersburg*" was dropped as too reminiscent of polemics (the *Review* was now published at Lancaster anyway) and the title now became the *Reformed Quarterly Review*, later the *Reformed Church Review*.

In the Fourth Series, started in 1897, there was more sociological and economic writing, and the circulation was considerably increased. The Fifth Series, started in 1922, was published under an endowment which was withdrawn four years later, and the magazine ended.

[6] *Mercersburg Review*, XIII, 317 (April 1861).

16

HARPER'S MONTHLY MAGAZINE [1]

IF WE were asked why we first started a monthly magazine, we would have to say frankly that it was as a tender to our business," Fletcher Harper once confessed.[2] The four Harper brothers had built up one of the largest publishing houses in the world. Its prosperity had been founded largely upon cheap reprints of English fiction, *Harper's Library of Select Novels* reaching a total of 615 volumes; but its business by 1850 was widely diversified, with an emphasis upon English novels, travel and exploration, school books, and history and biography. The idea behind the establishment of the magazine was that the wealth of contemporary English literature might well be presented in periodical form, together with a few pages of announcements of Harper books in an advertising section. In *Harper's Family Library*, with its monthly issues, the house had been approaching the idea of a periodical; but the *New Monthly* was to be a complete magazine — eclectic, to be sure, but a magazine with departments and variety. The advertising section was an important part of the plan; and in spite of the tempting offers from outside advertisers which were received

[1] TITLES: (1) *Harper's New Monthly Magazine*, 1850–1900; *Harper's Monthly Magazine*, 1900–current. Cover and half title 1925–current: *Harper's Magazine*. FIRST ISSUE: June 1850. Current. PERIODICITY: Monthly. Semiannual volumes. Vol. LXII (December 1880–May 1881) is Vol. I of the English edition. PUBLISHERS: Harper & Brothers, New York. EDITORS: Henry J. Raymond, 1850–56; Alfred H. Guernsey, 1856–69; Henry Mills Alden, 1869–1919; Thomas B. Wells, 1919–31; Lee Foster Hartman, 1931–current. INDEXES: General indexes, each cumulative to date, were published in 1870, 1875, 1886, and 1893. Also indexed in *Poole's, Readers' Guide, Poole's Abridged, Annual Library Index, Cumulative Index, Jones' Index, A. L. A. Portrait Index, Dramatic Index*. REFERENCES: J. H. Harper, *The House of Harper* (New York, 1912); Algernon Tassin, *The Magazine in America* (New York, 1916), Chapter X; H. M. Alden, "Fifty Years of Harper's Magazine," *Harper's*, CI, 947 (May 1900); H. M. Alden, "An Anniversary Retrospect," *Harper's*, CXXI, 38 (June 1910); Henry Seidel Canby, *Harper's Magazine — A National Institution* (New York, 1925); A. R. Hyde, *The Story of Harper's Magazine* (New York, 1931).
[2] Harper, *op. cit.*, p. 84.

later when the magazine gained a large circulation, this section was reserved strictly for Harper Brothers until the bars came down in the eighties.[3] "The intimacy between the magazine and the book-publishing department, never wholly broken, was closest in the first score of years after the establishment of the former," wrote Editor Alden fifty years later.[4]

The first number of *Harper's New Monthly Magazine* appeared in June 1850. It consisted of 144 octavo pages printed in small type in double columns on a good paper stock, enclosed in a light buff cover designed in imitation of the English *Bentley's*. The price was $3.00 a year. Two serials were begun: Charles Lever's historical romance, *Maurice Tiernay, Soldier of Fortune*, and Mrs. Anne Marsh's *Lettice Arnold*. There were three short stories, two of them by Dickens — one of his lesser-known Christmas tales and "A Child's Dream of a Star." There were biographical sketches, some travel essays, and popular articles on science — in all over sixty items, long and short, in great variety of subject matter. The periodicals most levied upon for this material were *Household Words*, *Bentley's*, the *Ladies' Companion*, and the *Dublin University Magazine*. Three departments appeared — a "Monthly Record of Current Events," giving an uncolored résumé of the happenings of the preceding month; "Literary Notices," giving brief announcements of new books; and two pages of fashions.[5] The only illustrations were three portraits of historians and five woodcuts of styles — all eight in the back of the book.

In "A Word at the Start" the publishers said:

The magazine will transfer to its pages as rapidly as they may be issued all the continuous tales of Dickens, Bulwer, Croly, Lever, Warren, and other distinguished contributors to British Periodicals. . . . The design is . . . to place within the reach of the great mass of the American people the unbounded treasures of the Periodical Literature of the present day.[6]

"Transfer" is probably the most delicious euphemism in all the apologetics of literary piracy. There can be no doubt that

[3] See Volume III, Chapter I.
[4] *Harper's Monthly*, CI, 947 (May 1900).
[5] A brief fashion department was carried until 1865.
[6] *Harper's Monthly*, I, 1 (June 1850).

A SATIRE ON THE HARPER "PIRACIES"

Henry L. Stephens drew this lively picture for *Punchinello*, which published it November 12, 1870. It shows a scene on the upper deck of "the piratical rover, *Harpy*," which has sighted the good ship *Author*, carrying a rich cargo. Thereupon the pirates make sure that everything to be seen above the gunwales should be sweetness and light, while the bloodthirsty villains hide by cowering low on the deck. Fletcher Harper commands them all, while George William Curtis, mounted on his "Easy Chair," plays a sweet air on the violin.

the Harpers, honorable men and good Methodists as they were, meant to take these "unbounded treasures" from the British periodicals without so much as a thank-you, precisely as they had pirated hundreds of novels for their various Libraries. But practical ethics are based upon custom; and it must be remembered that both English and American publishers in 1850, in the absence of any international copyright agreement, appropriated whatever they could use in transatlantic literary goods quite without scruple. It was a waste of breath for the jealous *Whig Review* to cry out at *Harper's*, "It is stealing!" [7] It was merely business.

Yet the outcry raised against the Harper piracies, by rivals and by disappointed American writers, may have had some effect; or there may have been a gradual awakening of the combined Harper mind to the fact that behind these "unbounded treasures" from overseas there were human beings who could do with a small share of profits. At any rate, when Dickens' *Bleak House* began its course through the magazine in 1852, newspapers announced that its author was being paid liberally for its use in the magazine and in book form. This custom grew year by year, until by the latter fifties, most of the serials were being paid for in the form of a price for the "advance sheets." These early proofs gave the purchaser a priority and a right which was usually recognized as "courtesy of the trade." The serials published in early volumes of *Harper's* were Dickens' *Bleak House* and *Little Dorrit*, Thackeray's *Newcomes* and *Virginians*, Bulwer's *My Novel*, George Eliot's *Romola*, as well as less-remembered novels by Trollope, Lever, Mrs. Craik, and others. Doubtless most of these, after the first three or four volumes of the magazine, were paid for through the purchase of advance sheets: we have the testimony of the Harpers that they paid $2,000 each for *Little Dorrit* and *The Virginians*.[8] In 1876 Joseph W. Harper stated that his house had paid a quarter of a million dollars to English publishers and authors for advance sheets.[9] In considering these prices, however, it must be remembered that they were paid for book rights as well as serialization.

[7] *American Whig Review*, XVI, 17 (July 1852).
[8] Harper, *op. cit.*, p. 115.   [9] *Ibid.*, p. 383.

The extra-legal "courtesy of the trade" rules did not always work. The following notice appeared at the top of the editorial columns of *Harper's Weekly* through several issues late in 1857:

Mr. Thackeray's new story, *The Virginians*, with many humorous illustrations by the author, is commenced in the December number of *Harper's Magazine*. It is printed from early sheets received from the author in advance of publication in England; for which the publishers pay Mr. Thackeray the sum of two thousand dollars. With the full knowledge of this arrangement, the proprietors of the *New York Tribune*, who have been leading advocates of an international Copyright Law, and profess the warmest regard for the interests of British authors in this country, have begun *to copy this story from our Magazine* into their paper. . . . The same parties, under the same circumstances, reprinted upon us Mr. Dickens' *Little Dorrit*, for which we paid the author two thousand dollars for early sheets of a foreign work which is instantly reprinted upon him by a rival in business. The course of the *Tribune* is therefore decidedly calculated to deprive the British author of the only compensation he can get in the present state of the Copyright Law.[10]

The *Tribune* replied with the sophistical defense that it did not reprint from *Harper's* but from the English periodical in which the story was appearing, whereupon *Harper's* laid a trap by changing a few words in the next installment and found that the *Tribune* followed the changes instead of adhering to the English version.[11] We should feel more sympathetic with the Harpers in their attempt to keep the expensive path of virtue did we not read in *Every Saturday* a few years later an accusation against them almost identical with their indictment of the *Tribune*; this time *Every Saturday* had paid for Charles Reade's *A Terrible Temptation*, and *Harper's Weekly* was reprinting it.[12] Osgood tried to get *Edwin Drood* for *Every Saturday*, but Harper got it and paid for it; nevertheless, *Every Saturday* printed it, too. Tit for tat.

There is no mystery in the preference for English literature

[10] Reprinted in Harper, *op. cit.*, p. 115.
[11] *Frank Leslie's Illustrated Newspaper* (V, 6, December 5, 1857) refuses to sympathize with the Harpers in this matter, because, it says, they had ruined Greeley's partner McElrath by pirating Dickens' *Hard Times* when McElrath had paid $1,500 for advance sheets of it.
[12] *Every Saturday*, Second Series, III, 19 (July 1, 1871).

shown by the Harpers. English literature had made their fortune. It was the day of the great popular English novelists. To say, as has been said repeatedly by apologists for *Harper's Monthly*,[13] that in 1850 America had "few eminent names" in literature is misleading. Emerson, Hawthorne, Melville, Longfellow, and Lowell were in their prime; *The Scarlet Letter* and *Representative Men* appeared in 1850, and *The Conspiracy of Pontiac* and *The House of Seven Gables* in 1851. But the point is that America had no great popular novelists like Dickens and Thackeray, proved and sure and profitable. Dickens, Thackeray, Bulwer, and Trollope were good business.

This policy laid the Harpers open to abuse on patriotic grounds, and their rivals made the most of the chauvinistic argument.

> *Harper's* is a good foreign magazine [said *Graham's*]. But no man can long continue to read John Bull's self-glorification without saying to himself, "Well, this is all right about Nelson, and Wellington and Bulwer and Southey, but what is Brother Jonathan about? What says the leading American magazine about the American flag, and Yankee Doodle, and Home Literature?" . . . The veriest worshiper of the dust of Europe will tire of the dead level of silly praise of John Bull upon every page.[14]

And letters of American authors are full of expressions of resentment against a policy which excluded them from Harper pages and money.

Harper's Monthly did not remain wholly eclectic, however. For the first year the names of the English magazines from which its articles were taken were printed conspicuously at the head of each; then these credit lines were suppressed. Enemies of the magazine said this made its thefts all the more heinous, but it also betokened a resolution to haul down the pirate's black flag and classify the magazine no longer as a mere eclectic. Non-English material crept it. Benson J. Lossing's articles on American places and American history were printed from 1851 on; a few American articles by Jacob Abbott appeared, with short stories by Caroline Chesebrough as early as 1852

---

[13] See Harper, *op. cit.*, p. 86; Canby, *op. cit.*, p. 3; Hyde, *op. cit.*, p. 3.
[14] *Graham's Magazine*, XXXVIII, 280 (March 1851).

and by Fitz-James O'Brien from 1853; and Strother's "Porte Crayon" articles came after 1853, and so on — scarcely enough to leaven the loaf for a decade or two, but a slowly growing infusion of Americanism.

The magazine's departments, originally not especially American, gradually came to be very much so. To the original three departments, a few pages called "Leaves from Punch" were added in the second volume, but they gave way in a year or two to original comic drawings. "The Editor's Drawer," *Harper's* famous department of humor, began in the third volume — the outcome, we are told, of certain foregatherings of Methodist preachers at the home of Fletcher Harper, where the guests were prone to tell good after-dinner anecdotes. When an especially good one convulsed the group, Harper would ask the narrator to write it out and put it in a certain drawer of his desk at the office: thence the name.[15] Lewis Gaylord Clarke, long editor of the *Knickerbocker* and conductor of its capital "Editor's Table," was the first editor of the "Drawer"; but one evening in 1854, presumably at such a gathering of the cloth as has been described, the Reverend S. Irenæus Prime, editor of a religious newspaper in New York called the *Observer*, objected to certain profanity and "matter not in the highest degree delicate" which had crept in, and Prime himself was made editor on the spot.[16] The "Drawer's" jokes were not always true to the name of its editor, however: "More melancholy reading than the facetiae of the 'Editor's Drawer' we have not often lighted upon," said the *Nation* once, and added the reflection that "the composition of such jokes must be an awful drain on any man's vitality." [17] This is one of the stories from the current issue that the critic had just been reading:

> During the early part of 1863, while the Union forces were before Charleston, a Union officer had a domestic parrot. The bird was kept near the trenches, and had learned from two negroes on the island to say, "O Lord! O Lord!" One day a stray shot wounded the poor bird, and it fluttered over to the enemy's works, crying, "O Lord! O Lord!" and breathed out its life with these earnest words.[18]

[15] Harper, *op. cit.*, p. 34.   [16] *Ibid.*, pp. 34–35.
[17] *Nation*, I, 316 (September 7, 1865).
[18] *Harper's Monthly*, XXXI, 538 (September 1865).

Nevertheless, "The Editor's Drawer" was a popular feature, with its odd anecdotes and Methodistic piety.

The best of the early departments, however, was the "Editor's Easy Chair," begun in 1851 and filled at first chiefly by Donald G. Mitchell, who had achieved fame the year before with his *Reveries of a Bachelor*. In 1853 George William Curtis joined Mitchell in writing the department, though he was also at the same time an associate editor of the rival *Putnam's*; and in 1859 Curtis settled into the Chair alone. For forty years Curtis made this section of *Harper's* the most delightful department in an American periodical.

It was the chief product of Mr. Curtis' pen [writes his biographer]; it was wrought in the pure literary spirit and was, as much as the work of any prose-writer of his time, literature. . . . There is something slightly pathetic and wholly beautiful in his spirit toward this curious *clientele*. It is absolutely free from any taint or suspicion of condescension. . . . Poetry, art, music, letters, the higher politics, take their place naturally beside social satire and reminiscence and anecdote.[19]

One other department was the "Editor's Table," also begun in 1851, to run for nearly twelve years. It was a repository for miscellaneous short pieces commenting on social matters of the day in a light manner. It was written by Tayler Lewis and A. A. Lipscomb, with a few pieces by Samuel Osgood, E. P. Whipple, and Theodore Sedgwick.

But the largest contribution to the early *Harper's*, next to the serials, was by an American about a Frenchman — the Reverend John S. C. Abbott's *History of Napoleon Bonaparte*. It was a stupendous serial, running through Volumes Three to Ten, inclusive. It took the French rather than the English view of the great commander, making him a very perfect hero. The "Napoleon Romance," as the *New York Post* was in the habit of calling it, though the product of laborious research, and an undoubted success with the magazine's readers in general, aroused vigorous dissent among the better informed; but when *Harper's* publishers tried to get the biographer to tone down his eulogies of the great Corsican, they met with complete rout.[20]

[19] Edward Cary, *George William Curtis* (Boston, 1894, American Men of Letters Series), pp. 322–325.   [20] See Introduction to this volume.

The Napoleon serial gained much of its appeal from the woodcuts which illustrated it. *Harper's* went on from those few pictures in the back of the first number to an extent of illustration that had theretofore been unknown in magazines. The increase was gradual through 1851–52; a common feature to lead off a number became the illustrated poem from older English literature — Gray's "Elegy," or something of the kind, taken from a Harper book. Later one or two travel articles would be illustrated, together with the "Napoleon." By 1861 there was fairly adequate illustration; though compared with the copious picturization of the magazine in the nineties, these early volumes, which so amazed contemporary readers by lavish use of woodcuts, were bare indeed. Some fifty cuts, including large and small, came to be the ratio per number in the later fifties.[21] The two pages of fashions were carried until 1865.

John Chapin was the early art editor, and pictures were drawn by Hoppin, Bellew, Darley, and others. Very passable wood engraving was done by John Andrew, James H. Richardson, Bobbett & Hooper, and N. Orr & Company. Lossing illustrated his own early pieces, Thackeray's original drawings went with some of his serials, and Daniel H. Strother's travel articles were accompanied by his own pictures. These Strother pieces, written and illustrated under the name of "Porte Crayon," were deservedly popular. They dealt first with Strother's native South, but later their crayon was carried to the West. Another artist-author was T. Addison Richards, who worked chiefly in New York and New England, with occasional excursions southward.

Many attempts have been made to explain *Harper's* phenomenal success in the fifties, but no such effort can be convincing which does not take into consideration the various elements just pointed out. It was the combination of popular English serials, variety of miscellany, the emotionally stirring Napoleon serial, and the unusual amount of illustration — all in a magazine of 144 closely packed pages instead of the customary 80 or 96 — which scored the greatest success in magazine history up to that time.

[21] See *Harper's Magazine*, XXXII, 11 (December 1865), where it is claimed that in the first fifteen and a half years the magazine published 10,000 cuts, at a cost of $300,000 for the drawing and engraving.

Starting with an edition of 7,500, within six months the magazine reached 50,000. Thence the circulation went up to around 200,000 by the beginning of the war — an unprecedented circulation for a three-dollar magazine. Its rivals, who paid it the compliment of abusing it, freely admitted its prosperity. "Probably no magazine in the world was ever so popular or so profitable," said *Putnam's*.[22] "There is not a village, there is scarcely a township in the land into which your work has not penetrated," said "An American Writer" in addressing a censorious "Letter to the Publishers of *Harper's Magazine*" in the pages of the *Whig Review*.[23] *Graham's Magazine* commented upon the unfriendly remark of an Ohio newspaper to the effect that *Harper's* was "a grand failure" as follows:

As to *Harper's* being a grand failure with 135,000 copies, it reminds us of the Dutchman's ruin when his barn was burned down but was insured for twice the amount. He delivered himself as follows: "Mr. Inshurance, I been ruined mit dis parn." "Ruined!" exclaimed the man of risks, "Why, haven't you got the money now in your hand?" "Oh, yaw! put money iss not de hay!" *Harper's* is not the hay — that is, it is not an original magazine, as it should have been, coming from the leading house in the trade, in facilities — but it is money! [24]

During these early years of *Harper's,* and indeed for its first quarter-century, the real editor of the magazine was Fletcher Harper. Until a year or two before his death in 1877, he personally attended to the larger questions of policy and many of the details of management. Curtis wrote of Fletcher Harper's magazine policy that he was "anxious above all that it should be popular in a high and generous sense. . . . He had in view 'the people,' 'the plain people,' and not philosophers and poets." [25] This was the key to which *Harper's* was pitched throughout at least its first half-century: it was the great successful middle-class magazine.

Working with Fletcher Harper was Henry J. Raymond, the first managing editor. How much time Raymond gave to the magazine is problematical. The *Whig Review* said he was paid

[22] *Putnam's Monthly*, IX, 293 (March 1857).
[23] *American Whig Review*, XVI, 12 (July 1852).
[24] *Graham's Magazine*, XLIII, 554 (November 1853).
[25] Harper, *op. cit.*, p. 405.

$100 a month "for pasting the 'Summary' into the *New Monthly*," and hinted that the publishers merely wanted his influence against the international copyright movement [26] — doubtless a base imputation. Raymond was an editor of the *Courier and Enquirer* in 1850, and the next year he organized the *New York Times*, of which he became editor. In 1856 he resigned from *Harper's* and was succeeded by Alfred H. Guernsey. Guernsey was a Hebrew scholar who had worked up in the Harper organization from compositor's stool to editor's chair. He had been doing "rewrite" work on the magazine since its first volume. "He possessed," says the historian of the house, "the exceptional ability to make a readable article of eight to twelve pages out of a two-volume historical or biographical work." [27]

The Civil War was a fiery ordeal for *Harper's,* as for many other magazines. It had eschewed all partisan and controversial questions and had managed to keep clear of the slavery debate and to hold its southern patronage until the military operations had set up an actual blockade. *Harper's,* said *De Bow's Review*, speaking for the South, was "more unexceptionable on the subject of slavery than any northern work of similar kind." [28] The Harpers were Democrats, but their magazine was earnestly nonpartisan. It was anything but a "journal of opinion," except when an opinion was almost universally acceptable. Indeed its pacific and agreeable spirit was one of the qualities most criticized by its enemies: "Every month it made its courtly bow; and, with bent head and unimpeachable toilet, whispered smoothly, 'No offence, I hope.' " [29] But this policy helped to build a big circulation in the South, as in all sections and in all parties. Then came the war, slicing off that southern list at one blow of the sword. The magazine continued without marked partisanship. Lossing's serial history of the War of 1812 was a concession to the martial spirit of the country, and later there were many sketches of life in camp. The "Monthly Record" dispassionately set down events, Brownell's "The Bay Fight"

[26] *American Whig Review*, XVI, 16 (July 1852).
[27] Harper, *op. cit.*, p. 158.
[28] *De Bow's Review*, X, 492 (April 1851).
[29] *Putnam's Monthly*, IX, 294 (March 1857).

painted its vivid picture, and there were a few other military and naval items; but as a rule *Harper's* was not very warlike. Its circulation during the war went down alarmingly; war prices forced an increase of the yearly price to $4.00; "the shrinkage of the subscription list was so great that Fletcher Harper seriously considered the advisability of terminating its publication." [30]

But just as English serials had made *Harper's* prosperity in the first place, so they renewed it now. In December 1864 the magazine began to print Wilkie Collins' *Armadale*; and from the very first installment of this story the old popularity began to flow back "until before the story was completed, the magazine had reached its former circulation." [31] Doubtless some of the credit for this new success belongs to Dickens' *Our Mutual Friend*, which was also running its course through *Harper's* in 1865. Many other English serials followed, most of them now forgotten, by Mrs. Craik, Justin McCarthy, Anthony Trollope, Miss Thackeray, R. D. Blackmore, William Black, and Thomas Hardy. And shortly after the war two serials by an American writer were published: the fortunate author was William M. Baker ("George F. Harrington"), whose *Inside, A Chronicle of Secession* had made a sensational hit in *Harper's Weekly*. But his two stories in the *Monthly* were less successful; and, with the single exception of Julian Hawthorne's *Garth* in 1874, no other American broke the succession of English fiction serials until the eighties.

But there were many American short stories in *Harper's*; indeed, after the middle fifties most of the magazine's short story writers were American. True, Charles Reade, protesting the while that "to write small stories is the small game" finan-cially,[32] furnished several; and Justin McCarthy accepted and filled a wholesale order for forty-five during his extensive first visit to America;[33] but the great bulk of them were American in authorship and scene. It would be pleasant to be able to say that these American short stories were all fresh and vital and

[30] Harper, *op. cit.*, p. 233.
[31] *Ibid.*
[32] *Ibid.*, p. 161.
[33] *Ibid.*, p. 224.

significant, but the sad fact is that a large proportion of them were sentimental balderdash. The reader of a series of them, written by T. S. Arthur, Jane G. Austin, Kate J. Neely, and D. R. Castleton, is driven to sympathize with the *Nation's* outburst against the characters in the *Harper* tales in 1866:

Where else may we look for the wondrous young gentlemen and ladies who love each other, and fill *Harper's* with a constancy that reminds us of Rochefoucauld's remark on that quality — that constancy is a fact, not a virtue? It would be pleasant to meet some of those Belles and Perditas and Helens and Lilies whom their relatives, we are told, call homely, but who have a way of putting a simple rose in their hair and walking off with the most eligible young gentlemen; whose father fails in business and leaves Margaret to keep school and a journal, from which latter we perceive that the writer is consciously unconscious of possessing all the virtues. Marcias are pretty common too: "As they drew near I noticed that Marcia had left off her deep mourning. She wore black silk, and looked regal in it." But her elegant figure and becoming dress do not prevent her dying with a moan on her lips for James Harris. It might not be so pleasant to meet the various males of this species — Howard, with the patch on his boot, and the grave, sweet smile, is apt to be priggish; Trehune has an artist nature and great means, but this is his way of talking to Margaret when he presses her hand and says goodnight, as the two return from a ball: "Whatsoever your hands find to do, do it with your might, and blossom into success as the rose blossoms, by natural impulsion, instead of grappling fortune by the throat and crying 'Stand and deliver!' like a highwayman." He gets his leg broken, though. . . . Then there is Hugh, . . . and Arthur, who has a misunderstanding with Ellery, and goes and gets himself made a colonel in the army, and by and by is shot in the shoulder at the head of his men, and, after "all the rest was a blank" opens his eyes upon the white face of Ellery, who is speechless with gratitude. She had shut her grief in her proud heart, and had gone to Washington as a nurse, where she casually heard of a mortally wounded colonel, and her heart told her it might be Arthur. This month we have a dozen or more of this sort of persons in half a dozen stories. It is difficult to say just what frame of mind the reading of them is apt to create. We can conceive that young people of unhardened hearts, and Henry Kingsley, might, after a steady perusal of these tales, find themselves in a state of what you may call toploftiness — going off in a gush of moral nobility on any little provocation, and delighting to martyrize themselves in a painted flame of self-sacrifice. It would tend, too, to marriages on a limited income, we should say, and preferably to marriages with artists and poets and persons with curly hair. It would not be true to say that these thousand and one tales have nothing good in them. Unless one's nature abhors a vacuum, there is not much fault to be found with them, and that in itself is something. Sometimes they are well enough written; but, as a general thing their nature is to run to this sort of writing (Gibraltar is to be described): "A huge lion, godhewn out of the solid rock, lying ever with its face turned to that land of mystic lore — the wonderful East — guards the narrow portal that leads thitherward." [34]

But while sentimentality and self-consciousness left their trail across much of the short fiction in the early *Harper's*, a considerable group of writers, increasing toward the seventies, had begun to contribute tales with more freshness of material and a surer art. Among them were Fitz-James O'Brien, most of whose stories were written for *Harper's*; Herman Melville, whose few tales attracted but little attention; Fitz-Hugh Ludlow, the hashish eater; John T. Trowbridge and Frederick Beecher Perkins, of New England antecedents; Charles Nordhoff, of the Harper organization; J. W. DeForest, the novelist; and a group of brilliant young women — Caroline Chesebrough, Elizabeth Stuart Phelps, Harriet Prescott Spofford, Louise Chandler Moulton, and Rose Terry.

Along with the fiction there was much travel literature, especially travel that was almost or quite exploration. The arctic regions, Africa, and Asia were favorite fields. "Hardly a spot on the habitable globe seems to have been left untouched by the travelers and narrators of the *Harper* staff," said the *Literary World* in 1870.[35] Science, too, was treated in many of its branches, first by Jacob Abbott, and later by better specialists. Spencer F. Baird, secretary of the Smithsonian Institution, had charge of the "Editor's Scientific Record," a department established in December 1869. History and biography, frequently condensed from contemporary books, filled many pages. Politics were left to the *Weekly*.

A new period in the history of *Harper's Magazine* began

about 1870. In the first place, a new set of editors took charge. Henry Mills Alden succeeded Guernsey as editor-in-chief in 1869; Charles Parsons had taken over the art department a few years before and now put Henry Sears in charge of the engraving; Colonel William A. Seaver, president of the Adriatic Insurance Company, took charge of the "Drawer" in 1868; Baird, as just noted, began the science department in 1869. Fletcher Harper's was still the guiding hand, but new vigor and freshness seemed to have come into the magazine after it had passed the crisis of 1865. Alden, who was to retain the editorship for a full half-century, was, like his predecessor, a scholar and a writer. A great-great-grandson of that John Alden who would not speak for himself, he had been educated at Williams and Andover, had contributed to the *Atlantic*, and had been literary editor of *Harper's Weekly* for a few years before he came to the editorship of the *Monthly* in his thirty-third year. He was a remarkable personality and a memorable figure in the history of American magazines. Part mystic, part man of affairs; a valetudinarian with an extraordinary capacity for work; a philosopher and scholar whose heart was always open to the appeal of primitive emotions — Alden was in many respects an ideal editor for a general magazine. John Corbin, a later member of his staff, wrote in an obituary sketch:

His kindness was as simple and frank as his pride, and pervaded every act of his daily life. I have never known, and fear I shall never know, a being so genial, so beneficent. . . . Above everything was his unfailing wisdom. . . . It was the wisdom of a sage among men.[36]

A second factor in the inauguration of a new period for the magazine was the coming of new competition. *Graham's*, *Putnam's*, the *Knickerbocker*, and the *Atlantic* had furnished competition in varying degree; but none of them had furnished at the same time the number of pages, the abundance of illustration, and the literary quality of *Harper's*. Of later comers, *Beadle's* was a flash in the pan, and neither the *Galaxy* nor *Lippincott's* could compete in the matter of pictures. But in 1870 *Scribner's Monthly*, backed by a publishing house which

[36] John Corbin, "Henry Mills Alden," *New York Times Book Review*, October 19, 1919.

rivaled Harper Brothers in resources, fully illustrated, and aiming at the same middle-class public, put *Harper's* on its mettle. Alden wrote years later:

If you are driving a mettlesome horse, and another spirited steed comes alongside, your horse (which would not otherwise have paid any attention to the other nor even so but for the fact that the other is *running the same road*) naturally leaps forward, rejoicing in a good race.[37]

It was in the art department that the race was most noticeable. "The competition between the magazines became so keen that at times we paid as high as five hundred dollars for an engraving for one page of our magazine," writes J. Henry Harper.[38] Parsons grouped about him such men as C. S. Reinhart, who was notable for forceful portrayal of characters, Edward A. Abbey, famous for his feathery line in black-and-white, and for his murals; John W. Alexander, the portrait painter, who did wash drawings for *Harper's*; A. B. Frost, the draughtsman of comedy; Howard Pyle, artist of historical romance; and F. V. DuMond, illustrator of Mark Twain's *Joan of Arc*. Besides these of the Parsons group, such well-known artists as H. L. Stephens, Sol Eytinge, A. R. Waud, Winslow Homer, F. O. C. Darley, and Augustus Hoppin should be listed as frequent contributors to *Harper's*. Parsons himself was a kindly critic, encouraging excellence in young artists.[39]

Both *Harper's* and the *Century* came to make so much of illustration that their authors sometimes felt rebellious. "The May *Harper's* will contain a gossipy sketch to illustrate some portraits of the London poets," wrote Stedman in 1882.[40] Lafcadio Hearn gave up his contract to write some articles on Japan for *Harper's* because he discovered during his passage thither that the artist who accompanied him, C. D. Weldon, was to receive more than double the pay allowed him for the text at two cents a word.[41]

[37] Harper, *op. cit.*, p. 601.
[38] *Ibid.*, p. 202.
[39] Charles D. Abbott, *Howard Pyle* (New York, 1925), p. 50; W. A. Rogers, *A World Worth While* (New York, 1922), pp. 37, 236.
[40] Laura Stedman and George M. Gould, *The Life and Letters of Edmund Clarence Stedman* (New York, 1910), II, 73. Letter dated March 31, 1882.
[41] Elizabeth Bisland, *Life and Letters of Lafcadio Hearn* (Boston, 1906), I, 97.

Fletcher Harper retired in 1875, two years before his death, and the hand of the man who had been much more than a mere publisher was thus removed from the helm. J. Henry Harper, grandson of Fletcher, who had been associated with the firm for the preceding six years, took a special interest in the magazine; but no other member of the family ever had quite the same connection with it as had Fletcher Harper.

In 1877 a better paper was introduced, and two years later the crowded effect that had always distinguished the *Harper* type page was relieved by slightly larger type. Paper, presswork and typography continued to improve throughout the eighties. David Lewis was the pressman in those years.

The editorial policy changed but little in the seventies and eighties; the most important shift was the introduction of occasional serial stories by American writers after 1880 — Howells, James, Warner, and Miss Woolson. English novelists continued, however, to furnish the greater number of the serials. In the later seventies there was a notable improvement in the quality of the short stories. The reason is doubtless to be found in the gradual decay of the old antebellum taste for sentimentalism, with the concurrent (perhaps resultant) appearance of a group of more brilliant and vital short story writers. At any rate, *Harper's* soon became an important factor in the development of the American short story.[42]

Most of the *Harper* short story writers contributed also to *Scribner's* (called *Century* after 1881). *Harper's* still specialized in distant travel, and in that department and in English fiction it exceeded its rival; but in biography and public affairs the *Century* had the advantage. *Harper's* had somewhat more variety. It published much concerning art, but not in series, as the *Century* did; and it was strong in history. In 1886 John H.

---

[42] Following are some of the writers of *Harper* tales, 1875–1900, not already mentioned as contributors to the early volumes: James Lane Allen, Alice Brown, John Esten Cooke, Rose Terry Cooke, "Charles Egbert Craddock," Stephen Crane, Rebecca Harding Davis, Richard Harding Davis, Margaret Deland, Hamlin Garland, E. E. Hale, Lafcadio Hearn, W. D. Howells, Henry James, Thomas A. Janvier, Sarah Orne Jewett, R. M. Johnston, Grace King, Brander Matthews, Thomas Nelson Page, Amélie Rives, Anne Trumbull Slosson, F. Hopkinson Smith, F. J. Stimson, Ruth McE. Stewart, "Octave Thanet," Maurice Thompson, Mary E. Wilkins, Owen Wister, Constance Fenimore Woolson.

Inman, the southern industrial magnate, was host to a Harper excursion party headed by Charles Dudley Warner; and out of this junket came the illustrated series on *The New South*. Another series, with letter press by Warner and pictures by Reinhart, on the summer resorts followed, and still another on *The Great West*.

In December 1880 *Harper's* inaugurated an English edition under the editorship of John Lillie. It differed, at first, from the American edition by the inclusion of some additional English materials. Within three years *Harper's* English edition had a circulation [43] of 25,000, and it continued to increase. Poultney Bigelow says of the early nineties: "In those royal days *Harper's* had more circulation, even in England, than any English magazine; indeed many English people spoke of *Harper's* as their own." [44] The fineness of the wood engraving, unlike anything in England, was much admired. In 1884 Andrew Lang became editor of the English *Harper's*.

The magazine began to accept advertising in the eighties, placing the announcements of the house in the front section, and the outside advertising at the back of the book. By the end of the decade it was carrying some forty pages of such paid advertisements a month.

In 1885 William Dean Howells undertook an editorial position on *Harper's*, founding a department of comment, chiefly literary, called the "Editor's Study." In this he waged for six years his campaign for the new realistic fiction, one of the most important series of controversial criticism in American periodical literature. John Kendrick Bangs became editor of the "Drawer" in 1888, continuing in that capacity and as a writer of the literary notices for over a decade. Charles Dudley Warner had been in charge of this important feature of the magazine (which Mark Twain once referred to as "that potter's field") since the death of Seaver in 1883, and he continued to contribute the introductory storiettes until he succeeded Howells in the "Editor's Study" in 1894. After that Thomas Nelson Page did the first article for a time; but Bangs was the editor of the department all the while, and it was he who changed it from a

[43] *Critic*, VI, 33 (January 17, 1885), quoted from the *Paper World*.
[44] Poultney Bigelow, *Seventy Summers* (New York, 1925), p. 309.

burial place for jokes to a really distinguished collection of pictorial and literary satire. Such artists as Du Maurier, Gibson, Oliver Herford, and Peter Newell contributed pictures; poets ranging from homely Riley to exquisite Aldrich were drawn upon for light verse; and Page, F. Hopkinson Smith, Richard Harding Davis, Kate Douglas Wiggin, Brander Matthews, and many others wrote humorous and satirical sketches for the new "Drawer." Bangs himself wrote some of his best farces for it.

Harper's reached its highest point as a general illustrated literary magazine in the nineties. One is tempted to say that it then attained the very zenith of success among the world's periodicals of that class; at any rate, no other magazine can be shown to have been markedly superior to it in literary quality, variety, illustration, and physical appearance.

The greatest serial success of the decade was Du Maurier's *Trilby*, printed in 1894 with the author's own matchless illustrations. The magazine had already serialized *Peter Ibbetson*, but it had been only mildly successful, so that some of the editorial staff opposed the publication of *Trilby* on the grounds that the author was not popular and, more especially, that the lax morals of the Latin Quarter would not be acceptable in *Harper* homes. But Alden overruled the doubters on the basis of his observation of "the increasing tolerance of our moral judgments as a people," and because it had novelty and "essential purity." [45] The story created a national sensation, and the "Trilby craze" did not subside until at last Trilby's perfect feet and Svengali's perfect villainy were forgotten in the interests aroused by the Spanish-American War. It was while the story was still running in the magazine that the publishers "received a pathetic letter from an afflicted mother telling us that her daughter was desperately ill and would probably survive but a few weeks, and that she was anxious to see the final chapters before she died." The request was granted. [46] Another spectacular success was Mark Twain's *Personal Recollections of Joan of Arc*, published in 1895–96. The anonymity of this serial was preserved throughout its publication, but the secret leaked out in a few months.

[45] John Corbin, *loc. cit.*
[46] Harper, *op. cit.*, p. 536.

Alden was not as liberal about Hardy's *Jude the Obscure*, serialized under the title "Hearts Insurgent," as he had been concerning *Trilby*. He wrote Hardy that the magazine was pledged to print nothing "that could not be read aloud in the family circle," and he made changes as the story ran its course, and even induced the author to rewrite one chapter.[47] A few years before, Henry James had been much disturbed by the omission, on religious grounds, of a whole chapter of his translation of Daudet's *Tarascon*.[48]

The magazine's contents were clearly brighter and more entertaining than ever before. Art, the theater, travel, and science competed with brilliant short stories and successful serials in interest. Woodrow Wilson, Theodore Roosevelt, Henry Cabot Lodge, and A. B. Hart wrote historical series. Andrew Lang's series on the Shakespearean comedies was beautifully illustrated by Edwin A. Abbey.

Half-tone illustration began to supplant the woodcut in *Harper's* in the early nineties, but woodcuts had for years been so delicate in their lines that the change was scarcely noted by most readers. Parsons was succeeded as art director by F. C. Schell in 1888, and he was soon followed by A. B. Turnure and later by Horace Bradley.[49] J. G. Smithwick was long manager of the engraving department. Howard Pyle, William T. Smedley, A. E. Sterner, and F. O. Small were among the newer recruits to *Harper's* art staff.

With the coming of the Spanish-American War, trumpets blared and swords flashed in the pages of the magazine. This effect came not from war material alone, but from the swashbuckling stories which were the fashion of the moment. The war scarcely was over when Lodge's history of it began to appear serially.

The Harper bankruptcy of 1900, the rescue of the House by Pierpont Morgan, and the coming of George Harvey to the presidency of the firm seem to have had little effect on the magazine. The chief change in *Harper's* at the turn of the century had no hint of financial troubles: it was found in the advent of color in the illustrations.

[47] *Ibid.*, p. 531.
[48] *Ibid.*, p. 620.   [49] *Quarterly Illustrator*, I, 60–62 (March 1893).

Howard Pyle's pictures, brilliant with crimsons, were perfectly adapted not only to his own dashing stories, but to the romantic early work of James Branch Cabell and to such pieces as Mark Twain's essay on "Saint Joan of Arc." Such pictures as Pyle's "Flying Dutchman" and "The Fishing of Thor and Hymir" in the number for January 1902 were very impressive. Elizabeth Shippen Green painted charming pictures for Josephine Preston Peabody's child verses. Sarah S. Stillwell and Jessie Wilcox Smith also did excellent work in color. The general character of *Harper's* color illustration changed about 1912, the gorgeous, romantic pictures being superseded by more realistic work by Howard Giles and C. E. Chambers; and yet N. C. Wyeth appeared occasionally in brilliant fancy.

After 1900, contemporary problems received rather more emphasis than formerly. "It must be timely," wrote Alden of the magazine in 1910. "Its field is the living present." [50] *Harper's* was by no means as journalistic, however, as some of its younger and cheaper competitors. British writers were still drawn upon copiously: Sir J. J. Thompson and Sir William Ramsay wrote on scientific matters; W. M. Flinders-Petrie discussed archaeology; Henry W. Nevinson told of his journey in the Congo; Mrs. Humphrey Ward, Israel Zangwill, and Gilbert Parker contributed serials. Among American writers of fiction, Mark Twain, Frank R. Stockton, Mary Johnston, and Mrs. Deland stood out. A little later came Booth Tarkington and Wilbur Daniel Steele. Woodrow Wilson's *History of the American People* ran its serial course in 1901; T. R. Lounsbury had two series on language problems; and Presidents Eliot and Hadley were prominent contributors on social and educational matters. Peary, Nansen, Stefansson, and Amundsen contributed articles on their explorations.

"The Editor's Study," which had been conducted by Charles Dudley Warner since 1894, was taken over by Alden after 1898. In 1901 Howells returned to *Harper's* to occupy the "Easy Chair," which had been vacant since the death of Curtis in 1892; he held this pleasant literary position until his own death in 1921, when the urbane E. S. Martin succeeded him, to be himself succeeded by Bernard De Voto in 1935.

[50] *Harper's Magazine*, CXXI, 39 (June 1910).

During the Great War, *Harper's* published some articles on the campaigns by English and French generals, several on the life of the soldiers and on various forms of mobilization, and a series on the German Kaiser by David Jayne Hill.

In 1919 Henry Mills Alden O.K.'d his last table of contents and passed to whatever reward there may be for faithful editors. For fifty years his unpretentious office, with no name upon its open door, had been the mecca of literary men and women of two continents. During this time, wrote Poultney Bigelow,

the greatest editor of his age educated the English-speaking world from an editorial sanctum so small that he could reach everything therein without moving from his chair. His table was not visible because of the papers upon it.[51]

On his seventieth birthday Carolyn Wells had written a toast to him:

> A health to H. M. Alden,
> Of editors the Dean!
> What does the "H. M." stand for?
> Why, *Harper's Magazine!*

> A health to H. M. Alden,
> The god of the machine;
> He is a Living Issue
> Of *Harper's Magazine!* [52]

Alden was followed by Thomas Bucklin Wells, vice-president of Harper & Brothers, and long an assistant editor. Wells succeeded in two great achievements: he reorganized Harper & Brothers, and he made a modern journal out of *Harper's Magazine.*

It was in 1921 that Wells refinanced the firm to take up over a million and a quarter of the Morgan bonds. There had been talk for twenty years of *Harper's* being "in Wall Street," though the influence of large financial interests is far from clear in the magazine. By 1925, however, there was no doubt of its independence, and it was ready for what one commentator,

[51] Bigelow, *op. cit.*, p. 308.
[52] *Putnam's Monthly*, I, 460 (January 1907).

impressed by the color of its new cover, called its "red revolution." [53]

It had been realized after the World War that the old type of general literary magazine was out of step with the times. For some years, liberals had been poking fun at *Harper's* conservatism: John Curtis Underwood had gone so far as to call it "a literary old woman's home." [54] Now, after careful investigation through questionnaires, it was decided to do two things: dispense with illustrations and devote the magazine to the interpretation and discussion of the modern scene. Abandonment of pictures, traditional basis of *Harper* popularity, was a startling change. Wells has explained that it was felt

that illustrations were no longer necessary in a high-quality magazine, owing to the fact that the large women's magazines had stolen our thunder by illustrating very elaborately in color, and had employed at fabulously high prices such illustrators as the advertisers were not employing at even higher prices. . . . I think we must all admit that illustration has become a highly commercialized business in this country, as it has in France, and that it is no longer possible to secure illustrations of the type for which *Harper's* and the *Century* were famous.[55]

And so, in September 1925 *Harper's* came out with no pictures except an art reproduction for a frontispiece, and in a brilliant orange cover, with a new, clear typography, and filled with provocative, distinctly liberal articles. The old inhibitions were swept away, and *Harper's* became a journal of diversified opinion, written by the leading thinkers of the new day — Charles A. Beard, James Truslow Adams, Count Keyserling, Bertrand Russell, James Harvey Robinson, Harold J. Laski, Harry Emerson Fosdick, and so on. Serial fiction has had but a small place since 1925, but short stories of freshness and distinction have appeared regularly: Aldous Huxley, Wilbur Daniel Steele, Ruth Suckow, Roark Bradford, and Katharine Brush have been among the contributors of this type of writing. Lee Foster Hartman, who had been an associate of Wells, became editor in 1931.

[53] *Survey*, LVII, 429 (January 1, 1927). Article "The Revolution on Quality Street," by Leon Whipple.
[54] J. C. Underwood, *Literature and Insurgency* (New York, 1914), p. 95.
[55] *Survey*, LVII, 431 (January 1, 1927).

In 1866 the *Nation* said:

To a large part of the American people, *Harper's* for many years has been English literature; and it has been so very successful that we may well consider it an index to the literary culture and general character of the nation.[56]

Doubtless *Harper's* has remained such an index during the years which have followed the *Nation's* observation, and in its latest phase it points to certain changes in the national character.

[56] *Nation*, II, 550 (May 1, 1866).

THE INTERNATIONAL MAGAZINE [1]

ONE month after the Harper Brothers issued the first number of their monthly magazine, Stringer & Townsend began the publication of their *International Weekly Miscellany*. In size, typography, and policy the two new periodicals were much alike, though one was weekly and the other monthly. When the *International's* publishers gathered its weekly parts together and issued them as a monthly, the number of pages was almost equal to *Harper's*; and after two months, weekly publication was abandoned entirely by the *International*, and both magazines were on the monthly basis. But Stringer & Townsend could not compete with *Harper's* in woodcuts; they had a few in the first volume and more in the second, but they were far behind their model.

Like *Harper's*, the *International* relied much on English serials.[2] Michael Scott's *The Green Hand* was not a particularly auspicious beginning, but it was followed by Bulwer's *My Novel* and by other works of Bulwer, Thackeray, G. P. R. James, Collins, and Dickens. American writers were recognized in the *International* more quickly than in *Harper's*: Bayard Taylor, R. H. Stoddard, Elizabeth Oakes Smith, A. B. Street, and Horace Greeley were in early numbers. The title was justified by many translations from French and German, and a little later by literary correspondence from Paris and Berlin. Be-

---

[1] TITLES: (1) *International Weekly Miscellany of Literature, Art, and Science*, July 1–August 26, 1850; (2) *The International Miscellany of Literature, Art, and Science*, October–November 1850; (3) *The International Monthly Magazine of Literature, Art, and Science* (running title omits *Monthly*), December 1850–April 1852.

FIRST ISSUE: July 1, 1850. LAST ISSUE: April 1852.

PERIODICITY: Weekly July–August 1850; monthly thereafter. I, July–November 1850; II, December 1850–March 1851; III, April–July 1851; IV, August–December 1851; V, January–April 1852.

PUBLISHERS: Stringer & Townsend, New York.

EDITOR: Rufus Wilmot Griswold.

INDEXED in *Poole's*.

[2] See p. 384.

sides fiction, there was a good deal of poetry, with many articles of a biographical sort, some travel accounts, and much literary criticism dealing with both American and foreign books. There were scientific notes, a "Historical Review of the Month" similar to that of *Harper's* in 1851–52, a department of necrology, and another devoted to the fine arts. Fashion notes with woodcuts were, again as in *Harper's*, placed at the end of each number. The two magazines were priced alike — at three dollars.

The editor of the *International* was Rufus Wilmot Griswold. He had held a similar position on *Graham's* for a short period in the early forties,[3] and he had become famous as the editor of *Poets and Poetry of America* and other anthologies. His assistant was young Charles Godfrey Leland, lately returned from study abroad.

Griswold's wide acquaintance with American men of letters and his liking for literary criticism made the *International* thoroughly literary in tone. The editor's department of literary comment was extensive and valuable. In spite of all that has been said against him by defenders of Edgar Allan Poe, Griswold was a fairly discriminating and honest critic.[4] He was not above literary logrolling himself and seems to have permitted it in his magazine.[5] His memoir of Poe, which had been printed in the *New York Tribune*, appeared in the *International* in October 1850; it was in bad taste, but one need not doubt its honesty. Griswold wrote many other brief articles on American authors for his magazine.

The number of original contributors increased in 1851. Besides those already named, there were John R. Thompson, Parke Godwin, Alice Cary, Constance Fenimore Woolson, George William Curtis, William Gilmore Simms, and so on. Hawthorne's "Feathertop" appeared in the penultimate number — that for March 1852.

The competition of *Harper's* was too much for the *Inter-*

[3] See Mott, *A History of American Magazines, 1741–1850*, p. 550.
[4] See a statement of his critical creed, *International Magazine*, II, 297 (February 1851).
[5] Note article on Boker by Taylor, IV, 156 (September 1851), followed by one on Taylor by Boker, V, 13 (January 1852).

national, and it was merged in its rival in May 1852. W. M. Griswold, son of the editor, wrote many years later that the immediate cause of the suspension of the dying magazine was its failure to obtain from Dickens' publishers advance sheets of a serial which the author had promised to *Harper's*.[6]

[6] *Passages from the Correspondence of Rufus W. Griswold* (Cambridge, Massachusetts: W. M. Griswold, 1898), p. 303.

A TYPICAL *GLEASON'S PICTORIAL* FIRST PAGE

The Boston Harbor cut was a part of the heading. The size of the type page of the original was 10½ x 13¾.

18

GLEASON'S (BALLOU'S) PICTORIAL DRAWING-ROOM COMPANION [1]

FREDERICK GLEASON, publisher of a successful Boston story-paper called the *Flag of Our Union*,[2] founded in 1851 a copiously illustrated family miscellany which he entitled *Gleason's Pictorial Drawing-Room Companion*. It was a well-printed small folio of sixteen pages and sold for $3.00 a year. Its editor was Maturin Murray Ballou, son of the Reverend Hosea Balou, founder of the *Universalist Review*.[3] Maturin Ballou had been in journalism (chiefly religious) ever since his teens and had developed a facility for writing travel sketches and for editorial management.

Five preliminary numbers in quarto, with only a few woodcuts, were issued before the *Pictorial* published its Volume I, Number 1, on May 3, 1851. It was modeled upon the *London Illustrated News*, and it was fortunate in having the former superintendent of the engraving department of that journal in its employ — young Frank Leslie, lately arrived on these shores, his mind already filled with ideas about publishing. From the first, the *Pictorial* covered eight pages — or one "side" of its paper — with woodcuts and only a little letterpress. These pictorial pages were devoted to the portrayal of aspects of travel both abroad and in America, natural history subjects, occasional sculpture, ships, and military scenes. G. T. Devereux, J. H. Manning, A. R. Waud, and A. C. Warren were among the

[1] TITLES: (1) *Gleason's Pictorial Drawing-Room Companion*, 1851–54; (2) *Ballou's Pictorial Drawing-Room Companion*, 1855–59. Half title and title page: *Gleason's* (later *Ballou's*) *Pictorial*.

FIRST ISSUE: May 3, 1851. (Five preliminary numbers were issued March 29–April 26.) LAST ISSUE: December 24, 1859.

PERIODICITY: Weekly. I, May–December 1851; II–XVII, regular semiannual volumes, 1852–59.

PUBLISHERS: Frederick Gleason, Boston, 1851–54; Maturin M. Ballou, Boston, 1854–59.

EDITOR: Maturin M. Ballou.

[2] See p. 35.

[3] See F. L. Mott, *A History of American Magazines, 1741–1850* (New York, 1930), p. 372.

leading artists for the paper; while Leslie, Henry Vizetelly, J. W. Orr, Samuel P. Avery, and John Andrew engraved blocks for it. Engravers on wood were none too plentiful in those days, and the *Pictorial* had to advertise for help in 1852.

The letterpress consisted of two serials, two or three short stories, a few poems, two pages of editorial miscellany, and the sketches to go with the pictures. All the authors and artists who contributed to the paper were Americans; and it made much of its pure brand of Americanism, as opposed to the practice of periodicals which pirated English works.

The serials came from the pens of Sylvanus Cobb, Jr. (at one time a member of the *Pictorial* staff), Ben Perley Poore, A. J. H. Duganne, Francis A. Durivage, Mrs. Caroline Orne, and others of that group of ready writers of the endless procession of romances which ran on and on through the pages of second-rate periodicals — and still runs. T. S. Arthur, the Reverend Hastings Weld, and the equally Reverend J. H. Ingraham wrote tales of moral import. These tales of the *Pictorial* sometimes had some excellent homely delineation of character — especially those of Alice B. Neal and Dr. J. H. Robinson. The Cary sisters, Thomas Buchanan Read, and Mrs. Sigourney were among the poets. There were various travel series, including work by the successive publishers, Gleason and Ballou, both of them inveterate travelers. Some of the earliest work of Horatio Alger, Jr., is found in the *Pictorial*; he was not yet writing juveniles. There was no attempt to portray current events either in pictures or articles.

The paper was very moral. In 1843 it printed an illustrated series on the churches and clergymen of Boston. Ballou liked to write little moral essays to hold the place of honor on his editorial page. The fiction may have been second- or third- or fourth-rate, but it was never either immoral or amoral. The periodical's conservatism extended to such questions as women's rights; in writing of "strong-minded women," Ballou said, "We tremble for their modesty, delicacy, and truthfulness to the sweet characteristics of their better natures." [4]

The *Pictorial* was a success. It began with an edition of 5,000, which, in consideration of the expense of its engraving,

[4] *Gleason's Pictorial*, V, 29 (July 9, 1853).

was far below the profit line. It raised its price to $4.00 in its second year, and its growth was gratifying. When it brought the price back to $3.00, its circulation mounted to over 100,000, and it made its publisher $25,000 a year.[5] In November 1854 Gleason sold it, along with the *Flag of Our Union*, to Ballou, declaring that he had "realized an ample competency" and now wished to "retire from business altogether." [6] It may be noted here that Gleason's subsequent life did not bring him the happiness in retirement to which he had looked forward. He lost much of his "competency," started *Gleason's Monthly Companion* (1872–87) and lost the remainder of it, and died in a home for the indigent.[7]

Meantime the *Pictorial* went on with high hopes. Francis A. Durivage became assistant editor, better paper was used, a fine new building was erected. Advertising was inserted during 1855, but some readers objected, and the attempt was abandoned. With the hard times of 1857, the circulation declined. The price was reduced to $2.50 in 1858, without beneficial result. Fortunately, Ballou had started a dollar monthly in 1855,[8] and it was booming; so he was not without resources. He discontinued the *Pictorial* at the end of 1859, following it for a short time with the *Welcome Guest*, a story-and-miscellany paper in mammoth folio.

In the last number of the *Pictorial*, Ballou gave some interesting figures. He said that the 451 numbers of the *Pictorial* had cost $767,000 — $423,000 for paper, $161,000 for drawing and engraving, and $28,000 for authorship. Apparently a circulation of forty or fifty thousand was required to make the paper pay — perhaps more in 1859. But what price authorship? Sixty-two dollars an issue! ·

As a postscript, it may be noted that Gleason and Ballou trained several future publishers in their establishment. Elliott, Thomes & Talbot, later publishers of several successful Boston story-papers,[9] were Gleason workmen. Leslie went from the

---

[5] George Waldo Browne, "Pioneers of Popular Literature," *Granite State Magazine*, III, 51 (February 1907). Gleason's statement is quoted.

[6] *Gleason's Pictorial*, VIII, 317 (November 18, 1854).

[7] Browne, *loc. cit.*   [8] See p. 31.

[9] *True Flag, American Union, Line-of-Battle Ship, Weekly Novelette*. See pp. 35–36.

Gleason office to New York in 1853 to work on the brief *Illustrated News* of Barnum and the Beaches; at the end of that year the *News* was merged in *Gleason's Pictorial,* but Leslie stayed in New York to begin the first of his long series of periodicals.[10]

[10] See p. 437.

BULLETIN OF THE AMERICAN GEOGRAPHICAL SOCIETY; GEOGRAPHICAL REVIEW

GEORGE BANCROFT was president of the American Geographical and Statistical Society in 1852, when it published the first number of its *Bulletin*,[1] and Francis L. Hawks became president soon afterward. The secretary was Elisha K. Kane, who was so much occupied with preparations for his fatal trip to the Arctic that he allowed many errors to creep into the second number. The magazine was issued very irregularly, with only four numbers in its six years; but there was some extremely interesting material in it. Kane had an article on polar exploration in the second number, and the Society's proceedings at the memorial meeting in his honor on February 26, 1857, are in the last number. Lieutenant M. F. Maury gave the annual address in 1854, and Henry V. Poor contributed a paper about a proposed railway to the Pacific to the third number. Professor A. D. Bache, Horatio Seymour, and George E. Waring, Jr., were other contributors.

After publication had lapsed for two years, it was resolved to make a new start with a monthly. Accordingly, the new *Journal*,[2] a square octavo of thirty-two pages, was issued in

[1] TITLE: *Bulletin of the American Geographical and Statistical Society.*
FIRST ISSUE: August 1852. LAST ISSUE: January 1857.
PERIODICITY: I, August 1852; January 1853; "for the year 1854." II, "for the year 1856," half title dated January 1857.
PUBLISHER: G. P. Putnam, New York, "for the Society."
EDITORS: Secretaries of the Society.

[2] TITLES: (1) *Journal of the American Geographical and Statistical Society,* 1859–70; (2) *Journal of the American Geographical Society of New York,* 1870–1900. (Quarterly parts were called *Bulletin of the American Geographical Society of New York,* 1877–1900.) (3) *Bulletin of the American Geographical Society of New York,* 1901–15.
FIRST ISSUE: January 1859. LAST ISSUE: December 1915.
PERIODICITY: I, 1859, monthly, except August, September; II, Part I (1860), report for 1860; Part II (1870), report for 1868–70; III, 1872, report for 1873; VI–XVIII, reports for 1874–86 in annual volumes; XIX–XXIX, quarterly parts, annual volumes, 1887–97; XXX–XXXV, five parts a year, annual volumes, 1898–1903; XXXVI–XLVII, monthly, annual volumes, 1904–15.
PUBLISHERS: American Geographical and Statistical Society, New York, 1859–70; American Geographical Society of New York, 1871–1915.

January 1859. There were articles on Canada and South America, on railroads and meteorology; there were maps and statistical tables. But after the first year, enthusiasm (and probably funds) waned; and in 1860 a single number was issued, giving the proceedings of the Society for that year, after which there was a silence for ten years. In 1870 the proceedings for 1868–70 were published, and then in 1872, under the presidency of Chief Justice Charles P. Daly, the state of New York took over the publication of the annual proceedings. The Society was required, under its charter, to make annual reports to the legislature; and these were published as "senate documents."

There was much of polar exploration in the early volumes, including an article by Dr. I. I. Hayes, a companion of Kane and later a leader of other expeditions, in 1860. African exploration was also featured, Stanley's letters to the *Herald* were reprinted, and the proceedings of a memorial meeting for Livingstone were published in the 1874 volume. George Kennan wrote on the eastern Caucasus in 1873, and later on Siberia. In the eighties there was more variety. Elial F. Hall was editor from 1875 to 1893; and the Society flourished under Judge Daly, whose early sea experience, scholarly mind, and wide acquaintance made him a good head for the organization. Men like Daniel Coit Gilman, Andrew D. White, John Bach McMaster, and the Earl of Dunraven contributed to the annual volumes.

In 1887 the *Journal* became a quarterly, and its separate issues were entitled *Bulletin of the American Geographical Society of New York*. A short department of "Geographical Notes" begun at the time became at length a thorough digest of the world's geographical publications. Indeed, the *Journal*, though it had started as the organ of a group of amateurs interested in exploration, became more and more a professional publication. There were many good maps, meteorological rec-

---

EDITORS: Daniel W. Fiske, 1859–70; E. R. Straznicky, 1870–71; Alvan S. Southworth, 1872–74; Elial F. Hall, 1875–93; Anton A. Raven, 1894–1907; George C. Hurlbut, 1908; Cyrus C. Adams, 1909–15.

INDEXES: *Poole's, Readers' Guide Supplement, Engineering Index, Annual Magazine-Subject Index.*

ords, data of geological surveys, and (after 1890) book reviews and a Washington letter. Robert E. Peary appeared in the magazine's pages first in 1889; he was later to be conspicuous there.

Judge Daly died in 1899, after having been president of the Society for over a third of a century. In 1904 the *Bulletin* changed to monthly publication. Among the more prominent contributors were Angelo Heilprin, G. W. Littlehales, Ellsworth Huntington, Edwin S. Balch, and Vilhaljmur Stefansson. Cyrus C. Adams, president of the American Association of Geographers, was editor 1909–15.

The Society had long before grown strong enough to dispense with state aid in the publication of its journal. In 1916 it broke even more sharply with its past by discontinuing the *Bulletin* and beginning in its place the *Geographical Review* [3] — a handsome, copiously illustrated large octavo. The moving spirit in the change was Isaiah Bowman, who had been a professor of geography at Yale and the leader of expeditions to Peru and the Andes, and who now came to the Society as director of its activities to remain as general editor of publications until 1935. G. M. Wrigley became editor of the *Review* in 1920. It has had a series of distinguished contributors and has at the same time maintained a high level of interest and good standards of scholarship. In 1921 it was changed from monthly back to quarterly publication.

[3] TITLE: *The Geographical Review.*
FIRST ISSUE: January 1916. Current.
PERIODICITY: Monthly, 1916–20, semiannual volumes, I–X; quarterly, 1921–current, annual volumes, XI–current.
PUBLISHER: American Geographical Society, New York.
EDITORS: Isaiah Bowman, 1916–20; G. M. Wrigley, 1920–current.
INDEXES: *International Index; Engineering Index;* Arthur A. Brooks, *Index to the Geographical Review,* Vols. XVI–XXV, 1926–35 (New York, 1936).

ARTHUR'S HOME MAGAZINE [1]

IN OCTOBER 1852 *T. S. Arthur's Home Gazette: A Journal of Pure Literature for Home Reading* was beginning its third year, and it occurred to Editor-Publisher Arthur that he might increase the profits on his weekly by reprinting its contents in a monthly. Thus was born *Arthur's Home Magazine*, destined to be dressed in the but slightly refashioned garments of an elder sister. In spite of its handicap, however, the monthly seemed to flourish, and at the end of 1854 the *Gazette* was abandoned, and its publisher's efforts were concentrated on the *Home Magazine*.[2]

Immediately the magazine was greatly improved. Virginia F. Townsend, only nineteen years old but showing precocious aptitude for writing that "pure literature" on which Arthur and his many readers doted, became editorial assistant and eventually responsible editor of the magazine. She and Arthur wrote most of the serials and many of the short stories. Woodcuts brightened the pages, and even hand-colored fashion plates were added after a year or two. The magazine was highly departmentalized, with sections devoted to fashions, a "Housekeepers' Friend," a "Boys' and Girls' Treasury," music and concert notes with (after 1860) a piece of music in each num-

---

[1] TITLES: (1) *The Home Magazine* (with running head *Arthur's Home Magazine*), 1852–53; (2) *Arthur's Home Magazine*, 1854–56, 1861–71, 1880–91; (3) *The Lady's Home Magazine* (with running head *Arthur's Home Magazine*), 1857–60; (4) *Arthur's Lady's Home Magazine*, 1871–73; (5) *Arthur's Illustrated Home Magazine*, 1874–79; (6) *Arthur's New Home Magazine*, 1891–98.

FIRST ISSUE: October 1852. LAST ISSUE: December 1898.

PERIODICITY: Monthly. I, October 1852–June 1853; II–XL, semiannual volumes, July 1853–1872; XLI–LXI, annual volumes, 1873–93; LXII–LXVII, semiannual volumes, 1894–98. Suspended February 1896–January 1897.

PUBLISHERS: T. S. Arthur, 1852–69; T. S. Arthur & Son, 1870–91; Arthur Publishing Company (E. Stanley Hart, president), 1891–94; Penfield Publishing Company, 1894–98.

EDITORS: T. S. Arthur, 1852–85 (with Virginia F. Townsend, 1855–72); Joseph P. Reed, 1891–94 (with Emily H. May, 1893–94); Roderic C. Penfield and Marion Alcott Prentice, 1894–98.

[2] See *Arthur's Home Magazine*, V, 148 (February 1855).

ber, an editor's department, book reviews, some art, science, and economics. A health department was added in 1860. There were patterns for fancywork, puzzles for the children, and many poems and tales.

Both name and contents indicated a women's and children's magazine, and it was for the family sitting room that this periodical was designed. The stories were highly moral, of course, illustrating the evils of flirtation, the folly of personal vanity, the dangers of ill-temper, the crime of intemperance. This last theme was naturally prominent in a magazine published by the author of *Ten Nights in a Bar Room*.

Few well-known names are found. For some years Arthur and Miss Townsend apparently did nearly all of the magazine themselves. Lucy Larcom, Helen L. Bostwick, "Clara Augusta," and J. Starr Holloway became prominent contributors in the sixties; and Julia C. R. Dorr and Louise Chandler Moulton came in during the following decade, with Alice Cary and Ella Wheeler, those ubiquitous magazine poets. An entertaining contributor to the "Home Life and Character" department was one "Pipsissiway Potts." Miss Townsend dissolved her connection with the magazine in 1872.

Arthur's chief competitor was *Peterson's*; each of them sold for $2.00 a year,[3] while *Godey's* kept to its $3.00 price. Among these three great Philadelphia women's magazines, *Arthur's* ranked third in circulation as in merit. Indeed the *Home Magazine* never attained a large circulation, ranging from ten to thirty thousand. But it was a cheap magazine to produce, except for the illustration; and it dropped its color fashion plates at the beginning of the war, which cut off the chief cost in that department. By the late seventies the number of woodcut illustrations substantially decreased. Several pages of advertising were carried from the beginning, and by the early seventies *Arthur's* was getting $100 a page for its space; but its advertising was light through that decade.

In the eighties, free dress patterns became the great circulation inducement among the women's magazines. *Arthur's*, which had no pattern designers of its own, relied at first upon the

---

[3] *Arthur's* sold for $2.50 until after the war, when it came to $2.00 — a price maintained until 1891.

Butterick patterns, which it reproduced in four pages of its advertising section; but in 1888 it adopted the McCall patterns and actually stapled into its own numbers James McCall & Company's monthly pattern and fashion periodical called the *Queen*, then in its fifteenth volume — though it had to fold the *Queen's* pink quarto pages to fit them to its own octavo size. A few years later it got the *Queen* on its own regular pages, though still in pink; by this time it was offering $3.00 worth of McCall patterns as a premium with a $1.50 yearly subscription.

Arthur had died in 1885, but his son continued the magazine until he sold it in June 1891 to E. Stanley Hart. Hart lowered the price, to meet the magazine competition of the times, first to $1.50 and then in 1893 to $1.00. It was now *Arthur's New Home Magazine*. Joseph P. Reed was editor, assisted by Emily H. May, who had long edited the women's departments in *Peterson's*. Competition with *McCall's* and the Butterick publications became so sharp that *Arthur's* turned to domestic patterns in 1893. The next year Roderic Penfield, who had acquired *Peterson's Magazine*, bought it. By this time it had declined pitiably in every respect; and though Penfield improved it, he was not able to put it on its feet. After a disastrous suspension in 1896–97, it ended in 1898.

Arthur's Home Magazine, though always a second-rate periodical, succeeded during its existence of nearly half a century in making many devoted friends who liked precisely what it gave them — fashions, patterns, miscellany, and mildly sentimental verse and fiction at a low price.

PUTNAM'S MONTHLY MAGAZINE [1]

THE original projector of *Putnam's* appears to have been
Charles F. Briggs, called "Harry Franco" by his
friends, from the name of an early novel of his. Briggs
had been the editor of the *Broadway Journal*,[2] on which he had
Poe for an associate, and later of *Holden's Dollar Magazine*,[3]
which had been suspended in the fall of 1851. In 1852 he
broached the project of a high-class literary magazine to be
issued by a leading book publisher to George William Curtis
and won his support.[4] The publisher he found was George
Palmer Putnam, a man of literary discrimination and culture,
and the publisher of Irving's works and of a number of popular
successes. Putnam was an energetic manager and obtained at
once promises to contribute to the new magazine from most of

[1] TITLES: (1) *Putnam's Monthly Magazine of American Literature, Science,
and Art*, 1853–57; (2) *Putnam's Magazine: Original Papers on Literature, Science, Art, and National Interests*, 1868–70; (3) *Putnam's Monthly and the
Critic: A Magazine of Literature, Art, and Life*, 1906; (4) *Putnam's Monthly:
A Magazine of Literature, Art, and Life*, 1907–08; (5) *Putnam's Monthly and
the Reader*, 1908–09; (6) *Putnam's Monthly: An Illustrated Monthly of Literature, Art, and Life*, 1909–10.
FIRST ISSUE: January 1853. LAST ISSUE: April 1910.
PERIODICITY: Monthly. [First Series] I–X, regular semiannual volumes, Janu-
ary 1853–September 1857; Vol. X ends the series with only three numbers.
New Series, I–VI, regular semiannual volumes, January 1868–November 1870;
Vol. VI ends the series with only five numbers. [Third Series, not connected
in any way with the numbering of earlier series] I–VII, October 1906–April
1910; each volume has six numbers except the last (VII), which has seven.
PUBLISHERS: G. P. Putnam & Company, New York, 1853–55; Dix & Edwards,
New York, 1855–57; Miller & Company, New York, 1857; G. P. Putnam & Son,
New York, 1868–70; G. P. Putnam's Sons, New York, 1906–10.
EDITORS: Charles F. Briggs (George William Curtis and Parke Godwin, asso-
ciate editors), 1853–57; Charles F. Briggs, 1868–69; Edmund Clarence Stedman,
1869–70; Parke Godwin, 1870; Jeanette Gilder and Joseph B. Gilder, 1906–10.
INDEXES: Poole's, Jones' Index, Readers' Guide.
REFERENCES: *Putnam's Magazine*, N. S., I, 1 (January 1868); *Putnam's
Monthly and the Critic*, I, 1 (October 1906); George Haven Putnam, *George
Palmer Putnam: A Memoir* (New York, 1912), Chapters IX and XVII.
[2] See Mott, *A History of American Magazines, 1741–1850*, p. 757.
[3] *Ibid.*, pp. 347–348.
[4] *Putnam's Magazine*, N. S., I, 5 (January 1868).

the leading American writers.[5] To Briggs and Curtis he added
Parke Godwin, of the *Evening Post*, as political editor, for it
was planned to combine the functions of a serious review with
those of a literary magazine. The subscription list of the
American Whig Review was purchased to swell *Putnam's*
initial circulation.[6]

The first number, dated January 1853, was a handsome, large
octavo of 120 double-column pages, with a pea-green cover
decorated with pictures of graceful stalks of corn and sugar
cane, and priced at twenty-five cents. Its contents were varied
and well written; if it had not been for the rule of anonymity
which prevailed, readers would generally have recognized the
names of most of the authors. Briggs had an introductory editorial, an article on the Uncle Tom craze, and a filler anecdote;
Curtis contributed no less than seven pieces in prose and verse
with his characteristic versatility; Longfellow and Lowell each
had poems in the first number, and Thoreau began his "Excursion to Canada"; Horace Greeley wrote on "Modern Spiritualism," Charles A. Dana on current French and German books,
and Augustus Maverick on current science; Richard B. Kimball
wrote the lead article — on Cuba; Francis L. Hawks discussed
John L. Stephens, the famous traveler, who had just died;
Fitz-James O'Brien wrote on Donald G. Mitchell in the first of
what promised to be a series on "Our Young Authors" but
reached only two numbers, the second being on Herman Melville; William North contributed a Poesque short story, and
Mrs. R. B. Hicks, of Richmond, the first installment of a continued story called "Virginia"; and the number was completed
by some personal recollections of Thorwaldsen by Professor
George W. Greene.

"A sort of American *Blackwood's*," said *Norton's Literary
Gazette*, when it noticed the first number.[7] But it was better
printed than *Blackwood's*; and if its fiction was not equal to
that of the English magazine, it was rather more mellow and
attractive. It was resolutely American: its stand for original
and American contributions was intended and received as a

[5] J. C. Derby, *Fifty Years Among Authors, Books and Publishers* (New York, 1884), p. 312.
[6] *Norton's Literary Gazette*, III, 1 (January 15, 1852).
[7] *Ibid.*

stinging rebuke to the disgracefully successful *Harper's,* with its "borrowed" English serials. The policy and attitude of *Putnam's* may have been formed somewhat on the *Blackwood* model, and (it may be noted in passing) when "Christopher North" died in 1854 *Putnam's* called him "the greatest of our tribe";[8] but the new magazine stood on its own feet, and that more firmly and with more *savoir-faire* than any other American magazine of its time.

Putnam's was lucky enough to make a "hit" in its second number. It printed an article by one Charles H. Hanson, a clergyman, attempting to prove that Charles Louis, the *dauphin* of pathetic memory, son of Louis XVI and Marie Antoinette, had been brought to America during the French Revolution, had been reared by the Indians, and, having taken orders in the Episcopal church, was now living as a missionary to the Indians under the name of Eleazar Williams. Twenty-seven points of evidence were adduced to show that Williams was "Louis XVII," including a childhood loss of memory, certain clothing and medals supposed to have come from Louis XVI, Williams' own story of efforts of French emissaries to make him sign away his rights to the French throne, and a strong Bourbon physical resemblance. Simon the Jailer is said to have exclaimed, upon seeing his picture, "My God, I know that face! It has haunted me through life!" The face was shown in a woodcut of *Putnam's*; and it must be admitted that the picture has a haunting quality and that profane exclamations about it seem not inappropriate. The fault is probably that of the engraver, however, for the Reverend Eleazar Williams was said by Curtis, who had a good look at him on one occasion when the man of mystery visited *Putnam's* office, to have been "quite as royal a looking gentleman as any king of his time." [9] The romantic story created a widespread furore, and the title of the article, "Have We a Bourbon Among Us?" passed into a current catch phrase; but the *Putnam* staff did not, apparently, take the Hanson-Williams claims very seriously, though they printed some "follow-up" material.[10] Williams was probably a

[8] *Putnam's Monthly,* III, 568 (May 1854).

[9] *Ibid.,* N. s., I, 6 (January 1868).

[10] The original article appeared in February 1853, and a second article by Hanson in the following April. See also Charles H. Hanson, *The Lost Prince* (New York, 1854).

great-grandson of that John Williams of Deerfield who wrote a classic story of his captivity among the Indians.[11]

But if the Reverend Mr. Hanson furnished the "very palpable hit" of the first volume, the associate editors also did much to popularize the new magazine.

One day [writes Curtis in his reminiscences] Mr. Franco said, in his crisp way, "There must be an article upon the present state of parties in the next number." Thereupon Godwin, who was our states-man and political thinker, dropped his modest eyes; but Mr. Franco added, "I don't mean political parties; I mean Brown's." Alas! it was in that manner that "our best society" was described. . . . The result of Mr. Franco's hint was Mrs. Potiphar's first appearance.[12]

Those satirical essays about Brown's parties and other social goings-on, later published as *The Potiphar Papers*, made an excellent magazine feature; they had enough of indignant ex-aggeration to make them the subject of controversy. They were followed in 1855 by the brief series of papers later collected as *Prue and I* — more urbane though perhaps more sentimental sketches of character and morals.

Godwin was only a little later than Curtis in catching the popular attention; he did it first by a political article in the September 1853 number. But as Curtis has told of the begin-nings of his own success in the magazine, so shall Godwin tell of his hit:

It happened while Mr. Curtis had been ministering to the delight of our readers in many ways and receiving showers of applause in return, that another one of the triumvirate, taken by Mr. Franco's suggestion, had written his version of the state of parties, and called it "Our New President." It was a criticism of Mr. Pierce, who had recently been elected, not for Democratic depravity in general, but for the reckless license he had shown in distributing the sacred trusts of office to a parcel of heelers and hoodlums. . . . This article raised a fierce out-cry of opposition; but Commodore Putnam, though he had values on board, was a brave soul, and said, "Brace up, my lads! Put her head one point nearer the wind and crowd on sail!" . . . A succession of

---

[11] *The Redeemed Captive* (Boston, 1707). Eleazar probably descended through John's daughter Eunice, who never returned to white civilization. See article in *Appleton's Cyclopaedia of American Biography*.

[12] *Putnam's Magazine*, N. S., I, 6 (January 1868).

papers on "Parties and Politics," perhaps more verjuicy than juicy; on "Our American Depotism," meaning slavery; on "Kansas — It Must Be Free"; and "The Two Forms of Society, Which?" only aggravated the original scream of protest into a fierce howl of rage.[13]

Godwin wielded a sharp pen, and he had command of an excellent vocabulary of invective, as when he described the political leaders of the day as "the flatulent old hacks, the queasy and prurient old bawds, who have so long had control of the old parties." [14] His reference to the "fierce howl of rage" elicited by his articles was not exaggerated. *De Bow's* called *Putnam's* "the leading review of the Black Republican party" [15] and never lost an opportunity to condemn it; in this attack it was joined by the *Southern Literary Messenger* and *Russell's Magazine*.[16] That *De Bow's* was correct in its designation of *Putnam's* as the organ of the new party is sufficiently proved by the fact that Godwin wrote the first platform of the Republican party, basing it on an article he had contributed to the magazine in January 1856.[17]

But although *Putnam's* made itself a political force, it was in the field of belles-lettres that it achieved its highest mark. The most famous writers who contributed to it with any frequency were Longfellow, Lowell, Thoreau, Melville, and Cooper. Longfellow was represented in the first number, with "The Warden of the Cinque Ports"; and he contributed several other poems at intervals, the best known of them being "My Lost Youth." Lowell was a close friend of the chief editor. He had a poem, "The Fountain of Youth," in the initial number; and three months later began the serial publication of a serio-comic poem in alexandrines, intended to chronicle discursively his thoughts and travels. It was called "Our Own: His Wanderings and Personal Adventures," that is, *Putnam's* "own" correspondent.

Alas, the wit was too forced, the poem was dull and somehow promised to be duller; and when the editor regretfully reported

---

[13] Parke Godwin, *Commemorative Addresses* (New York, 1895), p. 30, footnote.

[14] *Putnam's Monthly*, V, 97 (January 1855).

[15] *De Bow's Review*, XXII, 129 (February 1857).

[16] See *Southern Literary Messenger*, XXIV, 236 (March 1857) and *Russell's Magazine*, I, 82–85 (April 1857).

[17] George Haven Putnam, *Memories of a Publisher* (New York, 1915), p. 13.

to the author, after the third installment had appeared, that its reader-interest appeared to be practically nil, Lowell urged that it should be discontinued.[18] It was so ordered, and the poem still stands with a line "To be continued" at its close in the number for June 1853. "A Moosehead Journal" a few months later was much more successful; and in the spring of the next year "Cambridge Thirty Years Ago" appeared as a two-part article under the heading "Fireside Travels." Thoreau's "Excursion to Canada" appeared in the first three numbers of 1853, and his "Cape Cod" in three numbers of 1855. Melville contributed his *Israel Potter* to *Putnam's* in 1854–55, together with half a dozen or more of his *Piazza Tales*. Cooper's "Old Ironsides," one of his naval histories, was published posthumously. Bryant's "Robert of Lincoln" appeared in the June 1855 number, and other poems of his were contributed to the second series.

Other *Putnam* names are almost as well known. Bayard Taylor, John P. Kennedy, Charles Dudley Warner, Richard Henry Stoddard, Charles Eliot Norton, Henry James, and Francis H. Underwood may be listed. Arthur Hugh Clough, with his two "Letters of Parepidemus," in 1853, was the only foreign author printed; and he was admitted by virtue of his brief residence at Cambridge in Massachusetts. Richard Grant White contributed several papers dealing with Shakespearean criticism. Frederick S. Cozzens, New York wine dealer and wit, wrote on "American Wines" and later upon diverse topics in his delightful *Sparrowgrass Papers*. Frederick Beecher Perkins was another accomplished writer whose wit and urbanity helped to give the first series of *Putnam's* its high position as an essay magazine. Edmund Quincy contributed his serial novel, *Wensley*; and writers of tales were Calvin W. Philleo, C. M. Webber, "Frank Forrester," Fitz-James O'Brien, and William North. A story by the Reverend George W. Bethune was copied into the English *Eliza Cook's Journal* without credit; and when in that magazine it fell victim to *Harper's* free-borrowing habits. Another *Putnam* item that crossed the ocean twice was Longfellow's "Two Angels," which was pirated by *Bentley's* and then

<hr/>

[18] C. E. Norton, ed., *Letters of James Russell Lowell* (Boston, 1894), I, 199. Lowell's letter to Briggs dated June 10, 1853.

copied into the *Living Age* credited to the English magazine.[19]
Putnam's gave much attention to the West. "We believe in
the West," the editor had declared in his salutatory.[20] Western
travel and adventure and articles on western resources were
common. Perhaps the outstanding papers on this region were
those by Charles Dudley Warner. Nor was the South neglected,
in spite of the political bias of the magazine. The first fiction
serial was southern; and writers like Kennedy, Mrs. Hicks,
William Swinton, and Francis Lieber represented that region.
"Every number of this work, from the beginning, has contained
one or more articles from the pens of southern writers," wrote
the editor of *Putnam's* in its second year.[21] But in spite of these
efforts toward a national outlook, *Putnam's* had very much the
New York flavor. Clarence Cook's "New York Daguerreo-
typed," a series dealing with New York architecture, began in
the second number; George Pomeroy Keese wrote of the
theaters; and the music, the parks, and the society of the metropolis were exploited.

European affairs were not neglected; the war in the Crimea
was treated in various articles. Travel was a prominent feature
of the magazine's contents: Curtis, George H. Calvert, and
John M. Mackie were prominent writers about foreign lands.
Biography appeared occasionally; Caroline M. Kirkland's study
of Washington was a serial publication in 1856. The literary
criticism was of a distinctly high class. It was written by men
like Charles A. Dana, George Ripley, and those of the editorial
triumvirate; it was often incisive and acute and always seemed
to be above personal bias.

One fact that emerges from a study of the first *Putnam's* roll
of authors is that so many of them were newspaper men. Magazinists had in the past been recruited chiefly from the pulpits
and the law courts. *Putnam's*, too, had many friends among the
clergy; and the Reverend Francis L. Hawks, the publisher's
rector, was intimately associated with it. But the journalists,
who knew current interests and could write interestingly about
them, were drawn into the *Putnam* net in shoals. Briggs him-

[19] Putnam, *Memories*, p. 189.
[20] *Putnam's Monthly*, I, 2 (January 1853).
[21] *Ibid.*, III, 344 (March 1854).

self had been on the staff of the *Times* and later on that of the
Evening Mirror. Godwin came to the magazine from the *Evening Post*. The *Tribune* furnished many writers to *Putnam's* —
most conspicuously Greeley, Dana, Ripley, Clarence Cook (art
critic), versatile William Henry Hurlbert, and later the Swintons. And so on: a large proportion of *Putnam's* leading writers
had some connection with the daily press.

Whether the leaven of journalism had anything to do with it
or not, the fact seems undeniable that the first series of *Putnam's*, or at least the first half of that series, maintained consistently about the highest level which an American magazine
had reached up to that time.[22] The old *Port Folio* had been a
good journal for a time; *Graham's* had some high spots in spite
of its catering to the feminine; Lowell's very brief *Pioneer* was
of the first class; the *Knickerbocker*, too, sometimes reached a
high standard. But the early *Putnam's* was for some three years
edited with a degree of freedom from the inhibitory fears of the
times, with a certain sophistication, with a cultivation and intelligence, that would have given it standing in any period of our
history. That the editors felt strong resentment against current
irrational curbs upon thinking, feeling, and living is shown by
such an article as Godwin's "American Despotisms";[23] but for
the most part they were inclined not to rail against them in set
terms, but to satirize them, or merely to set them at naught by
their editorial policy.

But the magazine lost its publisher in 1855. Putnam had been
a most sympathetic manager and counselor from the first; in
his magazine's second year he wrote to a friend that he had
"assumed control more directly than before." [24] The first few
numbers had developed a circulation which seemed encouraging. Briggs wrote exultantly to Lowell that 20,000 copies of the
first number had been sold, but apparently that was the highest
point the circulation ever reached.[25] The publisher paid his

---

[22] This opinion is corroborated by that of the writer of the article on "American Periodicals" in the *New American Cyclopaedia* (New York, 1861), XIII, 141.

[23] *Putnam's Monthly*, IV, 524–531 (November 1854).

[24] *Putnam's Monthly and the Critic*, I, 11 (October 1906).

[25] H. E. Scudder, *James Russell Lowell* (Boston, 1901), I, 350. Putnam (*George Palmer Putnam*, p. 362) says the circulation varied from twelve to twenty thousand.

authors well, for the times: "every article that we published,"
wrote Putnam at the end of the first volume, "has been paid for
at a rate which its writer has thought liberal." [26] But there was
little advertising, aside from that of Putnam's books, and the
hard times of the middle fifties presented unexpected difficulties,
so that in 1855 Putnam had to dispose of the magazine to Dix &
Edwards. What happened then is related by the biographer of
Curtis:

> In the spring of 1856 he [Curtis] had put some money into the
> publishing firm of Dix, Edwards & Co., to whom had passed the
> ownership of *Putnam's Monthly*. They failed the next year in April,
> and in August Curtis, in a letter to Mr. Charles Eliot Norton, de-
> scribes his experience in business: "I was responsible as a general
> partner. To save the creditors (for I would willingly have called quits
> myself), I threw in more money, which was already forfeited, and
> undertook the business with Mr. Miller, the printer, who wanted to
> save himself. Presently Mr. Shaw [27] put in some money as special
> partner. But what was confessed to be difficult, when we relied upon
> the statements given us, became impossible when those statements
> turned against us, and last week we suspended. In the very moment
> of arrangement, it appeared that by an informality Mr. Shaw was
> held as a general partner: the creditors swarmed in to avail them-
> selves of the slip, and we are now wallowing in the law. Of course I
> lose everything and expected to, but there is now, in addition, this
> ugly chance of Mr. S.'s losing sixty or seventy thousand dollars, and
> all by an accident which the creditors fully comprehend." Without
> going into the details of the arrangement by which this trouble was
> finally settled, it is sufficient to say that Mr. Curtis assumed a large
> indebtedness for which he was not legally bound, and for nearly a
> score of years labored incessantly to pay it, devoting to that purpose
> the money earned by lecturing.[28]

The contents of the magazine remained excellent for some
time after Putnam's withdrawal. But its brilliance seemed to
dim somewhat by the end of 1856, while its political articles
became more radical. A new department called "The World of
New York" was added at the beginning of that year; it presented a remarkable picture of life in the metropolis, but it

---

[26] *Putnam's Monthly*, I, 704 (June 1853).
[27] Francis G. Shaw, whose daughter Curtis had just married.
[28] Edward Cary, *George William Curtis* (Boston, 1894), p. 106.

tended to overemphasize the relation of magazine and city. A humor department was added in March 1857, and woodcuts in the next month: both changes were clearly made to meet *Harper's* competition. It was in March of that year that *Putnam's* printed an article on *"Harper's Monthly* and *Weekly"* containing criticisms which, however just, were scarcely proper in a rival magazine. *Putnam's* itself had used woodcuts occasionally during its first year or two, for the illustration of articles on architecture, for example, and had later published some engraved portraits; but in the spring of 1857 it adopted woodcuts as a regular feature. As Godkin wrote to a friend in England: "After a brilliant career of a few years [*Putnam's*] was at last driven into that last haven of all crazy literary craft — 'first class wood engravings.' " [29] The book reviews were inferior, and the paper and printing poorer in that last year.

In October 1857 *Putnam's* was merged in *Emerson's United States Magazine*,[30] another *Harper* competitor, which was called for the next year *Emerson's Magazine and Putnam's Monthly*. In the very next month after the disappearance of *Putnam's*, the *Atlantic Monthly* was founded; and since it used some of the same contributors — particularly Parke Godwin on politics — and was of the same magazine type, it was sometimes regarded as a Boston successor of *Putnam's* first series.

A decade later Briggs and Putnam again embarked on a magazine adventure. The years immediately after the close of the war were boom years, offering a favorable opportunity to test an editorial policy in which they still believed. George Palmer Putnam's son, George Haven Putnam, was now associated with him and active in the firm's publications. Curtis, who had become associated editorially with *Harper's Weekly* even before the end of the first series of *Putnam's*, was not in the new combination; nor was Godwin, who was again connected with the *Evening Post*. But young Edmund Clarence Stedman was associate editor and book reviewer,[31] while S. S. Conant

[29] Rollo Ogden, *Life and Letters of Edwin Laurence Godkin* (New York, 1907), I, 222.
[30] See pp. 448–451.
[31] Laura Stedman and George M. Gould, *The Life and Letters of Edmund Clarence Stedman* (New York, 1910), I, 427.

conducted a department of the fine arts and V. B. Denslow a current events section.

The second series of *Putnam's* was apparently designed to be much the same kind of magazine as its predecessor. It was a little larger and sold for ten cents more. It was close to current affairs and much interested in manners. But it lacked the brilliance and gaiety of the first series; it needed Curtis. It gave space at the "back of the book" to a chronicle of current events, notices of new books and the fine arts, and a rather undistinguished department of "Table Talk." Perhaps its greatest strength was in its various articles on social questions.

Few of the writers for the first series are found in the revived *Putnam's*. Bryant and Taylor occasionally, H. T. Tuckerman oftener, George H. Calvert, F. B. Perkins, and Clarence Cook helped to carry on, and there was more posthumous Cooper; but it was a new post-war group in the main. Evert A. Duyckinck wrote a number of historical and biographical articles, including a series on "Out-of-the-Way Books and Authors." Charles Wyllys Elliott did an interesting series on "Life in Great Cities"; also, under the pen name of "Thom. White," he started a lively little controversy over women's rights. Political articles for the first year or two were written by Denslow. Among the short story writers were Caroline Chesebrough, young Frank R. Stockton, and Jane G. Austin; and Edgar Fawcett, Elizabeth Stoddard, A. B. Street, and J. J. Piatt furnished poems. There were many pages of travel accounts, including J. Bishop Putnam's "Letters from Japan" and George Kennan's eastern papers. A striking contribution to the first number was a Christmas story called "The Carpenter" by W. D. O'Connor, the Whitman disciple, in which Christ appears in a country home near Washington on the last Christmas Eve of the war — and the Christ bears a vague though undeniable resemblance to Whitman. Kimball, Miss Chesebrough, and Mary Clemmer Ames furnished serials. W. D. Howells, John Burroughs, and J. S. C. Abbott were other contributors.

Briggs dropped out after the first year of the new series and was succeeded by Stedman,[32] who held the helm until he was

---

[32] *Printers' Circular*, III, 370 (February 1869).

relieved by Godwin in April 1870.[33] Godwin gave the magazine more vigor, but not enough to save it. Departments in 1869–70 were commonly better than the articles; they were conducted by Taylor, Stedman, Conant, Stoddard, Cook, Perkins, Charlton T. Lewis, and Godwin.

The circulation of the second series never exceeded 1,500.[34] In the publisher's note to the last volume of the second series, the following balance sheet is presented:

To cash paid contributors	$30,000
By compliments to publishers	? ? ?
By profits on an outlay of $100,000	00,000
By balance	? ? ?[35]

With such a financial statement before them, it is not strange that the Putnams decided in November 1870 [36] to make that number their last and to merge the magazine in the new *Scribner's Monthly*. In receiving *Putnam's* into her bosom, *Scribner's* truly said that the older magazine had "embodied in its pages not only the old Knickerbocker culture and prestige, but the free spirit of modern progress and the broadest literary catholicity." [37]

It was a third of a century before the house of Putnam again attempted a general magazine. The third *Putnam's Monthly* was established as a successor to the *Critic*, a literary monthly which the Putnams had owned since 1898.[38] The *Critic* was discontinued in September 1906, and the next month appeared Volume I, Number 1, of *Putnam's Monthly and the Critic*, a fully illustrated general magazine of varied contents.

Jeanette Gilder had been founder and editor of the *Critic*, and she continued to edit the new monthly, with the aid of her brother Joseph B. Her special department, "The Lounger," in which she had long gossiped pleasantly of authors and their

[33] Stedman and Gould, *op. cit.*, I, 441.

[34] Putnam, *George Palmer Putnam*, p. 362.

[35] *Putnam's Magazine*, preface to Vol. VI (1870).

[36] A year before, it had been said in the *Nation* (November 25, 1869) that *Putnam's* was "hereafter to be published by an association of which it is announced that Mr. W. C. Bryant is a member." But the Putnams continued as publishers for another year.

[37] *Scribner's Monthly*, I, 105 (November 1870).

[38] See Volume III, sketch 35.

books, of art, and of actors, was continued, with copious illustration; it was the part of the magazine that many readers turned
to first.

The *Putnam's Monthly* of 1906 to 1910 was a very literary
magazine. It was concerned chiefly with authors and authorship, with books and publishing. True, it printed fiction, poetry,
travel essays, and art criticism; but it seldom wandered far from
literary subject-matter. Its biographical articles were of literary
folk; and its pleasant discursive essays, numerous and excellent,
were usually bookish. Many half-tone illustrations made the
successive numbers attractive.

There was not very much fiction at first — a serial most of
the time and a short story in each number. After a year or
more, however, the fictional content increased, with work by
Alice Duer Miller, Grace MacGowan, Basil King, Don Marquis,
Eden Phillpotts, and Henry James. Some humor enlivened the
magazine's pages, notably "The Emily Emmins Papers" by
Carolyn Wells in 1907, and poems by Gelett Burgess. Arthur
C. Benson's essays were a valued feature. Among other prominent contributors were Henry Holt, Gerald Stanley Lee, Herbert Quick, Guglielmo Ferrero, and H. W. Boynton. John G.
Neihardt's delightful *The River and I* was a serial in 1909–10.

The tone of the magazine was, on the whole, conservative in
criticism and in its occasional comment on society and politics.
It was not snobbish, but it had a high regard for what it conceived to be the best standards and for Culture with a capital.

It dropped the name of the *Critic* from its title at the beginning of 1907, only to add that of the *Reader* when it absorbed
that magazine in March 1908; but a year after that date it was
back to its proper title, *Putnam's Monthly*. The circulation ran
up to 120,000 in 1909; but that was not enough for an illustrated general magazine, and the Putnams abandoned their
third venture in the field of the popular monthly with the number for April 1910. The merger this time was with the *Atlantic
Monthly*.

THE COUNTRY GENTLEMAN [1]

THAT pioneer in agricultural journalism, Luther Tucker, was editing and publishing but one periodical in 1852. He was accustomed to drive a tandem, but he had recently disposed of his weekly *Horticulturist*, and this left him only the stalwart monthly *Cultivator* [2] to occupy his abundant energies. Clearly, this was unsatisfactory, especially since his son, Luther Junior, was now eighteen and in training for farm-paper work. A new agricultural weekly was therefore announced, to be published under the name of the *Country Gentleman*; and a preliminary number of it was issued November 4, 1852. This specimen copy demonstrated the plan of its publisher to divide the paper into five departments, devoted to the farm, the garden and orchard, the fireside, current events, and the produce markets.

The new paper was launched on January 6, 1853. A paragraph from Luther Tucker's salutatory address is worth quoting:

[1] TITLES: (1) *The Country Gentleman: A Journal for the Farm, the Garden and the Fireside*, 1853–65; (2) *The Cultivator & Country Gentleman*, 1866–97; (3) *The Country Gentleman: A Consolidation of the Genesee Farmer, 1831–1839, and the Cultivator, 1834–1865*, 1898–June 1911; (4) *The Country Gentleman: The Oldest Agricultural Journal in the World*, July 1911–current.

FIRST ISSUE: January 6, 1853. (There was a specimen number, November 4, 1852.) Current.

PERIODICITY: Weekly. I–XXXIV, semiannual volumes, 1853–69; XXXV–current, annual volumes, 1870–current.

PUBLISHERS: Luther Tucker, Albany, 1853–55; Luther Tucker & Son, Albany, 1856–1911; Curtis Publishing Company, Philadelphia, 1911–current.

EDITORS: Luther Tucker and John J. Thomas, 1853–73 (with Joseph Warren, 1853–54; Joseph Harris, 1855; Luther H. Tucker, 1855–73); Luther H. Tucker and Gilbert M. Tucker, 1873–97 (with John J. Thomas, 1873–94; Luther H. Tucker, Jr., 1893–97); Gilbert M. Tucker and Luther H. Tucker, Jr., 1898–1911; J. Clyde Marquis, 1911–12; Harry A. Thompson, 1812–17; Barton W. Currie, 1918–20; John E. Pickett, 1921–24; Loring A. Schuler, 1924–28; Philip S. Rose, 1928–current.

INDEXED in *Agricultural Index*.

REFERENCE: "The First Hundred Years," by E. H. Taylor in *Country Gentleman*, CI, 3 (March 1931).

[2] See Mott, *A History of American Magazines, 1741–1850*, p. 443.

Wherever the honest, earnest feeling of the heart finds utterance — wherever the deed of generous sympathy is performed — wherever the life is ruled by the principles of honor and religion, do we find the gentleman. . . . Country life is particularly adapted to inspire character of this sort. . . . We have placed a portrait of Washington in our vignette . . . a fit type of the American country gentleman.[3]

The paper was a sixteen-page quarto well printed on good paper with excellent typography. There were some woodcuts, including a series portraying country houses in 1853. The subscription price was two dollars, but it was advanced fifty cents during the latter years of the Civil War. The contents held closely to the departments promised in the specimen number. The farm section dealt with agronomy, stockraising, machinery, and meetings of agricultural societies; for the gardeners there was advice about methods, as well as information about new varieties of vegetables and fruits. A new seedling grape developed by E. W. Bull, of Concord, Massachusetts, to be known as the Concord grape, was announced by the *Country Gentleman* in its second year.[4] The Fireside Department contained entertaining reading, including excerpts from new books, and a Leisure Hour Column of selected poetry.

The editors at the beginning were Tucker, John J. Thomas, and Joseph Warren; and they wrote most of the paper. Professor S. W. Johnson, of Yale, was a valued contributor, and there were many who sent in smaller pieces. Joseph Harris was another important writer for the journal, and a contributing editor in 1855. When Luther H. Tucker was twenty-one, his father took him into partnership in both the editorial and publishing departments.

The *Country Gentleman* prospered in both circulation and advertising. In 1858 it boasted the truly phenomenal circulation of 250,000: this was greatly reduced during the war, however. Rowell's first directory (1869) quoted Tucker's paper at 13,000.

Tucker made a western trip in 1857, and several articles tell of what he saw there. "One of the advantages the prairie farmer possesses over his eastern brethren," he said, "is the peculiar

---

[3] *Country Gentleman*, I, 1 (January 6, 1853).
[4] *Ibid.*, III, 120 (February 23, 1854).

adaptation of his land to the use of labor-saving machinery." [5]
It was this interest in other regions than New York that made
the *Country Gentleman* a national journal and brought it such
a wide circulation. The Middle West was given special attention
through correspondents in the various states.

In 1866 the *Cultivator*, Tucker's fifty-cent monthly, which
had declined even more than the *Country Gentleman* during the
war, was merged with it under the name of the *Cultivator &
Country Gentleman* — the serial numbering of the weekly being
retained. The new arrangement brought back a taste of the
old-time prosperity. In the paper's file the interested reader
may follow the development of the western ranges, the improvement of farm stock, the coming of ensilage and silos, and the
growth of the Grange and the Farmers' Alliance. Luther Tucker
died in 1873; and Luther H. formed a partnership with a
brother, Gilbert M. Tucker. The veteran John J. Thomas remained with them until his death in 1894.

In the eighties the *Cultivator*, as it was now commonly called,
lost much of its ancient prestige. It continued to claim about
20,000 circulation, but the increase of state and regional farm
papers had forced it to draw in its lines and concentrate upon
its own local field.

Upon the death of the second Luther Tucker, a third —
Luther H. Tucker, Jr., — was taken into partnership with Gilbert M. At that time the old name of the *Country Gentleman*
was restored. The price was lowered to $2.00 and later to $1.50.

It was in 1911 that the Curtis Publishing Company purchased
the paper, and the first number under the new management was
issued from Philadelphia July 6 of that year. A succession of
editors, recruited chiefly from the *Ladies' Home Journal* staff,
held office for brief terms during the next decade or more. The
circulation upturn began at once. Within five years it had risen
to 300,000, and the price was lowered to a dollar; in the next
lustrum the circulation rose to about half a million. The paper
was made a national weekly, giving attention to the larger
phases of farming, of country life, and of outdoor living in
general. The tractor and power farming, road building, taxation and freight problems, rural schools, farm homes, and

[5] *Country Gentleman*, X, 116 (August 20, 1857).

women's helps were all major concerns. At the same time, the paper published good popular fiction — especially of the outdoor sort.

But it was not until the change was made to monthly publication and to the subscription rate of three years for a dollar that the new *Country Gentleman* became a record breaker. That was in September 1925, when the circulation was at 800,000; in five years it had doubled that figure, thus achieving the largest circulation ever reached by a farm periodical. Advertising, especially of automobiles and tractors, followed in quantity. In spite of the low price, the magazine was not cheap in appearance or quality. With attractive covers, superior make-up, and good illustration, it appealed to a large public which was not on the land at all. Fiction was important: Joseph C. Lincoln, Zane Grey, Corra Harris, Ben Ames Williams, and Courtney Riley Cooper were favorite authors. A staff of special-article writers included Stuart O. Blythe, Harry R. O'Brien, E. H. Taylor, J. Sidney Cates, and Paul de Kruif. Occasionally there were articles by men well known in public life. Some strictly agricultural articles were notable, as the campaign for lespedeza as a sour-soil crop.[6]

"The oldest agricultural journal in the world" — so runs the subtitle. The chief periodical to dispute the claim is the *American Agriculturist*,[7] which was founded in 1842. In deciding such matters, the ordinary procedure is to consult the serial numbering of the periodicals involved. If we do this, we find that Volume I, Number 1, of the *Country Gentleman* was issued on January 6, 1853, while Volume I, Number 1, of the *American Agriculturist* appeared April 1842. But there is another method of basing claims of priority: a periodical may choose to take over the beginning date of another publication which it has purchased and incorporated with itself. This is the method followed by the *Country Gentleman*. The Albany *Cultivator*, which it absorbed in 1866, was founded in 1834; and the *Gene-*

[6] See article on this campaign and on the history of the *Country Gentleman* by Ben Hibbs, associate editor of the paper, in the *Quill*, September 1934, p. 5. See also *Country Gentleman*, October 1937, p. 4.

[7] See Mott, *op. cit.*, p. 728. The *Southern Cultivator*, founded in 1843, might also dispute this claim, as well as the *Southern Planter*, founded in 1841, which in some respects has the best claim of all.

see Farmer, which the *Cultivator* had absorbed, was founded in
1831: hence the *Country Gentleman* fixes 1831 as its beginning
date. But it should not be forgotten, if we adopt such a method,
that the *American Agriculturist* absorbed the *American Farmer*
in 1897, and that the *American Farmer* was founded in 1819.

FRANK LESLIE'S MAGAZINES FOR WOMEN

THE first of that large brood of magazines fathered by Frank Leslie was a twenty-five cent monthly of sixteen large quarto pages called *Frank Leslie's Ladies' Gazette of Fashion and Fancy Needlework.*[1] Leslie had come to New York in 1853 [2] to engrave woodcuts for Barnum's ill-fated *Illustrated News.*[3] The end of that paper after a few months' trial could not really discourage such an ebullient spirit as Leslie's, and he immediately began to make plans to start a paper of his own. That he had no capital except his skill as an engraver, and his ambition and industry, appears to have been no obstacle. Looking about him, he decided that the fashion magazine promised the quickest returns in the periodical business: in Philadelphia two or three of them were coining money. He found Mrs. Ann S. Stephens, wife of a New York newspaper man and an editor of the Philadelphia *Peterson's,* who was willing to edit the new journal if her name was not printed. So in January 1854 the first number of Leslie's first magazine appeared, without a subscriber.

The *Gazette of Fashion* contained one very large and handsome hand-colored fashion plate; good woodcuts by Leslie & Hooper (who dissolved their partnership in 1854), and others; songs, music for the pianoforte, short stories by Mrs. Stephens, notices of the opera, theater, and art galleries, book reviews, a chess department, folded-in dress and embroidery patterns, and advertising of sewing machines, patent medicines, jewelry, etc.

---

[1] TITLES: (1) *Frank Leslie's Ladies' Gazette of Fashion and Fancy Needlework,* 1854–55; (2) *Frank Leslie's Ladies' Gazette of Fashion and the Beau Monde,* 1855–56; (3) *Frank Leslie's Gazette of Fashion and the Beau Monde,* 1856–57.

FIRST ISSUE: January 1854. LAST ISSUE: August 1857.

PERIODICITY: Monthly. Regular semiannual volumes, of which the last (VIII) contains only two numbers (July and August 1857).

PUBLISHER: Frank Leslie, New York.

EDITORS: Mrs. Ann S. Stephens, 1854–56; Frank Leslie, 1856–57.

[2] See pp. 411–412.

[3] See p. 45.

It was a really attractive periodical for its field. "We have promised," said the publisher in the first number, "that no inferior art shall encumber our pages";[4] and the illustration, with William H. Thwaites as the chief artist, was generally of a high class.

In the second number readers were informed that "three large editions" had been insufficient to meet the demand for the first issue;[5] and at the end of the first year Leslie wrote, "The great success of the Magazine has enabled us to set up our own steam presses."[6] Four pages were added to the monthly issue in 1855 and four more in 1857; the price was increased to thirty cents in 1856.

Mrs. Stephens left Leslie in 1856 to found her own magazine, but he seemed to get on quite as well without her. To be sure, book notices sounded rather too much like publishers' "blurbs," and the increase of anecdotes and small departments gave the magazine a very miscellaneous nature; but society news both from American cities and from abroad conferred a cosmopolitan air, and the art work kept up well. An attempt was made to emphasize American fashions — to improve them, indeed. Said the introductory statement:

Our object is to improve the standard of our own national fashions. . . . We design to carry the influence of our work into social life, manners, household habits, and the thousand elegant and useful trifles which make up the entire life of an intelligent and refined social system.[7]

The chief fashion plate was Parisian, but other styles were sometimes credited to London or New York; and the running title of the magazine the first year was *Frank Leslie's Ladies' Gazette of Fashions of Paris, London and New York*. But however patriotic an adherence to New York's styles might seem, Leslie soon found that what his readers wanted was the latest from Paris; and to Leslie the voice of his public was clearly *vox Dei*.

By 1857 Leslie had made a big success with his general weekly

[4] *Frank Leslie's Ladies' Gazette*, I, 37 (March 1854).
[5] *Ibid.*, I, 17 (February 1854).
[6] *Ibid.*, II, 217 (December 1854).
[7] *Ibid.*, I, 1 (January 1854).

LACES, RUFFLES, FLOUNCES, AND BOWS

These costumes were illustrated and described in *Frank Leslie's Gazette of Fashions* for September 1855. Of No. 1, the description says: "Nothing could be more superb than the decorations of the overskirt. Three falls of rich guipure lace extend round the skirt, and up the opening at the right side, connected by full bows and ends of purple ribbon." The skirt of the ball dress "is ornamented to within a few inches of the waist by a succession of narrow flounces in two shades of rose-color and white, giving it a cloud-like appearance." In the third dress the frills and bows of the sleeves harmonize with the flounces and bows of the skirt.

paper, besides experimenting with two or three other periodicals, and he now decided to incorporate the *Gazette* into a larger journal for the whole family. Accordingly, in September of that year, he founded *Frank Leslie's New Family Magazine*,[8] with a continuously paged supplement carrying the half title *Frank Leslie's Gazette of Fashion*.[9] This sixteen-page supplement was a continuation of the old *Gazette* and was intended as a women's department of the new magazine. "Our lady readers will observe," said the editor in his first number, "that the *Gazette* makes its appearance this month in a new and greatly improved form."[10] The department continued, with separate running title, throughout the life of the *Family Magazine*.

Frank Leslie's New Family Magazine was, of course, much more general in nature than the *Gazette* had been. It began with serials by Ouida and G. J. Whyte Melville, pirated from English periodicals; many travel articles, also "lifted" but very well illustrated, some natural history, and much wit and humor. There were woodcuts in great quantity, and a large hand-colored fashion plate of a quality quite equal to *Godey's*, and of a larger size because *Leslie's* page was larger. In June 1862 an extension plate was published showing twenty-nine figures: to get twenty-nine crinolines on one plate was a feat! This was a woodcut, but extension colored plates came later. The pictures, serials, and humor seem to have been the chief attractions in these first years. Serials were chiefly by English writers such as Wilkie Collins, Mrs. Henry Wood, Miss M. E. Braddon, Mrs. Annie Edwards — all a bit sensational for the times. *Lady Audley's Secret* was a hit of 1862.

The magazine also had something of current affairs. The war

---

[8] TITLES: (1) *Frank Leslie's New Family Magazine*, 1857–60; (2) *Frank Leslie's Monthly*, 1860–63; (3) *Frank Leslie's Ladies' Magazine*, 1863; (4) *Frank Leslie's Lady's Magazine*, 1863–82.
FIRST ISSUE: September 1857. LAST ISSUE: December 1882.
PERIODICITY: Monthly. I, September–December 1857; II–LI, regular semiannual volumes.
PUBLISHER: Frank Leslie, New York.
EDITORS: Frank Leslie, 1857–63; Miriam F. Squier (Mrs. Frank Leslie after 1873), 1863–82.
[9] The half title was carried through June 1866, and the running title to the end of the file.
[10] *Frank Leslie's New Family Magazine*, I, 81 (September 1857).

was followed with pictures and articles. It is clear that Leslie made an effort to hold his southern circulation by treating the secessionists handsomely. He wrote in May 1861 that his was "the only magazine which goes into every part of the Union, north, south, east, and west." [11] "Union" was perhaps an unfortunate word. But by October the magazine was calling the Confederates "rebels" and regarding them as enemies.

A sample number of *Frank Leslie's Monthly*, as it was called after April 1860, may be briefly analyzed. Of the ninety-six pages in the issue for July 1862, nineteen pages are given to serials — chiefly Lady Audley's inviolate mystery — and nearly fifteen to short stories. There are fourteen pages of fashions, and as much devoted to wit and humor and anecdote. Ten pages and a half are given to the war. There is a feature which takes five and a half pages — a lot of replies to a matrimonial advertisement inserted in the *New York Herald*. Four and a half pages are occupied by natural history, three and a half by travel, two by poetry, two by recipes, and one-half a page by puzzles. The measurements include the lavish illustration. Add a fashion plate, several pages of advertisements, and an attractive cover; and you have *Frank Leslie's Monthly* in war times, thirty cents.

In February 1863 it was made somewhat less general in nature and was called, after a little experimenting with the plural possessive, *Frank Leslie's Lady's Magazine*. It dropped its material about the war and became a bit less sensational in its features; otherwise it was much the same. Mrs. Miriam F. Squier, wife of a member of the staff of *Leslie's Weekly*, became the editor. Of Mrs. Squier it is difficult to speak with assurance of justice. That she was, in Gilbertian phrase,

> a lady with a record
> Whose career was rather checkered

cannot be disputed; but she was probably much maligned by the scandalmongers of the period.[12] The publisher and the lady editor fell in love, and after appropriate divorces they were married in 1873. What concerns us most is that Mrs. Squier

[11] *Frank Leslie's Monthly*, VIII, 478 (May 1861).
[12] See p. 461.

was an efficient editor and, after the death of Leslie, an efficient publisher.

The magazine tried hand-colored lithographs in 1864; it had published three in 1857, but now it tried them out for a year or two often in double pages. In 1866 it used chromolithographic frontispieces. By the seventies, however, it was back to the old-fashioned and prettier hand-colored steel plates, using three of them in an issue, but no folding inserts. These fashion plates were charming, but the drawing for the comics in the back of the book was very bad. Woodcuts continued to illustrate fiction and travel.

On March 4, 1871, a weekly for young women was begun, with Mrs. Squier as editor. Strangely enough, it did not have Leslie's name in its title, which ran: *Once a Week, the Young Lady's Own Journal*. After three months the word *Young* came out of the title, and after five months more (with Volume II, Number 10) the periodical was superseded by *Frank Leslie's Ladies' Journal*.[13] Each issue of the new weekly contained a beautiful hand-colored fashion plate measuring about twelve by eighteen inches, as well as handsome large woodcuts. It carried some of the usual Leslie fiction; but gradually it became the leading fashion periodical of the Leslie house, leaving general literature to the monthly *Lady's Magazine*.

The monthly had enjoyed a circulation of 50,000 shortly after the war, but it declined in the seventies. The weekly *Journal* reached some 30,000 by the middle seventies, but both woman's periodicals were down to 6,000 or 7,000 by 1880, when Leslie died. In 1881 Mrs. Leslie merged the *Journal* in the *Lady's Magazine*; and at the end of the next year she combined the *Magazine* with the periodical which was now chief of the Leslie monthlies — *Frank Leslie's Popular Monthly*, later to be called the *American Magazine*.[14]

[13] TITLE: *Frank Leslie's Ladies' Journal: Devoted to Fashion and Choice Literature*.
FIRST ISSUE: November 18, 1871. LAST ISSUE: October 8, 1881.
PERIODICITY: Weekly. Semiannual volumes.
PUBLISHER: Frank Leslie, New York.
EDITOR: Miriam F. Squier (Mrs. Frank Leslie after 1873).
[14] See sketch 26.

THE AMERICAN JOURNAL OF EDUCATION [1]
(BARNARD'S)

THAT Barnard's *American Journal of Education* is "by far the most valuable work in our language on the history of education" was the statement of the Ninth Edition of the *Encyclopaedia Britannica*.[2] The adjectives mon-

[1] TITLES: (1) *The American Journal of Education and College Review*, August 1855–January 1856; (2) *The American Journal of Education*, March 1856–1882. Commonly referred to as *Barnard's American Journal of Education*, and bound volumes are usually so stamped.

FIRST ISSUE: August 1855. LAST ISSUE: [no month] 1882.

PERIODICITY: Irregular quarterly. Suspended, 1874–75. [First Series] I, August 1855, and January, March, May 1856, with Supplement; II, July (called August in Table of Contents), September, December 1856; III, March, June 1857; IV, September, December 1857, and March 1858; V, June, September, December 1858; VI, March, June 1859; VII, September, December 1859; VIII, March, June 1860; IX, September, December 1860; X, March, June 1861. New Series, I–VI, (whole numbers XI–XVI), March 1862–December 1866 (regular quarterly, semiannual volumes). National Series, I (XVII), September 1867, and January, April, September 1868; II (XVIII), *American Year Book and Register* for 1869, with Supplement; III (XIX), *Special Report of Commissioner of Education on Public Instruction in the District of Columbia*, 1870; IV (XX), *Special Report of Commissioner of Education on National Education in Europe*, 1870; V (XXI), *Scientific and Industrial Education . . . in Different Countries in Europe*, 1870; VI (XXII), January 1871, and Nos. 67, 68, 69 [no months], 1871; VII (XXIII), Nos. 70–73 [no months], 1873, with Supplement; VIII (XXIV), March 15, June 13, October 15, December 15, 1873. XXV. (In regard to this volume, C. W. Bardeen, publisher of the final volume (XXXII), purchaser of the plates of the *Journal*, and the dealer who has supplied many libraries with files, issued a printed circular headed "Final Volume of Barnard's American Journal of Education," which says: "Some two-thirds of this volume [XXXII] was originally printed by Dr. Barnard for Vol. XXV of the *Journal*, and the matter is so indexed in the index volume issued by the bureau of education [and in Poole and Jones]. But the sheets so prepared were accidentally destroyed after one or two volumes had been bound up and removed, and the volume never came into circulation." In some sets, therefore, and properly in all but one or two, Vol. XXV is missing. It will be noted that in the numbering of volumes within series it is omitted. However, the Bardeen circular adds: "Dr. Barnard intended to reprint it, but in his straitened circumstances this was not easy, and he substituted for it in the series the *Report of the Commissioner of Education for 1879*. Most sets of Barnard's *Journal* contain this *Report* as Vol. XXV, but some libraries have preferred to leave that volume missing." As

umental, encyclopedic, and invaluable are commonly used in referring to it.[3]

Its editor, indeed, was accustomed to refer to it as "my encyclopedia of education." Henry Barnard was a native of Hartford and a graduate of Yale before he was twenty. Educated for the law, he had served in the Connecticut legislature, edited the *Connecticut Common School Journal*,[4] and headed the common schools of two states — Connecticut and Rhode Island —

---

a matter of fact, Bardeen also bound up some copies of the *Report of the Commissioner of Education for 1880* as Vol. XXV, and the Library of Congress cards specify the 1880 *Report* as Vol. XXV. The circular proceeds: "We have accordingly bound up this [final] volume in two forms, as Vol. XXXII for those who have the other Vol. XXV, and as Vol. XXV for those who have kept that place vacant." Bardeen later ceased to sell his final volume as XXV. There are therefore three variants of Vol. XXV on library shelves — the *Report of the Commissioner of Education for 1879*, that official's *Report* for 1880, and the final or Bardeen volume [XXXII] of the *Journal*. It is doubtful if there is justification for using a commissioner's report for Vol. XXV. If Barnard ever decided to do so, it must have been after he had passed his Vol. XXVIII, for not until then was the 1879 report issued.) International Series, I (XXVI), January, April, July, October 1876; II (XXVII), January, April, July, October, December (Supplement) 1877; III (XXVIII), March, July, October, December 1878, with Supplement; IV (XXIX), *Report of Commissioner of Education for 1877;* V (XXX), March, July, September 1880; VI (XXXI), March, July, September, December 1881. XXXII, Parts 1–5 [no months], 1882 [actual date of publication, 1902].

PUBLISHERS: N. A. Calkins, New York, August 1855, and January 1856; F. C. Brownell, Hartford, March 1856–1860 [F. B. Perkins was actual publisher 1859–60, though Brownell's name continues on the title page]; Henry Barnard, Hartford, 1861–66, 1868–82 [C. W. Bardeen was actual publisher of 1882 volume]; D. N. Camp, Hartford, 1867.

EDITOR: Henry Barnard (with Absalom Peters, Vol. I, Nos. 1 and 2 only).

INDEXES: "Analytical Index to Barnard's American Journal of Education," in *A Catalogue of Educational Literature* (Washington, 1892); volume indexes and classified general index in issue for January 1876; *Poole's* (except XXXI–XXXII); *Jones' Index.*

REFERENCES: Bernard C. Steiner, *Life of Henry Barnard* (Bureau of Education Bulletin, 1919, No. 8), Chapter VII; Will S. Monroe, *Educational Labors of Henry Barnard* (New York, 1893); Sereno Watson, "The American Journal of Education," *New Englander*, XXIV, 518–530 (July 1865); Sheldon E. Davis, *Educational Periodicals During the Nineteenth Century* (Bureau of Education Bulletin, 1919, No. 28), pp. 54–56.

[2] *Encyclopaedia Britannica* (Ninth Edition), article "Education," by Oscar Browning.

[3] See Paul Monroe in *The Cambridge History of American Literature* (New York, 1921), III, 404.

[4] See Mott, *A History of American Magazines, 1741–1850*, p. 694.

before he projected the journal which was to give him an international reputation. He

undertook in March, 1855, on his own responsibility, the publication
of a Journal and Library of Education. Arrangements were accordingly made in April to print the first number of the *American Journal
of Education*, in connection with the proceedings of the [American]
Association [for the Advancement of Education] for 1854, to be
issued on or before August, 1855.[5]

Learning, however, that the Reverend Absalom Peters was
about to begin a journal with similar aims, though with more
emphasis on the colleges and their work, he joined forces with
him, and together they issued two numbers of the new periodical
under the title of the *American Journal of Education and College Review*. After that the two editors agreed to disagree, and
Barnard proceeded with the work under the briefer name as
originally planned.

   Barnard had a fixed aim for his quarterly, and he adhered to
it without much variation throughout the *Journal's* career. In
his preface to the first volume he tells his readers that for many
years he had planned a periodical "devoted exclusively to the
History, Discussion and Statistics of Systems, Institutions, and
methods of Education in different countries, with special reference to the condition and wants of our own." Thus the history
of education, with accompanying biography, was very prominent, and ranged from systems in use under the Ptolemies in
ancient Egypt down to the methods being developed for the
education of the Cherokee Indians. One-third of the pages of
the *Journal* were devoted to educational history.[6] Much of the
source material for a general history of education was given
entire, and classics in educational theory from most of the
great reformers were reprinted. Memoirs of famous educators
were presented in great number, with portraits engraved on
steel by such artists as John Sartain, A. H. Ritchie, and J. C.
Buttre.

   Another feature promised by the prospectus was later carried
out with great thoroughness in the comparative studies in
foreign education. "Discussions of foreign education, often

[5] *American Journal of Education*, Preface to Vol. I.
[6] Davis, *op. cit.*, p. 54.

historical, occupy one-fourth of all the space," one statistical student of the file tells us, "German, British and French leading in the order named, but Holland, Canada, Sardinia, Norway, Sweden, Belgium, and Greece, as well as less important countries, not being forgotten." [7] Karl von Raumer's *Geschichte der Pädagogik* gave up many chapters to the *Journal*; all of Volume III of Savigny's *Geschichte des Römischen Rechts im Mittelalter* was translated; while much of Schmid's *Encyklopädie des gesammten Erziehungs und Unterrichtwesens*, then in course of publication, was likewise taken over. Translations were also made from French, Swiss, and Italian works (including Bonghi's *Publica Instruczione*).

Proceedings of educational societies, surveys of American and foreign institutions, reports of educational officers, bibliographies, and bodies of statistics also fill a large space. When Barnard became the first United States Commissioner of Education in 1867, he utilized the publications of his office to give completeness to his "encyclopedia" or "library" of education.

School architecture, upon which the editor was an authority, was treated at length, with woodcut illustrations. The education of the defective and the criminal, normal schools, college curricula, physical education, and the education of women were also prominent interests.

Among the names which appear as authors of special articles and addresses in the *Journal* are those of most of the educators of any prominence in America. Horace Mann, Francis Bowen, Edward Everett, Tayler Lewis, D. C. Gilman, William Russell, F. P. Huntington, Gideon F. Thayer, W. T. Coggeshall may be cited almost at random.

Educational leaders and the critics generally welcomed the *Journal* with enthusiasm, both in England and America. Of the first volume the *Westminster Review* said, "We received [it] with unmingled pleasure, save in the regret that England has as yet nothing in the same field worthy of comparison with it." But alas, merit and reward do not always go properly hand in hand, and at the end of the eighth volume, the editor confessed to "a formidable and increasing deficit."

[7] *Ibid.*, p. 55.

The first year's experience [he said] convinced me that a very small proportion of those engaged in teaching either high or elementary schools, or in administering State or city systems, or of professed friends of popular education, would labor, spend, or even subscribe for a work of this character; and indeed that the regular subscription list would not meet the expense of printing and paper.[8]

And yet by personal sacrifices, by subscriptions, and by the sale of sets, Barnard carried on until 1878, when he wrote to the educator R. H. Quick as follows:

The publication of the *Journal* has proved pecuniarily disastrous. The subscriptions paid in from year to year have never met the expenses of publication. My small income has been reduced by the deprivation of office and the pressure of the times. No publisher can be induced to undertake the responsibility of the *Journal*; and to carry on the work to a point where the encyclopedic scope of the undertaking could be seen and appreciated has involved my little property in mortgages and myself in obligations which I am now making a desperate effort to meet. If I am successful in disposing of enough sets or volumes of the *Journal* to meet the obligations which mature before the first day of May, I shall continue the publication to the end of Volume XVIII. If I am not successful, the plates (25,000 pages with more than 1000 illustrations of school structures) which have cost over $40,000 will go into the melting-pot . . . to meet my obligations; and thus will end with me an enterprise which has absorbed my best energies for the last twenty years.[9]

"I would as soon hear," exclaimed Mr. Quick in the circular he then addressed to New England superintendents, "that there was talk of pulling down one of our cathedrals and selling the stones for building material!" Friends rallied to Barnard's support, the crisis was passed, and the publication was continued four years longer. In the editor's old age a company was formed to take over the plates of the work and thus make Barnard's last years financially more comfortable. He lived to be nearly ninety, and after his death a final volume (XXXII), made up of some of his remaining papers, was added to the file of the *Journal*.

Remarkable as was Barnard's *Journal*, it should be pointed

out that it failed as a periodical. It stands primarily as a collection of monographs. Barnard was unable to muster a group of loyal contributors or to adhere to a regular system of editing and publishing. Typography and printing are often inferior. The lack of diversification and of the popular touch made it impossible for him to build up a large circulation.

Yet contemporary appreciations were not exaggerated. Two of them may be quoted. "He has done a work for which his country and coming generations ought to thank him and do honor to his name," wrote Ray Palmer of Barnard in 1874,[10] and two years later, in a survey of "Education in America 1776–1876" in the *North American Review*, President Gilman wrote of the *Journal*:

It is the best and only general authority in respect to the progress of education in America in the past century. The comprehensiveness of this work and its persistent publication under adverse circumstances entitle the editor to the grateful recognition of all investigators of our systems of instruction.[11]

[10] *International Review*, I, 65 (January 1874).
[11] *North American Review*, CXXII, 193 (January 1876).

THE UNITED STATES MAGAZINE [1]

THE *United States Magazine*, a dollar monthly, was founded in May 1854 by Alexander Jones, a New York journalist and financial writer. It was a quarto of thirty pages, printed on cheap paper, illustrated by a few wood-cuts, and of a "useful, practical, instructive character." [2] Its subtitle dedicated it to science, art, manufactures, agriculture, commerce, and trade; and its contents were even more varied than this catalogue would lead one to expect. "The publication of a single number has placed it on a paying basis," it boasted in June; [3] and in August the company was reorganized to publish three periodicals. These were the *Magazine*; the *United States Journal*, a monthly newspaper selling for twenty-five cents a year; and the *United States Weekly Journal*, a paper which reprinted the matter in the *Magazine* and the monthly *Journal*. The new organization was called J. M. Emerson & Company and included, besides the printer and publisher Emerson, Jones, David Bigelow (elder brother of John Bigelow, managing editor of the *New York Evening Post*) and Franklin Woods, another journalist.

An editor was hired in the person of Seba Smith. Smith's chief claim to fame was the creation of the Yankee comic character, Major Jack Downing, whose shrewd comments on poli-

[1] TITLES: (1) *The United States Magazine of Science, Art, Manufactures, Agriculture, Commerce, and Trade,* 1854–56; (2) *The United States Magazine,* 1856–57; (3) *Emerson's United States Magazine,* 1857; (4) *Emerson's Magazine and Putnam's Monthly,* 1857–58.

FIRST ISSUE: May 15, 1854. LAST ISSUE: November 1858.

PERIODICITY: Monthly. I, May 15, 1854–April 15, 1855; II, June 1855–April 1856; III–VI, regular semiannual volumes, July 1856–June 1858; VII, July–November 1858. No numbers issued for May 1855, May 1856, June 1856.

PUBLISHERS: A. Jones & Company, New York, 1854; J. M. Emerson & Company, New York, 1854–57; Oaksmith & Company, New York, 1858.

EDITOR: Seba Smith.

REFERENCE: Mary Alice Wyman, *Two American Pioneers: Seba Smith and Elizabeth Oakes Smith* (New York, 1927), pp. 141–150.

[2] *United States Magazine,* I, 27 (May 1854).

[3] *Ibid.,* I, 59 (June 1854).

tics and personalities had amused many thousands of readers when copied into other papers from his own *Portland Courier* and his later magazine, the *Rover*.[4] Smith did the editorial work on both the *Magazine* and the *Journal*,[5] using the scissors more or less, writing a great deal himself, and getting some contributions from members of J. M. Emerson & Company and others. Elizabeth Oakes Smith, wife of the editor and well known as a poet, lecturer, and critic, did some articles on New York theaters. There was a well-illustrated series on "Our Manufactories," as well as biography, travel, ornithology, archaeology, and anecdotes. As might be expected of its editor, humor was notable in the magazine. Smith's "Democritus Junior" perpetrated some good satires, especially the one in which the Yankee sailor Solomon Swop, who accompanies Commodore Perry to Japan, lays down the law to the Japanese "rats." [6] Later, in 1857–58, Smith reprinted in the magazine the first series of Downing letters, following them with the later series which had been appearing in the *National Intelligencer*, all under the title (itself a satire on Thomas H. Benton's autobiography) *My Thirty Years Out of the Senate*. There was much of the European war in 1854–55; and there were political articles, carefully nonpartisan, by the editor. Fiction was not prominent. Large woodcuts engraved by William Roberts and J. W. & N. Orr, and drawn by A. R. Waud and others, appeared, printed on colored stock.

In the middle of 1856, after missing a number, the *United States Magazine* changed to octavo size and raised its price to $2.00 a year. Mrs. Smith now became a leading contributor of poems, essays, and tales; there was better variety and better illustration; and an effort was made to compete with *Harper's*. The *United States Magazine* underbid Harper's, and for a time its illustration (which included fashions and comics) approached the *Harper* level; but it did not carry the popular English serials.

In October 1857 J. M. Emerson & Company took over *Putnam's Monthly*, a high-class periodical which had been founded

---

[4] See F. L. Mott, *A History of American Magazines, 1741–1850* (New York, 1930), pp. 365–366.

[5] Wyman, *op. cit.*, p. 142.

[6] *United States Magazine*, I, 288 (January 1855).

the year before the *United States Magazine*, and which was now ready to give up the struggle to get the balance on the right side of the ledger.[7] After the merger, the name was changed to *Emerson's Magazine and Putnam's Monthly*, which now claimed a circulation of 40,000. The editor's Downing letters, older tales and sketches by Mrs. Smith, now reprinted, and some serials translated from the French were among the leading features. Mrs. Smith also did dramatic criticism and wrote a life of Washington for the magazine. A serial description of the city of Washington was well illustrated. Advertising ran to ten or twelve pages.

The four sons of Seba and Elizabeth Oakes Smith joined their parents at the beginning of 1858, and under the name of Oaksmith & Company, bought the magazine from the Emerson group. Appleton Oaksmith, the eldest son, became publisher; and Edward wrote art criticism, while the other two sons, Sidney and Alvin, wrote on various subjects.[8] But the lack of funds to bring writers of the first class into the pages of the magazine made a popular success impossible, and in November 1858 *Emerson's Magazine and Putnam's Monthly* suspended publication.

Smith thought that failure was owing to the fact that both *Emerson's* and *Putnam's* were moribund when the merger had been made, and announced immediately that a new magazine would be begun the following January to be called the *Great Republic Monthly*.[9] It was to make a special effort to achieve national coverage and to be nonpartisan.

The new magazine was duly launched and was published for eleven months. The Oaksmiths conducted it, writing most of its articles, stories, and poems. Its chief feature was "Life and Travel in the Southern States," illustrated by woodcuts. An-

[7] See sketch 21.
[8] Wyman, *op. cit.*, p. 147.
[9] TITLE: *The Great Republic Monthly: A National Magazine Devoted to the Best Interests of American Literature.*
FIRST ISSUE: January 1859. LAST ISSUE: November 1859.
PERIODICITY: Monthly. I, January–July 1859; II, August–November 1859.
PUBLISHER: Oaksmith & Company, New York.
EDITORS: Seba and Elizabeth Oakes Smith.
REFERENCE: Wyman, *op. cit.*, pp. 148–150.

other travel series told of the West, and there were articles on the street life of New York: thus the magazine attempted to fulfill its promise. A serial history of America, Seba Smith's tedious three-part poems, musical and literary reviews, and fashions made up the contents. The periodical was in the form of a small quarto and left something to be desired in paper and presswork. With it the magazine publishing activities of the Oaksmiths ceased.

LESLIE'S WEEKLY [1]

IN 1848 there came to America, land of opportunity, an English wood engraver of twenty-seven named Henry Carter. He was an ambitious, lively fellow, quick to make both friends and enemies, at once visionary and practical. As a boy he had been attracted to art; but his father, an Ipswich mercer, could not understand and would not encourage such an idiosyncrasy. The boy thereupon smuggled some drawings through the mails to the London *Illustrated News*, concealing his identity, in case they should be accepted and published, under the *nom de guerre* of "Frank Leslie." They were published; and a little later young Carter went up to London, ostensibly to enter a dry-goods house as clerk, but really to be nearer the *Illustrated News*. Within a few years he was chief of the *News* engraving room.

Arrived in New York, Carter found work as an engraver; and when Jenny Lind came to America for her famous tour of 1849, he arranged with Barnum to issue illustrated programs for her various concerts, and followed her company about to

[1] TITLES: *Frank Leslie's Illustrated Newspaper*, 1855–91; *Frank Leslie's Illustrated Weekly* (folio captions omit *Illustrated*), 1891–94; *Leslie's Illustrated Weekly* (folio captions: *Leslie's Weekly*), 1894–95, 1907–12; *Leslie's Weekly*, 1895–1907; *Leslie's, the People's Weekly*, March–November 1912; *Leslie's*, 1912–14; *Leslie's Illustrated Weekly Newspaper*, 1914–22.
FIRST ISSUE: December 15, 1855. LAST ISSUE: June 24, 1922.
PERIODICITY: Weekly. Semiannual volumes, I–CXXXIV; volumes ran December–June and June–December until after Vol. LXXV (June 30, 1892–December 29, 1892), after which they were regularly January–June and July–December.
PUBLISHERS: Frank Leslie, New York, 1855–79; I. W. England, Assignee, New York, 1880–81; Mrs. Frank Leslie, 1881–89; Judge Publishing Company, New York (W. J. Arkell and Russell B. Harrison, 1889–92; W. J. Arkell, 1892–94; Arkell Weekly Company, 1894–98; John A. Schleicher, 1898–1909), 1889–98; Leslie-Judge Company, New York (John A. Schleicher), 1898–1922.
EDITORS: Frank Leslie, 1855–80 (managing editors, Henry C. Watson, 1855–61; Ephraim G. Squier, 1861–68 (?); J. C. Goldsmith, 1873–74); Mrs. Frank Leslie, 1880–89; John A. Schleicher, 1889–1922.
INDEXED in *Cumulative Index, Dramatic Index*.

various American cities and to Havana.[2] When *Gleason's Pictorial* was established in Boston, he removed to that city to take charge of its engraving; but after twelve months he was back in New York planning with Barnum and the Beaches for the founding of the *Illustrated News*.[3] This paper lasted only a few months.

By this time Leslie thought he knew enough about the business of publishing illustrated periodicals to succeed with one of his own. He chose the field of the fashion monthly for his first venture and began *Frank Leslie's Ladies' Gazette of Fashion and Fancy Needlework* [4] in January 1854. It went very well, and at the end of that year Leslie purchased the *New York Journal of Romance*, a story-paper, and revamped it with adequate illustration. But the project which the ambitious artist-publisher had planned for years was the founding of a weekly miscellany to be featured by news pictures like those of the great journal of his 'prentice days, the London *Illustrated News*.

Accordingly, after months devoted to the organization of an efficient art staff, *Frank Leslie's Illustrated Newspaper* was launched December 15, 1855. It was a small folio of sixteen pages, priced at ten cents a number, or four dollars by the year. The contents were highly miscellaneous. The news stories were illustrated by large, striking pictures which were nearly always lively and interesting and which usually followed the events they portrayed by about two weeks — a promptitude in news illustration never before known in America and not matched by any competitor until after the Civil War. Music, drama, the fine arts, the turf, sports in general, army sketches, book reviews, and serial fiction were among the earliest departments. "Frank Forester" edited a weekly "Sporting Chronicle" for some months, and there was an "Editorial Portrait Gallery" series in the first volume. Fashions were introduced in the second year. A religious news department also appeared in 1856, but it was later crowded out by fiction; Leslie was not very friendly to the

[2] See untitled and undated pamphlet headed "New York Common Pleas: Frank Leslie *against* Sarah Ann Leslie," p. 4.
[3] See pp. 409–412 for the *Pictorial;* and p. 45 for the *News.*
[4] See pp. 437–439.

churches and occasionally found opportunity to criticize the clergy. Reade, Lever, Dickens, Pierce Egan, and Miss Mulock were among the authors whose novels were printed serially in the *Newspaper*.

Jacob Dallas drew most of the large news pictures for earlier numbers; other artists were Samuel Wallin, John McLenan, Thomas Nast, and Charles Parsons. In order to prepare the big cuts in a hurry, Leslie would divide the block into as many as thirty-two sections by sawing, giving a section to each of his large force of engravers. Sometimes the joints would show white in the printing, but such defects were inconspicuous. The big cuts were all done by this method, and pictures grew larger and larger. Many of the illustrations bore no relation to news; they accompanied the fiction, or they portrayed subjects from nature or history or the home. A large engraving of "The Monarch of the Glen" appeared October 25, 1856, measuring about two by three feet; and one accompanying the number for March 7, 1857, picturing "General Wayne's Assault on Stony Point" was almost as large. These oversize illustrations had to be folded into the journal. Christmas brought a large pictorial extra. The leading engravers were Bobbett & Hooper, Bross & Bogart, Davis & Berlett, S. F. Baker, and J. W. Orr.

The news events which *Leslie's* chose for emphasis were, in the main, those of the more sensational kind. The Walker war in Nicaragua and the fighting in Kansas were good subjects. The Burdell murder was featured — the first but by no means the last of such cases to receive "a big play" in *Leslie's*.

A copiously illustrated weekly was very expensive to publish, and for the first few months the paper hesitated between success and failure. It is said that Leslie was ready to give up the struggle one day when two subscriptions came in with one mail, and he said to himself, "Well, there are those who think the *Newspaper* is going to last out the year! I'll justify their faith." [5] In six months subscriptions began flooding into the office, and in its third year the paper was claiming over 100,000 circulation. *Harper's Weekly* began in 1857, and bitter paragraphs criticizing the newcomer showed how much Leslie's felt its competition. But the older paper reduced its price to six cents a

[5] *Leslie's Weekly*, CI, 568 (December 14, 1905).

NEW YORK CITY.—ASSASSINATION OF COLONEL JAMES FISK, JR., BY EDWARD S. STOKES, AT THE GRAND CENTRAL HOTEL—THE SCENE OF THE TRAGEDY.—SEE PAGE 290.

FRONT PAGE OF *FRANK LESLIE'S ILLUSTRATED* SHOWING
ASSASSINATION OF COLONEL FISK

number and two dollars a year, and circulation continued to increase, reaching 164,000 before the war.[6] The success of the *Newspaper* "laid the foundations of Frank Leslie's fortune";[7] other periodicals were founded — *Frank Leslie's New Family Magazine* in 1857, *Frank Leslie's Budget of Fun*[8] in 1858, and so on. In 1857 the publisher legally acquired the right to the name "Frank Leslie," now so valuable to him, by an act of the legislature.[9]

The *Newspaper* published much travel material in these years. Such articles lent themselves well to illustration, and there were some interesting expeditions to chronicle — Kane's to the Arctic, Perry's to the Orient, and Livingstone's in Africa. The Crimean War and the Austrian War of 1859 were featured. The paper had a Paris correspondent in 1859. A series on "A Trip from Paris to China, by Our Own Correspondent" was published in 1857; and in that year there was also a series on America's own "Great West." But perhaps the paper did its best work in handling certain New York features: certainly its "City Gossip" was always readable; its continued story of Fernando Wood's troubles was really excellent; its pictures of New York life, such as that brilliant illustrated story of the Election Day of 1858,[10] were lively and vivid. There was a series on watering places in 1857. National events had their place, of course — the laying of the Atlantic cable, the panic of '57, the Lynn strike, pictures of Dred Scott and his family. Sports grew somewhat in importance, especially ballooning, prize fighting, and billiards. Michael Phelan began a billiard department in the paper in January 1859. Other new departments had come in a year or two before — "Progress of Science," "Housewife's Friend," "Family Medical Guide," puzzles. There was some humor — especially cacographic monstrosities.

Henry C. Watson, art and music critic, who had been associated with Poe on the *Broadway Journal*,[11] was for several years Leslie's managing editor, and Park Benjamin was a member of

[6] *Frank Leslie's Illustrated Newspaper*, IX, 145 (February 4, 1860).
[7] *Leslie's Monthly Magazine*, LIX, 358 (January 1905).
[8] See pp. 439–441 for the former; and p. 184 for the latter.
[9] See testimony in "Frank Leslie *against* Sarah Ann Leslie," p. 2.
[10] *Frank Leslie's Illustrated Newspaper*, VI, 367 (November 13, 1858).
[11] See Mott, *A History of American Magazines, 1741–1850*, p. 758.

the staff. E. G. Squier, who had been United States *chargé* to
the Central American states, and is remembered chiefly as an
archaeologist, became a member of Leslie's staff in the late
fifties and succeeded Watson at the beginning of the war.
Thomas B. Thorpe, "generally known as Tom Owen, the Bee
Hunter," was a member of the editorial corps for a year or two.[12]
Another humorist who contributed regularly was Mortimer
Thomson, known as "Q. K. Philander Doesticks, P. B."

The most exciting episode of the early history of *Leslie's* was
the campaign against the "swill milk" abuse. Shocking conditions had been allowed to develop in the dairies which supplied
most of New York City with milk. The cows were fed upon
refuse from the distilleries, with the result that sores developed
all over the animals' bodies, and their tails rotted off, though
the production of milk was stimulated almost up to the time
when the poisoned cows died. There had been some attempts
made to correct this incredible evil, but reformers soon found
that dairies and distilleries alike were allied with the city's
political machine and that nothing whatever could be done even
when the milk distributed to the children of New York was
shown to be filled with the germs of disease. The "swill milk"
business was profitable, and the politicians were committed to
protect the investments of their henchmen rather than the
health of the city's children.

Never were the powers of Frank Leslie better displayed than
in his fight against these vilest of corruptionists. He began the
attack singlehanded, though after a month or two other papers
came to his aid. "For the midnight assassin," he wrote, "we
have the rope and the gallows; for the robber, the penitentiary;
but for those who murder our children by the thousands we have
neither reprobation nor punishment."[13] But editorial comment, vigorous though it was, did not have half the effectiveness
that the picture campaign launched by *Leslie's* artists possessed.
The foul dairies and the diseased, stump-tailed, dying cows were
relentlessly pictured. The *American Medical Times*, in its account of the whole episode, printed three or four years later,
observed that "the delineations of Mr. Leslie, horrible as they

[12] *Frank Leslie's Illustrated Newspaper*, IV, 358 (November 7, 1857).
[13] *Ibid.*, V, 359 (May 8, 1858).

were, fell short of the truth." [14] Certainly the pictures were disgusting and revolting to a degree, but they could not fail to be effective in arousing public feeling. The Board of Health convened in alarm, pretending to investigate, issuing a reassuring report. "Every one of these cows has a vote!" cried Leslie's.[15] It hired detectives to follow the milk wagons and make a note of all the addresses at which milk was left, and then it published these addresses and warned the buyers that they were feeding poison to their children. "Shall these manufactories of hell-broths be permitted longer to exist among us?" Leslie asked.[16] His attacks finally forced a formal inquiry, which, like that of the Board of Health, was perfectly useless because the committee was dominated by the city machine. Chairman of the committee was one Tuomey, "a barefaced, shameless rascal," [17] seconded by Alderman Reed, who "in all that constitutes the scurrilous blackguard and mouthy poltroon," said *Leslie's*, "is Tuomey's superior." [18] And the paper printed a cartoon showing three aldermen whitewashing a stump-tailed cow. Of course, an attempt was made to indict Leslie for criminal libel; but after a hearing marked by violence the action was dismissed by the grand jury.

Leslie's was now deep in city politics. It attacked the whole administration — police, board of health, aldermen, and mayor. Reed, one of the whitewashers, was defeated for alderman that fall; *Leslie's* circulation grew apace; and the mayor was at length forced to appoint a committee from the New York Academy of Medicine to make a real investigation into the "swill milk" scandal. The report of this committee was made in the spring of 1859, and it fully justified Leslie's every contention. "It would be impossible to convey in language," said the doctors, "the sufferings imposed on infancy by this nefarious traffic." [19] This was the end of the war so far as *Leslie's* was concerned, though it took two more years actually to forbid the sale of milk from cows fed on distillery waste; the deed was

[14] *American Medical Times*, IV, 278 (May 17, 1862).
[15] *Frank Leslie's Illustrated Newspaper*, V, 379 (May 15, 1858).
[16] *Ibid.*, V, 385 (May 22, 1858).
[17] *Ibid.*, VI, 90 (July 10, 1858).
[18] *Ibid.*, VI, 120 (July 24, 1858).
[19] *Ibid.*, VII, 329 (April 26, 1859).

finally accomplished by the state legislature in the spring of
1861. But the "nefarious traffic" was practically dead before
this coup de grâce, and Leslie had slain the monster. A gold
watch and chain were presented to the victorious editor "in behalf," as the inscription set forth, "of the mothers and children
of New-York, as a grateful testimonial of his Manly and Fearless Exposure of the Swill Milk Traffic." [20] The lid was decorated with an engraving of the new press just installed for
Leslie's; the links of the chain represented the lost caudal
appendages of the stump-tailed cows; and on the charm was
engraved in miniature the now famous whitewashing cartoon.
The paper gave its readers pictures of the watch and a full
account of the presentation; and who shall say that Leslie's
pride in it all was not justifiable?

Less creditable, certainly, was the tendency of the paper to
feature crime news in these years. It was almost a police gazette
in 1859, with shrieking pictures and sensational stories. Popular
interest in the Daniel E. Sickles murder and the trial which
followed was the main reason for this emphasis. The Sickles
case brought *Leslie's* circulation up temporarily to 200,000.
But the paper was severely criticized for its sensationalism by
the New York press,[21] and it was chiefly *Leslie's* at which *De
Bow's Review* hit in its condemnation of New York illustrated
papers that succeeded "by lending a darker hue to the calendar
of crime." [22]

Prize fighting, then unlawful in most places, was also
"played" by *Leslie's*, though the paper had fits of righteousness
in which it condemned the sport.[23] It gave much space to the
Morrissey-Heenan bout in 1858; and when, two years later,
"Benicia Boy" Heenan went to England to fight Sayers, it followed the arrangements with many columns of letterpress and
pages of pictures. In connection with this contest Leslie
arranged one of the greatest feats of journalistic enterprise in
his career. He sent Dr. Augustus Rawlings, a staff writer, to
cover the fight, accompanied by one of his best artists, Albert

[20] *Frank Leslie's Illustrated Newspaper*, VII, 186 (February 19, 1859).
[21] *Ibid.*, VII, 280 (April 2, 1859).
[22] *De Bow's Review*, XXIX, 328 (September 1860).
[23] See p. 202.

"THE GREAT PRIZE-FIGHT BETWEEN MORRISSEY AND THE BENICIA BOY
AT LONG POINT, CANADA WEST"

Frank Leslie's Illustrated Newspaper, October 30, 1858.

Berghaus. These men made arrangements in London for engraving blocks in the Leslie sectional manner from the Berghaus drawings; twenty-four hours after the sensational encounter, fought desperately with bare fists at a place some thirty miles from London, they had an extra on the streets of the city, where it sold in large numbers, amazing the Londoners with Yankee speed; then they hurried the plates on shipboard, with 20,000 printed copies, and when they reached New York they were ready not only to "scoop" the town with the first complete story of the great fight, but also to furnish full-page pictures of it. The fight edition, dated May 12, 1860, sold 347,000 copies.

The arrival of the *Great Eastern* in September 1859 was the occasion for a special pictorial number. The visit of the Prince of Wales in the autumn of 1860 was chronicled with many illustrations of elegant social functions. The loss of the *Lady Elgin* in Lake Michigan was another sensational story in September 1860. Early in that year the Leslie publications had moved into a new five-story stone building in Park Place.

Meantime, war clouds grew darker and more threatening. *Leslie's* was strongly opposed to abolitionism; John Brown it denounced as a maniac.[24] But the raid on Harper's Ferry and the trial and execution of Brown and his band were big news, and the paper gave the whole episode much attention. Its pictures of the hanging of Brown made an indelible impression on many minds. Three months later *Leslie's* was berating Wendell Phillips for his Toussaint oration at Cooper Union.[25] Leslie aimed at nonpartisanship, only to find his paper criticized by both North and South.

After the first secessions, *Leslie's* at once arranged for correspondents in the South; and one of these dated his dispatches from "Charleston, Republic of South Carolina." Came the firing on Sumter, and a week later a four-page folding picture of the bombardment in *Leslie's*. The paper offered payment to soldiers "in either army" for sketches from which drawings could be made. But this transportation of water on two shoulders could not last, and by the middle of 1861 *Leslie's* was a good Union paper.

[24] See p. 146.
[25] *Frank Leslie's Illustrated Newspaper*, IX, 162 (February 11, 1860).

It became a great pictorial history of the Civil War. In this respect, as in most others, it was in direct competition with *Harper's Weekly*, to which it was inferior in literary excellence and dignity, but which it generally excelled in liveliness. It did not hesitate to issue extras for big events. It carried many full- and double-page action pictures of military engagements and an occasional four-page folding battle scene. Albert Berghaus, Joseph Becker, A. R. Waud, and many others contributed such work. At one time the paper had twelve correspondents at the front.[26]

We have had [wrote the editor at the end of 1864] since the commencement of the present war, over eighty artists engaged in making sketches for our paper, and have published nearly three thousand pictures of battles, sieges, bombardments, and other scenes incidental to the war.[27]

But increases in the costs of production brought the price of *Leslie's* back, by degrees, to ten cents a number and four dollars a year; by 1865 the circulation was down to 50,000. Though in the flush days after the close of the war and before the beginning of the depression of the seventies the circulation went up again, reaching 70,000 and more, it came down once more in the late seventies to less than 40,000. Yet this represented a fair prosperity, and the *Newspaper* and its half-score of associates — story-papers, women's journals, juveniles, and miscellanies — would doubtless have ridden the financial storms of those years if Leslie had interested himself more in them and less in real estate speculation and personal display.

Frank Leslie, now in his forties, was a remarkable man. Short and broad, with a great black beard and lively eyes, he had abundant energy, some degree of artistic ability, and much boldness and daring. He hated his enemies with all his heart, and he loved his friends with equal ardor. He took a personal interest in his employes, especially those of his art department — always the favorite and pivotal branch of his organization. In 1867 Leslie made a trip to the Paris Exposition, to which he had been appointed a commissioner for the United States. He

invited to accompany him on the junket two of his editors —
Ephraim G. Squier, managing editor through the war of the
Newspaper, and Mrs. Squier, editor of *Frank Leslie's Lady's
Magazine*. The supposedly scandalous behavior of Leslie and
Mrs. Squier on this holiday was afterward detailed in the courts
and the newspapers,[28] and it has no special relevance here. Mrs.
Squier was a woman of charm, ability, and a past. In 1873 she
divorced Squier and married her employer, who had in the
meantime arranged a divorce from the wife he had married in
his early London days.[29] The Leslies then built a magnificent
home at Saratoga, where they entertained lavishly; among their
distinguished guests were the Emperor and Empress of Brazil.[30]
In 1877 they made a grand tour to California in a private car,
accompanied by writers and artists.[31] Leslie's business would
probably have supported these and other extravagances, but it
was his speculation in Saratoga real estate which brought him
into bankruptcy in the year of his California trip.[32] He continued, however, to conduct his periodicals, under the watchful
eye of an assignee, until his death in January 1880. By this
time the circulation of the *Newspaper* was down to 33,000.

It had maintained much the same policy through the seventies
that it had formed during the war. Its artists were sent far
and wide on varied assignments. It was perhaps a little less

[28] These matters are set forth in a gay and careless article on Leslie by Fulton
Oursler in the *American Mercury*, XX, 94 (May 1930). Among other errors is
the consistent misspelling of the Squier name.

[29] See pamphlet referred to above, which contains Leslie's sworn statement,
with supporting affidavits, detailing the first Mrs. Leslie's elopement with another artist and subsequent difficulties. Apparently the long-suffering Sarah Ann
of Mr. Oursler's narrative is fictional. She certainly did not contribute to Leslie's
success. The pair were separated long before the Paris junket; Leslie began an
action for divorce the year before that trip, but later withdrew it. He began a
similar action in 1868, withdrawing it likwise two or three years later. The
affair was a tangled skein; there were accusations of adultery on both sides. See
records of appeals in New York court reports, dealing with temporary alimony,
etc.

[30] *Frank Leslie's Illustrated Newspaper*, XLIX, 381 (January 24, 1880).

[31] In Mrs. Leslie's account of this journey, *From Gotham to the Golden Gate*
(New York, 1877), she offended the Virginia City, Nevada, *Enterprise*, which
thereupon issued a scurrilous pamphlet attacking the Leslies. See *Territorial
Enterprise Extra. Containing a Full Account of " Frank Leslie" and Wife* (Virginia City, July 14, 1878).

[32] *Frank Leslie's Illustrated Newspaper*, XLIX, 381 (January 24, 1880).

sensational, but it was always lively. It fought Grant, using Joseph Keppler's cartoons as strong weapons of attack in the first campaign; while for the contest of 1872 it brought to America Matt Morgan, who had made a reputation for effectiveness on the London *Tomahawk*. Morgan, however, did not repeat his English success in America and soon returned to London. J. E. Taylor, John Hyde, Charles Kendrick, and Ben Day were other Leslie artists; Joseph Becker was manager of the art department from 1875 for a quarter of a century.

In its second decade *Leslie's* printed serials by both English and American writers, but they were far from measuring up to those being published in *Harper's Weekly, Appleton's Journal*, or *Every Saturday*. Anthony Trollope headed the Leslie list of authors, and Mary Elizabeth Braddon, who had communicated to the world that terrible secret of Lady Audley's, was prominent in the paper's columns. Edward S. Ellis, one of the best of the dime-novel writers, was a Leslie serialist. Harriet Prescott Spofford wrote many short stories for the paper in the late sixties, as did Richard B. Kimball a few years later. John Esten Cooke and G. J. Whyte-Melville contributed serials in the latter seventies. Thomas W. Knox, one of the foremost travel writers of the time, did many sketches for *Leslie's*. Bayard Taylor, William Winter, and Ella Wheeler were among the paper's poets. But there were also many little-known writers who contributed mediocre work, as well as a good deal of anonymous material; and belles-lettres were, in general, subordinated to the varied fare of politics, the record of amusements and theaters, the news features, and the "Town Gossip" which served, in the main, to set the table of *Frank Leslie's Illustrated Newspaper*.

When Leslie made his assignment, his periodicals were burdened with debts amounting to some $300,000. When he died in 1880, the debts had been reduced to about $25,000.[33] About half his papers had been discontinued. Mrs. Leslie succeeded to the management of the publishing house, bringing to it acumen, executive ability, and careful attention to details. She took the name of Frank Leslie by court order in 1882. Her first big success with the *Weekly* came when she broke up forms which were ready to go to press, in order to make room for the

[33] *Daly's Reports, New York Common Pleas*, X, 86–87.

pictures and story of the Garfield assassination. This coup is said to have made her a profit of $50,000.[34] She devised a decorative cover for the paper, used better stock, improved the printing of the woodcuts, attracted new writers, and raised the circulation in a year or two to nearly 50,000. She became a figure of legend in New York publishing circles. With her passionate past, her two or three divorces, her reputed Creole ancestry, her claim to the title of the Duchess of Bazus, and her publishing success, it was no wonder that she was the object of both respectful praises and satirical jibes. She helped to build her own legend by her dress and behavior: she sat at her desk

dressed in a French costume that is stayed and stiffened till it fits without a wrinkle or a crease. Her sleeves are poems, her back is a study, and her waist could be spanned by a necklace. She wears the tiniest of shoes, and carries a painted feather fan.[35]

Wilkie Collins and Walter Besant were among the writers of Leslie serials in the early eighties. Pictures taken from foreign illustrated periodicals furnished forth a department which had run through the preceding decade and still continued. Also carried over from the seventies was the policy of promoting "independent" political action.

In 1889 Mrs. Leslie sold the paper to W. J. Arkell and Russell B. Harrison, publishers of *Judge*; and it remained in Arkell's control for nine years, the name being changed in the nineties to *Leslie's Weekly*. The paper now became strongly Republican in politics. W. G. Sumner's gold-standard articles were a feature, and the paper gave its chief attention to politics and sports. For a few years serial fiction was abandoned; but in the middle nineties it was resumed, with stories by Julia Magruder, Gilbert Parker, and Conan Doyle. Arthur C. Grisson, E. F. Benson, and Cleveland Moffett were other frequent contributors. There was a children's department edited by Anne Rhodes and a women's department by Ella Starr. Arthur Hornblow did theaters and operas for a time, and increasing attention was

[34] *Leslie's Weekly*, CI, 568 (December 14, 1905).
[35] *Current Literature*, II, 104 (February 1889). See also *Journalist*, VIII, 3 (January 26, 1889).

given to the drama. Bernhard Gillam was art editor; Max Bachmann's clay-modeled cartoons were a feature, and contests in amateur photography excited much interest. Each Christmas brought a de luxe number.

John A. Schleicher, who had been editor of the paper since its sale to Arkell, bought it in 1898 and conducted it throughout the remainder of its life. He kept it consistently a party paper — expansionist, Rooseveltian, anti-Bryan. It furnished an excellent pictorial history of the Spanish-American War, with drawings by such artists as F. Cresson Schell, B. West Clinedinst, and G. A. Traver; and with correspondence from the front by Gilson Willets, Edwin Emerson, George Edward Graham, Teresa Dean, and others. Slashing big half tones from photographs were a feature, and there were many personal stories of the war.

Following the war, *Leslie's* had a boom in circulation, going to 75,000. Politics, sports, and the theater continued to be the leading topics; and there were book reviews, travel series, and much discussion of motors and motoring. Artists who helped make the magazine in these years were Opper, Miranda, Wales, and Christy. Charles Weber's series of New York society girls was a feature. The Boxer War furnished good copy in both pictures and articles.

Schleicher had, apparently, hit upon a winning editorial formula, for circulation steadily advanced until, in the first years of the World War, it was close to 400,000. This formula called for the exploitation in large pictures and short but interesting articles of the more important general news events, a similar treatment of sports and the theater, an emphasis on personalities in the news, a liberal dash of humor, and, in general, a lightness and ease of treatment which made the paper a good one to pick up to distract the mind when waiting in a dentist's office or to while away a railroad journey. The reader was given the satisfaction of thinking he was improving himself, while he was being mildly entertained and amused. It was a kind of tired business man's weekly.

But in the deflationary days following the war, *Leslie's* lost ground rapidly. It had raised its subscription price when it was booming, from the $4.00 rate to which it had adhered for half a century, to $5.00; now it was faced with the necessity of lowering the price. The *Bulletin of Bibliography*, that cynical chronicler of the ups and downs of magazines, printed its obituary: *"Leslie's Weekly* tried a reducer, and like many another seeker after a more 'compact' form, died under treatment. Funeral was June 24, 1922. *Judge* is the residuary legatee." [36]

Frank Leslie's motto was "Never shoot over the heads of the people." [37] From beginning to end, his *Weekly* lived up to that precept. As a result it was never profound and seldom very stimulating; but it was nearly always passably amusing, and in its earlier years especially it presented a vivid and lively picture of the American scene.

[36] *Bulletin of Bibliography*, XI, 138 (May–August 1922).

[37] Joseph Becker in the semicentennial number of *Leslie's Weekly*, CI, 570 (December 14, 1905).

THE BEADLE MAGAZINES

IN 1856 Erastus F. Beadle, who was later to become famous as a publisher of dime novels, began at Buffalo, New York, the publication of a monthly magazine for women called the *Home*.[1] Its editor was Mrs. H. E. G. Arey, a writer of verse and tales, who was also at that time in charge of Beadle's *Youth's Casket*,[2] a juvenile then four years old. Assisting her in the editorship was Mrs. C. H. Gildersleeve.

We shall [said the introductory editorial of the magazine] from time to time, devote our pages to a much neglected form of education — that of the heart. By this we mean the culture of those affections which are the light and peace of the family circle; those warm and earnest sympathies and feelings which bind heart to heart.[3]

Pursuant to this announcement, the *Home* proceeded to print serial stories of the type for which Mary Jane Holmes was just becoming famous; they were written by Mrs. Arey, Mrs. Metta V. Victor, Mrs. Helen L. Bostwick, Mrs. Frances F. Barritt (a sister of Mrs. Victor), and others. The Cary sisters wrote verse and tales for the magazine; William T. Coggeshall and Mrs. Caroline A. Halbert contributed biographical and historical sketches. There was a monthly "Digest of News," abandoned after the third volume, as well as a corner for book reviews and another for recipes, and an "Editor's Department." Fashions were disdained and openly flouted. Beginning with the third year there were a few steel engravings. The magazine

[1] TITLES: (1) *The Home: A Fireside Monthly Companion and Guide for the Wife, the Mother, the Sister, and the Daughter*, 1856–58; (2) *Beadle's Home Monthly: A Journal for the Fireside and Home Circle*, 1860.

FIRST ISSUE: January 1856. LAST ISSUE: June 1860.

PERIODICITY: Monthly. Regular semiannual volumes.

PUBLISHERS: E. F. Beadle, January–June 1856; Beadle and Adams, July 1856–June 1860. At Buffalo, 1856–58; New York, 1859–60.

EDITORS: Mrs. H. E. G. Arey, 1856–58; Mrs. Metta V. Victor, 1859–60.

REFERENCE: F. H. Severance's "Periodical Press of Buffalo, 1811–1915," *Buffalo Historical Society Publications*, 1915, XIX, 234.

[2] See p. 100.

[3] *Home*, I, 11 (January 1856).

contained forty-eight pages octavo, and the price was a dollar a year.

It may be noted that all the writers named above were Ohioans: Mrs. Arey herself had been a resident of Cleveland. But in 1859 the magazine was moved to New York, leaving Mrs. Arey behind. Beadle and his partner Robert Adams had gone to New York to carry on the publication of the dime books; and Mrs. Victor, who with her husband had cast in her lot with the Beadle concern, now became editor of the *Home*. The new editor had begun her career as a writer at the tender age of thirteen, she had contributed steadily to periodicals under the name of "Singing Sibyl," had published several volumes of verse and tales, and she had married Orville J. Victor in the year the *Home* was founded.

But the next year after its flitting, the magazine, having changed its name for a few months to *Beadle's Home Monthly*, was merged with the Reverend S. H. Platt's *Household Magazine*. Probably the absorption of the Beadle House in the production of the dime books had much to do with the abandonment of a venture which was comparatively unprofitable.

After the great success with the cheap novels, however, the Beadles made another experiment in the periodical field, this time with a general magazine called *Beadle's Monthly*,[4] begun in 1866. The newcomer was clearly planned in imitation of *Harper's Magazine*, the great success of the day. "It follows as closely as it can in the wake of *Harper's*," commented the *Nation*.[5] It was illustrated by woodcuts very much in the manner of its prototype; and the chief difference in contents was the lack of departments for "the back of the book" in *Beadle's*, and its failure to use English serials.

Orville J. Victor, general literary editor for the Beadle publications, had charge of the new magazine. He enlisted some competent writers. Harriet E. Prescott, Caroline Chesebrough, the veteran John Neal, and the tyro Frank R. Stockton fur-

---

[4] TITLE: *Beadle's Monthly: A Magazine of To-day.*
FIRST ISSUE: January 1866. LAST ISSUE: June 1867.
PERIODICITY: Monthly. Regular semiannual volumes.
PUBLISHERS: Beadle & Company, New York.
EDITOR: Orville James Victor.
[5] *Nation*, II, 281 (March 1, 1866).

nished short stories. A. B. Street, the Carys, Eben E. Rexford, and Kate Putnam Osgood, who had lately made a great hit in *Harper's* with her "Driving Home the Cows," wrote poetry for *Beadle's*. James Franklin Fitts's excellent war sketches appeared there, together with the reminiscences of Elizabeth Oakes Smith and those racy articles of western travel by Albert D. Richardson which later enriched the pages of *Beyond the Mississippi*.

But the name and imprint of Beadle were handicaps: they were connected ineradicably with dime novels. *Beadle's Monthly* was undoubtedly aiming higher, but it was inevitable that the public should carelessly suppose it to be designed for the devourers of yellowbacks. On the other hand, the Beadle public was disappointed in the more literary airs of the magazine. Thus *Beadle's Monthly*, after an existence of eighteen months, died of being misunderstood.

The weekly *Star-Journal* was founded three years later by the Beadles and continued, under Victor's management, to publish thrillers for many years. Other more short-lived weeklies were *Belles and Beaux*, *Girls of Today*, the *Young New Yorker*, and the *Weekly Novelette*.[6]

[6] For these periodicals, see Volume III, Chapter VII.

HARPER'S WEEKLY [1]

THE old files of *Harper's Weekly* are a delight to the casual reader and a rich treasury for the historical investigator. Here is a vital illustrated history of the years from 1857 to 1916. The combination of pictures, politics, essays, and fiction lends variety; and the frequent excellence of contributions in all these kinds, together with the known influence of the journal upon its times, gives first-rate importance to the *Harper's Weekly* files.

Fletcher Harper was responsible for the founding of the *Weekly*. It "became his pet enterprise," says his grandson, J. Henry Harper, "and until within a few months of his death the best energies of his controlling mind were devoted to it." [2] All those familiar with the affairs of the Harper publishing house agree that Fletcher Harper was the manager of the

[1] TITLE: *Harper's Weekly: A Journal of Civilization.*
FIRST ISSUE: January 3, 1857. LAST ISSUE: May 13, 1916.
PERIODICITY: Weekly. I–LVI, annual volumes, 1857–1912; LVII, January–August 9, 1913; LVIII, August 16, 1913–June 27, 1914; LIX–LXI, semiannual volumes, July 1914–December 1915; LXII, January–May 13, 1916. Supplements for 1870 have separate paging as follows: April 23, May 21, June 25, July 23, August 27, September 17, October 1, October 8, November 19, November 26, December 3. Supplement for December 10, 1870, was paged consecutively with the regular number, as were those in 1871–79 and 1885–91. Supplement for June 25, 1898, was unpaged.
PUBLISHERS: Harper & Brothers, New York, 1857–May 30, 1913; McClure Publications, New York, June 7, 1913–August 28, 1915; Harper's Weekly Corporation, New York, September 4, 1915–May 13, 1916.
EDITORS: Theodore Sedgwick, 1857–58; John Bonner, 1858–63; George William Curtis, 1863–92; Carl Schurz, 1892–94; Henry Loomis Nelson, 1894–98; John Kendrick Bangs, 1898–1901; George Harvey, 1901–13; Norman Hapgood, 1913–16. (Managing Editors: Henry Mills Alden, 1863–69; S. S. Conant, 1869–85; Montgomery Schuyler, 1885–88; John Foord, 1888–92; Richard Harding Davis, 1892–94. In other years the general editors were managing editors.)
INDEXES: *Poole's, Readers' Guide, Cumulative, Engineering, Annual Library, A. L. A. Portrait, Dramatic.*
REFERENCES: Fiftieth Anniversary Number of *Harper's Weekly* (LI, 1–34, January 5, 1907); J. Henry Harper, *The House of Harper* (New York, 1912); Edward Cary, *George William Curtis* (Boston, 1894); Albert Bigelow Paine, *Th. Nast, His Period and His Pictures* (New York, 1904).
[2] Harper, *op. cit.*, p. 152.

Weekly until his retirement in 1875. "Every Monday morning," writes one of his editors, "he brought me the scheme of the illustrated pages of the next number." [3] He bought much of the fiction, hired the editors of departments, and was in close touch with the political writers.[4] One of his sub-editors later wrote that Fletcher Harper was *the* editor, who, modestly pretending to be no more than a printer, or at the most a manufacturer, yet saw and examined, either in manuscript or in proof, all that went into the *Magazine* and the *Weekly* — except routine matters, and even on these he kept a sharp eye.[5] Fletcher was the youngest of the Harper brothers; like the others he was a trained printer, a shrewd and enterprising business man, and a good Methodist. He appears to have had somewhat more boldness than his brothers. "When you fight, fight," was his maxim, said George William Curtis, and added that his was "a sturdy and masterful nature." [6] But he was, withal, courteous, patient, and even genial toward his associates. Add to these qualities industry and ability to judge men and breadth of interests, and we have the chief characteristics of a successful editor.

Theodore Sedgwick, a lawyer and publicist to whom President Buchanan offered the mission to The Hague in 1857, did most of the political writing for the *Weekly* in that year and has therefore been called the first editor. It is doubtful if he did much or any office work, however; and when, early in 1858, he was appointed attorney for the Southern District of New York, he was succeeded by a member of the Harper organization, John Bonner, who acted as managing editor for the next five years.

The new periodical, subtitled *A Journal of Civilization*, was modeled to a certain extent upon the *London Illustrated News*; but the resemblance is not very striking, except perhaps in typography. It was doubtless suggested by *Frank Leslie's Illustrated Newspaper*, founded a little more than a year earlier. The news element was stressed, and the new journal was advertised as a "family newspaper": "in the first place and be-

---

[3] *Harper's Weekly*, LI, 11 (January 5, 1907).
[4] *Ibid.*, XXI, 458 (June 16, 1877).
[5] Charles Nordhoff, *Reminiscences of Some Editors I have Known* (San Diego, California, 1900), p. 5.
[6] Harper, *op. cit.*, p. 406.

fore anything else," said one announcement, "it is a first-class newspaper." [7] In size it was a small folio of sixteen pages. Editorials occupied the first page in the earliest numbers, but they were soon relegated to the second page in order to emphasize on page one the pictures which came to be an increasingly important feature of the *Weekly*. Editorials were followed by light essays, a department of "Chat" (later superseded by Curtis' "Lounger"), three columns of short and not very incisive book notices, and then nearly two pages of domestic and foreign news in small print. Notes and queries, agricultural items, a market summary, and a humorous column or two furnished the early departments. There was much miscellany from the fields of travel, biography, and general information, with some verse, and a page or two of advertising. After the new journal struck its stride, it was never without its serial, and sometimes two at once; in its first three volumes it printed Dickens' *Tale of Two Cities*, Collins' *The Woman in White*, Curtis' single venture in the novel, *Trumps*, and other serials by Bulwer, Reade, and Mrs. Gaskell. Some unsigned short stories by Nora Perry, Fitz-James O'Brien, and others appeared in these years; but they were not numerous.

The pictures in the first few issues were neither numerous nor important, but the number increased rapidly, and on April 11, 1857, appeared the first full-page engraving — a picture of President Buchanan and his cabinet. The opening of the second volume was signalized by the printing of three full-page woodcuts in one number; and on March 6, 1858, came the first double-page picture, a portrayal of the steamship *Leviathan*. Thwaites, Hoppin, Hitchcock, and Fredericks were among the artists employed. Homer and Hennessey made their beginnings here in the early years. The method of engraving the big cuts was to make the drawing upon the large block and then to saw it up and assign each section to a separate engraver, according to Frank Leslie's formula, thus making it possible to publish news cuts promptly in spite of the toilsome process of the graver. Neither draughtman's nor engraver's name was signed to most of this early work.

Nor were names commonly signed to anything in *Harper's*

[7] Note in Index of Vol. III.

Weekly in the antebellum volumes, except to serial fiction. This resulted in at least three controversies over authorship. The first of them raged over William Allen Butler's famous "Nothing to Wear," which appeared in the sixth number with pictures by Hoppin; of its swift popularity, wrote Howells later, "the prairie fire suggests but a feeble image." [8] The other two were John Whitaker Watson's "Beautiful Snow"; and "The Picket Guard," better known as "All Quiet Along the Potomac," signed E. L. B. (as for Ethel Lynn Beers) but actually a reprint, the authorship of which is not even now wholly settled.[9]

The *Weekly* had been designed largely as a vehicle for that political discussion which *Harper's Monthly* eschewed. The first article in its first number was an editorial some four thousand words long on the results of the recent election, presumably by Sedgwick. Editor and owners were good Democrats, and the *Weekly* expressed entire confidence in Buchanan, just elected after "a canvass angry and excited to an unusual degree" — a confidence in which only "partisan jealousy" could refuse to join. The central idea of the editorial was that the election had been a glorious triumph for the noble principles of Union and Compromise, Harmony and Concession. The words "conservative," "sound," "proper," occurred again and again in the editorial pages of the *Weekly* before the war. An advertisement in the second volume declared that

the object of the magazine will be to unite rather than to separate the views and feelings of the different sections of our common country. They [the publishers] will continue to fill the magazine with articles inculcating sound views in Life and Morals; leaving, as heretofore, the discussion of sectarian opinions in Religion, and sectional questions in Politics, to their own appropriate organs.[10]

But sectional questions were so much in the news that they could not be avoided: there was, for example, the John Brown episode, concerning which "Porte Crayon" was drawing a notable series of sketches for the picture pages. Could it be ignored in

---

[8] Quoted in J. A. Kouwenhoven's article about the poem, *Colophon*, N. s., II, 101 (Autumn, 1936).

[9] See *Southern Historical Society Papers*, VIII, 255, for claims of Thaddeus Oliver.

[10] *Harper's Weekly*, II, 271 (April 24, 1858).

the editorial columns? Certainly not; and accordingly the uprising was said to be "the work of a half-crazed white, whose views were, to say the least, vague and indefinite . . . horrors of servile war. . . . Mr. Brown will, we think, have cost the Republicans many thousand votes." [11] There were echoes in the columns of the *Weekly* of resentments which this compromise policy was bound to arouse among those whom the editor called "the ultras of both parties." Very early, *Putnam's Monthly*, actuated not wholly by jealousy of Harper success, remarked that "whoever believes in his country and its constant progress in developing human liberty will understand that he has no ally in *Harper's Weekly*," [12] and the *New York Tribune* was accustomed to refer to the new paper as the *"Weakly Journal of Civilization."* On the other hand, the growing anger of the South was not to be cooled by any middle-of-the-road policy. But the prosperity of the *Weekly* was evidence that extreme views were at least not universal. It went on from 60,000 circulation in May 1857, to 75,000 in November of the next year, and 90,000 in October 1859.

It published on January 7, 1860, full-page and double-page pictures of "the great Union meeting at New York" which had taken place six weeks before (for engraving and printing processes were slow at best). Its editorial on "The Nomination of Lincoln" was devoted to a discussion of the defeated Seward, who, it said, "towered head and shoulders above all competitors . . . in every quality which can fit a man for the presidency." [13] But there was practically no discussion of the campaign of 1860, doubtless because of the difficulties of the *Weekly's* position. Many editorials and very many pictures were given in 1860, not to the campaign, but to the visit of the Prince of Wales; and the leader the week before the election was headed "The Prince Among the Ladies." When South Carolina left the Union, the *Weekly* printed a picture of the seceding congressional delegation of that state, with eulogistic sketches of the members; [14] and this was followed by a similar treatment of the

[11] *Ibid.*, III, 690 (October 29, 1859).
[12] *Putnam's Monthly*, IX, 296 (March 1857).
[13] *Harper's Weekly*, IV, 338 (June 2, 1860).
[14] *Ibid.*, IV, 802 (December 22, 1860).

other seceding groups. January 12, 1861, it referred to its "illustrations of the pending Revolution." Immediately after Lincoln's inauguration it stated its conviction that "there can be no question but the enterprise of holding the union together by force would ultimately prove futile," and it still favored compromise.[15] But after Sumter and Lincoln's call to arms, the *Weekly* declared that "the northern blood is up. . . . As war has actually begun, and exists, what is the use of deprecating it?" [16] And the next issue found the blood of the *Weekly* up. "It is a question of whether northern men will fight." If they will, and "if Abraham Lincoln is equal to the position he fills," the war will be over in a few months. But "Mr. Lincoln must remember that this is no time for trifling." As for slavery, "this is a matter which concerns the southern states exclusively." [17] But the criticism of Lincoln which marked the 1861 and 1862 volumes changed to enthusiastic support by the end of 1863. Thus we have in outline the progress of a conscientious conservative in the days when the war clouds darkened and the lightning began.

A new epoch opened for *Harper's Weekly* in 1862. Not only did it find its true position in relation to the war about that time, but it brought to its support the two men who were to connect their names with its history most prominently — George William Curtis and Thomas Nast. Curtis had been an important contributor for some five years; indeed his notes on arts and manners under the heading of "The Lounger" had been a regular and attractive feature since the autumn of 1857. When he came to the post of political editor of the *Weekly* in 1862, he had won a reputation as an essayist and public speaker. He had been a Frémont Republican and had campaigned for Lincoln. Nast was a young artist of twenty-two who had worked on *Frank Leslie's Illustrated Newspaper* and the *Illustrated News*, the two competitors of *Harper's Weekly* in the field of illustrated journalism. He also was an ardent Lincoln admirer.

The combination of news and editorial features on the war with pictures by Nast, A. R. and William Waud, Theodore R.

[15] *Harper's Weekly*, V, 146 (March 9, 1861).
[16] *Ibid.*, V, 258 (April 27, 1861).
[17] *Ibid.*, V, 274 (May 4, 1861).

Davis, Robert Weir, Andrew McCallum, and A. W. Warren made a pictorial history of the war which was popular and valuable. Artists were early sent to the front with the armies, and Federal officers were enlisted in aid of the paper's effort to present full accounts of military operations by pen and pencil. This led to some difficulties, and at one time Secretary Stanton ordered the paper's suspension, alleging that it had been guilty of giving "aid and comfort to the enemy" by publishing pictures of the works before Yorktown, which McClellan was then besieging. Fletcher Harper went to Washington and by diplomatic handling of the matter received not only a revocation of the order but the informal thanks of the secretary for the *Weekly's* services.[18] Nast's war pictures were neither illustrations nor satirical cartoons, but imaginative works dealing with the feelings and sentiments of war time. "Santa Claus in Camp" in the Christmas number, 1862, is an example of one type; another kind foreshadows the fierceness of the later Nast in its severe and even brutal arraignment of southern atrocities in the border warfare. There can be no doubt that these pictures stimulated enlistments: Lincoln is reported to have said that "Thomas Nast has been our best recruiting sergeant." [19]

The editorial page now made up for earlier criticisms of Lincoln by its eloquent tributes to the "wisdom and passionless equity which have marked his official career." [20] It powerfully supported him in his campaign for re-election. Nast's "Compromise with the South," showing an exultant Confederate soldier clasping hands with a crippled and defeated Union soldier over a grave "To the Memory of Union Heroes in a Useless War," was the first of Nast's great political cartoons. An increased edition of the paper containing it was called for, and the picture was used as a campaign document. There was much also of the troubles with England, and later of reconstruction problems.

The war circulation of *Harper's Weekly* was larger than ever. It went to 120,000 by the end of 1861 [21] and stayed at a figure

---

[18] *Ibid.*, XXI, 458 (June 16, 1877). See also Harper, *op. cit.*, p. 181.
[19] Paine, *op. cit.*, p. 69.
[20] *Harper's Weekly*, VII, 818 (December 26, 1863).
[21] *Ibid.*, V, 818 (December 28, 1861). See also June 27, 1863.

above the 100,000 mark throughout most of the conflict — a very unusual circulation for that time. After the war, the sub-scription list, while it showed some decrease owing to slackened interest in public affairs and to the competition of the improved *Leslie's* [22] and other journals of opinion newly founded, did not experience the slump which came upon the *Monthly*.[23] By 1872 it had reached 160,000, and its three pages of advertising were highly remunerative.[24] The impeachment of President Johnson and the campaign of 1868 furnished matter of great popular interest: Curtis' editorials and, even more effectively, Nast's cartoons captured the attention of the time. Curtis, as always, was less radical than Nast and opposed the impeachment. "We believe that he is faithful to what he conceives to be the best in-terests of the country," wrote Curtis of the President. "And while upon this question we wholly differ from him, we differ with no aspersion or suspicion." [25] Nast, on the other hand, cartooned "Andy" as Iago, Nero, a bully, a Ku-Kluxer, a would-be king. This disharmony between editor and leading cartoonist was to reappear from time to time, but Fletcher Harper insisted that "the *Weekly* is an independent forum. There are many contributors. It is not necessary that all should agree." [26] During Grant's campaign, however, editor and car-toonist were happily united. Curtis was a Grant elector. Grant was Nast's great hero, Nast was pleased with a new contract from the Harpers calling for $150 a double-page,[27] and Sey-mour furnished a target for bitter cartoons which was utilized pitilessly.

In the meantime, the *Weekly* was not all politics. The English serials continued, by Dickens, Reade, Collins, Lever, and the rest.[28] Reade's *Terrible Temptation*, which shocked the paper's readers by introducing the mistress of a London society man,

---

[22] *The Land We Love* thought the *Weekly's* "popularity is monthly waning before the reconstructed *Leslie's*" (V, 79, May 1868), and it had no predilection for the latter.

[23] See p. 393.

[24] See p. 14.

[25] *Harper's Weekly*, March 3, 1866; December 15, 1866.

[26] Harper, *op. cit.*, p. 241; Paine, *op. cit.*, p. 123.

[27] Paine, *op. cit.*, p. 120.

[28] For financial arrangements with English writers and pirating difficulties ex-perienced by *Harper's Weekly*, see p. 386.

as well as by using the lady's boudoir as a setting, brought much censure upon the Harper brothers. Some newspapers went so far as to leave out all mention of the *Weekly* as a mark of their disapproval — a kind of journalistic banishment to Coventry. Two Americans were represented by serials in these years — Fitz Hugh Ludlow and William M. Baker. The latter's *Inside: A Chronicle of Secession*, written under the pen name of "George F. Harrington" (though at first unsigned), achieved a real success. Justin McCarthy, Mrs. Piatt, Harriet Prescott, and J. Ross Browne contributed signed pieces, but most articles were anonymous. A travel and adventure sequence by Sir Samuel Baker and literary reminiscences by S. C. Hall were notable serials. In 1870–71 the Franco-Prussian War occupied much space.

The pictures, now a large part of the contents of the *Weekly*, included illustrations of events, places, and persons in the news, social cartoons by such artists as Charles G. Bush and Thomas Worth, comics, and (until the *Bazar* was started in 1867) some fashion plates. W. J. Linton, writing of the art work done for the *Weekly*, found it hasty and journalistic through the war. But "by 1871 the improvement is very noticeable. Designs and engravings assume a more ambitious character, both in size and effect. But the engraving is not much improved." [29] Linton's prejudice against the *Weekly*, which had become by the time of his writing a leading exponent of the "new school" in engraving,[30] prevented him from doing for that journal more than his stern critical sense demanded as minimum justice; but he praises the portraits of the seventies and notes the great staff of designers and painters built up by the house of Harper — Abbey, Reinhart, Shirlaw, Church, Perkins, Julian Scott, E. W. Perry, Eytinge, Champney.[31] Woodcuts by Frederick Juengling and George Kruell were of paramount importance in the work of the more resourceful engravers who were becoming prominent. An artistic feature of 1872 was the publication of Doré's London, with the French blocks. There were frequent maps, bird's-eye views, and so on, published as folded supplements. In 1876

[29] W. J. Linton, *History of Wood-Engraving in America* (Boston, 1882), p. 29.
[30] See Volume III, Chapter VII.
[31] Linton, *op. cit.*, p. 43.

there was a full pictorial record of the Centennial Exposition at Philadelphia.

Thomas Nast's greatest work came in the seventies; it consisted of a campaign against the famous Tweed ring which was then in absolute control of New York's government. Probably no group of political corruptionists ever gained greater power in America than the Tweed ring, and no cartoon campaign has ever been so effective as that of Nast against Tammany. Later investigation has established the astounding fact that Tweed and his fellow-thieves robbed the city of $200,000,000.[32] Many devices were employed in these robberies, but the courthouse in process of erection in 1870 was perhaps the juiciest plum the gang ever bit into. The record which was finally shown to an incredulous world disclosed that one plasterer supposed to be working on that building had received $50,000 a day for an entire month; the total received by this Andrew J. Garvey, "Prince of Plasterers," for his season's job was $2,870,464.06, and the *New York Times* appropriately suggested that he could afford to donate the extra six cents to charity.[33] When Nast, in *Harper's Weekly*, took up his pencil for relentless war on the carnival of graft, he was supported only by the *New York Times*: other papers kept under cover. In the days of the first pictures of misgovernment and of the cartoons of Tweed as the power behind the throne, the arrogant chief could ask, "What are you going to do about it?" And since the city government's records were unobtainable, the question seemed pertinent. Tweed, however, was able to strike at the Harpers, who had been furnishing the textbooks for the city schools; early in 1871 he threw out all the Harper books and installed a set printed by a Tammany-owned company. This was indeed a solar plexus blow, and a majority of the Harper firm wished to surrender at once. When affairs reached a crisis, Fletcher Harper saved the day by seizing his hat in the midst of a conference of the firm and saying, as he stood at the door, "Gentlemen, you know where I live. When you are ready to continue the fight against these scoun-

[32] Matthew J. O'Rourke in the *New York Herald*, January 13, 1901, quoted in Paine, *op. cit.*, p. 177.
[33] Paine, *op. cit.*, p. 176. Of course, it was the Ring, not Garvey, who received nearly all of this money.

HARPER'S WEEKLY.

A JOURNAL OF CIVILIZATION

Vol. XV.—No. 773.]   NEW YORK, SATURDAY, OCTOBER 21, 1871.   [WITH A SUPPLEMENT. PRICE TEN CENTS.

Entered according to Act of Congress, in the Year 1871, by Harper & Brothers, in the Office of the Librarian of Congress, at Washington.

THE ONLY THING THEY RESPECT OR FEAR.

"We presume it is strictly correct to say that the one consequence of thieving which —— would now dread is a violent death. Public scorn, or even the penitentiary, has little terrors for them."

"We do not know how the affair may end, but we do know that if —— close their careers in peace, and ease, and affluence, it will be a terrible blow to political and private morality."—*The Nation.*

NAST SHOWS THE TWEED RING COWERING BENEATH THE SHADOW OF THE GIBBET

The quotation from the *Nation*, which says that the only punishment which Hall, Tweed, and Connolly fear is "violent death," was attacked by the *New York Sun* as an incitement to riot when it first appeared in the *Nation*, but was reiterated by that periodical.

drels, send for me. Meantime I shall find a way to continue it alone." But they did not let Fletcher Harper go, and the fight against the scoundrels went on even more relentlessly.[34] "Tweedledee and Sweedledum" — Tweed and Sweeny — were pictured passing out banknotes from the looted treasury; the city of New York was shown under the gigantic thumb of "The Boss." At last, in July 1871, the city records, which had been obtained through a trick, were published, and Tammany began a disorderly retreat. Nast, who had been threatened repeatedly and had actually removed his residence from the city, was now offered $100,000 by a Tammany banker to take a trip to Europe "to study art." "Do you think I could get *two* hundred thousand?" asked Nast. "Very possibly. You have great talent," said the emissary. Nast, having a curiosity to know what his absence was worth, bid the banker up to half a million and then said to him: "Well, I don't think I'll go to Europe. I made up my mind not long ago to put some of those fellows behind the bars, and I'm going to put them there!"[35] The great "Let us Prey" cartoon, showing Tweed, Sweeny, Connolly, and Hall as vultures on the mountainside with the lightning flashing about them, appeared September 23, 1871; and "The Tammany Tiger Loose," showing the tiger in a Roman amphitheater tearing the prone figure of the Republic, while Tweed as emperor, surrounded by his henchmen and the crowds, looks on, came on November 11. This was the first prominent appearance of the Tammany tiger in a cartoon. The two cartoons just referred to not only were powerful in meaning, but were admirable pictures. Two others must be mentioned: the one showing the shadow of the gallows above the cowering or mock-defiant gangsters (October 21) and " 'Twas Him," showing fifteen of the looters in a circle, each pointing to his next neighbor in answer to the question, "Who stole the people's money?" Finally the gang went to pieces. Some confessed, some fled to Europe, some died in prison. Tweed, who escaped from an American jail, was later captured in Spain by a Spanish official who identified him by means of a Nast cartoon in the *Weekly*, and who, though he had no idea of the real nature of the man's offense, could see by the

[34] *Ibid.*, p. 159.
[35] *Ibid.*, p. 181.

picture that he was an undesirable.[36] Tweed died in the Ludlow
Street Jail in 1878.

The wide significance of this great fight had made it a national
rather than a municipal episode. The *Weekly's* circulation
trebled; Nast had won undeniable fame. The next chapter of
the journal's greater political achievement belongs to the history of the national campaign of 1872, in which Nast cartooned
Greeley unmercifully. Greeley was undoubtedly a figure of
mirth in some respects, but the cruelty of Nast's attacks aroused
some resentment. Bellew, in the *Illustrated News*, showed
Curtis and Nast mixing a tremendous bowl of mud in the
Harper's Weekly office, while the Harper brothers look on with
mingled horror and amusement. Nast is spitting in the filthy
broth, while Curtis, his hands full of mud, says: "Don't spit in
it, Thomas; it is not gentlemanly." As a matter of fact, the
gentle and aristocratic Curtis was much distressed by Nast's
cartoons of certain of his friends who were supporting Greeley.
"To Curtis," says Paine, "the cartoon was not a gentleman's
weapon — at least not a weapon to be used on a gentleman." [37]
Undeniably it was sometimes brass knuckles as Nast used it.
As time went on, the breach between the *Weekly's* editor and
cartoonist was reopened frequently. "Nast and George William
Curtis are rival editors on the same journal," said the *Chicago
Inter-Ocean* in 1876.[38] Nast had plenty of issues — the defense
of Grant, the skeleton army, the Hayes-Tilden campaign — and
on all questions he was extraordinarily effective. It was Nast
who invented the Republican elephant as a symbol of the Republican party, and who popularized the donkey as the emblem
of the Democrats.[39] He first made the donkey famous in this
connotation by his cartoon rebuking the "Copperhead Press"
for its attacks on the memory of the dead Stanton: the picture
was based on the Aesopian fable of "The Live Jackass Kicking
a Dead Lion," which appeared January 15, 1870. The elephant
was the symbol of "The Republican Vote," which had lately
been so large, and it was first shown as frightened by the Demo-

[36] Paine, *op. cit.*, p. 336.
[37] *Ibid.*, p. 244.
[38] *Ibid.*, p. 321.
[39] For earlier Democratic donkey cartoons, see William Murrell's "Rise and
Fall of Cartoon Symbols," *American Scholar*, IV, 312 (Summer, 1935).

cratic ass in a lion's skin and about to fall into a hidden trap of Repudiation, Reconstruction, and Southern Claims Chaos. The elephant first appeared November 7, 1874.

When it came to the Garfield-Hancock campaign, Nast's liking for Hancock and his dislike of Garfield had to be adjusted to the *Weekly's* needs; and as a result his cartoons lacked the customary vigor, and Gillam, Rogers, Thulstrup, and others supplemented his work.

Blaine was a bête noire to Curtis, Nast, and the whole Harper organization, and when he was nominated for president in 1884 the *Weekly* supported Cleveland throughout that acrimonious campaign. "We calculated when we decided to oppose the Blaine ticket," says a member of the firm, "that it would cost the House about a hundred thousand dollars in business losses; but in reality that figure was largely exceeded." [40] The fact is that, although the *Weekly* had always claimed to be nonpartisan, it had been consistently supporting the Republican party, Curtis had been an active leader in that party, and a subscription list had been built up which depended much on Republican support. Thousands of protests were received by the publishers and editors, and an avalanche of partisan attacks was loosed against the journal by the Republican press. Moreover, as it happened, Gillam assailed Blaine more effectively in *Puck* than Nast did in the *Weekly*.[41] Nast's old friend Petroleum Vesuvius Nasby, satirizing at once the artist's fondness for classical subjects, his apostasy, and his decline, wrote:

Mr. Nast had better quit taking Roman subjex and fly back to the tropix [where the elephant and tiger were at home]. The best thing he can do is to fall back on his regular pictur of an elephant with his back broke by somebody's climin' onto it, with the legend under, "Broken at last." [42]

Frank Beard, A. R. Waud, and others cartooned Curtis and Nast repeatedly in the Republican *Judge*.

This was Nast's last presidential campaign; after its close he drew some pictures, including a few strong comments on the labor troubles which occupied much of the *Weekly's* attention

[40] Harper, *op. cit.*, p. 503.
[41] See Volume III, sketch 30.
[42] Paine, *op. cit.*, p. 496.

and a powerful cartoon against the Chicago anarchists; but in 1887 — ten years after Fletcher Harper's death — he retired from the journal to which he had made such important contributions. "In quitting *Harper's Weekly*," said Henry Watterson long afterward, with some exaggeration, "Nast lost his forum: in losing him, *Harper's Weekly* lost its political influence." [43] He later acquired a paper of his own, but it was unsuccessful, and he died a consul to Guayaquil, Ecuador, whither he went, he told his friends, "to learn how to pronounce its name." He was probably America's greatest cartoonist. His success came largely from his fire and boldness, united with a fine sincerity, an ardent imagination, and strong feeling. His pictures, said James Parton (who was related to him by marriage), "were as much the expression of heartfelt conviction as Mr. Curtis's most impassioned editorials, or Mr. Lincoln's Gettysburg speech." [44]

Harper's Weekly never regained the circulation it lost in the campaign of 1884. It had for several years been missing the magical names of the group of English novelists who had passed; Farjeon, Payn, and Braddon could not equal Dickens, Reade, and Collins. Hardy, Besant, and others came on in the eighties; and William Winter wrote much on dramatic themes in the latter part of the decade. In the nineties the journal improved greatly in appearance, with calendered paper and big half tones. Lafcadio Hearn's *Youma* appeared serially in 1890, with short stories by the sensational Kipling, and Frederick Remington's articles illustrated by himself. John Kendrick Bangs was a frequent contributor of prose and verse. His *Houseboat on the Styx* was a success of 1895. James M. Barrie, Conan Doyle, Jerome K. Jerome, Henry James, and Hamlin Garland came in 1891, while in the following years of the decade Richard Harding Davis, Owen Wister, Brander Matthews, Israel Zangwill, Julian Ralph, and many others wrote short stories; and such serials were published as Henry B. Fuller's *Cliff Dwellers* (1893), Mary E. Wilkins' *Pembroke* (1894), Stanley J. Weyman's *Red Cockade* (1895), Henry James's *Awkward Age* (1898), and several novels by William Dean Howells, including two of his best — *A Hazard of New Fortunes* (1889) and

---

[43] Paine, *op. cit.*, p. 528.
[44] James Parton, *Caricature and Other Comic Art* (New York, 1877), p. 327; also in *Harper's Monthly*, LII, 40 (December 1875).

The Landlord of Lion's Head (1896). In the nineties John Corbin discussed dramatics weekly, Edward S. Martin edited his pleasant and wise department called "This Busy World," and Caspar Whitney conducted a page dealing with amateur sports which was influential in combatting the element of professionalism in college athletics.[45] There was a fine pictorial record of the Columbian Exposition at Chicago in 1893; and the Spanish War was adequately recorded by the artists and by Caspar Whitney, John Fox, Jr., John R. Spears, O. K. Davis, Richard Harding Davis, John F. Bass, and Harold Martin as correspondents at the various fronts.

In the meantime, illustration was, as always, a main support of the journal. The pictures of Abbey, Smedley, and Pyle were enough to distinguish any periodical. R. F. Zogbaum's war drawings attracted wide attention. W. A. Rogers was the leading cartoonist, and his pictures against the free-silver craze were powerful arguments. The *Weekly* joined in the mania for colored illustrations in 1898. After the turn of the century Charles Dana Gibson's pictures of the American girl became very popular, and James Montgomery Flagg's double-page drawings were a feature. Much attention was given to discussions of art from the time of the World's Fair on, Sydney Brooks, Edward Hungerford, and William Inglis being among the writers on the subject.

Curtis remained with the *Weekly* until his death in 1892, maintaining the attitude of a sincere independent. He supported Cleveland again in 1888, and there was much of civil service reform, Curtis' chief political interest, as there had been almost from the first of his editorship. His death brought many tributes to his character as a Christian scholar and gentleman, an able and eloquent writer and speaker, an unselfish reformer, and a chivalric fighter. Richard Henry Stoddard wrote in the *Independent*:

> What Sidney's fame was his shall be —
> A gracious name to men,
> With more than Sidney's chivalry,
> And more than Sidney's pen.[46]

---

[45] *Bookman*, XII, 361 (December 1900).
[46] *Independent*, XLIV, 1277 (September 15, 1892).

The loss of Curtis was deeply felt by the readers of the *Weekly*, for he had maintained an almost personal relationship with them. A fellow editor wrote of him:

He won and has kept the enthusiastic personal support and admiration of his audience, as no other editor has succeeded in doing, with the single exception of Horace Greeley.[47]

Curtis, recognized as the editorial head of the paper, was in reality purely a political editor. He was responsible for two or three editorials a week, and he did this work without assuming "the least trouble or responsibility for the details of the paper, and with no necessity of even being at the office." [48] During his service with the *Weekly*, therefore, a succession of managing editors attended to such details — Henry Mills Alden, later editor of the *Monthly*; S. S. Conant, who mysteriously disappeared in 1885; the Reverend Montgomery Schuyler, and John Foord. After the death of Curtis, his friend Carl Schurz, an independent of somewhat the same stamp, was employed to contribute the leading political editorials; and Richard Harding Davis, who had supplied fiction and articles for some years, took over the post of managing editor.

Davis kept the position only two or three years and then gave way to Henry Loomis Nelson. Nelson was a general editor and Schurz's position became merely that of an editorial contributor. These were the days of the free-silver campaign and the agrarian revolt in the Middle West. The *Weekly*, though it opposed the McKinley tariff, fought Bryanism even more strenuously by the pen of Schurz and the pencil of W. A. Rogers. Just before Harper & Brothers' failure in 1899, Schurz severed his connection with the paper because of a disagreement with the management over the "imperialism" issue,[49] and Nelson retired to teach politics at Williams College. Thereupon, John Kendrick Bangs, who had been known to the *Weekly's* readers chiefly as a humorist, was made editor. Bangs in the editorial columns and Rogers in the cartoon pages made a good team. Bangs wrote of being "a forced convert to Republican

[47] *Century*, XXV, 581 (February 1883). Article by S. S. Conant.
[48] Cary, *op. cit.*, p. 191.
[49] Carl Schurz, *Reminiscences* (New York, 1908), III, 434.

principles," [50] but he supported McKinley and Roosevelt vigorously in the 1900 campaign and guided the *Weekly* in its discussion of the Boer War, imperialism, and Cuban affairs. He went to Cuba to view the situation there at first hand and became an ardent believer in General Wood and his policies — a faith expressed in a series of papers on "The Cuban Situation" in 1901. It may be that a disapproval of this position by the president of the publishing company had something to do with the retirement of Bangs as editor in this year; he remained, however, as a contributor of hundreds of pieces, long and short, under a variety of pen names, for several years. [51]

Throughout the whole of the existence of *Harper's Weekly* there had been a remarkable correlation between owners, editors, and political writers. Up to Fletcher Harper's retirement in 1875 he had been the guiding spirit of the periodical; following that year Joseph W. Harper, Jr., had general supervising charge for about ten years; then J. Henry Harper came to fill that position. At the time of the reorganization of the Harper company in 1900, George Harvey became president. He took much interest in the *Weekly* and in 1901 himself assumed the editorship. Harvey's natural force, his journalistic training, and his personal ambition made him a vigorous and picturesque editor, though his connections with Wall Street brought some criticisms upon the paper, and though most of the editorial work was performed by Edward S. Martin, George Buchanan Fife, and other members of the staff. Harvey's championship of Woodrow Wilson was notable, and once again *Harper's Weekly* was found following a Democratic leader. Indeed, it was Harvey, in the *Weekly*, who first definitely and prominently suggested Wilson's nomination March 10, 1906. [52] *Life*, presumably by the pen of Martin, summed up Harvey's editorship admirably in a post-mortem on the paper in 1916. Harvey, we are told, did "some memorable things" with the *Weekly*;

especially he used it to make Dr. Wilson president. He had a lot of fun with it, made it an interesting paper, and did almost everything

---

[50] *Harper's Weekly*, LI, 31 (January 5, 1907).

[51] Francis H. Bangs, son of the editor-humorist, has afforded the author valuable help in the preparation of this chapter. See *Yale University Library Gazette*, VII, 53 (January 1933).

[52] See Willis Fletcher Johnson, *George Harvey* (Boston, 1929), p. 114.

he should have done, except to make it pay. . . . Colonel Harvey might have made it pay but for two things: he didn't know how, and he had too much else to do. In order to make a paper pay, somebody who knows how must put his very soul into it.[53]

In 1913, the year after Wilson's election to the presidency, the Harpers sold the *Weekly* to the McClure organization. It had been unprofitable, according to Harvey's statement after the sale, for twenty years past.[54] Harvey's farewell editorial sounded like a dare to his successors, Norman Hapgood, Charles R. Crane,[55] McClure, and their associates, to make the old Journal of Civilization pay. They took up the dare, but they lost. Hapgood, who had made a spectacular success as editor of *Collier's*, gave the *Weekly* a lightness and verve it had never known before; but it was the feverish agitation of approaching dissolution. Let us quote *Life* again:

When the paper was sold to Mr. Hapgood, there was a chance for it. Mr. Hapgood is an able man. . . . To the consternation of the *Weekly's* old friends, he took the first turn to the left, and drove the dear old paper down the hill. He also tipped her over and tipped out most of the old subscribers.[56]

There were many other comments upon the reasons for the failure of the "grand old weekly," doubtless called forth by Harvey's own remarks on the subject. They were bad advertising. Such post-mortems, indeed, are generally unprofitable. Magazine success comes from editorial genius, plenty of luck, and a good advertising manager; magazine failure is followed by interment, and "there's an end on 't."

In 1915 the *Weekly* was sold to a new organization, Hapgood remaining in control, but after eight months it was merged in the *Independent*.

From the literary point of view, *Harper's Weekly* must be conceded to have enjoyed a certain importance; but it is as a vigorous political journal of conservative tendencies that it was

[53] *Life*, LXVII, 899 (May 11, 1916).
[54] *Harper's Weekly*, LVII, 3 (May 31, 1913).
[55] Hapgood calls Crane "the leading support of *Harper's Weekly* during the years that I edited it." Norman Hapgood, *The Changing Years* (New York, 1930), p. 196.
[56] *Life*, LXVII, 899 (May 11, 1916).

most noteworthy. Henry Mills Alden was accustomed to call it "the fighting arm" of the House of Harper, and its great fights for Lincoln, for the people of New York against Tammany, for Grant, for Cleveland, for the gold standard, and for Wilson are the achievements by which it deserves remembrance. Besides this, its record in text and picture of the events of sixty years make it a contemporaneous history of the highest value.

RUSSELL'S MAGAZINE [1]

CHARLESTON was one of the chief cultural centers of the South in the days before the Civil War, and in Charleston the chief gathering place for the literary and scientific was John Russell's bookstore. Russell had sold books in Charleston for many years, knew all the literati of the place well, and was a witty conversationalist and a man of wide information. He was friendly and generous, and his patrons liked to call him "Lord John." [2] His bookstore had a big plate-glass window in front; and in the rear, seats were provided for the more frequent visitors, so that the place became a kind of club. Here William Gilmore Simms often spent an afternoon with such men as James L. Petigru, the state's best-known lawyer; Mitchell King, another literary lawyer and wit; Basil L. Gildersleeve, leonine young graduate of Göttingen; Dr. Samuel Henry Dickson, of the Charleston Medical College; William R. Taber, editor of the *Charleston Mercury*; Dr. John Dickson Bruns, a young poet; Samuel Lord, Jr., a third young lawyer of literary leanings; and two "literary bohemians" named Henry Timrod and Paul Hamilton Hayne.[3]

Of this group Simms was the acknowledged leader; and its members were often invited to the "Wigwam," as Simms called his home, for a supper and an evening of talk. It was at one of these suppers that *Russell's Magazine* was projected.[4]

[1] TITLE: *Russell's Magazine.*
FIRST ISSUE: April 1857. LAST ISSUE: March 1860.
PERIODICITY: Monthly. Six semiannual volumes.
PUBLISHERS: Russell & Jones, Charleston.
EDITOR: Paul Hamilton Hayne.
REFERENCES: Fronde Kennedy, "Russell's Magazine," *South Atlantic Quarterly*, XVIII, 125–144 (April 1919); Sidney J. Cohen, *Three Notable Ante-Bellum Magazines of South Carolina* (Bulletin of the University of South Carolina, No. 42, Part II, July 1915), pp. 38–62.
[2] See Hayne's "Memories of Charleston," *Southern Bivouac* (November 1885).
[3] See William Peterfield Trent, *William Gilmore Simms* (Boston, 1892), pp. 228–229.
[4] *Southern Bivouac*, IV, 327 (October 1885).

"Lord John," the bookseller, took the financial responsibility of the magazine. W. B. Carlisle, a Charleston journalist, was announced as co-editor with Hayne; but he proved a disappointment to Russell and Hayne, and after the second number Russell himself became an associate editor.[5] Late in the magazine's second year, George C. Hurlbut, subsequently secretary of the New York Geographical Society, was added to the staff.[6]

The first number was issued for April 1857. It was modeled, as it frankly acknowledged, upon *Blackwood's*, typographically and otherwise; a neat, thin octavo, it was priced at twenty-five cents. Its contents were varied — politics, literature, art, fiction, poetry, and so on, with a department of book reviews and an "Editor's Table." The magazine was welcomed by a chorus of praise from the southern press, most of which it deserved; but there was not then or ever any great influx of subscriptions.

Russell's never aspired to be a national periodical. In some respects it was a local Charleston magazine, telling of Charleston culture and Charleston events. The opening of an art gallery in that city, the appearance of Rachel at the Academy of Music there, and the literary activities of Charleston writers furnished themes for many pages. But its aim was to be a magazine for the whole South and to speak with the voice of the South. It was filled with sectional feeling. In one of its last few issues Hayne wrote: "It is not the province of this magazine — at least in its editorial department — to touch, however superficially, upon the question of politics." [7] But its writers of articles had done so many times, and nearly always in order to sound the sectional note and defend the southern position. The aim of the magazine was named in its first editorial as the "expression of southern thought and feeling"; it was reiterated on the cover: "To give utterance and circulation to the opinions, doctrines, and arguments of the educated mind of the South."

The leading article of the first number was an attack on antislavery doctrinaires called "The *Edinburgh Review* Reviewed";

---

[5] *Russell's Magazine*, III, 79 (April 1858).

[6] *Ibid.*, IV, 378 (January 1859). Hurlbut joined the staff with the number for December 1858.

[7] *Ibid.*, VI, 360 (January 1860).

it was by William J. Grayson, a South Carolina planter and former congressman and a leading apologist for slavery, and it developed the argument for the "peculiar institution" (as *Russell's* was fond of calling it) at length. In August 1858 Grayson again based a defense of slavery upon a discussion of the views of foreign abolitionists, and he repeatedly returned to the attack in the six volumes of the magazine. A favorite doctrine of Grayson was the one that Carlyle later expressed so forcibly in his "Shooting Niagara" pamphlet — that the state of the hireling was worse than that of the slave. But Grayson was by no means the only defender of slavery in *Russell's Magazine*. Proslavery arguments were presented separately and serially, in articles, book reviews, fiction, and poetry.

Poetry occupied a position of prominence in the magazine. Hayne's own work, that of his friend Timrod and his mentor Simms, together with verse by minor poetasters — J. Wood Davidson, Howard H. Caldwell, and many others — made *Russell's* an unusually poetical magazine; but as it happened, no very distinctive or outstanding verse reached its pages. Perhaps an exception should be made of a sonnet or two of Timrod's which stand among his best work. There was also much discussion of poetry — a two-part article by the editor at the end of 1857 on "The Poets and Poetry of the South" and his article on the sonnet in the second number, an article by Professor Davidson on Poe,[8] one by Caldwell on French writers, and Hayne's own book reviews, for example.

There was less fiction than in most general magazines of the time. Two of the chief writers of short tales, sketches, and serial fiction were Mrs. H. C. King and Miss Essie Cheseborough. Mrs. King did such society sketches as were prominent in the women's journals of the day, showing the bad end that flirts, coquettes, and gossips come to; her stories dealt with social situations and taught what she was sure were good lessons. Miss Cheseborough was more sentimental; her work was in the worst perfervid style of the broken-heart school.

Some translations from the French gave variety to the magazine; and there were hitherto unpublished revolutionary papers,

---

[8] *Russell's Magazine*, V, 83 (April 1859).

much biography, occasional addresses by educators, a few travel articles, and many discussions of southern resources. Simms had a two-part article on General Marion in the issues for October and November 1858, and Professor William J. Rivers furnished a number of articles dealing with South Carolina history. A curious controversy which arose in the magazine in 1857 dealt with the rights and wrongs of dueling: Dr. Dickson defended the custom, and Grayson attacked it.

The "Editor's Table" was always readable. Hayne's own gentle character and fine sensibility are reflected there; and he gathered together curious bits, quaint essays, and light verse which preserve something of the aroma of the Old South. The book reviews were written by various members of the Charleston group. When prejudice did not enter, they were often good. That Hayne attempted to keep his literary judgments free of sectional hatreds is evidenced by an editorial statement:

It seems to us that when a work is purely *literary*, interfering in no degree with the "peculiar institution," or our rights under it, common honesty requires that it should be reviewed without reference to the birthplace of its author or the locale of its publication.[9]

Even this, however, was a difficult degree of aloofness from the strained emotions of the moment, for a southern magazine on the eve of the war. "The Southern States," said the editor at the beginning of 1860, "are standing on the verge of a revolution."[10] It was inevitable that everything should be seen through an unreal haze of political passion.

It was two months after this observation about the impending "revolution" that *Russell's* published its last number. "Other and superior interests require our attention," wrote Hayne;[11] but it is clear that the magazine had become a financial burden to its publisher. In later reminiscences Hayne wrote that "our small and audacious craft . . . at the close of the fourth volume struck upon breakers and sank, like a shot, to Davy Jones' locker."[12]

---

[9] *Ibid.*, II, 182 (November 1857).
[10] *Ibid.*, VI, 360 (January 1860).
[11] *Ibid.*, VI, 565 (March 1860).
[12] *Southern Bivouac*, IV, 334 (October 1885).

On the whole, *Russell's* was a good magazine — elevated in tone, varied, usually well written and always well printed. It was the best of the Charleston monthlies and superior to the *Southern Literary Messenger* of its time. In calmer weather it might have had a longer voyage; but however that may be, the six volumes as they stand afford a good view of thought and feeling in antebellum South Carolina.

THE ATLANTIC MONTHLY [1]

THERE have always been some irreverent ones to dispute the primacy of the *Atlantic Monthly* among American literary magazines, but throughout all of its nearly eighty years of existence it has not lacked readers who have believed it the beneficiary of a kind of divine election to leadership in American letters. In the terminology of an older

[1] TITLES: (1) *The Atlantic Monthly: A Magazine of Literature, Art and Politics*, 1857–September 1865; (2) *The Atlantic Monthly: A Magazine of Literature, Science, Art and Politics*, October 1865–current.

FIRST ISSUE: November 1857. Current.

PERIODICITY: Monthly. I, November 1857–May 1858; II, June–December 1858; thereafter regular semiannual volumes. Supplements to L and LVIII.

PUBLISHERS: Phillips, Sampson & Company, 1857–October 1859; Ticknor & Fields, November 1859–June 1868; Fields, Osgood & Company, July 1868–1870; James H. Osgood & Company, 1871–73; H. O. Houghton & Company, 1874–77; Houghton, Osgood & Company, 1878–79; Houghton, Mifflin & Company, 1880–July 1908; Atlantic Monthly Company (Ellery Sedgwick, president), August 1908–current.

EDITORS: James Russell Lowell, 1857–June 1861; James T. Fields, July 1861–July 1871; William Dean Howells, August 1871–January 1881; Thomas Bailey Aldrich, February 1881–March 1890; Horace E. Scudder, April 1890–July 1898; Walter Hines Page, August 1898–July 1899; Bliss Perry, August 1899–July 1909; Ellery Sedgwick, August 1909–June 1938; Edward A. Weeks, Jr., July 1938–current. (Among the assistant editors have been Francis H. Underwood, Susan M. Francis, William Dean Howells, George Parsons Lathrop, M. A. DeWolfe Howe, Walter Hines Page, William Belmont Parker, Harry James Smith, Ferris Greenslet, Florence Converse, John Gilman D'Arcey Paul, Francis Lester Warner, Charles Rumford Walker, Frederick L. Allen, Joseph Barber, Jr.)

INDEXES: *Index . . . I–XXXVIII* (Boston, 1877); *The Atlantic Index* (Boston, 1889, vols. XXXIX–LXII); *The Atlantic Index Supplement . . . 1889–1901* (Boston, 1903, vols. LXIII–LXXXVIII); *Poole's, Poole's Abridged, Readers' Guide, Review of Reviews Index, Contents-Subject Index, Annual Library Index, Cumulative Index, Jones' Index, Engineering Index.*

REFERENCES: M. A. DeWolfe Howe, *The Atlantic Monthly and Its Makers* (Boston, 1919); Fiftieth Anniversary Number, *Atlantic Monthly*, C, 577–720 (November 1907); Bliss Perry, *Park Street Papers* (Boston, 1908); Caroline Ticknor, *Hawthorne and His Publisher* (Boston, 1913), Chapter XVI; Algernon Tassin, *The Magazine in America* (New York, 1916), Chapter VII; Horace E. Scudder, *James Russell Lowell* (Boston, 1901), Chapter IX; Charles Eliot Norton, ed., *Letters of James Russell Lowell* (Boston, 1894), Chapters IV–V; Ferris Greenslet, *The Life of Thomas Bailey Aldrich* (New York, 1908), Chapter VI; Edward Everett Hale, *James Russell Lowell and His Friends* (Boston, 1899), Chapter X; Bliss Perry, *And Gladly Teach* (Boston, 1935), Chapter VIII.

New England, the *Atlantic* may be said to have enjoyed a perpetual state of literary grace, so that for a large section of the American public, whatever the *Atlantic* printed was literature. Moreover, the student of American magazines since 1857, whatever his predilections, is forced to agree that throughout much of its career it has maintained a higher literary standard than its contemporaries.

The *Atlantic Monthly* was founded in 1857 by Moses Dresser Phillips, of the Boston publishing firm of Phillips, Sampson & Company. Francis H. Underwood, literary adviser for this firm, was the originator of the project and did much of the preliminary work on it; he has been called the true founder of the magazine. He planned it first in connection with John P. Jewett, who had made large profits in the publication of *Uncle Tom's Cabin*, but lost them before the proposed magazine could be started.[2] Edward Everett Hale was also an early counselor in the matter. A biographer says that Hale was living in the same house with Mr. Phillips in 1857, "and Mr. Phillips used to say if it had not been for his interest he would not have attempted the magazine."[3] Emerson, Longfellow, Lowell, Holmes, Cabot, and Motley were brought into formal counsel, besides many others with whom Underwood communicated. When Lowell was fixed upon as the first editor, he expressed the view that Holmes would have been a better choice[4] and accepted only on condition that the latter contribute faithfully. This condition resulted in the renewal in the *Atlantic* of the *Autocrat of the Breakfast-Table* papers — a series which had been begun in Buckingham's *New England Magazine* twenty-five years before and abandoned, and which was now resumed with a nonchalant "As I was saying —." Dr. Holmes was also godfather to the

[2] Ticknor, *op. cit.*, p. 284.
[3] *Century*, XXIX, 340 (January 1885). Professor Gohdes advances the theory that the *Atlantic's* establishment was "in a way" connected with the *Massachusetts Quarterly Review's* discontinuance in 1850. See Clarence L. F. Gohdes, *The Periodicals of American Transcendentalism* (Durham, North Carolina, 1931), pp. 191–193. But Theodore Parker's discouraging letter written to Underwood in 1853, when the latter was first trying to promote the new journal, shows clearly that he did not look upon it as the successor to the *Review* which he had hoped for. For the letter see *Atlantic Monthly*, C, 660 (November 1907).
[4] Underwood in *Scribner's Monthly*, XVIII, 121 (May 1879). Underwood says it was he who nominated Lowell as editor.

magazine, calling it the *Atlantic* in preference to "The Orient." "I suppose I have made more money and reputation out of it than anybody else," he wrote of the *Atlantic* early in 1861, in a letter to Motley. "I have written more than anybody else, at any rate." [5]

That the early *Atlantic* was sectional and provincial cannot be denied. Note the New England, even the Bostonian, character, which is given to its first number, not so much by the subject matter as by the contributors and tone. Emerson contributed four poems and an essay, Longfellow two poems, Holmes an installment of the *Autocrat*, and a poem; Lowell an amusing poem, a sonnet, and an editorial essay; Motley an article on Florentine mosaics; Norton an article on the Manchester art exhibition; Trowbridge a short story satirizing a reformer turned spiritualist; C. C. Hazewell, the Boston journalist and student of history, an article on British India; Harriet Beecher Stowe a New England sketch; Rose Terry the first of a long line of New England stories; C. W. Philleo, of Hartford, the first installment of a serial story with New England setting; [6] Parke Godwin, of New York, a financial article; and the English James Hannay an article on Douglas Jerrold. Only the two last-named contributors, it will be seen, mailed their contributions from outside the New England group of states. Throughout the first fifteen years of the *Atlantic*, about two-thirds of its contributors were from New England, and far more

---

[5] See J. C. Derby, *Fifty Years among Authors, Books and Publishers* (New York, 1884), p. 523, regarding the name. "The Orient" had been proposed by William Lee, later of Lee & Shepard, but then a member of Phillips, Sampson & Company, and enthusiastic about the plans for the new magazine. For the letter to Motley see John T. Morse, Jr., *Life and Letters of Oliver Wendell Holmes* (Boston, 1896), II, 156.

[6] Calvin Wheeler Philleo was a young Hartford lawyer, who had written a novel *Twice Married* and had been a contributor to *Graham's*, *Putnam's*, and *Harper's* before he undertook *Akin by Marriage* for the *Atlantic*. The story was to be written Dickens-fashion, number by number, but when only three installments had appeared and the story was but well started, the author was taken ill and a few months later died, at the age of thirty-six, without having been able to finish the novel. The curious reader never learned whether Laura Stebbins was actually forced to marry the pimply young minister against her will, or what were the "momentous results" promised in the fourth installment. For sketch of the author see D. H. Van Hoosear, *The Fillow, Philo, and Philleo Genealogy* (Albany, 1888).

than two-thirds of its pages were filled with their writing. Scudder, in his index, was able to identify fifty-six of the contributors to the first volume.[7] Over two of these the waters of oblivion seem to have closed effectively and finally, but the others may be placed geographically as follows: New England, 35; New York, 10; foreign countries, 6 (this includes one Anglo-Italian temporarily in America and one American permanently resident in Europe); the South, 2 (P. H. Hayne, of Charleston, and O. Tiffany, of Baltimore); the West, 1. Of 122 assignable contributions, 3 are by untraced writers, 90 of the remaining 119 by New Englanders, 16 by New Yorkers, 10 by writers from abroad, 2 by Southerners, and 1 from west of the Alleghenies.

How great a fault this apparent provincialism was, or whether, strictly from the magazine's point of view, it was a fault at all, is questionable. It seems certain that Lowell and Fields, the first two editors, had little thought of any necessity for drawing contributions from outside of New England. It was natural for them to take what was near at hand, just as it was natural to use the picture of a New England hero-saint, John Winthrop, on the cover. What they tried to obtain was good literature, and no reader can deny that those early volumes, filled as they were with Emerson, Longfellow, Whittier, Lowell, Holmes, Higginson, Hale, and Mrs. Stowe, set a high literary standard. It was the period of New England supremacy in American letters, and most of the better writers were New Englanders. "There was in those days very little good writing done beyond the borders of New England," wrote Howells;[8] and in another place he asserted that "outside of New England, or at the farthest New York or Philadelphia," there was "little

[7] Early volumes of the *Atlantic* did not contain the names of the authors. Beginning with December 1862, there were a few signed articles from time to time, but not until July 1870 was the custom of signing adopted for all, or nearly all, contributions. From the beginning the authorship of *Atlantic* pieces was an open secret, however. The prospectus contained a list of authors. The publishers did not hesitate to give out the names and were soon furnishing printed lists of them with each copy sent to the reviewers. Beginning with the tenth volume (1862), semiannual indexes contained the names of the authors of the various contributions. Authorship of some reviews and poems has, however, never been ascertained. See Perry's *Park Street Papers*, pp. 249–250.

[8] W. D. Howells, *Literary Friends and Acquaintance* (New York, 1900), p. 115.

writing worth printing" in the *Atlantic*.[9] "Occasionally," he wrote in *Literary Friends and Acquaintance*, "there came a poem from Bryant, at New York, from Mr. Stedman, from Mr. Stoddard and Mrs. Stoddard, from Mr. Aldrich, and from Bayard Taylor. But all these except the last were not only of New England race, but of New England birth. I think there was no contributor from the South but Mr. M. D. Conway." [10] Professor Bliss Perry, a later editor, believes that in the earlier years of the *Atlantic* "a majority of the best-known American writers were living within twenty-five miles of the Massachusetts state house." [11] He denies that "any of its conductors have ever purposed to make it an organ of Bostonian or New England opinion," [12] and Howells went further when he asserted that "the editors of the *Atlantic* had been eager from the beginning to discover any outlying literature." [13]

This eagerness, however, was not always apparent to would-be contributors from outside of New England. Stedman, in New York, wrote to Taylor, in Pennsylvania:

> The Boston house, naturally, drive apace every steed that wins a heat. But when a man's pace is slow, though sure, they don't make much of him unless he is "in their midst." . . . They never ask me for anything and have declined what little I have sent them. I have this week hit upon a magnificent subject, but when done, I shall not have the courage to send it to the *Atlantic*.[14]

There is no evidence that either of the first two editors was so alarmed about the possibility of a narrowing provincialism due to inbreeding that he solicited outside aid. "He had little to do in the way of foraging for matter," [15] says Scudder of Lowell.

---

[9] *Atlantic Monthly*, C, 600 (November 1907).

[10] Howells, *op. cit.*, p. 114. A slip of memory causes Howells to overlook three little poems of Paul Hamilton Hayne that Lowell printed, one of them in the first volume. O. Tiffany, of Baltimore, a writer for several magazines, was, as has been noted, a contributor to the first volume, and Francis Lieber to the third, J. P. Kennedy to the sixth, etc. But Howells' main contention — that there was very little representation of the South — is of course correct.

[11] Perry, *Park Street Papers*, p. 9.

[12] *Ibid.*, p. 8.

[13] Howells, *op. cit.*, p. 115.

[14] Laura Stedman and George M. Gould, *Life and Letters of Edmund Clarence Stedman* (New York, 1910), I, 449. Letter dated January 8, 1871.

[15] Scudder, *op. cit.*, I, 247.

Emerson, however, seems to have had some fear of a narrow policy. Writing to Furness at Philadelphia in January 1858, he says, "I am glad if you like the *Atlantic*. We hope that it shall be better. . . . I believe that we have not yet had a single correspondent from Philadelphia. I hope that we shall yet supply these deficiencies." [16] In his journal he wrote: "Great scope and illumination ought to be in the Editor, to draw from the best in the land, and defy the public." [17]

While one must not, of course, expect any magazine to publish all the good authors, yet in view of what the *Atlantic's* apologists have said of the dearth of good writing outside Boston, it may be noted that Irving, Simms, Timrod, Willis, Paulding, and Halleck were alive and all writing more or less in 1857 and were never *Atlantic* contributors; that Lanier was cavalierly rejected by the *Atlantic*;[18] that Bryant had but one poem in the first twelve volumes, Hayne only three in the first twenty-nine, and Walt Whitman but two poems in the whole file.[19] The list might of course be greatly extended. It would still remain true, however, that no other American periodical has a table of contents that will compare in distinction (so far as American writers are concerned) with that of the *Atlantic Monthly*, in spite of the geographical narrowness of its first twenty volumes.

The Brahminism of the *Atlantic* did not go unchallenged, even among its neighbors. The *New Englander*, published at New Haven, remarked "a certain peculiar tone" about its Boston contemporary "which after a while gets to be a little dull and monotonous, and any introduction of talent from the wide outside world is something of an event in its history, and a great

---

[16] But Howells writes in *Literary Friends* (p. 12), "Philadelphia had long counted for nothing in the literary field."

[17] E. W. Emerson and W. E. Forbes, eds., *Journals of Ralph Waldo Emerson* (Boston, 1909–14), IX, 118.

[18] See E. P. Kuhl, "Sidney Lanier and Edward Spencer," *Studies in Philology*, XXVII, 462 (July 1930); and A. H. Starke, "William Dean Howells and Sidney Lanier," *American Literature*, III, 79 (March 1931).

[19] As to Whitman, it may be added that Burroughs grew indignant because "Willie" Howells would not use articles about the poet. See Clara Barrus, *Life and Letters of John Burroughs* (New York, 1925), I, 116. Letter to Benton, March 20, 1866. See also Portia Baker, "Walt Whitman and the *Atlantic Monthly*," *American Literature*, VI, 283 (November 1934).

relief to its readers." [20] Probably a dislike of the *Atlantic's* fondness for Harvard College had something to do with the antipathy of Yale's *New Englander* as well as with that of the *Church Review*, which was naturally allied with Columbia. "The University at Cambridge," as Fiske calls it, received much consideration; many of the more important contributors to the *Atlantic* were officially connected with it. Subscribers to the magazine received as a supplement to the fifty-eighth volume Lowell's oration and Holmes's poem commemorating Harvard's 250th anniversary. The important curricular reforms at Harvard were dealt with in two articles in 1867. Even in Boston this Harvard alliance was not always acceptable, and Parkman wrote to Underwood in 1875, by way of consolation for the fact that the *Atlantic* had never given the latter anything of the fame or opportunity he seemed to deserve as its true founder, "Those who are neither Harvard men nor humbugs may be said to be the victims of their own merit, having neither the prestige of the one nor the arts of the other." [21]

The manifest danger in all this was that the national character of the magazine should be impugned. Its founders had intended that it should exert a wide political influence. On the cover of its first issue is the legend, "Devoted to Literature, Art, and Politics," and on another page of the cover is stated this aim, among others:

In politics the *Atlantic* will be the organ of no party or clique, but will honestly endeavor to be the exponent of what its conductors believe to be the American idea. It will deal frankly with persons and parties, endeavoring always to keep in view that moral element which transcends all persons and parties and which alone makes the basis of a true and lasting national prosperity. It will not rank itself with any sect of anties, but with that body of men which is in favor of Freedom, National Progress, and Honor, whether public or private.[22]

[20] *New Englander*, XXIV, 319 (April 1865). It was the *New Englander* which rebuked the *Atlantic* for the theology of "The Professor at the Breakfast Table" series in a full-length article, XVII, 771 (August 1859).

[21] Perry, *Park Street Papers*, p. 270.

[22] The remainder of this statement of aims runs: "In Literature, to leave no province unrepresented, so that while each number will contain articles of an abstract and permanent value, it will also be found that the healthy appetite of the mind for entertainment in its various forms of Narrative, Wit and Humor,

In short, though in true transcendental fashion it refuses to commit itself to any reform party, it wishes to stand for a broad and general idea of Americanism which is expressed rather vaguely by the watchwords "Freedom, National Progress, and Honor." The abstraction and generality foreshadowed in this announcement were realized less in the first editorship than in some that followed. Lowell had pronounced political views, and Underwood, his assistant,[23] was an ardent antislavery man and believed the *Atlantic* to be quite as important in its political phase as in its more purely literary work. Writing to Higginson, Underwood had called the projected periodical "the new literary and anti-slavery magazine." [24] As a matter of fact, its antislavery sentiment was pronounced enough to make it soundly hated in the South. The *Southern Literary Messenger* introduced the new magazine to its readers as "a work engaged in the systematic defamation of everything southern." [25]

Many years later, Underwood wrote: "Every number contained a political article by Parke Godwin or by Lowell, and the public understood and felt that this was the point of the plough-share that was to break up the old fields." [26] The proportion of political articles indicated by this statement was scarcely maintained, however, after the first volume. Godwin may have been offended by editorial additions to an article on Buchanan in April 1858; at any rate, after contributing one more article already contracted for, he never again wrote for the *Atlantic*.[27] Very little notice was taken of politics in 1859, and in 1860 the politics dealt largely with Pan-American relationships, except for Lowell's strong article on the election in November. The four political articles by Lowell in 1861 which mark the end of his editorship are fine examples of political

---

will not go uncared for. . . . In the term Art they intend to include the whole domain of aesthetics, and hope gradually to make this critical department a true and fearless representative of Art, in all its various branches, without any regard to prejudice, whether personal or national, or to private considerations of what kind soever." — Statement of publishers on fourth page of cover of first number.

[23] William Winter in his recollections called *Old Friends* (New York, 1909), p. 55, says, "The *Atlantic Monthly* was started in 1857 with Frank Underwood as editor." Underwood was what is sometimes called the "office editor."

[24] Mary T. Higginson, *Thomas Wentworth Higginson* (Boston, 1914), p. 155.

[25] *Southern Literary Messenger*, XXV, 472 (December 1857).

[26] F. H. Underwood, *John Greenleaf Whittier* (Boston, 1884), p. 216.

[27] See Edward G. Bernard in *New England Quarterly*, X, 337 (June 1937).

writing, though the expression of dissatisfaction with Lincoln and the clarion calls for leadership strike strangely upon ears habituated to unvaried praises of the Great Emancipator. On the whole, Lowell's political articles in the *Atlantic* were brilliant rather than acute and incisive, general rather than specific. Scudder, who made an admirable analysis of Lowell's political writing, called it "coruscating" but not "direct." [28]

Lowell was undoubtedly one of the great magazine editors of his times. He had his shortcomings, to be sure; but his own writing ability, his critical acumen, and his sure taste were just what were necessary in the special situation in which he found himself, to make him an ideal editor for the *Atlantic*. In the single field of the short story, for example, he made his magazine a great force for the more realistic, vital fiction by printing the work of Rose Terry, Rebecca Harding Davis, and other honest writers.[29]

Sometimes Lowell's collaboration with his authors was of great value. Perhaps the most notable of which we have record is his suggestion of dialect for the refrain of Whittier's "Old Flud Oirson" ballad.[30] But not infrequently there was resentment at interference with the freedom of authorship (if there is such a thing).

I wish to be understood as giving a suppressed but audible growl at the chopping knife which has made mincemeat of my sentences [wrote Thomas Wentworth Higginson to the *Atlantic*]. It isn't pleasant to think that my sentences belong to such a low order of organization that they can be chopped in two in the middle and each half wriggle away independently.[31]

Thoreau quarreled with Lowell about the omission of a sentence from an article of his, and never offered the *Atlantic* another contribution while Lowell was editor.[32] Whitman objected to Lowell's deletion of two lines from his "Bardic Symbols":

See from my dead lips the ooze exuding at last!
See the prismatic colors glistening and rolling!

[28] Scudder, *op. cit.*, II, 13.   [29] See p. 173.
[30] Scudder, *op. cit.*, I, 418.
[31] Higginson, *op. cit.*, p. 158.
[32] Frank B. Sanborn, *Thoreau* (Boston, 1882, American Men of Letters Series), p. 300.

but he submitted to the editor's insistence.[33] It is amusing to find our careful copyreader writing Emerson about his diction, yet gracefully conceding his elder's right to use words as he pleases "until we find someone who writes better English to correct you." [34] Lowell wrote Whittier finding fault, justly enough, with his assonances.[35] He said to R. H. Stoddard, of Mrs. Stoddard's first story:

I am not altogether pleased with the story as it now stands. Would Mrs. Stoddard be willing to modify it in certain respects? If so, I will send it back with my criticism in detail. It is unpleasant, this playing Rhadamanthus all the time, and I do not wish to judge unless I am asked.[36]

Mrs. Stoddard of course changed the story, probably for the better; Lowell's judgment of short stories, as is shown by the files of the early *Atlantic*, was excellent.

But we find a hint in this letter to Stoddard, and in other letters as well,[37] that the head that wore the crown was sometimes uneasy; indeed we can be sure that it was sometimes scratched in anxious indecision. It is a mark of the sincerity of the man that, much as he hated the drudgery of his task, he did his editing with the most scrupulous care.

Toward the end of 1859 the death of Phillips precipitated a bankruptcy which had been hanging over the firm of Phillips & Sampson, and the *Atlantic* was purchased by Ticknor & Fields, rather reluctantly, it seems. The assignee had asked various publishers for bids on the property, to be opened on a day set. The day came, but no bids. The assignee dropped into the Ticknor & Fields office and remarked that he had not yet received the bid of that firm. "No," replied Mr. Ticknor, "and you will not, for we do not care to undertake it." The assignee urged the value of the *Atlantic* and then, pointing to the clock on Old South Church, said, "I am about to go to my office to

[33] Copy of autograph letter, Catalogue 2297, Anderson Galleries (New York, 1928), p. 15.
[34] Scudder, *op. cit.*, I, 416.
[35] *Ibid.*, I, 418.
[36] R. H. Stoddard, *Recollections Personal and Literary* (New York, 1903), p. 104.
[37] Norton, *op. cit.*, I, 285.

open the bids, and I am sure that Ticknor & Fields will be sorry if I find none from them." After a period of reflection, Mr. Ticknor turned to his desk, wrote a line on a sheet of paper, and handed it to the assignee; and that gentleman returned to his office, opened the one and only bid in due form, and declared the property sold to Ticknor & Fields [38] for $10,000. Fields, who was absent in Europe, was displeased when he heard of the purchase,[39] but made the best of it, and in 1861 himself succeeded Lowell in the editorial chair; Fields's wide acquaintance and literary judgment made a hired editor, as the publishers thought, an expensive luxury.

Fields was the war editor of the *Atlantic*. One finds comparatively little of battle in his volumes, however. The reader who turns to the Civil War volumes of any general monthly magazine of the time expecting to find them filled chiefly with war literature will be disappointed. Those magazines fulfilled a duty in offering the minds of the people some relief from the burdens of the war as well as in helping to guide public opinion through the perils of the day. Higginson's "Ordeal by Battle," Emerson's "Emancipation Proclamation," and Wasson's "Shall We Compromise?" were notable political articles. C. C. Hazewell wrote then and later a number of political essays. Hawthorne's fault-finding "Chiefly of War Matters," with adverse "editorial" footnotes by himself, is interesting to students both of Hawthorne and of the historical period. The *Atlantic* very early concerned itself with reconstruction matters, printing in 1861 an article by Judge Hoar entitled "Where Will the Rebellion Leave Us?" and continuing the treatment of that subject by Senator Sumner, Frederick Douglass, E. P. Whipple, Carl Schurz, and others through some ten years. Notable articles on the relations of England and America were contributed by Goldwin Smith, W. M. Rossetti, and others. In belles-lettres also the *Atlantic* occasionally reflected the war. With characteristic verve and charm Theodore Winthrop tells of the march of his New York regiment to Washington in the number for June 1861; it was one of his first published writings and was to be the initial chapter in a series of war sketches which unfor-

[38] Ticknor, *op. cit.*, p. 289.
[39] *Ibid.*, p. 21.

tunately reached only the second number: just one year from the time of their beginning their author was shot in action. Julia Ward Howe's "Battle Hymn of the Republic," Whittier's "Barbara Frietchie," Emerson's "Voluntaries," Lowell's "Commemoration Ode" and Second Series of the "Biglow Papers," Holmes's "Hunt After the Captain," and Hale's "The Man Without a Country" [40] are among the war contributions to the *Atlantic*.

Fields followed closely in Lowell's editorial footsteps. In his diary we find, among others, this entry: "Letter from ————, saying his article in the A. M. was shamefully mutilated. ————, standing by, says it is the editor's *duty* to cut off people's heads." [41] Yet Fields did not enjoy the "duties" of Lord High Executioner, being a friendly and gentle soul. In the main, he was an editor loved by his contributors as he had been a publisher loved by his editors. Edward Everett Hale called him "the prince among editors." [42] Like Lowell, Fields kept closely to New England for his contributors, retaining, for the most part, those who had become identified with the magazine during his predecessor's administration. Of these the chief, in point of space, were Lowell himself, Holmes, and Higginson. The last was a great favorite with Fields. Howells later named these eight as the most memorable *Atlantic* contributors before his time: Longfellow, Emerson, Hawthorne, Whittier, Holmes, Lowell, Mrs. Stowe, and Bryant.[43]

---

[40] This famous story had a political purpose. It was directed against the southern sympathizer Vallandingham, who was the Democratic candidate for governor of Ohio in 1863. But though the story was in type before September, it was not printed until after the election, so Hale could claim no part in the overwhelming defeat of Vallandingham. "I had a standing agreement with Fields," writes Hale in his *Memories of a Hundred Years* (II, 218) "that I would write for the *Atlantic* articles to keep up people's courage. This was when people felt very blue in the middle of the war. There appeared 'A Man Without a Country,' 'Northern Invasions,' 'How to Use Victory,' 'How Mr. Frye Would Have Preached It.' This last story covers in a parable the relations of General Butler with General Banks."

[41] James T. Fields, *Biographical Notes and Personal Sketches* (Boston, 1881), p. 86.

[42] Hale, *op. cit.*, p. 151.

[43] *Atlantic Monthly*, C, 594 (November 1907). He then proceeds to name alphabetically the following contributors: Agassiz, Mrs. Akers, Alden, Aldrich, Baker, Burroughs, Alice Cary, Caroline Chesebrough, Mrs. Child, Z. Clark,

During the latter part of Fields's editorship, which extended from 1866 through 1871, he was frequently an absentee editor, leaving the magazine in charge of his assistant, William Dean Howells. It was during his absence in Europe that Mrs. Stowe, who was scarcely to be refused in the *Atlantic* office, submitted her Lady Byron article, which was published simultaneously in the English *Macmillan's* and the *Atlantic*. "Mrs. Stowe intended," wrote Professor Youmans in *Appleton's Journal*, "to arrest Byron's influence upon the young by overwhelming him with moral reprobation; instead of that, she has raised the interest in Byron to sevenfold intensity." [44] *Harper's Weekly* compared the sensation made by this article to that created by *Uncle Tom's Cabin*.[45] The *Nation*, while condemning the outburst, insisted that "as a magazine article it is one of the greatest successes ever achieved in any country." [46] Perhaps, temporarily; but a very large number of readers stopped their subscriptions because of the scandal, says Howells. *Rowell's Newspaper Directory* bears him out, for it shows a decrease from 50,000 to 35,000 in the course of 1870.[47] This was not easily recovered, for the hard times of 1873 were coming on, and successive numbers of Rowell's annual show a steady decline. Houghton took over the publication in 1874, when 20,000 was the figure given,

Conway, Rose Terry Cooke, Cranch, Curtis, DeForest, Mrs. Diaz, Rebecca Harding Davis, Mr. and Mrs. Field, Henry Giles, Annie Douglas Green, E. E. Hale, Lucretia Hale, Henry James, father and son, Lucy Larcom, Fitz Hugh Ludlow, Donald G. Mitchell, Walter Mitchell, Fitz-James O'Brien, J. W. Palmer, Parkman, Parsons, Norah Perry, Mr. and Mrs. Piatt, Buchanan Read, Epes Sargent, Mrs. Spofford, W. J. Stillman, Mr. and Mrs. Stoddard, W. W. Story, Bayard Taylor, Celia Thaxter, Thoreau, Trowbridge, Elizabeth S. P. Ward, Wasson, Whipple, R. G. White, Mrs. A. D. T. Whitney, Forceythe Wilson, Theodore Winthrop.

[44] *Appleton's Journal*, II, 247 (October 9, 1869).

[45] *Harper's Weekly*, XIII, 579 (September 11, 1869). See *The Stowe-Byron Controversy: A Complete Résumé*, by the Editor of *Once A Week* (London, n. d.).

[46] *Nation*, IX, 167 (August 26, 1869). The English *Tomahawk* doubted "whether the whole annals of literature contain anything at once so cruel and so painful," and cartooned Mrs. Stowe as a snoopy old woman opening the door of a closet to reveal the skeleton in it (V, 3, September 11, 1869).

[47] Apparently the *Atlantic's* circulation had climbed to that 50,000 mark steadily. Fields wrote in his diary in 1863: "It has a subscription list, daily increasing, of 32,000." Fields, *op. cit.*, p. 84. The decrease of 1870 may have been in part owing to new competition.

and soon thereafter the publishers refused to state their circulation. Apparently it continued to decline. *Ayer's Directory* gives it as 12,000 in 1881; it was certainly not more than that. Of course Mrs. Stowe is not to blame for this steady decline in circulation, though her foolish Byron article doubtless had an initial influence. The real reason was the competition of the new magazines of the postbellum period and the increasing popularity of the great illustrated magazine. The *Atlantic* did not again reach its circulation of 1869 until nearly forty years after Mrs. Stowe's article.

Begun at a subscription price of $3.00 a year, the magazine had, like most of its class, increased its rate during the war; and it had remained at $4.00 ever since. It carried some advertising from the beginning — six pages to twelve pages an issue during the fifties and early sixties.[48] It was a fair paymaster to its contributors, its "mean rate" of payment being $6.00 a page.[49]

A change came over the spirit of the *Atlantic* with what Howells calls his own "suzerain" — the seventies, by the middle of which the magazine had become a much more truly American periodical than it had been in its earlier years.

> The fact is [wrote Howells in the Anniversary Number many years later] we were growing, whether we liked it or not, more and more American. Without ceasing to be New England, without ceasing to be Bostonian, at heart, we had become southern, mid-western, and far-western in our sympathies. It seemed to me that the new good things were coming from those regions rather than from our own coasts and hills.[50]

[48] See p. 13.
[49] See pp. 20–21.
[50] *Atlantic*, C, 601 (November 1907). In addition to some named in a preceding list, Howells here cites the following contributors during his control of the *Atlantic*: William M. Baker, William Henry Bishop, H. H. Boyesen, Clemens, Philip Deming, Dickens, George Cary Eggleston, Edgar Fawcett, Fiske, Alice French, Harte, Hay, Hayne, Helen Hunt Jackson, Sarah Orne Jewett, Mrs. Kemble, Clarence King, George P. Lathrop, S. Weir Mitchell, Louise Chandler Moulton, Mary N. Murfree, Robert Dale Owen, Parton, Thomas Sergeant Perry, Frances N. Pratt, Reade, Stedman, C. W. Stoddard, Maurice Thompson, George E. Waring, Warner, Mrs. Wharton, Mrs. Wister, Constance Fenimore Woolson. See also, regarding "the broadening of the *Atlantic's* phylacteries," *Every Saturday*, N. s., I, 588 (May 23, 1874).

Though Howells did not lack in veneration of the New England literary tradition, doubtless his own midwestern birth and rearing had something to do with this willingness to receive gentiles into the holy of holies. The wider horizon, moreover, was characteristic of the times. But the tradition of tyrannical editorship was maintained, and authors were sometimes "corrected" to their displeasure.[51]

Several new departments were introduced.[52] Howells' own contributions, both in serial fiction and in literary criticism, added much to the *Atlantic's* charm, in his as well as in other editorships. Though book reviewing was not a pleasure to him,[53] his work in that kind was a delight to his readers. Indeed, the *Atlantic's* book reviews had always been good. Lowell and Fields had taken especial pride in that department of the magazine. Under Howells, the "literary notices," writes a critic in the *Nation*, "are sure to contain some of the most graceful and sedulously finished writing of the month." [54] And again, "It is seldom that the critical department is not the most profitable part of the magazine." [55]

The greatest hit of Howells' administration, as indeed the greatest story hit of the magazine's history, was Aldrich's "Marjorie Daw." It had a tremendous popular success. It was printed in 1873, a year of financial troubles, but it was the boast of the publishers in their advertising that Marjorie Daw had "taken the edge off the panic." The magazine critic of the *Nation* already quoted,[56] himself an admirer of the story, noted, six months after its publication, that "Marjorie Daw has had a poem addressed to her, and we presume a colossal statue,

[51] See Volume III, Chapter I.

[52] A section of book reviews was printed from the beginning. In 1872 departments of recent literature (with a French-German section under the care of Thomas Sergeant Perry), science by John Fiske, music by William Foster Apthorp, and politics by A. G. Sedgwick were added to the magazine. The science and politics departments were dropped at the end of 1873; music was carried to July 1877, with occasional original songs printed with musical scores. A department of education, begun May 1874, was carried through several years, irregularly at the last. "The Contributors' Club" was begun in January 1877 and still flourishes.

[53] *Atlantic Monthly*, C, 596 (November 1907).

[54] *Nation*, VII, 355 (October 29, 1868).

[55] *Ibid.*, X, 77 (February 3, 1870).

[56] It was probably John R. Dennett.

equestrian, is next in order." [57] The immaterial nature of the subject, however, probably precluded this final tribute.

Another adventure of Howells' early connection with the *Atlantic* was the serial publication of Charles Reade's novel *Griffith Gaunt*. It was the *Atlantic's* first English serial, though there had originally been no thought of eschewing English writers. A statement had appeared in the prospectus in 1857 promising that

while native writers will receive the most solid encouragement, and will be mainly relied upon to fill the pages of the *Atlantic*, they [the publishers] will not hesitate to draw from the foreign sources at their command, as occasion may require, relying rather on the competency of an author to treat a particular subject, than on any other claim whatever.

Norton, who was in England when plans for the magazine were being made, and Underwood, who was sent over in 1857, scouted for English manuscripts. Norton tells in the Fiftieth Anniversary Number of the magazine how the trunk which contained most of the collected manuscripts was lost and never recovered. To the fortunate episode of the lost trunk may be due, in part at least, the fact that the *Atlantic* was written almost wholly by Americans.

It may be noted in passing, however, that the magazine was held rather firmly in the European literary tradition. If, as may well be contended, nonconformity and even iconoclasm are marks of a distinctively American literature, the *Atlantic*, which refused to countenance Whitman and Lanier and neglected Melville, was, in that respect at least, less American than its contemporary, the *Galaxy*, for example. But when American magazines were printing serial fiction by English writers, the *Atlantic* remained faithful to the American novel, except for her one flirtation with the seductive Charles Reade — a flirtation which, truth to tell, turned out rather scandalously.

For when *Griffith Gaunt* was published, it was immediately and violently attacked on the ground of its morals, or its lack of them. Among the critics was the lively *Round Table*, of New York, which headed its article "An Indecent Publication," and

[57] *Nation*, XVII, 294 (October 30, 1873).

called the story "one of the worst novels that has appeared during this generation . . . an unpardonable insult to morality," and added that it had been "declined by some of the lowest sensational weekly papers of New York."[58] Reade retorted upon his critics with his famous phrase "prurient prudes," wrote an angry reply to them in the *New York Times*,[59] and caused suit for libel to be brought against the *Round Table*.[60] It seems strange that this publicity did not increase *Atlantic* sales. Reade said that *Griffith Gaunt* "floated the Argosy," his newly launched English magazine; but Howells tells us that though he had looked to Reade for prosperity, he was "disappointed of it."[61] He had paid £3 a page for the serial.[62] Augustin Daly produced the story in dramatic form at the New York Theater in November 1866, while it was still running in the *Atlantic*. A Dickens novelette, *George Silverman's Explanation*, which cost the publishers of the *Atlantic* $1,000 in advance sheets, excited less comment but was similarly unprofitable.[63]

Among the new departments that Howells started when he took charge of the magazine was one devoted to politics, in charge of Arthur George Sedgwick. It was not greatly distinguished and was dropped after two years. In spite of a somewhat fortuitous early consulship, Howells was never much occupied with politics.

In the early days of the magazine, dinners at the Porter House, attended by a group of contributors, became almost an

[58] *Round Table*, III, 472 (July 28, 1866).

[59] Published in both the *Times* and the *World* October 6, 1866.

[60] See Volume III, sketch 1.

[61] *Atlantic Monthly*, C, 601 (November 1907).

[62] So it was testified in the Reade-*Round Table* suit. See *New York Tribune*, March 2, 1869, p. 5.

[63] *Griffith Gaunt* was published in England in the *Argosy*, and *George Silverman's Explanation* in *All the Year Round*. Tennyson's "The Victim" was printed in the February 1868 number of the *Atlantic* and had appeared in the January number of *Good Words*. Three poems by Browning — "Prospice," "Gold Hair," and "James Lee's Wife" (called "Under the Cliff") — are believed to have had their first publication in the *Atlantic* of May and June 1864. See the bibliography in Thomas M. Parrott's *Examination of the Non-Dramatic Poems in Robert Browning's First and Second Periods* (Leipzig, 1892). George Eliot's poems "Agatha" and "The Legend of Jubal" appeared first in the *Atlantic*, and her "Armgart," a one-act play in verse, was published simultaneously in the *Atlantic* and *Macmillan's*. Clough's "Amours de Voyage" was first published in the *Atlantic*.

510 A HISTORY OF AMERICAN MAGAZINES

institution; but it was not until Henry O. Houghton became publisher that these occasions were given a dignity that attracted public attention. The first of the more formal series was in honor of the new ownership and was given December 15, 1874. Later Houghton instituted the pleasant custom of the *Atlantic* birthday dinners.[64] The first was given to John G. Whittier December 17, 1877, on the occasion of the poet's seventieth birthday and the *Atlantic's* twentieth. The *Atlantic's* great were all there (except the ladies, who thought Mr. Houghton was unkind not to invite them), and poems for the occasion were read by Whittier and Holmes. A similar occasion was the Holmes breakfast two years later. At the birthday party given Mrs. Stowe in 1882 the recent deaths of Emerson and Longfellow cast a certain gloom upon the festivities.

In 1881 Howells resigned his editorship in order to devote more of his time to writing, and the office devolved upon Thomas Bailey Aldrich, who had been editor of another Houghton publication, *Every Saturday*. Aldrich's attitude was more Brahminical than that of Howells; he belonged more to the Lowell tradition. He was "a little less accessible to new and unknown talent," says his biographer Greenslet, "than Mr. Howells had been. . . . He was not a militant editor, and was not greatly concerned about political affairs." [65] It is as if the magazine continued to carry the word "politics" in her subtitle merely to have it ready for subsequent editors. But Aldrich was a careful editor, and his taste was critical and exquisite. Holmes (who is absent from only four of the first sixty volumes of the *Atlantic*), Whittier, and Lowell remained faithful contributors. James, Crawford, and Bishop wrote two or three serials each, and Miss Jewett, Miss Murfree, and Mrs. Oliphant each one.[66]

[64] Accounts of these dinners are found in Derby, *op. cit.*, pp. 280–290. A fuller history is in Arthur Gilman's "*Atlantic* Dinners and Diners," *Atlantic Monthly*, C, 646 (November 1907). See also T. W. Higginson, *Cheerful Yesterdays* (Boston, 1898), p. 178.

[65] Greenslet, *op. cit.*, p. 146.

[66] Among other frequent contributors were Parkman and Fiske in history, George F. Parsons and J. B. Harrison in sociology, William H. Downes in art, Herbert Tuttle in international affairs, William C. Langdon on Italy, William C. Lawton on classical subjects, Edmund Noble on travel, Edward Payson Evans on oriental topics, Richard Grant White on Shakespeare, and White, George E.

Horace E. Scudder, who had taken charge of the magazine during Aldrich's absences in Europe, became the latter's successor. He was industrious, contributing "more pages to the *Atlantic* than any other writer," and the magazine in an obituary article commended his "prudent and high-minded conservatism."⁶⁷ Bliss Perry thought him more "resourceful" than his predecessor, and adds the comment: "He was the only magazine editor I ever knew who read Greek and Latin authors for a half hour each morning in order to keep his ear attuned to style."⁶⁸ Scudder was especially interested in education, and discussion of social topics was frequent in his editorship. Theodore Roosevelt's articles on the civil service and machine politics attracted much attention. The circulation of the magazine at this time appears to have been less than ten thousand.⁶⁹

The *Atlantic* had now been going along for many years with a small circulation, certainly making no money for its publishers, but maintaining a high character and a reputation for conservatism. Sometime in the nineties young John Adams Thayer, later to make such a sensational success with *Everybody's*, breezed into the *Atlantic* office and offered to take over the management, put in illustrations, fill the magazine with matter that would get it talked about, clothe it in a picture-cover, and "push the circulation to the hundred thousands." Would they do it? They would not. In his well-named autobiography, *Astir*, Thayer tells us all about it. "To change the magazine in any way — never! It was Boston."⁷⁰ Young Mr. Thayer was lucky not to be taken in charge by the janitor and

Woodberry, Miss Preston Scudder, and Lathrop on the new books. Some other poets should be named, as Helen Gray Cone, Julia C. R. Dorr, Helen Hunt Jackson, Father Tabb, and Edith Thomas; and some essayists, such as Agnes Repplier, Elizabeth Robins, Olive Thorne Miller, N. S. Shaler, and Warner.

⁶⁷ *Atlantic Monthly*, LXXXIX, 433 (March 1902).
⁶⁸ Perry, *And Gladly Teach*, p. 165.
⁶⁹ Rowell complained in 1907 that he had never had a satisfactory circulation statement from the *Atlantic*. But in that year his *Directory* gave the figure as 25,000, and an *Atlantic* advertisement in the same volume said there had been a 20 per cent increase in 1900, 21 per cent in 1901, 12 per cent in 1904, and 12 per cent in 1905 — which would place the figure for 1899 at 14,000, and Rowell actually quotes 14,000 in 1899. If Page's biographer is right in his claim that the circulation doubled under Page's editorship, it was 7,000 in 1897. Perry quotes the circulation under Page as 11,000 to 12,000 (*And Gladly Teach*, p. 174).
⁷⁰ J. A. Thayer, *Astir: A Publisher's Life-Story* (Boston, 1910), p. 112.

thrown not only out of the *Atlantic* office, but out of Boston. But when Walter Hines Page became a very active assistant editor in 1896 and then succeeded Scudder in 1898, the consternation was not very much less than it would have been if Thayer himself had begun to give orders. This aggressive young Southerner had come to the *Atlantic* from the *Forum*, where he had made a big success. He disturbed the order and peace of the *Atlantic* régime with his ideas and enthusiasms. A later editor lists his characteristics: "an uneasy, often explosive, energy, a disposition to underrate fine-drawn niceties of all sorts, ingrained Yankee commonsense checking his vaulting enthusiasm, enormous self-confidence, impatience of failure." [71]   Under Page and his successor, Bliss Perry, the *Atlantic* bore some small part in the muckraking campaign which was the most distinctive feature of periodical literature at the turn of the century. John Jay Chapman's "The Capture of the Government by Commercialism" in February 1898 and his "Between Elections" in January 1900, Everett P. Wheeler's "The Unofficial Government of Cities" in March 1900, and Francis C. Lowell's "The American Boss" in September of that year are examples. Roosevelt, Wilson, E. L. Godkin, and William Allen White were contributors of political articles. Page himself contributed "The Autobiography of a Southerner" under the name of "Nicholas Worth." Moreover, Page startled the Boston anti-imperialists by displaying a war flag on the *Atlantic's* cover in 1898; he developed a liking for political controversy; he got Booker Washington and Jacob Riis to write about their social work. Best, or at least most remunerative, of all, he printed Mary Johnston's *To Have and to Hold*, which is said to have doubled the magazine's circulation — though even then it was very small.

Page was soon called to other duties, leaving the *Atlantic* to Bliss Perry, who retained his professorship at Princeton during his first year as editor. Under his management there were a good many more or less abstract disquisitions on politics — like the series by Woodrow Wilson, and Grover Cleveland's "The Independence of the Executive" (June–July 1900) — which

[71] B. J. Hendrick, *Life and Letters of Walter Hines Page* (New York, 1924), I, 55, 62; B. J. Hendrick, *The Training of an American* (Boston, 1928), p. 273.

gave an appreciable boost to circulation.[72] But there was a nearer approach to that wide interest in the problems of the modern world which characterized the magazine under later management; and by no means abstract were William Vaughn Moody's "Ode in Time of Hesitation" (May 1900) and the editorial article demanding facts on the Philippine situation (March 1901). The open letter to President Roosevelt in March 1905 was greeted with an angry reaction in the White House; and Editor Perry thought it best to place his resignation in the hands of the publishers, but he was persuaded to remain.[73] A later troublemaker was the "bedroom scene" with which May Sinclair began her serial "The Helpmate" and which cost the magazine "many subscribers." [74] During the editor's absence in Europe for six months of 1906, Ferris Greenslet was in charge.

Professor Perry was succeeded in 1909, after precisely ten years of editorship, by Ellery Sedgwick, who had in the previous year joined with MacGregor Jenkins in organizing a company to purchase the magazine and publish it, under the name of the Atlantic Monthly Company. The coming of Sedgwick and the dissolution of the connection with a book-publishing house, marked a new era for the magazine. Sedgwick had gained the newer outlook from his work with *Leslie's Monthly*, the *American Magazine*, and *McClure's*. Jenkins, who had been with Houghton Mifflin for some years, was an acute student of reader-interests. Under the new management the *Atlantic* showed a sense of the profound importance of the economic, social, and political changes in contemporary life, all of which it reflected with dignity and frequently with literary charm. "Of late years the appeal which the *Atlantic* makes to men active in commercial life has widened and deepened," said the prospectus for 1913. Notable also was the magazine's increased interest in contemporary science and its intelligent discussion of religious topics. "There is no arguing the question," declared the *New York Times Book Review* in 1922,

. .*. the *Atlantic Monthly* is not the staid magazine that refreshed our grandfathers. Its has grown lively during recent years; it has

---

[72] This issue sold 23,000 copies. Perry, *And Gladly Teach*, p. 174.
[73] *Ibid.*, p. 184.   [74] *Ibid.*, p. 195.

moved with the times and, finely enough, yet retained that dignified composure that is associated with it. In other words, the editors have brought it up to date, but have done it in such a skillful manner that old readers will hardly guess that the magazine is moving on from their conservative views.[75]

To show the contrast between the Lowell-Fields method of editing the magazine and that of Sedgwick, the following lines by a former assistant may be quoted:

Sedgwick's method of editing was — and is — simple. He keeps a sharp lookout for promising material among manuscripts submitted to him, never forgetting that even in an unpromising manuscript there may be the germ of a valuable feature. He reads thoroughly the New York *Times* and the London *Times*, keeps thus abreast of the news of the world, and makes up his mind what are the vital problems to which the *Atlantic* must address itself. He dines out frequently, listens to the talk, and notices what active-minded people are thinking about. And he keeps up a voluminous correspondence with writers, newspaper correspondents, statesmen, and men of affairs on two or three continents. . . . Thus he is able to sit at an editorial desk in Boston, keep his finger on the pulse of the world, and when he wants a given article written, reach out and find the man to do it.[76]

A good example of the Sedgwick editorship was the publication, during the campaign preliminary to the nomination of Alfred E. Smith for the presidency, of an "Open Letter" to him frankly stating the disabilities which many of his opponents believed his Catholic faith would place upon him. The article was written by Charles C. Marshall, a New York attorney who specialized in canon law. Smith wrote a reply for the next number.[77] The exchange was not only "an historic incident," as the editor suggested, but it was "spot news" for the daily papers. Other notable articles of recent years were Felix Frankfurter's discussion of the Sacco-Vanzetti case (March 1927); William Z. Ripley's "From Main Street to Wall Street" (January 1926), which resulted directly in reforms by the New York

---

[75] *New York Times Book Review*, January 15, 1922.

[76] Frederick L. Allen, "Sedgwick and the Atlantic," *Outlook*, CL, 1407 (December 26, 1928). See also Leon Whipple's "The Revolution on Quality Street," *Survey*, LVII, 122–124 (November 1, 1926).

[77] *Atlantic Monthly*, CXXXIX, 540, 721 (April, May 1927).

Stock Exchange; and Rear Admiral William S. Sims's criticism of the system of naval promotions (September 1935), which brought wide repercussions.

Sedgwick made many visits to Europe on missions connected with his editorship, and during his later absences his place in the office was taken by Edward A. Weeks, Jr. In June, 1938, Sedgwick, though he retained financial control, resigned the editorship to Weeks.

Under the Sedgwick management, the circulation of the *Atlantic*, which passed the 100,000 mark in 1921, has remained remarkably stable even through years of financial upset. Its circulation statements of recent years recall the verses written by Oliver Wendell Holmes for the *Atlantic* dinner of 1874, and cause the observer to wonder if the time may not yet come when

> The roughs, as we call them, grown loving and dutiful,
> Shall worship the true and the pure and the beautiful,
> And, preying no longer as tiger and vulture do,
> All read the *Atlantic* as persons of culture do!

31

THE AMERICAN PRESBYTERIAN REVIEW [1]

AN orthodox Calvinistic journal called the *American Theological Review* was begun in 1859 to effect, according to a "Notice" in the first number, "a union between Boston and New York . . . on the common doctrinal basis of Congregationalism and Presbyterianism contained in the Westminster Assembly's Shorter Catechism." It was to be published in the two cities simultaneously, but its owners were Boston men. The *Independent*, smelling what it called a "heresy hunt," sounded the alarm, and, according to its later claim,[2] caused an abortion of the deep-laid plot. At any rate, after the issue of only one or two numbers in Boston, New Yorkers got control and spirited the new journal off to their own metropolis and put it in charge of Henry B. Smith, of Union Theological Seminary, a gifted scholar and theologian. Too late the American Theological Review Company, the body originally formed to manage the *Review* but now bereft of its progeny by the bold coup of the New York kidnapers, met and resolved "that in our judgment the proprietorship of the *Review* should be returned to Boston." Passing resolutions would not bring it back, however, and the *Boston Review* [3] was immediately started in its place.

Meanwhile, the *American Theological Review* was winning high praise as an able journal. The Appleton *Annual Cyclo-*

---

[1] TITLES: (1) *The American Theological Review*, 1859–62; *The American Presbyterian and Theological Review*, 1863–68; *The American Presbyterian Review*, 1869–71.

FIRST ISSUE: January 1859. LAST ISSUE: October 1871.

PERIODICITY: Quarterly. Annual volumes. [First Series], I–IV, 1859–62; New [Second] Series, I–VI [V–X], 1863–68; New [Third] Series, I–III [XI–XIII], 1869–71.

PUBLISHERS: Charles Scribner, Boston and New York, 1859; J. M. Sherwood, New York, 1860, 1863–71; W. H. Bidwell, New York, 1861–62.

EDITOR: Henry Boynton Smith (with J. M. Sherwood, 1863–71).

INDEXED in *Poole's*.

[2] *Independent*, January 10, 1861.

[3] See sketch 32.

paedia says that it "at once took the front rank in theological science." [4] It became a leading advocate of reunion of Old and New School Presbyterianism, but soon came into collision with the *Princeton Review* on this great controversy; and Smith measured lances with Charles Hodge, the *Princeton's* great theologian. Smith's historical learning, his ability in dialectic, and his independent position gave great force to his articles.

In 1863 the *Presbyterian Quarterly Review*,[5] of Philadelphia, like-minded on the subject of reunion, was merged with the New York journal, and the name was changed to the *American Presbyterian and Theological Review*. J. M. Sherwood, experienced on several other periodicals, became joint editor, as well as publisher; and a board of associate editors was set up.[6]

After the reunion in 1869, a new series was begun, and the name of the journal was mercifully shortened to the *American Presbyterian Review*; but it continued under the same management. The *Princeton Review* was presently moved to New York; there were now no differences between the two journals, and there seemed to be no room for both, so at the end of 1871 Sherwood purchased the *Princeton* and combined the two under the name of the elder.[7]

The *American Presbyterian Review* was, throughout its thirteen years, almost wholly a theological journal. Literature, philosophy, and science were discussed sometimes, but chiefly in their relation to the theology expounded. The review was distinctly heavy. W. G. T. Shedd, of Union Theological, and President John Bascom, of the University of Wisconsin, were leading contributors; and in its last years, President James McCosh, of Princeton.

[4] *American Annual Cyclopaedia*, 1861, p. 422.
[5] See p. 62.
[6] This board consisted of R. D. Hitchcock, Albert Barnes, Thomas Brainerd, John Jenkins, J. B. Condit, and George E. Day.
[7] See Mott, *A History of American Magazines, 1741–1850*, p. 534.

THE BOSTON REVIEW [1]

AFTER the *American Theological Review* [2] was spirited away to New York in 1859, Boston supporters of orthodox theology no sooner recovered from their amazement than they proceeded to start another review, this one to be named after their own city so nobody could move it off the grounds. The New York *Independent* announced the journal thus:

> The theological world is startled by a new divisive movement and a conspiracy to agitate the churches of New England with cries of heresy and demands of more stringent measures to guard the Old Theology. [3]

There was a good basis for the *Independent's* fears; the *Boston Review* did turn out to be a lively controversialist, attacking the "Beecher theology," the *Independent* (edited then by another Beecher), and the New School generally. The quartet of clergymen in charge, headed by Joshua T. Tucker, managed to impart to the *Review* a brilliance and ease unusual among polemical journals. It consciously tried to be "spicy, possibly peppery," and at times it was liberal enough with the pepper.

The *Review* printed some literary criticism, usually with a strong theological flavor, and an occasional poem. In 1865–66 it published Willard Barrows' picturesque sketches of his western travels, later given book form as *The General*.

---

[1] TITLES: (1) *The Boston Review: Devoted to Theology and Literature,* 1861–67; *Congregational Review,* 1867–71.
FIRST ISSUE: January 1861. LAST ISSUE: November 1871.
PERIODICITY: Bimonthly, 1861–65, 1868–71; quarterly, 1866–67. Regular annual volumes. Vols. X–XI also called Second Series, I–II (1870–71).
PUBLISHERS: John M. Whittemore & Company, Boston, 1861–64; E. P. Marvin, Boston, 1865–69; Boston Review Company, Chicago, 1870–71.
EDITORS: William Barrows, J. C. Bodwell, E. P. Marvin, and J. T. Tucker, 1864–67; E. P. Marvin, E. Cutler, and J. E. Rankin, 1867–69; A. L. Chapin, G. F. Magoun, S. C. Bartlett, and G. S. F. Savage, 1870–71 (with W. A. Nichols, 1871).
[2] See sketch 31 for *American Presbyterian Review.*
[3] *Independent,* January 10, 1861.

But the journal did not prosper. It tried quarterly publication in 1866, but at the end of that year it admitted editorially that "for several years" it had been "a dead loss to its proprietors." [4] At the beginning of the next year it therefore put its controversial past behind it, changed its name to the *Congregational Review*, and made trial again with a new set of editors. "We see no longer any necessity for polemical discussions. . . . We intend to give a good proportion of our columns to general literature," [5] said the new editors. Their "general literature" was not of a very distinguished kind, however, and the editorship was rather less brilliant than before.

In 1870 a group of western Congregational leaders obtained control of the *Review* and moved it to Chicago. Long-suffering Boston, robbed first by New York and now by Chicago, had no word to say about the injustice of it this time, for she had failed to support her *Review*. The new editors were President G. F. Magoun, of Grinnell College; President A. L. Chapin, of Beloit College; Professor S. C. Bartlett, of Chicago Seminary (later president of Dartmouth); and the Reverend G. S. F. Savage. But the church had little opportunity to see what a western *Congregational Review* could do, for the great Chicago fire of 1871 burned the roof over its head. Its number for November 1871 was printed by friends in Detroit.

This was the last issue. Its proprietors decided to give up the fight and merge it with the *New Englander*, most flourishing of the Congregational magazines. On the whole, its career was unsuccessful: its reactionary polemics had not been widely popular, and its later attempts in the field of general literature had been undistinguished.

[4] *Boston Review*, VI, 620 (October 1866).
[5] *Congregational Review*, VII, 146 (January 1867).

VANITY FAIR [1]

W E WERE all very merry at Pfaff's," begins a poem by Thomas Bailey Aldrich in the first number of *Vanity Fair*. This best of early comic papers was born in Pfaff's cellar, bohemian gathering place of the wits of the fifties.[2] There George Arnold the poet, Fitz-James O'Brien the short story writer, "Queen" Ada Clare, Frank Wood, and Artemus Ward (after he came to town in 1861) drank Charley Pfaff's lager beer, coined epigrams, talked interminably of letters and the arts, and admired one another's cleverness.

But it is doubtful if the wits at Pfaff's would have made the idea of a new comic any more than a comic idea if agreeable entrepreneurs had not come along. It took the Stephenses to make the paper a reality — Henry Louis Stephens, the cartoonist, and his brothers Louis Henry and William Allan. Of these, Henry Louis became the art editor, William Allan the general editor, and Louis Henry the publisher. The "angel" was Frank J. Thompson, an intimate friend of H. L. Stephens, who had made money as a merchant in Baltimore and, after spending some of it on *Vanity Fair*, invested the remainder in travel and adventure in many parts of the world.[3]

The first number of the new paper, published on the last day

[1] TITLE: *Vanity Fair*.

FIRST ISSUE: December 31, 1859. LAST ISSUE: July 4, 1863.

PERIODICITY: Weekly, except for two monthly numbers, January and February 1863. I–VI, regular semiannual volumes, 1860–62 (December 31, 1859, included with Vol. I); VII, January, February 1863, and May 2–July 4, 1863.

PUBLISHER: Louis Henry Stephens, "for the Proprietors" (Frank J. Thompson and, later, William Camac).

EDITOR: William Allan Stephens. Managing editors: Frank Wood, 1859–60; Charles Godfrey Leland, 1860–61; Charles Farrar Browne, 1861–62; Charles Dawson Shanly, 1862–63.

REFERENCES: Don C. Seitz, *Artemus Ward* (New York, 1919), Chapter IV; Franklin J. Meine, "American Comic Periodicals. No. 2 — *Vanity Fair*," in the *Collector's Journal*, IV, 461 (January–March 1934); William Murrell, *A History of American Graphic Humor* (New York, 1933), pp. 209–211.

[2] See p. 39.

[3] For this information and some other data about staff personnel the author is indebted to W. P. and Frank Stephens, sons of H. L. Stephens.

of 1859, was excellent. It was a small quarto of sixteen pages, not unlike the London *Punch* in appearance, with a full-page unbacked cartoon by H. L. Stephens facing page eight. It began with a preface asserting that "gentleness is quite compatible with courage, and, depend upon it, more can be accomplished by good-humored raillery than envenomed wit," and continuing:

But Momus as well as Janus has two faces: one smiling and kindly, ready to laugh down Folly and cheer on Merit; the other stern and frowning, in whose glance Vice and Falsehood wither. . . . We can assume a very unpleasant expression when we are face to face with political tricksters, venal editors, public charlatans, silly authors, and all people whose stupidity necessitates their being treated as criminals.[4]

Having thus made its bow in form, though saying no more of pith or consequence than salutatories usually do, the number gives us an opening poem on food adulteration by George Arnold, entitled "The Modern Mithridates."

> Ho! Bring my breakfast — give to me
> Bread that is snowy and light of weight —
> Of alum and bone-dust let it be,
> Chalk, and ammonia's carbonate.[5]

And he proceeds to order up a full breakfast poisoned by adulterants. "Poisons? yes! yet one and all are found on every grocer's shelves!" The illustration shows a skeleton in cook's apron stirring a hell's broth. On the next page is a skit by Ada Clare detailing the troubles caused by "A Home-Made Shirt": Ada Claire did not believe in homemade shirts. If Arnold's poem was hard on the grocers, Ada's was good business for the haberdashers. Follows an illustrated satire on the folly of opening Congress with prayer, and then comes a series of small pictures by Frank Bellew illustrating some of the humors of Christmas. The big cartoon deals with John Bull's jealousy over America's diplomatic overtures to China. "A Walking Gentleman" then complains, as so many have before and since, of the dangers of pedestrianism on Broadway. "Pendennis" starts a

[4] *Vanity Fair*, I, IV (December 31, 1859).
[5] *Ibid.*, I, 5 (December 31, 1859).

VANITY FAIR'S PORTRAIT GALLERY.

We publish this week the second of this series of portraitures of
MEN BEFORE THE COUNTRY
By one of the best Caricaturists in America. They will represent the originals, not as they are popularly supposed to be—but as they are seen through THE SPECTACLES OF VANITY FAIR.

VOL. 5   NO. 123

Saturday,

MAY 3,

1862.

PRICE THREE DOLLARS PER ANNUM-SINGLE COPIES SIX CENTS.

WILLIAM CULLEN BRYANT

AS HE APPEARED WHILE ENRAPTURED WITH THE LOVELY WATERFOWL TO WHICH HE SUBSEQUENTLY ADDRESSED A POEM.

A POET POSES FOR *VANITY FAIR*

series on the follies of "The Town," and that is followed by Aldrich's very sentimental little set of verses beginning with the reference to Pfaff's. A political article commences with: *"Vanity Fair* looketh on all politics as vanity, and will therefore persistently intermeddle therewith"; and it then proceeds to declare itself against all disunionists. On the last page is an elegiac sonnet on Washington Irving by the editor, and good foolery on some orotund periods of the *Tribune's.* The price is ten cents, or three dollars a year, and there are three pages of advertising on the self-cover.

Altogether, it was an auspicious beginning. The woodcuts, while not numerous, were plentiful enough and of high quality, and continued so throughout the life of the periodical. Stephens was the leading illustrator, but Frank Bellew and Ned Miller were also on the staff; and John McLenan, Edward F. Mullen, and J. H. Howard drew occasional pictures for the paper. George Wevill, the engraver for the first volume, was a brother-in-law of H. L. Stephens. Andrew and Filmer cut the blocks for the second volume, and Bobbett-Hooper did the chief pieces thereafter. Beginning in June 1861, a large cartoon, usually political, appeared on the cover page; in the latter part of 1862 some excellent *portraits chargés* appeared in this position. The caricatures of H. L. Stephens in *Vanity Fair* entitle him to be ranked at or very near the top of the list of cartoonists who were prominent before Nast and Keppler. He had good ideas, and he drew smoothly; but he lacked the vigorous feeling of Nast and the action and robust comedy of Keppler.

Politics were indeed "persistently intermeddled with." "King Buck" Buchanan, Douglas, and Greeley were frequent objects of satire. *Vanity Fair* had no sympathy with the Negro's situation and thought that too much fuss was being made over slavery; in the number for March 3, 1860, Stephens pictured "Sambo Agonistes" trying to push apart the pillars of the Constitution. Lincoln was shown three months later as Blondin crossing over Niagara on a rotten rail, carrying a carpetbag containing a pickaninny, while Greeley calls from the shore, "Don't drop the carpetbag!" [6] Attacks on Lincoln ceased in the

---

[6] *Vanity Fair,* I, 377 (June 9, 1860). Doubtless it was this cartoon that suggested the comparison of himself to Blondin which Lincoln used in an interview

summer of 1860, however. Perhaps the accession of Charles Godfrey Leland to the managing editorship, which occurred in July 1860, had something to do with this change.[7] Frank Wood had been the first managing editor; but "there was some difficulty between Wood and Mr. Stephens, the *gérant* of the weekly," wrote Leland,

and Wood left, followed by all the clan [of Pfaff's cellar]. I was called in in the emergency, and what with writing myself, and the aid of R. H. Stoddard, T. B. Aldrich, and a few more, we made a very creditable appearance indeed. Little by little the bohemians all came back, and all went well. . . . The manager of *Vanity Fair* was very much averse to absolutely committing the journal to Republicanism, and I was determined on it. I had a delicate and very difficult path to pursue, and I succeeded, as the publication bears witness. I went several times to Mr. Dana, and availed myself of his shrewd advice.[8]

The paper was scarcely as thick-and-thinly Republican as this would indicate. It was content to thump the other candidates and to rejoice over James Gordon Bennett's discomfiture on Lincoln's election; and after Leland left *Vanity Fair* at the end of about ten months' editorship in order to conduct a magazine in which his Republican sympathies could have free play,[9] the paper "backslid" into a lukewarmness toward Lincoln and a hatred of the "nigger." The fact is that the Stephenses were Democrats — not "Copperheads" by any means, but consistent "War Democrats." They now opposed emancipation as vigorously as their former editor was urging that policy. By the middle of 1862, however, *Vanity Fair* had come to a better understanding of Lincoln, though it still urged that Stanton be thrust aside.[10]

Vanity Fair was full of the war. It was critical of the war

with the committee of senators who urged him to interfere with Stanton's policies. See James M. Scovel's "Recollections of Lincoln," *Lippincott's Magazine,* LXIII, 278 (February 1899). For reproduction of this cartoon, see p. 153.

[7] Laura Stedman and George M. Gould, *Life and Letters of Edmund Clarence Stedman* (New York, 1910), I, 217. Stedman noted the fact in his diary under date of July 18.

[8] C. G. Leland, *Memoirs* (London, 1893), II, 19, 22.

[9] The *Knickerbocker Magazine.* A little later he edited the *Continental Monthly,* an immediate-emancipation magazine; see pp. 540–543.

[10] See *Vanity Fair,* VI, 36 (July 19, 1862).

policies of the government at Washington and quick with its blame. A satirist of John Bull before the war, the Mason and Slidell episode made it an ardent hater of England and its government. Army contractors were directly in *Vanity Fair's* line of fire from the beginning of the war. But besides these regular satirical themes, the paper was full of war features: a humorous treatise on military tactics called "Hardee Made Easy," a series of "Humors of the War," elegies of the famous dead. Of these last, perhaps the most notable is that which mourned the death of one of its own group — Fitz-James O'Brien.

But the paper was not wholly or even chiefly concerned with politics and war. Notable personalities of those years received attention; favorite objects of attack were James Gordon Bennett and Henry Ward Beecher. The arrival of the steamship *Great Eastern* in the summer of 1860, the welcome to the prize fighter Heenan, and the visits of the Japanese embassy and the Prince of Wales were events which were "played up" in the journal. There were reams of "Prince-of-Walesiana," of which Stedman's poem "The Prince's Ball," published in two parts in October 1860, with Stephens' illustrations, was the crowning feature. It was not particularly inspired, as Stedman admitted; but it "trebled the usual edition of *Vanity Fair*" and "saved the paper." [11] Stedman's "Peter Stuyvesant's New Year's Call" in the number for December 29, 1860, is a better ballad but made less of a "hit."

But more important, and one of the two chief attractions of the paper's entire table of contents, was George Arnold's series of "McArone" papers (originally spelled "McAroni") burlesquing war correspondence. They began in December 1860 and ran through to the end. The pseudonym arose from the fact that the papers originally dealt with the Italian war; but after Sumter, "McArone" shifted the field of his investigations to the war at home, under the heading, "Our War Correspondence." A sample at random:

Dear *Vanity*: Me and McClelland has got a new water-base, and things are going on all right.
. . . Keep dark.

[11] Stedman and Gould, *op. cit.*, I, 218.

The enemy met us in superior force, as usual.

We repulsed him at all points, and retreated towards Richmond, extending our lines to within a rod, or a rod and a half, of the city.

The Rebels made a furious attack upon our position in the Chickahominy swamps, took everything they found there. . . .

They didn't find anything there.

Then they pushed on, and after a desperate struggle — through the swamps — they succeeded in reaching the White House, killing and capturing all the soldiers in the place. . . .

There were no soldiers in that place.

On this, they attacked the rear of the Army, still retreating, and nearing Richmond.

Here they took all they could get.

. . . It was a thrashing.

I rode, dear *Vanity*, upon a little dapple-grey cockhorse, the gift of Lou. Napoleon. I rode at the head of my troops, with a rose in my mouth, occasionally humming the Hallelooyer chorus or swearing at my staff. I am an awful fellow, I tell you. We newspaper correspondents always are.

. . . And the correspondent of the *Chicago Tribune*, too.[12]

It may sound flat now; but in the days when dispatches from the front were read with suspense and avidity, these burlesques of their style and stock phrases and exaggerations caught the popular fancy. Arnold was a member of the staff and the most faithful of *Vanity Fair's* contributors in prose, as H. L. Stephens was in art. After the paper died, "McArone" continued in the *New York Leader*.

Another of the paper's big drawing cards and probably most important of them, was the series of contributions by Charles Farrar Browne, writing under the name of "Artemus Ward." Browne had already achieved a national reputation by his showman's letters when he began to send pieces to *Vanity Fair* at $10 apiece. These contributions caused a break with the *Cleveland Plain Dealer*, of whose staff the humorist had been a member, because its publisher was unwilling to share the showman's letters with any other publication.[13] Consequently, Browne gravitated to New York, where he went to work as Leland's assistant on *Vanity Fair*, January 2, 1861, at

[12] *Vanity Fair*, VI, 28 (July 19, 1862).
[13] Seitz, *op. cit.*, p. 63.

$20 a week.[14] Probably nothing in the whole file of the paper surpasses in actual cachinnatory effectiveness those early "wards" — as Browne called his showman's letters. The new editor also wielded the shears, wrote some clever book reviews and paragraphs on shows, and did other odds and ends. When Leland left the paper in May 1861, Browne stepped into his shoes and continued as managing editor until his restlessness and his growing success as a lecturer led to his withdrawal early in 1862, though the paper published occasional pieces from his pen after that. His chief contributions in the latter part of his incumbency were serial travesties upon the popular romances of the *New York Ledger* and such story-papers. These had such titles as "Moses the Sassy," "The Fair Inez," and "Washy-Boshy; or, the Prestidigitating Squaw of the Snakeheads."

Other serials there were of varying worth. Leland's "Telegraph Tour" seems rather tiresome. The "College Department" was an attempt to catch the interest of a class from which much was hoped but little realized. Shanly's "Mrs. Mehitable Ross" papers were usually amusing; but, as in Perley C. Tucker's "Letters from a Country Editor," the misspelling then believed so necessary to such writing is really a handicap to the enjoyment of them. Matthew Whittier, brother of the poet, contributed some letters in New England dialect, dealing with public affairs and signed "Ethan Spike," in the summer and fall of 1862. Fitz Hugh Ludlow's serial story called "The Primpenny Family" was published in the early months of 1861. William Winter did occasional poems and prose pieces, as did Richard Henry Stoddard.

Puns, the main reliance of so many early American comics, were not slighted by *Vanity Fair* contributors. The author of a serial discussion of this form of wit declared in 1860:

I would restrict the allowance of a punster in good health to eighty or ninety a day, certainly not more than a hundred. I frequently make six or seven hundred before dinner, but then everybody has not my constitution.[15]

A later writer confessed that "the wear and tear of intellect on *Vanity Fair* is so enormous that the most brilliant writer lasts

[14] *Ibid.*, p. 73.　　　　[15] *Vanity Fair*, I, 395 (June 16, 1860).

only three months, at the end of which time he becomes either idiotic or consumptive." [16] The obvious unkind rejoinder is that some seem idiotic to begin with. Must we make allowance for the strain of constant punning — and of punning purely for the pun's sake? "The man who neglects his hair early in life," writes a star contributor, "will have toupée for it." Puns are permissible only when they seem spontaneous, but the early comics made a business of them.

Charles Dawson Shanly succeeded Browne as managing editor of *Vanity Fair*. The number of pages had been reduced to twelve in the middle of 1861, and later the price was reduced to two dollars a year. There was some advertising, chiefly of books and patent medicines. Few contributions to *Vanity Fair* are funnier than some of the serious testimonial advertisements of Brandreth's pills to be found in it:

. . . When twenty Pills had been taken, and from twelve to fourteen hours from the attack of intense pain, something gave way in the region of the heart with a sound like that of a pistol-shot. He laid his hand on his side, and thought he was about to die, but he sunk off into a sweet and quiet sleep, little thinking that he was cured of a supposed incurable affection; but it was so.[17]

Mounting prices of materials in the face of a lowered subscription price probably caused the demise of *Vanity Fair*. But it had never attained popularity. Contemporary commentators were inclined to praise it, but its enemies were legion. A satirical paper must select its butts carefully, and *Vanity Fair* was on the losing side when it devoted so large a part of its energies to decrying, however cleverly, the abolitionists and the Negro. That might have done five or ten years earlier, but not during the war. In his preface to the sixth volume the editor wrote:

In the past six months we have received several bushels of anonymous letters, expressing the most exaggerated hatred, intensified abhorrence, and unmitigated malevolence toward us. . . . [They] appear to emanate from lunatics connected with the so-called "abolition press." . . . We think the nation is, at present, of more consequence than the negro.[18]

[16] *Vanity Fair*, III, 131 (March 16, 1861).
[17] *Ibid.*, V, 30 (January 18, 1862).
[18] *Ibid.*, VI, 3 (July 5, 1862).

Through the latter part of its life, William Camac, a wealthy Philadelphian, succeeded Thompson as the chief financial backer of the paper. At the beginning of 1863 it resorted to monthly publication, giving the paper shortage as the reason.[19] After issuing two monthly numbers, *Vanity Fair* seemed to be dead; but (whether through the agency of Brandreth's pills or a new "angel") it was resurrected on May 2 for what proved to be a final series of ten weekly numbers. In this postscript the chief topics were the "Copperheads," resentment against British aid to the South, the pneumatic tubes recently installed in London, and the water cure.

All of *Vanity Fair* is included in seven thin volumes. We cannot object to the shortness of the file, however, when we remember what brevity is the soul of.

[19] *Ibid.*, preface to Vol. VII. See also references to the paper shortage in the number for January 1863.

THE NATIONAL QUARTERLY REVIEW [1]

I N THE midst of the gathering clouds of civil war, Edward I. Sears, a professor of languages in Manhattan College, a New York Catholic institution, set up a quarterly review in that city. The review was to be general in scope, touching on politics, the arts, economics, education, letters. It was to be national, as its title indicated — "American in the broadest and most legitimate acceptation of the term" — and not merely Bostonian, as the *North American Review* was conceived to be.

Sears was an Irishman, a graduate of Trinity College, Dublin, and a man of strong character, positive views, and scholarly mind. He had come to America in 1848, a young man of twenty-nine, and had done journalistic work for the *Herald* and the *Times*. The breadth of his interests is demonstrated by his review, for he wrote a large part of it himself.

The *National* was a quarterly review of classic form, frankly modeled upon the famous English reviews. Its articles had weight and substance. No matter what the subject, the writer felt the necessity of leading to it by tracing it down from the beginning of history, and of citing classical and European authors upon it before getting to the crux of the discussion. However heavy the articles were, they were nevertheless frequently relieved from dullness by the native pungency of Professor Sears's wit. He was disposed to be severe with writers, politicians, and financiers alike; he always spoke from the

[1] TITLE: *The National Quarterly Review.* Nickname: "Sears' Review."
FIRST ISSUE: June 1860. LAST ISSUE: October 1880.
PERIODICITY: Quarterly. [First Series], I–XXXIV, June 1880–March 1877; Second Series, I–VII (XXXV–XLI), July 1877–October 1880.
PUBLISHERS: Pudney & Russell, 1860; Edward I. Sears, 1860–76; David A. Gorton & Company, 1877–79; *National Quarterly Review*, 1880. All of New York.
EDITORS: Edward I. Sears, 1860–76; David A. Gorton, 1876–80; C. H. Woodman, 1880.
INDEXED in *Poole's, Jones' Index.*
REFERENCE: "Impressions and Reminiscences of Edward I. Sears," *National Quarterly Review*, XXXIV, 197 (March 1877).

tripod, and sometimes almost as if he had a personal grudge against the object of his attack.

His delight [wrote an admirer] to prick a bubble or to expose a sham, his hatred of quackery and ill-founded pretension, the satisfaction he derived from ventilating the dark ways and doings of men — in unmasking the hypocrite and in unraveling the mercenary and over-reaching designs of individuals and corporations — more especially those of educational institutions — kept him always busy.[2]

The *National* contained many reviews of educational institutions, some of them including severe strictures upon scholarly inadequacies. The drift away from the classics, the failures of the common school system, and educational fads were condemned. Textbooks were frequently reviewed with considerable authority.

Sears was a strong critic of monopolies. America, he said in 1869 in an article entitled "Our Millionaires and Their Influence," was ruled by "an oligarchy whose only claim to power is money."[3] In the year of his death he wrote an article called "Our Railroad Monopolies and Monopolists," in which he asserted that "No nation on earth is less free . . . the American people are farmed out to monopolies."[4] These strong statements were backed, in the Sears fashion, by statistics and arrays of facts.

The editor apparently had a flair for economics. The *National* started out with special attention to insurance — clearly an effort to capitalize upon the remarkable growth of that industry and the increasing interest in it. Sears did his best to keep the insurance companies in the strait and narrow path, and that perhaps prevented his review from becoming what he seems to have intended — an authoritative insurance organ. It printed regular insurance supplements for some years.

There was a political article in nearly every number. Sears opposed Lincoln in both his campaigns because he did not believe the candidate possessed the qualities and training necessary for the presidency. The *National* was loyal to the North,

[2] *National Quarterly Review*, XXXIV, viii (1876–77).
[3] *Ibid.*, XX, 130 (December 1869).
[4] *Ibid.*, XXXII, 345 (March 1876).

however, and gave considerable attention to the war. It was strongly opposed to Secretary Seward, and later to Grant the politician, but it rallied to the defense of President Johnson. European politics were also given much attention.

Sears's quarterly was not distinguished in literary criticism. Its standards were classical; it abhorred romantic extravagances, and it had an especial hatred for "puffery." It watched over the morals of literature: of George W. Carleton & Company, who had published such questionable foreign writers as Balzac and Swinburne in the United States, it declared, "No publisher in this country has so flagrantly offended public decency." [5] After the death of Sears, the journal contained more criticism of books and much more comment on art subjects.

Who Sears's collaborators were is not always easy to determine, since articles were uniformly unsigned. Karl Blind was a valued contributor on European politics; and Dr. R. S. Mackenzie, a fellow countryman of Sears, journalist and cosmopolite, wrote on European politics and literature. John T. Morse, Jr., contributed some historical articles, and David Trowbridge wrote on astronomy. John Pyne's fields were history and comparative theology, and that of Professor Charles Morris archaeology. The moral and literary essays of Henry Giles furnished perhaps as near an approach to sustained brilliance as the *National* afforded.

Sears died in 1876, and the *Review* came into the hands of Dr. David A. Gorton, who was its editor for the next four years. There was little change in policy — perhaps more emphasis on the arts and less on economics. Anonymity, by this time abandoned by other American reviews, was still clung to: "The editor deems it unwise to depart from a usage . . . still maintained by the best quarterlies in our language, to yield to the popular demand for the names of contributors." [6] In 1879 the name of one contributor was printed, however: the leading article for the March number of that year, on "Ideal Commonwealths," turned out to have been stolen bodily from the *Demo-*

[5] *National Quarterly Review*, XIV, 151 (December 1866).
[6] *Ibid.*, XXXVII, ii (1878).

cratic Review for 1846, and the *National* later pilloried the name of the plagiarist.

In 1880 Gorton turned the review over to his associate editor, C. H. Woodman; but it was discontinued at the end of that year. In the last few issues articles were signed. The *National's* circulation had always been small, though it had made Sears "a respectable living." [7] With Sears's personality removed, it declined. Besides, the *North American* had come to New York and renewed its youth, while the conservatism of the *National* found fewer and still fewer admirers.

In the middle seventies, however, it had occupied a high place in the esteem of many good judges. The *London Spectator*, reviewing American journals, voted it "at once the most learned, most brilliant, and most attractive of all their periodicals." [8] Unquestionably Sears's passion for justice and truth, with his native wit and his acquired wisdom, made it for a time an important journal.

[7] *Ibid.*, XXXIV, 207 (March 1877).
[8] Quoted *ibid.*, XXXIV, 205 (March 1877).

THE DIAL [1]
(of Cincinnati)

MONCURE D. CONWAY, liberal, reformer, and talented author, came to Cincinnati as minister of the First Congregational Church when he was twenty-four years old. Within three years he had aroused widespread controversy by his defense of Thomas Paine, his sympathy with strange creeds, and in general his freedom from the trammels of strait orthodoxy. "The papers teemed with controversial letters," wrote Conway later in his *Autobiography*, "and a magazine became inevitable." [2] Thus spake the born publicist.

In his preface, in January 1860, the editor called the *Dial* "a legitimation of the Spirit of the Age, which aspires to be free: free in thought, doubt, utterance, love, and knowledge." [3] And so it was: the contents of the twelve monthly numbers were instinct with the spirit of free inquiry. Many were the creeds, systems, and theories touched upon, always with an open mind. Doubtless the chief influence upon Conway's *Dial* was that of Theodore Parker, whose bold spirit seems to pervade its pages.

The leading item of its contents was a serial essay on "The Christianity of Christ" by O. B. Frothingham, devoted largely to showing the perversions of the religion of Jesus worked, through the centuries, by dogma. This serial ran through nine of the twelve numbers and occupied one-sixth of the volume. Conway himself wrote a considerable proportion of the magazine, including essays on abolition and John Brown, commentary on science, sermons made over into articles, and an

---

[1] TITLE: *The Dial: A Monthly Magazine for Literature, Philosophy and Religion.*
FIRST ISSUE: January 1860. LAST ISSUE: December 1860.
PERIODICITY: Monthly. One annual volume.
EDITOR AND PUBLISHER: Moncure Daniel Conway.
REFERENCES: M. D. Conway, *Autobiography, Memories and Experiences* (London, 1904), I, 272–279; Clarence L. F. Gohdes, *The Periodicals of American Transcendentalism* (Durham, North Carolina, 1931), Chapter IX.
[2] Conway, *op. cit.*, I, 272.
[3] *Dial*, I, 11 (January 1860).

excellent series of "Critical Notices" of recent books. Next to Conway in quantity of contributed material was Marx E. Lazarus, of North Carolina, who wrote on phrenology, emancipation, spiritualism, and so on, and translated a number of pieces from the French. An early lecture of Emerson's on West Indian emancipation was reprinted, and the lecture on "Domestic Life" made its first appearance in print in the *Dial*. An interesting department was that called "Catholic Chapters," modeled to some extent upon the "Ethnic Scriptures" of the Emerson-Fuller *Dial*. It contained passages from the great leaders in philosophy and religion, classified one month under "Worship," another under "Religion," and so on.

Some excellent poetry was printed in the *Dial*. Most notable were "The Sacred Dance" and twelve quatrains by Emerson. Frank Sanborn and Myron Benton (a brother of Joel Benton) contributed verse very much in the transcendental vein. Several Ohio poets were represented — young W. D. Howells, W. W. Fosdick, and others.

There was also an occasional piece of fiction. Conway wrote at least one story, of a didactic nature; and there were some translations from Balzac.

"The *Dial* was well received, had a large subscription list — the Jews especially interesting themselves," wrote Conway later.[4] "Large" probably means several hundred. The magazine was a well-printed octavo of sixty-four pages, with a subscription price of $2.00. Howells wrote an enthusiastic notice of it for the *Ohio State Journal* at Columbus. "That men should say what they think, outside of Boston, is of course astonishing," he began.

. . . If Cincinnati can place herself beside Boston on this serene eminence, she will accomplish a thing nobler than pork, sublimer than Catawba, more magnificent than Pike's Opera House. The *Dial* is an attempt on the part of intellectual Cincinnati to do this, and the attempt is a noble one.[5]

It is a pity the attempt succumbed at the end of twelve months. In his last number the editor said he was unable to continue the

[4] Conway, *op. cit.*, I, 272.
[5] *Ibid.*, pp. 272–273.

labor entailed.[6] He made an attempt, however, to change to quarterly publication, without success. He wrote Benton on January 9, 1861:

> Subscribers are coming in very slowly. . . . I do wish I could interest the rising thinkers and singers of this generation in the great importance of having a free and bold quarterly which shall be the organ of thought elsewhere suppressed.[7]

In his *Autobiography* Conway says that the hurly-burly of political debate just before the Civil War made it impossible for the *Dial*, speaking in the gentler tones of philosophy and literature, to be heard.[8] A year or so later he went back to Concord to start an immediate-emancipation weekly called the *Commonwealth*, in which some of his old *Dial* contributors found a welcome.

[6] *Dial*, I, 713 (December 1860).
[7] *Troutbeck Leaflets*, no. 9 (Amenia, New York, 1925), p. 7.
[8] Conway, *op. cit.*, I, 276.

DANVILLE QUARTERLY REVIEW [1]

THE *Danville Review* was founded by a group of professors in Centre College and Danville Theological Seminary in order to provide a Presbyterian quarterly more
centrally located than those of the eastern states. It was "designed mainly for the exposition, advancement and defence of
the Christian Religion, considered in its purely Evangelical
sense." [2] It was Old School in its alignment, and strongly opposed the Congregational "heresies" which were rife. It began
in March 1861, with a circulation of less than four hundred,
at $3.00 a year.

But though the *Danville Review* never forgot its theological
controversies, and though Robert W. Landis' serial discussion
attacking Hodge's position on the doctrine of Imputation doubtless had some importance, the journal is chiefly significant for
its political articles. It was published in the heart of that border-
land in which the question of secession was most violently debated, and its first number was issued a month before the firing
on Fort Sumter. For that first number, the chief editor, Robert
J. Breckinridge, wrote an article on the state of the country in
which he advocated adherence to the Union with vigor and eloquence. At the same time he defended slavery as a policy and
attacked the Lincoln doctrines, though he thought Lincoln personally "able, honest and patriotic." Fanaticism, anarchy, and
the flouting of the Constitution had led, he wrote, to recent secessions; but he expected counter-revolutions in the seceded states.[3]

[1] TITLE: *Danville Quarterly Review*. (Covers and half titles: *Danville Review*.)
FIRST ISSUE: March 1861. LAST ISSUE: December 1864.
PERIODICITY: Quarterly. Regular annual volumes.
PUBLISHERS: Richard H. Collins, Danville, Kentucky, and Cincinnati, 1861;
Moore, Wilstach & Company, Danville and Cincinnati, 1862–64.
EDITORS: Robert J. Breckinridge, Edward P. Humphrey, Stephen Yerkes,
James Matthews, Jacob Cooper, Robert W. Landis, 1861–64 (with Joseph T.
Smith, John M. Worrall, Robert L. Breck, 1861; Robert L. Stanton, 1862–64).
INDEXED in *Poole's*.
[2] *Danville Quarterly Review*, I, 1 (March 1861).
[3] *Ibid.*, I, 73–115 (March 1861).

For nearly every issue thereafter Breckinridge wrote a political article. In the second number he told of "the majestic reappearance of the American Nation in the mighty scene," [4] and anticipated the speedy end of that chaos in affairs which had developed. Kentucky he believed to be Union in sentiment. In the fourth number he urged the "imperative duty to crush this Rebellion, and preserve the Federal Union and Constitution." [5] In 1862 he published serially his "The Secession Conspiracy in Kentucky, and Its Overthrow," a vigorous, if prejudiced, story of those troublous times. In December of that year he pleaded against the proposal to emancipate the slaves by Federal proclamation.[6]

Breckinridge was a son of Senator John Breckinridge, a famous advocate of states' rights, who had died while serving as attorney general in Jefferson's cabinet. He had himself been educated in law and had been a member of the state legislature, advocating at that time the emancipation of slaves in Kentucky; but he had turned to the church in 1829 and was at this time serving as professor of didactic and polemical theology at the Danville Seminary.

Three of the original "Association of Ministers" who were to have been responsible for the *Review* resigned before the publication of the first number because of their sympathy with secession. At the end of the first year two more (Worrall and Breck) withdrew because of disagreement with Breckinridge on political questions. Two others (Landis and Matthews) were with the Confederate forces as chaplains, and still another (Smith) resigned for reasons not given. Moreover, at the end of the first volume there was trouble with the publisher, whom Breckinridge accused of secession sympathies.[7] In the course of attacks on Breckinridge by seceding editors, he was accused of using the funds and prestige of the seminary for political effect. Thereupon Breckinridge appealed to the General Assembly of the church and resigned his chair; but his resignation was declined, and he was commended for "his bold and patri-

[4] *Danville Quarterly Review*, I, 295 (June 1861).
[5] *Ibid.*, I, 639 (December 1861).
[6] *Ibid.*, II, 670–713 (December 1862).
[7] *Ibid.*, II, 141 (March 1862).

otic stand in reference to the great conflict now in progress." [8]
These disputes, which were aired in the papers, increased the
Review's circulation appreciably.

The original plan was for the board of twelve editors to write
the journal; and though Breckinridge did more than his share,
the defection of a part of the board brought into play the writing abilities of most of the remaining members. The articles
were chiefly theological and political, but other fields were entered occasionally.

In its March 1864 number the *Review* carried an article by
James Cooper on "The Loyalty Demanded by the Present
Crisis," in which it was asserted that there were now only two
parties — those of secession and union — and that Abraham
Lincoln should be nominated to succeed himself. Breckinridge
was chairman of the national Republican convention at Baltimore which renominated him.

The June 1864 issue was delayed by the departure of the
printers for the scene of war; after the hundred-days volunteers
had gone, the publishers had no workers available. Humphrey
and Yerkes resigned from the editorial board at the end of 1864,
and the announcement was made that the *Review* would be
temporarily suspended. It was, however, never resumed.

[8] *Ibid.*, II, 361 (June 1862).

THE CONTINENTAL MONTHLY [1]

JAMES ROBERTS GILMORE was born in Boston, but entered business in New York, where he became head of a cotton-buying house and made a fortune before the beginning of the Civil War. His intimate acquaintance with the South gave him strong opinions on the sectional conflict. He was an ardent advocate of emancipation as a war measure; and when he purchased the old and declining *Knickerbocker Magazine* in 1861,[2] he put the staunchly Republican Charles Godfrey Leland in editorial charge and inspired him to urge immediate emancipation. He soon decided, however, that his new wine needed new bottles; and in January 1862 he founded in the city of his birth a new magazine which he called the *Continental Monthly* and of which he made Leland editor.

The *Continental* was a well-printed royal octavo of 120 pages, priced at thirty-five cents. Said the editor in the first number:

We see a new time forming, new ideas rising, and would give it and them a voice in such earnest and energetic tones as the people love. . . . Write and publish; the public is listening. Now is the time, if it ever was, to develop an American character. . . . We hope to make a bold step forward, presenting in our columns contributions characterized by vigor, variety, and originality. . . . We shall advocate the holy cause of the UNION with might and main. . . . We believe in Emancipation. . . .[3]

The political articles were usually by the editor. They strongly urged emancipation as a war measure; they told of

[1] TITLE: *The Continental Monthly: Devoted to Literature and National Policy.*

FIRST ISSUE: January 1862. LAST ISSUE: December 1864.

PERIODICITY: Monthly. Six regular semiannual volumes.

PUBLISHERS: J. R. Gilmore, Boston, 1862; John F. Trow, Boston, "for the proprietors," 1862–64. (Proprietors were James R. Gilmore, 1862–63; Gilmore and Robert J. Walker, 1863–64.)

EDITORS: Charles Godfrey Leland, 1862–63; Mrs. Martha Elizabeth Duncan Walker Cook, 1863–64.

INDEXED in *Poole*.

[2] See Mott, *A History of American Magazines, 1741–1850*, pp. 606 n., 612.

[3] *Continental Monthly*, I, 99 (January 1862).

southern spies in the North, and they reported mutilations of northern dead by southern ogres. Leland later declared that the magazine had been

a something more than semi-official organ. Mr. Seward contributed to it two anonymous articles, or rather their substance, which were written out and forwarded to me by Oakey Hall, Esq., of New York. We received from the Cabinet at Washington continual suggestions, for it was well understood that the *Continental* was read by all influential Republicans.[4]

Leland believed that the magazine was very effective and that it "advanced the time of the Declaration of Emancipation." [5]

Leland's reputation at this time was chiefly that of a humorist. His "Hans Breitmann's Party" had been immensely popular, and the later Breitmann pieces and those devoted to Meister Karl and Mace Sloper only a little less so. Though a brilliant writer, it had been his fortune to be connected with unsuccessful magazines — *Graham's* and the *Knickerbocker* in sad later years, and Barnum's short-lived *Illustrated News*.[6] He gave the *Continental* exactly the character he had promised to give it in his salutatory — vigor, variety, originality, with a strong political flavor. Most of the articles were short. Wit and humor were prominent, both in verse and prose. Leland's own "Editor's Table" was lively and fresh; to illustrate the sort of fare it set forth, we may specify the story of the coming of an itinerant troupe of actors to a country village with the temperance drama, "Down the Hill." Their posters were their undoing:

Unparalleled Attraction!
On Monday Evening
The Youthful Roscuss!
Eglantine Mowbray!!
Will Appear in His Great Rôle
DOWN THE HILL.

The audience of the first night angrily demanded its money back after the show, because the youthful "Roscuss" had not rolled

---

[4] Charles Godfrey Leland, *Memoirs* (London, 1893), II, 31.

[5] *Ibid.*, p. 42. It must be recognized that Leland seems to exaggerate his own achievements and to underestimate those of his associates.

[6] For the Barnum paper see pp. 43–44; for *Graham's* see Mott, *op. cit.*, p. 554.

down the hill at all; so, the next night, after taking his last drink, he rolled spectacularly from a high painted rock into a painted abyss whence issued red and green flames. It was a great success.[7]

Gilmore, the publisher, took an active part in the management of the magazine, and he wrote for it, under the pen name of "Edmund Kirke," its most successful fictional offering. This was the serial *Among the Pines*, a vivid story of southern life and character; issued in book form, it became a best seller of 1863. "Kirke" followed it in 1862–63 with the serial *A Merchant's Story*, which also had a southern setting but was much less successful.

Leland's acquaintances among journalists and Gilmore's among public men helped to make the list of contributors to the *Continental* a distinguished one. Horace Greeley, George C. Boutwell, Henry Carey Lea, C. C. Hazewell, George H. Boker, John G. Nicolay, Henry T. Tuckerman, Delia M. Colton, N. L. Frothingham, and C. S. Henry were among them. Richard B. Kimball, versatile magazinist, novelist, lawyer, and railroad builder, and a good friend of the editor of the *Continental*, contributed an interminable serial that ran through most of the magazine's file, called *Was He Successful?*

After the Emancipation Proclamation was issued, the *Continental* afforded only the heartiest support to the administration at Washington. "Don't grumble!" advised Leland.

Don't be incessantly croaking from morn till night at the war and the administration and the generals and everything else! Things have been going better on the whole than you imagine, and your endless growling is just what the traitors like.[8]

This was Leland's last number — that for April 1863. Gilmore had brought in Robert J. Walker to take a half-interest in the magazine; and Walker's sister, Martha E. D. Walker Cook, was made editor.

Leland claims that the venture made only its bare publishing expenses and that he never received a cent for his services.[9] It

---

[7] *Continental Monthly*, I, 612 (May 1862).
[8] *Ibid.*, III, 505 (April 1863).
[9] Leland, *op. cit.*, p. 42.

had begun amid great interest and with encouraging prospects,[10] but with the rising costs of war times it undoubtedly failed of the prosperity its projector had hoped for. Walker's help must have been welcome. He had been a United States senator, secretary of the treasury under Polk, and governor of Kansas Territory; and the articles which he now contributed to the magazine were both vigorous and illuminating. Even when he went to Europe as financial agent for the United States, he continued his political articles for the *Continental*. His arguments for the re-election of Lincoln in 1864 were particularly cogent.

It must be admitted, however, that the magazine was less lively after Leland left it. Comment on the conduct of the war continued, but it seems less acute. There were some stories from the field in the latter part of 1864. The editor herself contributed poems, tales, and translations to the magazine. There were some articles on theological subjects by Philip Schaff, Asa L. Colton, and others. Caroline Chesebrough and Caroline M. Kirkland wrote stories and sketches. The poet Alfred B. Street and Professor Andrew TenBrook were frequent contributors. A series on "The English Press" by Nicholas Rowe, of London, appeared in 1864.

At the end of that year the *Continental Monthly* was discontinued. The economic pressure of the times was undoubtedly too great for it. Though it had many interests outside of the Civil War, it was essentially a war magazine; and finally it was itself a war casualty.

---

[10] See *Knickerbocker Magazine*, LIX, 316 (March 1862).

THE OLD GUARD [1]

We began the work in the midst of the reign of terror, when every man who ventured to adhere to the principles of democracy was threatened, not only with incarceration in a bastile, but with summary hanging by the "Loyal League" mobs. We have many times been followed in the streets of this city by a crowd of from one to five hundred of these infuriated fanatics.[2]

THUS the Reverend C. Chauncey Burr wrote of the early days of the publication of the *Old Guard*, the only consistently anti-Lincoln magazine published in the North during the war. "Copperhead" its enemies called it and the movement of which it was the organ, after the name of a certain species of poisonous snake; but the editor of the *Old Guard* preferred to believe that the nickname came from "the copper head of Liberty on the old cent of the United States."

It began in June 1862 as a pamphlet of twenty-four pages and published three numbers in that year under the warning of the postmaster general against treasonable utterances. Burr, who was both editor and publisher of the early numbers, was dissatisfied with the enforced moderation of the 1862 issues;[3] but in the freer times which came with the next year, he could give his political passions free rein. He had the devil's gift of scur-

---

[1] TITLE: *The Old Guard.* Subtitles: *A Monthly Journal, Devoted to the Principles of 1776 and 1787*, 1863–64. *A Monthly Magazine, Devoted to Literature, Science, and Art, and the Political Principles of 1776 and 1787*, 1865–70.

FIRST ISSUE: June 1862. LAST ISSUE: December 1870.

PERIODICITY: Monthly. Three 1862 numbers were originally called Vol. I; and January and February 1863 were called Vol. II, Nos. 1 and 2; but it was then decided to leave the three initial numbers out of the file and begin it with January 1863. March–September are therefore Nos. 3–9 of Vol. I; the remainder of the pages required for Vol. I were then issued without date, repeating much of the three initial numbers. Vols. II–VIII, regular annual volumes of twelve monthly issues each, 1864–70.

PUBLISHERS: C. Chauncey Burr, New York, 1863; Van Evrie, Horton & Company, New York, 1863–70; English & Company, New York, 1870.

EDITORS: C. Chauncey Burr, 1863–69; Thomas Dunn English, 1870.

[2] *Old Guard*, II, 281 (December 1864).

[3] *Ibid.*, I, 23 (January 1863).

rilous phrase, and a grandiloquence which, spurred with exclamation points and capitals, often had the effect of tearing a passion to tatters.[4]

The *Old Guard* defended slavery and the right of secession, attacked President Lincoln violently in every number, and urged the cessation of the war. It was, it claimed, "the only magazine published in the United States which is devoted to a fearless and uncompromising exposure of the monstrous crimes and frauds of the party in power."[5] It argued that the North was waging "a war for abolition and plunder,"[6] and it called the federal forces "the Abolition Army" and the whole conflict "the Lincoln War." Lincoln himself was usually referred to as "Abraham I."; and two years after the assassination Burr published an article on "Abraham Lincoln's Place in History," in which he pictured Lincoln as a weakling who was never strong enough to be more than a tool of vice and conspiracy.[7]

Each of the 1863 numbers was adorned with an engraved portrait; the leaders so honored were Horatio Seymour, C. S. Vallandingham, Joel Parker, Daniel Voorhees, James A. Bayard, Fernando Wood, B. Wood, and George W. Woodward. The magazine promoted all the peace movements of 1863 and in the next year became a campaign journal for the opposition party. Even after the war was over, it continued to attack the memory of Lincoln and to defend the Confederacy. "The magazine contains nothing but vulgar ribaldry concerning whatever is best and purest in our national life; in a word, it is Copperhead," said the *Nation.*[8]

The size of the magazine was enlarged in the first year after the war, a Richmond edition was begun, and its pages were embellished with pictures of the southern military leaders. No longer was it purely political, though most of its fiction and poetry was unimportant. Poems by William Gilmore Simms appeared in 1866, and two serials by him were printed — *Joscelyn* in 1867 and *The Cub of the Panther* in 1869. Other contributors besides Burr were John Esten Cooke, John R. Thompson, and James W. Wall. Dr. J. H. Van Evrie, who had

[4] See p. 154.
[5] *Old Guard*, I, 288 (undated, 1863).
[6] *Ibid.*, II, 1 (January 1864).
[7] *Ibid.*, V, 207–217 (March 1867).
[8] *Nation*, II, 25 (January 4, 1866).

become publisher of the *Old Guard* in the latter part of 1863, also wrote for the magazine.

In 1870 Dr. Thomas Dunn English became editor and owner. Politics were still present, bitter enough, but less of them. There were some woodcuts. The McDoodle Club, which gossiped about politics and personalities in dialogue form, was pretty bad. The best thing in the magazine was the editor's own "Down Among Dead Men" — a series of anecdotes of persons the writer had known, including some derogatory stories of Poe. English doubtless remembered that Poe had once "done him brown" in a magazine;[9] now he gets revenge by calling the dead poet "a moral idiot." [10] Christian Reid and Mrs. Burton Harrison were contributors during English's editorship. There was much abuse of A. D. Richardson in connection with the famous McFarland trial for murder. The magazine ended with the 1870 volume.

That Burr was sincere in his propaganda one need not doubt. His periodical is an interesting presentation of a point of view. But the whole file, under both Burr and English, displays too much ill nature to win sympathy for its cause.

[9] See Mott, *A History of American Magazines, 1741–1850*, p. 347.
[10] *Old Guard*, VIII, 466 (June 1870).

ARMY AND NAVY JOURNAL [1]

PROMPTED by the expressed belief of certain patriotic societies in the North that "journals and documents of unquestioned loyalty" ought to be distributed among the soldiers of "the armies now engaged in the suppression of the rebellion," [2] young Captain William C. Church, a soldier fresh from campaigns with Generals W. T. Sherman and Silas Casey, founded in New York in August 1863 the *Army and Navy Journal*. Associated with him in the publishing side of the work was his brother, Francis P. Church, later his partner also in the publication of the *Galaxy*; [3] but William C. was the editor of the *Journal*, and he continued in that capacity for over half a century, until his death in 1917. The partners were sons of the Reverend Pharcellus Church, founder of the *New York Chronicle*, a Baptist newspaper, and had been trained in journalism in the office of the *Chronicle*, now newly merged with the *Examiner*.

Though by no means without competition, [4] the *Army and Navy Journal* soon became and has long remained the great weekly unofficial spokesman of the military establishment of the United States. The editor wrote at the beginning of his second year that he had "labored to make the journal worthy

---

[1] TITLES: (1) *The United States Army and Navy Journal, and Gazette of the Regular and Volunteer Forces*, 1863–1921; (2) *American Army and Navy Journal and Gazette of the Regular and Volunteer Forces*, 1922–25; (3) *Army and Navy Journal, Gazette of the Land, Sea and Air*, 1926–current. (Of these, the first and second are title-page titles; after 1925 title pages were discontinued. Half titles, running heads, etc., have been, throughout, *Army and Navy Journal*.)

FIRST ISSUE: August 29, 1863. Current.

PERIODICITY: Weekly. Annual volumes ending in August.

PUBLISHERS: W. C. and F. P. Church, New York, 1863–1921; Franklin Coe, New York, 1921–25; John Callan O'Laughlin, 1925–current.

EDITORS: William Conant Church, 1863–1917; Willard Church, 1917–21; Henry J. Reilly, 1921–25; John Callan O'Laughlin, 1925–30; LeRoy Whitman, 1930–current.

[2] *Army and Navy Journal*, LIV, 1262 (May 26, 1917).

[3] See Volume III, sketch 6.

[4] See p. 150 of this volume, and Chapter V of Volume III.

of the pride of military men and truly representative of the honor and dignity of the profession of arms." [5]

The first two volumes present a detailed history of the closing phases of the Civil War. Editorially the *Journal* opposed the talk of an armistice which was not uncommon in 1864, noted the increase of public confidence after Sherman's capture of Atlanta and the victory at Mobile Bay, and interpreted the defeat of McClellan in the fall elections as the collapse of the "immediate armistice" propaganda. It grew enthusiastic about Sherman's march to the sea: its heroes were Sherman, Farragut, and Grant. So excited was it about the fall of Richmond that its half-page map of the "Scene of Conflict" was placed in the forms upside down.[6] But rejoicing soon gave place to mourning; and Lincoln, in the *Journal's* funeral eulogy, was compared to King Henry of Navarre. Already, before the war was over, careful histories of the various campaigns had been begun, with technical analyses.

In its first number the paper had declared that "the one permanent aim of this journal" was to protect the nation against antimilitary propaganda and to maintain the military and naval estblishments.[7] In pursuance of that duty, it began immediately after the surrender to protest against too rapid a reduction of the forces. From that day to this it has consistently advocated expansion of the land, sea, and air strength of the United States, and has attacked what it called in 1890 "an ignorant hostility to the maintenance of an efficient military establishment." [8] It has followed with care the progress of all military and naval legislation in congress. When that body in 1877 refused to make the regular military appropriation, the *Journal* interested J. Pierpont Morgan in the plight of the army and aided in the formation of a bankers' syndicate to lend money to army officers.

The *Journal* followed the Indian fighting in the West in detail, especially the Custer campaign. It reported foreign military activity from week to week, giving special attention to inter-

---

[5] *Army and Navy Journal*, II, 8 (August 27, 1864).
[6] *Ibid.*, II, 513 (April 8, 1865). File in the John Crerar Library.
[7] *Ibid.*, I, 8 (August 29, 1863).
[8] *Ibid.*, XXVIII, 264 (December 13, 1890).

national relations. Mechanical inventions for war, new improvements in tactics, the development of rifle matches, the progress of military education, and militia and G. A. R. news were all prominent features. The paper has always been a military and naval gazette, publishing official orders, announcements, casualties, and stations, as well as much personal news of officers. Advertising was chiefly of firearms and personal equipment. Colonel Church's editorials were consistently well written — clear, lively, direct.

The *Journal's* file affords an excellent detailed history of the Spanish-American War. Though always somewhat more military than naval, and more devoted to the regular than to the volunteer forces, the paper now reported faithfully and discussed lucidly all phases of the conflict, giving especial attention to such professional questions as that involved in the Schley controversy and trial.

The Spanish War marked the beginning of a new era of prosperity for the *Army and Navy Journal.* Its circulation had been under 5,000; now it increased to 7,000, and with the absorption of the Washington *Army and Navy Gazette* in 1899 and the Philadelphia paper of the same name a few years later it rose to over 10,000. Its price ever since its second year had been $6.00 a year.

During the World War, circulation more than doubled. Again the *Journal* followed the military operations in detail, publishing orders, appointments, casualties, etc. It became more distinctively than ever a newspaper for the services, with a few magazine features. Only a few weeks after the entry of the United States into the war, Colonel Church died; and his son Willard, who had for some years borne the burden of the work, became editor.

A few years after peace was declared, Franklin Coe bought the *Journal* and made General Henry J. Reilly editor. Its circulation declined somewhat, and its page size was reduced during the years 1923–26. In 1925 John Callan O'Laughlin purchased it and moved it to Washington, where he edited it until he installed LeRoy Whitman in the editorial chair in 1930. The page size was again reduced to small quarto in 1932.

THE UNITED STATES SERVICE MAGAZINE [1]

MUCH more than a technical military journal, the *United States Service Magazine* published not only such articles on military and naval affairs as were required for the basis of a service periodical during the Civil War, but fiction, poetry, stories of the war, and articles on literary and artistic subjects. Its scope and excellence reflected credit on the military and naval services, and the *Nation* pronounced it "one of the most valuable results of the war." [2]

Without question, its quality was owing largely to its editor, Professor Henry Coppée. Coppée had the breadth of interests and the richness of experience so often found in the effective magazine editor. Born in Georgia, he was educated at Yale, after which he studied engineering and helped build the Georgia Central Railroad. Then he entered West Point and was graduated in time to serve through the Mexican War. Then he was called to the professorship of history, geography, and ethics at West Point, and later resigned from the army to become professor of English literature at the University of Pennsylvania — the position he occupied while he was editor of the magazine in question.

The first number of the *United States Service Magazine*, a well-printed octavo of 120 pages, was issued by Charles B. Richardson in New York in January 1864. Three years of the war were past; it was after Gettysburg but before Sherman's march to the sea. The professional military and naval articles occupied the more important place in the magazine, and there were some twenty-five pages of "official intelligence." Military

[1] TITLE: *The United States Service Magazine.*
FIRST ISSUE: January 1864. LAST ISSUE: June 1866.
PERIODICITY: Monthly. Regular semiannual volumes.
PUBLISHER: Charles B. Richardson, New York.
EDITORS: Henry Coppée, January 1864–January 1866; Richard B. Irwin, February–June 1866.
INDEXED in *Poole's* and *Jones' Index.*
[2] *Nation*, I, 317 (September 7, 1865).

operations were carefully traced through the last third of the conflict.

But the more literary phases of the magazine were also important. Charles Godfrey Leland's "Ana of the War" was an excellent miscellany in 1865; but Leland had been a contributor before that, his "War Songs in History" in the first number being notable. Louisa M. Alcott's story, *Love and Loyalty*, appeared serially in 1864. Coppée's Philadelphia friends were well represented: besides Leland there were George H. Boker, S. Austin Allibone, and Mrs. Lucy H. Hooper. Among other well-known contributors were Charles Astor Bristed, the Reverend E. A. Washburn, James G. Wilson, and Charles D. Gardette. There were capable book reviews and occasional portraits on steel.

Early in 1866 Coppée was made president of Lehigh College, and his new duties made it necessary for him to resign his editorship. He was succeeded by Colonel Richard B. Irwin, with Dr. Ben Ellis Martin as associate editor; but after a few months the magazine was suspended. Doubtless competition with the growing *Army and Navy Journal*, a weekly, made existence difficult for it. It was felt, too, that the magazine had been born of the war and had little reason for existence now that the war was over. "The mission of a military magazine is ended," it said in its last number, "and it, too, is mustered out."

CHRONOLOGICAL LIST

CHRONOLOGICAL LIST

PERIODICALS founded 1850–1864 and mentioned in the text are here arranged under the years in which they were begun. The end-date follows the place of publication. Only the most important changes of title are noted here. In some cases a part of the title carried throughout only part of the file is included in parentheses.

1850

American Vegetarian and Health Journal. Philadelphia. 1854.
Arthur's Home Gazette. Philadelphia. 1852.
Buffalo Christian Advocate. 1894.
Catholic Mirror. Baltimore. 1908.
Choral Advocate, later *New York Musical Review*, etc. 1873.
Christian World. New York. 1884.
Columbian and Great West. Cincinnati. 1854.
Deseret News. Salt Lake City. Current.
Dye's Counterfeit Detector. Philadelphia. 1910.
Family Visitor. Cleveland, Hudson (Ohio). 1853.
Farmer and Planter Monthly. Pendleton, Columbia (South Carolina). 1861.
Figaro! New York. 1851.
Fonetic Propagandist. New York. 1852.
Harper's (New) Monthly Magazine. New York. Current.
Humphrey's Journal of Photography. New York. 1870.
Insurance Advocate and Journal. Chicopee (Massachusetts). 1850.
International Magazine. New York. 1852.
Lorgnette, or, Studies of the Town. New York. 1850.
Mrs. Whittelsey's Magazine for Mothers. New York. 1852.
New Hampshire Journal of Medicine. Concord. 1859.
New Orleans Christian Advocate. 1926.
New York Colonization Journal. 1863.
New York (later American) Medical Gazette. 1861.
Presbyterian Monthly Record. Philadelphia. 1886.
Spirit Messenger and Harmonial Guide. Springfield (Massachusetts). 1851.
Templar's Magazine. Cincinnati, Philadelphia. 1874.
Waverley Magazine. Boston. 1908.
Whitaker's Magazine. Charleston. 1850.

1851

American Miscellany. New York. 1852.
California Christian Advocate. San Francisco. 1931.

Carpet-Bag. Boston. 1853.
Circular. Oneida (New York). 1876.
Dollar Weekly Mirror. Manchester (New Hampshire). 1863.
Foreign Missionary Journal. Richmond. 1916.
Gleason's (Ballou's) Pictorial Drawing-Room Companion. Boston. 1859.
Hombre. San Francisco. 1851.
Illustrated American News. New York. 1852.
Literary Advertiser. Cincinnati. 1856.
Magnolia. Richmond. 1851.
Nashville Journal of Medicine and Surgery. 1920.
North American Journal of Homoeopathy, later *Pan-Therapist.* New York, Chicago. 1933.
North American Miscellany. New York. 1852.
Ohio Farmer. Cleveland. Current.
Opal. Utica (New York). 1860.
Pacific. San Francisco. 1928.
Photographic Art Journal. 1860.
Presbyterian Magazine. Philadelphia. 1860.
Republic. New York. 1852.
Reveille. New York. 1854.
Shekinah. Bridgeport (Connecticut). 1853.
Soil of the South. Columbus (Georgia). 1857.
St. Louis Christian Advocate. 1928.
True Flag. Boston. 1908.
Whitaker's Southern Magazine. Columbia (South Carolina). 1853.
White Banner. New York. 1851.

1852

American Celt. Boston, Buffalo, New York. 1857.
American Journal of Photography. New York. 1867.
American Law Register and Review, later *University of Pennsylvania Law Review.* Philadelphia. Current.
American Telegraph Magazine. New York. 1853.
Child's Paper. New York. 1897.
Christian Recorder. Philadelphia. Current.
(Church's) Bizarre. Philadelphia. 1855.
(City) Budget. New York. 1854.
Crystal Fountain. Allegheny (Pennsylvania). 1852.
Diogenes hys Lanterne. New York. 1853.
Dwight's Journal of Music. Boston. 1881.
Farmer's Journal. Bath (North Carolina). 1854.
Ford's Christian Repository. Louisville, St. Louis. 1905.
Genius of Liberty. Cincinnati. 1854.
Golden Era. San Francisco, San Diego. 1893.
Humbug's American Museum. New York. 1852.
Ink Fountain. Philadelphia. 1856.
Ladies' Pearl. St. Louis. 1870.

Literary Budget. Chicago. 1856.
Mountain Cove Journal and Spiritual Harbinger. Mountain Cove (Virginia). 1853.
National Magazine. New York. 1858.
New-York Quarterly. 1855.
Northwestern Christian Advocate. Chicago. 1932.
Ohio Journal of Education, later *Ohio Educational Monthly.* Columbus. 1933.
Pennsylvania School Journal. Lancaster, Harrisburg. Current.
Pick. New York. 1854.
Pioneer and Woman's Advocate. Providence. 1853(?).
Presbyterian Banner. Philadelphia, Pittsburgh. Current.
Presbyterian Quarterly Review. Philadelphia. 1862.
Revolution. New York. 1852.
Schoolmate. Boston. 1855.
Southern Parlour Magazine. Mobile (Alabama), Memphis (Tennessee). 1856.
South-Western Monthly. Nashville. 1852.
To-Day. Boston. 1852.
Tuckett's Insurance Journal. Philadelphia. 1861.
Yankee Notions. New York. 1875.
Yankee Privateer. Boston. 1860(?).
Young Sam. New York. 1852.
Youth's Casket. Buffalo. 1857.

1853

American Cotton Planter. Montgomery (Alabama). 1861.
American Polytechnic Journal. Washington. 1854.
(Arthur's) Home Magazine. Philadelphia. 1898.
Beloit College Monthly. Beloit (Wisconsin). 1875.
Bubble. New York. 1853.
Christian Times. Chicago. 1867.
Church Journal. New York. 1878.
Country Gentleman. Philadelphia. Current.
Eclaireur. New York. 1857.
Everybody's Own. Buffalo. 1853.
Freewill Baptist Quarterly. Providence. 1869.
Genius of the West. Cincinnati. 1856.
Illustrated Monthly Magazine of Art. New York. 1854.
Illustrated News. New York. 1853.
Iowa Medical Journal. Keokuk (Iowa). 1869.
Kentucky Garland. Covington. 1853.
Metropolitan. Baltimore. 1859.
Mining Magazine. New York. 1861.
Monitor, later *Insurance Monitor,* later *American Insurance Digest.* New York. Current.
New-Church Independent and Monthly Review. Chicago. 1904.

New York Clipper. 1923.
New York Journal, later *Frank Leslie's New York Journal of Romance, General Literature, Science, and Art.* 1857.
New York Time-Piece. 1853.
O. K. New York. 1853.
Parlor Magazine. Cincinnati. 1854.
Pen and Pencil. Cincinnati. 1853.
People's Journal. New York. 1854.
Pioneer Farmer. Des Moines (Iowa). 1861.
Pittsburgh Legal Journal. Current.
Putnam's Monthly Magazine. New York. 1857.
Quarterly (later *Monthly*) *Journal of the American Unitarian Association.* Boston. 1869.
Railroad Record. Cincinnati. 1873.
St. Nicholas. Oswego (New York). 1853.
Saturday Evening Mail. Philadelphia. ?
Seer. Washington. 1854.
Sloan's Garden City. Chicago. 1854.
Southern Eclectic. Augusta (Georgia). 1854.
Spiritual Telegraph. New York. 1857.
Una. Providence. 1856(?).
Weekly News and Southern Literary Gazette. Charleston. 1856.
Western Home Visitor. Mt. Vernon (Ohio). 1855.
Western Literary Cabinet. Detroit. 1854.
Young America. New York. 1854.
Zion's Advocate. Washington. 1923.

1854

American Israelite. Cincinnati. Current.
American Jubilee. New York. 1855.
American Medical Monthly. New York. 1862.
Arkansas Magazine. Little Rock. 1854.
California Farmer. San Francisco. 1884.
Christian Spiritualist. New York. 1855.
Churchman's Monthly Magazine. New York. 1859.
Cozzens' Wine Press. New York. 1861.
Curiosity Shop. San Francisco. 1854.
(Emerson's) United States Magazine, later *Great Republic.* New York. 1859.
Fireman's Journal, later *California Spirit of the Times.* San Francisco. 1894.
Forrester's Playmate. New York. 1864.
Frank Leslie's (Ladies') Gazette of Fashion. New York. 1857.
Hall's Journal of Health. New York. 1894.
Harvard Magazine. Cambridge. 1864.
Herald of Freedom. Lawrence (Kansas). 1860.
Hint. New York. 1854.

Journal of Medical Reform. New York. 1857.
Life Illustrated. New York. 1861.
Little Pilgrim. Philadelphia. 1875.
Pioneer. San Francisco. 1855.
Protestant Episcopal Quarterly and Church Register. New York. 1861.
Railroad Advocate. New York. 1857.
Sacred Circle. New York. 1856.
Southern Episcopalian. Charleston (South Carolina). 1863.
West American Review. Cincinnati. 1855.
Western Democratic Review, later *National Democratic Review.* Indianapolis, Washington. 1856.
Wide West. San Francisco. 1858.

1855

Anglo-Saxon. New York. 1857.
Atlanta Medical and Surgical Journal. 1899.
Ballou's Dollar Monthly Magazine. Boston. 1893.
(Barnard's) American Journal of Education. New York. 1882.
Comic World. New York. 1855.
Crayon. New York. 1861.
Criterion. New York. 1856.
Family Newspaper. New York. 1856(?).
Frank Leslie's Illustrated Newspaper, later *Leslie's Weekly.* New York. 1922.
Hardware Man's Newspaper, later *Iron Age.* New York. Current.
Illinois Teacher. Peoria. 1873.
Inventor. New York. 1857.
Monthly Trade Gazette. New York. 1872.
New-Church Messenger. Chicago, New York. Current.
New England Spiritualist. Boston. 1856.
New Western Magazine. Cincinnati. 1855.
New York Musical Pioneer. 1871.
North Carolina Christian Advocate. Greensboro. Current.
Panorama of Life and Literature. Boston. 1857.
Practical Farmer. Philadelphia. 1922.
Quampeag Coyote. Mokelumne Hill (California). 1855.
Radical Abolitionist. New York. 1858.
Shanghai. Ellicott's Mills (Maryland). 1856.
Southern Baptist Review and Eclectic. Nashville (Kentucky). 1861.
Southern Times. Montgomery (Alabama). 1855.
Squatter Sovereign, later *(Freedom's) Champion.* Atchison (Kansas). 1909.
Student and Schoolmate. Boston. 1872(?).
Typographic Advertiser. Philadelphia. 1892.
United States Insurance Gazette and Magazine. New York. 1882.
Western Art Journal. Cincinnati. 1855.
Western Standard. San Francisco. 1857.
Woman's Advocate. Philadelphia. 1860.

1856

Billiard Cue. New York. 1874.
Central Christian Advocate. St. Louis, Kansas City. 1932.
Cincinnatus. Cincinnati. 1861.
College Journal of Medical Science. Cincinnati. 1869.
Hebrew Observer. San Francisco. 1890.
Home, later *Home Circle.* Buffalo, New York. 1860.
Hutchings' Illustrated California Magazine. San Francisco. 1861.
Indiana School Journal. Indianapolis. 1900.
Journal of Agriculture. St. Louis. 1921.
Kaleidoscope. Petersburg (Virginia). 1857.
Manford's Magazine. Chicago, St. Louis. 1896.
Moravian. Bethlehem (Pennsylvania). Current.
Mrs. Stephens' Illustrated Monthly. New York. 1858.
National Journal of Finance. New York. 1866.
New York Weekly. 1914(?).
Nick Nax. New York. 1875.
Northern Independent. Auburn (New York). 1861.
Northwestern Farmer. Indianapolis. 1871.
Northwestern Farmer and Horticultural Journal, later *Iowa Homestead.* Dubuque, Des Moines. 1929.
North-Western Home Journal. Chicago. 1862.
Pacific Christian Advocate. Portland. 1932.
Pen and Pencil. Chicago. 1856.
Porter's Spirit of the Times. New York. 1859.
Quarterly Reporter of Y.M.C.A.'s in North America, later *Young Men's Christian Journal.* Buffalo. ?
Round's Printer's Cabinet. Chicago. 1888.
Rural American. Utica (New York), New York. 1869.
San Francisco News-Letter. 1928.
Sibyl. Middletown (New York). 1864.
United States Railway and Mining Register. Philadelphia. 1915.
University Literary Magazine, later *University of Virginia Magazine.* Charlottesville. 1929.
Wisconsin Journal of Education. Racine, Madison. Current.
Yankee Doodle. New York. 1856.

1857

Age of Steel. St. Louis. 1902.
American Church Monthly. New York. 1858.
American Druggists' Circular and Chemical Gazette. New York. Current.
American Quarterly Review of Freemasonry. New York. 1859.
Atlantic Monthly. Boston. Current.
Banner of Light. Boston. 1907.
Catholic Youth's Magazine. Baltimore. 1861.
Chess Monthly. New York. 1861.
Chicago Record, later *Church Record.* 1862.

Clark's School Visitor, later *Schoolday Magazine*. Philadelphia. 1875.
Frank Leslie's New Family Magazine, later *Frank Leslie's Lady's Magazine*. New York. 1882.
Harness and Carriage Journal. New York. 1883.
Harper's Weekly. New York. 1916.
Herald of Light. New York. 1861.
Historical Magazine and Notes and Queries. Boston, New York. 1875.
Jewish Messenger. New York. 1903.
New Hampshire Journal of Agriculture. Manchester. 1863.
Norton's Literary Letter. New York. 1860.
Philadelphia Intelligencer. 1920.
Russell's Magazine. Charleston (South Carolina). 1860.
Scottish-American Journal. New York. 1865.
Shoe and Leather Reporter. New York, Boston. Current.
Tablet. New York. 1890.
Weekly Novelette. Boston. 1862.
(Western) Railroad Gazette. Chicago, New York. 1908.

1858

American Christian Review. Cincinnati. 1886.
American Homoeopathic Review. New York. 1866.
Catholic Guardian. Louisville (Kentucky). 1862.
Coach-Makers' Magazine. New York. 1871.
De Bow's Weekly Press. New Orleans. 1858.
Douglass' Monthly. Rochester (New York). 1860.
Firelands Pioneer. Norwalk (Ohio). 1878.
Frank Leslie's Budget of Fun. New York. 1896.
Gleason's Line-of-Battle Ship. Boston. 1859.
Hesperian. San Francisco. 1862.
Household Monthly. Lynn, Boston. 1860.
Journal of Materia Medica. New Lebanon (New York), Terre Haute (Indiana). 1896.
Laws of Life. Dansville (New York). 1893.
Literary Locomotive and Phonetic Paragon. Newburgh (New York). 1859.
Mathematical Monthly. Cambridge, New York. 1861.
Medical and Surgical Reporter. Philadelphia. 1898.
Military Gazette. New York. 1861.
Mount Vernon Record. Philadelphia. 1860.
North Carolina Presbyterian, later *Presbyterian Standard*. Fayetteville, Wilmington, Charlotte. 1931.
Oregon Farmer. Portland. 1861.
Pacific Medical Journal. San Francisco. 1917.
Peterson's Counterfeit Detector. Philadelphia. 1889.
Printer. New York. 1875.
Rutgers College Quarterly. New Brunswick (New Jersey). 1861.
Saturday Press. New York. 1866.

Social Republic. New York. 1860.
Texian Monthly Magazine. Galveston. 1858(?).
Wang Doodle. Chicago. 1859.

1859

American Gas-Light Journal and Mining Reporter, later *American Gas Journal.* New York. Current.
American Life Assurance Magazine and Journal of Actuaries. New York. 1878.
American (Presbyterian and) Theological Review. Boston, New York. 1871.
American Railway Review. New York. 1862.
American Stock Journal. New York. 1864.
Anglo-African Magazine. New York. 1860.
Baltimore Methodist, later *Washington Christian Advocate.* 1928.
Bulletin of the American Geographical Society, later *Geographical Review.* New York. Current.
California Police Gazette. San Francisco. 1877.
Christian Banner and Tract Journal. New York. 1872.
Comic Bouquet. Philadelphia. 1859.
Comic Monthly. New York. 1881.
Congregational Herald. Lawrence (Kansas). 1863.
Congregational Quarterly. Boston. 1878.
Dental Cosmos. Philadelphia. 1936.
Essex Institute Historical Collections. Salem (Massachusetts). Current.
Female Student. Louisville (Kentucky). 1860.
Gardener's Monthly and Horticultural Advertiser. Philadelphia. 1888.
Hall's Fireside Monthly. New York. 1861.
Home Monthly. Buffalo. 1860.
Hub, later *Automotive Manufacturer.* New York. Current.
Iowa Instructor. Davenport. 1877.
Kentucky Family Journal, later *Educational Monthly.* Louisville. 1860.
(Legal and) Insurance Reporter. Philadelphia. 1899.
Metropolitan Record. New York. 1873.
National Democratic Quarterly Review. Washington. 1860.
New York Illustrated News. 1864.
Phunny Phellow. New York. 1876.
Principia. New York. 1866.
Southern Field and Fireside. Augusta (Georgia). 1864.
Southern Literary Companion. Newnan (Georgia). 1864.
Southern Musical Advocate. Singer's Glen (Virginia). 1869.
Sunday School Times. Philadelphia. Current.
Vanity Fair. New York. 1863.
Voice of Masonry. Louisville, Chicago. 1899.
(Wall Street; New York) Weekly Underwriter. Current.
Water-Cure Monthly. Yellow Springs (Ohio). 1860.
(Wilkes') Spirit of the Times. New York. 1902.

1860

American Medical Times. New York. 1864.
American Register and International Journal. Boston. 1861.
Boston Musical Times. 1871.
Dial. Cincinnati. 1860.
Father Abraham. Lancaster (Pennsylvania). 1860.
Gleason's Literary Companion. Boston. 1870.
Herald of Progress. New York. 1864.
Home Monthly. Boston. 1908.
Household Journal. New York. 1862.
Household Magazine, later *American Monthly.* New York. 1860.
Illustrated Police News. Boston. 1904.
Innocent Weekly Owl. New York. 1860.
Irving Magazine. New York. 1860.
Lincoln Clarion. Springfield (Illinois). 1860.
Methodist. New York. 1882.
Mining and Scientific Press. San Francisco. 1922.
Momus. New York. 1860.
National Educator. Quakertown, Williamsport, etc. (Pennsylvania). 1905.
National Quarterly Review. New York. 1880.
Pacific Methodist. San Francisco. Current.
Plantation. New York. 1860.
Saints' Herald. Lamoni (Iowa). 1923(?).
United Presbyterian Quarterly Review. Pittsburgh. 1861.
(United States) Medical Investigator. Chicago. 1892.
University Quarterly. New Haven. 1861.
Water-Cure World. Brattleboro (Vermont). 1861.

1861

American Bee Journal. Philadelphia, Washington, Chicago. Current.
American Churchman. Chicago. 1871.
Boston Review. 1871.
Camp Kettle. Camps of 100th Pennsylvania Infantry. 1862.
Church Monthly. Boston. 1870.
Countryman. Eatonton (Georgia). 1865.
Danville Quarterly Review. Danville (Kentucky). 1864.
Legal Adviser. Chicago. 1920.
Lutheran and Missionary, later *Lutheran.* Philadelphia. Current.
Philobiblion. New York. 1863.
Southern Monthly. Memphis (Tennessee), Grenada (Mississippi). 1862.

1862

American Exchange and Review. Philadelphia. Current.
American Journal of Ophthalmology. New York. 1864.
American Odd Fellow. New York. 1874.

American Spirit and Wine Trade Review, later *Western Spirit,* later *American Wine and Spirit Review.* Chicago. 1886.
Army and Navy Gazette. New York. 1863.
Boston Commonwealth. 1896.
Continental Monthly. Boston. 1864.
Dental Quarterly. Philadelphia. 1867.
Eclectic Medical Journal of Pennsylvania. Philadelphia. 1880.
Harry Hazel's Yankee Blade. Boston. 1894.
Jolly Joker. New York. 1877.
Magnolia (Weekly). Richmond. 1864.
New England Insurance Gazette. Boston. 1876.
New York Insurance Journal. 1910.
Northwestern Church. Chicago. 1865.
Southern Illustrated News. Richmond. 1865.
Stockholder. New York. 1911(?).
Trade of the West, later *American Manufacture and Iron World,* later *Steel and Iron.* Pittsburgh. Current.
Western Farmer. Dixon (Illinois). 1882.
Western Rural. Chicago. 1901.

1863

Annals of Iowa. Iowa City, Des Moines. Current.
Army and Navy Official Gazette. Washington. 1865.
Bohemian. Richmond. 1863.
Bugle-Horn of Liberty. Griffin (Georgia). 1863.
California Teacher. San Francisco. 1876.
Chicago Journal of Commerce, later *Iron and Steel,* later *Iron and Machinery World.* 1906.
Child at Home. New York. 1873.
Christian. New York. 1869.
Connecticut War Record. Hartford. 1865.
Financier, later *Bank Director and Financier.* New York. Current.
Fincher's Trades Review. Philadelphia. 1866.
Frank Leslie's Boys of America, later *Frank Leslie's Boys' and Girls' Weekly.* New York. 1878.
Frank Leslie's Ten-Cent Monthly, later *Frank Leslie's Pleasant Hours.* New York. 1896.
Grierson's Underwriter's Weekly Circular. New York. 1873.
Herald of Life. New York, Springfield (Massachusetts), Hartford, New Haven. 1931.
Illustrated Mercury. Raleigh. 1864.
(International) Iron Molders' Journal. Cincinnati. Current.
Kansas Farmer. Topeka. Current.
Merryman's Monthly. New York. 1877.
Millers' Journal. New York. 1886.
Mirror and Farmer. Manchester (New Hampshire). 1918.
Musical World. Cleveland. 1890.

Old Guard. New York. 1870.
Portrait Monthly. New York. 1864.
Round Table. New York. 1869.
Sanitary Commission Bulletin. New York, Philadelphia, Washington. 1865.
Seminary Magazine, later *Old Dominion.* Richmond. 1873.
Southern Punch. Richmond. 1864.
Sportsman. New York. 1863.
Theological Eclectic. Boston. 1871.
(United States) Army and Navy Journal. New York. Current.
Western Homoeopathic Observer. St. Louis. 1871.

1864

Age: a Southern Eclectic Magazine. Richmond. 1865.
American Artisan and Patent Recorder. New York. 1875.
American Educational Monthly. New York. 1876.
American Homoeopathic Observer. Detroit. 1884.
American Mining Gazette and Geological Magazine. New York. 1868.
Brainard's Musical World. Cleveland. 1888.
Californian. San Francisco. 1868.
Christian (Evangelist). Kansas City, St. Louis. Current.
Cigar Makers' Official Journal. Chicago. Current.
Confederate States Medical and Surgical Journal. Richmond. 1865.
Drumbeat. Brooklyn. 1864.
Family Treasure. Pittsburgh, Cincinnati. 1869.
Freedman's Friend. Philadelphia. 1883.
Haversack. Philadelphia. 1864.
Herald of Truth. Elkhart (Indiana). 1908.
Kansas Educational Review. Leavenworth, Emporia, etc. 1874.
Lady's Friend. Philadelphia. 1873.
Maryland Farmer, later *Farmer's and Planter's Guide.* Baltimore. 1902.
Our Daily Fair. Philadelphia. 1864.
Pacific Index, later *American Mining Index.* San Francisco, New York. 1867.
Philadelphia Photographer, later *Wilson's Photographic Magazine,* later *Photographic Journal of America.* Philadelphia, New York. 1923.
Smith and Barrow's Monthly. Richmond. 1864.
Spirit of the Fair. New York. 1864.
Swamp Angel. Charleston. 1864.
Telegrapher. New York. 1877.
United States Service Magazine. New York. 1866.
Watson's Weekly Art Journal. New York. 1905.
Workingmen's Advocate. Chicago. 1879.

INDEX

INDEX

Eads, James Buchanan, 318.
Eagle, Edward E., 325n.
Eaton, William O., 36n.
Eclaireur, 150.
Eclectic Magazine, 129, 192.
Eclectic Medical Journal, 85.
Eclectic Medical Journal of Pennsylvania, 85.
Eclecticism in magazines, 129, 264, 383.
Eddy, Richard, 72n.
Edinburgh, Review, 129, 130, 221.
Edison, Thomas Alva, 318, 324.
Editorial Practices. Censorious editing, 26; of *North American Review*, 233–34; of *Atlantic Monthly*, 500–02, 507, 514.
Editorial salaries, 24–25, 42, 368, 369, 391–392, 526–27.
Edmonds, John Worth, 208, 209.
Education. Periodicals devoted to, 96–98; magazine comment on, 314, 343–44, 444–45, 507n, 531. *See American Journal of Education.*
Educational Monthly, 59.
Edwards, Mrs. Annie, 439.
Egan, Pierce, 454.
Eggleston, Edward, 374.
Eggleston, George Cary, 506n.
Elder, John A., 113.
Eliot, Charles William, 376.
"Eliot, George." *See* Cross, Mary Ann Evans.
Eliot, Samuel Atkins, 233.
Eliot, William, 402.
Ellet, Mrs. Elizabeth Fries, 308, 352.
Elliott, Charles, 67n.
Elliott, Charles Wyllys, 429.
Ellis, Edward S., 171, 462.
Ellis, George Edward, 128, 241.
Ellis, Rufus, 72n.
Elwell, E. H., 36.
Emancipator, 369.
Emerson, Edwin, 464.
Emerson, George H., 57, 72.
Emerson, J. M., 32.
Emerson, Ralph Waldo, as contributor, 20, 33, 175, 238, 244, 253, 387, 495, 502, 503, 504, 535; criticism of, 166–167; 147, 169, 494, 498, 510.
Emerson's United States Magazine. See United States Magazine.

England. Circulation of American magazines in, 130; American magazines reprinted in, 322, 399; American political relations with, 127–28; antislavery activities of, 282, 284, 289. *See* English Literature; English Magazines.
England, Isaac W., 452n.
England, (Bishop) John, 76.
Englehardt, George W., 95n.
English, Thomas Dunn, 181, 544n, 546.
English Literature. Criticisms of English writers, 159–62, 230–31, 236; serials by English novelists, 129, 172, 386ff, 393ff, 406, 421, 508; reprints of English novels, 383.
English Magazines. Circulated in United States, 13, 129–30; used as models by American magazines, 130, 221, 357, 409, 420, 452, 470, 489, 521, 530.
Engraving, Copper and steel, 116n, 58, 192–3, 303, 308, 309, 310, 315, 345, 441, 466.
Engraving, Wood. *See* Woodcuts.
Enterprise, 461n.
Episcopalian, 70n.
Episcopalian Periodicals. *See* Protestant Episcopal Periodicals.
Episcopal Recorder, 70.
Ericsson, John, 318.
Erskine, John, 260.
Essex Institute Historical Collections, 176.
"Estelle." *See* Bogart, Elizabeth.
Eude, Louis-Marie, 355.
Evangelical Messenger, 68.
Evangelical Repository, 63n.
Evangelical Review, 73.
Evangelist, 18, 63, 140, 369.
Evans, Augusta Jane, 171.
Evans, Edward Payson, 510n.
Evans, Hugh Davey, 69.
Evarts, Jeremiah, 233.
Everett, Alexander Hill, 218n, 227, 229, 232, 234.
Everett, Charles Carroll, 243.
Everett, Edward, 23–24, 149, 220n, 226ff, 232, 238, 360, 361, 445.
Everett, Oliver, 227.
Evergreen, 69.
Every Saturday, 386, 462, 510.

INDEX

Wagner, Richard, 253.
Wagner, Samuel, 91.
Wales, George E., 464.
Wales, Salem Howe, 316n, 319.
Walker, Charles Rumford, 493n.
Walker, J. Bernard, 323.
Walker, Robert John, 540n, 542, 543.
Walker, Wareham, 65n.
Wall, James Walter, 545.
Wall Street Underwriter and the Joint Stock Register, 94n.
Wallace, Benjamin J., 62n.
Wallace, J. M. Power, 93n.
Wallace, William, 93n.
Wallace's Farmer, 90n.
Wallin, Samuel, 454.
Walsh, Robert, 221.
Wanamaker, John, 75n.
Wang Doodle, 185n.
"Ward, Artemus." *See* Browne, Charles Farrar.
Ward, Elizabeth Stuart Phelps, 267, 395, 505n.
Ward, Mrs. Humphry, 402.
Ward, Julius Hammond, 249.
Ward, William Hayes, 367n, 374, 376, 377, 378.
Ware, John, 228.
Waring, George Edwin, 413, 506n.
Warner, Charles Dudley, 398, 399, 402, 424, 425, 506n, 511n.
Warner, Francis Lester, 493n.
Warner, Susan, 171.
Warren, A. C., 409.
Warren, A. W., 475.
Warren, Joseph, 432n, 433.
Warren, J. L. L. F., 90.
Warren, O. G., 209.
Washburn, Edward Abiel, 551.
Washburn, Emory, 235.
Washington, Booker Taliaferro, 271, 512.
Washington Christian Advocate, 67n.
Wasp, 118n.
Wasson, David Atwood, 152, 503, 505.
Watchman and Reflector, 64, 266.
Watchman of the Prairies, 65n.
Water-Cure Journal, 87.
Water-Cure Monthly, 87.
Water-Cure World, 87.
Watervillonian. See Yankee Blade.
Watson, Henry Cood, 452n, 455.

Watson, James V., 67.
Watson, John Whitaker, 472.
Watson, William, 211n.
Watson's Weekly Art Journal, 197.
Watterson, Henry, 251.
Wattles, John D., 75n.
Waud, Alfred R., 45, 397, 409, 449, 460, 474, 481.
Waud, William, 474.
Waverly Magazine, 41–42, 100.
Wayland, Francis, 154.
Webb, Charles Henry, 118.
Webb, James Watson, 282.
Weber, Charles, 464.
Webster, Daniel, 227, 290.
Webster, John White, 228.
Webster's Dictionary, 177.
Weekly Journal of Free Opinion, 367n.
Weekly News and Southern Literary Gazette, 110n.
Weekly Novelette, 36, 411, 468.
Weekly Periodicals. In the period, 33–45; home weeklies, 57–58; literary weeklies, 172; religious weeklies, 61, 103; 150, 178, 206.
Weekly Recorder, 63n.
Weekly Review, 379.
Weekly Underwriter and the Insurance Press, 94n.
Weeks, Edward Augustus, Jr., 493n, 515.
Weir, Robert, 475.
Welcome Guest, 411.
Weld, Horatio Hastings, 410.
Weldon, Charles Dater, 397.
Welford, B. R., 346.
Wellman's Literary Miscellany, 116.
Well-Spring, 101.
Wells, Carolyn, 431.
Wells, Herbert George, 257.
Wells, Thomas Bucklin, 383n, 403.
Wells, William Harvey, 303.
Wells and Lilly, 221, 227.
Wellstood, William, 303.
Wentworth, E., 301n.
West. Periodicals of, 116–18; comment on, 119–21, 206, 425, 548–49. *See* Middle West.
West American Monthly, 115n.
West American Review, 115n.
Western Art Journal, 194n.
Western Baptist Review, 63.